Introduction to the New Testament

"The Word Became Flesh"

THE MACMILLAN COMPANY, NEW YORK

COLLIER-MACMILLAN LIMITED, LONDON

Introduction
to the
New Testament
"The Word Became Flesh"

Donald J. Selby

CATAWBA COLLEGE

This book and its companion, *Introduction to the Old Testament: "Hear, O Israel,"*
by James King West are available in a one-volume edition entitled *Introduction
to the Bible,* by Donald J. Selby and James King West,
copyright © 1971 by The Macmillan Company.

The Scripture quotations in this publication are from the Revised Standard Version
of the Bible, copyrighted 1946 and 1952, by the Division of Christian Education,
National Council of Churches, and used by permission.

The Macmillan Company
866 Third Avenue, New York, New York 10022
Collier-Macmillan Canada, Ltd., Toronto, Ontario

Library of Congress catalog card number: 71-152822
FIRST PRINTING

Dedication

To Allene, Robert, and Donald

Preface

Modern New Testament scholarship had its beginnings in certain historical questions arising from the conflict between traditional Christianity and the "age of reason." The documents of the New Testament were treated, for that reason, primarily as sources for the recovery of history. The Gospels, for example, were subjected to the most intensive historical and literary criticism in order to reconstruct a life of "the Jesus of history" as distinguished from "the Christ of Faith." Paul's Epistles and Acts were subjected to minute scrutiny for signs of conflict in the original Jewish Church, Hellenistic influences on Paul, and other clues which might account for the theology of the later Church.

Although neither of these enterprises reached undisputed conclusions or came out quite as their sponsors had hoped, they nevertheless produced a wealth of data and knowledge which fully justified the countless man-hours they had cost.

When scholarly interest turned to a preoccupation with the New Testament itself, it had in hand a highly useful body of knowledge for reconstructing the history of the nascent church out of which the New Testament came. Many deservedly well-known introductions to the New Testament came from this period. It was characteristic of the method and presuppositions of the scholars in this period that their books were organized around chronological considerations. Because they were the earliest of the New Testament documents to be written, Paul's letters were frequently the first books to be treated. The current development, particularly in the study of the Gospels, which attempts to understand the purposes, methods, and thought of the final authors, is a natural outgrowth of the earlier programs of research in the New Testament. Redaction or composition criticism, as this development is known, is both dependent upon and a correction of previous methods. Its work must, at every point, take into account historical and literary findings of its predecessors; but not infrequently it is able to set problems in a new perspective and bring new insights to bear on problems which have refused to yield to other approaches.

For the reader of the New Testament whose interest is in understanding the book as he has it, however, this approach has the added feature of meeting more directly his needs. In a sense it brings to a meaningful conclusion the several approaches which for some two centuries now have occupied the specialists. For that reason this book follows the program of composition criticism.

Since the goal is to help the reader understand the New Testament as he finds it, and since the history of the writing of the documents which comprise it is secondary, I have followed essentially the Canonical order. Not only does this order begin where the study must begin, with Jesus Christ who is in one way or another the subject of the entire New Testament, but it also helps the reader to see the significance of the shape which the Church has given its sacred writings. For similar reasons I have omitted any attempt to reconstruct a "life of Jesus." Because the goal in this study is to understand the interpretations of Jesus which each of the writers was concerned to provide for the church of his own time, it seems inappropriate to add another, modern interpretation. Without entering into the debate, which is by no means over, as to whether a reconstruction of the "Jesus of history" is possible, this study has assumed the more modest task of helping the reader to a better understanding of the witnesses to Jesus written by these men of faith, and leaves it to him to discover in his own response who HE is.

There are, of course, many able treatments of the questions surrounding the life of Jesus. The footnotes and reading lists will direct the reader to these and to important works on the many other facets of New Testament study. Insofar as possible I have confined my references to books available in English. Happily, the "language gap" has narrowed in recent years, and in a few instances I have been able to modify the footnotes with translations which have appeared since this work was begun. This book was written to guide the reader in his own understanding of the New Testament. He is expected therefore to follow in the New Testament the passages under discussion. The many references which clutter the pages throughout are included to help the reader to keep in touch with these passages. If through a better understanding of its making and meaning he comes to discover the joy of reading the New Testament, this book will have accomplished its purpose.

Acknowledgments

Writing acknowledgments is always difficult because one becomes aware that the magnitude of his indebtedness cannot be so easily cataloged. Among those who deserve special thanks are my colleagues in the Department of Religion at Catawba College. This book was written as a companion volume to *Introduction to the Old Testament:"Hear, O Israel,"* by my colleague, Dr. James King West, and in another edition the two are combined in a single volume. The benefit of his excellent judgment and scholarship which this relationship has brought me is hard to overestimate. Our colleague Dr. Richard Schiemann, who spends his summers in archaeological exploration in Israel, has placed us heavily in his debt, not only by the pictures which, as the credits show, he provided for our use—most of them taken especially for our project—but also by his willingness to bear a disproportionate load of departmental responsibilities while we were "scribbling." The administration of the college, President Martin Luther Shotzberger, Vice President Charles Turney, and former Dean Daniel E. Kirk, have been most helpful in protecting our time.

Mr. Charles E. Smith, Editor of the College and Professional Division of The Macmillan Company, has not only been most patient, but has given most liberally of his time and wisdom to help in bringing this project to completion. The Rev. John N. McAllister, Rector of St. Mark's Episcopal Church in Gastonia, North Carolina, has read and discussed with me several key sections of this work. To him, and to the many students who in class dialogues helped to formulate my thinking at many points, I offer my thanks. Our student assistants, Mr. George Fouts, Mr. Gary C. Hauze, and Mr. Gerald D. Fuss, gave hours of work to cataloging and arranging the illustrations. Professors William Wilson and Frances Wentz of the college library staff have been most helpful. Professor Charles G. Eagan helped in locating some of the illustrations. For the illustrations in this volume I gratefully acknowledge the kindness of Mr. Charles R. Hoskins, director of the Money Museum, The National Bank of Detroit; a former student, Mr. Don R. Smith; Mr. and Mrs. David W. Roderick and Catawba College; Israel Government Tourist Office; The Vatican Library; The John Rylands Library; and The University of Michigan Library. Assisted by two of my students, Mr. Jack B. Blanks and Mr. William J. Harrold, Professor James O. Morris compiled the General Index.

Mrs. Mary Ellen King has helped with the typing. My wife, in literally hundreds of hours of work in producing the typescript, has shared with me once more in another of our many projects together. In whatever virtues this book has these people, and others, have had an important share; for its weaknesses I must bear full responsibility.

Eastertide
Salisbury, N.C.   D. J. S.

Contents

Chapter Two

As They Were Delivered to Us, 82

Chapter Three

That You May Have Life, 197

Part II

That Together We May Share
in a Common Life, 265

Chapter Four

To the End of the Earth, 267

Chapter Five

Chapter Six

In Imitation of Paul, 406

xx

Contents

Lists

Maps

Tables

Illustrations

Abbreviations

ASV	*The American Standard Version,* based on the *RV,* made in 1901
AV	*The Authorized Version,* English translation of the Bible published in 1611
HDB	*Harvard Divinity Bulletin*
HTR	*Harvard Theological Review*
IB	*Interpreter's Bible*
ICC	*International Critical Commentary*
IDB	*Interpreter's Dictionary of the Bible*
JAAR	*Journal of the American Academy of Religion*
JBL	*Journal of Biblical Literature*
JBR	*Journal of Bible and Religion*
JJS	*Journal of Jewish Studies*
JR	*Journal of Religion*
JTS	*Journal of Theological Studies*
MNTC	*Moffatt's New Testament Commentary*
RSV	*The Revised Standard Version,* based on the *RV* and *ASV,* in 1946 and 1952
RV	*The English Revised Version,* a revision of the *AV* made in 1881

Introduction

Although it is little more than one fourth the length, and written during a much briefer period of time, the New Testament, like the Old Testament, is a collection of writings of several literary types which grew out of the life, experiences, and needs of a community of faith. This community, furthermore, grew up within the larger context of Judaism and, therefore, claimed the same books of the Law, Prophets, and Writings for its Sacred Scriptures as did its parent religion. The writings which were to become the New Testament appeared at first, consequently, not as Scripture, but, at the most, as interpretations or midrashim on Scripture. Only gradually did they assume the position of a supplement to Scripture and, finally, the position of a conclusion or climax to Scripture.

The New Testament also has its roots in the same soil as the Old Testament. For the beginnings of the Christian movement in the story of Jesus and his disciples transpired in the same land which saw the coming of Abraham and the long history of Israel from Joshua's invasion to the return from the Babylonian Exile under Persian protection. Yet the world of the New Testament was far different from that which Nehemiah found when he arrived from the Persian capital to begin his reforms. In a sentence, the land we call Palestine, which had in Old Testament times been the western end of an eastern world, was now the eastern end of a western world. The story of how this change came about will help to provide a necessary background for understanding the beginnings of Christian literature.

ALEXANDER AND HIS SUCCESSORS

Alexander's far-flung conquests are familiar to every student of world history: the crossing of the Hellespont and the sweep through Asia Minor in 334; the victorious march down the Mediterranean Coast, bringing Phoenicia, Palestine, and Egypt under his control (333–332 B.C.); the campaign eastward across Mesopotamia, which saw the crushing defeat of the Persian army at Gaugamela (331 B.C.), the capitulation of Babylon, Susa, and Persepolis, and the end of all active resistance to the invincible Greeks. Only after reaching the Indus Valley (326 B.C.), where legend has it that he wept for want of more worlds to conquer, did Alexander finally

1

Silver tetradrachma of Alexander the Great. Obverse, head of the god Heracles; reverse, Zeus on his throne. This was one of the coins minted for the new Hellenistic world following the conquests of Alexander. (Courtesy of the Money Museum, National Bank of Detroit.)

turn again westward. His premature death in Babylon at thirty-three years of age (323 B.C.) cut short his illustrious and unparalleled career.

So great was Alexander's devotion to Greek culture, that each new territory he entered became at once a ripe field for Hellenization—the dissemination of Greek ideals, learning, dress, and customs. Greek festivals

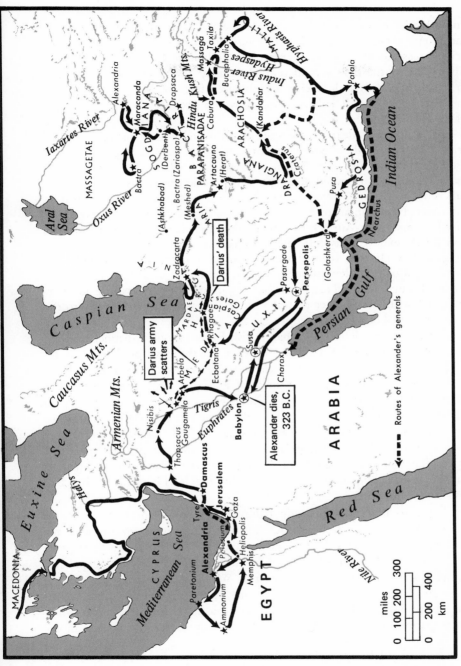

The conquests of Alexander the Great. (Adapted with permission of The Macmillan Company from *Macmillan Bible Atlas* by Y. Aharoni and Michael Avi-Yonah. Copyright © 1968 Carta, Jerusalem. © Copyright 1964 by Carta, Jerusalem. © Copyright 1966 by Carta, Jerusalem.)

3

and athletic contests became common, and the Greek language was made the lingua franca of the realm. The Egyptian city of Alexandria, in particular, was founded as a showplace of Hellenistic learning and culture. There, during the next several centuries, many Jews would be introduced to Hellenistic ideas and develop a Hellenized form of Judaism; there, too, the Greek-speaking Jewish community would produce the Greek version of the Old Testament.

At Alexander's death, his empire was divided among his several generals. The two of these whose dynasties were to have lasting importance for Palestinian affairs were Ptolemy (Lagi) and Seleucus (I). The Ptolemaic dynasty was centered in Egypt, with Alexandria as its capital. For a full century, from 301 to 198 B.C., the Ptolemies held a firm grip upon the coveted Palestinian corridor. Seleucid control extended over Syria and Mesopotamia, with Antioch as capital. Our knowledge of Jewish fortunes under Ptolemaic rule is extremely limited, but such evidence as there is suggests few changes from the conditions that prevailed throughout the Persian period.[1] Hellenization doubtless continued in Palestine, as elsewhere throughout the Near East, but apparently there was little interference in Jewish affairs other than the monetary exactions and loyalty to the crown required of a subject people.

It was under Seleucid rule that Jewish fortunes took a distinct turn for the worse. This did not happen, however, in the days of Antiochus III (223–187 B.C.), the strong Seleucid king whose victory over Ptolemy V in 198 B.C. gave the Seleucids control of Palestine. The crisis came rather in the reign of his younger son, Antiochus IV (175–163 B.C.), who assumed the name "Epiphanes" ("the manifest [God]"). Antiochus Epiphanes is depicted in Jewish writings[2] as the most infamous tyrant ever to rule over the Jewish people. Whether or not one accepts that verdict at face value, there can be no doubt that he displayed an utter lack of feeling for the Jewish religion and made inevitable the Jewish revolt of 167 B.C. and succeeding years.

Eager to unify his unsteady realm and thereby offset the growing threat posed by Rome, Antiochus surpassed Alexander in his zeal for cultural solidarity—based, of course, on Greek models. Among those Jews for whom Greek culture held a strong attraction, his Hellenizing policies initially met with little or no resistance. Within these circles the gymnasium and Greek dress were popular; some Jewish males even submitted to surgery to disguise their circumcision and thus avoid embarrassment when participating in sports in the nude.[3] Membership in the gymnasium, more-

---

1. John Bright, *A History of Israel,* (London: SCM Press, 1962), pp. 397–399.
2. I and II Maccabees, and Josephus, *Antiquities of the Jews.*
3. I Maccabees 1:14–15.

Coin of Antiochus IV (Epiphanes). (The American Numismatic Society.)

over, involved a recognition of the Greek gods who were its patrons.[4]
When Antiochus replaced the legitimate high priest Onias with the latter's Hellenizing brother Jason, he gained an active supporter for his
policies. After three years, however, Jason was supplanted by yet another

4. John Bright, *A History of Israel*, p. 404.

Hellenizer named Menelaus, who was able to outbid Jason for the office. Antiochus, hard-pressed for funds, had the cooperation of Menelaus in his act of looting the temple.

Jews faithful to the ways of their fathers found these practices appalling, and with good reason. In all fairness to Antiochus, however, he probably failed to understand the uncompromising character of Jewish monotheism, its inability to pay allegiance to other gods or to a king who claimed divine honors. Thus, as Jewish resistance to his policies stiffened, sterner measures were enacted. The final break came in 168 B.C., shortly after Antiochus' humiliating withdrawal from Egypt on Roman orders. Treating Jerusalem as an enemy city, his loosed his army upon it, resulting in widespread death, looting, and destruction. A citadel, called the Acra, was erected there and garrisoned with Syrian troops. Soon after, an edict was issued forbidding the practice of Judaism in all its traditional forms: temple sacrifices, circumcision, Sabbath observance, and possession of sacred books. Jews were compelled to eat foods forbidden by the Torah and to sacrifice at pagan altars erected throughout the land. Failure to comply with any of these demands carried the death penalty. The crowning affront came in December, 168 B.C., when an altar to Zeus was set up in the temple and swine's flesh sacrificed upon it. This act of desecration became known in Jewish circles as the "abomination of desolation."[5]

Open rebellion broke out in 167 B.C., at the village of Modein, near Jerusalem. Mattathias, a local priest of the family known later as the Hasmoneans, flatly refused the order to sacrifice to the Greek gods and struck down the king's officer sent to enforce it. Together with his five stalwart sons, foremost among whom was Judas, Mattathias summoned all who were zealous for the faith to join in a war of resistance to Antiochus. Support came quickly from the group known as the Hasidim ("the pious" or "loyal ones," from the same verb root as *hased,* "steadfast love"), the probable forerunners of the later Pharisees and Essenes. Although Mattathias died shortly after the incident at Modein, leadership was ably borne by Judas, whose nickname "Maccabeus" (probably "Hammerer") became synonymous with the revolt. Pressing their skill in guerilla tactics and abetted by Antiochus' occupation with affairs in the East, the Maccabeans administered successive defeats to the forces dispatched by the king. In December, 164 B.C., three years to the month after the Temple's profanation, Judas entered Jerusalem, fortified and garrisoned the city, and cleansed and rededicated the Temple—the event celebrated ever since in the Feast of Hanukkah.

With the restoration of the Temple and the death of Antiochus the following year, much of the support for the Maccabees among the Hasidim

5. Dan. 9:27; 11:31; 12:11; I Macc. 1:54.

Bronze coin minted by the Jewish revolutionaries ca. A.D. 67–68. The obverse bears the date and an amphora; the reverse contains the vine branch and leaf. (Courtesy of the Money Museum, National Bank of Detroit.)

began to melt away. About this time, furthermore, the Hasidim themselves, by name at least, disappeared from history. So while, as the military fortification near the Temple continually reminded them, the danger of Syrian interference remained, the sons of Mattathias found themselves continuing the campaign with only a fraction of their original army (I Macc. 9:5). With the death of Judas at Elasa (161 B.C.) the original phase of the revolt was over. The contest between Judea and Syria which had raged for seven years had reached a standoff. The elusive troops of the Maccabees at home among the wadys of the Judean hills were impossible to crush; the detested citadel hard by the Temple and the ring of fortified cities set up by the Syrians (I Macc. 9:50–53), on the other hand, stood between Judea and her coveted independence. In the meantime Judas had taken one action which forebode the end of the Jewish independence for which he fought. Shortly before the fatal battle of Elasa Judas had sent a delegation to Rome to conclude a treaty with this burgeoning power in the West (I Macc. 8:17–32). He could not know that before a century had passed Rome would succeed where Syria had failed and bring Judea under subjugation and eventual destruction.

THE HASMONEAN DYNASTY

In the subsequent development three important factors were at work: (1) From the death of Antiochus IV the Seleucid throne was constantly under dispute by rival pretenders, and consequently the once formidable power of the Syrian kingdom declined until it, along with Judea, lost its independence altogether and its territory was annexed as a Roman province. (2) The Hellenism which had been largely responsible for the conflict with Syria from the outset, emerging once more in the person of the high priest Alcimus, showed itself to be a force to be reckoned with in Israel. (3) The Maccabean leaders themselves began to find the fresh taste of power to their liking, and their interests began to shift from the freedom from the Syrian invaders to the establishment of what became known from Hasmon, Mattathias' ancestral name, as the Hasmonean dynasty.

The first of these factors, the instability of the Syrian government, allowed the Jewish forces under Jonathan, Judas' younger brother, to survive the defeat in which Judas had been killed, and later under Simon, the last surviving son of Mattathias after the treacherous elimination of Jonathan (I Macc, 12:39–13:24), to overthrow the remaining Syrian fortifications and proclaim at last (143–142 B.C.) the long-coveted Jewish independence (I Macc. 13:41–53). Because of the second factor Jonathan had found it necessary to assume the vestments of the high priest, ironically under the authority of a pagan contender for the Syrian throne (I Macc. 10:1–21), and thus had established the Hasmonean high priesthood, which subsequently served as an effective basis for the power of that dynasty. An early result of the third factor was the intrigue which accomplished the death of Simon and all his sons except John Hyrcanus (usually known as Hyrcanus I to distinguish him from the later high priest) at the hands of his ambitious son-in-law Ptolemy (I Macc. 16:11–

The Hasmonean kingdom. (Adapted with permission of The Macmillan Company from *Macmillan Bible Atlas* by Y. Aharoni and Michael Avi-Yonah. Copyright © 1968 Carta, Jerusalem. © Copyright 1964 by Carta, Jerusalem. © Copyright 1966 by Carta, Jerusalem.)

24). John who fortunately had been occupied elsewhere at the time, warned by the news of the treachery, entered Jerusalem and assumed his father's leadership.

Although, according to Josephus the accoutrements of royalty did not appear until the reign of his son Aristobulus, John Hyrcanus became for all practical purposes the first king to reign in Jersualem since the fall of Zedekiah in 586 B.C.[6] There is no need to recite here in detail the checkered history of the Hasmonean kings, in whom the noble patriotism and valor of Judas Maccabeus degenerated into political ambition and murderous intrigue. Three items of importance, however, should be noted concerning this period (143–63 B.C.). First, John Hyrcanus I deepened Israel's fateful involvement with Rome by renewing the treaty which Judas Maccabeus had made with the Roman Senate.[7] Second, he began a program of expansion which, by the destruction of the temple on Mount Gerizim in the course of his Samaritan campaign, intensified the age-old hostilities between the Jews and the Samaritans, and, by the forcible proselyting of the Idumeans during his southern campaign, set the stage for the rise of Antipater and the Herodian kings. Third, it is during his rule, in connection with his transfer of loyalties from them to the Sadducees, that we first hear of the Pharisees and, except for the contention between the earlier Hellenizers and the loyal Hasidim, the appearance of competing parties within Judaism.

The Pharisees Quite possibly the Pharisees, whose name apparently derives from the Hebrew word *perisha,* meaning "separate" or "separated ones," developed as a movement from the Hasidim, who withdrew from Judas Maccabeus after the restoration of the Temple. Because of their influence in shaping the Rabbinic Judaism which survived the Fall of Jerusalem in A.D. 70, the appearance of the Pharisees at this point is important to the later history. On the premise that God's providential care, and therefore Israel's fate, was conditioned upon faithful obedience to his Torah, the Pharisees came to be the leading exponents of its study. They believed that Torah contained all knowledge necessary to right living and, therefore, required only a correct exegesis to discover the appropriate rule for every occasion. While they would insist that they were only making explicit what was already implicit in Torah, this concern to interpret and reapply the Torah to the changing needs of their people made them the progressive party of Judaism. As opposed to the conservative Sadducees, for example, they taught a doctrine of a general resurrection and a corresponding system of rewards and punishments in "the age to come," which links them in several ways with the apocalyptists. Their belief in angels and demons also may reflect the persistence among them of the earlier Persian influence from the post-Exilic period. Although the strained exegesis sometimes required to extract an applicable rule for a new situation and the meticulous legalism for which they were noted sometimes ex-

6. *Antiquities of the Jews,* XIII, 11, 1.
7. Josephus, *Ant.,* XIII, 9, 2.

posed them to ridicule, they took their religious responsibilities very seriously. In spite of the unfortunate prejudice which has made their name a
synonym for hypocrisy, they wielded the most significant religious influence
of their time. Their utter reliance on divine providence gave their political
views a passive turn which distinguished them to a considerable degree
from the apocalyptists and the Qumran community, and which may help
to explain their uneasy relationship to the Maccabean movement. As the
pious interpreters of Torah they represented and enjoyed the sympathy of
the large, pious middle class of Judaism. John Hyrcanus' renunciation of
the Pharisees in favor of the Sadducees, therefore, probably reflects more
than his displeasure with one of their number who had made an unfortunate comment on his ancestry.[8]

The Sadducees   The Sadducees, a name probably derived from Zadok,
Solomon's high priest, were the wealthy minority of the landed gentry who
controlled the Temple priesthood.[9] Basically conservative, they had little
interest in adding interpretations to Torah. Hence they rejected the growing body of tradition known as "oral Torah." They rejected also all belief
in angelic beings and the resurrection. Divine retribution was for them
confined to this life. Although they enjoyed little support among the
common people and were forced by popular opinion to follow the direction of the Pharisees in performance of the Temple rituals, their position
gave them considerable power. In the later Roman period, as we shall see,
this power placed them in an advantageous position with respect to the
Roman government—a position which was to increase popular animosity
toward them. In embracing the Sadducees Hyrcanus was turning his back
on the popular support to which the earlier Maccabean movement had
owed so much for its success. What had begun as a popular movement
among the pious common people had now become the ruling aristocracy.

Hyrcanus' change of loyalties, however, had serious consequences.
After the brief and unimportant reign of John Hyrcanus' eldest son
Aristobulus, a younger son, Alexander Jannaeus, came to the throne to
continue his father's policies. After being bombarded with citrus fruit
while presiding at the altar and being subjected to a subsequent revolt
that nearly succeeded, both of which were instigated by the disaffected
Pharisees, he crucified some eight hundred of them and hacked their wives
and children before their eyes.[10] The mounting pressure against him,
abetted by the Pharisees, became so great that on his deathbed he willed
his kingdom to his wife Alexandra with the advice that she make peace
with them lest they become her downfall. It is possible that at this time,

8. See Josephus, *Ant.,* XIII, 10.
9. See J. King West, *Introduction to the Old Testament,* (New York: The Macmillan
   Company, 1971), p. 337.
10. Josephus, *Ant.,* XIII, 13–14.

as some scholars believe, a group of pious Jews, usually identified with the Essenes, withdrew to Qumran above the shores of the Dead Sea to form a monastic community whose library was the subject of the dramatic discoveries of 1947 and succeeding years. Although a few scholars still question this identification of the Qumran community with the Essene sect known to us from Josephus, Philo, and a brief mention in Pliny's *Natural History,* its probabilities are sufficient to warrant a brief sketch here of the sect and its literature.

The Qumran Sect   The Dead Sea Scrolls, as the Qumran library has come to be known, provides vivid evidence of the radical eschatology that flourished within some Jewish groups of this period.[11] From the sect's beginnings until the destruction of its desert headquarters by Vespasian's armies in A.D. 68, its members lived in daily expectation of the great apocalyptic battle described in detail in one of their writings, "The War of the Sons of Light Against the Sons of Darkness."[12] Believing themselves to be God's righteous "volunteers," living under instructions laid down by their "right teacher" (or Teacher of Righteousness) and set forth in a Manual of Discipline, they were assured that through their efforts an atonement was being made for the apostate land and a ready army kept on stand-by for God's awaited signal.

In contrast to the Zealot groups that arose during the Roman period, the Qumran Essenes instigated no nationalistic uprisings. Rather, consistent with their eschatological orientation, the warfare for which they prepared awaited that precise and predestined moment when God himself and his hosts of angels would intervene decisively on behalf of the righteous cause. Until then, the group's preparedness consisted of a constant study of Torah, the copying and maintenance of their sacred books, and a strict regimen of purificatory baths, ritual meals, and prayers. Demanding perfection of conduct, enforced by rigorously defined penalties for offenses, the community's ethical stringency appears to have exceeded that of the Pharisees.

The sect's prolific literary activity produced a collection of commentaries on Old Testament books, one of which, "The Habakkuk Commentary," describes in cryptic terms the hostilities which led to the

11. Cf. Krister Stendahl's *Introduction to The Scrolls and The New Testament* (New York: Harper & Brothers, 1957), and Frank Cross, *The Ancient Library of Qumran and Modern Biblical Studies* (Garden City, N.Y.: Doubleday and Company, 1958), ch. 5.
12. English translations of the best-known Scroll texts are available in Millar Burrows, *The Dead Sea Scrolls* (New York: Viking Press, 1955) and Millar Burrows, *More Light on the Dead Sea Scrolls* (New York: Viking Press, 1958); Geza Vermes, *The Dead Sea Scrolls in English* (Baltimore: Penguin Books, 1962); and A. Dupont-Sommer, *The Essene Writings from Qumran* (Oxford: Basil Blackwell, 1961; New York: World [Meridian], 1962).

group's separation from Jerusalem Jewry. Unfortunately, the veiled language and the poorly preserved state of the text prevents certainty concerning the identification of such intriguing figures as "the right teacher," who is persecuted by a "wicked priest" and his followers. Hyrcanus, Aristobulus, Jannaeus, and a host of other historical persons have been cast in the role of the "wicked priest" by the flood of conflicting theories developed since the scroll discoveries. Particularly vexing is the question of whether the teacher—himself a priest and presumably the sect's founder—died as a martyr and thereby became a redeemer figure for the group. Theories that appeared shortly after the publication of the Scrolls, so characterizing the teacher and identifying him as Qumran's Messiah, have long since been revealed as hasty and inconclusive, based as they were on conjectured reconstructions of crucial textual lacunae. It is apparent, however, that the sectarians' eschatology included the expectation of a messiah—in fact, two messiahs, one priestly and the other a prince —who would officiate at the community's future eschatological banquet.

Some of the Qumran literature may represent the work of the teacher himself, though this, too, is open to question. The Manual of Discipline speaks authoritatively not only in the sphere of community regulations, but as to the theological dogmas to which the sect subscribed. These included a metaphysical dualism, involving an Angel of Light and a Prince of Darkness, reminiscent of the patterns familiar in Iranian religions. A collection of Thanksgiving Psalms (Hodayoth), similar to though scarcely the equal of the Old Testament Psalter, bear the stamp of a sensitive poet (or poets), acutely conscious of man's natural perversity and his corresponding dependence upon God's righteousness and forgiveness. Employing phrases strikingly like those of St. Paul, the Qumran Hymns attest the coexistence within this stream of intertestamental Judaism of a radical eschatological ethic and a clear-cut theology of grace.

UNDER ROMAN OCCUPATION

With Alexandra's death the Hasmonean throne became the object of contention between her two sons, John Hyrcanus II and Aristobulus. In this struggle two new figures emerged. The first was the native governor of Idumea, Antipater. Since he along with his countrymen had been forcibly proselyted to Judaism, he decided by placing his influence behind John Hyrcanus, the weaker and more pliable of the brothers, to gain for himself the real control of Palestine. As a result of his influence, Hyrcanus with assistance from the Arabian king Aretas began to make progress against Aristobulus. At this point both brothers appealed to the Roman commander Pompey who at that time was in the process of organizing the newly subdued kingdom of Syria into a Roman province. Pompey, deciding in favor of John Hyrcanus II, marched to Judea, took Jerusalem, and left him in charge as high priest and "ethnarch" (roughly equivalent to "prince"); whereas Antipater becoming his advisor was enabled to cultivate invaluable influence with Rome. Judea's brief period of independence was over. Finally freed from Greek (Syrian) domination in 143 B.C., this unhappy land was now, in 63 B.C., under the control of the burgeoning Empire of Rome.

By the time of the assassination of Antipater in 44 B.C., vast changes had taken place in the Mediterranean world. Only a few months earlier the assassination of Julius Caesar had ended the famous First Triumvirate, which itself had marked the end of the old senatorial republic, and the kaleidoscopic series of events was now in full motion toward the new Augustan Age. Herod, Antipater's famous son, had been serving under his father as governor of Galilee and had managed by an incredible series of political juggling acts—a talent he inherited from his father—to stay on the side of the winner until he had obtained an appointment from Anthony and Octavian (later Augustus Caesar) as "King of the Jews." After two unsuccessful attempts he managed at the head of Roman legions to reenter Judea from which he had been driven by Antigonus, the son of Aristobulus, who was bent on avenging his father's loss to John Hyrcanus. After a bloody siege which nearly ruined his capital, Herod found himself established on the throne in Jerusalem in 38 B.C. Antigonus was beheaded and John Hyrcanus II, having been mutilated in order to render him eligible to continue as the high priest, was finally mercilessly executed. With the defeat of Anthony at Actium and his reconfirmation by Augustus, Herod's power and position were secure.

In spite of the stability Herod brought to Palestine and his strenuous efforts to ingratiate himself with them, the faithful of Judaism continued hostile to him to the end. Even though he was a product of the proselyting campaign of John Hyrcanus I, they regarded him still as an Edomite and, therefore, far from the scion of David which pious expectations had taught them to await. More serious was the fact that he was a client king whose reign, however effective, represented the subjugation of Israel to a pagan foreign power. Finally, of course, Herod's vast building program, including pagan temples and Hellenistic gymnasia, clearly placed him among the hated Hellenizers who had played so malevolent a role in Israel's troubles during the preceding century. It is not surprising, therefore, that his one great contribution to Judaism, the rebuilding of the Temple, should be received with such mixed feelings.

More splendid and costly even than the original Temple built by Solomon, and built with the utmost attention to the scruples of Jewish laws regarding the protection of the sacred precincts from foreign contamination, Herod's Temple was rejected completely by the Qumran sect and regarded with such half-hearted devotion by the Pharisees that it helped pave the way for the survival after its destruction of the rabbinic Judaism of the synagogue which has come to be known as "normative Judaism." It is a tragic irony that, within a decade after the last construction on the Temple precincts was complete, this splendid gift of a Roman client king was destroyed by the Roman legions.

The Fourth Philosophy The animosity toward Herod stimulated the growth of a movement which after his death became a factor of fatal importance in the history of Palestine. With the dream of restoring the Davidic monarchy rekindled by the Maccabean victories and fanned into flame by Herod's reign, these men came to believe that by throwing off the Roman yoke and placing on Herod's throne the true messianic scion of David they could realize the golden age, Israel's destiny of ancient promise. Although Josephus regarded them as basically akin to the Pharisees in belief and practice, their real interests seem to have been much more political and mundane.[13] Because of their increasingly violent revolutionary activities, these men, whom Josephus calls "the Fourth Philosophy," came later to be known as Zealots or sicarii (dagger men).[14] The series of revolutions they fomented brought on the contest with Roman might that ended in the fall of Jerusalem in A.D. 70.

Following Herod's death in 4 B.C. and as a result of his will, his territory was divided among his three sons who ruled, in consequence, as tetrarchs (Greek: *tetrarches,* lit. ruler of a fourth of a country, hence a minor prince). Philip was given a heterogeneous region northeast of the Sea of Galilee which became known as the territory of Caesarea Philippi, its capital city; Herod Antipas was given Galilee and Perea; and Archelaus received Samaria, Judea, and Idumea. Ten years later constant agitation and complaints, together with his frantic misrule, accomplished Archelaus' downfall. His territory was placed in the hands of procurators, i.e., Roman military governors of equestrian rank (knights). In connection with the accession of Coponius the first of these, Quarinius, the governor of Syria—the "eyes and ears of the Emperor" in the East—was ordered to take a census of the territory. The ancient Hebrew aversion to "numbering the people" (cf. II Sam. 24) along with rising indignation over this reminder of Roman occupation and taxation combined to trigger a rebellion led by a Galilean patriot named Judas. His rebellion was soon crushed but his cause was far from forgotten.[15]

Some years later Antipas' brother-in-law Agrippa contrived by a piece

13. *Wars,* II, 8, 1; IV, 3, 9. For a good study of the development of this party see W. R. Farmer, *Maccabees, Zealots and Josephus* (New York: Columbia University Press, 1956), esp. ch. VIII, pp. 175–204.

14. See *Wars,* II, 8, 1; Iv, 3, 9.

15. Josephus, *Ant.,* XVIII, 1, 1.

of chicanery to unseat Antipas and, thanks to Claudius, to regain the territory and title of king once held by Herod the Great (A.D. 41–44). Although more successful than Herod in gaining the favor of the Jews, Antipas managed to arouse such suspicion in his Roman overlords that, but for his unexpected death after only three years of rule, he might well have followed Antipas into banishment. Following his death Judea was returned to the supervision of procurators, and eventually, under Nero, his son Agrippa II became ruler of parts of Galilee and Perea.

The appearance, shortly after Agrippa's death, of two more rebels with messianic pretentions indicates something of the deteriorating political situation in Jerusalem.[16] The great revolt (A.D. 66–70), consequently, which was brought on by the egregious misrule of Florus, the last of the procurators, and aggravated by no fewer than three rival rebel leaders, was virtually inevitable. As the war raged beyond the control of local Roman authorities, Nero dispatched his star commander Vespasian to end it. Having been proclaimed Emperor to succeed Nero (following, of course, the three unsuccessful pretenders in the "year of four Emperors"), he left the battle in the hands of his son Titus. In a little more than a year Titus was victorious, the city was demolished, the Temple destroyed, and he was on his way back to Rome, where the memorial of his victory celebration the following year is still preserved on his Triumphal Arch.[17]

In the course of the siege of Jerusalem, a rabbi by the name of Johanan ben Zakkai contrived to escape the city by having himself carried through the gate in a coffin. Having obtained permission from Titus, he established a Sanhedrin (council) at Jamnia (Jabneh) which in time established Phariseeism as the norm for Judaism. From this Sanhedrin came the finally fixed form of the Hebrew Canon. The Mishnah, the Talmuds, and the entire production of the Tannaim rabbis, furthermore, were the result of the influence of Johanan's community of scholars.

In the meantime, the turbulent political fortunes of Palestine under the Roman overlords stimulated the revival of apocalyptic literature. As such writings as Daniel and Enoch appeared in the time of the Seleucid tyrants, so now works like the assumption of Moses, only part of which is still extant, IV Esdras, and the Apocalypse of Baruch began to appear. At the same time, the more militant messianism of the rebel leaders continued to smoulder beneath the surface until, in response to Roman strictures against circumcision and Hadrian's decision to rebuild Jerusalem as a pagan city named Aelia Capitolina, it burst into flame once more in the ill-starred rebellion of Bar Cochba (Bar Kozibah) in A.D. 132–135. When the final defeat of his armies and his treacherous assassination

16. Josephus, *Ant.*, XX, 5 and 8; *Wars*, II, 13.
17. The whole tragic story is the subject of Josephus' work, *The Wars of the Jews*.

Coin of Vespasian bearing his likeness and celebrating the capture of Judea by Titus in A.D. 70. (Courtesy of the Money Museum, National Bank of Detroit.)

brought the rebellion to an end, the land of Israel, now ironically renamed Palestine after the ancient Philistines, was in the hands of gentiles; and the Jews scattered throughout the world became a people without a homeland save "the Portable Fatherland of the Torah."

THE BEGINNING OF CHRISTIANITY AND THE NEW TESTAMENT

The Christian story begins during the latter half of the reign of Herod Antipas with the baptism of Jesus by a wilderness prophet named John.

Scene on the Arch of Titus depicting Roman soldiers carrying away the holy objects, including the menorah or seven-branch lampstand, from the Temple. This triumphal arch was erected in the Roman Forum to celebrate Titus' victory over Jerusalem. (Courtesy of Alinari-Art Reference Bureau.)

When, following the imprisonment of John, Jesus came into Galilee proclaiming a call to repentance in preparation for the approaching Kingdom of God and gathering about him a community of disciples, he did so in the context of Israel's age-old hopes and beliefs. Back of that proclamation was God's ancient promise to Abraham eschatologically understood and shaped by the expectations which II Isaiah had stirred in the hearts of the exiles returning from Babylon. Although it was variously interpreted with a range of ideas running all the way from the cataclysmic judgment and renovation of the world expected by the apocalyptists to the militaristic triumphalism modeled on the monarchy of David and inspired by the success of the Maccabean revolt, these expectations received new impetus as the Jews began more and more to chafe under the Roman occupation of their land (cf. Lk. 3:15).[18]

After the Passion and Resurrection of Jesus, the community of his followers continued the proclamation in a new dimension. In his Resur-

18. For a good summary of the historical, geographical, and economic factors in first century Palestine see Frederic R. Crownfield, *A Historical Approach to the New Testament* (New York: Harper & Brothers, 1960), pp. 82–103.

rection they saw the beginning of the promised eschatological events—his Resurrection was, proleptically, the beginning of the resurrection of God's people. The community understood itself, therefore, in terms of I Isaiah's prophecy as the nucleus of the righteous remnant to whom the Kingdom would come. It was the Church, the *Ecclesia* (Greek, meaning the called-out ones), the New Israel whose task was to proclaim the gospel around the world before the eschaton arrived (Mk. 13:10). Jesus as the Messiah, the eschatological man, was the fulfillment, and therefore, the meaning of prophecy. As the Church's thinking progressed, this Christological interpretation of Scriptures took on larger dimensions. All Scripture found its final meaning in him (Jn. 5:39–47); he was the embodiment of Israel's true hope and destiny.

Three factors conspired to turn the Church in an unexpected direction. First was the increasing opposition to the movement which began with the Temple officials, but for several reasons spread to the synagogues until before the end of the first century the Church and Synagogue were separated into bitter opponents. Each of them charged the other with apostasy, and the Church now claimed to be not only the New Israel but exclusively the True Israel. Second was the development of the gentile mission. Following the inspiration of the universalism of II Isaiah the Church developed the belief, which it found expressed in several places in the later writings of Israel's Scriptures, that the eschaton would bring the nations to obedience to Israel's God. The result was that the mission progressed with so much greater success among the gentiles that they came to dominate it. In the third place, the eschaton, which, following the Resurrection, the original disciples had expected almost momentarily, began to recede into the future, requiring new adjustments in the Church's life and theology.

One conclusion which the Church drew from this delay was a larger understanding of its world mission. In the course of that mission literary developments began to appear which were to eventuate in the New Testament. There were two sides to these developments. On the one side, the memorabilia of Jesus, which from the outset played an important role in the preaching, teaching, and worship of the Church, came to be collected and written down in a process that, as we shall see, eventually produced the four Gospels.

In the meantime Paul, "the Apostle to the Gentiles," began writing letters to meet the various needs of his scattered churches. His instructions that these letters be read in the respective churches apparently were carried further than their original intent. Before the end of the first century his letters had been collected and circulated among the churches generally. Thus the Church found itself with two kinds of material supplementing the Law and the Prophets which were, of course, still its acknowledged Bible. As the breach between the Church and Synagogue widened, and as the Church developed its understanding of Jesus to be the summation and embodiment of all the meaning and institutions of Israel, these materials became more and more the equivalent of Scriptures.

When, in the middle of the second century, the heretic Marcion attempted to purge the Church of its Hebraic heritage in favor of gnosticism, he chose an attenuated version of Luke's Gospel and ten letters of Paul to replace the Law and the Prophets as the Scripture for his churches. In doing so he forced the Church to reconsider the place of its writings with respect to the Scriptures. The result was that the four Gospels and Paul's letters became recognized as the Scriptures of the "New Covenant" (Testament) as the climax, summation, and conclusion to those of the Old Covenant. There were by this time, of course, other documents to be considered. Luke's second volume, the Acts of the Apostles, for example, did not apparently share at first the acceptance accorded his Gospel. By A.D. 200 the Letter to Philemon and the Pastoral Epistles were still kept outside the Canon because they were regarded as merely personal letters. The story of these and the remaining books, sometimes called the Deuterocanon of the New Testament, we shall consider in more detail later. For now it is important to note that the two-part shape of the New Testament was by this time determined.

As a part of its legacy from Judaism the Church had been from the beginning accustomed to a two-part Canon which found expression in the Torah (or Seder) and the Haftarah (or Prophet) lessons in the synagogue. With the Old Testament as its model, along with the two kinds of material it had in hand, it was inevitable that the Church should organize its new Scriptures in the same way. Thus we find in the early liturgy four lessons: The Law, the Prophets, the Epistle, and the Gospel. Later the first two were reduced to one lesson from the Old Testament and finally were dropped in favor of a two-lesson schedule consisting in the Epistle and Gospel with the Old Testament appearing only occasionally in place of the Epistle. The current trend toward increasing Old Testament readings in Christian liturgies is, therefore, a movement toward the ancient practice.

The similarities between the Canonical structures of the two Testaments, however, go farther. As the Gospel stands at the head of the New Testament in both position and importance in a way comparable with the Torah in the Old Testament, and Paul's letters occupy a position and relationship to the Gospels analogous to the Latter Prophets, so the Book of Acts, which finally found a place between the Gospels and "the Apostle," functions as an historical background and introduction for the Epistles in much the same way as the historical books, Joshua, Judges, Samuel, Kings—the Former Prophets—link the Torah with the Latter

Prophets. The comparison can be carried farther. The Catholic Epistles at the end of the New Testament and the third division of the Hebrew Canon, the Writings, stand last in position and relatively late in time both in writing and canonization. There is, as we shall see, a pronounced similarity between two of these Epistles and the Wisdom Literature in the Old Testament Writings. Each of the Testaments also includes an apocalypse, Daniel and Revelation, in this third level. It may not be carrying the analogy too far to compare Paul's Letters in the relationship to the Deutero-Pauline Epistles, the Pastorals and Ephesians(?), and Hebrews with the Major and Minor Prophets. It is interesting also to note the contrast between the Tetrateuch and Deuteronomy in comparison with that between the Synoptics and John.[19] The chart on page 22 will illustrate the striking similarities in the structure of the Two Testaments.

Undoubtedly, some of these similarities are incidental, perhaps we should say accidental. Others, especially the two-part structure, may reflect the almost unconscious influence of the Old Testament. The early Christians were so saturated with the Scriptures, as the many quotations, allusions, and the like within the New Testament show, that their very diction, their patterns, motifs, and style were colored thereby. If this influence can be observed in detail in individual passages, we must expect to see its effect in the shape of the whole literature. In a deeper sense, nevertheless, the shape of both Testaments was made almost inevitable by the common elements in their making. Given the ethical monotheism, the faith in God's saving activity in history, the concept of the covenant which constituted the People of God and bound them to him, the story of a central drama and teaching followed by a history and by prophetic exhortations, interpretations, and attempts to interpret the ultimate dimensions of the destiny of that People is a natural, if not inevitable, pattern for the literature of that People to take.

From another standpoint it will be worthwhile to note that the twenty-seven books of the New Testament include five types of material. The Gospel is, of course, a literary form which originated with the Christian movement. A second type is represented by Paul's letters, which although not written to individuals but to churches were, nevertheless, real letters. A third type of material, popular in antiquity, was a result of the influence of Paul's letters. The epistle, as distinguished from the genuine letter, is a literary tract or treatise using the letter form as a literary device. The Pastorals and the Catholic Epistles are epistles in this sense. There are three documents in the New Testament which must be classed as books in the ancient sense of the word. Luke's Book of

19. See pp. 43–44.

Comparison of the Canonical Structures of the Old and New Testaments

	Seder		**Haftarah**	
OLD TESTAMENT	Torah (Tetrateuch-Deuteronomy)	Former Prophets	Latter Prophets (Major and Minor Prophets)	Writings (and Apocalypse of Daniel) (Deuterocanon)
	Gospel		**Epistle**	
NEW TESTAMENT	The Gospels (Synoptics and John)	Acts	Pauline Epistles (Letters and Deutero-Pauline Epistles)	Catholics (and Apocalypse of John)

22

Acts, for example, reflects the form of Greek history writing. Hebrews and I John also lack the devices of the epistle and therefore must simply be called books. Finally, there is the Apocalypse which, like the Gospel, is a peculiar kind of literature whose content gives it a form of its own. We shall examine these literary characteristics in greater detail in the course of our study.

Selected Readings

Here, and at the end of each of the following chapters, the reader is provided with a short classified bibliography for further study in the areas covered therein, and there is in the Appendix a general bibliography of useful books applying to the New Testament as a whole. Compiling reading lists is not easy. To be useful a reading list must be reasonably short and, therefore, highly selective. It must reckon with the wide variety of holdings in those libraries to which various readers have access. Subjective judgments enter into the selection to no small degree, so that care must be taken to make the lists balanced. The most troublesome difficulty is the very vastness of the literature. Surely no one who has undertaken to compile such a list has finished without another list of books he wishes he could have included, or without a sense of the arbitrariness involved in many of his choices.

On the other side of the ledger, many of the books included in these lists contain bibliographies of their own. Along with the footnotes these lists can beckon the willing reader along a virtually unending road of literature on Biblical studies. There are, furthermore, books and journals of bibliographical references and lists such as Bruce M. Metzger, *New Testament Tools and Studies,* vols. 1, 6, and 7 (Leiden: Brill, 1960–66; Grand Rapids, Mich.: Wm. B. Eerdmans Publishing Company), the journal, *New Testament Abstracts,* Weston College School of Theology, Cambridge, Mass., and the *Quarterly Check-List of Biblical Studies,* of the American Bibliographic Service, Darien, Conn. There is even a bibliography of bibliographies: J. C. Hurd, Jr., *A Bibliography of New Testament Bibliographies* (New York: Seabury Press, 1966)! The lists herein included contain some of the more important classical studies along with more recent works which present the clearest statements of developments in the field and exemplify the divergent trends in current scholarship. Specific volumes from the standard sets of commentaries are cited only when they are of special importance or are particularly well known.

THE JEWISH BACKGROUND TO THE NEW TESTAMENT

Burrows, Millar, *The Dead Sea Scrolls* (New York: The Viking Press, 1955).

————, *More Light on the Dead Sea Scrolls* (New York: The Viking Press, 1958).

Daniel-Rops, Henri, *Daily Life in the Time of Jesus,* tr. Patrick O'Brian (New York: New American Library of World Literature, 1962).

Enslin, Morton Scott, *Christian Beginnings,* Part I (New York: Harper & Row, 1938).

Finkelstein, Louis, *The Pharisees,* 2 vols. (Philadelphia, The Jewish Publication Society of America, 1962).

Herford, R. Travers, *The Pharisees* (Boston: Beacon Press, 1962).

Moore, George Foot, *Judaism,* 3 vols. (Cambridge: Harvard University Press, 1930).

Part I

This Life Was Made Visible

This life was made visible; we have seen it and bear our testimony; we here declare to you the eternal life which dwelt with the Father and was made visible to us.
I John 1:2

Chapter One

To Compile a Narrative
The Study of the Gospels

Inasmuch as many have undertaken to compile a narrative of the things which have been accomplished among us. . . . Luke 1:1.

W hen we open the New Testament between the fourth Gospel and the Book of Acts we discover that we have opened it almost in the middle. Only slightly less (in Nestle's Greek text about 296 pages of a total of 657 pages) than half of the entire New Testament is occupied by the four Gospels, which is one reason that the next three chapters of our study will be occupied with the first four of the twenty-seven books of the New Testament. Following is a table of statistics comparing the four Gospels which will be useful for our study later in the chapter:

Statistics of the Four Gospels

	Mark	John	Matthew	Luke
Gospels in order of length				
Number of chapters	16	21	28	24
Number of verses*	661	860	1068	1149
Average number of verses per chapter	41½	41	38½	48
Number of lines in Nestle's Greek Text	1,524	1,976	2,499	2,668

* Based on the critical texts. The text from which the Authorized Version was made contains 5 verses in Mark, 3 verses in Matthew, 2 verses in Luke, and 13 verses in John which are not supported by the best ancient texts known to us.
Note that Luke is almost twice the length of Mark. The line count is given in order to emphasize the fact that chapters and verses vary in length and comparisons based on

A second reason for giving so much attention to the Gospels is that to understand the remainder of the New Testament requires a knowledge of Jesus which they give us. The New Testament falls, as we have seen, into two distinct parts: the Gospels and the Epistles. The Gospels are the heart of the New Testament upon which the Epistles function as a kind of commentary. This is true not only because the subject matter, the stories of Jesus, involves the center of interest of the whole New Testament, but also because the Gospels grew quite naturally and, we might almost say, inevitably at the center of the life, worship, and work of the nascent Church.

THE GOSPELS AS SCRIPTURE

To understand correctly the growth of the Gospels, we need to remember that the Scripture of the New Testament Church was what we have come to call the Old Testament. In the Law and the Prophets, as the Old Testament was known, the early Christians heard the Gospel. From Moses to Daniel they found Jesus promised or foreshadowed. In Luke's story (4:16–30) of Jesus in the synagogue of Nazareth we may catch a glimpse of the earliest beginnings of the Gospel material:

> And he came to Nazareth, where he had been brought up; and he went to the synagogue, as his custom was, on the sabbath day. And he stood up to read; and there was given to him the book of the prophet Isaiah. He opened the book and found the place where it was written, "The Spirit of the Lord is upon me, because he has anointed me to preach good news to the poor. He has sent me to proclaim release to the captives and recovering of sight to the blind, to set at liberty those who are oppressed, to proclaim the acceptable year of the Lord." And he closed the book, and gave it back to the attendant, and sat down; and the eyes of all in the synagogue were fixed on him. And he began to say to them, "Today this scripture has been fulfilled in your hearing." And all spoke well of him, and wondered at the gracious words which proceeded out of his mouth; and they said, "Is not this Joseph's son?" And he said to them, "Doubtless you will quote to me this proverb, 'Physician, heal yourself; what we have heard you did at Capernaum, do here also in your own country.'" . . . "And there were many lepers in Israel in the time of the prophet Elisha; and none of them was cleansed, but only Naaman the Syrian." When they heard this, all in the synagogue were filled with wrath.

---

them are only approximate. Matthew, for example, has four more chapters than Luke but has 219 fewer lines. Similarly, Mark has two thirds as many chapters as Luke but it is only 190 lines more than half the length of Luke.

> And they rose up and put him out of the city, and led him to
> the brow of the hill on which their city was built, that they
> might throw him down headlong. But passing through the
> midst of them he went away.   Luke 4:16–23; 27–30.

A Jewish follower of "the Way," being invited to read the lessons in
the synagogue service and deliver the homily thereupon would follow
the reading with a picture of Jesus as the ultimate fulfillment of the
meaning of the passage. This homily would include recitation of an
appropriate story of Jesus. As he himself repeatedly demonstrates in his
stories in Acts of the beginnings of the Church, Luke's story was a model
for early Christian practice. Similarly, Jesus' expulsion from the synagogue (vss. 28–30) becomes a harbinger of the later expulsion of the
Church and final break with synagogue.

By this process the Church came very early to see Jesus as the ultimate fulfillment and embodiment of every Jewish institution, indeed, of
Judaism itself. The memorabilia of Jesus became, therefore, the final
interpretation and commentary (the Hebraic terms are *targum* and
midrash) on Scripture. As the break between Church and Synagogue
became wider and more irreparable, this material became more than midrashim or targumim, and the final step of canonizing the Gospels as
Scripture became inevitable. Thus the later practice of the Church in
reading four lessons beginning with the Law and concluding with the
Gospel is significant of more than the mere addition of the new Christian
Scriptures to the older Jewish ones; it expressed the theological relations
among them. The Law and the Gospel are the beginning and end of
divine revelation to which the Prophets and Epistles stand related as
commentary. The Gospels, therefore, represented the position of Jesus as
God's final climactic act for the deliverance of his people. The rituals
which separated and emphasized the reading of the Gospel in the later
liturgies dramatized the significance of this arrangement. So from fragmentary supplements to Scripture they gradually moved to the position as
the climax of Scripture,[1] a position which they enjoy in Christian liturgy
to this day.

The Gospels are a unique literary form. The word means good news.
The Greek word *evangelion,* so translated, originally meant a reward for
the bearer of good news. Our English word, from *godspell,* probably
originally meant God's story, although it is usually taken to be from the
Old English meaning good story.[2] Although they are stories of Jesus and
contain most of the information about Jesus we have, they are not bi-
ographies in either the ancient or modern sense of the word. If they

1. See F. C. Grant, *An Introduction to New Testament Thought* (New York: Abingdon Press, 1950), p. 81.
2. See article "Gospel," *IDB*, Vol. II.

are to be understood as their writers intended, their unique genre must be appreciated and understood. The term "Gospel" seems to have been derived from the opening words of Mark, "The beginning of the gospel of Jesus Christ." Whether Mark intended this phrase as a title of his work is a matter of dispute, but it finally provided the name universally applied to all the writings in this new genre. It may be worth noting that none of the other Gospels uses the term in this way. Matthew begins his work with the words, "The book (*biblos*) of the genealogy of Jesus Christ," which obviously has immediate reference to the genealogical table which follows in verses 2–17. The phrase can, nevertheless, be as appropriately applied to the entire work as Mark's opening phrase can to his. Luke refers to his undertaking (probably including Acts) as "an orderly account" (*kathexas*) and calls the work of his predecessors in this enterprise a "narrative" (*diagasis*). Later, in the Preface to Acts, he refers to his Gospel as a "treatise" (*logos*, lit. word. This term, in Greek literature a reference to a "book" of a larger work, is equivalent to our word volume.). The author of the fourth Gospel calls his work simply a book (*biblos*), 20:30. His opening words, "In the beginning," recall to the reader's mind, however, the same opening of the Torah (Gen. 1:1) and suggest something of what John means by the word "book." Justin Martyr, as late as the middle of the second century, could refer to the Gospels as the "memoirs of the apostles," indicating that the term for these works was still fluid at that time.[3] Clearly, then, the word Gospel as an accepted title for this kind of literature was unknown to the writers of the Gospels themselves.

THE GOSPELS AND THE GROWTH OF THE CHURCH

We must keep in mind throughout this part of our study that the earliest New Testament documents written as we have them are not the Gospels but the letters of Paul. Since, however, the process of reciting, collecting, and recording the stories which resulted in our canonical Gospels began almost immediately after the Passion and Resurrection, and Paul's Letters probably were not collected and placed in circulation until the latter part of the first century, these two parts of the New Testament may be viewed as the result of parallel processes.[4] The difference is that

3. *First Apology*, 66 and 67. On this whole question see *IDB*, Vol. II., article on "Gospels."
4. The dates for the writing of New Testament documents can only be approximated. The estimates on some of them vary widely among the scholars. For our purposes the following will suffice: Paul's letters, the earliest documents in the New Testament, were written between A.D. 48 and A.D. 64. Some would place them all in the decade between A.D. 50 and A.D. 60. The Gospels are usually placed between A.D. 65 and A.D. 110, with Mark the earliest and John the last of the four. The Pastoral Epistles were probably written at the end of the first century or early in the second. He-

the documents themselves were produced as the beginning of the process in the case of Paul's Letters and at the conclusion of it in the Gospels. Neither of these processes, of course, took place in a vacuum. Both are closely related to and grew out of the life and needs of the nascent Church. A brief sketch of the growth of the Church during its first stages therefore will be useful for our study.

In the first period which followed the events of the Passion and Resurrection the community of believers settled in Jerusalem apparently in expectation of the almost immediate return of Christ to end this present evil age and usher in the Kingdom of God. (Cf. Acts 1–12, which is our main source of information for this period.) Their activities revolved around the Upper Room and the Temple.[5] Undoubtedly, too, their activities included weekly attendance at a synagogue. So far as their relation to the larger world, especially to the gentiles, is concerned, they probably conceived it in terms of Zechariah 8:23 and passages in Isaiah such as 60:3, "And nations shall come to your light, and kings to the brightness of your rising." They were in the Holy City, the capital of Judaism and therefore the focal point of the cosmic drama soon to reach its climax in the Judgment and final resurrection to the new age to come. Here on the Temple porches they stood proclaiming the Gospel, calling the world to repentance, and, as evidence of the truth of their message, witnessing to the Resurrection of Jesus.

For this act of proclamation the New Testament uses a Greek word meaning to announce or proclaim, which in its substantive form is *kerygma*. The term refers primarily to the act of proclaiming or speaking, but by inference may be made to include the content of the proclamation. In this latter sense it has been widely adopted as a technical term for the message, hence the distinctive beliefs, of the Primitive Church. C. H. Dodd, who did much to popularize the term, posited an outline of the contents which with only minor variations he believed was the fixed form of this message.[6] Such a stereotyped concept, however, has been seriously questioned and modified in recent years.[7] The suggestion is sometimes made

---

brews and the Catholic Epistles belong to a period perhaps beginning as early as A.D. 65 and extending to the middle of the second century, with Hebrews, James, and I Peter appearing in the early part of this period and II Peter and Jude near its end. Revelation was probably written in the time of Domitian at the end of the first century.

5. For a different understanding of the relationship of the Apostles to the Temple see Ernest Lohemeyer, *The Lord of the Temple*, tr. Stewart Todd (Richmond, Virginia: John Knox Press, 1962), esp. pp. 111ff.
6. See *The Apostolic Preaching* (New York: and London: Harper & Brothers [1936], 1951).
7. See Henry J. Cadbury, "Acts and Eschatology," in W. D. Davies and D. Daube, *The Background of the New Testament and Its Eschatology* (Cambridge: At The

that we should distinguish between the "Gospel" as the proclamation of the coming kingdom and the "kerygma" as the recitation of certain historical facts concerning Jesus as sustaining evidence of the truth of the Gospel.[8] Such a distinction is difficult to support, however, either etymologically or exegetically. The Primitive Church regarded the events of Jesus as part of the eschatological program itself and would hardly distinguish them from the "good news." The two terms are, in fact, approximately synonymous; the word gospel emphasizes the content of the preaching, while kerygma emphasizes the act.

This kerygmatic activity, from the beginning a very central part of the life and meaning of the Church, soon began to cause trouble. Opposition grew into persecution which, following the martyrdom of Stephen, scattered many of the believers in several directions. As these followers of "the Way" "went everywhere preaching" (Acts 8:4 A.V.) they brought an end to this chapter of the Church's story.

Very little information has survived concerning the spread of the Church in the eastern and southern regions. Presumably Luke's story of the conversion of the Ethiopian eunuch (Acts 8:26–39) accounts for the Church in that country. We find believers in Damascus, and hear of converts in Samaria and Caesarea, and of preaching in Phoenicia, and Cyprus, and a reference to men of Cyrene. Acts 11:20–26 provides us a more detailed picture of the founding in Antioch of that most important church. There were Christians in Rome to whom Paul addressed his longest and most important letter. When this Church was founded we cannot guess; it was there before Paul. As meager as these hints are, they nevertheless indicate an astonishing burst of activity. With the conversion of one of the Church's chief persecutors, Saul of Tarsus, these first evangelists gained an ally of the greatest importance. Within little more than two decades, the "Apostle to the Gentiles" had planted the Church in the Roman provinces of Galatia and Asia in eastern and western Asia Minor, in Macedonia and Achaia on the Greek peninsula, and had written letters destined to dominate and shape the second half of the New Testament.

Paul's work almost immediately had one effect which was to have far-reaching consequences. However much effect the experiences with gentile converts in Caesarea (Acts 10) and Antioch (Acts 11:20ff.) may have had on the Church's attitude, it was Paul who made the Church face the issue of the gentile mission. The moment the Church agreed to admit gentile converts without requiring of them the rites of a proselyte to Judaism, its own ultimate break with institutional Judaism became inevitable. If we may judge from the prosecutions in Jerusalem, the break

University Press, 1956), pp. 313–314. Also C. F. Evans, "The Kerygma," *JTS*, VII, 1956, pp. 25–41.
8. Typical of this position is O. A. Piper's article, "Gospel," *IDB*, Vol. II, p. 444.

would likely have occurred sooner or later anyway. As it was, Paul's churches, which came to exert more and more influence in shaping the future of Christianity, had from the start a decidedly gentile character.

Thus in the period following the outbreak of persecution in Jerusalem the Church reversed its understanding of its role in the world. No longer content to seek from the Temple porches to call Israel to repentance and preparation for the coming Kingdom, it became aggressively missionary and sought out believers in the synagogues of the diaspora across the ancient world. Its eschatology was altered accordingly. Instead of waiting patiently in Jerusalem for the return of Christ as the heavenly Messiah, the Church was now spurred to its world mission by its conviction that "the gospel must first be preached to all nations" (Mk. 13:10). Although the mission began with the synagogues it did not end there. The pattern so basic to the structure of Acts, of starting in the synagogue and moving into a gentile setting, is too widely reflected throughout the New Testament to be regarded as a concept peculiar to Luke. Christians therefore found themselves establishing their own synagogues wherever they went—an action which could only serve to widen their breach with organized Judaism.

In the meantime conditions in Jerusalem steadily worsened. Tensions between the Jews and authorities of the Roman occupation were leading inevitably toward the crisis which in A.D. 70 brought about the fall of the city and the destruction of the Temple. In this context the fortunes of the Jerusalem Christians became increasingly precarious. In A.D. 44 near the end of the brief reign of the client king of the Jews, Herod Agrippa I executed one of the apostles, James son of Zebedee—and probably others. Peter was imprisoned but miraculously escaped execution. A few years later, following a riot, Paul's arrest at the Temple site began the chain of events which finally brought him to Rome and to his martyrdom in A.D. 64. Eusebius tells us that, obedient to a revelation, the Christians in Jerusalem fled to Pella in northern Perea, but not before their leader, James the Just, was brutally murdered in the streets.[9] With these events the leadership of Jersualem over the Church was at an end. We hear occasional references later to a conservative Jewish-Christian sect in Palestine known as Ebionites, but the difficulty with which church historians piece together the available fragments of information into a coherent picture indicates that it stood outside the mainstream of Christianity. Although few followers have been won for the view, J. L. Teicher identifies the Qumran sect as an Ebionite community.[10] The Church even more than

9. *Church History* (hereafter: *H.E.*), II, 23.
10. See Millar Burrows *The Dead Sea Scrolls* (New York: The Viking Press, 1955), pp. 295ff., also bibliography, p. 433, listing his articles in *JJS*, 1951–1955. On the Qumran sectaries see above, pp. 12–13.

Judaism was now a part of the world at large without a geographical center in the city of its birth.

The Church fared little better at the hands of the gentiles. The process of separation of the Church from Judaism lost to it whatever advantages it may have enjoyed from the privileged status of the Jews in the Empire.[11] In Paul's speech to the Athenians, Acts 17:22–31, Luke gives us an important picture of the skepticism with which the Gospel was greeted among much of the gentile intelligentsia. That Paul included in his list of trials suffered for the sake of the Gospel numerous imprisonments and three beatings with rods, a Roman punishment, shows how from the beginning of the mission to the gentiles they proved as capable of persecuting the Church as was Judaism. In I Thessalonians 3:14–15 Paul compares the persecution of his church there at the hands of their fellow citizens with the Jewish persecutions in Jerusalem.

The great fire in Rome and the despicable executions under Nero which followed it established a pattern of periodic outbreaks of harassment which became a fact of life for the Christians until the Edict of Milan, A.D. 312. Although writing many years later in the early years of the second century, Tacitus' utter contempt for the Christians as he records the Neronian persecution (A.D. 64) is probably an accurate estimate of official feelings toward the Church.[12] It is in this period that the process of using and preserving the traditions about Jesus began to issue in the production of our canonical Gospels.

To summarize we may note four important developments in the Church during its first period. (1) The waiting community in Jerusalem became an aggressive missionary movement with no less a goal than the evangelization of the world. (2) The return of its Lord to bring the end of world history and establish the Kingdom of God, at first expected almost daily, receded into the future and now awaited the completion of the world mission. In some quarters, as we shall see, the hope appears to have become even more distant. (3) Persecution at first encountered at the hands of the Jewish hierarchy met the Christians in their gentile mission and became an inescapable part of their existence. (4) Finally, the tensions between the followers of Jesus and their parent faith increased steadily to result in a complete and bitter separation. With the fall of Jerusalem and the resulting loss of the leadership of the Church there the future course of Christianity as an essentially gentile world religion was set. It is out of this transitional period that our Gospels come.

11. For the special decrees of Julius Caesar in behalf of the Jews see Josephus, *Antiquities of the Jews,* XIV, 10. For an excellent examination of the whole question of Christianity and the Roman Empire see Robert M. Grant, *The Sword and the Cross* (New York: The Macmillan Company, 1955).
12. *Annals,* 15, 44.

With this brief sketch of the development of the Primitive Church in mind we may list at least five reasons why the traditions of Jesus were recorded in a process that finally produced the four Gospels:

1. The expansion of the Church into the distant regions created the need for a way of transmitting the tradition which could only be met by written materials.
2. The increasing predominance of gentiles in many congregations made the oral transmission of the tradition, so congenial to the Jewish mind, impractical. The pagan world had not been conditioned by the oral tradition as had the Jews.
3. The delay of the return of Christ (the parousia, from the Greek word for coming) soon made it apparent to the Church that its sojourn in this present age would be longer than it had supposed and therefore it would have longer need for the memorabilia of Jesus and, consequently, a more careful and permanent means of preserving them.
4. Martyrdom soon began to make inroads on the original band of Jesus' disciples, and, as their number decreased, it became more imperative for the sake of the Church which followed to crystallize the teaching and witness of those "who had been with Jesus."
5. As the Church moved into a gentile milieu heretical teachings and fanciful expansions of the tradition began to appear. The publication and canonization of Gospels bearing the explicit approval of the Church and an unquestionable connection with the original apostles became necessary as a protection from such errors.

1. *Why Four Gospels?*

If one were to come to the New Testament with no prior knowledge of it, one would doubtless be quite surprised to find four books comprising four parallel stories of Jesus. One would naturally expect the Gospels to present a single, consecutive story in four parts, but instead they actually compete. Except for the infancy narratives in the two opening chapters of Matthew and Luke, and the Prologue of John (1:1–18), they all begin with the ministry of John the Baptist and conclude with the Passion and Resurrection. The natural question with which to begin the study of the New Testament is: Why four Gospels?

THE ANCIENT COLLECTION

The question is, in fact, a very old one. In a well-known passage, St. Irenaeus, Bishop of Lyons in Gaul and one of the most important Christian writers of his time, writing near the end of the second century, says

It is not possible that the Gospels can be either more or fewer in number than they are. For, since there are four zones of the world in which we live, and four principal winds,[13] while the church is scattered throughout all the world, and the "pillar and ground" of the Church is the gospel and the spirit of life; it is fitting that she should have four pillars, breathing out immortality on every side, and vivifying men afresh.[14]

Irenaeus continues his argument with an appeal to the apparently already familiar connection between the Gospels and the four cherubim of Revelation 4:6ff. and a quotation from Psalm 80:1b. On this basis he outlines the individual characteristics of the Gospels by means of their opening themes: John's opening Logos theme establishes "His original, effectual, and glorious generation from the Father" as the Gospel's emphasis. By beginning with the priesthood of Zacharias, Luke represents Jesus' priestly character. The genealogy which opens Matthew reveals this Gospel's emphasis on Jesus' humanity. Mark's reference to the prophet Isaiah suggests his concern with prophetic aspect of the Gospel. Irenaeus sums up his argument with an appeal to four covenants God has given to man: one with Adam, Noah, Moses, and Christ. Appropriately, then, the quatriform Gospels correspond to the four cherubim and four covenants. The four Gospels are thus justified by a need for universality and by Scripture. The cherubic symbols in which Mark is represented by a lion, Luke by an ox, Matthew by a human face, and John an eagle are still a familiar part of Christian art.[15]

Tertullian, a native of the Roman province in North Africa and a leading apologist for Christianity at the beginning of the third century, offered another, and to us more meaningful, explanation. In answer to the arch-heretic Marcion, who in promoting his deviant version of Christianity had rejected the Old Testament entirely and established a canon of his own consisting exclusively of ten letters of Paul and a truncated version of Luke, Tertullian appealed to the corroborative witness to the truth of two apostles, Matthew and John, and two "apostolic men" (i.e., disciples of

13. Irenaeus' original words here are "catholic spirits" (*katholika pneumata,* the latter word means both spirit and wind). This may be a deliberate play on words.
14. *Against Heresies,* III, 11, 8. The translation is taken from *The Antenicene Library, The Writings of Irenaeus,* tr. by Rev. Alexander Roberts, D.D. and Rev. W. H. Rambaut, A.B. (Edinburgh: T. & T. Clark, 1868), Vol. I, p. 293.
15. The application of the symbols to the respective Gospels was not always uniform among the Fathers. Cf. Irenaeus, *Against Heresies,* Bk. III, I, 1; The Commentary on the Revelation of John by the third-century bishop, Victorinus, bishop of Petau, which appears to be following the lead of Irenaeus in his explanations but makes the identifications in the usual order; and St. Augustine, *The Harmony of the Gospels,* I, 6, 9, where he challenges the usual order on the basis of the fact that the beginnings of the Gospels do not necessarily reflect their "full design."

Matthew

The four evangelists seated on their symbols. Illuminations from a twelfth-century manuscript of the Gospels made in England. (Courtesy of the Pierpont Morgan Library.)

apostles), Luke and Mark.[16] A fragment of a document on the New Testament books approved to be read in the churches at Rome, called after

16. *Against Marcion*, IV, 2.

Mark

the eighteenth-century scholar who discovered it, the Muratorian Fragment, written shortly before Tertullian's work *Against Marcion,* sums up the matter:

> And hence, although different points (*principia*) are taught us in the several books of the Gospels, there is no difference

Luke

as regards the faith of believers, inasmuch as in all of them all things are related under one imperial (*principali,* leading) spirit, which concern the (Lord's) nativity, His passion, His resurrection, His conversation with His disciples, and His two-fold advent,—the first in the humiliation of rejection,

John

which is now past, and the second in the glory of royal power, which is yet in the future.[17]

Eusebius, the Bishop of Caesarea in Palestine to whose *Church History* we are heavily indebted for our knowledge of the early Church, writing in the early part of the fourth century, after stating that John's Gospel was

17. *The Antenicene Library, Irenaeus,* Vol. II, *Hippolytus, Vol. II,* Fragments, tr. Rev. Alexander Roberts, D.D., and Rev. W. H. Rambaut, A.B., "Fragments of Caius," p. 160.

written to supply an account of Jesus' activity before John the Baptist was imprisoned, concludes

> One who understands this can no longer think that the Gospels are at variance with one another, inasmuch as the Gospel according to John contains the first acts of Christ, while the others give an account of the latter part of his life. And the genealogy of our saviour according to the flesh John quite naturally omitted, because it had been already given by Matthew and Luke and began with the doctrine of his divinity, which had, as it were, been reserved for him, as their superior, by the divine Spirit.[18]

Eusebius' theory that John and the other Gospels are treating different periods in Jesus' life is true in only small part. He here calls attention, nevertheless, to the striking contrast between John and the other three Gospels with which we will be concerned at the conclusion of this section.

A very different approach to the problem of the four Gospels was introduced during the latter part of the second century by a Syrian Christian named Tatian. The *Diatessaron,* as he called it, interwove the materials of the four Gospels into a single continuous work.[19] It survived in Syria for about two centuries, but, as Eusebius indicates, Tatian's orthodoxy came under serious question and his work was finally rejected. This solution seems not to have found much appeal beyond the Syrian churches.

The Gospels each came into being separately and, in a sense, independently in certain important centers of Christianity for use in the churches of the area. As they came to receive wider circulation, they became parts of a collection which was soon canonized. Thus the Church found itself with the four Gospels as we have them. Beside the Church's natural conservatism which would hesitate to discard anything traditional, two motives appear to have led the Church to retain the four separate records of the tradition: (1) the apologetic value of the corroborative witness of the separate books believed to come, either directly or through a disciple, from the apostles; (2) the recognition that these works not only supplement one another but each of them presents the tradition from a different theological perspective. The happy accident that the number of Gospels came to four, the symbol of catholicity, served to reinforce the conviction of men like St. Irenaeus that the four were divinely intended.

18. *H.E.,* III, 24, 13. *The Nicene and Post-Nicene Fathers,* Second Series, Eusebius, tr. The Rev. Arthur Cushman McGiffert, Ph.D. (New York: The Christian Literature Company, 1890), p. 153.
19. Eusebius, *H.E.,* IV, 24. A Latin and an Arabic Diatessaron are extant which apparently go back in the main to Tatian's work. Otherwise only fragments of it have survived.

A COMPARISON OF THE GOSPELS

From our modern perspective we may for other reasons be grateful for the survival of the separate Gospels. In the first place, by comparing them we can learn much about their sources and the ways in which the authors used these sources, a discovery of great importance in knowing how to understand and interpret them and their subject, Jesus Christ. Second, since they come from different areas and different periods in the growth and development of the early Church they reflect in their treatment of the tradition the needs, problems, and faith of their own time. The knowledge gained from a study of the Gospels from this point of view is of indispensable aid in filling in the gaps in what is otherwise an obscure period in the history of the Church.

Our first step, then, in studying the Gospels is to examine them comparatively. When we do, one important fact immediately emerges: Three of them have much in common, whereas the fourth, John, stands apart in striking contrast. Because the first three follow the same general pattern, have so much material in common—even to the wording in many cases—and therefore can be arranged in parallel columns for comparison they are called the Synoptic Gospels (from Greek *synopsis,* viewing together, a general or unified view). The fourth Gospel,[20] on the other hand, differs radically both in order and content from the other three. The Church Fathers, as the great Christian writers of the early centuries of our era are known, were aware of the uniqueness of John's Gospel.[21] Eusebius, as we have seen, attempted to solve the chronological problems by a theory of an early Judean ministry and regarded it as John's divinely ordained mission "as their superior" to set forth "the doctrine of his divinity" as a climax to the Gospels. Elsewhere he quotes the words of Clement of Alexandria so frequently cited in this connection:

"But, last of all, John, perceiving that the external facts had been made plain in the Gospel, being urged by his friends, and inspired by the Spirit, composed a spiritual Gospel."[22] From the tone of both of these statements it is clear that they regarded John as not only the latest but the superior

20. A technical term for John's Gospel. Some scholars protest its use on the ground that its use tends to overemphasize the differences at the expense of the very real bond that does exist between John and the Synoptics. The term tends also to be pejorative with regard to authorship and reliability. See John A. T. Robinson, *Twelve New Testament Studies* (London: SCM Press Ltd., 1962), p. 95.
21. The Fathers of the Church are usually divided into three groups: the Apostolic Fathers who belong to the first period following the generation of the original apostles; the ante-Nicene Fathers, a larger group, usually including the Apostolic Fathers, who wrote before the time of the Council of Nicea (A.D. 325); the post-Nicene Fathers include the writers for the next several centuries following the Nicene Council.
22. *H.E.*, 14, 7. Translation from *The Nicene and Post-Nicene Fathers*, Second Series, Vol. I, p. 261.

Gospel. The Muratorian Fragment goes even farther to suggest that not only did John write at the instigation of his fellow apostles but that they shared in the enterprise by contributing what was "revealed" to them.[23] Such statements as these indicate how important apostolic witness as a guarantee of orthodoxy and authenticity had become.

To gain an idea of how the four Gospels are related to one another, we may compare the units into which the Synoptic Gospels are divided in the *Gospel Parallels* (RSV).[24] In this comparison the fourth Gospel presents a slight problem. Since it is not capable of comparison on the same basis with the other three, we do not have it broken into comparable units. Indeed it is significant of our point that John scarcely lends itself to such division. For our present purpose, however, the paragraphing in the RSV will suffice.

Out of the 103 units into which Mark is divided, 100 are paralleled in whole or in part by Matthew and/or Luke; 144 of Matthew's 167 units are paralleled by the other two; and Luke is paralleled in 126 of the 164 units in his Gospel. John's Gospel, on the other hand, has parallel material to the Synoptic Gospels in only 36 of its 130 paragraphs. The following graph will demonstrate something of the similarity of the Synoptics, on the one hand, and the uniqueness of John, on the other. This comparison is not, of course, precise. It takes no account, for example, of the question of verbal agreements which would make the contrast between the Synoptics and John even greater. We will be concerned with such a more exact comparison in the next section. The extent of similarity also varies greatly. Some scholars for good reason regard Matthew's parable of the weeds, 13:24–30, as a rewriting of Mark's parable of the mysterious growth of seed, 4:26–29. Yet the difference is great enough so that these parables were not included in the comparison. It might be argued, on the other hand, that the differences between the story of Bartimaeus, Mark 10:46–52, and the two blind men, Matthew 20:29–34, is too great to warrant counting them as parallels. The same might be said for the parables of the talents and the pounds, Matthew 25:14–30 and Luke 19:11–27. In several instances, furthermore, only part of a unit contains material paralleled in other Gospels and at the same time such a unique story as Mark's flight of the young man, 14:51–52, because it is part of a larger unit, is included in the parallels. These units are more closely alike, nevertheless, than are most of the Johannine parallels to any of the Synoptic Gospels. These observations help to indicate the very complicated

23. *Canon Muratorianus,* 1.
24. J. B. H. Throckmorton, Jr. (New York: Thomas Nelson & Sons, 1949). This indispensable tool for the student of the English Bible is based on and in its arrangement faithfully follows the Greek Huck-Lietzmann, *Synopse Der Drei Ersten Evangelism.* 9th ed. (Tubingen: J. C. B. Mohr, [Paul Siebeck], 1936).

Comparison of Material in Common Among the Four Gospels

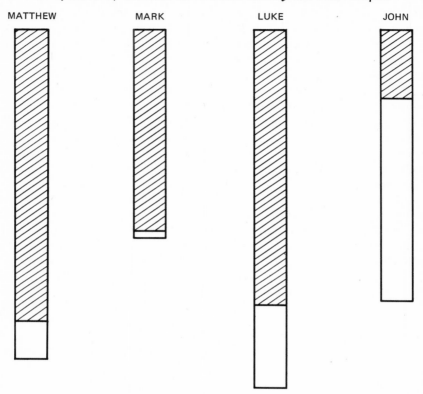

nature of the relations among the Gospels. We are concerned to see here only a general picture of the closeness of the Synoptics to one another and the wide divergence of John from all of them.

The comparison of parallels does not by any means show all of the important differences between John and the Synoptics. More than half (20) of the 36 paragraphs in John which can be paralleled in the other Gospels are in the Passion and Resurrection. More significant are the important items in the story of Jesus which John omits. Although Jesus comes to John the Baptizer in Judea and John witnesses the descent of the Holy Spirit upon him, the baptism is omitted and the voice from heaven now comes through the mouth of the Baptizer. There is no temptation in the wilderness; the mount of transfiguration is reduced to a heavenly voice in Jerusalem. Gone is the story of Caesarea Philippi and the agony in the Garden. The order of events in John differs radically from the general pattern agreed upon by the Synoptic writers. John appears anxious to push back everything he can to the beginning of his Gospel. Thus Jesus is in the first chapter identified as "the Lamb of God, who takes away the sin of the world" (cf. Mk. 10:45). Also in the first chapter is the renaming of Peter (cf. Mt. 16:18). Perhaps the most prominent and best known of these relocations is the cleansing of the Temple in chapter 2 (cf. Mk. 11:15–17 and para. Also 2:19ff. with Mk. 14:58 and Mt. 25:61). Instead of a single Galilean ministry ending with the journey to Jerusalem for the Passover which leads to the Passion, John has three Passovers. Thus according to the Synoptics Jesus' ministry could have occupied a year or less, but John's arrangement requires more than two years.

Throughout the Gospel of John, Jesus moves with a precise dignity that leaves no doubt as to who he is. There is no "messianic secret" as in Mark.[25] The story moves on a veritable timetable. At several points the phrase "my hour has not yet come" punctuates the narrative. Then the hour does come and Jesus, always in full control of the situation, moves with profound dignity to his "glorification" on the cross. In another chapter, as we seek to understand the method and thought of John, we will note a number of other characteristics which set this Gospel apart from the other three. In some ways the "Synoptic Problem," to which we must now turn, is the problem of the fourth Gospel. The complex problem of the relationships among the first three Gospels is set in sharper relief by the contrast between them and this Gospel, so different in order and content and yet with a vague familiarity which meets the reader in virtually every chapter.

2. The Quest for Sources

Because of the ways in which John's Gospel stands apart from the rest, we shall lay it aside for the time and turn our attention to a matter concerning the other three which has come to be known as the Synoptic problem. This problem arises from the extensive amount of correspondence among the first three Gospels which extends beyond agreement in content, in many instances, to word-by-word agreement. These verbal agreements are too extensive and complex to be accounted for by a theory of well-memorized oral tradition or by independent writings of eye witnesses. They indicate a literary relationship of dependence either on common sources or on one another. At the same time, the Synoptics cannot be related as simply expanded or condensed versions of one another. Rearrangements in the order of the material they have in common, variations in the amount of verbal agreement, and the fact that in places each of them may be compared with one of the other Gospels to the exclusion of

25. On the "Messianic secret" see below, pp. 101–102, 499. For a good statement of the contrasts between John and the Synoptics see Donald T. Rowlingson, *Introduction to New Testament Study*, (New York: The Macmillan Company, 1956), pp. 42–56.

the third, all indicate that Luke's frank admission in the Preface to his Gospel to dependence on written sources is true also of the other Gospels. That more sources than one are involved is evident both in the considerable amount of material common to Matthew and Luke not found in Mark and in the material peculiar to each of them. The Synoptic problem, then, is to give an account of Gospel origins which will satisfactorily explain these facts. The problem and its significance are far more than a matter of academic curiosity and not unlike those which may be observed in the study of the Pentateuch.[26] Any discovery concerning the sources used by the Gospel writers will be of considerable importance in evaluating and interpreting their work.

THE PRIORITY OF MARK

That almost all of Mark is found in one or both of the other two Gospels and constitutes the major part of the material common to them places the second Gospel in a peculiar position as a middle term in Synoptic relations. This position is all the more significant when compared to the sizable body of material independent of Mark in common between Matthew and Luke. The quest for sources must therefore begin with the question of the place of Mark among the Synoptics. It will be useful at this point to make a more detailed analysis of the relationships of these Gospels. Following is a graph comparing by verses each of the Synoptic Gospels with the other two.

A graph of this sort, of course, fails to reveal how complicated the matter of Synoptic relationships actually is. The ratios, to begin with, are not exact because of the variation in the length of the verses and the problem of how to reckon the fractions of verses involved. Second, there is a wide variation in the closeness of verbal agreement among the passages. Between Matthew 12:19–20 and Luke 11:27–28, for example, the verbal agreement is virtually total. Except for Matthew's unimportant omission of a particle at the beginning and one insignificant transposition of word order, the only difference, which undoubtedly represents a deliberate change, is the word "spirit" in Matthew and "finger" in Luke. In contrast, Luke 14:26–27 agrees with its parallel in Matthew 10:37–38 in less than one third of its wording. Or, to take another example, in one section of the Little Apocalypse, Mark 13:5–8, nine tenths of Mark's words are identical with nearly five sixths of the corresponding passage in Matthew 24:4–8 and with more than one half of Luke 21:8–11. On the other hand, less than one fifth of Mark's words in the story of the healing of the epileptic son, 9:14–29, corresponds to one third of those of Matthew 17:14–21 and slightly more than one fifth of those in Luke 9:37–43.

26. See West, *Introduction to the Old Testament*, pp. 35–49.

Comparison of Material in Common Among the Synoptic Gospels

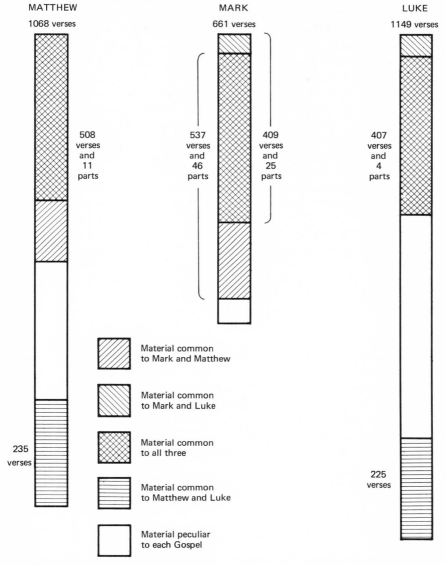

MATTHEW
1068 verses

MARK
661 verses

LUKE
1149 verses

508 verses and 11 parts

537 verses and 46 parts

409 verses and 25 parts

407 verses and 4 parts

235 verses

225 verses

Material common to Mark and Matthew

Material common to Mark and Luke

Material common to all three

Material common to Matthew and Luke

Material peculiar to each Gospel

This latter example leads us to two further observations: First, verbal agreement in parallel passages is significantly greater in sayings material than in narratives. This difference is not only evident in the comparison of the sayings from the Little Apocalypse with the story of the healing of the epileptic son, but also in the fact that in the latter story the two points at which the greatest amount of verbal agreement occur are where Jesus speaks. Second, in a number of important narratives Matthew and, to a slightly lesser degree, Luke are more condensed than Mark. In the healing of the epileptic son, for instance, Mark is two and a half times longer than Matthew and more than twice as long as Luke. The impression that Mark is the middle term in Synoptic relations is further confirmed by the consistency of the characteristic ways in which Matthew and Luke each differ from Mark. Matthew often condenses Mark by omitting unimportant details and especially his many redundancies. Matthew retains considerably more of Mark's vocabulary,[27] but adds variety and complexity to the sentences by turning finite verbs into infinitives and participles. Where Matthew expands Mark he does it either by adding new supplementary material or further details which sharpen the narrative.

Luke, on the other hand, more radically edits the Markan material. He especially enriches Mark's rather impoverished vocabulary by use of synonyms. Sentence structures are modified to produce a considerably more literary style. (The historic present, so prominent a feature of Mark's style, is largely eliminated by both Evangelists.) We are concerned here purely with matters of literary style. In the next chapter we will observe the ways in which the writers clarify and reinterpret their material by editorial modifications.

Another indication of the position of Mark in Synoptic relations is the variations in the ordering of Mark's material in the other two Gospels. Both Matthew and Luke depart from Mark's order but not at the same points and, therefore, do not agree against Mark in doing so.[28]

The search for sources of the Gospels must begin therefore with the question of Mark's relation to the other two Gospels. It will be useful to observe a long-standing convention which designates the material in common between Mark and the other two Synoptics as "triple tradition."

Until the nineteenth century the tradition concerning Mark for the most part followed unquestioningly the lead of St. Augustine:

> For Matthew is understood to have taken it in hand to construct the record of the incarnation of the Lord according to

27. The English reader may gain a fairly accurate picture of these matters from Walter E. Bundy, *A Syllabus and Synopsis of the First Three Gospels* (Indianapolis: The Bobbs-Merrill Company, 1932), in which the words in common among the three Gospels are printed in boldface type. By using the American Standard Version, which is one of the most literal of the translations, and insofar as feasible uses the same English word for the same Greek word, this book represents the situation in the Gospels as well as possible for those not able to read Greek.

28. For an excellent chart showing not only the proportions of material in common among the Gospels versus that peculiar to each, but also the distribution of the several materials, transpositions of order, and other matters relevant to the Synoptic problem see Allan Barr, *A Diagram of Synoptic Relationships* (Edinburgh: T. & T. Clark, n.d.).

the royal lineage, and to give an account of most part of His deeds and words as they stood in relation to this present life of men. Mark follows him closely, and *looks like his attendant and epitomizer.* For in his narrative he gives nothing in concert with John apart from the others: by himself separately, he has little to record; in conjunction with Luke, as distinguished from the rest, he has still less; but in concord with Matthew, he has a very large number of passages. Much, too, he narrates in words almost numerically and identically the same as those used by Matthew, where the agreement is either with that evangelist alone, or with him in connection with the rest.[29]

Toward the end of the eighteenth century new investigations of the Gospels began to challenge the Augustinian assumption. Among the hypotheses attempted was the suggestion that Mark was the earliest Gospel and therefore a source for Matthew and Luke, which manifestly set Mark in the middle of the problem. Experiments continued, nevertheless, with notions of a primitive Aramaic "handbook" created for use by early evangelists, which being enlarged and supplemented independently became finally our Synoptic Gospels, or of collections of fragmentary traditions oral or written which served as sources for our Gospels. Such hypotheses in the forms in which they were presented finally proved untenable and gave way before the growing consensus that Mark is the key to the common tradition among the three Gospels. When the "tendency criticism" of the Tübingen School, which attempted to restore the Augustinian position on the theory that Mark was a harmonizing Gospel intended to mediate the antagonism between the Jewish-Christian Matthew and the gentile Luke, finally gave way under repeated attack, the way was clear for the triumph of the doctrine of the priority of Mark.[30] This doctrine has become so well established that occasional attempts to dispute it which still appear are given little notice by the majority of New Testament scholars.

It is important to note that the priority of Mark rests not on any abstract historical theory but on critical literary analysis. The essence of the matter is the difficulty of explaining how an epitomizer could produce a document which on every count appears more primitive than its sources.

29. *The Harmony of the Gospels,* tr. the Rev. S. D. F. Salmond (Edinburgh: T. & T. Clark, 1873), p. 142. (Italics mine.)

30. See Bernhard Weiss, *A Manual of Introduction to the New Testament,* tr. A. J. K. Davidson (New York: Funk & Wagnalls, Publishers, 1889), Vol. II, pp. 203–263. This old work provides an excellent summary of the history of nineteenth-century research on Mark and the Synoptic problem by a scholar who himself made significant contributions to the theory of the priority of Mark which eventually prevailed. See further James Hastings, ed., *A Dictionary of the Bible* (New York: Charles Scribner's Sons, 1902), Vol. III, pp. 258–260; and IDB, Vol. IV, pp. 491–495, and Vol. III, pp. 269–270. Also B. H. Streeter, *The Four Gospels,* rev. ed. (London: Macmillan & Co., Ltd., 1930), p. 164.

The characteristic differences between Mark and Matthew and Luke which we have noted, for example, are most understandable if Mark was the source, but virtually impossible to explain in reverse. It is difficult, furthermore, to understand how Mark, as an epitomizer, could have omitted what he did and reshuffled the remaining material to create the Gospel as it stands.[31]

Whether the copies of Mark used by Matthew and Luke were identical with our canonical Gospel, however, is another question. Some of the variations in agreement, condensations, the omission of Mark 4:26–29, 7:32–36, 8:22–26, and similar alterations of Mark by Matthew, the significantly smaller amount of verbal agreement between Mark and Luke and the larger amount of Mark's material which Luke omits, especially Mark 6:45–8:26, commonly called "Luke's great omission," have suggested to some scholars that Matthew and Luke were working from different earlier versions of Mark. To solve some difficulties in relating our Gospel to the work, parts of which have been preserved in Eusebius' *Church History,* in which the second-century Bishop of Hierapolis, *Papias,* said Mark wrote what he had heard Peter teach but not in order,[32] a theory of a primitive form of the Gospel which was called *Ur-Markus* had been advanced fairly early in the investigation. The combination of these theories led to elaborate and complicated hypotheses of successive editions of Mark, which by the very weight of their complexity became self-defeating. The basic problem itself arose, of course, because of a too mechanical conception of the editorial work of Matthew and Luke. When it was recognized that the latter writers were exercising appropriate freedom in adapting their sources to their own purposes, the problems disappeared and the Ur-Markus theory in its various forms was abandoned.[33]

Not inappropriately the question of what sources were used by Mark has been raised. If we take Papias' statement seriously and assume that the writing to which he refers is essentially our Mark, Peter becomes the sole and direct source of the Gospel. A number of investigators have questioned Papias' reliability, however, and have noted groupings of material which appear to have come to Mark in small collections. We may observe some of these, for example, in the following passages:

1. A day in Capernaum, 1:21–34
   (perhaps 2:1–12 belongs here also).

31. For a detailed analysis of this point see Bernhard Weiss, *A Manual of Introduction to the New Testament,* II, p. 242, n. 1. For an able answer to the latest of recent attempts to challenge the priority of Mark see the review in *JBL,* Vol. LXXXIV, Sept. 1965, pp. 295–297, by F. W. Beare of W. R. Farmer's book, *The Synoptic Problem: A Critical Analysis,* (New York: Macmillan, 1964).
32. For the full statement by Papias and its significance see pp. 70–73.
33. For a good critique of the Ur-Marcus theory see B. H. Streeter, *The Four Gospels,* p. 181, *passim.*

2. Parables about seed, 4:3–20, 26–32.
3. Controversies, 2:1–3:6 (or 2:13–3:6).
4. Stories involving boats, 3:7–10, 4:1–2, 4:35–6:56. (Perhaps there is here a larger complex involving the Sea of Galilee: 1:16–20, 2:13; 3:7–12; 4:1–44; 5:1–19, 21–23; 6:45–54; 7:31–37; 8:13–21.)
5. The traditions of John the Baptist, 1:2–11; 6:14–29.
6. The predictions of the Passion, 8:31ff.; 9:31–32; 10:32b–34.

Along with the Passion story, often described as the oldest extended body of written materials in the Gospels, an apocalyptic tract presumed by some commentators to underlie the Little Apocalypse (ch. 13), and a possible collection of Old Testament proof texts for use by early Christian preachers and teachers, these groups of material may provide a clue to the sources from which Mark wrote his Gospel.[34] Whether any or all of these were in written form, or how extensively Mark may have modified them are questions we cannot answer with any certainty.

THE TWO-DOCUMENT HYPOTHESIS

We must now return to the question of the double tradition (i.e., material occurring only in Matthew and Luke) designated on the graph (p. 47) by the horizontal shading at the bottom of the outside columns. Some of the closest agreements among the Synoptics are in this material. If therefore literary interdependence is indicated anywhere in the Gospels it is indicated here. Early attempts to explain these agreements by Luke's use of Matthew as well as Mark ran into the difficulty of explaining how, if he was dependent on Matthew for the double tradition, Luke remained so little influenced by Matthew's modifications of Mark. This difficulty, the fact that the double tradition is fairly homogeneous and consists almost exclusively of teaching, the large difference in their order and use of the material, and the fact that Matthew and Luke differ in the double tradition in a way quite consistent with their differences in the triple tradition, make it reasonably certain that they are using another common source much as they used Mark.[35] Because this source is now lost and can only be conjectured from the double tradition, it is simply called Q, from the German word *Quelle,* meaning source. The use of a German term reflects the fact that the hypothesis was established largely through the studies of German

34. See C. H. Dodd's modification of this theory, advanced originally in Rendal Harris, *Testimonia,* in his *According to the Scriptures.* (New York: Charles Scribner's Sons, 1953). Cf. T. H. Gaster, *The Dead Sea Scriptures* (Garden City, N.Y.: Doubleday & Company, 1956), pp. 335ff. See F. C. Grant, *The Gospels: Their Origin and Growth* (New York: Harper & Brothers, 1957), ch. IX, pp. 108–116. Also Vincent Taylor, *The Gospel According to St. Mark* (London: Macmillan & Co. Ltd., 1959), pp. 67–77.
35. A few scholars have remained unconvinced, however. See Morton Scott Enslin, *Christian Beginnings* (New York: Harper & Brothers Publishers, 1938), pp. 433–434.

scholars. Papias' mention, in the quotation to which we have already referred, of *logia* which he said Matthew had written in Hebrew (probably meaning Aramaic) has frequently been taken to refer to Q and therefore to identify it. If the *logia* was Q, it must have been translated into Greek before our Evangelists used it or else it cannot account for the verbal agreements. On the whole this identification raises more questions than it answers.[36] Whatever its identity, Q cannot be regarded as a Gospel. If the double tradition in any way reflects its content, it not only was void of narratives of the life of Jesus but had no Passion story. It is unlikely that a "Gospel" would omit the Passion. Q was more than likely a catechist's handbook of teachings of Jesus. The combination Q and Mark then became the two identifiable sources from which, along with other fragments available to each writer independently, the later Synoptic Gospels were composed. This theory, widely accepted at the end of the nineteenth century, was known as the two-document hypothesis.

Because of problems such as the juxtaposition of Markan and Q materials within the same passages in several places in Matthew (e.g., Mt. 6:14–15, 9:37–38, 12:27ff.), sayings in Mark which are in effect parallel to sayings in the other Gospels and similar in character to Q material but with so little verbal agreement that they appear to have come to the other Gospels from another source, it has been suggested that Mark also knew and used Q.[37] That there are other equally plausible explanations for these phenomena, and that it is hard to explain why Mark, if he knew it, made so little use of Q, kept this theory from gaining much acceptance.

THE FOUR-DOCUMENT HYPOTHESIS

The achievements of Synoptic research up to this point originated largely in Germany. About the turn of the century, however, Dr. William Sanday, of Oxford University, assembled a seminar in his home which undertook a prodigious investigation of the Synoptic problem during the next several years.[38] From these studies several important points emerged.

36. Cf. Morton S. Enslin, *Christian Beginnings,* p. 431.
37. See Moffatt, *Introduction to the Literature of the New Testament* (New York: Charles Scribner's Son's, 1922), pp. 194–206, for a good discussion of the Q document including sixteen reconstructions of its content, and the question of its use by Mark. See also Streeter, *The Four Gospels,* pp. 187ff., 242ff., on Mark and Q. On the problem of the unity and reconstruction of Q see ch. X, and p. 291. On the possibility of two rescinsions of Q see pp. 235ff. A good brief summary of the question of Q may be found in H. D. A. Major, T. W. Manson, and C. J. Wright, *The Mission and Message of Jesus* (New York: E. P. Dutton and Co., Inc., 1938).
38. Beside the very important work of B. H. Streeter, *The Four Gospels,* which we have cited above and on which the following paragraphs depend, at least two other significant books came out of this Seminar: William Sanday, ed., *Studies in the Synoptic Problem* (Oxford: At the Clarendon Press, 1911); and John C.

First, the single tradition in Matthew and Luke requires a more elaborate source theory than the two-document hypothesis. Second, differences between Matthew and Luke in their relation to Mark had not been sufficiently accounted for. Finally, the question of the relation of the emerging Gospels to the life of the churches, in other words, the provenance of the Gospels, required more attention.

In 1924, B. H. Streeter published his famous study, *The Four Gospels,* which attempted the ambitious undertaking of drawing the mass of data accumulated as a result of the Sanday seminars into a coherent hypothesis.[39] Observing "Jewish atmosphere" in Matthew's single tradition, Streeter concluded that it displayed sufficient homogeneity to represent an independent written source which he designated "M." Similarly, the material peculiar to Luke, which he designated "L," he took to represent a separate source. Streeter did not simply add the two sources, M and L, to the two-document hypothesis to replace the fragments assumed by the German scholars to have been used. Noting that Q and L are often intertwined in Luke, that not only is less of Mark used but it appears in Luke in blocks rather than interwoven throughout the Gospel, and that Luke's outline is relatively independent of Mark, Streeter assumed that a version of Luke once existed without the Markan material. This version he called Proto-Luke and assumed it to be comprised of Q and L. The effect of Streeter's hypothesis can be seen from his diagram:

Streeter's Four-Document Hypothesis

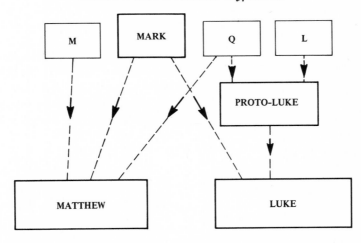

Hawkins, *Horae Synopticae* (Oxford: At the Clarendon Press, 1909). A survey of these three books will indicate how nearly exhaustive were the examinations of the evidence in the Gospels.

39. See *The Four Gospels,* pp. 149–270. For the complete diagram see p. 150.

The theory of Proto-Luke admittedly solves several problems. For one thing, although the Q material is distributed fairly well throughout Luke, Markan material is separated by two extensive non-Markan sections.[40] These have usually been called the lesser and greater interpolations: Luke 6:20–8:3 and 9:51–18:14. There are brief scattered bits of material parallel with Mark in the latter, but the verbal agreements are not significantly close. Streeter has called attention to a third such block of "interpolated" material in Luke 3:1–4:30. By regarding the Markan material as the interpolation, his Proto-Luke theory reverses the matter. Luke's Passion story stands in sufficient contrast to that of Matthew and Mark as to suggest that it is based on an independent tradition which would be understandable if Luke was a complete Gospel before the insertion of Mark's material. Luke's disuse of Mark in the "great omission" also becomes more understandable if Mark was a later addition rather than a primary source.

The problems of parallel passages with little verbal agreement, minor agreements in passages which are not otherwise parallel, and the like are explained by Streeter by "overlapping of sources." Thus the occasional parallels with Mark found in Q material do not indicate Mark's use of Q but independent strands of tradition which are bound to overlap in places. Since similar overlapping must be presumed with M and L, neither these documents nor Q can be supposed to correspond exactly to the double and single traditions in Matthew and Luke.[41] In this aspect of his theory Streeter has given impetus to the many attempts at reconstructions of these sources.[42]

Anyone who works through Streeter's large volume cannot help being impressed with the ingenuity of his hypothesis. Its popularity, attested by allusions to it in almost all treatments of source criticism since its publication, suggests that it is probably about as far as one can go in solving the Synoptic problem on the basis of written sources. The theory, nevertheless, has not been without its critics. The idea of a Proto-Luke has come under the strongest and most frequent attack.[43] Diagrams of the four-document theory, in consequence, frequently omit Proto-Luke. The homogeneity of M also has been questioned.[44] That Streeter had to assume an occasional bit of oral tradition coming directly into the Gospels points to a number of problems which lie beyond the reach of any source theory. Unless one is to

40. A glance at the chart in Barr, *A Diagram of Synoptic Relationships* will show the contrast between the distribution of double and triple tradition in Luke.

41. For a contrary opinion see F. C. Grant, *IDB*, "Matthew, Gospel of," Vol. III, p. 305.

42. Cf. Albert E. Barnett, *The New Testament: Its Making and Meaning* (New York: Abingdon-Cokesbury Press, 1946), ch. 9.

43. For one of the most recent of these, see Hans Conzelmann, *The Theology of St. Luke,* tr. Geoffrey Buswell (New York: Harper & Brothers, 1960), pp. 22 n. 1, 29 n. 52ff. and notes, *passim.*

44. For example Barnett, *The New Testament,* p. 115.

assume that most improbable theory that written accounts of Jesus were created on the spot, a significant period of oral transmission must be accounted for. That oral tradition played an important role and continued into the second century alongside the written Gospels is attested to by Papias in his famous statement of a preference for the "living and abiding voice" over "the books" (our canonical Gospels?).[45] By locating the origin of Mark in Rome, Matthew in Antioch of Syria, Luke in Caesarea of Judea and Corinth, and John in Ephesus, Streeter called attention to the important role of the leading churches in producing the Gospels, but can we narrow so much the lines of influence? Such problems have led to further elaborations of source theories interlocked with studies of oral tradition. One of the most recent of these by Pierson Parker posits an earlier Palestinian document as a source for both Mark and Matthew.[46] None of these has fully succeeded in supplanting Streeter's hypothesis. For the question of oral tradition we must turn to another development in Synoptic studies.

3. Crystallized Memories

From the very beginning of modern studies in the Gospels, the existence of a period of oral transmission of the tradition has been assumed. We have already mentioned early attempts to solve the Synoptic problem by theories of oral tradition. With the advance of source criticism such theories were laid aside, but in the early years of this century, as scholars applied themselves to the task of examining the gap between the life of Jesus and the earliest written documents, interest in them was revived.

This new study arose out of the collapse of the Markan hypothesis. At the beginning of the century Wilhelm Wrede, by an analysis of the messianic secret motif, succeeded in showing that Mark's Gospel was organized on dogmatic lines, and no more represents a simple biography of Jesus than do the other Gospels.[47] In 1919 two important books appeared which launched the study of oral tradition as a distinct, clearly defined discipline. In one of these Karl Ludwig Schmidt confirmed Wrede's judgment on Mark's Gospel and established the method of distinguishing the editorial "cement" created by the Evangelist from the units of the tradition from which he compiled his Gospel.[48]

45. See Eusebius, *H.E.*, III, 39, 4.
46. Pierson Parker, *The Gospel Before Mark* (Chicago: The University of Chicago Press, 1953). Cf. F. C. Grant, *The Gospels: Their Origin and Their Growth.*
47. On Wrede's work see p. 101. For a more recent appraisal of the issue of the Messianic secret see Lewis S. Hay, "Mark's Use of the Messianic Secret," *JAAR*, Vol. XXXV, No. 1, March, 1967, pp. 16–27.
48. *Der Rahmen Der Geschichte Jesu* (Berlin: Trowitzch, 1919). For a good survey of the initial development of this method written at the time, see Henry J. Cadbury, "Between Jesus and the Gospels," *HTR*, Vol. XVI, Jan. 1923.

MARTIN DIBELIUS

The other work, *Die Formgeschichte Des Evangeliums,* became the charter of the new discipline.[49] In it, Martin Dibelius adapted the methods, developed by Herman Gunkel for Old Testament study,[50] to the analysis of the oral period of Gospel tradition. The study concentrates on the individual units, called *pericopae* (from the Greek word, *pericopto,* meaning to cut around or cut away), and by an analysis of their forms attempts to discover the *Sitz im Leben* (situation in life) which shaped them. Dibelius credits Edward Norden, who used the word in the subtitle of his book, *Agnostos Theos,* with the title *Formgeschichte* which by his use in the title of his book Dibelius established as the name of the new discipline.[51] The term has become in English "form criticism." In what he called his "constructive method" Dibelius began by a search for the activity in the Primitive Church which characterized its life and therefore shaped its traditions of Jesus. He found that activity in the Church's mission in which the sermon played the key role. Assuming, then, that sermons were the formative *Sitz im Leben* of the traditions, he proceeded to reconstruct from Acts and Paul's Letters an outline of the pattern which these sermons assumed.[52] With this pattern as a basis, Dibelius examined the Synoptic material to discover therein three principal types of "unliterary" literature which betrayed their oral history: (1) *The paradigm,* or example-narrative, is a self-contained, compact story that focuses attention upon a saying of Jesus for the edification of the hearers in a form useful for preaching.[53] Dibelius lists eight examples of noteworthy purity: Mark 2:1ff., 18f., 23ff., 3:1ff., 3:20f., 30ff., 10:13ff., 12:13ff., 14:3ff. (2) *The tale,* or *novelle,* is more worldly, more literary, displays more secular motives such as interest in miracles for their own sake, and follows closely the form of the pagan stories of miracles. Its purpose is to show Jesus as the miracle-worker. Thus it begins with a "history of the illness," describes the technique of the healer, the success of the miracle, and the amazement of the witnesses. As clear example of this form Dibelius lists Mark 1:40–45, 4:35–41, 5:1–20, 21–43, 6:35–44, 45–52, 7:32–37, 8:22–26, 9:14–29. (3) The term *legend,* which Dibelius employed for the third category, is used in its medieval sense of pious stories of the acts and lives of holy men. They are of two kinds, etiological (i.e., intended as an explanation of a doctrine or practice) and personal, although ultimately the personal legend is not without etiological motive. Legends are clearly distinguished from the

49. In English, *From Tradition to Gospel,* tr. Bertram Lee Woolf, 2nd ed. rev. (New York: Charles Scribner's Sons, n.d.).
50. See West, *Introduction to the Old Testament,* pp. 13, 46, 385.
51. See Dibelius, *From Tradition to Gospel,* p. 4.
52. *From Tradition to Gospel,* p. 13, and pp. 17ff. This chapter closely anticipates C. H. Dodd's theory of the Kerygma. Above, pp. 31–32.
53. *From Tradition to Gospel,* pp. 37–132.

other forms in the Gospels by the way in which biographical interests, otherwise notably subordinate, come to the fore. They are, nevertheless, religious in character. According to Dibelius legends are distinguished from paradigms and tales, which deal with divine manifestations in human form, by their concern with a human life under the direction of God. Thus legends emphasize special signs accompanying the birth and death of the hero, miraculous and beneficent exploits, and the like. The controlling factor in the legend is that particular quality of the hero which is to be honored. The edifying element is to be found in the way the story focuses attention upon that quality as something to be admired, adored, and in some way to be emulated. In the Gospel material legends, although scattered throughout, are secondary and often in modified form. Dibelius regards the story of Jesus' visit to the Temple at the age of twelve (Lk. 2:41ff.) as the clearest example of a legend in the Gospels. In a sense, the Passion story is a cult legend, and the birth stories consist of a series of such legends. That legends in the Gospels are not confined to Jesus can be seen in such stories as Peter's attempt to walk on the water (Mt. 14:28–33), the calling of Zacchaeus (Lk. 19:1–10), Mary and Martha (Lk. 10:38–42). It is important to note that for Dibelius the question of historical reliability of legends is not automatically determined by their form. As with other forms each pericope must be critically examined on its own merits.

Beside these three principal forms Dibelius lists two others. The first of these, the sayings or exhortations, were brought together for hortatory purposes and consist in "maxim, metaphor, parabolic narrative, prophetic call (beatitude, woe, eschatological preaching), short commandment, extended commandment."[54] Dibelius finds only three clear examples of myth, the second of these additional forms: "the baptismal miracle, the temptation of Jesus, and the Transfiguration." This is not to say that there are no other mythical elements in the Gospels, but that elsewhere these elements are subordinated to other motives and forms. By his definition, myths are stories *"which in some fashion* tell of many-sided doings of the gods." The form of mythology appears in the Gospel accounts, in other words, at the point at which an episode of Jesus' life is viewed for its own sake as a strictly divine act.

RUDOLF BULTMANN

Two years after Dibelius' work appeared, Rudolf Bultmann published his monumental *Die Geschichte Der Synoptischen Tradition.*[55] In general,

---

54. *From Tradition to Gospel,* pp. 233–286.
55. Published in English many years later under the title *The History of the Synoptic Tradition,* tr. John Marsh (Oxford: Basil Blackwell [1921], 1963). See also his article, "The New Approach to the Synoptic Problem," *JR,* VI (1926), pp. 337–62,

his methods and findings are similar to those of Dibelius. He comments in the introduction on the necessarily circular reasoning involved in the method of form criticism, which must move between the literary forms on the one side and the needs and concerns of the community that determined the forms on the other. That Dibelius begins with the community and proceeds to an interpretation of the forms, whereas Bultmann uses the literary forms as a starting point for understanding the community does not place them in opposition. Rather, as Bultmann points out, the two approaches are complementary and mutually corrective. The essential difference between the two is that Bultmann, unlike Dibelius, believes that form criticism is capable of making historical judgments on the content of the material. To a great extent, therefore, his interest in form criticism is determined by his concern with the relationship between Palestinian and Hellenistic Christianity.[56]

Bultmann discerned four basic forms of material in the Gospels. (1) *Apophthegms* (from the Greek word meaning a terse, pointed saying) correspond in general to Dibelius' *paradigms*. They are "sayings of Jesus set in a brief context," but this context turns out upon examination to be secondary.[57] One important difference between Dibelius and Bultmann lies in their conclusions concerning the *Sitz im Leben*. Whereas Dibelius finds it principally in the mission, hence the preaching, of the Church, Bultmann finds it in the Church's apologetic and polemic needs, especially in the controversies between Church and Synagogue. The situations therefore which provide the framework of the *apophthegms* were generated by the sayings to give them point and color and particularly to make clear their applicability to the current needs of the Church. Not only the narrative framework but the dialogues themselves manifest a "productive power." If we ask how to determine the original saying of Jesus around which the Church constructed the *apophthegms* we are given no certain answer: "If any part of these controversy dialogues does go back to Jesus himself, it is, apart from their general spiritual tenor, the decisive saying. . . . Yet we must also freely recognize that we may find Church formulations even among the arguments themselves." The skepticism is only slightly relieved by his concession:

> Yet in face of the entire content of the Tradition it can hardly be doubted that Jesus did teach as a Rabbi, gather disciples and engage in disputations. The individual controversy dialogues may not be historical reports of particular incidents in the life of Jesus, but the general character of his life is

reprinted in *Existence and Faith*, Shorter Writings of Rudolf Bultmann (New York: Meridian Books, Inc., 1960).
56. *The History of the Synoptic Tradition*, p. 5.
57. *The History of the Synoptic Tradition*, pp. 11ff., 69ff., 209ff., 244ff.

rightly portrayed in them, on the basis of historical recollection.[58]

Bultmann's actual working assumption becomes clear in his comment on the historicity of Luke 13:1-5: "On the other hand we must admit that such a dialogue could easily contain an historical reminiscence, and the less the specific interest of the Church were expressed, the more likely that it would be."[59] The more clearly a pericope is seen to have served the needs of the Primitive Church, in other words, the more remote is the authentic voice of Jesus.

The same method and conclusions appear in Bultmann's treatment of the other three forms. The dominical sayings (sayings of the Lord) he subdivides into five subdivisions: (1) Logia are proverbial sayings in the manner of the Hebrew *mashal*.[60] (2) Prophetic and apocalyptic sayings. Here one is surprised to find, having followed Bultmann's method in treating the other forms, that these sayings, though they do not appear so clearly to serve the interests of the Church, cannot be traced to Jesus with much more confidence than can the rest. (3) The legal sayings and Church rules display the marks of the creative developments of Church tradition and are among the earliest of such developments. (4) The "I- sayings," although they began in the Palestinian Church, developed mainly in the Hellenistic churches. (5) In the similitudes and similar forms the allegorical expansions are most obviously the work of the Church, and consequently in many instances the original meaning has been lost.

The remaining two forms, the miracle stories, and historical stories and legends, are concerned with the narrative material per se. The miracles he divides into four groups: (1) exorcisms of demons; (2) other healings; (3) raisings from the dead; (4) nature miracles. Bultmann's analysis of the form of the miracle stories, following much the same pattern, is more detailed and elaborate than that of Dibelius. These stories, he believes were developed either from popular folk tales, elaborations of sayings of Jesus, or misplaced Easter stories.

In contrast to miracle stories, legends are more concerned with what is religiously edifying. While actual historical events may lie back of legends, the legend form is not essentially concerned with history, nor can legends be distinguished with any certainty from historical stories. Both Dibelius and Bultmann supplement their studies by extensive parallels from both Jewish and pagan sources and have shed invaluable light on the study of the Gospels. It may be said, in fact, that they did their work so well that,

58. *The History of the Synoptic Tradition*, p. 50.
59. *The History of the Synoptic Tradition*, p. 55, *passim*.
60. On the Mashal and Wisdom tradition see West, *Introduction to The Old Testament*, p. 399.

insofar as the analyses and identifications of the forms of the pericopae are concerned, there has been comparatively little room for change.

FURTHER DEVELOPMENTS

That Bultmann's disturbingly negative conclusions regarding the historical validity of the tradition provoked vigorous reaction was inevitable. Along with German works of such scholars as M. Albertz and E. Fascher, there appeared during the next decade a number of English and American books, of which we need only notice a few. In 1928 Burton Scott Easton published his *The Gospel Before the Gospels,*[61] in which, while appreciative of the insights into the history of the tradition furnished by form criticism, he nevertheless chided its authors for attempting to press into the service of historical judgments this method which cannot by its own nature do more than disclose formal characteristics. From instances in which the Church could have served its own interests by modifying several traditions but did not do so, Easton went on to argue that the Church was in fact quite conservative in its handling of its traditions.

Charles Fox Burney, in a slender volume entitled *The Poetry of Our Lord,* made a valuable study of the poetic forms of the sayings material in the Gospels. Burney held this rabbinic characteristic of considerable mnemonic value to be a mark of authenticity.[62] Henry J. Cadbury, in 1927, published his well-known volume, *The Making of Luke-Acts,*[63] in which his effective but judicious use of form criticism did much to give balance and perspective to the new method. A few years later, in 1933, Vincent Taylor published his lectures, given at the University of Leeds the previous year, as a sympathetic critique of the new discipline.[64] Along with a valuable survey of the developments in Gospel research and a critical appraisal of the function and limitations of form criticism, Taylor made contributions of his own to the method, not the least of which was a simplification of the terminology. For Dibelius' *paradigmn* and Bultmann's *apophthegmata* he suggested the term "pronouncement stories." To Dibelius' *novellen* he preferred Bultmann's "miracle stories." Myths and legends Taylor believed were question-begging terms to which he preferred the

---

61. New York: Charles Scribner's Sons, 1928.
62. Oxford: Oxford University Press, 1925.
63. New York: The Macmillan Co., 1927.
64. *The Formation of the Gospel Tradition* (London: Macmillan & Co. Ltd. [1933], 1957). Also his, *The Life and Ministry of Jesus* (New York: Abingdon Press, 1955), pp. 13–50, which contains a good summary of English reaction to the skepticism produced by form criticism. See further Major, Manson, and Wright, *The Mission and Message of Jesus,* pp. 8–12. For examples of American reactions cf. S. J. Case, *Jesus: A New Biography* (Chicago: University of Chicago Press, 1927) with Dwight Marion Beck, *Through the Gospels to Jesus* (New York: Harper & Brothers, 1954).

simple title, "stories about Jesus." Dominical sayings are classified simply as "sayings and parables." Taylor also refuses to surrender altogether the Markan hypothesis. Still adhering to the essential reliability of the Papias tradition, he insisted that Mark's chronological order is based on apostolic recollection and is therefore generally reliable. In 1939, E. Basil Redlich published a small volume, entitled *Form Criticism,*[65] which along with a very useful survey of the history and method of the discipline presents an incisive scrutiny of its assumptions and conclusions. More recently, Joachim Jeremias, in his *The Parables of Jesus,*[66] subjected the parables to a thorough analysis with respect to their use and contexts in the Gospels and the *Sitz im Leben* which they implied. By this means he developed a method which he believed would distinguish the original parables of Jesus from the developments to which they were subjected by the Church.

Objections to form criticism have been made mainly at three points. (1) The *Sitz im Leben* has been too hastily established or assumed. Without doubt the history of the pericopae is far more complicated than the pioneer form critics assumed, and they must have been subject during their formative period to varying situations including, in many of them at least, the ministry of Jesus himself. That a pericope proved useful to the Church's immediate needs and may have been shaped and crystallized by such use by no means excludes or renders more doubtful its basic historicity. (2) There are few items in the Gospels which manifest any of the forms in a pure state.[67] Also there is a significant amount of material which is difficult to fit into any of the categories of oral forms.[68] These observations point to the singular brevity of the period, unlike the long history of the Old Testament traditions, during which the Gospel tradition developed. The short distance in time and the comparatively small group of persons involved place decided limits on the development and modification of the Church's tradition. (3) While discerning the formal characteristics of the tradition is very useful in reconstructing its history, it is only one step in the process of historical criticism and must be used under the control of other disciplines to make valid historical judgments.

When the significance of the forms is properly assessed and the study is placed in proper conjunction with other methods of study applied to the history of the beginnings of Christianity and the production of the Gospels, form criticism plays a very helpful role. As the study has developed we can discern at least five uses in the Primitive Church to which the traditions were put which contributed to their shape: (1) worship,

65. London: Duckworth, 1939.
66. New York: Charles Scribner's Sons, 1963.
67. Bultmann acknowledges this point but denies that it in any way affects his conclusions. *The History of the Synoptic Tradition,* p. 245, n. 2.
68. See Taylor, *The Formation of the Gospel Tradition.* Ch. VII, "Formless Stories," pp. 180–197.

(2) catechetical instruction, (3) the mission of evangelizing the world, (4) apologetics (a reasoned defense of Christianity, particularly in the worsening relations with the Roman Empire), and (5) polemics (controversy over doctrine and practice, especially in the increasing tension between Church and Synagogue).

4. A Connected Narrative

Because the studies which developed form criticism had also challenged the credibility of the Markan hypothesis, they put the question of the motives and methods of the final writers of the Gospels into a new perspective. If Mark was working only with isolated units of tradition and had no more than the most general knowledge of the chronology of the life of Jesus to guide him, by what plan did he put his Gospel together? The Gospel moves with too great an impelling force and displays too much underlying unity to have resulted from a haphazard collection of disparate materials. The other Gospel writers, as we have seen, show by their careful and extensive editing of their sources that they, too, are authors and not mere editors. These observations make it obvious that any study of the process which produced the Gospels must take careful account of the final writers.

Before we pursue these questions, however, we must take notice of some parallel developments which had considerable influence on the next stage in Gospel research.

THE PROBLEM OF ESCHATOLOGY

Literary criticism is not alone responsible for challenging the picture of Mark, the simple dragoman of Peter, faithfully if not skillfully recording the Apostle's reminiscences. One of the major turning points in the history of Gospel research occurred with the publication, in 1906, of Albert Schweitzer's *Von Reimarus Zu Wrede.* Translated by W. Montgomery and published in English under the title, *The Quest of the Historical Jesus,*[69] it became one of the best-known and most significant works in the New Testament field to be written in this century. The bulk of *The Quest* consists of an historical survey of studies in the Gospels and the life of Jesus from the middle of the eighteenth to the end of the nineteenth century, in the course of which Schweitzer shows how the persistent question of eschatology had either to be excised, suppressed, or rationalized in the attempts to write a life of Jesus acceptable to the modern point of view. The controlling goal of the scholars whom he surveyed was to find

69. With Introduction by J. M. Robinson (New York: The Macmillan Company, 1968).

an accommodation between Jesus in the Gospels and the rationalistic world view shaped by the emerging scientific age. This accommodation took the form of an attempt to liberate the historical Jesus from the dogmas of orthodoxy. Or, to use the figure of one of their last and greatest exponents, they sought to extract the "kernel" of the abiding validity of Jesus' religion from the "husk" of ancient, temporally conditioned dogma.[70] Appropriately they came to be known as "liberals." From this survey he proceeds to show that the Jesus for whom the "liberals" were searching never existed. Taking as his key Matthew 10:23, "You will not have gone through all the towns of Israel, before the Son of Man comes," Schweitzer argued that Jesus had identified himself with the eschatological Son of Man and expected the arrival of the new age of the Kingdom of God before his disciples could complete their mission. When the Kingdom failed to materialize, Jesus set himself to go to Jerusalem, and, by dying there, to bring onto himself the eschatological woes, and thus precipitate the coming of the Kingdom. In a startling and vivid metaphor Schweitzer describes his view of Jesus:

> There is silence all around. The Baptist appears, and cries: "Repent, for the Kingdom of Heaven is at hand." Soon after that comes Jesus, and in the knowledge that He is the coming Son of Man lays hold of the wheel of the world to set it moving on that last revolution which is to bring all ordinary history to a close. It refuses to turn, and He throws Himself upon it. Then it does turn; and crushes Him. Instead of bringing in the eschatological conditions, he has destroyed them. The wheel rolls onward, and the mangled body of the one immeasurably great Man, who was strong enough to think of Himself as the spiritual ruler of mankind and to bend history to His purpose, is hanging upon it still. That is His victory and His reign.[71]

Schweitzer's book had declared the illegitimacy of the liberal quest for the historical Jesus; form criticism, little more than a decade later, declared its impossibility. The easy distinction between the "Jesus of History" and the "Christ of Faith," by which liberal scholars over more than the last half of the nineteenth century had sought to extract a believable, human biography of Jesus from records overlaid by religious credulity, was no longer possible. Jesus remained a stranger bound to his own century, and the records persisted in witnessing only to what the Church saw and believed in him.[72] Among many scholars it became fashionable to say that

70. Adolf Harnach, *What Is Christianity?* (New York: Harper & Brothers, 1957), see especially "Lecture VIII," pp. 113–151.
71. *The Quest of the Historical Jesus*, pp. 370–371.
72. See Henry J. Cadbury, *The Peril of Modernizing Jesus* (New York: The Macmillan Company, 1937).

it is no longer possible to write a life of Jesus. The "quest" was over. Yet there were clear gains to be derived from the debacle.[73] The nature of the documents was better understood, and, if that nature is such that they can no longer be expected to answer many of our questions, at least we can be more sure of our ground in evaluating what they do tell us. The theological issues, also, have been clarified. Doctrinal interests, of course, have never been absent in the study of Jesus and the Gospels.[74] The goal of nineteenth-century liberal scholarship was to free what they conceived to be the simple religion of Jesus from the heavy hand of an alien ecclesiastical theology. Now it is clear that Jesus' religion was not so simple nor the Church's theology quite so alien.

DEMYTHOLOGIZING

At this point in Gospel studies Bultmann took steps to go beyond the negative results of his form critical research by introducing his program for "demythologizing" the New Testament. The program was launched by a paper he published in the early forties under the title, "New Testament and Mythology."[75] Since the controlling perspective of both Jesus' ministry of proclaiming the Kingdom of God and the Church in preserving and recording the tradition was eschatological, any adequate treatment of them must deal with the theological dimensions of eschatology and the consequent messianic claims made for Jesus. Starting from the observation that not only eschatology but also the entire world view of the Bible is mythological, and that "for modern man the mythological conception of the world, the conceptions of eschatology, of redeemer and of redemption, are over and done with," Bultmann refuses, nevertheless, to salvage Jesus' ethical teaching at the expense of his eschatology, or to transform the Kingdom of God into a social gospel. Instead he sets himself to the task of discovering the deeper meaning hidden beneath these mythological concepts.[76] This task of demythologizing he carries through by identifying the mythical elements and, having carefully analyzed them to discover their essential meaning, translating them through an existentialist interpretation into terms intelligible to modern man. In the briefest possible terms the kerygma means that through the proclamation of the historical Jesus man

73. An excellent resumé of the development of New Testament studies in the twentieth century is found in Reginald H. Fuller, *The New Testament in Current Study* (New York: Charles Scribner's Sons, 1962).
74. For a survey of the history of interpretations of the Kingdom of God which illustrates this point see Gösta Lundström, *The Kingdom of God in the Teaching of Jesus*, tr. Joan Bulman (Richmond, Va.: John Knox Press, 1963).
75. Reprinted in *Kerygma and Myth*, Hans Werner Bartsch, ed., tr. by Reginald H. Fuller (New York: Harper & Brothers, 1953) (Torchbook ed., 1961).
76. *Jesus Christ and Mythology* (New York: Charles Scribner's Sons, 1958), pp. 17–18. This work consists of his Shaffer Lectures at Yale University Divinity, School and his Cole Lectures at Vanderbilt University, both in 1951.

is being called to repent and forsake his false existence in this evil world and, being delivered from bondage to his past, to find his authentic life in a new eschatological existence open to the future.[77] The New Testament understanding of existence confronts that of modern man in the preaching of the word and demands a radical decision. If one responds in a decision of faith, "he is already above time and history" and now being "in Christ" is "a contemporary of Christ, and time and the world's history are overcome."[78] Bultmann's project for demythologizing almost immediately met with a storm of debate, but for that very reason came to dominate New Testament research for the next two decades. Those who did not share his orientation toward the existentialism of Martin Heidegger objected to his project on philosophical grounds. Others took issue with what in the tradition he identified as myth. Two of the most serious and persistent criticisms of his theory concern the meaning of history, which by the results of his method appears to be left very much in doubt, and the significance of the Church as a community of the People of God.[79]

For our purposes it will not be necessary to follow the debate over demythologizing, but two consequences which follow from it are significant for the later developments in Gospel study: In the first place Bultmann established the point that the mythology in the Gospels is not a dispensable "husk" which may be shucked away to expose the "kernel of timeless truth" or the "real Jesus," but is itself a form of theological truth and therefore requires to be understood and interpreted. Second, he focused attention on the witness of the Gospel writers themselves and demanded that they be studied for their own sake. The Church's faith remains the only vehicle of Jesus' Gospel to us. If Jesus' history cannot be reconstructed with confidence, we can at least hear the testimony of the Church to him and with profit acquire a new understanding of the nature of her faith in him.

Scholars could hardly be content to rest with the negative conclusions concerning our knowledge of Jesus at which Gospel research had arrived. The inevitable renewal of interest in the history of Jesus arose within a group of Bultmann's former students who, joined by others attracted to the

77. See *Jesus Christ and Mythology*, ch. V. Bultmann carried through his project effectively and consistently in his monumental study of the teaching of Jesus: *Jesus and the Word,* tr. Louise Pettibone Smith and Erminie Huntress Lantero (New York: Charles Scribner's Sons, [1934], 1958).

78. History and Eschatology (New York: Harper Torchbook. 1957) pp. 152–153. This book consists of the Gifford Lectures at the University of Edinburgh for 1955.

79. It is to this problem of history that his Gifford Lectures in 1955 at the University of Edinburgh were addressed. First published under the title, *The Presence of Eternity,* they have been reissued in paperback with the new title, *History and Eschatology.* For further on Bultmann's debate with theologians and philosophers see *Kerygma and Myth* and *Myth and Christianity* (New York: The Noonday Press, 1958).

new movement, became known as the "post-Bultmannians." The "new quest of the historical Jesus," as it was called, proceeded with more modest goals and more cautious use of evidence.[80]

Two proposals furnished the support for the new quest: (1) that there is an essential continuity between Jesus' proclamation and the kerygma of the Church, so that the latter is accounted for in some way by the former; (2) that Jesus' actions and conduct were the original context of his proclamation and message—indeed, in a sense, must be said to be a part of it. As the first major result of the new enterprise one of Bultmann's former students, Günther Bornkamm, published, in 1956, a life of Jesus—a rare event in German scholarship since the end of the original quest.[81] Instead of issuing in a renewed production of "lives of Jesus," however, the "new quest" turned scholarly energies to another investigation. That investigation takes us back to the question with which we began this section: How are we to understand the message and meaning the canonical Gospels intend to convey?

COMPOSITION CRITICISM

The question of the theology of the Gospels is, of course, not a new one. By focusing attention on the messianic claims made for Jesus and the corresponding problem of eschatology, Wrede and Schweitzer had established the theological character of the Gospels. Bultmann had, in the course of his analysis of mythology in the Gospels, developed exegetical skills useful in defining and clarifying their theological patterns.[82] Each of the pioneer studies in form criticism had included a chapter

80. See James M. Robinson, *A New Quest of the Historical Jesus,* Studies In Biblical Theology No. 25 (Naperville, Ill.: Alec R. Allenson, Inc., 1959). Especially important for the resumption of the Quest was Ernst Fuchs' article, "Die Frage nach dem historischen Jesus" reprinted in his *Zur Frage Nach Dem Historischen Jesus* (Tubingen: J. C. B. Mohr [Paul Siebeck], 1960). See also Reginald H. Fuller, The New Testament in Current Study, pp. 25–53; and W. D. Davies, *Christian Origins and Judaism* (Philadelphia: The Westminster Press, 1962), pp. 1–17. For an essay critical of the movement see, Carl E. Braaten and Roy A. Harrisville, *The Historical Jesus and the Kerygmatic Christ* (New York: Abingdon Press, 1964), pp. 197–242.

81. *Jesus of Nazareth,* tr. Irene and Fraser McLuskey with James M. Robinson (New York: Harper & Brothers, 1960). Ethelbert Stauffer's *Jesus and His Story,* tr. Richard and Clara Winston (New York: Alfred A. Knopf, 1960), which appeared the next year (1957 German ed.) should be noted here. On the basis of the verisimilitude he professes to find in John's Gospel in connection with Jewish legal provisions regarding heretics Stauffer has elevated John to the position of a first-rate source for the life of Jesus, and produced an astonishingly detailed biography. The book goes even beyond many of the ambitious attempts in the peroid of the original quest. Needless to say, Stauffer's work has not met with much approval among scholars.

82. For the fruitfulness of these skills in his own writing see Rudolf Bultmann, *Theology of the New Testament,* tr. Kendrick Grobel (New York: Charles Scribner's Sons, 1951, 1955).

on the final composition of the Gospels which attempted at least a provisional answer to the question. By his delineation of Mosaic and Pentateuchal motifs in Matthew, Benjamin W. Bacon anticipated and helped to prepare the way for the new investigation.[83] Although his thesis that Matthew was attempting to present a new Christian Torah from Jesus, the new Law Giver, has generally been discarded, his emphasis on the five-fold structure of the Gospel as a clue to its meaning has called attention to the importance of the structure and patterns of all the Gospels for their interpretation. Similarly, Ernst Lohmeyer[84] laid the groundwork for another important aspect of the new study by examining the role geography plays in the structure of the Gospels. Beginning with the variant traditions of the appearances of the Risen Lord in Galilee or Jerusalem,[85] Lohmeyer reasons that the two districts represent centers of divergent forms of Christianity and therefore have theological significance. It is not necessary to subscribe to this thesis to appreciate the importance of the geographical symbolism in the Gospels to which Lohmeyer has called attention.

Numerous other studies in the theology of the Gospels, primarily concerned with Christology, have focused attention on the titles applied to Jesus by the Gospel writers.[86] The publication of a very modestly sized monograph in 1956 by Willi Marxsen may be taken as the formal opening of the school concerned with the composition of the Gospels.[87] At any rate, this book seems to have established the technical name *Redactionsgeschichte,* which in English becomes redaction criticism. Marxsen, in his

---

83. *Studies in Matthew* (New York: Holt, 1930). On his theory of Matthew as a new Christian Pentateuch and criticisms of it see below, pp. 112–113 and notes.
84. *Galiläa und Jerusalem* (Gottingen, Vandenhoeck & Ruprecht, 1936). For a summary and evaluation of Lohmeyer's theory see F. C. Grant, *The Earliest Gospel* (New York: Abingdon Press, 1943) ch. VI, pp. 125–147. See also R. H. Lightfoot, *Locality and Doctrine in the Gospels* (New York: Harper & Brothers, 1938).
85. Cf. Mk. 16:7–8; Mt. 28:7–20; Lk. 24:8–53; John 20:1–29; 21:1–23.
86. H. B. Sharman, *The Son of Man and Kingdom of God* (New York: Harper & Brothers, 1943); Rudolph Otto, *The Kingdom of God and the Son of Man,* tr. Floyd V. Filson and B. L. Woolf (London: Tutterworth Press, 1943); J. Y. Campbell, "The Origin and Meaning of the Term 'Son of Man,'" JTS, Vol. XLVIII, 1947, pp. 145ff. Reprinted in his *Three New Testament Studies* (Leiden: E. J. Brill, 1965) pp. 29–40. Among the books which in one way or another have either anticipated or helped to shape the study of the composition of the Gospels are B. W. Bacon, *The Gospel of Mark* (New Haven: Yale University Press, 1925); B. W. Bacon, *The Beginning of the Gospel Story* (New Haven: Yale University Press, 1909); James Hardy Ropes, *The Synoptic Gospels* (Cambridge: Harvard University Press, 1934); F. C. Grant, *The Earliest Gospel,* chs. VII and VIII; R. H. Lightfoot, *The Gospel Message of St. Mark* (Oxford: At the Clarendon Press, 1950); James M. Robinson, *The Problem of History in Mark* (London: SCM Press LTD, 1957), G. D. Kilpatrick *The Origins of the Gospel According to St. Matthew* (Oxford: At the Clarendon Press, 1946); Krister Stendahl, *The School of St. Matthew* (Philadelphia: Fortress Press, 1968).
87. *Mark the Evangelist,* tr. Roy A. Harrisville (Nashville, Tenn.: Abingdon Press, 1969).

introduction, protests the prevailing impression left by the form critics that the final compilers of the Gospels were mere "scissors and paste" editors and convincingly argues that they each were creative authors with a theological viewpoint to present. At about the same time Günther Bornkamm and two of his students at the University of Heidelberg, Gerhard Barth and Heinz Joachim Held, were writing studies (the latter two were doctoral dissertations) which were later combined and published under the title (of the English translation) *Tradition and Interpretation in Matthew.*[88] Shortly afterward, Hans Conzelmannn published his definitive study, *The Theology of St. Luke.*[89] Both of these works significantly advanced both the method and results of Marxsen's approach to the Gospels.

That the Gospel writers do in fact present a theology we have already seen. We have observed also that Matthew and Luke felt quite free to modify the order, and even the content, of both Mark and Q. That they were guided in a creative way in their editing by motives of their own and that the same motivation must be allowed Mark is therefore hardly deniable. Redaction is, for that reason, not an accurate description for their activity. Composition criticism, used in some quarters as an alternate, is a more accurate title for this method of Gospel study.

It is important to notice that composition criticism cannot be merely tacked onto the end of Gospel research as a final stage. If the editors were authors in any real sense, their individual motives must be taken into account in dealing with the problems of both source and form criticism. Quite possibly many of these hitherto stubborn problems will yield to the new approach.[90] This possibility was anticipated by Morton Scott Enslin who, in 1938, wrote

> It appears to me that a frank recognition of the fact that both of these writers (Matthew and Luke) were authors in the truest sense of the word—but authors who lived in the first century, not the twentieth—deprives the argument that each must have worked independent of the other, because of their omissions and substitutions, of most of its force, and enables us to see the matter of their so-called agreements in a different light.[91]

88. Tr. Percy Scott (Philadelphia: The Westminster Press, 1963).
89. The German title, *Die Mitte der Zeit* (The Middle of Time), is more descriptive of Conzelmann's thesis than the subtitle used as the title in the English edition. Dibelius' essay, "Style Criticism of Acts," published in 1923, although not concerned with the Gospels, anticipated these studies by focusing attention upon Luke's role as an author and the freedom he exercised in handling his material. See pp. 280–287.
90. We have already noted that Conzelmann, on the basis of his study of Luke's theological purpose, rejected Streeter's theory of Proto-Luke. See p. 54.
91. *Christian Beginnings,* p. 432. This whole chapter would bear rereading in the light of the newer direction in Gospel study.

Miracles which appear as pronouncement stories, mixed forms, the so-called "formless" stories, and the like may not in all cases require the fortuities of their oral history to account for their present condition.

Composition criticism, without ignoring the results of source and form criticism, concentrates on the Gospels in their present form. Patterns of organization and outline, especially as they represent modification of their sources, are revealing of the authors' emphases and purposes. Similarly geographical data disclose symbolic meanings; changes of locale serve to divide materials and indicate changes of themes. By the use of Old Testament quotations, allusions, and motifs, not only are prophetic patterns of "promise and fulfillment" delineated, but other Old Testament doctrines and interpretations are introduced. Of particular importance for composition criticism are the alterations made by Matthew and Luke in their use of Mark, and their differences in their use of Q. These differences concern both the modifications of the pericopae and rearrangements of the materials. Repetitions and doublets reveal not only modifications of interpretation and emphasis but associations of ideas and themes running through the Gospels whose meanings are developed by the various relationships that are thus established. Groupings and rearrangements of materials can be seen to modify the meaning of their components. In observations such as these the interpreter can follow the mind of the authors in tracing out the ways in which they were able, without drastically rewriting their sources, to make the traditions speak to their own time and needs and to affirm the Gospel as they understood it.

As scholars have observed, the methods of the Gospel writers disclosed by such analyses are not unlike those of rabbinic tradition. Jewish *haggadah* and *halakah* both find their parallels in the Gospels. It is not denying the uniqueness of the literary genre of Gospels, nor an inaccurate comprehension of their character, to describe them as Christian *midrashim*. The emphasis in the Gospels, however, is eschatological and therefore, as Stendahl has pointed out in his study of Matthew, they are more interested in the fulfillment of Old Testament prophecies than in elaborating rules of conduct. In this regard the Gospels stand closer to the *midrash pesher* of the Qumran scrolls than to the rabbinic teaching later incorporated in the Mishnah.[92]

Although during the period in which the Gospels were being produced the gentile element was becoming increasingly predominant, the presence in the Church of Judaic ideas and thought forms was by no means confined to the use of the Old Testament as the Scripture of the Church. The Christian movement was born in Judaism, its traditions grew and developed in a Jewish context, and it insisted that it was the "New Israel," the true con-

92. *The School of St. Matthew* p. 35. See especially his section, "The formula quotations of Matthew and the Habakkuk Commentary from Qumran," pp. 183ff.

tinuity of the People of God. A comprehensive knowledge of Jewish traditions, literature, and logic is therefore manifestly of great value to understanding the Gospels. A beginning was made in this direction around the
turn of the century by such scholars as Hermann L. Strack, Paul Billerbeck,
and Alfred Edersheim.[93] Composition critical studies have been greatly
aided by a new impetus in Judaic studies. The Dead Sea documents, needless to say, have proved invaluable in this connection as have all the rapid
developments in Biblical archaeology. Nothing that increases our understanding of the Old Testament generally, and the history of late Judaism
in particular, is unimportant in New Testament studies. The appearance
therefore of such midrashic studies as those of Peder Borgen, John Bow-
man, and Geza Vermes[94] has been a welcome aid to the composition
critics and has added a new dimension to the study of the Gospels.

THE QUESTION OF AUTHORSHIP

Before we turn to a survey of the message and contents of the Gospels,
we must concern ourselves briefly with the thorny questions of the identity
of the authors of the Gospels and the dates and places of their composition. We must, of course, keep in mind that the captions of the books of
the Bible are not a part of the texts themselves but were supplied by the
Church, probably because bringing them together into a single collection
made it necessary to distinguish them from one another. They therefore
do not necessarily represent the claims of the documents themselves and
are, especially in the case of the Gospels, nothing more than later tradition
which was more concerned to enhance their authority than to determine
their actual history.

Matthew   It is customary in connection with these introductory questions
to begin by citing the well-known quotation, found in the *Ecclesiastical
History* of Eusebius, Bishop of Caesarea (ca. A.D. 324), from the second-
century Christian writer, Papias:

> This also the presbyter said: Mark, having become the inter-
> preter of Peter, wrote down accurately, though not indeed in
> order, whatsoever he remembered of the things said or done
> by Christ. For he neither heard the Lord nor followed him,
> but afterward, as I said, he followed Peter, who adapted his
> teaching to the needs of his hearers, but with no intention

93. Cf. Herman L. Strack, *Introduction to the Talmud and Midrash* (New York:
Meridian Books, Inc., 1959). Herman E. Strack and Paul Billerbeck, *Kommentar
Zum Neuen Testament aus Talmud und Midrasch* (Munich: C. H. Beck, 1922–
28); Alfred Edersheim, *The Life and Times of Jesus the Messiah* (New York:
Longmans, Green, and Co. [1883], 1899).
94. *Bread From Heaven* (Leiden: E. J. Brill, 1965); *The Gospel of Mark* (Leiden:
E. J. Brill, 1965); *Scripture and Tradition in Judaism* (Leiden: E. J. Brill, 1961).

of giving a connected account of the Lord's discourses, so
that Mark committed no error while he thus wrote some
things as he remembered them. For he was careful of one
thing, not to omit any of the things which he had heard, and
not to state any of them falsely . . . so then Matthew wrote
the oracles in the Hebrew language, and every one interpreted
them as he was able.[95]

The importance of this passage lies in the fact that, if we can assume
that Eusebius quoted Papias accurately, it is the earliest statement we have
on the origin of the Gospels. It raises about as many questions, however,
as it answers.[96] What, for instance, did Papias mean by the word "oracles"?
Many have taken the word to mean sayings and have identified it with Q.
Thus Matthew's name came to be attached to the Gospel, on this theory, by
its author's use of Q. That a document such as Matthew should be credited
to the author of one of its sources is, on the face of it, unlikely.[97] Ancient
tradition is explicit, moreover, in ascribing the canonical Gospel itself to
Matthew and declares it to have been written in Hebrew (Aramaic).[98]
Since source criticism, on the basis of the verbal agreements among the
Synoptics (in Greek), has established that not only the Gospel itself but
the Q source as used in it were written in Greek, Papias' tradition is relatively worthless. The Q document may indeed have been written in
Aramaic, but if so, it was translated before it came into the hands of the
author of Matthew. Although it may help to account for the ancient tradition of Matthean authorship, the substitution of the name Matthew for
Levi in Matthew 9:9 (cf. Mk. 2:14 and Lk. 5:27) as a cryptic signature
of the author can hardly be taken seriously. The author's extensive use of
sources, which would not be necessary for an eyewitness, the ways in which
he reflects the life and problems of the post-Pauline Early Church, and
the difficulties involved in taking the ancient traditions literally all make
it clear that we simply do not know who the author was nor how Matthew's name became attached to the Gospel.

A more fruitful suggestion on the question of the authorship is Krister
Stendahl's thesis that the Gospel was the product of a "school" of Christian
scribes utilizing the Old Testament in their interpretations of Jesus with
much the same methods as those of the Qumran sectarians.[99] Whether this

95. Eusebius, H. E., III, 39, Quoted from The Nicene and Post-Nicene Fathers, 2nd
    Series, Vol. I, pp. 172–173.
96. Kirsopp Lakes's sage observation is worth quoting: Unfortunately many of the
    early 'traditions' of gospel origins were derived . . . not so much from apostolic
    tradition as from postapostolic guesses." Quoted from F. C. Grant, The Gospels,
    p. 65.
97. Cf. Henry J. Cadbury, The Making of Luke-Acts, pp. 105–106, with B. H. Streeter,
    The Four Gospels, p. 501.
98. E.g., Eusebius, H.E., III, 24, 6; V, 8, 2; VI, 25, 4.
99. The School of St. Matthew, especially pp. 28–29.

school and the church within which it functioned can be in any way associated with the apostle Matthew must remain an open question.

On the question of the provenance of Matthew, scholarly opinion generally agrees in locating it in Syria, perhaps Antioch itself. Its striking "Jewishness" and yet its universalism suggest a place in the East and one like Syria in which the streams of Semitic and Hellenistic culture met. That St. Ignatius of Antioch seems to have known the Gospel adds weight to this opinion.[100]

We can scarcely be more precise as to the date of Matthew. Since Mark served as a source for this Gospel, and it is likely, as we shall see, that Mark was written in Rome ca. A.D. 65–70, the time necessary for a copy of Mark to reach Syria would make a date earlier than A.D. 75–80 unlikely. This conclusion is reinforced by the reference to the "angry king" in Matthew 22:7, which, as many commentators suggest, may be an illusion to Titus' destruction of Jerusalem in A.D. 70. The character of the content in Matthew requires, if anything, an even later date. The resurgence of eschatological interest, the strong ecclesiastical concern, as well as the highly developed exegetical and theological tradition place Matthew clearly in the second-generation Church. If, on the other hand, St. Ignatius knew the canonical Matthew, a date after the end of the first century is not likely. Because there is no clear evidence as to whether Matthew was written before or after Luke, we can hardly date it more exactly than A.D. 80–100.

Mark   Papias' statement, quoted above, is hardly more helpful in accounting for Mark's Gospel. It confronts the fact, to begin with, that Mark's Gospel manifests characteristics which show him to be far more than a recorder of Peter's preaching. Form criticism has shown the evidence of considerable development which could scarcely have taken place if Mark had received his material directly from Peter. The Gospel shows a theological purpose which is too well organized and consistently carried through to be the incidental result of recording an Apostle's preaching. What Papias meant by the phrase "but not in order" is impossible to tell, but it does not describe the structure and organization of Mark.

So little has Papias' statement corresponded to what modern studies have found in Mark that some scholars have discarded it altogether. Noting that Eusebius regarded Papias as not very bright,[101] these scholars have concluded that the entire statement is nothing more than an inference from I Peter 5:13 designed to save Mark's place in the Canon alongside the other more popular Gospels. Such a conclusion, however, is too sweeping. Surely the author of this Gospel was named Mark. The importance of apostolic authority for canonicity was too great for a book to bear a non-

---

100. See B. H. Streeter, *The Four Gospels,* 500ff.; also F. C. Grant, *The Gospels,* pp. 140ff.
101. *H.E.,* III, 39, 13.

apostolic name unless its authorship was too well known to do otherwise. Papias therefore, in associating Mark's writing with Peter, may have been attempting, on the basis of I Peter 5:13, to give this Gospel its needed apostolic authority. That the Mark in question was the John Mark in Acts 13:13, 15:37, *passim,* is another matter. The name was quite common. It is a fair question to ask if a native of Jerusalem (Acts 12:12) would commit the geographical blunder of having Jesus go through the Decapolis on his way from Sidon to the Sea of Galilee (Mark 7:31).[102] Assuming that I Peter was written by the apostle—an assumption many scholars would not make—the identity of the Mark mentioned at the end of that Epistle with the one in Acts is no more than conjecture. (Cf. the tradition that Mark worked in Alexandria in Egypt, Eusebius, *H.E.,* II, 16, 1.) That the Gospel was written in Rome is intrinsically not unlikely. Although the Latinisms it contains are of little or no significance,[103] the persistent association with Mark and Rome of a Gospel, vying with its larger and more popular competitors for its place in the Canon, must have had a more solid base than the guesswork of Papias.[104] Fortunately, the questions of authorship and provenance are not so important as that of date for interpreting Mark.

If Papias' statement about the authorship of the second Gospel be accepted as essentially true, the date of its writing would be shortly after the death of Peter which is usually assumed to have occurred during the Neronian persecution in A.D. 64. This approximate dating can, fortunately, be accepted on quite other grounds. In the first place, Mark was used, as we have seen, as a source by both Matthew and Luke. It must therefore be earlier than either. Both Matthew and Luke appeared not later than the last two decades of the first century. Some time must be allowed for Mark to have been circulated widely enough—especially if it originated in Rome—and to have become sufficiently well known to have been so used by the other two Gospels. A date much later than A.D. 70 would not meet these requirements. On the other hand, the manifest development during their oral history which many of the pericopae display cannot be accounted for if we push the date back much farther than the seventh decade.

---

102. For opposite view see Branscomb, *The Gospel of Mark,* (MNTC) xxi-viii.
103. Joachim Jeremias does, however, find "the Roman division of the night into four watches (Mark 13:35, cf. 6:48), based on the requirements of Roman military service (cf. Acts 12:4)), instead of the Palestinian division into three" to be "one of the numerous indications that the second Gospel was written in Rome." *The Parables of Jesus,* p. 27. James L. Price regards such matters as the "martyr motif" in Mark as important evidence of its Roman provenance. See *Interpreting The New Testament* (New York: Holt, Rinehart and Winston, 1961), pp. 183ff.
104. That the appearance of Matthew and Luke pushed Mark into the background is shown by the fewer textual accommodations it suffered in comparison to the other two. For demonstration of this point see B. H. Streeter, *The Four Gospels,* rev. ed., (London: Macmillan & Co. Ltd., 1961), pp. 63–64, 341.

Alongside these general considerations is one more specific clue which some interpreters regard as decisive. This clue concerns the relation of the Little Apocalypse, chapter 13, especially verses 14–20, to the fall of Jerusalem in A.D. 70. A few scholars regard this passage as a reference to the later event written after the fact and read back into Jesus' teaching, which would mean that Mark could not have been written before A.D. 70.[105] A comparison of this passage with its parallel in Luke 21:20–24 has led others to conclude that Luke's more vivid and specific references to the catastrophe resulted from looking back upon the event which the writer of Mark 13:14ff. was anticipating in the immediate future. Parts of Mark 13, including these verses, as we shall see, very probably came from a brief apocalyptic tract circulated to warn Christians of the imminent danger in the rapidly deteriorating situation in Jerusalem. The tract must have been written shortly before the siege of Titus. Mark incorporated it into his Gospel not long afterward but before the fall of the city—or at least before news of the fall had reached him in Rome. Such reasoning would limit the composition of the Gospel to the seventh decade. We may therefore be allowed the educated guess that Mark was written by a Christian by that name in Rome ca. A.D. 65–70.

Luke We must always keep in mind in discussing Luke's Gospel that it is the first part of a two-volume work which we may designate, following Henry J. Cadbury's happy device, by the hyphenated title, Luke-Acts. The two volumes taken together represent the largest amount of material by one author in the New Testament (52 chapters out of a total of 260). If the unity of style, method, point of view, and the like were not enough to establish the unity of these two New Testament books, the Prefaces, Luke 1:1–4 and Acts 1:1, make that unity explicit.[106] This unity means for our present purpose not only that any decision we make concerning the origins of one immediately applies to the other, but also that any pertinent evidence found in either applies to both.

We may begin with another quotation from the Muratorian Fragment we mentioned earlier, which is probably the oldest extant statement on the authorship of Luke-Acts, and represents ancient opinion at least from the second century:

> The third book of the Gospel, that according to Luke, the well-known physician Luke wrote in his own name in order after the ascension of Christ, and when Paul had associated him with himself as one studious of right. Nor did he him-

---

105. For example, B. Harvie Branscomb, *The Gospel of Mark* (*MNTC*), pp. xxx–xxxi.
106. See Henry J. Cadbury, *The Making of Luke-Acts*, pp. 7–11. For opposite opinion see Albert C. Clark, *The Acts of the Apostles* (Oxford: At the Clarendon Press, 1933), pp. 393–408.

self see the Lord in the flesh; and he, according as he was able to accomplish it, began his narrative with the nativity of John. . . Moreover, the acts of all the apostles are comprised by Luke in one book, and addressed to the most excellent Theophilus, because these different events took place when he was present himself; and he shows this clearly (i.e., that the principle on which he wrote was to give only what fell under his own notice) by the omission of the passion of Peter, and also of the journey of Paul, when he went from the city (Rome) to Spain.[107]

That the author's name was Luke may be granted for the same reason that Mark is most probably the name of the author of the second Gospel. The question is, who was he? The name is common and in two forms occurs five times in the New Testament. One of them, Acts 13:1, refers to a Lucius of Cyrene who is not likely to be identical with the others.[108] The other four references are in letters bearing Paul's name: Romans 16:21, Colossians 4:14, Philemon 24, and II Timothy 4:11. That Colossians 4:14 calls Luke "the beloved physician" has generated considerable search for medical language and interests in Luke-Acts in order to confirm the statement of the Muratorian Fragment identifying the author with the Colossian Luke. The search, however, has not been very successful.[109] As the Fragment indicates in its reference to Acts, the matter hinges on Luke's association with Paul. The question is two-pronged: Was the author of Luke-Acts associated with Paul? If so, was that companion the same as the physician in Colossians? We obviously cannot take seriously the suggestion of the Muratorian Fragment that, in contrast to his dependence upon tradition in writing the Gospel, the author was a witness to all he included in Acts. Yet there is one piece of evidence that suggest the author was for a time Paul's traveling companion. In three passages the narrative abruptly turns from the usual third person to the first person plural. These so-called "we" sections, Acts 16:10–17, 20:5–21:18, 27:1–28:15, except for the journey to Jerusalem and finally to Rome, are limited to Troas and Macedonia, and therefore simply suggest that the author of Acts had joined Paul's party at those points in the story.[110] Because of historical dfficulties

107. Translation from *The Ante-Nicene Library,* Vol. IX, Fragments, pp. 159–161. See above, pp. 37–40.
108. Cf. Henry J. Cadbury, in Foakes Jackson and Kirsopp Lake, *Beginnings of Christianity,* (London: Macmillan & Company, 1922), Vol. V, pp. 489–495; A. C. Clark, *The Acts of the Apostles,* pp. 391–392.
109. On this whole question see Henry J. Cadbury, *The Making of Luke-Acts,* pp. 354ff. Also Foakes Jackson and Kirsopp Lake, *The Beginnings of Christianity,* Vol. II, pp. 209–250. Also A. H. McNeil, *An Introduction to the Study of the New Testament,* 2nd ed., rev. C. S. C. Williams (Oxford: At the Clarendon Press, 1953), pp. 103–123.
110. See pp. 279–281. Cf. Irenaeus, *Against Heresies,* III, 14.

between the earlier story of Paul in Acts 11–15 and Paul's own account in Galatians 1–2, a number of scholars contend that a companion of Paul could not have been the author of the entire book, and therefore the "we" sections represent a diary used by the author as a source. Since there is no discernible difference of style between these sections and their context, we are left with the difficult question, why the author would so thoroughly assimilate this source to his own style yet leave the first-person pronouns standing.[111] As an argument in this same direction we should note that the historical problems in the earlier part of Acts are not quite so insurmountable as was once supposed.[112] More difficult is the question why in Acts there is no mention of Paul's letters. It may be answered, of course, that since they had not yet been collected and circulated, Luke did not regard them germane to his story. Yet it remains strange that Luke should reflect so little influence of Paul's theology. The argument, on the other hand, that being an occasional traveling companion of Paul would not necessarily acquaint Luke with the peculiar subtleties of Paul's theology or oblige him to reflect them merits serious attention. Martin Dibelius, for example, contends for the traditional view of the authorship of Luke-Acts on the ground that the dedication to Theophilus indicates that the work was intended for the book market at large and must therefore have borne the author's name. That the name of the author would be lost while that of the patron was retained would, under such circumstances, be highly improbable. To the objections based on discrepancies between Acts and Paul's letters, Dibelius replies that both the discrepancies and the necessary influence of traveling companionship have been exaggerated, and that Luke, in accordance with the practices of ancient historiography, would feel free to shape his materials to his own purposes and point of view.[113] The weakness in this argument is that it establishes the name of the author but his identity as Paul's companion remains no more than a possibility. The case is not proved in either direction. That the author was the Luke of Colossians 4:14, furthermore, may be no more than an inference from the fact that it is difficult to find anyone else in Paul's letters to qualify for the identification. The suspicion cannot be altogether allayed, therefore, that the tradition presented in Muratorian Fragment may have been arrived at by inferences based on the "we" sections and a coincidence of names. In a word, we cannot say with any certainty who was the author of Luke-Acts.

If the discussion of the identity of Luke is indecisive, identifying the place of writing of Luke-Acts must be more so. There is no clear tradition

---

111. Henry J. Cadbury, *The Making of Luke-Acts,* p. 358.
112. Below, pp. 311–314. Also Donald J. Selby, *Toward the Understanding of St. Paul* (Englewood Cliffs, N.J.: Prentice-Hall, 1962), pp. 117–122, 176–178, 203–204.
113. *Studies in the Acts of the Apostles,* ed. H. Greeven, tr. M. Ling (New York: Charles Scribner's Sons, 1956), pp. 135–137, *passim.*

on the question ancient enough to be of any significance. That the first Epistle of St. Clement ca. A.D. 95 echoes a few passages in Acts does suggest a Roman provenance, but it is equally possible that the book, written elsewhere, had migrated by that time to Rome. B. H. Streeter believes that Luke began collecting the material for his work in Caesarea while Paul was imprisoned there. But this theory depends on the assumption that the author was the companion of Paul. For the final edition of Luke-Acts, Streeter cautiously follows St. Jerome in assigning the Gospel to Greece (Corinth?) and Acts to Rome.[114] This is perhaps as good a guess as any, but it is hardly more than a guess.

The curious fact that Acts makes no mention of Paul's letters provides some basis for fixing some approximate dates for the writing. That Luke regarded Paul's letters as of no importance to his purpose, since they were concerned only with the immediate problems of the churches receiving them, may explain why a companion of Paul would fail to mention them. If, however, the collected letters were already in circulation and receiving the attention we know they did receive at the end of the first century, the silence of Acts is completely inexplicable. Luke-Acts must, then, have been written before that collection was made.[115] The supposed dependence of Acts upon Josephus, which would have required a date at the earliest not before the very end of the first century, has not survived more careful scrutiny. We may therefore assume that Luke-Acts was written sometime before A.D. 90. That Luke 21:20ff. reflects knowledge of Titus' siege of Jerusalem and consequently requires a date after A.D. 70 is likely but not important. Luke's use of Mark would hardly allow a date earlier than A.D. 75 anyway. A date, therefore, between A.D. 75 and 90 seems a safe conclusion for the writing of Luke-Acts.

John   Like Luke's Gospel, the Gospel of John is linked to writing on the Epistle side of the New Testament. Five books bear the name of John: the Gospel, three Epistles, and the Revelation. The last of these, however, was shown by a remarkable piece of ancient literary criticism to be by a different hand from the Gospel and the Epistles. In the fourth century Dionysius of Alexandria analyzed the style of the Revelation and the Johannine Gospel and first Epistle to draw the conclusion, which must still be recognized as valid, that two authors are represented by this literature.[116] His conclusion that, although the Revelation was written by another John,

114. *The Four Gospels,* 534f. the entire chapter XVIII.
115. Edgar J. Goodspeed, *The Formation of the New Testament* (Chicago: The University of Chicago Press, 1926), pp. 20ff., suggests that it was the publication of Acts which instigated the collecting of Paul's letters.
116. Eusebius, H.E., VIII. 25. It should perhaps be noted that Dionysius was not without dogmatic motives. As an Alexandrian he found the crude materialistic eschatology of Revelation objectionable. Yet he did admit the possibility of a hidden meaning which he had not perceived.

the Gospel and Epistle were written by the disciple, John bar Zebedee, is less likely. That Dionysius was unsuccessful in persuading the Church of the nonapostolic authorship of the Revelation is clear from its presence in the Canon. The opposition to it would otherwise have been enough to keep it out.

In truth there is scarcely a more obscure problem in New Testament introduction than the provenance of the Johannine literature.[117] As Dionysius tells us there were many who bore the name John. He also tells of two monuments to John in Ephesus which both he and Eusebius take to refer to different men by that name.[118] Following the clue of the references to "the Elder" in the salutations of the second and third Epistles some scholars have supposed an Ephesian presbyter named John, and a disciple of the Apostle, to be the author of the Gospel and Epistles. The problem is complicated by the possibility that III John may be from a different author from the others. This meaning of the two tombs in itself only a guess, and any theory built on it cannot be more certain. The suspicion can never be removed, furthermore, that John bar Zebedee was martyred at the same time as his brother (Acts 12:2). The saying about sharing Jesus' cup and baptism, in Mark 10:30, certainly implies that he was.[119] Tradition is both confused and divided on the question to such a degree as to be virtually worthless as historical evidence. Except for some possible echoes of the Gospel in a few instances such as the letters of St. Ignatius,[120] it bursts on the scene rather suddenly in the latter part of the second century. As we have seen in the quotations earlier in this chapter, at that time its authorship by John bar Zebedee was positively affirmed—indeed a little too positively. The pronounced differences between John and the Synoptics and some suspicions of heresy had generated opposition to the Gospel. The insistence by the Gospel's champions on apostolic authorship, therefore, was hardly unbiased and should be taken *cum grano salis.*

Internal evidence, the character of the Gospel itself, is of little help. John's name appears nowhere in it, nor does the name of his brother James for that matter. (There is, of course, a reference to the "sons of Zebedee" in the appendix, 21:2). This fact, coupled with mysterious allusions to a "beloved disciple" in 13:23, 19:26, 20:2, 20, has led to the suggestion that the latter is a cryptic "signature" of the author, John bar

117. See B. W. Bacon, *The Fourth Gospel in Research and Debate* (New York: Moffat, Yard and Company, 1910); William Sanday, *The Criticism of the Fourth Gospel* (New York: Charles Scribner's Sons, 1905); B. H. Streeter, *The Four Gospels,* ch. XV, pp. 427–461, for a history of modern debate on this issue. For more recent works on the Gospel see references in chapter 3.

118. Eusebius, *H.E.* VII, 25, 16; cf. III, 36, 6.

119. For further on this question see McNeile, *An Introduction to the Study of the New Testament,* pp. 287–291.

120. C. K. Barrett, *The Gospel According to St. John* (New York: The Macmillan Company, 1957), pp. 92ff. lists these "echoes."

Zebedee.[121] Lacking more concrete evidence such suggestions are purely fanciful. Three verses do appear to represent the author. In 19:35 the words "He who saw it has borne witness" seem to claim the author to be an eyewitness of at least the Crucifixion. At the end of the appendix,[122] 21:24–25, there occurs another reference to a disciple "bearing witness to these things, and who has written these things." Few interpreters, however, would question that these verses, especially 21:24–25, are a later addition.

The style and character of John, on the other hand, provide presumptive evidence against apostolic authorship. Its language is, for the most part, Hellenistic Greek; its vocabulary and realm of ideas are a strange mixture of Judaism and Greek; the problems to which it addresses itself are those of a time and place later and considerably removed from the Apostle John.[123] We may conclude therefore that John bar Zebedee was probably not the author. To say, on the other hand, who did write the Gospel will probably never be possible.[124]

As to the place of origin little more can be said. Ephesus has been the traditional location assigned to the Gospel, but if St. Ignatius knew it, as some have claimed, why did he avoid mentioning it in his letter to the church there? Frankly, we are left without a clue to this question.[125]

We are in little better circumstance in the question of the date of the writing. In the enthusiasm aroused by the discovery of the Dead Sea Scrolls—an enthusiasm natural to so monumental a find—some have found sufficient similarity between the atmosphere of the Scrolls and John to conclude that the latter could have arisen early and in Palestine.[126] Whereas such observations should dampen the ardor of some scholars for late dates, the weight of evidence is still against a date much earlier than the end of the first century. If we take the "echoes" in St. Ignatius' letters seriously, we cannot date John much later. A fragment of John 18:31–33, 37–38, dated ca. A.D. 125–140, found in the upper Nile and published in 1935, confirms a date not later than the early decades of the second century.[127]

The indecisiveness which an honest examination of the evidence in

---

121. See J. H. Bernard, *The Gospel According to St. John, ICC,* Vol. I, pp. xxiv–xxvii.
122. On the relation of chapter 21 to the rest of the Gospel, see p. 218.
123. For the theology and point of view of John, see pp. 202–208, 219–230.
124. One scholar, almost playfully, has suggested the author may have been John Mark, and therefore the Fourth Gospel may be what Papias was referring to in his famous statement on Mark's Gospel! (Above, pp. 70–71.) Pierson Parker, "John and John Mark," *JBL,* Vol. LXXIX, Pt. II, June, 1960, pp. 97–110.
125. See F. C. Grant, *The Gospels,* pp. 172ff.
126. For example, Oscar Cullmann, "The Significance of the Qumran Texts for Research into the Beginnings of Christianity," *JBL,* Vol. LXXIV, Pt. IV, Dec. 1955, pp. 213–226.
127. P 52 published by C. H. Roberts and now in the John Ryland's Library. See *IDB,* Vol. IV, p. 595.

Fragments of the Gospel of John (18:31–33, 37, 38), technically designated as p⁵², found in Egypt and dating from early in the second century. It was apparently used as a talisman to ward off evil spirits. (Courtesy of the John Rylands Library, Manchester, England.)

these introductory matters we have been surveying requires of the student is frustrating, but there should be real comfort in the fact that, as helpful as a firm knowledge of author, date, place, and the like would be, such knowledge is not essential to an understanding of the message and meaning of the Gospels. We can afford to leave the introductory questions open, not only as a matter of intellectual honesty, but also because, as the original writers indicate by their deliberate anonymity, the "good news" of Jesus Christ which they endeavor to proclaim remains for the reader to understand and obey.[128]

Our survey of the history and methods of Gospel study comes now to a close. It is always easy in telling a story such as this to leave the impression that the story has finished, that scholarship "has arrived." That we are forced by the paucity of good evidence to leave so many questions open at the conclusion of our survey may therefore be fortunate. These open questions may, then, become a symbol of the tentativeness with which

128. Cf. Henry J. Cadbury, *The Making of Luke-Acts,* pp. 360–368, and F. C. Grant, *The Gospels: Their Origin and Growth,* pp. 7–10.

scholarship must always regard its conclusions. In every aspect of New Testament study, not alone that of the Gospels, the task is far from finished. Each new discovery requires adjustments of theories in other areas. New insights come, problems shift, and new methods are born bringing with them a fresh understanding of Scripture bearing with it its own reward. To the serious student of the Bible such rewards are ample enough, but they are double-edged. For no sooner do they come than they beckon him on to new research. Such is the way it is, indeed, in every quest for truth.

Selected Readings

HISTORICAL AND SOURCE CRITICISM

McCown, Chester C., *The Search for the Real Jesus* (New York: Charles Scribner's Sons, 1940).

Schweitzer, Albert, *The Quest for the Historical Jesus,* with Intro. by J. M. Robinson (New York: The Macmillan Company, 1968).

Streeter, B. H., *The Four Gospels,* rev. ed. (London: Macmillan and Co., Ltd., 1930).

FORM AND REDACTION CRITICISM

Bultmann, Rudolph, *The History of the Synoptic Tradition,* tr. John March (Oxford: Basil Blackwell, 1963).

Burney, Charles Fox, *The Poetry of Our Lord* (Oxford: Oxford University Press, 1925).

Dibelius, Martin, *From Tradition to Gospel,* tr. Bertram Lee Woolf, 2nd ed. rev. (New York: Charles Scribner's Sons, n.d.).

Easton, B. H., *The Gospel Before the Gospels* (New York: Charles Scribner's Sons, 1928).

Koch, Klaus, *The Growth of the Biblical Tradition,* tr. S. M. Capitt (New York: Charles Scribner's Sons, 1969).

Redlich, E. Basil, *Form Criticism* (London: Duckworth, 1934).

Robinson, J. M., *The New Quest of the Historical Jesus* (Naperville, Ill.: Alec R. Allenson, Inc., 1959).

Taylor, Vincent, *The Formation of the Gospel Tradition* (London: Macmillan and Company, Ltd., 1957).

Via, Dan O., ed., *Guides to Biblical Scholarship,* New Testament Series (Philadelphia: Fortress Press): Edgar V. McKnight, *What Is Form Criticism?* (1969); Norman Perrin, *What Is Redaction Criticism?* (1969); William A. Beardslee, *Literary Criticism of the New Testament* (1970).

For more studies in redaction criticism see Marxsen, Conzelmann, Bornkamm, Barth, and Held in the list at the end of the next chapter.

Chapter Two

As They Were Delivered to Us:

The Synoptic Gospels

*Just as they were delivered to us by those who
from the beginning were eyewitnesses and
ministers of the word, it seemed good to me also,
having followed all things closely for some time
past, to write an orderly account for you. . . .*
Luke 1:2

Each of the Gospel writers was in his own right and way an author
and interpreter of the traditions about Jesus. This distinctiveness of
perspective and purpose applies to the authors of the Synoptic
Gospels as well as to John. We therefore must not allow the discussion of
the Synoptic problem to obscure a fundamentally more important concern
for us: the character and message of the individual Gospels. In this chapter,
therefore, we turn our attention to the separate Gospels and with the aid
of the methods discussed in chapter 1 we will seek to understand what each
of them has to say.

Since, as we have seen, Mark served as a source for Matthew and Luke,
it will be helpful to depart from the canonical order and beginning with
Mark to study the Gospels in chronological order.[1]

1. See Preface.

1. *The Beginning of the Gospel: Mark*

To summarize our conclusions in the previous chapter, the second Gospel was written about A.D. 65 by a Christian named Mark and was early associated with the Church in Rome and may have been written there. Although there probably were earlier writings containing memorabilia of Jesus, some of which were likely used as sources by Mark,[2] this Gospel was probably the earliest attempt at a comprehensive statement of the tradition about Jesus. In a sense not intended by Mark we may use his opening words "The beginning of the Gospel" to describe his work.

GROUPINGS OF MATERIAL

In the previous chapter we noted several clearly defined groups of material in Mark which have inspired attempts to apply source criticism to the structure of the Gospel. Early fragmentary documents may be reflected by these groupings and therefore serve as clues to the sources used by Mark, or they may have been formed much as they are in the course of their oral history. Some of them, on the other hand, may have been so arranged by Mark himself. These groups do, however, point to an important observation about Mark: A significant amount of his material is topically arranged. The Gospel, therefore, cannot be regarded as a simple day-by-day chronicle of the ministry of Jesus. At several points editorial summaries serve to interpret the foregoing material for the reader, indicating thereby Mark's concern with something more than a collection of stories. The predominance of Jesus' Passion is most significant of Mark's meaning and purpose. From the ominous phrase "the days will come, when the bridegroom is taken away from them, and then they will fast in that day" (2:20) to the Passion narrative itself the reader is made aware, as the shadows of death deepen, of the impending Crucifixion. The control which this Passion theme exercises over the movement of the whole Gospel shows that Mark is far from a mere collection of "pearls on a string" which, should the string break, might as easily be strung in another order. In several other ways the Gospel displays a consistent pattern which moves swiftly from beginning to end. So pronounced is that pattern, in fact, that an earlier generation of scholars assumed it to be a faithful reflection of the actual chronology of Jesus' life. Closer examination, however, has shown that the Markan hypothesis, as it was called, is a misunderstanding of Mark's nature and purpose. The structure of the Gospel manifests, far more than biographical interests, the needs and concerns of the community of faith in Mark's own time. It is in this direction that we must look if we are to find the key to the Gospel's meaning and purpose.

2. See pp. 50–51.

Organizing Principles Several organizing principles manifest themselves in the Gospel. There are, for example, *double parables,* i.e., pairs of parables or similes which make the same point, such as the parables of the patch of unshrunk cloth on an old garment, the new wine in old wineskins (Mk. 2:21–22), and parables of the kingdom and the house divided against themselves (Mk. 3:24–25).[3]

Catchwords are used to join pericopae into a connected series. With exception of the brief similes of the lamp and measure, the collection which comprises the fourth chapter of Mark is linked by the word seed. The name Elijah ties together the transfiguration and the following discussion of his eschatological role (9:2–8 and 11–13). The word translated "sin" (A.V. offend, Greek: *skandalidzo,* lit. to trap or snare) in 9:42–47 forms the link for the sayings about the "little ones" and the offending members of the body. Sometimes the link is formed by synonyms or words that suggest one another. Thus the miraculous harvest in 4:20 may have suggested the inclusion of the saying about the lamp "under a bushel" in verse 21, which in turn suggested the inclusion of the saying about the measure in verse 24. Perhaps there is a similar link in 9:35–42 from the word "servant" in verse 35, to "child" in verse 36, the root of which also means servant, and finally to the "little ones" in verse 42.[4]

Occasionally *a parable is used to interpret another,* as the twin parables of the patch on the garment and new wine in old wineskins, for example, are used to elaborate the point of the parable of the wedding guests and the bridegroom (Mk. 2:19, 21–22), or as the parable of the strong man serves to interpret the twin parables of the divided kingdom and house (Mk. 3:24–25, 27). In other instances *sayings of Jesus are used to interpret parables.* Thus the saying that "there is nothing hid, except to be made manifest . . ." is used to interpret the parable of the lamp (Mk. 4:21–22) and "For to him who has will more be given . . ." interprets the parable of the measure (Mk. 4:24–25).[5]

Perhaps the most intriguing patterns of organization are those based on *repetition,* which is used in Mark in several ways. The familiar "rule of three," for instance, appears in the three predictions of the Passion to define and give unity to the section, 8:27–10:45. Mark skillfully uses *anticipation,* for another example, to aid the understanding or heighten the interest of the reader. The crowd coming to John the Baptizer from Judea and Jerusalem in 1:5 anticipates the crowd which in 3:7–8 came

---

3. Jeremias includes a third pair, the lamp and the measure (Mk. 4:21, 24) in this category. *The Parables of Jesus,* tr. S. H. Hooke (New York: Charles Scribner's Sons, 1963), pp. 90–91.
4. Bultmann, *History of the Synoptic Tradition,* pp. 149–150, 325–326.
5. These sayings are included by Jeremias in a long list of "secondary generalizing conclusions" found in the Synoptics. *The Parables of Jesus,* pp. 110–112.

to Jesus from Galilee, Judea, Jerusalem, Idumea, beyond the Jordan, and Tyre and Sidon. The plotting of the Pharisees with the Herodians in 3:6 is the first of a series of such anticipations, each succeeding one of which adds something to the reader's understanding of the Crucifixion. By this means Mark is able to provide a commentary on the Crucifixion without interrupting the narrative itself. The mention of the boat in the call of the sons of Zebedee (1:19) helps prepare the reader for the role played by boats in the section from 4:35 to 8:26. Jesus' retreat to the sea in 3:7–9 also serves the same purpose (cf. 4:1). In 3:31 the reference to Jesus' family anticipates the story of his rejection in "his own country" in 6:1–16. The geographical list in 3:7–8 anticipates the movements of Jesus in 4:35–8:26, especially 6:45ff. Although serving to locate the beginning of Jesus' Galilean ministry, the mention of the imprisonment of John the Baptizer in 1:14 also prepares the reader for the story of his execution in 6:14–29; while the latter anticipates the Passion and burial of Jesus. That the story of John's death ends as it does with his burial further accents the subordinate role of John and places Jesus' Resurrection in sharp contrast. The amazement of the crowd in 1:27 anticipates the section 4:35–7:37 in which it is a dominant refrain. There is a double anticipation of the mission of the twelve (6:7–13, 30) in the calling of disciples in 1:16–20 and 4:14–19. In the four passages on opposition to Jesus, 2:1–3:6, 7:1–23, 10:2–9, 11:27–12:44, tension is heightened in anticipation of Jesus' arrest, trial, and Crucifixion in chapters 14 and 15.

Among the most important patterns created by repetition are the recurring refrains or themes. Perhaps the most famous is the so-called "messianic secret," the injunctions to silence, in other words, which occur in 1:25, 34, 44, 3:12, 4:11, 5:43, 7:36, 8:30 leading to their climax in the conclusion to the story of the Transfiguration, 9:9. We will return to these injunctions later. Descriptions of *Jesus as a teacher* form another thread running through the Gospel. While the content of Jesus' teaching is given comparatively little space in Mark, his role as a teacher is emphasized in 1:21–22, 2:13, 4:1–2, 6:2, 6, 34, 10:1. References to the synagogue in the story of the healing of the man with the unclean spirit, 1:21ff., and his teaching in "his own country," 6:2ff., reinforce the connection between Jesus' teaching and healing and serve to tie the ministry of Jesus to that of the disciples. They also accent the origins of the church within the bosom of Judaism.

Alongside such general themes which run through a large part of the Gospel several *refrains* appear, in the manner of antiphons, to underscore the significance of smaller segments of Mark. Some of these are

1. The spread of Jesus' fame, 1:28, 2:7, 16, 18, 24.
2. The four questions in 2:7, 16, 18, 24 which challenge the authority and actions of Jesus and issue in the plot against him in 3:6.

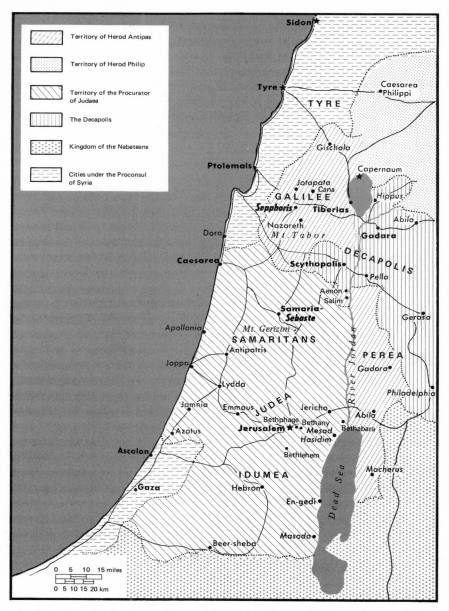

The Holy Land in the time of Jesus. (Adapted with permission of The Macmillan Company from *Macmillan Bible Atlas* by Y. Aharoni and Michael Avi-Yonah. Copyright © 1968 Carta, Jerusalem. © Copyright 1964 by Carta, Jerusalem. © Copyright 1966 by Carta, Jerusalem.)

3. The misunderstanding of Jesus by his friends in 3:21, the scribes from Jerusalem in 3:22, and his own family in 3:31, which leads to Jesus' statement about his true family in 3:34–35.
4. The place of parables in Jesus' teaching, 4:2, 11, 34 which alternates with the challenge to hear, 4:9, 23, 33.
5. Amazement at the mighty works of Jesus in 4:41, 5:20, 42, 6:2, 51, 7:37.

Finally there are *doublets,* the most familiar example of which in Mark are the two stories of the miraculous feeding of the multitude, the five thousand in 6:35–44, and the four thousand in 8:1–10. That each of these stories is followed by a boat scene, rebuke of the disciples and scribes and Pharisees, a saying about bread, and a healing, and that the first of these sequences is followed in the sixth chapter of the fourth Gospel with surprising faithfulness have caused a number of scholars to regard the entire sequences from 6:35–7:37 and from 8:1–26 as a single pair of doublets.[6] The two stories of a storm at sea, 4:36ff. and 6:45ff., in spite of important differences, are probably to be regarded as doublets. Attention is often called to the similarities between the story of the healing of the man with an unclean spirit in 1:23–26 and the healing of the son with a dumb spirit in 9:17–27. Probably we should also classify these stories as doublets. Jesus' words on true greatness in 9:35–36 and 10:42–44 furnish an example of double versions of a saying which has been placed in two different settings.

There are, in addition to these examples, a few places where features of one story are borrowed to serve as a framework for another.[7] These stories are too dissimilar in content and purpose to be regarded as true doublets, and yet for that very reason they may furnish a clue to a better understanding of doublets. Two examples of such related stories are the two disciples sent for the colt in 11:2ff. versus the two disciples sent to arrange for the upper room (14:13ff.); and the healing of the deaf mute, 7:32, and the blind man of Bethsaida, 8:22ff., both of whom were healed with spittle. Since this word in the New Testament occurs only here and in the story of the man born blind in John 9:1ff., its repetition is significant.

The importance of *geography* as an organizing principle in Mark may be seen in the fact that outlines of this Gospel almost invariably are based, in large part at least, on the division of Jesus' ministry between Galilee and Judea. On another level, however, geography lends structure to several smaller sections. Capernaum forms a link between the stories in 1:21–34,

---

6. For a full discussion of this question see Vincent Taylor, *The Gospel According to St. Mark* (London: Macmillan & Co. Ltd., 1959), pp. 628–32.
7. This borrowing of frameworks is one use the Gospels make of the Old Testament. Cf. pp. 98–99, 107–108, 125–126, 128–129.

2:1–12, and 9:33. The sudden frequency of place names, otherwise comparatively rare in Mark, characterizes the section from 6:45 to 7:37; whereas the large body of materials from 4:35–8:26 is bound together by the Sea of Galilee, which is mentioned only in four places (two of which are doublets and serve to anticipate this material) outside this section. A corollary to the role of the sea in this section is the frequent mention of boats. Fifteen out of the nineteen occurrences of the word in Mark are found here.

Jerusalem plays a part in the Gospel from the very beginning. People come out from Jerusalem to be baptized by John (1:5) and to hear Jesus (3:8); scribes come from Jerusalem to challenge Jesus' authority (3:22) and to dispute his neglect of the ceremonial laws (7:1ff.). It is to Jerusalem that Jesus must go for his Passion (10:33); and from the triumphal entry to the Crucifixion Jerusalem and Bethany form the two poles around which the narratives are organized.

THE STRUCTURE OF MARK

From the structures displayed by the organizing systems we have surveyed, something of the complexity of this apparently simple Gospel can be seen. Unquestionably a number of the collections of materials which we have noted came to Mark, some in oral tradition and others likely in brief written documents, much as they stand. We must not, however, deprive Mark of the credit due him as an author.[8] What is made of these segments and patterns in Mark depends in large degree upon our interests. If we seek to penetrate back of Mark's material to the history of Jesus, the structure of Mark will be of little chronological assistance. Each pericope will require analysis to recover so far as possible its original setting and meaning.[9] The collections will be of interest chiefly for their information about the history of the developing tradition. A prior and equally important question, certainly, is the message of Mark himself. As his title invites us to do, we must give our first attention to "the beginning of the Gospel of Jesus Christ" as Mark proposes to proclaim it. In this approach the structures, collections, patterns, and the like become significant of Mark's message.

Outlines of Mark In spite of the way in which the Gospel moves swiftly and directly toward its climax in the Passion, Mark is not easily outlined. The traditional outlines have been based on the geographical division of the story of Jesus between Galilee and Jerusalem, the well-defined sections on the rise of opposition, and the wider range of Jesus' journeys near the

8. See pp. 66–70.
9. This process has been carried through for the parables in an admirable way and with gratifying results by Joachim Jeremias in *The Parables of Jesus*.

middle of the Gospel. Interpreters have usually been content to list the individual pericopae within this essentially geographic framework. A number of years ago C. H. Dodd pointed out that the kerygma corresponded in pattern remarkably well with the structure of Mark and suggested that Mark was really an expanded version of the apostolic preaching.[10] Neither of these methods, however, has succeeded very well in elucidating the Gospel. More recently, Chalmer E. Faw undertook an outline of Mark based on some of the characteristics we have noted. Observing correctly that "chronology and geography as such are not the dominant interests of the author," he found that the Gospel could be divided into distinct sections each of which displayed a common mood or emphasis underscored by repeated structural forms or refrains and ending in a climactic saying, story, or editorial summary. These sections are further defined, according to Faw, by a sudden shift in locale.[11] The resulting outline makes considerable progress in exposing Mark's literary characteristics and purpose. This outline, nevertheless, encounters difficulties. Faw is obliged to subdivide the fifth section into four subdivisions which do not altogether conform to the mood he has assigned to that section. Some of the important themes and motifs cross these sectional lines, and some of the larger patterns are obscured. Because at many points it does serve to reveal the significance of Mark's structure, Faw's outline will be helpful in the remainder of the our analysis of Mark.

The truth is that Mark can scarcely be outlined in the forms to which we are accustomed. Patterns are started and dropped; motifs cross and recross one another; and patterns of repetition appear to compete with one another in a manner reminiscent of the kaleidoscope whose exquisite patterns are produced by repeating with mirrors the casual arrangements of miscellaneous bits of colored glass. There is a persistent and direct movement, nevertheless, which controls the Gospel and shows that it was not the product of ineptitude or carelessness on the part of its author. The summary and editorial statements further serve notice of a serious theological intent. When these statements are pursued, other evidences of Mark's theological purposes appear. Perhaps the best way to study Mark is by pursuing motifs by means of some such items as the organizing principles we have observed.

Parables and Mark's Message   Let us begin our quest for Mark's message with the parables. The word parable is sometimes loosely used of all comparisons and illustrations in the Gospels, but more exactly a parable is "an extended metaphor, or simile, frequently becoming a brief narrative." It is customary, also, to distinguish between parables and allegory; the

10. *The Apostolic Preaching,* pp. 46–52. On the question of the significance of the kerygma see above, pp. 31–32.
11. "The Outline of Mark," *JBR,* Vol. XXV, No. 1, 1957, pp. 19–23.

former being "a brief narrative which forcefully illustrates a single idea," whereas in the latter the literal meaning is abandoned for symbolic meanings attached to the several parts of the narrative. When the similes, metaphors, and parables are taken together there are some twenty of them in Mark.[12] At least two of these, however, are metaphors, several more are clearly similes, and most of the remainder, sometimes called parabolic sayings, are on the borderline. From the standpoint of length only five of these are of more than one verse and only three, the sower (4:3–8), the mysterious growth of seed (4:26–29), the wicked tenants (12:1–9), occupy more than two verses. The second of these, like the parable of the mustard seed, is attached by the catchword, seed, and is therefore subordinate to the parable of the sower. In only three places in Mark is attention directed to the parables themselves. Elsewhere they are incidental to a controversy or discussion to which they are entirely subordinate. The three instances in which Mark directs attention especially are therefore noteworthy. In all three instances they are introduced by an announcement (the sower, 4:2–3a; on defilement, 7:14, the wicked tenants, 12:1). In the first two the key parable or the parabolic saying is accented by a private interpretation to the disciples, and the third parable is associated with the Passion by the comment in verse 12. The first and last of these parables, the sower and the wicked tenants, furthermore, are significantly longer and are the only two narrative parables in the Gospel.

Insofar as the parables are concerned, these two are of primary importance for Mark's meaning and purpose. They stand, to begin with, in dominant positions in the two main divisions of the Gospel, and second, their subject matter is intimately related to these divisions. In the interpretation of the sower by which he underscores the parable, Mark is speaking to the problems of the mid-century Church in its own proclamation of the Gospel. It must not be discouraged, for did not Jesus himself predict such varied response to the Word? The parable of the sower and the mission of the twelve are both lessons for the beleaguered Church of Mark's day. The parable of the wicked tenants, on the other hand, which is one of several interpretations Mark provides for the Passion, reflects the growing tension between the Church and the Jewish communities. By means of the quotation from Psalm 118:22–23 which Mark has supplied

12. The list is as follows: 2:17; 2:19–20; 2:21; 2:22; 3:24; 3:25; 3:27; 4:3–8; 4:21; 4:24; 4:26–29; 4:31–32; 7:15; 7:27; 8:15; 9:50; 10:25; 12:1–9; 13:28; 13:34. For a discussion of the nature and form of a parable see *IDB*, Vol. I, p. 82, and Vol. III, p. 649. T. W. Manson offers this definition. "A parable is a literary creation in narrative form designed either to portray a type of character for warning or example or to embody a principle of God's governance of the world and men. It may partake of both natures." *The Teaching of Jesus* (Cambridge: At the University Press [1931], 1963), p. 65. See pp. 57–66.

as one of his interpretations of this parable, he is able to show the necessity of the Crucifixion and its outcome as the final expression of the motif of the reversal of fortunes.[13] The second interpretation, the attempt by the Pharisees to arrest Jesus because they understood the parable to be against them, supplied in verse 12 makes a direct connection with the plotting of the Pharisees and Herodians in 3:6 and therefore with the section on the rise of opposition, 2:1–3:6. From the point of the parable of the wicked tenants the Gospel moves swiftly to the climax in the Passion.

In view of the position of these two parables it is clear that the geographical divisions, Galilee and Judea, far more than mere factual data or literary convenience are symbols of the two facets of the meaning of Jesus which Mark has set out to portray.[14] Galilee represents the proclaimer-teacher-healer, the prototype of the apostolate. Jerusalem represents the Passion, at least one of whose meanings is found in the prototype of the Christian martyr (cf. I Pet. 2:21).

That the Galilean section of Mark is intended as a geographic symbol of Jesus' ministry can be shown by the following outline of the first part:

Introduction: Jesus and Disciples
The spread of Jesus' fame, ch. 1
The rise of opposition, ch. 2:1–3:6
The community of faithful as Jesus' true family, 3:7–35
The parables of the mission, 4:1–34

The Galilean Ministry: The Mission
The mighty works, 4:35–5:43
The apostolic mission, 6:1–56
Jesus and the Law, 7:1–37
Bread and faith, 8:1–26

Transition: The Predictions of the Passion, 8:27–10:45[15]

Here is seen a well-rounded topical description of Jesus' ministry, but a closer look reveals from the very beginning a parallel interest: the role of the disciples.

A Paradigm of Apostleship At the very beginning of Jesus' ministry, after the generalized description of Jesus' proclamation of the Kingdom of God, there follows the story of the calling of the four fishermen-disciples, Simon, Andrew, James, and John, three of whom are to become the so-called "inner circle" (1:16–20). The association of the disciples with Jesus' ministry is further underscored in verses 36–38. The second call of a dis-

13. Cf. pp. 126, 171, 178, 184.
14. See p. 106.
15. This is essentially the outline of Chalmer E. Faw. See p. 89, and note 10.

Fishing in the Sea of Galilee. This casting net (Greek: *amphiblestron*) is the type which Simon and Andrew were using when Jesus called them (Mk. 1:16–18). (Courtesy of the Israel Government Tourist Office.)

ciple, Levi, follows in 2:13.[16] In the appointment of the twelve (3:13ff.) and the description of Jesus' true family as those who do the will of his Father (3:33–35) both of these calls reach their climax and are interpreted. Three purposes for their appointment are given: (1) to be with him (to learn), (2) to be sent out to preach, (3) to have authority over demons. The parallel between these purposes and Mark's treatment of Jesus' ministry is not accidental. Each of these four introductory sections has a significant reference to disciples. When later in 6:7ff. the twelve are sent out on their own mission with a charge which sounds very much like an early Christian sermon to missioners, the significance of this material is completed. That it is scattered throughout the developing story of Jesus' own ministry serves to expose the intimate and necessary connection between the two. When we turn to the section, the predictions of the Passion (8:27–10:45), by which Mark makes the transition from Galilee to Jerusalem, the full challenge of discipleship comes into view. Immediately after Jesus' first prediction of his Passion three items follow (8:34–9:1): the cost of discipleship, the cost of not being a disciple, and a picture of the eschatological judgment which reinforces the latter. These items establish a close and significant relationship between the Passion and discipleship. Both the word "cross" and "ashamed" point ominously to the early Christian martyr and probably also to those who had renounced their faith under the pressures of ostracism and threat.

Immediately following the second prediction of the Passion in this section is the story of the dispute over greatness which ends with the saying, "If anyone would be first, he must be last of all and servant of all" (9:35), and the example of the child accompanied by the saying, "whosoever receives one such child in my name receives me . . ." (9:37). That the relationship between these two sayings is not at first apparent ceases to be a problem when we see that Mark is commenting on the leadership of the early Church. The role of a servant and receiving children in whom one receives Jesus stands parallel to the call of the cross in 9:34ff. In a similar manner the third prediction of the Passion is followed by the story of the ambition of James and John and Jesus' answer, which here becomes a definition of discipleship, bringing together the two themes (under the figures of the cup and baptism) of the cross and service. The key word "servant" in both of these passages is *diakonos*, the Greek equivalent of our word "minister" or "deacon." We will meet similar strictures against ambition, which must have been a serious problem in the early Church, in

16. Levi is not included among the twelve by name. Although it is customary, following the parallel story in Matthew 9:9, to identify him with the apostle Matthew, it may be that Mark intends this story to parallel the treatment of the Tribe of Levi in Numbers 1. See Dorothy M. and Gerald H. Slusser, *The Jesus of Mark's Gospel* (Philadelphia: The Westminster Press, 1967), pp. 65–68.

Paul's Letters to Corinth (II Cor. 10–13. Cf. I Pet. 5:3). Significantly, this section ends immediately after this saying with Mark's key definition of the meaning of the Passion: "For the Son of man also came not to be served but to serve, and to give his life as ransom for many" (10:45). It is important to notice that the two themes of the cross and service are in this passage, 10:35–45, jointly applied to Jesus and the disciples. The point is the same as in the words of the Risen Lord in John 20:21, "As the Father has sent me, even so I send you."

That the connection of Jesus' disciples with the leaders of the early Church is represented by the mission of the twelve, 6:7–13, 30, is shown by the use of the word "apostle" which occurs only here in Mark and is confirmed by the way Matthew (10:16–23) understands the story.[17] This connection is reinforced by the conclusion of the story of the Gerasene demoniac who is sent home to witness among his own people, 5:19, and the saying about the unauthorized exorcist in 9:38–40.

Related Themes   Several related themes parallel this motif of discipleship. One of these concerns the *authority of apostolic teaching.* We have already seen the allusion to teaching the disciples in 3:13–14, cf. Matthew 5:1–2. This theme becomes explicit in the treatment of parables in the fourth chapter. If we start from verse 22, "For there is nothing hid, except to be made manifest; nor anything secret, except to come to light," Jesus' private explanation of the parables to the disciples (4:10–13, 34) becomes a clear reference to the apostolic authority in the teaching of the Church. The irony in verse 12, "that they may indeed see but not perceive . . ." (cf. Isa. 6:9–10), reflects, undoubtedly, more of the bitter experiences of the early Christian teacher with such problems as are reflected in the "interpretation," verses 14–20, than Mark's historical estimate of Jesus' teaching. The refrain, "He who has ears to hear, let him hear" (4:9, 23, 33), becomes a bid to heed the apostolic teacher. Thus the entire section, 4:10–34, following the parable of the sower becomes a commentary thereupon, beginning and ending with the peculiar authority of the disciples, because of the private instruction they had received, to interpret Jesus' parables. That the two parabolic sayings concerning the lamp and the measure and the accompanying explanations apparently ill fit the context has long been noted. If, however, this section is viewed, not as a random sample of Jesus' teaching, but as an essay on Jesus teaching the Church in and through his disciples, the unity is apparent. The three "seed" parables are related by something of more substantial significance than a trite use of catchwords. The interpretation of the sower, surely originating in and reflecting the problems of the early Church, provides encouragement and

17. If the alternate reading "whom also he named apostles" in 3:14 is allowed, it only
    serves to reinforce this point, since that pericope is an anticipation of the mission.

reassurance in the face of varied responses to the Word with the promise of the eschatological harvest symbolized by the amazing yield. The relation of Jesus' private instruction to the teacher in the early Church is represented by the figure of the lamp; and the necessity for faithfully handing on the teaching is stated in the figure of the measure. That Jesus' Resurrection is the point of transition from Jesus' teaching to the teacher in the Church is shown later in his charge to secrecy about the Transfiguration (9:9) "until the Son of man should have risen from the dead." The failure of the disciples to understand the second prediction of the Passion (9:32) should be read in the same light (cf. 8:15–18; 10:24–26), as should Jesus' rebuke of the disciples in 10:14. Is this last reference an allusion to the question of children born into gentile Christian families? If so, its liturgical use in infant baptism has particular significance.

That the responsibility for the harvest rests in the mysterious Council of God is the theme of the following parable of the mysterious growth of seed (4:26–29). In the parable of the mustard seed we can see the small and humble beginnings of the Church which, nevertheless, must look forward in faith to the greatness of the coming Kingdom of God. That the mustard plant being an annual does not in fact grow large enough for bird's nests indicates that here as in the fantastic harvest in 4:8, 20, attention is being directed away from the mundane to the supernatural reference of the parable. This device of exaggeration is not uncommon in the Gospels. Similarly the theme of apostolic teaching is carried forward to be applied to ethical problems of the Church in 7:17–23, 10:10–12, and to the interpretation of the messiahship of Jesus and his Passion in 8:27–9:13; 9:31ff.; 10:32–45.

Mark prefaces the story of the mission of the twelve by a reference (6:6b) to Jesus teaching from village to village which apparently neither connects with what has gone before or what follows. The reference in verse 30 to what the apostles had taught, the further reference to Jesus' teaching in verse 34, and the setting of this story within the context of Jesus' mighty works, however, relates the disciples' mission to both the teaching and healing miracles of Jesus. The reference in 6:6b to the teaching, therefore, is intended to show that connection. As the disciples are an extension of Jesus' ministry so the Church is a continuation of that of the disciples.

Mark draws no hard and fast lines between the proclamation of the Gospel of the kingdom and the teaching and the healing ministries. Jesus' healing ministry is related in the same way as his teaching to the ministry of the disciples and that of the post-Resurrection Church. That the disciples are by their relation to Jesus being given *authority to exorcise demons* is specifically stated in 3:15. In the theological meaning applied to Jesus' exorcisms (3:22–30), that in them Satan's kingdom is being invaded and overcome, we are to see also the meaning of the disciples' authority over demons. The well-known difficulties in the story of the Gerasene demoniac (5:1–20) may well indicate its character as a veiled allegory of the Church's use of exorcisms in the course of the gentile mission. Phrases such as "the other side of the sea," the reference to swine, and the locality itself set this story in a gentile milieu. In the matter of the name of this territory the text is confused. Some manuscripts read Gergesenes or Gadarenes. It may not be too far fetched to see allegorical elements in the references to tombs (the city of the dead), "bruising himself with stones" (pagan rites, cf. Dan. 4:33–34, I Kings 18:28), legion (6,000 men, unit of the Roman army). The swine are a well-known Judaic symbol of gentile uncleanness. The healed demoniac sent home to witness to his own becomes here a symbol of the gentle mission under gentile leadership. The role of exorcism in the gentile mission is again symbolized in the Syrophoenician woman's retort concerning the children's crumbs[18] (cf. the unauthorized exorcist in 9:38). That Mark makes a point of the way in which only Peter, James, and John were permitted to accompany Jesus in the raising of Jairus' daughter may represent a connection between the miracles of Jesus and those which were regarded as marks of the apostolic leadership of the early Church (cf. Acts 3:1–16, 4:10, 5:12–16, II Cor. 12:12, James 5:13–18). This connection is explicitly reinforced in the story of the mission, 6:7, 13. In the case of the demoniac whom the disciples could not heal (9:14–29) we are probably to see a commentary on some of the difficulties encountered by early Christian exorcists. (See esp. vss. 28–29. Note also how the words, "O faithless generation," in vs. 19 bring this story into connection with the story of the storm at sea, 4:40.) This theme of faith and the disciples' ministry concludes with the saying about faith which can move mountains (11:22–23).

Another aspect of the motif of discipleship can be seen by comparing the two references to Jesus' natural family in 3:31 and 6:3 with the saying in 10:28–31. As Jesus had left his family for the sake of the Gospel, so must the disciples; as he had found his *true family* among those who do the will of God, so will they.

Finally, the aspect which is not only central to the motif of discipleship but which is also significantly related to one of Mark's main interests in the story of Jesus and which serves to tie together the two main parts of Mark is that of the *disciples' share in Jesus' opposition, rejection, and Passion.* This theme which has its explicit and central expression in the call of the cross, 8:34ff., is suggested in the mission of the twelve, 6:11. Immediately preceding the mission is the story of Jesus' rejection at Nazareth ending

18. On the figure of the crumbs compare Romans 11:25–32; 15:26–27. "To the Jew first and also to the Greek" (Rom. 1:16) is a stock formula for the gentile mission in the New Testament. It furnishes, for example, one of the controlling patterns for the Book of Acts.

with the words, "And he marveled because of their unbelief," but the reader has been prepared for this rejection by the stories of Capernaum in 1:21ff. and 2:1–3:6. It was at Capernaum that Jesus' fame as a teacher and healer began, but at Capernaum also his opposition arose. The points of that opposition are instructive: (1) the blasphemy of forgiving sins, (2) the defilement of eating with tax collectors and sinners, (3) the impiety of neglecting the fasts, (4) the breach of the law of the Sabbath. The connection of these charges with the conflicts between Judaism and the early Church is obvious. Now in his home town Jesus has been rejected and the mission with its reference to possible rejection follows. The parallel between this pattern and that in Acts 8:1–4 is worthy of note.

Almost like an interlude of ominous music to cover the time during the mission Mark digresses to relate the story of the beheading of John the Baptizer.[19] That the story of John's death ends with a burial scene serves both to anticipate the story in 15:43–47 of the burial of Jesus and, by means of the Resurrection, 16:1–8, to place John and Jesus in contrast. The position of the story here, however, focuses attention upon the theme of rejection. Jesus has been rejected in his home village, the disciples have been warned of their rejection on their mission, now John's rejection reaches its conclusion in his death. That death is the presentiment of Jesus' Crucifixion and the martyrdom of the disciples. This theme carries us into the second part of the Gospel, but before we pursue it to that point let us turn to the way in which the Galilean ministry and its corollary the motif of discipleship concludes.

Doublets   It is clear now that the story of Jesus and his disciples in Galilee is a *paradigm of discipleship* for the early Church. By means of this story the Christians in the Church of Mark's time could learn the language of the faith and life of their own discipleship. But the post-Resurrection Church is not left to its own resources in pursuing its apostolate any more than were the disciples, for as Jesus was with them so is he with his Church. To see how Mark makes this point we turn to the doublets which stand in the Gospel in an interesting interrelationship. We must not suppose that the doublets in Mark are the result of his carelessness or naivete. The variations between them are neither accidental nor meaningless to Mark's organization, as they would be if they were simply the same stories which had come to Mark in such varied forms as to lead him to suppose them to represent separate episodes. Mark's doublets are part of the pattern of repetitions by which he organized his material, on the analogy of a kaleidoscope, to represent the transition across the dividing line of the Resurrection, from Jesus and his disciples to *Christ and his*

19. On the death of John see Josephus, *Ant.* XVIII, 5, 2.

N.T. *98*

As They Were Delivered to Us

Church. There are, for example, two stories of the disciples in a storm at sea, 4:35–41 and 6:45–53. The chief difference between them is that in the first one Jesus is with the disciples in the boat, whereas in the second they are alone, which provides the occasion for Jesus' walking on the sea. The absence of Jesus accounts for the fright of the disciples even though they had been delivered from a similar peril shortly before. Commentators have long suspected a doctrinal motive at work in this story, some relating it to a Passion allegory, others have suspected docetic influence. Those who see here a Resurrection motif are nearest to Mark's intention. The most puzzling element in the second story is the explanation for their astonishment: "For they did not understand about the loaves." Yet this phrase is the key to the meaning of the story. Following as it does the feeding of the five thousand, this phrase obviously refers to that story, but not in the sense that they had questioned Jesus' power. Whether the two feeding stories are to be regarded as Eucharists, they certainly, for Mark, as for John, have Eucharistic reference and here serve at least in an anticipatory way to represent it. That the disciples were frightened was due to their failure to discern the presence of Jesus in his physical absence. Jesus' ghostly appearance represents an anticipation of his Resurrection existence and relation to his Church (cf. Mt. 28:20; Lk. 24:37ff.). By this device Mark is able to represent the connection between the disciples who during Jesus' earthly ministry were delivered in a storm and the Church after the Resurrection discerning in the bread of the Eucharist the assurance of the presence in saving power of her Risen Lord. Probably also the feeding, by its Eucharistic reference, represents the Passion which separated the disciples from the early Church. The symbolism of boats and the sea, of which Mark was so fond, was surely not lost on Mark's ancient readers, nor would they fail to see in the storm a reference to the waves of ostracism and persecution which threatened to swamp the Church.[20]

There remains the question of the doublets on the feeding of the multitude. That these stories have a number of symbolic elements can be seen in such items as the numbers, the arrangement of the crowd in fifty groups of one hundred each, and the actions of presentation, distribution, and collection. Undoubtedly we are to see in these actions the Eucharistic practices of the early Church. That the mention of fish is omitted in 6:44 and the fish added in an awkward afterthought in 8:7 has suggested to some commentators a liturgical influence.[21] Reference to the green grass has sometimes been taken as a deliberate indication of the Paschal season. The miraculous multiplication of food recalls the stories of Elijah and

20. The Old Testament background for this symbolism is abundant. See Jonah 1:4–2:10; Isa. 17:12–14; Nahum 1:4; Ps. 18:16f.; 65:5–7; 69; 89:9; 93:3.
21. Cf. *IB,* Vol. VII, p. 742.

Elisha in I Kings 17:8–16 and II Kings 4:2–7, 42–44, much as John (6:49–50)[22] and Paul (I Cor. 10:1–5) associated the Eucharist with the manna in the wilderness. The first feeding is prefaced by a reference to Jesus' compassion on the crowd "because they were like sheep without a shepherd" (6:34), a phrase which, in one form or another, occurs in several significant places in the Old Testament. In Numbers 27:17 Joshua is commissioned as Moses' successor in order "that the congregation may not be as sheep which have no shepherd"; Michaiah the Prophet described his ominous vision of Ahab's defeat with the words, "I saw all Israel scattered upon the mountains, as sheep that have no shepherd" (I Kg. 22:17 and II Chron. 18:16); In a more extended metaphor, Ezekiel develops the figure to blame Israel's kings for the Exile (ch. 34, cf. Zech. 10:2; 11:5; 13:7). The figure was established, therefore, as a symbol of Israel's leadership and consequently carried in later times a messianic meaning. The picture here, then, is that of the shepherd messiah faithfully teaching and feeding his people (cf. Isa. 40:11). The "lonely place," or wilderness, setting completes the picture of eschatological anticipation which coincides with the emphasis of the Last Supper (cf. 14:25). By repeating the note of compassion in the introduction to the second feeding, Mark includes both feedings within this meaning (cf. Jn. 10:1–18, 27–30).[23] There is a striking and significant similarity, furthermore, in the words describing Jesus' action in blessing, breaking, and delivering the bread in the two stories in 6:41 and 8:6 and the narrative of the Last Supper in 14:22.

To recognize that these two stories are intended, at least by anticipation, as Eucharistic references does not, however, explain the doublets. The answer to that question is to be sought in two significant differences between them. The most prominent of these differences is the number of baskets of food left over: twelve in the first instance (6:43) and seven in the second (8:8). In order that the reader not miss these numbers Mark has brought them together in the discussion on the "leaven of the Pharisees" which takes place in the boat scene immediately following the second feeding. The dialogue is uncommonly difficult to follow. What the disciples are failing to understand is not immediately clear, but must be understood in connection with the similar saying at the end of the feeding in 6:52. The numbers are to be interpreted, in all probability, as are the twelve and seventy in Luke's familiar doublets of the apostolic mission (Lk. 9:1–10 and 10:1–20) to represent, respectively, the twelve tribes of

---

22. Cf. Peder Borgen, *Bread From Heaven.*
23. For a valuable discussion of this point in connection with the development of New Testament Christology see Sherman E. Johnson, "The Davidic-Royal Motif in the Gospels," *JBL,* Vol. LXXXVII, Pt. II, June 1968, pp. 136–150.

Judaism and the gentile nations.[24] The second difference is more subtle but nonetheless significant. The word blessed in the first story (6:41) is *eulogesen,* from which our word eulogy is derived, and is the same as the blessing of the bread in the Last Supper, 14:22 (and Matt. 26:26), whereas in the second story (8:6) the word is *eucharistesas,* from which is derived our word eucharist, which all of the Synoptic Gospels use in reference to the cup and which Paul uses exclusively in I Cor. 11:23–25, and which became a standard term in the early Church for the Lord's Supper. Yet in the parenthetical sentence about the fish (8:7), Mark returns to *eulogesen.* The second story, therefore, uses the common word in the Eucharistic prayer of the early Church (more congenial to gentile understanding), and the first story uses the word closer to the Jewish idiom. That the doublets on feeding the multitude are separated by the story of Jesus' walking on the sea, which as we have seen has a post-Resurrection reference, and the section on the controversy over Jewish ceremonial regulations shows that like the storm stories the repetition of the feeding of the multitude represents the transition from the disciples and Jesus' earthly ministry to the post-Resurrection Church and enlarges the connections between the two. Here are seen the sign and seal of the continuing presence of Christ in his Church. Also this device serves to connect the Christian cultus in both meaning and authority with the Galilean ministry as well as the Passion.

After the second story of feeding the multitude and the controversy over the leaven of the Pharisees and forgetting the bread, the great central section of Mark comes to its end with the healing of the blind man of Bethsaida (8:22–26). The story follows immediately—almost as an answer—the question, "Do you not understand?" and is likely therefore intended as a commentary thereon. If Bethsaida was within the Tetrarchy of Philip as seems likely, Mark may have intended the reader to understand the blind man to be a gentile. If he was a gentile, sending him home connects this story with the conclusion of that of the Gerazene demoniac (5:19). At any rate the slow cure becomes a symbol of the slow growth of faith and comprehension. This story is related to the story, just before the feeding of the four thousand, of the cure of the deaf mute by the use of spittle (7:32–37). The relation of these stories to one another and their symbolic meaning are indicated by the question in 8:18 which stands between them: "Having eyes do you not see, and having ears do you not hear?" (Cf. 4:11–13 *passim*). That these two similar stories frame the feeding of the four thousand enhances their significance. By the power of the presence of Christ signified in the Eucharist, ears are opened to hear

24. The symbol of seventy to represent the gentile nations probably goes back to the genealogy of the nations in Genesis 10. See *IDB,* Vol. IV, p. 296 (Article: The Seven). Mark simply reduces the number to seven in the interest of realism.

and tongues to speak the Gospel; eyes are opened to see and the healed return home to witness. This hearing and seeing are what is meant by understanding.[25]

The Call to Faith   Through all of the Gospel there runs a strain of ambiguity. Neither the witness of John the Baptizer, the preaching and teaching of Jesus, nor his miracles are irrefutable proof of his Gospel. Thus the opening section on Jesus' fame is followed by the section on opposition. His healings can be credited to Beelzebub (3:22 and 29) as well as to the Holy Spirit. The parables may obscure rather than clarify his meaning.[26] The Gerasene countrymen plead with Jesus to depart from their neighborhood. The predictions of the Passion meet with either outright contradiction (8:32ff.) or misunderstanding (9:32). At Caesarea Philippi only Peter recognizes that Jesus is the Messiah and even he fails to understand what that messiahship meant. On the Mount of Transfiguration Peter babbles meaninglessly, "for he did not know what to say." Confronted by the demands of the Gospel the rich man "went away sorrowful."

All of these negative responses to Jesus are related to the *"messianic secret."*[27] One of the most debated problems in Mark, this motif has sometimes been understood as a device by which the early Church was able to read back into the story of Jesus messianic claims which he never made for himself.[28] This theory has engendered considerable debate, and several alternates have been advanced. The rebuke of the devils (e.g., 1:25, 34, 3:11) may be because they were attempting a "reverse magic."[29] In other places Mark uses the command to silence to underscore the rising fame and popularity of Jesus (e.g., 1:36, 44–45; 7:36). That the term messiah was subject to misunderstanding and involved dangerous political implications may explain Jesus' charge to secrecy concerning Peter's confession in 8:30. These explanations, however historically sound, do not exhaust the list nor do they explain Mark's purpose in this motif (cf. 5:43; 9:30). The key to the "messianic secret" motif is rather to be found in the climactic instance: "he charged them to tell no one what they had seen,

---

25. Cf. Ernest Best, *The Temptation and the Passion in Mark* (Cambridge: Cambridge University Press, 1965), pp. 107–108, *passim.*
26. Although the saying in 4:11–12 is said in irony, Mark seems to imply that the obscurity of the parables is deliberate on Jesus' part. Some interpreters see a connection between this theme and the theory of Paul that the hardening of Israel was to bring about the gentile Church (Rom. 11:25–26).
27. See p. 499.
28. This theory was advanced by Wilhelm Wrede in *Das Messiasgeheimnis in den Evangelien* (Gottingen: Vandenhoeck & Ruprecht, 1901). For a good English summary and criticism of this work see William Sanday, *The Life of Christ in Recent Research* (Oxford: At the Clarendon Press, 1907), pp. 69–77.
29. See Sherman Johnson, *The Gospel According to St. Mark* (New York: Harper & Brothers, 1960), p. 48. Cf. Mark 5:7.

until the Son of man should have risen from the dead" (9:9). Until the Resurrection had taken place neither the person nor the ministry of Jesus could be understood. In the Resurrection the "strong man" had been bound and now his house was being invaded (3:27). By means of the Resurrection the dull-witted disciples became the apostolic teachers.

Mark is well aware, on the other hand, that the Resurrection does not force assent to the faith. The issue still rests on a decision of faith, a decision not always easy to make, and one moreover which could exact a heavy price in courage and endurance. The humble prayer of the demoniac's father becomes a model for the Christian convert: "I believe; help my unbelief" (9:24). In a sense, therefore, the messiahship of Jesus is still a secret of faith.

With the end of the transition section on the predictions of the Passion and the call of the cross (8:27–10:45), during which the journey to Jerusalem takes place, Mark turns abruptly to the Jerusalem ministry and Passion. This division of the Gospel is in four sections:

> Controversies, 10:46–12:44
> The Little Apocalypse, ch. 13
> The Passion, chs. 14–15
> The Resurrection, ch. 16

The reader has been well prepared by the anticipations, interpretations, and symbolic representations for this concluding division. All the themes of the Galilean division have led to it, require it, and are summed up in it.

In this division, as the key parable of the wicked husbandmen (12:1–9) indicates, the mood is one of conflict. The Passion and Resurrection dominate, and thereby the reader senses that the conflict, far more than the carping of pedantic scribes, is a titanic struggle between the forces of Satan and the Son of God. Mark has already, in the first division, provided a commentary upon and therefore prepared the reader to understand the Passion and Resurrection. This division, consequently, moves swiftly and dramatically to its climax and thereby brings the whole Gospel to its logical conclusion.

In order that the essential unity of Jesus' meaning in both his Ministry and Passion (symbolically represented by Galilee and Jerusalem) be made clear, Mark carries through into this division the principal motifs of the first. Jesus' fame meets us immediately in the story of Bartimaeus (10:46–52). The triple cry of the beggar recalls the liturgical *Kyrie Eleison* and may be related to it. That the beggar received his sight surely carries symbolic overtones, and therefore his following Jesus "on the way," which leads directly to the story of the triumphal entry, symbolizes a conversion.

Irony   There is a strain of irony running through this division which focuses attention upon the paradox of the humility of the hidden Son of

God and the servitude of the "King of the Jews." It begins with the triumphal entry. Although Mark does not, as does Matthew, quote Zechariah 9:9, that verse with its incongruity of a king making his parousia on an ass is clearly in the background.[30] The cries of "Hosanna" to one who is in reality making a death march sustains the irony. Likewise the irony in Jesus' words at the cleansing of the Temple, "Is it not written, 'My house shall be called a house of prayer for all nations'? But you have made it a den of robbers." (11:15–19), is inescapable as is the irony in the dispute over the authority of Jesus versus that of John the Baptizer (11:27–33). They dare not dispute the authority of John, yet Jesus' authority was from the same source. The strain of irony—the failure of the People of God to recognize his action in their midst—runs through the parable of the wicked husbandmen, the controversy over tribute to Caesar, the condemnation of the ostentation of the scribes, the widow's mite, the anointing at Bethany, Judas' kiss, and Peter's denial after his loud protestations of loyalty to the death, the sleeping disciples whose "spirit is willing but the flesh is weak." It is not difficult to see the application of these words to lapsing Christians under persecution. The story of the release of Barabbas and the taunts hurled at Jesus on the cross are heavy with irony. In the accusation against Jesus, 14:61–64, this irony comes to focus: Jesus is the Christ (Messiah),

Bronze coin (Latin: *quadrans*; Greek: *kodrantes* or *dilepton*) issued by Pilate under Tiberius, A.D. 30–31. The smallest coin issued by the Romans which represented the combined value of the two coins, *leptons*, cast into the treasury by the poor widow (Mk. 12:42). (Courtesy of the Money Museum, National Bank of Detroit.)

30. We should note also, however, that the ass is a symbol of peace, see R. M. Lightfoot, *The Gospel Message of St. Mark*, p. 45.

yet by no means the kind of rebel messiah who would warrant execution by Pilate.

In the irony of the final chapters of Mark the motifs of the messianic secret and the dullness of the disciples find their conclusion and significance. This note of irony is not absent in the messianic secret motif itself. That the demons should recognize the true authority of Jesus while the Pharisees credit it to Beelzebub is the height of irony, but now in the conclusion of the Gospel its nature and meaning are brought to light. Through the lens of the Passion and Resurrection the disciples could look back on Jesus' ministry with understanding. Only then does the hidden become manifest, the secret come to light (4:22), and Jesus' private teaching of the disciples bear fruit. The apostolic authority in the Church, therefore rests on the two pillars of their training by Jesus and their witness to the Resurrection.

The motif of opposition to Jesus introduced in chapter 2 is likewise carried to its conclusion in the Passion. In the plot of the "chief priests and the scribes" to arrest and kill Jesus (11:18, 12:12, 14:1–2), the theme of threat against Jesus' life in 3:6, which culminates in his arrest and trial, is resumed. The controversies of chapter 2 have their counterpart in the questions put to Jesus in 11:28, 12:13–17, and 18–27. Even the circle of Jesus' followers does not escape the jarring note of controversy. In the story of the anointing at Bethany the complaint at the waste of valuable ointment serves as a foil to the strong overtones of symbolism. Here again there are ambiguity and irony. Anointing means kingship but Jesus makes it mean a preparation in advance for his burial. The reader knows that these meanings are not mutually exclusive but rather complementary. The pathos in the story, however, belongs to those who could see in the episode only a waste. They were the hopeless blind who would not see. Significantly, this story is followed immediately with Judas' bargain to betray Jesus.

Closely associated with the motif of opposition is that concerning Jewish religious institutions. This motif which occurs twice in Mark's first division, in the controversy stories in 2:1–3:6 and the subsection, 7:1–37, on Jesus versus the traditions is brought to its climax in the cleansing of the Temple. That Mark has framed this story with the cursing of the fig tree makes it mean something more than a rebuke of abuses in the Temple. The reader is to see in the death of the tree the Temple's fate. That the fig tree becomes the harbinger of the eschaton in the Little Apocalypse (13:29–30) serves to tie together the cleansing of the Temple, its destruction (13:1f.), and the eschaton. As the following apparently tangential discourse (11:22–26) shows, Jesus has established a new basis and dimension for faith, prayer and forgiveness. That Jesus becomes in himself the Temple's replacement is the point of the accusation at the trial (14:48): "he said, 'I will destroy this temple that is made with hands, and in three days I will build another, not made with hands!' " The irony of a saying which the reader knows is true but not in the sense intended by the speaker is one more instance of the ironic strain we have observed all through this division. Because of the prediction of the destruction of the Temple at the beginning of the apocalyptic discourse, 13:1f., the reader knows how to understand the accusation in 14:58. The testimony is false because it takes literally a symbolic saying which has reference both to Jesus' death and the Temple. By two devices here Mark indicates the symbolic reference: (1) the contrast between the temple "made with hands" and that "not made with hands"; (2) the word for temple is more properly translated "sanctuary" as contrasted with the word used in 11:15ff. and 13:1f. which refers to the Temple complex as a whole. These three Temple sayings must be taken together as the development of a single theme. The coming of Jesus and the approaching Kingdom of God mean the end of the age of the Temple.[31] The time has come for the new wineskin and the new garment (2:21–22).

In a similar way, in Jesus' answer to the scribe's question concerning the greatest commandment, 12:28–34, the *Shema,* the traditional Jewish confession of faith is replaced by an essentially new one. By replacing all but the first two sentences of the original *Shema* (consisting of Deut. 6:4–9 to which were added 11:13–21 and Num. 15:37–41) with the command from Leviticus 19:18 to "love your neighbor as yourself," Mark not only set aside Jewish legalism but redefined the meaning of love to God which now must include the neighbor.[32] The traditional concept of the messiah as the scion of David is likewise reinterpreted in 12:35–37. This pericope together with the triumphal entry and the question of tribute to Caesar makes the added point: "My kingship is not of this world" (John 18:36). It is significant that, except for the question of the first commandment, in the disputes which indicate the replacement of Jewish institutions Jesus takes the initiative and in 12:38–40 the institution of the scribes is condemned. Jesus, who teaches with authority, has taken their place. Perhaps, too, the "widow's mite" has taken the place of the Jewish Temple tax.[33] The Last Supper which continues in the Christian Eucharist replaces

31. The parenthetical interpretation in John 2:21f. coincides with Mark's meaning. It is worthy of note that the preceding verses, John 2:13–20, combine all three of these passages in Mark. The divinely built new messianic temple was an established figure in Jewish apocalyptic. Cf. Rev. 3:12; 21:2. See pp. 478–479.
32. This is the point of the "new commandment" which is yet "no new commandment" in I John 2:7–8. John finds it difficult, however, to bring himself to speak so boldly of love to God. I John 2:7–8 refers back directly to John 13:34 where the command is rephrased to say: "that you love one another as I have loved you." (But cf. I Jn. 4:21.) Cf. Rom. 13:8–10; Gal. 5:14 for Paul's understanding of love as the new way of life which is no longer "under the law."
33. Cf. Matt. 17:24–27, also the mustard seed Mk. 4:30–32. Here we may see a picture of the humble beginnings of the Church. Cf. also I Cor. 1:26; II Cor. 8:2.

the Passover; as the Lord's Day, i.e., the first day of the week on which the Resurrection occurred, replaces the Sabbath. The meaning of this judgment on the institutions of Judaism and their replacement by Jesus is made clear in the parable of the wicked husbandmen: "What will the owner do? He will come and destroy the tenants, and give the vineyard to others" (12:9).

We have already noted that the theme of the rejection and martyrdom of the disciples, developed in the Galilean division, is carried over into the second part of the Gospel to parallel the Passion story. This theme appears principally in two places: the Little Apocalypse and the parallel stories of Judas' betrayal and Peter's denial. It has long been the prevailing opinion that Mark 13 is a combination of sayings of Jesus and an apocalyptic tract often identified with the "revelation" to the church in Jerusalem just before the siege of Titus mentioned by Eusebius.[34] Although opinions differ on the exact extent of the original apocalypse we can make a good estimate of it by selecting verses 7–8, 14–20, 24–27, 30–31. Several characteristic elements are lacking, yet these verses taken together are homogeneous and typically apocalyptic. What remains when these verses are removed reads much more like an instruction to the disciples. Matthew has, in fact, transferred a considerable part of this material to his version of the mission discourse (cf. Mk. 13:9–12 with Mt. 10:17–22). The instructions include warnings against apostasy (being led astray); instructions on how to face arrests, trials, and punishments by hostile authorities; predictions of betrayal by families and friends; and exhortations to watchfulness. By placing these final apostolic exhortations in this apocalyptic context, Mark is able to indicate the eschatological significance of the apostolic mission (13:10) and of the persecutions. By placing the discourse as a whole just before the Passion story he relates the sufferings of the apostles with the sufferings of Christ and makes the latter a model for the faithful Christian martyr. The troublesome problem of unsuccessful rebel messiahs becomes likewise a warning against heresies and apostasies in the early Church. The tension between the statement, "this generation will not pass away before all these things take place," in the apocalypse (vs. 30) and the words, "But of that day or that hour no one knows," in the apostolic discourse (vs. 32) reflects and is intended to explain the eschatological tension in the Church in Mark's time.[35] Mark saw himself and his generation living on the edge of the eschatological event which required a constant expectancy and readiness.

In the dark hues of the Passion Mark paints his final pictures of the meaning and demands of discipleship. The sleeping disciples in Gethsemane reinforce the warning to watchfulness (13:33–37). Jesus' example becomes the ideal of prayerful, obedient watching. The flight of the

---

34. *H.E.*, III, 5, 3.
35. For a different explanation of this problem see Lightfoot, *The Gospel Message of St. Mark*, p. 54.

disciples and of the naked youth (14:50–52) are lessons addressed to lapsing and defecting Christians. The young man clad only in linen which he abandoned in flight may be an allegory on defecting Christians (cf. Rev. 19:8). In fleeing the Church the defector loses the linen garment of righteousness and is therefore naked before God (cf. II Cor. 5:3ff.; Mt. 22:11ff.).

In the story of Peter's denial there is both warning and encouragement. How quickly Peter's self-confidence faded into cowardice! Yet if "the Rock" (the name Peter means rock) himself could so weaken under duress and still find repentance and restoration, the fearful Christians of weaker character can take heart; there is hope for them also. Judas, whose story deliberately parallels that of Peter, on the other hand, provides an ominous judgment upon the traitorous informer. Perhaps this is why there are so few clues as to Judas' motives. The horrendous evil of betraying Christ or the community is neither to be excused nor in any way softened. Mark's interpretation of the meaning of the Passion and Resurrection is now complete. By introducing it with the Little Apocalypse Mark has indicated its eschatological significance as well as its meaning for Christian suffering and martyrdom. Both the messianic woes and the eschatological resurrection have begun in Jesus. Finally, as the conclusion of the transitional section (10:45) makes clear, in the Passion Jesus became, by giving "his life as a ransom for many," the ultimate servant.

The Passion Whetted and shaped by years of recitation,[36] the story of Jesus' death moves swiftly and with dramatic power from the agony in the garden and the arrest to the caucus before the high priest, the hearing before the Sanhedrin, and the trial before Pilate. In the choice Pilate required of the Jews between Jesus and Barabbas is symbolized the whole challenge of the Gospel. It is parallel with the choice between Caesar and God (12:13–17), and amounts to a choice between Jesus, the true eschatological Messiah, and the rebel leaders of Jewish nationalism. Appropriately the story of the cross itself is told in the framework of Old Testament quotations among which Psalm 22 is prominent.[37] Polemic motives in response to growing antagonism between Church and Synagogue and increasing tension and persecution from the Empire are evident in the tendency to emphasize the responsibility of the Jewish hierarchy and Pilate's reluctance in the condemnation of Jesus. There is a touching note in the story of Simon of Cyrene which undoubtedly establishes a direct, personal connection in the persons of Alexander and Rufus between Mark's

36. For suggestions as to additions Mark may have made to this material see F. C. Grant, *IB*, Vol. VII, p. 866.
37. For the suggestion that Psalm 41 (LXX, Psalm 40) has provided the framework for Mark 14:1–25 see Frederick W. Danker, "The Literary Unity of Mark 14:1–25," *JBL*, Vol. LXXXV, Pt. IV, December, 1966, pp. 467–472.

"Gordon's Calvary," one of two sites shown to travelers as the location of the Crucifixion, so called after Charles Gordon who in the late nineteenth century argued its authenticity on the basis of its skull-like appearance (Golgotha is a Greek transliteration of the Aramaic word for skull) and the proximity of the "garden tomb" (see p. 146). (The Roderick Slide Collection, courtesy of Catawba College.)

generation and the Crucifixion, very probably prominent members of the Church, whose father had carried Jesus' cross (that is, the cross bar which the victim was required to carry to the scene). We cannot miss the symbol of true discipleship in the bearing of Jesus' cross here (cf. 8:34). As in Matthew's Passion this Gospel records only one "last word" from the cross: the so-called cry of dereliction. This "word" being the opening sentence of Psalm 22 reinforces the appropriateness of that Psalm to interpret the meaning of the cross. With the rending of the Temple curtain (15:38), the theme of Jesus replacing the Temple is completed. The author of Hebrews understands this tradition in the same way when he interprets this story in terms of the Christian cultus as a symbol of the Crucifixion the true sacrifice which has gained access for us to the true Holy of Holies, the presence of God himself (Heb. 10:19–20). Cultic also are the notes on the time of day (15:25, 33–34). The darkness at midday is an obvious reference to prophetic sayings which had long been interpreted eschatologically (see Amos 8:9; Jer. 15:9; Joel 3:16). The story closes as it opened with words acclaiming Jesus as the Son of God. God's announcement of Jesus as his Son in the voice from heaven, 1:11, is acknowledged, significantly, by a gentile Roman military officer (15:39).[38] That the divine voice in 1:11 quotes from the coronation Psalm (2:7), to which the centurion's saying is the appropriate response, and from Deutero-Isaiah's reference to his ordination as a prophet (Isa. 42:1) makes the latter a particularly apt and significant climax to the Passion story as well as to the story of Jesus' earthly ministry.

The Resurrection In Mark's final division on the Resurrection, chapter 16, we encounter one of the most difficult and insoluble problems in the entire Gospel. On the basis of both the evidence of ancient texts and literary considerations only the first eight verses belong to the original Gospel. Verses 9–20 in the Authorized Version as well as the so-called "shorter ending" found in some manuscripts are attempts to supply what has been felt from ancient times to be a lost ending. Some scholars contend that verse 8 is the original end as Mark intended it. Others, however, point out that it is difficult to believe that Mark would end his Gospel with the word "for." Almost certainly the grammar calls for something more. Whether that something more was simply a conclusion to the final sentence, an explanation of why the women were afraid and did not fulfill their mission to tell the disciples, or whether it contained an account, such as that in Matthew 28:9–20 and John 21, of Jesus' appearance in Galilee to the disciples we cannot say.[39] It is not unlikely that only a few words have been lost and therefore what we have is substantially the complete Gospel. Further we cannot go.

It is worthy of note that the emphasis falls not on the empty tomb but on the witness of the "young man" (probably intended to mean an angel).[40] Even such a supernatural witness, however, is not enough to quell fear and produce understanding. That the women fled in fear echoes again the theme which we discussed in connection with the messianic secret, the dull-witted disciples, and the irony in the Jerusalem ministry and Passion: the need to see and hear in faith in order to understand. It was the disciples'

38. Cf. Johannes Weiss, *Earliest Christianity* (New York: Harper & Brothers, 1959), Vol. II, p. 691.
39. Edgar J. Goodspeed has attempted a reconstruction of the lost ending based on the theory that Matthew has been following Mark closely up to verse 8 and therefore followed him approximately as closely through the remainder of the twenty-eighth chapter. This theory probably deserves more consideration than it has received, but it is nevertheless not without its difficulties. See *An Introduction to the New Testament* (Chicago: The University of Chicago Press, 1937), pp. 144–145.
40. See Taylor, *The Gospel According to St. Mark,* pp. 606–607.

encounter with the Risen Lord, not the women's witness to the empty tomb, that gave authority to the apostolic preaching. Mark had no need for a long story of the Resurrection; in several ways he had already prepared the reader to expect and understand it. This preparation is evident, for example, in the story of the raising of Jairus' daughter; by contrast, in the burial of John the Baptizer; Jesus walking on the sea; the predictions of the Passion; the Transfiguration; and Jesus' dispute with the Sadducees over the resurrection. As the fourth Gospel puts it, Jesus is the Resurrection and Life. (Jn. 11:25). The women mentioned three times, 15:40, 47, and 16:1–8, serving to tie together the Crucifixion, Burial, and Resurrection, are the last of the series of repetitions by which Mark has organized and structured his Gospel.[41] From such passages as 8:38, 13:26–27, and 14:62 we know that Mark's gaze was not finally backward to the Resurrection but forward to the *parousia.* That his Gospel should so end as to leave the reader in suspense as though the story is not yet finished is altogether consonant with Mark's faith and purpose. The story will not end, cannot end until God's Kingdom be fully come.

Structure of Mark

INTRODUCTION: JESUS AND DISCIPLES
Spread of Jesus' fame, ch. 1
Rise of opposition, 2:1–3:6
The community of faithful as Jesus' true family, 3:7–35
Parables of the mission, 4:1–34

THE GALILEAN MINISTRY
The mighty works, 4:34–43
The apostolic mission, ch. 6
Jesus and the Law, ch. 7
Bread and faith, 8:1–26

TRANSITION: THE PREDICTIONS OF THE PASSION, 8:27–10:45

JERUSALEM: THE PASSION AND RESURRECTION
The controversies, 10:46–12:44
The Little Apocalypse, ch. 13
The Passion, chs. 14–15
The Resurrection, 16:1–8

2. *He Taught Them, Saying . . . :* Matthew

Matthew's Gospel has aptly been called an expanded version of Mark. As we have already noted all but eleven pericopae of Mark are paralleled in Matthew, and, although the latter is less than two thirds longer, and

---

41. But cf. *IB,* Vol. VII, p. 908, for another interpretation of the significance of this repetition. That women should end this Gospel is surprising in view of their relative rarity here in comparison, for example, to Luke.

Matthew drastically condensed several of Mark's longer stories, those parallels comprise nearly one half of it.[42] That Matthew is something more than Mark in an enlarged edition appears, however, both in the way he handles the Markan material and in the nature of what he adds to it. It may be well, therefore, for us to be begin our analysis of Matthew by observing some of the more general differences which distinguish it from Mark, its principal source.

MATTHEW'S USE OF MARK

The most important distinction of Matthew is the predominance of teaching material. There are not only five major discourses which, as we shall see, give the Gospel its structure, but much of the intervening material contains parables, short sayings, and the like which serve as examples of the teaching to which Mark so frequently alludes without quoting. That Jesus' teaching is important to Matthew's purpose is evident also in the way in which he virtually turns a number of the miracles into pronouncement stories, by condensing them so as to place the emphasis on a saying at the conclusion. To the comparatively small amount of teaching material he found in Mark, which he rearranged and expanded, Matthew added Q and a sizable body of material (M) peculiar to his Gospel.[43]

There is only a negligible amount of narrative in Q,[44] and outside the birth stories and Passion there are only three narratives in M (Peter's attempt to walk on the water, 14:28–31—actually an addition to a narrative taken from Mark; the renaming of Peter, 16:17–19; and the shekel in the fish's mouth, 17:24–27). For Matthew, therefore, the main function of the Markan source is to provide the narrative framework, while Q and M furnish most of the parables and sayings that give Matthew its emphasis on Jesus' teaching.

A second pronounced difference between Matthew and Mark appears in the way in which the two Gospels open and close. Mark begins abruptly by introducing John the Baptizer and, after a brief recital of Jesus' baptism and temptation, launches into Jesus' Galilean ministry which began at the imprisonment of John. Matthew, on the other hand, takes his two opening chapters to introduce a genealogy and narratives of the infancy of Jesus. We have already examined the problem of the apparently truncated end of Mark which leaves the story of Jesus' Resurrection appearances

---

42. See p. 46–48. On the comparative length of Mark and Matthew, in Nestle's Greek Text Mark has 1524 lines to Matthew's 2499. A table of word counts for Matthew's condensations can be found in Hawkin's *Horae Synopticae,* (Oxford: At the Clarendon Press, 1909), pp. 158–160.
43. See pp. 51–54.
44. The healing of the centurion's servant, Mt. 8:5–13; Lk. 7:1–10, is the major exception. The three temptations, Mt. 4:3–10; Lk. 4:3–12, and the healing of the dumb demoniac, Mt. 9:32–33; Lk. 11:14, should probably also be mentioned, although the lack of close verbal agreement raises some doubt that they should be included in Q.

hanging. Matthew carries the story forward to a meeting in Galilee of Jesus with the disciples and the climax in the great commission.

A third difference between the two Gospels can be seen in Matthew's emphasis on the Old Testament. There are, of course, many echoes, allusions, and quotations of the Old Testament in Mark, but seldom are they labeled as such. Especially noticeable and important in Matthew is the motif of fulfillment of prophecy. In eighteen passages an Old Testament quotation is cited with a formula such as: "This was done that it might be fulfilled" or "as it is written in." Beside these there are some thirty-five quotations from the Old Testament used in ethical admonitions, polemical discourse, and the like. These quotations are usually introduced by such phrases as "It is written," "you have heard that it was said," "have you not read," or "learn what this means." In more than eighty instances may be found indirect quotations, allusions, motifs, and patterns which shape the dialogue, are echoed in sayings, or otherwise furnish the framework for a pericope. When we include some twenty-seven instances which require an Old Testament passage to explain an allusion, custom, law, and the like, the number of Old Testament passages involved rises to more than one hundred and sixty. It is clear then that Matthew, more than sharing with the other Gospels a common body of Testimonia, has a special interest of his own in the Old Testament. Professor Krister Stendahl has shown by a careful analysis of the quotations in Matthew that an intensive special study of the Old Testament in relation to Jesus lies back of this Gospel; and on that basis he proposes the theory that the Gospel is the product of a school of Christian scribes much like the students of Torah in Judaism.[45] The treatment of Scripture in the Qumran community has thrown considerable light on this aspect of Matthew. That Matthew is the most Jewish of Gospels, furthermore, has often been noted. When these characteristics are taken together, we are probably justified in seeing an autobiographical reference in the words at the very end of the discourse in chapter 13, "Therefore every scribe who has been trained for the kingdom of heaven is like a householder who brings out of his treasure what is new and what is old."[46] It may not be going too far to take these words as a deliberate indication of the purpose of Matthew.

Some Organizing Principles   When we look for clues to the ways in which Matthew has organized his material the most obvious one we encounter is the five-part structure created by the discourses: chapters 5–7, 10, 13, 18, and 23–25. That these sections are important to the structure of Matthew is evident both by the key positions they occupy and the way in which they are marked off from and related to their contexts. Each of them ends with the formula "And when Jesus had finished . . ."; each

45. Krister Stendahl, *The School of St. Matthew.*
46. Stendahl, *The School of St. Matthew,* p. 30. Also W. D. Davies, *The Setting of the Sermon on the Mount* (Cambridge: At the University Press, 1964).

is preceded by a summary statement or a climactic story and is introduced with a definite setting appropriate to its content. From the fivefold structure which results, several scholars have concluded that the Gospel was intended as a new Christian Torah—a Pentateuch—and therefore Jesus is here being interpreted as a new Moses.[47] The word Torah, of course, means more than "Law." Perhaps authoritative teaching would better translate it; hence Moses as the giver of Torah is more accurately called teacher than lawgiver. The obvious correspondence between the story of Herod and the slaughter of the Holy Innocents in chapter 2 and the story of Moses in Exodus 1:15–2:15, the wilderness temptations of Jesus and the children of Israel, and the mountain setting for the Sermon (chs. 5–7), in which Jesus' sayings are deliberately contrasted with quotations from the Pentateuch, make this theory attractive. Certainly these correspondences are not accidental.

This theory, nevertheless, leads us astray from the actual structure and intention of Matthew. That the fivefold structure of the Gospel relates it to Hebrew literature is clear. As is apparent in such instances as the five books of the Psalms and the five poems in Lamentations, as well as several extracanonical writings, the fivefold structure was popular. This fact alone warns against making too much of the Pentateuch as Matthew's model. Critics of the theory point out that the legal instruction in the Pentateuch falls into two large sections (Ex. 20–Num. 10 and the book of Deut.) rather than five as in Matthew. The narrative sections could have been made to conform much more closely to the Pentateuchal pattern had this been Matthew's purpose.

With exceptions of the first, chapters 5–7, the five discourses are based on Markan material. The Sermon is placed in the Markan framework at the point of Jesus' retreat (Mk. 1:35–38). By omitting the story of the healing in the synagogue of the man with the unclean spirit and rewriting the story of the retreat he has made a place for it. The only other connection of this discourse with Mark is the reference to the mountain as the setting which he has borrowed from Mark 3:13. In the Sermon itself there are a few scattered parallels, but the verbal agreements are not impressive. The other four discourses are, in contrast, based on or at least take their departure from Mark. The second discourse, Chapter 10, for example, amounts to an expansion of Mark's story of the Mission of the Disciples (6:7–13). A significant part of this expansion consists in a section transposed from Mark's Apocalypse.

An even clearer instance of the relation of these discourses to Mark is found in the seven parables of the kingdom (13:1–52). If we allow that Matthew's parable of the tares (13:24–30) is actually an elaboration of

47. E.g., B. W. Bacon, *Studies in Matthew* (New York: Henry Holt and Company, 1930), ch. VI. For a cogent recent criticism of this theory see, W. D. Davies, *The Setting of the Sermon on the Mount*, ch. II, pp. 14–93.

Mark's parable of the mysterious growth of seed (4:26–29),[48] all of Mark's collection of parables on seed in chapter 4 reappear in this discourse and in Mark's order. Only two significant alterations occur. First, Matthew has removed Mark's section on the secret being made manifest which intervenes between the interpretation of the parable of the sower and the mysterious growth of seed. The two similes, the lamp and the measure (Mk. 4:21–25), he has used in the two previous discourses; and the remaining material has been added to the sayings on Jesus' use of parables which in both Matthew and Mark separate the parable of the sower from its interpretation. Second, Matthew has added the parable of the leaven just before the summary on Jesus' parabolic teaching. In the introduction to the parable of the leaven Matthew imitates the formula introducing the two previous parables, which indicates, as does the change of locale (vs. 36) separating these parables from what follows, that he was intent on keeping this collection intact. The word "again" which links the remaining three parables suggests that Matthew found this sequence in another similar collection.

Matthew places the fourth discourse at Jesus' return to Capernaum in Mark 9:33ff. He has partially obscured the setting by the story of the coin in the fish's mouth, but obviously intends the words "At that time" (18:1) to reestablish it. Although a considerable part of Mark's material reappears here, Matthew's additions and reorganization modify its interpretation. To this material he has added material from Q and M to form the body of the discourse.

The heart of the final discourse is Mark's Little Apocalypse (ch. 13). This apocalypse Matthew has allowed to stand where it occurs in the framework of Mark. As in the latter, the cleansing of the Temple and subsequent controversies lead into this discourse. He has, however, expanded Mark 12:38–39, largely from Q material, into an introductory section of seven woes on the Pharisees (ch. 23). A change of the setting separates these woes from the apocalypse itself. The three parables of chapter 25 comprise a fitting conclusion for the apocalypse. We can see from this survey of Matthew's organization that even in the discourses he is conscious of Mark's framework.

This last observation raises the question of Matthew's handling of Mark throughout the Gospel. It is commonly observed that he is far more faithful to and dependent upon Mark's order than is Luke, and that the major alterations he makes are in the earlier parts of both Gospels. It will be worthwhile to observe these alterations to discover what effect they have on the meaning and emphasis of Matthew.[49]

48. See p. 134.
49. We have already noted that the theory of an earlier version of Mark, which might account for these alterations, is improbable. See p. 50.

He Taught Them, Saying...

Beginning in chapter 3 Matthew follows and expands Mark's first twenty verses. At this point, as we have seen, he inserts the Sermon on the Mount. Omitting Mark's story of the healing in the synagogue (1:23–27), he utilizes most of the remainder of the first chapter, the second chapter (except the pericope on plucking grain on the Sabbath, 2:23–28), the last pericope of the fourth chapter, and chapter 5; all of which, rearranged and combined with Q material, make up the familiar section of ten miracles (chs. 8–9). Matthew then skips to Mark 6:6b–11 which, along with Mark 3:14–19, he uses as the basis for his mission discourse (ch. 10). The final pericope of chapter 2 and the rest of chapter 3 become the basis of Matthew's section between the mission discourse and the parables of the kingdom (chs. 11–12). In the latter most of Mark's fourth chapter is found. Matthew then returns to the remainder of Mark's sixth chapter (1–6a, 14ff.) and follows Mark with only minor rearrangements to the end. The following table will show Matthew's use of Mark in greater detail:

Matthew's Use of Mark°

Mark	Matthew
	1–2
1:1–20 (1:28, 39)	3–4
3:13	5–7
1:40–44 1:29–34 4:35–41 5:1–21 2:1–22 5:22–42	8–9
6:6b–7 3:16–19 6:8–11	10
2:23–28 3:1–12 3:22–35	11–12
4:1–34	13
6:1–6a 6:14–16:8	14–28

* This table is intended only to compare the main facts concerning Matthew's use of Mark. It takes no account of minor omissions, condensations, repetitions, and the like.

Matthew's purpose in these rearrangements seems to have been to set the Sermon on the Mount in as prominent a position as possible, to create the group of ten miracles following it, and to transpose the parables and mission of the disciples so that the parables become the climax to the division. The Sermon and the miracles thus become an expansion of the summaries of Jesus' ministry (8:23–25; 9:35–38) which introduce and define the mission, as the seven parables serve as a concluding commentary on it. Matthew omits only ten or eleven of Mark's pericopae (depending on whether we regard the parable of the tares, Mt. 13:24–30, as a revision of Mark's mysterious growth of seed, Mk. 4:26–29).

One other note on Matthew's rearrangements will be in order. We noted in the previous section how Mark has inserted certain pericopae within others as an interpretive device. Several of these "envelopes" Matthew has removed. Although he has left the healing of the woman with a hemorrhage in the middle of the story of the healing of the ruler's daughter, he removed the beheading of John the Baptist from the story of the mission (Mk. 6:7–30) to a position following the third discourse. By omitting any reference to the return of the apostles he destroyed the "envelope" altogether and thus avoided making Jesus' discourse on John a replacement. Similarly, the cursing of the fig tree in Matthew no longer surrounds but follows the cleansing of the Temple.

To summarize, Matthew has structured his Gospel in well-defined sections which succeed one another in a logical progression. He has, to a large degree, obscured Mark's patterns of concurrent themes running through the Gospel. Certainly one of the reasons for Matthew's rearrangements is his interest in Jesus' sayings, and especially the prominence he wishes to give to the five discourses. A closer examination of Matthew's changes in Markan material would, of course, reveal a number of reinterpretations and additions of meaning.

Another of Matthew's more noticeable characteristics is his interest in numerical arrangements. The five discourses are, as we have seen, basic to the entire structure of the Gospel. This characteristic, however, appears in several of the subordinate units. At the very opening of the Gospel, for example, Matthew places considerable emphasis on the *three* divisions of *fourteen* generations each in the genealogy. The introductory section, chapters 1–4, contains *seven* references to fulfillment of Old Testament prophecy. There are *three* temptations in the wilderness. In the Sermon on the Mount there are *nine* beatitudes, *six* comments on Torah, *three* sayings on true piety, and *seven* petitions in the Lord's Prayer. The section intervening between the Sermon and the mission discourse (chs. 8–9) consists principally of *ten* miracles; there are *seven* parables of the kingdom (ch. 13), *seven* woes to the Pharisees in chapter 23, and *three* great parables of the final judgment in chapter 25. In a few places Matthew has doubled the characters in stories taken from Mark.[50] There are, for example, *two* Garazene demoniacs (8:28–34), *two* blind men (9:27–31), *two* animals on which Jesus rode in the triumphal entry (21:1–11). We should not look for cryptic symbolic meanings in all these numbers. Probably many of them are no more than mnemonic devices or literary habit. Where Matthew wants the reader to take special note of the numbers, he employs effective ways of calling attention to them.

There is some evidence that these numerical arrangements are not all Matthew's doing. That the third group of fourteen generations in the genealogy contains only twelve names (thirteen, if Jesus himself is counted) is well known. Since Matthew is careful to call attention to the numerical scheme, a later textual error is quite possibly involved here. The Sermon on the Mount, on the other hand, displays evidence of an earlier numerical arrangement which Matthew's construction has partially obscured. There is good reason to believe, for example, that the original number of the beatitudes was seven rather than nine.[51] The last two beatitudes, on persecution, are surely doublets, and probably the third beatitude is a doublet (based on Ps. 37:11) of the first. Of the comments on Torah (5:21–48), the third, concerning divorce (5:31–32), because the phrasing of its opening words bears the marks of imitation, is probably also an addition suggested by the preceding saying on adultery. The resulting numerical scheme, when the doublets and additions are removed, is *seven* beatitudes (5:3–4, 6–10), *two* metaphors on discipleship (5:13–15), *five* comments on Torah (5:21–30, 33–45), and *three* sayings on true piety (6:1–18). To the seven parables of the kingdom in chapter 13 there is added the metaphor of the householder which would bring the number of parables to eight. Both the wording and structure of the discourse, however, make it clear that this metaphor is not intended to be included among the parables but stands as a summary and conclusion at the end of the discourse. Such difficulties as these in numerological schemes, however, are not unknown in Biblical, and apocalyptic and rabbinic literature as the "extra" 151st Psalm in the Septuagint and the beast which "is an eighth but it belongs to the seven" in Revelation (17:11) illustrate.

Matthew's difficulty in his numerical schemes arises partly from his method of expanding his material by agglomeration. This important aspect of Matthew's method may be illustrated from the structure of the Sermon. It is noteworthy that, except for four beatitudes and the Lord's Prayer, all of the significant parallels between the Sermon and Luke's Gospel follow the three sayings on true piety (6:19–7:29), and that this parallel material (i.e., Q material) comprises almost all of the remainder of the Sermon. If our suggestion above for restoring the original numerical form

50. See pp. 129–130, 142. Also Bultmann, *The History of the Synoptic Tradition*, pp. 314–317.
51. See Bultmann, *The History of the Synoptic Tradition*, p. 356.

of the first part of the Sermon is allowed, it is clear that Matthew has constructed the Sermon by a combination of two bodies of material: The first a body of sayings in the form of Semitic parallelism[52]; the second a collection or collections from Q. This would help to explain the discrepancy between 5:1 and 8:1 in which Jesus is privately instructing the disciples and 7:28–29 where Jesus is teaching the crowds. It may be worthy of note that the parabolic material is nearly all from Q (cf. Mk. 4:34). These are distinctly different settings belonging originally to the separate collections.

The first part of the Sermon, then, originated in a series of sayings in Semitic parallelism, arranged in meaningful numerical groups. With exception of four of the beatitudes, the metaphors of salt and light, and the last of the comments on Torah ("You shall love your neighbor and hate your enemy," 5:43ff), all of this material belongs to the M source. To these balanced sayings Matthew has added a considerable amount of material, some of it his own and some from Mark and Q. Because it upsets the balance and symmetry, the agglomeration is easily separated from the original. What Matthew has added is both supplemental and commentary. The ninth beatitude, on the theme of persecution (5:11–12), for example, is obviously an amplification from the alternate version in Q of the eighth. Verses 13b, 15, and 16 are expansions on the metaphors of salt and light. The section which follows, 5:17–20, is Matthew's commentary designed to interpret this entire collection of sayings. The two sayings on reconciliation (vss. 23–24 and 25–26); the Markan material on mortifying the flesh (vss. 29–30) and on divorce (vss. 31–32); at least verse 37 and perhaps most of 34b–36 on swearing; the sayings on turning the other cheek, the second mile, etc. (vss. 39b–42); the sayings on loving and saluting those who love and salute you, etc. (vss. 45–48); the saying on empty phrases; and Lord's Prayer; and forgiving others (6:7–15) are all additions suggested by similarities of thought. It should be noted, however, that this expansion is more than mere topical arrangement. In each case the additions serve to further define, apply, and interpret the saying.

If, as is often assumed, Luke's order of Q material more nearly represents the original, a comparison of the second half of the Sermon, 6:19–7:27, will show a similar method of compilation by association of ideas. Although almost all of this part of the sermon is paralleled in Luke very little of it is in the same sequence. It is, in fact, in Luke scattered among chapters 6, 11, 12, 13, and 16. The only extended sequence which appears the same in Luke is the section on anxiety, 6:25–33. That this section is a closely knit, characteristically rabbinic homily probably accounts for its appearance in both Gospels intact.[53]

52. See Burney, *The Poetry of Our Lord.*
53. On the structure of the homily in Judaism see Peder Borgen, *Bread from Heaven,* ch. II, p. 28–58.

There is also in Matthew a pronounced interest in mountains. Seven mountains mark important points in the Gospel: temptation, 4:8; the Sermon, 5:1; prayer, 14:23; feeding the multitude, 15:29; Transfiguration, 17:1; Mount of Olives (which is the scene of three episodes: the beginning of the triumphal entry, 21:1; setting for the Apocalypse, 24:3; and Gethsemane, 26:30); and the great commission, 28:16.

Mount Tabor in southern Galilee, traditional site of the Transfiguration. (Courtesy of the Israel Government Tourist Office.)

We may note, finally, Matthew's use of doublets and repetitions.[54] Some of these, of course, he has taken over from Mark. Unlike the series of motifs which Mark has woven through his Gospel, Matthew's repetitions are mostly in pairs. There are some thirty-four such repetitions, most of which, also, are sayings, and at least seven of these occur the first time in the Sermon. As in Mark, these repetitions serve to establish connections within the Gospel and, hence, are important for Matthew's interpretation of the meaning of Jesus. The proclamation of the Kingdom, for example, is first placed in the mouth of John the Baptist (3:2), then is made by Jesus (4:17), and finally given to the apostles as their mission (10:7). Matthew alone identifies the message of John and Jesus in this way. The

54. For a list of these items see p. 500.

continuity thus indicated is one of Matthew's basic interests. That the time of judgment for Israel has come is announced both by John (3:10) and Jesus (7:19). Between the Sermon and the mission discourse a tie is established by the repetition in the summaries which precede them (4:23 and 9:35). Both the Sermon and the mission discourse in turn are related to the discourse on Church order (ch. 18) by repetitions; the first by the sayings on mortifying the flesh (5:29–30 and 18:8–9) and forgiveness (6:15 and 18:35), the second by the saying, "He who receives you receives me" (10:40 and 18:5). The connection which we noted in Mark between the mission of the disciples and the apocalypse is reinforced in Matthew by the repetition of the warning of arrest and trial in Mark 13:9–13 (10:17–22 and 24:9, 13). Like the thrice-repeated proclamation of the Kingdom, the saying on true greatness, which is also basic to Matthew's understanding of discipleship, occurs three times (18:1–5; 20:26–27; and 23:11–12). The repetitions, which in a number of instances occur, on the one hand, in the discourses and, on the other hand, in the narrative sections, not only give the Gospel a greater unity and underscore some of Matthew's major emphases, but by the connections they establish also provide a subtle but significant interpretation of their contexts.

THE PATTERN OF THOUGHT IN MATTHEW

From our analysis of Matthew's method of organization and structure we can see that the five great discourses are basic to the meaning and purpose of his Gospel. Yet it is equally clear that the Gospel is more than a series of five discourses using a presumably chronological narrative of Jesus' ministry for a convenient setting. The narratives as well as the discourse are topically compiled and are in Matthew, no less than in Mark, paradigms of discipleship. As such they picture situations in the Church of Matthew's time for which the discourses provide extended instruction. As settings for the discourses, the narratives interpret not only the ministry and Passion but also the teaching of Jesus. The discourses are therefore more than catechetical material (though some of the material may have been transmitted through catechetical instruction), they are rather intended to inform the Church of Matthew's time across the whole range of its life by means of Jesus' teaching.

The Prologue   The Sermon on the Mount, standing as it does in the place of prominence at the beginning, is rightfully regarded as the characteristic and most significant part of the Gospel.

The customary title for the first discourse in Matthew is not altogether fortunate. Matthew himself introduces it as teaching. The word "sermon" had not, in antiquity, acquired the technical meaning it has for us. "The

Discourse on the Mount" would be more accurate and consonant with ancient usage and Matthew's intention. The setting for the Sermon is provided by a prologue consisting in the first four chapters.[55] This section is in three movements: (1) the birth stories, chs. 1–2; (2) the baptism and temptation, 3:1–4:11; (3) the opening of the Galilean ministry, 4:12–25. A series of seven citations of Old Testament prophecies tie the section together as a unit.

In the first movement the advent of Jesus is firmly grounded in the history and destiny of Israel not only by five of the seven prophecies but also by the use of Old Testament traditions and motifs. The genealogy, with which the Gospel opens, serves to establish this point at the outset. By introducing the genealogy with the names of Abraham and David, Matthew recalls to his readers two great covenant figures of Israel's history. In Genesis 12:2–3 Abraham is promised, "I will make of you a great nation" and "by you all the families of the earth will bless themselves." Matthew's readers would not fail to recall Isaac "the child of promise," nor would they overlook the parallel between the angel's announcement to Joseph, 1:20–21, and the annunciation to Abraham in Genesis 18:1–15, as well as the parallel of the providential miracle of Isaac's birth to the aged couple, Gen. 21:1–7, with the virgin birth of Jesus. The second part of the promise referring to "all the families of the earth" is reinforced by the inclusion of four women in the genealogy: Tamar, Rahab, Ruth, and Bathsheba, all of whom were foreigners.[56] Thus the beginning of the Gospel anticipates the universality of the great commission at its conclusion. Jesus, the ultimate Son of Abraham, becomes the realization of this promise.

Attention has often been called to the fact that the numerical value of the Hebrew name David is fourteen, and the three fourteens of the genealogy, therefore, may be Matthew's way of underscoring Jesus' Davidic lineage. That this emphasis may be something more than an appeal to popular messianic expectations appears in two promises in the Davidic covenant passage, II Samuel 7:14 and 16. With reference to David's son through whom the promises would be fulfilled God says, "I will be his father, and he shall be my son." By means of characteristic scribal exegesis Matthew would have no difficulty in finding the true fulfillment of these

55. On the question of the extent of Matthew's prologue see Edgar Krentz, "The Extent of Matthew's Prologue," *JBL*, Vol. LXXXIII, Dec. 1964, pp. 409–414. For the structure and use of the Old Testament see also Helen Milton, "The Structure of the Prologue to St. Matthew's Gospel," *JBL*, Vol. LXXXI, June 1962, pp. 175–181. The following analysis of Mt. 1–2, is indebted at several points to the latter article.

56. Bathsheba, the wife of Uriah the Hittite, would be presumably a Hittite. The inclusion of these women in the genealogy has often been interpreted as an attempt to offset Jewish calumny against Jesus' birth. On this interpretation see W. D. Davies, *The Setting of the Sermon on the Mount*, pp. 65–66.

promises in the ultimate Son of David who was conceived of the Holy Spirit, and therefore the Son of God (cf. 3:17; 4:3, 6; 8:29; 11:27; 16:16; 17:5; 27:54). Similarly, the second promise to David, "Your throne shall be established forever," would for Matthew refer to Jesus who as Messiah is the ultimate king. Thus both covenant traditions find their ultimate fulfillment in Jesus.[57]

The two covenant traditions find a parallel in the two names for Jesus that Matthew provides: Jesus (Greek form of Joshua) and Emmanuel. By the name Jesus, which in Hebrew means "Yahweh is salvation," he is designated the ultimate deliverer and, as Matthew's translation points out, Emmanuel (God with us) indicates him as the realization of the eternal presence of God with his people (cf. 28:20b).

In a similar fashion the second chapter carries through the story of Herod, the wise men, and the settlement of the Holy Family in Nazareth in the framework of Old Testament motifs. On one level this chapter is Matthew's explanation of how it happens that Jesus, although born in Bethlehem, was known as a native of Nazareth. But this explanation can hardly be Matthew's real concern. Of the seven prophecies of the prologue, the four that are located in this chapter underscore Matthew's determination to place Jesus within as well as at the end of Israel's history and tradition. The wise men's inquiry of Herod (2:2) recalls Naaman's visit to the king of Israel in II Kings 5:1–7. Herod's slaughter of the Holy Innocents (2:13–18) as a parallel to Pharaoh's order for the death of male Hebrew babies and the birth of Moses (Exod. 1:15–2:10) is one of the most familiar and transparent examples of Matthew's use of an Old Testament motif.[58] In so doing he has introduced Moses as a third figure antecedent to Jesus. To make Jesus a "new Moses" on this basis is to narrow too much Matthew's purpose and thought and to fail to grasp the paradigmatic function of the Old Testament motif. Jesus for Matthew is no more a "new Moses" than a new Abraham or David. It would be more accurate to say that he is the ultimate teacher as he is the ultimate Son of Abraham and ultimate king. The two prophetic quotations in 2:15 and 18 refer in their original setting to Israel's Exodus from Egypt and the Babylonian Exile, respectively. Matthew's readers might well recall II Isaiah's announcement of the end of the Exile which was soon to be brought about by Cyrus of Medo-Persia whom he called "God's Messiah" (Isa. 51:10). Probably Matthew by this means intends for his readers to see Jesus' coming as the ultimate deliverance.

The second and third movements of this section each begin with one

---

57. Cf. Heb. 1:5ff. For a stimulating modern application of this concept see Donald T. Rowlingson, *Jesus the Religious Ultimate* (New York: The Macmillan Company, 1960).
58. On the significance of the Pentateuchal motifs in Matthew's Prologue see Davies, *The Setting of the Sermon on the Mount*, ch. II, pp. 14–108.

of the two remaining prophetic quotations. These quotations underscore the prophetic roles of John the Baptizer and Jesus which are here paralleled and contrasted. Jesus is thus placed in the continuity of Israel's prophetic tradition. The first and most important of these parallels is the proclamation of the approaching Kingdom of Heaven which is given, as we have seen, by John and Jesus and later by the apostolic mission. Jesus' repetition of several items in John's teaching carries this parallel further (cf. 3:7 with 12:34; 3:10 with 7:19, and 3:12 with 13:30). In a later section, 11:2–19, Matthew completes his development of this comparison of prophetic roles. There it becomes clear that John stands climactically at the end of the prophetic tradition. Yet Jesus, while belonging to and fulfilling the continuity of that tradition, nevertheless stands over against it as something new and greater. He is, in other words, the ultimate prophet. The significance of this comparison of Jesus with John the Baptizer is evident in the fact that each of the narrative sections which link together five discourses have some sort of reference to John the Baptist.

The contrast in prophetic roles, by which Matthew has prepared for Jesus' discourse on John the Baptist in chapter 11, is indicated first by John himself in his announcement of the Coming One who will baptize "with the Holy Spirit and with fire." More than an apology for Jesus' submission to John's baptism of repentance, his protest "I need to be baptized by you, and do you come to me?" and Jesus' answer "Let it be so now; for thus it is fitting for us to fulfill all righteousness" (3:14–15) serve to interpret and define the continuity and contrast between Jesus and John. Both the continuity and contrast are confirmed by the descent of the Spirit and the voice from heaven.

There follows the familiar story of three temptations in the wilderness. The forty days may recall Moses' flight to Midian until recalled to Egypt to lead his people to freedom, his fast on Mount Sinai (Exod. 34:28), or perhaps they may echo Israel's sojourn in the wilderness.[59] The temptations serve several functions here. For one thing they underscore the righteousness of Jesus which has already been asserted in the story of his baptism (3:14–15, cf. Heb. 2:17–18; 4:15). Second, they represent Jesus' authority over satanic powers, an authority grounded in the Law. They serve to define, in other words, the messiahship of Jesus. One scholar has offered the interesting suggestion that the temptations reflect Jesus' question about his own messiahship. The devil, therefore, is tempting Jesus to put God to the test, as ancient Israel had done in the wilderness, to see if he really is God's "Beloved Son."[60]

---

59. The number forty in the Old Testament symbolizes trial, temptation, and the like. Matthew need not have had any particular antecedent in mind here. See Davies, *The Setting of the Sermon on the Mount,* pp. 46, 57, and n. 1.
60. J. A. T. Robinson, *Twelve New Testament Studies,* pp. 53–60.

The third movement of Matthew's prologue begins with the imprisonment of John the Baptist. This event not only marks the beginning of Jesus' Galilean ministry, it is, as we learn later in 11:7–15, the great dividing line in the history of salvation. John the last and greatest in Israel's noble prophetic tradition has fulfilled the ultimate function of prophecy, the announcement of God's Messiah, and has begun the proclamation of the approaching Kingdom of Heaven. Jesus, as the ultimate prophet, marks both the fulfillment and the end of the prophetic tradition as he takes up the task of proclaiming the Kingdom. In him the "light has dawned." With the call of the four fishermen disciples his ministry is established. From the beginning, as in Mark, the disciples form a parallel to the story of Jesus. A summary of Jesus' ministry as teaching, preaching, and healing (based on Mark 6:6b), and a description of his fame and popularity close the prologue and introduce the Sermon on the Mount.

The Sermon on the Mount In the prologue the frame of reference and the perspective for understanding the Sermon are given. The Sermon, therefore, is not to be read as a universal ethic, a body of sublime teaching of timeless, self-evident validity. This teaching, in the first place, is inseparable from the Kingdom of God whose nearness was Jesus' proclamation. Second, as the Kingdom stands at the end as fulfillment of Israel's sacred history, so the teaching stands related to Israel's Torah as its fulfillment. It would not be accurate to call the Sermon "New Torah" any more than Jesus can be called a "New Moses."[61] It is rather the final midrash, the final definition of God's will for his Kingdom for which all previous teaching was a preparation.

The key to understanding the Sermon is to be found in the parenthetical section on Jesus' relation to the Law in 5:17–20.[62] The paradoxes herein are intentional. In the paradox that the Law is permanent and yet a new superior righteousness is demanded both the continuity and uniqueness of Jesus' teaching are defined. Israel's Scripture cannot be repudiated except at the expense of the continuity of the Church with the history of Israel. (The "Law and the Prophets" was the accepted name for the Old Testament. The reference here is not primarily to the commandments but to Israel's Sacred Writings as a whole.) Yet in Jesus something new has entered history, something which completes and fulfills the real purpose and intention of the old and is therefore in continuity with it. The commandments are therefore not to be relaxed but rather deepened.

From this perspective the Sermon is a commentary upon the way the believer's righteousness must exceed "that of the scribes and Pharisees."

61. See Davies, *The Setting of the Sermon on the Mount,* pp. 93–108.
62. On the problem of this passage see W. D. Davies, *Christian Origins and Judaism,* pp. 31–66.

The ethics of the Sermon are, in other words, the ethics of the Kingdom of God. So the hearer is commanded to "seek first his kingdom and his righteousness" (6:33). But the believer, just because he by faith has accepted it, becomes a citizen of this Kingdom, and consequently comes proleptically under its ethical demands. The demands are absolute: "You, therefore must be perfect, as your heavenly Father is perfect" (5:48)!

If the Sermon stood alone, its forbidding absoluteness would render it impotent; it must be read in the context in which Matthew has put it: the call to repentance and faith proclaimed with the approaching Kingdom, on the one hand, and the theme of forgiveness of sin which appears repeatedly throughout the Gospel, on the other hand. The theme of divine forgiveness, in fact, occupies a place of prominence in the middle of the Sermon itself, where the petition for forgiveness in the Lord's Prayer receives the added comment, "For if you forgive men their trespasses, your heavenly Father also will forgive you" (6:12, 14–15).[63]

Matthew's solution to the question of the place of Torah in the Church's faith and life stands in rather sharp contrast to that of Paul. As we shall see in a later chapter, Paul saw the Law as ended with the advent of Christ, and a new age of the Spirit inaugurated. Such an abrupt abandonment of the Law could easily be taken to mean a repudiation of Israel's history as the People of God. Indeed, the heretic Marcion in the second century was to take Paul to mean exactly that. To solve this problem of continuity between Israel's sacred history and the Church, Paul declared that the believer is a child of Abraham by faith. Faith, therefore, not Torah, even in Israel's history, is prior. Matthew's position is more conservative. Torah for Matthew is the expression of God's eternal will rather than, as Paul taught, an interim provision because of man's perversity (Gal. 3:15–29, Rom. 7:7–14). Hence for Matthew Torah had the same preparatory and paradigmatic value that he found in the rest of the Old Testament.

The word "fulfill" in Matthew means several things. It means, first of all, the correspondence of certain actions or events in the story of Jesus to their Old Testament paradigms. Matthew intends more here than simply the apologetic value of an ancient prediction coming true. Nor does Matthew use this word to refer to the arrival of a particular climactic moment of time; he, in fact, carefully omits Mark's use of the word in just that sense in reference to Jesus' preaching (cf. Mt. 4:17 with Mk. 1:15). The Old Testament is the record of God's self-disclosure within history of what he had done or would do for his people. Therefore within the Old Testament are disclosed characteristic patterns of divine action

63. See further 9:2–9, 13; 12:31; 16:19; 18:15–35. For a penetrating and valuable study of the whole problem of Jesus' absolute ethic see John Knox, *The Ethic of Jesus in the Teaching of the Church* (Nashville: Abingdon, 1961).

toward man. Fulfillment means for Matthew, then, that in Jesus these patterns are repeated on the ultimate level. Thus the patterns are brought to their final and ultimate meaning. For this reason fulfillment does not mean conclusion in the sense of finishing something so that it may now be laid aside or dispensed with. Jesus fulfilled the Law and the Prophets by bringing to them their final realization, by filling them with their ultimate meaning. In him their eternal valadity is disclosed. The word fulfill is very important to Matthew. He uses it no fewer than sixteen times throughout his Gospel. His use of it here places Jesus' teaching among those messianic acts which signal the approach of the Kingdom and the final realization of God's purpose for his people. This is how the Sermon is to be understood. We must now briefly survey the pattern and content of this most important section of Matthew.

The Sermon begins, like the Book of Psalms, with the word "blessed." Indeed it may not be too far fetched to regard Matthew's beatitudes as miniatures of the First Psalm which celebrates the man "whose delight is in the Law of the Lord." They differ from the Psalm and Old Testament beatitudes in general, however, in that their consequent rewards are eschatological rather than temporal. This eschatological emphasis accounts for their paradoxical quality. It is just those who appear to be the most unfortunate who are blessed because of what is in store for them in the Kingdom. The beatitudes are therefore both a list of the qualifications for entrance into and a description of the Kingdom. They fall into three groups, the first of which (vss. 3–5) is based on the motif of the reversal of fortunes.[64] In the second group (vss. 6–8) those longing for true piety are promised satisfaction, and in the third (vss. 9–12) a reward in heaven is promised the faithful under persecution.

The beatitudes are followed by two metaphors of salt and light on the function of the disciples as witnesses in the world. After the pronouncement on the Law and Prophets and the righteousness demanded by the Kingdom, which we discussed above, the Sermon moves to a series of six sayings concerning the Law (5:21–48). Three are from the decalogue (vss. 21, 27, 33), and the key phrase of the last one is not found in the Old Testament at all (vs. 43). They follow a simple but definite form: "You have heard that it was said . . . but I say to you. . . ." What follows in each of the first four pushes the moral issue back of the act to the motives and character from which the act arises. We are not, however, to read these sayings as a reduction of ethics to a matter of disposition and general principles. They are no less specific than the commandments in Torah on which they are commentary.[65] The last two, however, have the effect of nullifying or basically altering the statement in favor of a mandate

64. Cf. 19:30; 20:16; Lk. 1:46–55; 6:20–23; 16:19–31, *passim*. On Beatitude in the Bible, see *IDB*, Vol. I, pp. 369–371.
65. Amos Wilder, "The Sermon on the Mount," *IB*, Vol. VII, pp. 161–162.

of love which must include one's enemies. This law of love, the reader senses, is really the underlying principle of the whole Sermon. That impression is confirmed when, in 22:34–40, the law of love reappears in explicit form as that on which hangs all Scripture. The section reaches its climax in the summary command: "You, therefore, must be perfect, as your heavenly Father is perfect." That this command is a paraphrase of the theme of the Holiness Code (Lev. 19:2 and 20:26) emphasizes again the relation of this section to the Torah.

The final section in the first half of the Sermon consists of three sayings on true piety (6:1–18). The form, though rather complicated, is adhered to very consistently in treating three basic acts of piety: almsgiving, prayer, and fasting. The thrust of these sayings is that one's actions are performed before God and should not be done "to be seen by men." This theme, which also applies to the Sermon as a whole, appears again later in the Gospel in the seven woes against the Pharisees (ch. 23). Three additional items, a saying on "empty phrases," the Lord's Prayer, and a saying on forgiving, serve to expand the theme of prayer.

The second half of the Sermon might be called "The New Wisdom." Its character is not unlike the Wisdom Literature.[66] After three sayings (6:19–24) on treasures, a sound eye, and serving two masters, Matthew has included a short homily on anxiety (6:25–34). Matthew's interest in this homily is the concluding saying on seeking first the Kingdom, which is the Christian alternative to anxiety.

Chapter 7, after two sayings in judging, casting pearls before swine (which, because it partly contradicts the preceding saying on judging, serves to qualify it), includes a short homily (vss. 7–12) on asking, seeking, and knocking which concludes with the very important "Golden Rule." T. W. Manson has described this, which is probably the best known of Jesus' sayings, as "a rule of thumb for the guidance of those who are already presumed to have the root of the matter in them" (i.e., the law of love, Mt. 22:37–40).[67] The final section (7:13–27) is concerned with the way into the Kingdom. The narrow and broad ways and the danger of following false prophets lead to the concluding parable of rock and sand foundations with which the Sermon reaches its climax and conclusion.

Scattered throughout the Sermon are several epigrammatic sayings which accent and sum up the key points. Taken together they form an impressive summary:

> 5:16 Let your light so shine before men, that they may see your good works and give glory to your Father who is in heaven.

---

66. J. King West, *Introduction to the Old Testament*, pp. 391–392.
67. *The Teaching of Jesus* (Cambridge: At the University Press [1931], 1963), p. 307. Note that both the Golden Rule and the Law of Love are equated with the "Law and the Prophets."

5:20 For I tell you, unless your righteousness exceeds that of the scribes and Pharisees, you will never enter the Kingdom of heaven.

5:48 You, therefore must be perfect, as your heavenly Father is perfect.

6:1 Beware of practicing your piety before men in order to be seen by them; for then you will have no reward from your Father who is in heaven.

6:21 Where your treasure is, there will your heart be also.

6:33 But seek first his kingdom and his righteousness, and all these things shall be yours as well.

7:12 So whatever you wish that men would do to you, do so to them; for this is the law and the Prophets.

7:21 Not every one who says to me, 'Lord, Lord,' shall enter the kingdom of heaven, but he who does the will of my Father who is in heaven.

Ten Miracles and Discipleship The narrative section which links the Sermon to the discourse on the mission of the twelve is dominated by ten miracles. Matthew is clearly at some pains to have ten miracles, which has suggested to some commentators the influence of the saying concerning the number ten in the Talmudic tractate, *Pirqe Aboth* (5:5): "Ten miracles were wrought for our ancestors in Egypt and ten at the Sea" (cf. 5:1–7).[68] Other interpreters, however, point out that the miracles are broken into groups by the two sections concerning disciples. Since the first two groups contain three miracles each, it is suggested that Matthew regarded the healing of the woman with the hemorrhage and the story of the healing of ruler's daughted within which it is enclosed as one miracle, and so intended nine miracles in groups of three.[69] The arrangement of these groups of miracles certainly has significance for Matthew. It is not therefore unlikely that he took advantage of the unity which Mark had given the stories of the ruler's daughter and the woman with the hemorrhage so as to have it both ways: ten miracles and yet arranged in groups of threes.

In the first three miracles (8:2–17) one of those healed is a Jew (a leper), one is a gentile (the centurion's servant), and one a member of the family of a disciple (Peter's mother-in-law). Thus Jesus' healing ministry is made to take on significance for all mankind, and the prophecy (Isa. 53:4) which concludes the editorial summary on healings in the evening (8:16–17) is made to apply to Jew, gentile, and disciple alike.

68. Judah Goldin, *The Living Talmud* (Chicago: University of Chicago Press, 1957), p. 186; Hawkins, *Horae Synopticae*, pp. 166–167; See *IB*, Vol. VII, p. 336.

69. Willoughby C. Allen, *The Gospel According to St. Matthew* (*ICC*), pp. 73–94, classes the miracles under the following titles: three miracles of healing, three miracles of power, and three miracles of restoration. W. D. Davies argues convincingly for the number ten. See *The Setting of the Sermon on the Mount*, pp. 86ff.

To underscore this point Matthew has virtually turned the healing of the centurion's servant, the longest and most prominent of the three, into a pronouncement story. The climax of the story is in the saying, "I tell you, many will come from east and west and sit at table with Abraham, Isaac, and Jacob in the kingdom of heaven, while the sons of the kingdom will be thrown into the outer darkness" (8:11–12).

A change of locale in 8:18 indicates a change of theme. Jesus and the disciples are on the point of crossing the Sea of Galilee but before they can leave two would-be disciples appear. To the scribe who would follow him Jesus said, "the Son of man has nowhere to lay his head"; and the disciple who would first bury his father is told to "leave the dead to bury their own dead." By these stories Matthew pictures the utter abandon demanded of the true disciple under the pressure of proclaiming the kingdom.

The story of the stilling of the storm which follows is a commentary on these demands of discipleship and the faith required of disciples. As in Mark's version, the stormy sea and the boat symbolize the Church in a hostile and evil world.[70] Matthew's readers would hardly fail to note the similarity of this story to that of Jonah; nor would they fail to recall in that connection Jonah's mission to Ninevah and see therein an Old Testament justification of the gentile mission.

Matthew has turned Mark's story of the Gerasene demoniac, who became a witness to his own country, into a stark picture of gentile rejection of the mission. He has intensified the story by adding a second demoniac but has otherwise drastically abbreviated it. Many details such as the chains, the slashing, and the legion, are gone, but more significantly in the conclusion the demoniacs are lost sight of. Only the perverse plea of the swineherds and the populace of the city that Jesus "leave their neighborhood" remains.

The final story in this group is again separated by a change of locale. The authority of Jesus and, through him, of his disciples to forgive sins is the point of the story of the paralytic. The reader must recognize that the scribes are basically correct: Mere man has no authority to forgive sins. Thus they are being challenged to recognize who Jesus is. The "authority" of Jesus both to heal and to forgive sins is that of the Son of Man. The plural "men" at the end of verse 8 extends to the Church Jesus' authority to forgive sins (cf. 16:19; 18:18). The word "authority" (*exousia*) here derives from the preposition (ek) "out of" or "from" and the verb (*estin*) "to be." It means the freedom of choice, or freedom to dispose of one's property, and the like. It does not primarily refer to power, strength, or

70. On the meaning of this story see Bornkamm, Barth, and Held, *Tradition and Interpretation in Matthew,* pp. 52–57.

skill, but to the right to exercise such. Bultmann suggests "authorization."[71] Ultimately all authority belongs to God, therefore Jesus is exercising God's prerogative here. The same issue is joined in the five questions in Matthew 21:23–22:46.

Another change of locale introduces the story of the calling of Matthew (both Mark and Luke call him Levi), which again focuses attention on the role of the disciples. As in chapters 3 and 4, Jesus and John the Baptist are contrasted. Here the issues are eating with outcasts and neglecting the fasts. By means of the quotation from Hosea 6:6 (repeated again in 12:7) and the twin parables of the patch and the wineskins Matthew interprets the ministry of Jesus—and therefore that of his disciples—as being a fulfillment of Israel's role as the People of God and yet at the same time something new. Thus "both are preserved" (vs. 17c).

The healing of the woman with a hemorrhage, a paradigm of faith, is joined with the healing of the ruler's daughter which presages the Resurrection, the ultimate healing. Two more changes of locale lend an increasing tempo as the section comes to a close. A healing of two blind men (Matthew has again abbreviated and intensified, by doubling the characters, a story from Mark) provides another example of true faith; astonishment and healing of a dumb demoniac lead to the concluding summary.

The first part of the summary, which concludes this section of narratives and introduces the discourse on the mission, is a deliberate repetition of the summary introducing the Sermon at the end of the fourth chapter. By this means these two discourses are placed in a significant parallel. The second parts of these summaries are likewise significantly different. 4:24–25 recounts Jesus' fame and the crowds which followed him; whereas 9:36–38 recounts Jesus' compassion and the prayer for laborers. It is this prayer which anticipates and is interpreted by the mission in chapter 10.

The Discourse on the Mission of the Disciples With the commission taken from Mark 6:7 as a setting, Matthew introduces the mission discourse by a list of the twelve disciples from Mark 3:16–19. The material that follows reflects several stages of the mission. Verses 5–15, which come from Mark's story of the mission with the addition of two or three verses from Q, picture the original mission of the disciples. As the reference to "testimony before . . . the Gentiles," verse 18, in contrast to the command in verse 5 to "go nowhere among the Gentiles," makes clear, the section from verses 16–23 is addressed to the early apostolic mission. This latter section is taken almost totally from Mark's Apocalypse (Mk. 13:9, 11–13). The concluding saying, "I say to you, you will not have gone through all the towns of Israel, before the Son of man comes" (vs. 23b),[72] un-

---

71. See *Theology of the New Testament*, Vol. I, p. 342.
72. This verse was the basis of Albert Schweitzer's theory of "thoroughgoing eschatology." See pp. 62–64.

doubtedly comes from the early Palestinian mission and reflects the vivid apocalyptic eschatology which characterized their outlook. Matthew by including it is simply updating and reapplying it to the Church's mission of his own time. The remaining material in the discourse is largely from Q with a few scattered verses from Mark and two sentences from Matthew's own sources.

The entire discourse gives the appearance of a characteristic instruction to early Church evangelists based on the tradition of Jesus' instructions to the disciples. As it stands, the discourse falls into four parts, the first of which (vss. 5–15), after the commission to go only "to the lost sheep of the house of Israel" preaching, healing, raising the dead, cleansing lepers, and exorcising demons, emphasizes the haste the urgency of the mission demands. The second part (vss. 16–23) is concerned with how to meet persecution, and the third (vss. 24–33) carries the theme farther by comparing the opposition to the disciples with that to Jesus. The disciples are to proclaim from the housetops without fear what they have learned privately from Jesus. The promise of God's providential care in time of persecution is coupled with the warning that failure to witness will bring far more serious consequences than the persecutions which await the faithful witness. Beginning with a repetition of the paraphrase of Micah 7:6 in verses 21 and 22, the final verses, 34–42, picture the divisions created by radical decision called for by the Gospel. A statement of the blessedness of those who receive the disciples brings this discourse to a close.

Woe to this Evil Generation The two chapters which intervene between the mission discourse and the seven parables of the Kingdom are a commentary on the mission and its reception. Although the pericopae are in narrative form and setting, this section is dominated by sayings of Jesus. Even the actual narratives are pronouncement stories, so that if it were not for the settings, dialogue character of the sayings, and Matthew's organization, this section would differ little from the discourses. At least part of the reason for the predominance of sayings in this section is that much of it is Q material. Chapter 11 and nearly the last half of chapter 12 come from Q, while the first 32 verses of chapter 12 utilize the material from chapters 2 and 3 of Mark which Matthew had omitted in the earlier part of the Gospel.

The section falls into two distinct parts which divide between chapters 11 and 12. In chapter 11 the emphasis is on preaching, and in chapter 12 it is on healing. That neither healing nor preaching is lost sight of in either chapter indicates again how closely these are related in Matthew's concept of the mission.

That the Gospel of the Kingdom had not met with wholesale repentance and preparation either in Judaism or among the gentiles was a fact of which Matthew's Church was painfully aware. It would help them to accept and, to a degree at least, to understand the rejection of the Gospel to know that their Lord had experienced similar disappointment and to read his comments on it.

John's question, sent from prison by his disciples, "Are you he who is to come, or shall we look for another?" (11:3), and Jesus' rather oblique answer in the form of a paraphrase of Isaiah 35:5–6 introduce Jesus' discourse on John the Baptist. The similarity of this answer to the commission to the disciples in the mission discourse (10:7–8), which is especially marked by the reference to raising the dead, is not accidental but underscores the connection between Jesus' ministry and that of his disciples. The speech, built around the quotation from Malachi 3:1 which Mark used at the opening of his Gospel, serves two purposes. First, it climaxes Matthew's treatment of the role of John in relation to the Kingdom of God: The last and greatest of the Old Testament prophets, in fact the expected Elijah *redivivus,* is less than the "least in the kingdom of heaven" (11:11). The second and more basic purpose of this speech is its commentary on a generation which has the enviable privilege of hearing the announcement of the coming Kingdom but which perversely spurns the message. The woes that follow in verses 20–24 drive the point home (cf. the repetition of this theme in 12:41–42, and the seven woes in 23:13–39). In contrast, Jesus' prayer of thanks in the next paragraph recognizes those who have humbly obeyed Jesus' call. Verse 27 contains the saying concerning the relationship between the Father and the Son which has often been called the Johannine saying because of its similarity to the language and thought of the fourth Gospel. Concluding and climaxing this series of pericopae is the beautiful and familiar great invitation, "Come to me, all who labor and are heavy-laden. . . ." Apparently this invitation stands in the place of Mark's story of the return of the disciples. The meaning for Matthew's Church of such a change is both clear and forceful and anticipates the concluding great commission at the very end of the Gospel: The mission was not finished; it continues in the life of the Church.

Two Sabbath stories and the story of the healing of the dumb demoniac introduce the subject of chapter 12, which in pattern and theme is parallel to the eleventh chapter. Although the latter two are healings, Matthew uses them as pronouncement stories to focus attention upon two points of conflict. The first of these, the proper observance of the Sabbath (vss. 1–21), was the hallmark of Judaism. Both the opposition of the Pharisees and the reference to the gentiles in the quotation from Isaiah 42:1–4 thus reveal the judgment upon Judaism. The sign of the true Israel is not the Sabbath but the mission to the gentiles. In the second conflict (vss. 22–42), crediting Jesus' exorcisms to the power of Beelezebub, the nature of the Pharisees' fatal perfidy becomes clear. They have confused divine activity with the demonic, good with evil; they are therefore themselves evil. As in the climax of the previous chapter, the argument is concluded by contrasting this evil generation with previous generations. Two items conclude the section. To the parable of the return of the unclean spirit with seven more evil spirits (vss. 43–45), which Matthew has taken from Q, he adds the phrase, "So shall it be also with this evil generation," which directs the parable against the generation rather than the individual. As chapter 11 concluded by calling attention to the "babes" and the humble who, in contrast to the representatives of this generation, are receptive to the Gospel so this chapter, and therefore the section, ends (vss. 46–50) with the Markan saying on Jesus' true family: "Whoever does the will of my Father in heaven is my brother, and sister, and mother."

Seven Parables of the Kingdom Two emphases meet in this discourse. One is the final judgment from which the Church is by no means exempted. As the Gospel brings about a division among men between those who accept and those who reject the Kingdom, which Matthew has shown in chapters 11 and 12, so the final Judgment will separate the faithful from the unfaithful in the Church. In this regard the discourse becomes a midrash on the words in the Sermon: "For I tell you, unless your righteousness exceeds that of the scribes and Pharisees, you will never enter the kingdom of heaven" (5:20. cf. 7:24–27, 10:33, 25). The problem of lax members in Matthew's Church is prominently reflected in this theme which runs through the Gospel. From the standpoint of the other emphasis, the absolute value of the Kingdom, the discourse may be regarded as a midrash on the command in the Sermon: "But seek first his kingdom and his righteousness..." (6:33).

The third discourse is built, as we have already observed, upon Mark's section on parables (4:1–34). Matthew's modifications and additions are therefore particularly significant of his purpose. His addition of the quotation from Isaiah 6:9–10 on hearing but not understanding is not only in line with his general emphasis on fulfillment of prophecy, but is also a way of making explicit the Old Testament passage which lies back of verse 13 taken from Mark 4:12. He thereby underscores the irony in Mark and at the same time places in contrast the blessed who truly see and hear (vs. 16). Matthew's second addition on the prophets and righteous men who longed to see what Jesus' hearers are seeing (vss. 16–17), which comes from Q, states once more, as in the woes of 11:20–24 and the perverse sign-seeking generation in 12:38–42, the uniqueness of the time. In Jesus the Messiah has come, the Kingdom has drawn near, and the Judgment, which occupies so much of Matthew's attention, lies therefore in the near future.

By changing the plural pronouns in Mark's interpretation of the sower to the singular (vss. 18–23, cf. Mk. 4:13–20), Matthew shifts the emphasis in the parable to the contrasting destinies of the fickle and the faithful converts. He has also rewritten the simple parable from Mark (4:26) of the mysterious growth of seed to turn it into a parable of judgment which cautions against a rigorous attempt to purify the Church by excluding unfaithful members (the weeds). That responsibility is to be left to the final Judgment: "Let both grow together until the harvest" (vs. 30 cf. 7:1–5). By a change of locale and an interpretation (vss. 37–43), which he has supplied from his own sources in manifest imitation of the interpretation of the sower, Matthew lends emphasis to the parable of the wheat and weeds. In this interpretation the theme of judgment is picked up from the parable and underscored. The theme of judgment within the Church is repeated once more in the parable of the net full of good and bad fish, verses 47–50.

The parable of leaven (vs. 33 from Q) was added simply as an expansion of the theme of the growth of the Church in the preceding parable of the mustard seed and affirms more explicitly the final and complete triumph of the Kingdom: "till it was all leavened." The remaining two parables added by Matthew, the treasure in the field and pearl of great price (vss. 44–45), emphasize the absolute value of the Kingdom for whose sake everything else is to be surrendered. The simile of the householder (vs. 52) not only summarizes this discourse, but serves as a minor conclusion for the first half of the Gospel. By reference to Jesus' family the conclusion following the discourse echoes the pericope on Jesus' true family which introduces it. The bitter proverb, "A prophet is not without honor except in his own country . . ." reflects the disappointment of the Church over its Jewish mission.

The Church in a Hostile World   With the conclusion of the discourse on the parables we come to a major division in Matthew's Gospel. The brief transitional passage, 13:53–58, ends with a comment on the unbelief the ministry encountered. Such lack of faith is one of Matthew's main concerns. After the introduction of Jesus, chapters 1–4, and the new interpretation of Torah and the new righteousness in the Sermon, the attention of the Gospel has been upon the mission of Jesus and the Church as interpreted in the discourse of chapter 10. Chapters 8 and 9 introduced it and chapters 11 and 12 commented on its results. The parables of chapter 13 conclude the matter with observations on the value and demands of the Kingdom which the mission proclaims and, conversely, the judgment awaiting those who reject or abandon it.

The controlling theme of the Gospel thus far may be called "the mission and the teaching." The new turn which the Gospel takes at this point and continues to the end may be entitled "the mission and the cross." Several characteristics significant of this change of emphasis appear in this half of the Gospel. The narrative sections which separate the remaining two discourses are twice as long as those separating the previous ones. The eight chapters of narrative between the parable discourse and the final discourse are separated by the shortest of the five discourses, chapter 18. It is at this point also that Matthew picks up the thread of Mark's narrative and follows it with only a few minor rearrangements to its end. We may note, too, that with this closer attention to Mark's order Matthew moves correspondingly closer to the theme of the Passion which in Mark is prominent virtually from the beginning.

By opening the second half of the Gospel with the story of John the Baptist's death at the hands of Herod, Matthew establishes the somber mood which dominates until the joy of the Resurrection floods the scene with its light. The rearrangement of this scene, which we have already outlined,[73] and the addition of the report to Jesus of John's death changes the retreat, verse 13, from a retreat of Jesus with his disciples after their mission (cf. Mk. 6:32–34) to one by Jesus alone in response to the news. This arrangement intensifies the significance of John's execution as an anticipation of the Crucifixion.

The narrative section between the discourse on parables (13:1–52) and that on church discipline (ch. 18) falls into two subdivisions. The first includes the two stories of feeding the multitude, the story of Jesus walking on the water, and the controversies with the Pharisees (14:1–16:12). The second includes Peter's confession, the Transfiguration, and their sequels (16:13–17:23). Three healing editorial summaries (14:14, 34–36; 15:30–31) and three retreats by Jesus alone (14:3, 23; 15:29) lend unity to the first subdivision. That two of the healing summaries are created by Matthew out of Markan material to a different effect indicates something of the importance Matthew attaches to these summaries. The first summary, 14:14, is in Mark a reference to Jesus' teaching (cf. Mk. 6:34); the third summary, 15:30–31, is created from Mark's story of the healing of the deaf mute with spittle. A secondary motive for Matthew's change here may be to eliminate the healing with spittle which he found objectionable and unnecessary. (Only Mark and John refer to Jesus' use of spittle in healing.)

The three retreats introduce and, therefore, underscore the two feedings and the story of Jesus walking on the water. Matthew has created two of these solitary retreats also by altering Markan material. The first instance, 14:13, we have already observed. In the other instance, 15:29, Matthew has substituted a retreat to the hills for Mark's geographically awkward

73. See p. 116.

reference to "the regions of the Decapolis." That the reference to the hills, Jesus' sitting down, and the crowds coming to him, which provides the occasion for the second feeding, reminds the reader of the introduction of the Sermon (cf. 5:1–2) was probably intended by Matthew. This association suggests a subtle connection between the teaching and sacrament in the Church. Similarly, the reader should find the meaning of the crowd's amazement at the healings, 15:31, in Jesus' reply to John's disciples, 11:4–6.

In Peter's confession which opens the second part of this section Matthew comes to a point which is basic to his whole Gospel. By thrusting his special material on the blessing and renaming of Peter and the giving of the keys, between Peter's confession and the charge to secrecy, Matthew has radically altered the rather negative slant in Mark's version of this story. Mark focuses attention on the paradox, which Peter misunderstood, of a crucified messiah; Matthew confines Peter's misunderstanding to the Passion; his misunderstanding and rebuke is thus clearly detached from his confession.[74] Mark's story had the effect of suggesting that the confession was premature, but in Matthew it is most closely and basically related to the founding of the Church. Significantly, here is the first of the only three occurrences of the word "church" in the Gospels. The other two occurrences follow in the discourse in chapter 18. Matthew's addition of the phrase, "the Son of the living God," in verse 16, and his subordination of the charge to secrecy completes his reinterpretation and anticipates his theme of the hidden (to the hostile world) messiah in the next narrative section.

The three predictions of the Passion, 16:22; 17:12, 22, hold this part of the section together and point forward to the Passion narrative. (Note that Matthew has added the second prediction, 17:12, to the Markan material.) By two minor changes Matthew has accommodated the story of Jesus' Transfiguration to his emphasis in this section. First, the addition of the phrase, "and his (Jesus') face shone like the sun" (vs. 2), and the obeisance of the disciples (vs. 6) underscore the messianic significance of the story. Verse 2 is probably a reference to Exodus 34:29–35 where Moses' face shone after being on Mount Sinai. Moses' face no longer shines! (cf. II Cor. 3:7–18.) Second, by omitting the phrase, "he did not know what to say," (Mk. 9:6), Matthew removes this reflection on Peter which would otherwise detract from the role Matthew has given him at Caesarea Philippi. The story of the healing of the epileptic boy, 17:14–21, has been drastically reduced to give added prominence to Peter's confession and the Transfiguration.

---

74. For an excellent discussion of this passage see Bornkamm, *Tradition and Interpretation in Matthew,* pp. 46ff.

Except for the important change of emphasis in the story of Peter's confession, the material in this section has much the same paradigmatic meaning for Matthew as for Mark. By noting some of Matthew's more important additions, we may discover Matthew's own emphasis. There are, for example, three short additions from Q. The sayings about blind guides in 15:14 intensifies the conflict with the Pharisees over ritual washings, and similarly the saying about interpreting the weather, 16:2–3, underscores the perversity of sign-seekers. The whole saying, 16:1–4, by repeating the theme of the sign of Jonah (cf. 12:38–42) relates this section with the earlier narrative section, chapters 11 and 12, on this evil generation. The world's hostility to the Church is based, therefore, on this generation's rejection of the Kingdom. By adding the saying about faith as a grain of mustard seed, 17:20, Matthew calls attention once more to the problem of the disciple's lack of faith.

Aside from four brief interpretive notes in 15:12–13, 22b–23; 16:12; 17:13, Matthew's additions from his own special material concern Peter. There are three of these: Peter's attempt to walk on the water, 14:28–31; the blessing and renaming of Peter at Caesarea Philippi, 16:17–19; and the shekel in the fish's mouth, 17:24–27. Matthew is not only underscoring Peter's position of leadership among the disciples and therefore in the Early Church, but he is also using Peter as a symbol to dramatize certain important truths about the Church. This symbolic use of his name becomes especially clear in the play on words in the naming of Peter: "You are Peter (*Petros,* masculine), and on this rock (*Petra,* feminine) I will build my church" (16:18). In his attempt to walk on the water Peter depicts the constant problem of weak faith. Only the gracious coming of the Lord to his Church can save it from being drowned in the storms which assail it. It is by divine revelation that the Church follows Peter in confessing Jesus to be the Christ and becomes invincible even before the gates of death. The keys given to Peter (16:19) become the possession of the Church (18:18). In the third passage, the question of the Temple tax, 17:24–27, Peter represents somehow the Church's relation to traditional Judaism. We should note that institutional Judaism is not here disowned, but the Church is, nevertheless, free and its participation voluntary. The final phrase, "for me and yourself" is surprisingly exclusive in view of the general treatment of the disciples as a group in the Gospel. Perhaps Matthew intends by this means to represent the Jewish membership to whom alone the Temple tax would apply. This pericope on the relation of the Church to institutional Judaism raises the question of other relationships and so introduces the fourth discourse.

On Church Life and Discipline The theme of the fourth discourse is established by the opening question: "Who is the greatest in the kingdom

Tyrian sheckel, apparently preferred for payments to the Temple because of its superior silver content. The image of the god Heracles was, of course, offensive to the religion of Judaism, but since Israel minted no silver coins until the revolt of A.D. 66–70, this coin was no more objectionable than others which were available. (Courtesy of the Money Museum, National Bank of Detroit.)

of heaven?" In one way or another the entire discourse answers this question. As the question implies a dispute among the disciples (cf. Mk. 9:33–34), it raises the issue of relationships and discipline within the community of disciples. Although the question points to the Kingdom, Matthew's treatment of it is manifestly in reference to the present life of the Church. This does not mean that Matthew has abandoned the distinction between this age and the age to come, or that he has identified the Kingdom with the Church. Matthew is rather working on the assumption that the age of the Church is the age of preparation and lives always under the shadow of the final Judgment and the coming Kingdom. Hence Matthew can speak of the Kingdom in the present tense. As the Kingdom of Heaven was proleptically present in the action of Jesus (12:28), so it is in the Church. Matthew has gone considerably farther than Mark in this use of the term. The question to which this discourse speaks therefore concerns the present life of the Church but at the same time has grave implications for the future.

Matthew has stripped Mark's story of the dispute along the way (Mk. 9:33–37) of its local references and omitted the pericope of the strange exorcist, making the question and discussion of who is the greatest more clearly addressed to the Church. The discourse is in two parts: (1) the lessons of the child, and (2) on forgiveness. Three points are made from the child figure. First, the believer is to imitate the child's humility (vss. 3–4). Second, he is to "receive" such children as receiving Jesus himself (vss. 5–6). Here the thought anticipates the parable of the Judgment, 25:31–46. By using the synonym "little ones" in verse 6, Matthew is able to make the transition from a literal child in verses 2–5 to the figurative use of child to indicate the weaker believers. That such "little ones" must not be caused to stumble (or sin) interprets what it means to "receive" such an one. The expansion on this theme which follows (vss. 7–9) concludes with what appears to be an oblique reference to Judas' betrayal (cf. 26:24), and a connection with the Sermon by repeating in extended form the saying about removing the offending eye or hand (5:29–30). The third point concerning the child figure, following closely the thought of the second, is the command not to "despise one of these little ones." This point is interpreted by the pericope from Q of the lost sheep.

The second part of the discourse begins with a prescription for dealing with a recalcitrant church member (vss. 15–20). Beginning with a Q saying (cf. vs. 15 with Lk. 17:3), it concludes with two affirmations of the authority of the Church: the saying on binding and loosing, originally addressed to Peter at Caesarea Philippi (16:19); and the saying about two or three agreeing on a matter, which includes the presence of the Lord in such agreement. This passage clearly reflects early Church problems and practices. (Compare Paul's instructions concerning the incestuous man in I Cor. 5:1ff.)

Peter's question, possibly from Q, as to how many times to forgive and Jesus' answer, which practically removes any limitation to the responsibility to forgive, introduce the parable of the unforgiving debtor (vss. 23–35) as the conclusion of the discourse.

The Hidden Messiah   The final narrative section in the body of the Gospel begins with a very brief note of the journey from Galilee to Judea. The setting for the entire section is therefore in Judea and especially Jerusalem. An editorial summary on Jesus' healings (which, like the healing summary in 14:14 above, has been created from a teaching summary in Mark) and a fourth prediction of the Passion (corresponding to Mark's third, cf. 20:18–19 with Mk. 10:32–34) provide a bond of continuity with the preceding narrative section, chapters 14–17.

Like the section (chs. 11–12) between the second and third discourses, this one actually contains very little narrative. With the exception of the two brief travel notes in 19:1 and 20:17, which anticipate the triumphal entry, the only episodes in this section are the blessing of the children, 19:13–15 (Perhaps the attempt of James and John through their mother to acquire the highest seats, 20:20–28, should be counted as an episode. If so it is, nevertheless, a pronouncement story.); the healing of the two blind men of Jericho, 20:29–34; the triumphal entry, 21:1–11; the cleansing of the Temple, 21:12–17; and the cursing of the fig tree, 21:18–22

(Matthew makes this also into a pronouncement story). Most of this section, then, is teaching material in the form of Jesus' responses to questions or controversies.

There are only two passages from Q included in these chapters, the brief saying about the disciples sitting on twelve thrones in the Kingdom, 19:28—which is for Matthew an explanation of the significance of the twelve disciples—and the parable of the unwilling guests (22:1–14). To the latter Matthew has added two parables within the parable: The abuse and killing of the messengers which the king avenged, probably a deliberate doublet from the parable of the wicked tenants (cf. vss. 6–7 with 21:33–43), and the man without the wedding garment (vss. 11–14).

Most of the remaining material is from Mark and carries much the same significance. Matthew's additions and alterations are, again, the key to his meaning. Some early tendencies toward celibacy, for example, with which the Church became so preoccupied in later times may be seen in Matthew's addition of the passage on the three kinds of eunuchs (19:10–12). The parable of the laborers in the vineyard (20:1–15) reinterprets, by emphasizing the grace (generosity) of God, Mark's saying about the last being first. Matthew underscores the prophetic significance of the triumphal entry by supplying the quotation from Zechariah 9:9 which Mark only implied. By means of the parable of the two sons (21:28–32), Matthew again defines the righteousness superior to that of the scribes and Pharisees (cf. 5:20). The point is reiterated once more in 21:43. "Therefore I tell you, the kingdom of God will be taken away from you and given to a nation producing the fruits of it." The parable of the man without a wedding garment (22:11–14) repeats the theme—so prominent in the discourse of parables of the Kingdom—of judgment within the Church.

As the two previous narrative sections, this one falls into two parts: (1) the journey to the Temple, and (2) controversies in the Temple. Three travel notes in 19:1, 20:17, and 29, lead to the climax of this part of the section. The reader is to see the symbolism in this action: The Messiah, the scion of David, is approaching the royal city and the holy shrine. It is only against this background that the awful judgment and desolation in Jesus' lament over Jerusalem and the Temple and his leaving the Temple (23:37–24:1), which link the two parts of the final discourse, can be understood.

The second part of this section is structured around debate of five questions, the first four of which are put to Jesus. Although these questions appear together in Mark in the same order, Matthew has rewritten the editorial links to give them a new prominence. This is an excellent example of his editorial method. As a climax the final question is put by Jesus to his challengers. The questions are (1) "By what authority are you doing these things?" (21:23–27). The three parables of the two sons

(21:28–32), the wicked tenants (21:33–43), and the unwilling guests (22:1–14) serve to interpret this question and its answer. It should be noted that, although the parable of the wicked tenants stands in relatively the same position it does in Mark, the restructuring of the section around the five questions and addition of the other two parables reduce this parable from its predominance in Mark to a secondary position. (2) "Is it lawful to pay tribute to Caesar, or not?" (22:15–22). (3) "In the resurrection, therefore, to which of the seven will she be wife?" (22:23–33). (4) "Which is the greatest commandment in the law?" (22:34–40). (5) Jesus' question to the Pharisees: "What do you think of the Christ? Whose son is he?" (22:41–46). The questioners in each instance are from a different segment of Judaism: (1) chief priest, (2) Pharisees, (3) Sadducees, (4) lawyer (he is, of course, a Pharisee, but at the same time represents the scholarly inner circle). Jesus' final question is, in a sense, addressed to all four groups.

Running through this section as the underlying motif is the theme of the hidden, or unrecognized messiah. The hiddenness is not the doing of Jesus but the perversity of those who will not see. At least three reasons are given for this perversity: a misguided loyalty to Jewish traditions, wealth, and mistaken notions of the role of the messiah. Thus in the opening pericope Jesus is tested by a comparison with Moses who for the teachers of Judaism was the absolute authority. The Pharisees' question on divorce (19:3–9), which led to Jesus' deliberate qualification of Moses' teaching, anticipates the first of the five questions in the second part of the section: What is Jesus' authority? (21:23–27). This discussion is a doublet of that in the Sermon (5:31–32) where Jesus' authority to reinterpret is explicit. (Notice that Matthew contrary to Mark has the Pharisees raise the question of Moses' provision. In Mark the deliberate modification of Moses' teaching is not so prominent.)

The question of Jesus' authority could not have been asked by anyone who recognized him as the Messiah. Hence the three parables which follow the question all depict willful disobedience and rejection of God's action. In contrast Jesus supplies the true meaning of Scripture in response to the question of the greatest commandment. This summary of the Law completes Matthew's theme of the new righteousness and understanding of Torah which began in the Sermon.

That the conservative Sadducees by rejecting the Pharisaical doctrine of the resurrection have placed themselves even farther outside the truth is the burden of the debate in 22:23–33. They "know neither the scriptures nor the power of God" (vs. 29). The tragedy of riches which blind their possessor to the true wealth of rewards in the Kingdom and therefore cause them sadly to reject the Messiah is vividly pictured in the story of the rich young man and the discussion which follows (19:16–30). That

Matthew has modified Mark's question, "Why do you call me good?" to remove any reflection on the character of Jesus is well known. By adding the question, "What do I still lack?" Matthew points back to the theme of the superior righteousness in 5:20, as the word "perfect" (vs. 21) does to 5:48. The parable of the laborers in the vineyard, in which the wages are paid on the basis of the owner's goodness rather than the relative merits of the workers, is a concluding commentary on the point.[75]

Misunderstandings of the meaning of Jesus' messiahship began, in the previous section, with Peter's rebuke in response to the first prediction of the Passion. The theme is developed in this section by the story, which follows the final prediction of the Passion, of James and John seeking the highest seats in the coming Kingdom (20:20–28). As is often suggested, Matthew may have introduced their mother here to soften the reflection on the character of James and John implicit in the story.[76] Even the disciples fail to understand Jesus' messianic role. The definition of Jesus' messianic mission at the conclusion of the story, "Even as the Son of Man came not to be served but to serve, and to give his life as a ransom for many" (20:28), which in Mark is a pivotal passage, completes Matthew's definition of Jesus' mission. The Pharisees' share in this misunderstanding becomes evident in their question concerning tribute to Caesar. A political revolutionary bent on freeing his land of the hated Roman overlords could hardly approve paying the imperial tax.

Jesus' question, "What do you think of the Christ?" (22:42) brings the section to its climax and conclusion with the paradox of the Son of David who is also David's Lord. To understand this paradox enables the believer to understand the other paradoxes Jesus embodies, such as the triumph of the cross, the servant Lord, and the new teaching which is nevertheless in continuity with the Mosaic Torah.

There were, on the other hand, those for whom the Messiah was not hidden: The children to whom "belongs the kingdom of heaven" (19:13–15) (Matthew's omission of the saying on receiving the Kingdom like a child, Mk. 10:15, and changing Mark's "touch" to "lay his hands on them" makes this contrast clearer.); the two blind men of Jericho (20:29–34) (Note that Matthew intensifies this story by doubling the number of blind men.); the shouting crowd at the triumphal entry (21:1–11) (Although, like the disciples, their understanding is far from complete as they call him "the prophet Jesus."); and the blind and lame healed and "children crying out in the Temple" (21:14–16, cf. the "babes," 11:25; the "child," 18:2–14). Here in the final narrative section we are given a picture and an explanation of the division which Jesus promised in the discourse on the

---

75. On the meaning and significance of this story see Bornkamm, *Tradition and Interpretation in Matthew*, pp. 96ff.
76. See W. C. Allen, *The Gospel According to St. Matthew* (ICC), p. 216.

mission (10:34–39) and which is reflected in numerous ways throughout the Gospel. This division in turn anticipates and becomes the basis of the ultimate Judgment which is to come and which is the subject of the fifth discourse.

The Judgment to Come Where the fifth discourse begins is not so easy to determine as it is with the other discourses. Some scholars confine the discourse to chapters 24 and 25. Others include the twenty-third chapter. A case could be made for beginning it with 21:23. The establishment of a setting at this point is similar to that in the previous discourses and what follows contains no actual narrative but is built around five questions. That the continuity is sustained by dialogue in which the reader is invited to see a controversy with institutional Judaism, however, suggests that Matthew did not intend this material to be part of the final discourse but rather as an elaborate setting for it. With chapter 23, on the other hand, the dialogue vanishes, specific opponents no longer stand before Jesus, and the setting is altered by the inclusion of the disciples who are a part of the setting of each of the other four discourses. The change of locale in 24:1 makes no sharper break in the unity than the similar change in the third discourse, 13:36. We may include, therefore, chapter 23 as the actual beginning.

The discourse falls into three parts: (1) seven woes on the Pharisees (ch. 23), (2) the Apocalypse (ch. 24), (3) three parables of judgment (ch. 25). Based on the brief criticism of the hypocrisy of the scribes in Mark 12:37–40, the introduction, condemning the scribes and Pharisees for failing to practice what they teach, establishes the theme of the first part. Matthew's attitude toward the Law and concern to preserve the continuity of the Church with Israel shows itself in the admonition to "practice and observe whatever they tell you, but not what they do" (23:3, cf. 5:17–20), as well as in the comment, "these you ought to have done, without neglecting the others" (23:23b). The seven woes condemn the Pharisees for hypocrisy, superficiality in religious observance, and persecution of the truly righteous. The seventh woe against those who "build the tombs of the prophets" at the same time that they are showing themselves to be true "sons of those who murdered the prophets" (vs. 31) leads to a passage of bitter recrimination in which we see a picture of persecutions endured by the early Church. Jesus' lament over Jerusalem forms the climax and conclusion to this part, while the ominous words "Behold, your house is forsaken and desolate" introduces the Apocalypse in chapter 24.

In the words "Jesus left the Temple" the reader is to see more than a change of locale. The Temple is now abandoned, the glory (Shekinah) has departed, and the statement in the lament, 23:38, has come true. The prediction of the destruction of the building which follows is a judgment on institutional Judaism. Except for the passage concerning arrests and trials before authorities which he transposed to the mission discourse, Matthew has followed Mark relatively faithfully in this chapter. One apparently slight change, however, stands out. Whereas in Mark the Apocalypse of chapter 13 is entrusted to Peter, James, John, and Andrew, Matthew by simply substituting the word "disciples" for these names makes the apocalyptic secrets the possession of the whole body of the disciples, hence the whole Church. Otherwise only the parable of the man going on a journey (Mk. 13:33–37), for which Matthew has substituted that of the householder and the thief, is omitted.

The additions which Matthew makes (mostly from Q, with a brief paraphrase of Daniel 7:13) are warnings against false prophets (vss. 10–12 and 26–28), exhortations to watchfulness including the analogy of the days of Noah and the householder and the thief (vss. 37–41, 43–44, cf. I Thess. 5:2ff. and Rom. 13:11ff.), and a call for endurance using the parable of the wise and wicked servants (vss. 45–51). The sentence, "But he who endures to the end will be saved" (vs. 13), repeated from the mission discourse (10:22b), not only underscores the eschatological significance of the mission but also expresses Matthew's main concern in the Apocalypse.

Of the three parables of judgment (ch. 25), the first and last are from Matthew's special source. Each of them picks up and emphasizes themes in the Apocalypse and earlier in the Gospel. In the parable of the wise and foolish virgins two themes are joined: watchfulness and endurance. That the foolishness of the five virgins consists in their overestimating the nearness of the Kingdom may reflect a problem in Matthew's church with some overenthusiastic (or disillusioned) apocalyptists.[77] This parable strongly resembles Mark's analogy of the man on a journey and may explain why Matthew omitted the latter. The parable of the talents is little more than an expansion of the analogy in the Apocalypse (24:45–51) of the wise and wicked servants (or is the latter a condensation?), both of which are probably from Q. The parable of the great judgment, which concludes both the fifth discourse and the body of the Gospel, picks up the note in the early part of the fourth discourse, "Whosoever receives one such child in my name receives me" (18:5), as well as the judgment theme in such parables as the weeds and net (13:24–30, 36–43, 47–50). Probably in the plight of the "brethren," hungry, thirsty, sick, and imprisoned we are afforded a glimpse of the sufferings and troubles of the early Church. By bringing together the themes of the eschatological judgment and concern for the unfortunate, the dispossessed, the poor this parable becomes a forceful climax to the body of the Gospel.

77. See Bornkamm, *Tradition and Interpretation in Matthew*, p. 23.

The Passion Matthew has followed Mark's Passion story very faithfully, omitting only a few brief sentences (14:35b, 40b, 51–52, 58b–59, 65b, 72a; 15:15a, 25, 42, 44–45a) and altering two or three other verses (cf. Mk. 14:13–15 with Mt. 26:18). His additions, on the other hand, lend dramatic emphasis at several significant points. The most prominent and extensive of these concern Judas' betrayal. In 26:15 Matthew expands the account of Judas' bargain with the chief priests with a question which implies greed as a motive (cf. Jn. 12:6; 13:21–30). Again, in verse 25, Judas repeats the disciples' question, "Is it I," and is identified by the same answer Jesus later gave to Pilate's question (27:11), "You have said so" (present tense in Greek: "you say so"). In the story of the arrest Matthew adds the ironic question, "Friend, why are you here?" (26:50). The major addition is the story of Judas' suicide (27:3–10; cf. Acts 1:18–19). Thrust into the story of the trial under Pilate, the picture of a Roman governor and a miserable, remorseful informer must have been all too familiar to many early Christians.

The three guard stories, at the cross, 27:36, at the tomb, 27:62–66, and climaxed in the failure and the bribing of the guards in 28:4, 11–15, reflect the increasing polemic on the Resurrection with which Matthew's Church had to contend. By several additions of details, Matthew has intensified the drama of the Passion. Caiaphas, who is not otherwise named in the Passion in any of the Synoptics, is named here twice: 26:3, 57. (He is named, however, in Luke 3:2.) That Jesus went willingly to his death in fulfillment of his mission (cf. 20:28) and of Scripture is highlighted by Jesus' reference to the more than twelves legions of angels at his disposal were he to ask for them, 26:52–54. Pilate's wife's dream, Pilate's own question, "Why, what evil has he done?," his act of washing his hands in protest of innocence, and the horrendous cry of the people "His blood be on us and on our children." are all part of Matthew's contribution to a noticeable tendency in the succeeding Gospels to shift more and more of the blame for the Crucifixion onto the Jews and correspondingly to minimize the role of the Roman governor. The practical and apologetic importance of this tendency to the Church's relations with the Empire is obvious. Evangelistic interests may be reflected in the choice between Barabbas and Jesus which is accented by the repetition of Pilate's question (27:17 and 21). Both the redemptive power of Jesus' death and the coming Resurrection as a "first fruit" (cf. I Cor. 15:20) of the believer's resurrection are dramatized in the story of the opened tombs and resurrected saints, 27:5–57.

Matthew has added six direct questions to those in the Passion story which he found in Mark while dropping one of Mark's. The result is two series of ten questions which add movement and drama to the two main parts of the story. Taken together they form a dramatic outline of the

The "garden tomb," near "Gordon's Calvary" (see p. 108), designated by Charles Gordon as the place of Jesus' burial (Jn. 19:41). Excavations have shown, however, that the ancient city wall did not encompass the site of the Church of the Holy Sepulchre, making that traditional site more probable than was once thought. Jesus could not, of course, have been buried within the city. (The Roderick Slide Collection, courtesy of Catawba College.)

Passion. In the first part, which includes the anointing at Bethany, the Last Supper, the prayer in Gethsemane, and the arrest:

1. The indignant disciples at the anointing: "Why this waste?"
2. Jesus' reply: "Why do you trouble the woman?"
3. Judas to the chief priests: "What will you give me if I deliver him to you?"
4. The disciples to Jesus: "Where will you have us prepare for you to eat the Passover?"
5. The disciples on Jesus' announcement of the betrayal: "Is it I, Lord?"

He Taught Them, Saying...

6. And Judas: "Is it I, Master?"
7. Jesus to Peter in Gethsemane: "So, could you not watch with me one hour?"
8. Later to the disciples: "Are you still sleeping and taking your rest?"
9. To Judas at the arrest: "Friend, why are you here?"
10. "Do you think that I cannot appeal to my Father, and he will at once send me more than twelve legions of angels? But how then should the scriptures be fulfilled, that it must be so?" . . . "Have you come out as against a robber, with swords and clubs to capture me?"

In the second part, which includes the trials before Caiaphas and Pilate and the Crucifixion:

1. The high priest to Jesus: "Have you no answer to make? What is it that these men testify against you?"
2. The high priest to the council: "Why do we still need witnesses? You have now heard his blasphemy. What is your judgment?"
3. To Jesus at the mocking: "Who is it that struck you?"
4. The chief priests to Judas at his repentance: "What is that to us?"
5. Pilate to Jesus: "Are you the King of the Jews?"
6. Again: "Do you not hear how many things they testify against you?"
7. Pilate to the people: "Whom do you want me to release for you, Barabbas or Jesus who is called Christ?"
8. Again: "Which of the two do you want me to release for you?"
9. Again: "Then what shall I do with Jesus who is called Christ?"
10. Again in response to their cry for crucifixion: "Why, what evil has he done?"

The Resurrection   Although obviously built on Mark's attenuated story of Jesus' Resurrection, Matthew's final chapter actually owes its source only five verses. Matthew's additions are concerned with three points. The first of these, 28:2–4, picks up the story of the guard at the tomb and recounts how that guard was foiled. These verses, at the same time, are a midrash on Mark 16:3–5, which they replace, to explain how the stone was rolled from the door of the tomb and to identify the "young man" who in Mark is seen sitting in the tomb. The motif of the guards at the tomb is concluded in a story (vss. 11–15) of obvious apologetic and polemic value which tells how they were bribed by the chief priests to claim that Jesus' body was stolen.

A midrash on the conclusion of Mark's story comprises Matthew's second addition, verses 9 and 10. In this addition Jesus himself meets the women and repeats the command of the angel. The silence of the women is removed and the fear is modified by adding the phrase, "and great joy." By clarifying the meaning of the Galilean reference these verses prepare for the final scene of the Risen Lord with his disciples, verses 16–20, with which the Gospel closes. Some scholars have taken Mark's reference to

Galilee (16:7) to refer to the parousia. If so, Matthew's addition represents a deliberate alteration of Mark's eschatology.

As the body of the Gospel began so it ends: on a mountain. There is more than historical interest in the brief clause at the end of verse 17, "But some doubted." The hortatory usefulness of these words is not hard to imagine. As with the blind man of Bethsaida, Mark 8:22–26, faith's vision is not always restored at once. Each of the Gospels contain a similar picture. In Mark the women "said nothing to anyone, for they were afraid." When Jesus appeared to the group in Jerusalem, according to Luke 24:36ff., even though they had been told of his appearance to the couple on the way to Emmaus, "they were startled and frightened, and supposed that they saw a spirit." John's Gospel concludes the story of doubting Thomas (20:24–29) with the words: "Do not be faithless, but believing." And then in response to Thomas' answer of faith come the words which include all the faithful of the ages since: "Have you believed because you have seen me? Blessed are those who have not seen and yet have believed."

In Jesus' farewell speech Matthew's story is complete. "All power" is now his. He is the ultimate king. The mission once restricted "to the lost sheep of the house of Israel" (10:6) is now to "make disciples of all nations." And the perpetual guiding and enabling presence of their Lord is assured even as symbolized in the storm (14:23–33), promised in the discourse on Church discipline (18:20), and sealed in the Eucharist. To the end of the age he is Emmanuel, God with us (1:23). Nor is the new righteousness lost sight of, for they are to teach "them to observe all that I have commanded you." And for this task Matthew has provided in his Gospel a most useful instrument.

Structure of Matthew

I. The Mission and Teaching, chs. 1–13

PROLOGUE
The birth of Jesus, chs. 1–2
Baptism, temptation, call of disciples, chs. 3–4

FIRST DISCOURSE: The Sermon on the Mount, chs. 5–7
Ten miracles and disciples, chs. 8–9

SECOND DISCOURSE: The mission of the disciples, ch. 10
This evil generation, chs. 11–12

THIRD DISCOURSE: Seven parables of the Kingdom, ch. 13

II. The Mission and the Cross, chs. 14–28
The Church in a hostile world, chs. 14–17

FOURTH DISCOURSE: Church discipline, ch. 18
The hidden messiah, chs. 19–22

FIFTH DISCOURSE: Apocalyptic Judgment, chs. 23–
The Passion, Resurrection, Commission, chs. 26–2

3. *A Gospel for Theophilus: Luke*

The observant reader approaching Luke's Gospel will immediately notice the way in which the preface (1:1–4) sets Luke apart from the other Gospels. In contrast to the scriptural quotation with which Mark begins and the genealogy which opens Matthew, Luke's preface impresses the reader with its self-conscious literary intention. That the only other book in the New Testament with such a preface is thereby linked to this Gospel as a second volume is further evidence that Luke is writing on a literary level different from the others.

Other evidence in the Gospel confirms this impression. Luke's good idiomatic Greek, for example, compares favorably with the literature of his time.[78] Where Semitic idioms appear, they are probably due either to his sources or a sense of appropriateness for the setting of his narrative at that point.[79] Even in English translation, the greater breadth of his vocabulary and his consistent modification of his sources for the sake of rhetorical improvement are clearly observable. Perhaps more significant is way in which Luke has recast the general structure of his work to conform more closely to the patterns of historical writing of his time. Although not insensitive to the patterns and structures of Scriptural and rabbinic writing, a considerable amount of which appear in his Gospel, he nevertheless imposes on his material a sense of movement and a chronological framework which are clearly inspired by the literary conventions of his world. Throughout both books journeys, which provide the dominant motif, give his work a character reminiscent of the popular ancient travelogue form. Similarly the miracles recall popular pagan stories of miracle workers.[80]

The distinctiveness of Luke, however, goes farther than literary characteristics. Luke's awareness of and sensitivity to the larger Graeco-Roman world around him, abundantly clear in Acts, become evident in the opening section of his Gospel by the way he sets the birth and ministry of both John the Baptizer and Jesus within the chronological framework of the

---

78. On the character and quality of Luke's language see J. de Zwaan, "The Use of the Greek Language in Acts," Foakes-Jackson and Lake, *The Beginnings of Christianity*, Vol. II, ch. II pp. 30–65.
79. See the excellent discussion of Luke's style and literary method in Henry J. Cadbury, *The Making of Luke-Acts*, especially chapter XVI, pp. 213–238.
80. For the travelogue cf. Apuleius, *The Golden Ass*, Petronius, *Satyricon*. For the miracle worker cf. Philostratus, *Apolonius of Tyana*. Cf. also Herodotus, *Histories*, although here the author himself is the "traveler," and Xenophon, *Anabasis*.

Augustan Age (2:1–3; 3:1–2). Whether Theophilus was a high-born Christian, a Roman official to whom Luke addresses his work as an apology for the faith, or a happy epithet for all devout Christians who may hear or read it, the presence of his name in the prefaces of Luke-Acts represents both Luke's literary intention and his cosmopolitan interests.[81] In our study of these two volumes we must be alert to observe the ways in which these interests have influenced the author's version of Christian origins.

LUKE AND ACTS

We have already noted that Luke is associated with Acts not only by common authorship, but also as the first of at least two volumes of a single work.[82] If there were no other reasons, the prefaces (Lk. 1:1–4 and Acts 1:1ff.) would, in the absence of evidence to the contrary, establish their relationship. That Luke's Gospel is the first half of a single two-volume work is significant of more than matters of date, style, authorship, and the like. By viewing these works together we can learn much of the author's method of organization and handling of his sources, his over-all plan and purpose, and his presuppositions and point of view. The very attempt to encompass in a single writing the story of Jesus and his disciples and the beginnings and spread of Christianity says a great deal about what Luke believed about these events.

There are several cross references, repetitions, and the like which not only indicate the unity of Luke-Acts, but illustrate also the author's attitude toward and use of his sources. He omits, for example, items in his Gospel which appear in parallel passages in the other Gospels, but uses them instead in Acts. The suicide of Judas in Matthew 27:3–10 appears in a variant form in Acts 1:18–19. The charge in the Passion story in both Mark (14:58) and Matthew (26:61) that Jesus threatened to destroy the Temple, Luke postpones to the beginning of his story of the martyrdom of Stephen (Acts 6:14). Similarly, Mark's warning that "no one knows" the time of the eschaton except the Father (13:32) is paraphrased in Acts 1:7 (cf. Mk. 13:10 with Acts 1:8). Among the cross references are the list of the twelve in Acts 1:13, which is repeated from Luke 6:13–16 (minus Judas Iscariot, of course) including the substitution,

81. For a detailed analysis of the prefaces see the article by Henry J. Cadbury in Foakes Jackson and Lake, *The Beginnings of Christianity,* Vol. II, pp. 489–510. Attention is frequently called to the prefaces of ancient Greek and Latin writers in this connection. Thucydides, I, 20 contains, for example, an interesting comment on the speeches he has included in his work (see pp. 285–286). Cf. also the beginning of Bk. II of his *History* with Acts 1:1. Arrian's *Alexander,* I, provides us with a comment on predecessors which compares interestingly with Lk. 1:1. See Cadbury, *The Making of Luke-Acts,* pp. 194–204.

82. See p. 74. On the question whether Luke intended a third volume to follow Acts, see p. 307.

peculiar to Luke, of "Judas of James" for Thaddeus (cf. Mk. 3:16–19 and Mt. 10:2–4); the promise of Jesus (Lk. 10:19), elsewhere in the Gospels only in the spurious end of Mark, that serpents, scorpions, and the like will not harm the apostles, which is fulfilled in the story of Paul on the Isle of Malta, Acts 28:3ff.; the charge in Jesus' trial that he opposed Caesar, found only in Luke and John (Lk. 23:2; Jn. 19:12), is reiterated in Acts 17:7; and the charge to remain in the city until the coming of the Holy Spirit (24:49), which is repeated in Acts 1:4 and fulfilled in 2:1ff.

In the course of the speeches in Acts a number of details of the Passion story reappear. Jesus' trial before Herod, peculiar to Luke's Gospel, is alluded to in the Church's prayer, 5:27. This reference to Herod (Lk. 23:6–12) and the two in Luke 9:7ff. and 13:31ff. which anticipate it point forward to the murder of James by Herod Agrippa I and the latter's own gruesome death as well as Paul's trial before Agrippa II. The "murderer" in 3:14 recalls Luke's emphasis on that characterization of Barabbas in the Gospel (cf. Lk. 23:19, 25 with Mk. 15:7ff. and Mt. 27:15). Stephen's vision of Jesus at the right hand of God, Acts 7:55, answers to Jesus' statement before the Council, Luke 22:67. That the Crucifixion was the work of ignorance on the part of the Jews and their leaders, but at the same time a matter of divine necessity in fulfillment of Scripture, is reiterated in Acts 2:23; 3:17–18, and 13:27–29, cf. Lk. 24:34; 9:22; 17:25; 24:7, 26, 44. Jesus' prayer for his executioners, exclusive to Luke, 23:34, is echoed in Stephen's prayer, Acts 7:60 (cf. Lk. 23:46 with Acts 7:59). Perhaps we should notice also the similarity in Luke's treatment of Joseph of Arimathea and Gamaliel (cf. Lk. 23:50–53, esp. vs. 51, with Acts 5:34. Note the emphasis in comparison with the parallels: Mk. 15:42ff.; Mt. 27:57ff. esp. the latter).

The summary of Jesus' post-Resurrection appearances in Acts 1:3–4 assumes that they were in Jerusalem as Luke, ch. 24, in contrast to Matthew and Mark, describes them (cf. Jn. 21). The reference in Acts 10:41 to eating and drinking with Jesus after the Resurrection obviously points back to Luke 24:30, 43. In Jesus' farewell speech, Luke 24:44–49, Luke establishes the pattern and theme of the apostles' kerygmatic sermons which form such a prominent and important part of Acts (cf. Acts 2:14–40; 3:11–26; 4:8–12; 5:29–32; 7:2–53; 10:34–43; 13:16–41). As we shall see later, there are several key words and themes, such as the Temple, synagogues, and witnesses, which, running through both books tie them together as two parts of a single work, and in doing so help to reveal Luke's meaning and purpose.

The Ascension story, Acts 1:9–11, represents both a repetition and an apparent contradiction of that in Luke 24:50–51. Even though the words, "And was carried up into heaven," found in some manuscripts are probably not original, this passage must be taken as an Ascension story rather than a temporary departure such as might be implied in Acts 1:3.[83] The differences in both time and location of the Ascension in the two accounts seem, therefore, to weigh against the unity of Luke-Acts.

The general pattern of the two stories, without parallel in the other Gospels, indicates, in spite of the differences, a common authorship. Perhaps Luke had come upon the tradition of the "forty days" between his completion of the Gospel and the beginning of Acts.[84] It is more likely that, in his interest in the topical sequence, he was unconcerned with the chronological inconsistencies he created by his introductory summary in Acts. His Gospel contains other examples of this unconcern. Because he has rearranged Mark's story of the call of the fishermen disciples, for example, Luke is forced to drop James and John from the story of the healing of Simon's mother-in-law, also taken from Mark, and since no disciples have yet been introduced, it is not clear who Simon is. An even greater difficulty of the same sort has resulted from Luke's moving the story of Jesus' rejection in Nazareth, Mark 6:1–6, back to a position before the healing in the synagogue at Capernaum. In speaking of works done in Capernaum, Luke 4:23, Jesus is made to refer to what apparently has not yet happened but follows in 4:31ff.

It may be worth noting, furthermore, that Luke 24 presents chronological problems when taken by itself. The Emmaus disciples walked the eight miles back to Jerusalem after the evening meal and apparently all that follows to the end of the chapter happened the same evening which would make a very long day. It is more likely, therefore, that Luke is not interested in literal chronology here, but links the sequences together as closely as possible for the sake of its meaning and dramatic effect as the climax of his Gospel. In his resume at the beginning of Acts his purpose and interest are different, so he can introduce the forty days without, from his standpoint, any inconsistency. Similarly, the discrepancy between Bethany, Luke 24:50, and the Mount called Olivet, Acts 1:12, has a precedent in the way Luke appears to bring Jesus to the Temple without entering Jerusalem (cf. 19:41, 45; 20:1; 21:37 with 22:10ff.; also Mk. 11:15). As Conzelman suggests, the meaning of Jerusalem for Luke is confined to the Passion (cf. Lk. 9:51 and 13:33) so he brings Jesus to the Temple without mentioning the city until the opening of the Passion story.[85]

Much the same sort of thinking seems to be involved here. Luke mentions Bethany as the beginning of the entry, 19:29, but even where it appears in his source (cf. Mk. 11:11–12 with Lk. 21:37), he omits any

83. Alfred Plummer, *The Gospel According to St. Luke, ICC*, p. 565.
84. M. S. Enslin, *Christian Beginnings*, p. 413.
85. Hans Conzelmann, *The Theology of St. Luke*, pp. 75ff.

further mention of it until the conclusion of his Gospel in the Ascension scene. That Luke understood Bethany to be located by Mount Olivet (19:29) is of little consequence. These places in his work play symbolic roles, and these roles explain the apparent discrepancy. This is why no place at all is mentioned in the Acts Ascension story until the disciples return to Jerusalem by exactly the same route over which their Lord made his way to his Passion.

LUKE AND THE OTHER GOSPELS

As the unity of Luke-Acts furnishes us with a perspective for better understanding the author's over-all plan and purpose, so a comparison of his Gospel with the other three, by giving us an insight into his way of using his sources and his direction and place in the developing tradition, will provide a basis for understanding his thought and emphases.

Mark That Luke uses less of Mark than Matthew does we have already noted. We have observed also that he has inserted what he uses from Mark in blocks separated by sections compiled from Q and his own source, and that in doing so he has disturbed noticeably less than has Matthew the order of Mark's pericopae. Although Mark's material is too well imbedded in the basic structure of Luke's Gospel to have been thrust into it as an afterthought, as Streeter's Proto-Luke theory suggests,[86] Mark has had no such influence on the organization and shape of Luke as it has on Matthew. The difference is not due so much to the proportionately smaller amount of Mark which Luke has used, as it is to the way he has used it. The following table will show the place of the Markan material in the general plan of the Gospel:

Luke's Use of Mark

Mark		Luke	
1:2–3:19	=	3:2–6:16	with minor disarrangements
(————		6:20–8:3	Luke's lesser interpolation)
4:1–6:44	=	8:4–9:17	
(6:45–8:26		————	Luke's omission)
8:27–9:41	=	9:18–50	
(————		9:51–18:14	Luke's greater interpolation, except for isolated agreements)
10:13–16:8	=	18:15–24:9	combined with considerable amount of L

Two facts are immediately apparent: (1) Most of the material Luke has omitted is in a single block in the heart of Mark's important center

86. See pp. 53–54.

section; and the omission takes place in the middle of the longest passage in which Luke is consistently following Mark. (2) Except for isolated fragments and a short passage near the end, the great section on the journey to Jerusalem, so important to Luke's plan, avoids Mark as consistently as the immediately preceding section follows him. These two observations help to explain how Matthew, while more extensively rearranging his material, can be called, in contrast to Luke, an expanded version of Mark.[87]

Another, and perhaps more significant, way by which Luke has effected this contrast appears in the few changes he has made in Mark's order. Four of the changes will be worth our attention here. In the first one, Luke has moved Mark's story of Jesus' rejection at Nazareth, 6:1–6, back to the beginning of his story of Jesus' ministry, 4:16–30. His expansion of Mark's story indicates how important it has become for the general plan of his work. The points of contact between his version and Mark's are the opening scene in which Jesus enters the synagogue and begins to teach (cf. Mk. 6:1–2 with Lk. 4:16, 21a); the congregation's astonishment (cf. Mk. 6:2b with Lk. 4:22a); the question, "Is not this the carpenter?" (cf. Mk. 6:3 with Lk. 4:22b); the saying about the prophet in his own country (cf. Mk. 6:4 with Lk. 4:24); and Jesus' failure to do mighty works in his home town (cf. Mk. 6:5 with Lk. 4:23).

That Mark is in this pericope calling particular attention to Jesus' teaching and its effect provides the basis for Luke's expansion, which in turn furnishes an explanation for the puzzling incongruity in Mark between the people's amazement, "What mighty works are wrought by his hands!" (cf. vs. 2b with 3b), and their taking "offense at him" (cf. Lk. 4:22 with 28). Mark's explanation, based on the proverb, that Jesus was a local carpenter is replaced by a speech which, because of its rejection of Jewish exclusiveness, had given offense.

By adding another proverb, "Physician, heal yourself," and comment, Luke resolves another difficulty in Mark: If Jesus "could do no mighty work" in Nazareth, by what mighty works were the people amazed? The problem was, of course, no less acute for Luke since he has, by placing this story at the beginning of the ministry, eliminated any miracles preceding it. This comment, pointing forward to the Capernaum story (4:31–37), replaces Mark's reference to the mighty works and anticipates the gentile mission.

Three items are added by Luke: (1) an extended Scriptural quotation, (2) a speech in the form of a synagogue homily, (3) the ejection of Jesus from the city and attempt on his life. Possibly we are to understand

---

87. For an analysis of Luke's editorial method by a form critic, see Bultmann, *The History of the Synoptic Tradition*, pp. 361ff.

this story as an attempted stoning; if so, its connection with the story of Stephen becomes more obvious and significant.[88] The setting is significantly similar to the story of Paul in Antioch of Pisidia (Acts 13:14–50), and the Scripture, speech, and expulsion anticipate the latter as well as Peter's speech at Pentecost (Acts 2:14–29) and Stephen's speech and stoning (Acts 7:2–53).

In the second transposition of Mark's order (cf. Mk. 1:16–20 with Lk. 5:1–11) Luke has moved the calling of the fishermen disciples, which in Mark opens Jesus' ministry, forward to a point corresponding roughly to Jesus' tour of Galilee in Mark and the Sermon on the Mount in Matthew. This change allows him to present Jesus teaching, healing, preaching, and at prayer independent of the disciples. Delaying the call of the disciples requires him to drop James, John, and Andrew from the story of the healing of Simon's mother-in-law, to leave Simon temporarily unidentified (cf. Mk. 1:29 with Lk. 4:38), and to change "Simon and those who were with him" to the indefinite phrase, "the people" (cf. Mk. 1:36 with Lk. 4:42).

Whether Luke's story of the miraculous catch of fish is his own re-modeling of Mark's call of the fishermen, or one which came to him in his exclusive source (L) is impossible to say. Luke's story, as it stands, has several points of contact with the other Gospels. The opening scene, which appears at first to be extraneous to the story, corresponds to the introduction to the parable of the sower in Mark 4:1. The remainder of both stories is organized around the saying about catching men (cf. Mk. 1:17 with Lk. 5:10b). The presence of two boats and James and John, and the conclusion in which they abandon their boats and follow Jesus furnish further points of similarity. Both stories perform the same function of introducing disciples into the narrative.

That Luke omits Andrew probably reflects the tradition of the three members of the inner circle, Peter, James, and John, and is a little surprising in view of his comparative neglect of that tradition elsewhere.[89] There is, in Jesus' command to let down their nets (Lk. 5:4), a reminiscence of Matthew's parable of the net (13:47–50, cf. the story of the shekel in the fish's mouth, 17:27), as there is also in Peter's reaction to Jesus (5:5, 8) and Matthew's story of Peter's attempt to walk on the water (Mt. 14:28–31). The miraculous quantity of fish recalls the miraculous harvest in the parable of the sower (Mk. 4:2–9), for which the fruitless night of fishing and the fruitless soil provide appropriate contrasts.

Whether the story of the woman anointing Jesus' feet (Lk. 7:35–50)

88. On the method of stoning see *The Mishnah,* Sanh. 6, 1–4. Also Foakes Jackson *The Beginnings of Christianity,* Vol. IV, p. 85. For more on the significance for Luke of this connection see below, pp. 294, 298–299.
89. See pp. 158–159.

is Luke's adaptation and transposition of Mark's story of the anointing at Bethany, or an independent tradition from Luke's special source is a matter of dispute. Either way Luke has replaced and transposed Mark's version with this one, hence it has the effect of a transposition of Mark's order. Certainly the differences in the stories appear more deliberate than accidental. The host in both cases is named Simon, whereas the woman remains nameless. (In John's version she becomes Mary, sister of Martha and Lazarus, cf. 12:2–3.) In Luke's version, however, there is a reversal of characteristics; Simon is no longer a leper but a Pharisee, and the woman becomes a "sinner," i.e., an immoral woman. In contrast to Mark's story, the woman in Luke anoints not Jesus' head but his feet. Although the alabaster box of ointment occupies a similar position at the beginning of both stories, in Luke it is replaced as the center of attention by the parable of the two forgiven debtors. His version, in fact, is built around the parable.

These differences reflect, and are produced by, the different use to which the two authors have put the story. In Mark it dramatizes the irony of Jesus' messiahship, as his "anointing" becomes a preparation for burial; in Luke it is a vehicle for his important theme of Jesus' attitude, in contrast to that of the Pharisees, toward sinners and outcasts. So Mark must use the story as the prologue to the Passion. Luke, on the other hand, moves the story back to the middle of his version of the Galilean ministry, and thus balances his similar interest, in the later division of his Gospel, in the parables of recovery (ch. 15).

As Luke has moved Mark's story of the anointing of Jesus back from the Passion to the Galilean ministry, so he has moved forward Mark's story of the dispute over greatness from the journey to Jerusalem to the end of the Last Supper in his Passion story. His version omits the request for chief seats by James and John and consequently turns the indignation of the other disciples into a general dispute. The correspondence of the wording of Jesus' saying in the two passages leaves little doubt that Luke is using Mark here. This relocation moves the saying closer to the Passion itself, which it is the function of the saying in both Gospels to interpret.[90] It is significant of Luke's method that two items from the omitted story of James' and John's request are found in other pericopae in his Gospel. The variant of the dispute over chief seats is found in the parable on choosing places of honor (Lk. 14:7–14), and Jesus' saying about his baptism (Mk. 10:38–39) becomes an independent saying in Luke 12:50.

Finally we should notice the way in which, by modifying the editorial links, Luke has detached a number of Mark's pericopae from specific locations and temporal sequences. Where Mark locates the healing of the

90. On Luke's change in the concluding sentence see p. 190.

paralytic, for example, by the editorial note, "And when he returned to Capernaum after some days," Luke says simply, "On one of those days, as he was teaching." Similarly, the phrase, "beside the sea," (Mark 2:13) is omitted. (Cf. Mk. 3:1 with Lk. 6:6; Mk. 3:7, 13, 19b–21 with Lk. 6:17, 12; 11:14; Mk. 4:1, 35; 8:27 with Lk. 8:4, 22; 9:18. Contrast Mk. 9:2 and Lk. 9:28, 37 where Luke is at pains to preserve the chronology.)

Matthew Luke's relation to Matthew, being based on the common use of Mark and Q as sources, is, of course, indirect. Because he has made fewer modifications in Mark's order than has Matthew, we may conjecture that his treatment of Q was similar, and his Gospel, therefore, reflects more closely the original order of Q. Several other comparisons between Luke and Matthew may be of interest. Each of them has material from his own special source which provides some of the best-known and treasured material in any of the Gospels. The first half of Matthew's Sermon on the Mount, for example, which is paralleled in Luke very little, is the best-known and most often cited part of that discourse (except, of course, for the Golden Rule, 7:12). The parables of the laborers in the vineyard, wise and foolish virgins, and the great judgment are also among the most familiar in Matthew. The parables of the prodigal son and the good samaritan, surely two of the most popular parables of Jesus, are correspondingly found only in Luke.

Most obvious among the similarities between Luke and Matthew is the fact that only these two Gospels have stories of the birth of Jesus. The similarity, however, goes little farther. That Jesus was born of the Virgin Mary in Bethlehem under Herod the Great, and that he grew up in Nazareth both agree. Beyond these general statements the two stories are quite independent. Each has a genealogy of Jesus, but from David to Jesus they are unrelated. On the other end of the Gospels they both differ from Mark by extending stories of Resurrection appearances to a climax in a commission of the disciples to their world mission. Here again the similarity ends.

In contrast to Mark, both Gospels have extensive blocks of teaching material, but while Matthew organizes his Gospel around five blocks of this material Luke scatters it more loosely throughout his work which he has organized around a journey motif. Both Gospels place great emphasis on the fulfillment of Scriptural prophecies, while differing equally as much in the way they do it. Matthew is oriented toward rabbinic literature; Luke is, as we have seen, much more under the influence of Greek historical literature.

John We observed in chapter 11 that the fourth Gospel stands apart, both in content and style, from the other three.[91] Yet several characteristics

91. See pp. 43–45.

of Luke's Gospel make a comparison of the two worthwhile. In more than its position in the Canon Luke's Gospel stands between the other Synoptics and John. Among the more conspicuous similarities between Luke and John in contrast to the other two Gospels are the appearances of the Risen Lord to the disciples in the "upper room" in Jerusalem (note also the eating of bread and fish in Lk. 24:30, 43 and in Jn. 21:12–13); only one feeding of the multitude and one story of a storm on the Sea of Galilee. (We should note, however, that while both use Mark's feeding of the five thousand, they use different storm stories. Luke uses the stilling of the storm from Mk. 4:35ff. and John uses the walking on the water, Mk. 6:45ff.); the elimination of all but two of the scenes involving the Sea of Galilee and boats, one of which—the miraculous catch of fish—has no parallel in Mark or Matthew (cf. Lk. 5:1–11 with Jn. 21:1–8); greater interest in Samaria (mentioned only once in Matthew 10:5, and not at all in Mark); and mention of Mary, Martha, and Lazarus (although the latter plays a different role in the two Gospels).

There are other less obvious but equally significant similarities. Luke has, for example, a third more material in pericopae peculiar to him than does Matthew (Mark, of course, has only four or five such pericopae). While this material, less than one fourth of the Gospel, represents far less unique material than the more than two thirds of John which consists of such items, yet when considered in conjunction with Luke's greater freedom in modifying his sources it becomes impressive. The result of these two factors, in fact, is that at least forty-four per cent of Luke's verses are not paralleled in the other Gospels.

Like John, Luke involves Judea in Jesus' ministry virtually from the beginning (note 4:44, 7:17, 23:5),[92] and both Gospels introduce the Temple and Jerusalem in their opening sections. The discourses, also, become longer, and especially in the journey section, are less well defined. Largely because of these blocks of teaching material Luke's motif of the journey to Jerusalem appears to be rather artificially constructed in a way quite reminiscent of John.

Several shifts in emphasis move Luke closer to John. John the Baptizer's part in the baptism of Jesus, omitted in the fourth Gospel, is minimized as much as possible by Luke. John the Baptizer's role as Elijah, omitted in Luke, is denied in John (note the omission of Mk. 9:11–13 in the conclusion of Luke's version of the Transfiguration, 9:36–37). There is less emphasis in Luke on the "inner circle," Peter, James, and John, which in John disappears altogether. Items that suggest human emotions, or leave Jesus' destiny or Lordship in question, are repressed. Thus in the

---

92. On Luke's intention here and the textual problem involved see Conzelmann, *The Theology of St. Luke,* pp. 40–41.

story of Peter's confession, his rebuke is omitted by Luke (cf. Mk. 8:32–33; Mt. 16:22–23 with Lk. 9:22 and John 6:66–69).

By replacing Mark's "messianic secret" with his motif of misunderstanding, Luke moves closer to John's theme of the obstinacy of the Jews. Miracles become more important for their evidential value. This point can be seen particularly in Jesus' power to restore the dead. While in Mark (5:39) and Matthew (9:24) it is possible to take literally Jesus' words, "The child is not dead but sleeping," Luke precludes such an interpretation by adding, "knowing that she was dead" (8:53). The story of Jesus' raising the son of the widow of Nain (Lk. 7:11–17) stands closer to John's story of the raising of Lazarus (11:1–45) than to anything in the other Gospels. Luke's reference to Peter's restoration (22:32) seems to assume the story in John 21:15–17.

In Luke's version of Jesus' prayer before his arrest, which John omits entirely, the Garden of Gethsemane is omitted, and emphasis on the agony is reduced. The prayer is said only once, the "inner circle" disappears, all the disciples are equally involved, and the saying at the beginning and end underscores the danger of temptation to the disciples. Similarly, at the arrest (Lk. 22:47–53) Jesus, with Johannine dignity and language, submits to his captors saying, "But this is your hour, and the power of darkness." In both Gospels Jesus is charged with subversive opposition to Caesar, which although it may be implied in the title King of the Jews, is not stated in Mark or Matthew (Lk. 23:2; Jn. 19:12. Cf. Acts 17:7 but cf. Mk. 12:13–17 and parallels). On the cross, the cry of dereliction, Ps. 22:1, the only "Last Word" in Matthew and Mark, is omitted; and the three "Words" given by Luke lend to the death, in contrast to the intense drama of Mark and Matthew, a dignity which again places Luke closer to John. Throughout both his Gospel and Acts, Luke emphasizes, in a way that anticipates John's treatment of the Jews, the culpability of the Jewish leaders in Jesus' rejection and death (cf. 7:29–30, 19:47, 21:37–22:2, 22:52).

LUKE'S PLAN AND ORGANIZATION

Something of the breadth of Luke's plan and interests can be seen in the geographical scope of his story beginning with Zechariah in the Temple at Jerusalem and ending with Paul in his own hired house in Rome. Indeed, the travel involved in this geography and the discourses which predominate throughout the work are basic to Luke's entire program. His words in Acts 8:4 "Now those who were scattered went about preaching the word" express quite well the controlling mood of Luke-Acts. Thus the discourses of Jesus, which the hymns in the birth stories and the discourse of John the Baptizer anticipate, dominate the story beginning with the opening of his ministry in Nazareth (4:21–27) to the end of the Gospel. In the speeches of Peter, Paul, and Stephen, representing the apostolic witness, Jesus' discourses have their counterpart and extension. Approximately thirty-eight per cent of the Gospel is comprised of Jesus' discourses, and the apostolic speeches (including that of Stephen) occupy about twenty-eight per cent of Acts.[93]

The journeys follow patterns which are controlled by certain key geographical points. At the center of these patterns are Jerusalem and the Temple. In its broadest outline the movement in Luke is from Nazareth to the Temple and Jerusalem and in Acts from Jerusalem to Asia Minor, Greece, and Rome. Three times Jesus comes to Jerusalem: once as an infant for his presentation in the Temple; again at the age of twelve; and finally the great journey, taking up more than a third of the Gospel, which brings him to Jerusalem and the Passion. In Acts, correspondingly, three succeeding and widening arches bring Paul to Rome.

In several other ways the structures in Luke and Acts parallel each other. Jerusalem and the Temple are prominent in the opening scenes of both books. Throughout the first major division of each, the movements are confined to local areas. In the Gospel Jesus' travel is confined, except for one editorial comment in 4:44, to a few Galilean towns, including Nazareth, Capernaum, Nain, Bethsaida, and Lake Gennesaret. (Luke prefers this term to "the Sea of Galilee." He never uses the word "sea" in referring to this body of water.) There is a rhythm in this part of the Gospel between Jesus' tours from village to village (4:43; 8:1) and the flow of crowds "from every village of Galilee and Judea and from Jerusalem" to him (5:17b; 8:4). Until the death of Stephen, the scene in Acts is set—except for the Ascension from the Mount of Olives—in Jerusalem and the Temple. Here, too, the scene alternates between the Temple and the upper room or their homes (1:13; 2:46 *passim*). Even after Stephen's martyrdom the "scattered" believers make their way only to surrounding Judea, Samaria, and finally to Antioch of Syria, which for Luke was still within the eastern world to which Judea belonged. At 9:51 in the Gospel and 13:1 in Acts parallel changes take place. Jesus' journey to Jerusalem prepares the reader for the corresponding journeys of Paul.

Luke has a way of developing his themes not only through such parallel patterns by which his narratives are structured, but also by introducing items early in his story which are later developed into major themes. These items sometimes occur in pairs, sometimes in threes, and a few of major importance more often.[94] Luke attaches his own symbolic meanings

93. On the speeches in Acts, which in all consist of more than thirty per cent of the book, see pp. 282–287.
94. For an interesting list of examples of the pairs see Cadbury, *The Making of Luke-Acts*, pp. 233–235.

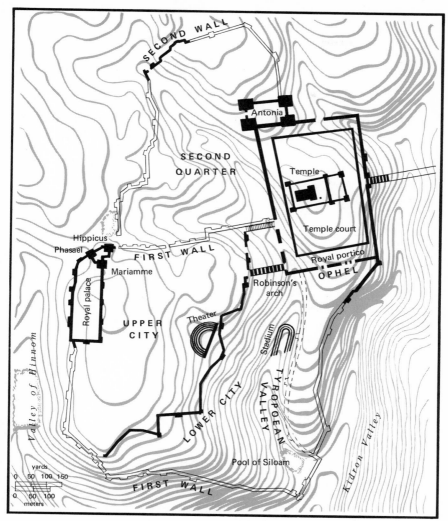

Jerusalem and the Temple. (Adapted with permission of The Macmillan Company from *Macmillan Bible Atlas* by Y. Aharoni and Michael Avi-Yonah. Copyright © 1968 Carta, Jerusalem. © Copyright 1964 by Carta, Jerusalem. © Copyright 1966 by Carta, Jerusalem.)

to geographical data which interpret the journeys. These meanings govern his use of geographical names and much of the structure of his work.

Fulfillment of Scripture is as important for Luke as for Matthew. They differ, however, in the way they use and understand this motif. In contrast to Matthew's formula quotations, Luke often includes his most important proof texts without identifying them in any way. When, in his Gospel, he does use something like Matthew's formula, he usually refers to the Scriptures in general without indicating any particular passage. One noteworthy exception is Jesus' homily in the synagogue of Nazareth (4:18–21), which anticipates and establishes the basis of all such references to follow. In developing this motif Luke prefers the term "it is necessary" to Matthew's word "fulfilled." The term translates the impersonal Greek verb, *dei,* and is frequently used in Greek literature with reference to divine destiny or unavoidable fate. From the verb, *deo,* meaning I bind or tie, probably derived metaphorically from reference to the thread of life spun by the fates in Greek mythology, it occurs eighteen times in Luke's Gospel (twenty-four times in Acts), in contrast to six occurrences in Mark and eight in Matthew. Appropriately, the motif receives its greatest emphasis in the sermons in Acts, but the basis for this emphasis is laid in the Gospel by such references to the Passion as 13:33; 22:37; 24:6–7, 25–26, and 44.

Luke's fondness for the word "necessary" points to another difference from Matthew's use of the Old Testament. Central to Luke's interest in "Moses and all the Prophets" is his need to show that Jesus' Crucifixion, far from being a miscarriage of the messianic program, was in fact included in the divine plan as predicted in Scripture, hence a necessity. In that he nowhere provides a reason for this "necessity," Luke comes much closer to an outright apologetic appeal to prophecy. Whereas in Matthew "fulfillment" means that the cycle of promise and fulfillment has now found its ultimate realization in Jesus, in these passages in Luke it means turning an apparent liability into an asset. The very Crucifixion which would seem to discredit the messianic claims for Jesus, because it corresponds to Scriptural predictions, actually proves them.

The Prologue We must make a distinction in this Gospel between the preface (1:1–4) and the introduction (1:5–4:15). In the preface, which except for the corresponding opening verse of Acts is a literary form not found elsewhere in the New Testament, Luke addresses himself directly to Theophilus (his patron?) to state his purpose and method. The remainder of the prologue parallels that of Matthew and serves to introduce not only the Gospel but his entire work. A primary concern in the prologue is the establishment and definition of the Church's continuity with Israel.[95] Luke achieves this point in two ways: by elaborating the role of John the Baptizer as the climax of Israel's prophetic tradition and by using a number of Scriptural quotations and motifs.

The prologue contains two basic divisions: the birth stories (chs. 1–2)

95. On the significance of the birth stories for Luke's theology see Paul S. Minear, "Luke's Use of the Birth Stories," in Leander E. Keck and J. Louis Martyn, *Studies in Luke-Acts* (Nashville: Abingdon Press, 1966), pp. 111–130.

and the initiation of Jesus' ministry (3:1–4:15). The opening chronological reference, "In the days of Herod, king of Judea "(1:5a, cf. Mt. 2:1a), one of the few points of contact between the birth stories of Luke and Matthew, is the first of three such references in the prologue (cf. 2:1–2 and 3:1–2a) by which Luke fixes his narrative firmly in the history of his time. His program of elaborating the role of John is apparent immediately in one of the most obvious differences between the opening chapters of Luke and Matthew, the story of John's birth which precedes that of Jesus. Because of the addition of this material and a few scattered references in Acts, even though the story of his death is reduced to one sentence, Luke-Acts contains nearly half of the material on John the Baptizer in the New Testament.

Luke has not only elaborated the role of John, but by the way in which he has intertwined the stories of their births, has brought it into the closest possible connection with Jesus. This section is elaborately structured with four items forming the basic outline: the annunciations by the angel Gabriel to Zechariah and to Mary, followed by the births of John and Jesus. The latter, occupying all of chapter 2, is amplified to make the birth of Jesus the appropriate climax to the section. Thus even in their conception John the Baptizer becomes the herald of Jesus. The angel Gabriel, who furnishes an additional tie between John and Jesus, is mentioned elsewhere in Canonical literature only in Daniel 8:16 and 9:21. In the latter reference Gabriel comes to Daniel "at the time of the evening sacrifice" (cf. Zechariah's occupation with the offering of incense which probably was the evening offering). Luke here seems to be establishing a connection between John and the priestly cultus, the prophetic tradition and eschatological view of history in Israel. At least seven hymns accentuate the pattern. (This includes Elizabeth's blessing of Mary, 1:42–45, and counts 1:32–35 and 2:29–35 as one hymn each.) In the four principal hymns of the first chapter the order is reversed to form a chiasm (a rhetorical construction in which parallel items are repeated in reverse order. The term derives from the Greek letter Chi): (a) the annunciation to Zechariah; (b) to Mary; (b) the hymn of Mary; and (a) of Zechariah. Mary's journey from Nazareth to Judea for her visit with Elizabeth, which separates the two pairs of hymns, introduces the dominant journey motif and anticipates the later journey of Mary and Joseph to Bethlehem for the birth of Jesus, for which the remaining two hymns, that of the angelic chorus to the shepherds and Simeon's hymn in the Temple, provide an appropriate emphasis.

Within this framework several points not found elsewhere are added to the tradition. John the prophetic herald of the Messiah is, for example, like Jeremiah and Ezekiel, of priestly lineage. The kinship of Elizabeth and Mary make John and Jesus related by more than their roles in the coming Kingdom of God. Just what this kinship was is not clear. The word is sometimes translated cousin, but is not a precise term and may not mean more than a common family or clan. That Jesus was born in Bethlehem but grew up as a native of Nazareth is explained, not as in Matthew by a migration of the Holy Family because of the hostility of Archelaus, but by the journey of Mary and Joseph required by the census.

Luke's chronological note, in 2:1–2, associating Jesus' birth with the census under Quirinius who became governor of Syria in A.D. 6 creates some problems. There is no evidence for either an earlier census or prior governorship of Quirinius. That it is the census of A.D. 6–7 which Luke had in mind seems all the more likely from his reference in Acts 5:37 to the census in connection with the revolt of Judas the Galilean, which according to Josephus took place at that time.[96] Since Herod the Great died in 4 B.C., Luke's reference to the census not only brings him into conflict with Matthew, who by his reference to Herod's slaughter of infants "who were two years old or under" (2:16) implies a date for Jesus' birth around 6 B.C., but also makes him contradict his own reference to Herod in 1:5. How much blame for this confusion his sources must bear, and how much is Luke's own doing, is impossible to say. It is possible, of course, that Luke possessed a tradition of a journey of the Holy Family at the time of the census which he took to be the occasion of the birth of Jesus but which was actually associated with the story of Jesus in the Temple (2:42–51). The coincidence of the discrepancy of about twelve years and the age of Jesus in the latter story lends some plausibility to the suggestion that the two journeys are doublets. As we will observe later, a similar possibility of doublets occurs in Acts.[97] That Luke is patently modeling his narrative on the story of Samuel's birth in I Samuel 1–3 makes this suggestion, however, no more than a guess.

Although Luke apparently knows the tradition that identifies John as Elijah, he reduces it to the phrase, "in the spirit and power of Elijah" (1:17), and later eliminates from his source the passage which explicitly makes that identification (cf. 9:36–37 with Mk. 9:11–13). By this means he reassesses the eschatological significance of John who now becomes only an anticipation of the arrival of Elijah "before the great and terrible day of the Lord" (Mal. 4:5), and whose real significance is a share in the prophetic ministry of Jesus (cf. 7:16, 39ff.; 13:33; 24:19; Acts 3:22–23; 7:37 with 7:26, 28; 16:16; 20:6). The coming of Elijah and the eschaton are thus moved into a more indefinite future. As central as eschatology is to the New Testament, it is nevertheless a movable partition, and a clear

96. *Antiquities*, XVIII, 1, 1.
97. See pp. 289–290, 313.

pattern of change in eschatological expectations is discernible in the New Testament.[98]

In Simeon's hymn in the Temple, the last of the series, Luke introduces the mission to the gentiles (2:31–32). Since all of the hymns but this final one have been concerned exclusively with Israel, the introduction of the gentiles here presents the sequence so basic to Luke's concept of sacred history: from Israel to the gentiles. In the same way, Jesus' birth in a manger, "because there was no place for them in the inn," anticipates the later expulsion of Jesus and the apostles from synagogues and the Temple. The shepherds who come to pay homage to the infant Jesus represent, in contrast to Matthew's magi, Luke's great concern for the common people.

Seven times in the first two chapters the Holy Spirit is mentioned, the last three of which, 2:25–27, refer to the endowment of Simeon for his prophetic pronouncement upon the infant Jesus. There are, in fact, as many references to the Spirit in Luke as in Mark and Matthew combined. Along with five more such references in the second part of the prologue, 3:16, 22; 4:1 (twice), 14, they complement the story of Pentecost and the dominant emphasis in the opening section of Acts, and introduce another of Luke's principal themes. The description of the descent of the Holy Spirit at Jesus' baptism "in bodily form" (3:22, cf. "tongues as of fire," Acts 2:3–4) underscores both his emphasis on the Spirit and the distinction between John's baptism and that of Jesus (cf. Acts 18:24–19:6).

The three scenes in the Temple: the annunciation to Zechariah; the purification of the Virgin, sacrifice of the firstborn, and prophecies of Simeon and Anna; and Jesus' visit to the Temple at the age of twelve place in the foreground another of Luke's major interests. They anticipate the scenes in the Temple in the final chapters of the Gospel, of Jesus' teaching, including Luke's version of the apocalyptic discourse (note especially the final verse of the Gospel, 24:53) and the prominent role of the Temple in Acts. Luke is at pains to show that Jesus' followers remained faithful to it until they were expelled and it was destroyed (cf. Acts 7:12–14, 58; 21:27–30; and Lk. 21:5ff.). His purposes in this treatment of the Temple are probably both theological and apologetic. Christianity is legitimately rooted in and the climax of the best of Israel's priestly and prophetic life, and neither violated nor despised its valid traditions.

The first two chapters of Luke are literally saturated with Old Testament language and quotations. Of controlling influence are I Samuel

---

98. See Donald J. Selby, "Changing Ideas in New Testament Eschatology," *The Harvard Theological Review*, Vol. L, No. 1, Jan. 1957.

1–3 (cf., for example, the three refrains, "and the child grew," 1:80; 2:40, 51, with the three refrains in I Sam. 2:21, 26; 3:19) and Judges 13, but many other passages are represented. The Magnificat, 1:46–55, and the Benedictus, 1:68–79, are catenae of such passages.[99] Hannah's song in I Samuel 2:1–10 provides the framework of the former, whereas the Psalms dominate the latter. Gabriel's hymn of annunciation to Zechariah is compiled from Judges 13:2 and Malachi 4:5–6; his annunciation to Mary echoes Isaiah 9:6–8; and Simeon's Nunc Dimittis paraphrases Psalm 98:2 (Isa. 52:10?) and Isaiah 49:6 (cf. Isa. 42:6). An atmosphere of worshipful awe and wonder hovers over the entire story, which explains why, of the two, Luke's Christmas story is the favorite. Added to the predominant Temple setting, the witness of angels and prophets, the Old Testament fabric of these chapters provides the link for the Church's continuity with Israel, which Luke is so concerned to establish, and defines Jesus as the climax of God's mighty saving acts in behalf of his people.

By this means also Luke places the birth of Jesus, and that of John which prepares for and introduces it, in the continuity of the providential births of Isaac (Gen. 18:11ff.), Samson (Judg. 13:2ff.), and Samuel (I Sam. 1:2ff., cf. Gen. 25:21; 29:31; 30:22). It is in the context, then, of Israel's beginnings that Luke interprets the virgin birth of Jesus as the appropriate and marvelous climax of God's providential actions for the salvation of his people. Matthew seems more concerned in his version of the virgin birth to expound a connection of Jesus with the Emmanuel of Isaiah 7:14, whereas Luke is concerned with the continuity and climax of the history of the redemption of the world.

In the second division of the prologue, John the Baptizer again precedes and introduces Jesus. John anticipates and prepares for Jesus in two ways, in his prophetic role and his baptism with water which anticipates the messianic baptism "with the Holy Spirit and with fire." The most elaborate chronological notes in the entire work preface Luke's account of John's ministry and, by their association with the reference to the age of Jesus at the beginning of his ministry (3:23), serve also to date the latter.

With his reference to "the fifteenth year of the reign of Tiberius Caesar" Luke appears again in chronological difficulty. Unless one counts the two years of his association with Augustus, which it is unlikely that Luke intended, Tiberius' reign dates from A.D. 14. John began his ministry, then, in A.D. 29. If Jesus' ministry is dated from approximately the same time and we take the "thirty years of age" strictly, this date, while it accords with the basis of our present calendar, fits neither with his

99. For a complete schedule of these passages see Alfred Plummer, *The Gospel According to St. Luke* (ICC), pp. 30–31, 39.

birth under Herod who died in 4 B.C. (cf. Mt. 2:1ff; Lk. 1:5), nor, on the other hand, with the known census under Quirinius (A.D. 6). If Luke understood John's ministry prior to Jesus' baptism to have been in progress for sometime and intended the "thirty years" somewhat loosely, the latter date could be reconciled. This reckoning, however, places the Crucifixion so late as to put a strain on the chronology of Paul.[100] It is clear from these difficulties that any chronology based on Luke's evidence must remain tentative and approximate.

Except for Matthew's addition of Jesus' discussion with John on his baptism, 3:14–15, and of Jesus' withdrawal to Capernaum and accompanying prophetic quotation, Luke includes in this division of the prologue virtually all of the parallel material in Mark and Matthew. His additions and rearrangements, however, are interesting. He has extended Mark's quotation of Isaiah 40:3 to include verses 4 and 5. To John's "brood of vipers" speech he has added a much more irenic discourse to the multitudes, the tax collectors, and soldiers, offering practical moral advice which serves to interpret the meaning of John's call to repentance. Here Luke's great concern for the common people, social outcasts, and the like shows itself again. By introducing John's announcement of Jesus with a description of the mood of expectancy that prevailed among the people, he not only provides historical background for the popular following which Jesus encountered, but by raising the question, reminiscent of the treatment of John in the fourth Gospel, whether John might be the Messiah, he provides a smoother and more meaningful setting for that announcement.

Instead of the brief note of John's imprisonment with which Mark and Matthew introduce the opening of Jesus' ministry, Luke imports the explanation of Herod's action from Mark's story of John's beheading (Mk. 6:17–18). By placing the reference to John's imprisonment before Jesus' baptism and omitting any direct mention of John in that connection, even though the phrase "when all the people were baptized" obviously refers to John's baptism, he has disassociated John from the baptism of Jesus as far as possible.[101] Characteristically, Luke places the emphasis in the story on the bestowal of the Holy Spirit. Baptism and prayer simply precede the Spirit's descent. The reference to prayer is the first of seven such references which form an important motif, comparable to Matthew's seven mountains, throughout the Gospel. The remaining six are prior to forgiving the sins of the paralytic 5:16; the appointment of the twelve, 6:12; Peter's confession, 9:18; Transfiguration, 9:28–29; teaching of the Lord's Prayer, 11:1; the Crucifixion, 22:39–46.

100. On the whole question of New Testament chronology see James Hastings, *A Dictionary of the Bible,* pp. 403–425.
101. See p. 123, and p. 235.

We have already noted that there is no direct relationship between the two versions of the genealogy of Jesus in Luke and Matthew. That they agree as far as David means only that David's genealogy is easily available from the Old Testament.[102] Many interpreters find an indication of his universal outlook in the fact that, unlike Matthew who begins his genealogy with Abraham, Luke runs his back to Adam. Perhaps its position in the middle of the prologue and at the introduction of Jesus' ministry between his baptism and temptation reinforces this interpretation. The reversed order of the second and third temptations, making Jesus return to Galilee from the Temple, rather than from the Jordan as in Mark and Matthew, reflects once more his interest in it. (Perhaps Matthew is the one who has altered this Q material to avoid such a program.) Luke adds that the devil "departed from him until an opportune time," which, when taken with the reference to Satan (unique to Luke) in 22:3, connects the Passion with the temptation and interprets them both as demonic attempts to thwart or subvert the Gospel. Thus Luke lays the foundation for his interpretation of the Crucifixion.

The Beginning of Jesus' Ministry By a deliberate rearrangement of Mark's material, Luke presents Jesus in a brief ministry without disciples. Since we hear nothing of disciples of John the Baptizer until they come to Jesus on behalf of their imprisoned leader (from Q, see Matt. 11:2–19; Lk. 7:18–35), this rearrangement increases the parallels between John and Jesus. When taken with the call of the fishermen disciples in 5:1–11, this section manifests a pattern paralleled at the opening of the Gospel's second main division, 9:51ff.: a rejection, departure, proclamation, and call of disciples.[103] The proclamations complement one another and, in a way reminiscent of Mark, underscore Luke's interest in the example of Jesus for the Church's mission: "I must preach the good news of the Kingdom of God to other cities also" (4:43a); "No one who puts his hand to the plow and looks back is fit for the Kingdom of God" (9:62).

Two scenes in synagogues control this section. The first in Nazareth and the second in Capernaum represent Jesus' ministry, like Paul's (Acts 9:20), as beginning in the synagogue. Thus Luke introduces his basic concept of the development of Christianity. Temple and synagogue are linked by their roles in the beginnings of the Church. As the Temple, the center of Israel's cultic life, provides the setting for the essential beginning of both volumes, and again near the end, for the prelude to the Passion of Jesus and the trials of Paul, so the synagogue, the center of Israel's communal life, provides a focal point of the ministries of Jesus and Paul. In the three references in the Gospel, after these initial scenes,

102. See Gen. 5:3–32; 11:10–26; Ruth 4:18–22; I Chron. 1:1–4, 24–28; 2:1–15.
103. Hans Conzelmann, *The Theology of St. Luke*, p. 64.

Present-day city of Nazareth. (Courtesy of the Israel Government Tourist Office.)

to Jesus' teaching in the synagogues, 4:44; 6:6; 13:10, they represent outlying Judaism in its homeland; the ten or more synagogues in the story of Paul in Acts represent the diaspora.

The scenes in the synagogues of Nazareth and Capernaum, therefore, are basic to Luke's understanding of the relationship between Judaism and Christianity. Jesus' rejection in his home synagogue (cf. Jn. 1:11–12) anticipates and explains Paul's controversies in the synagogues and his turning to the gentiles (cf. especially Acts 13:45–46, 18:4–5, 28:25–28). Capernaum is a reminder, on the other hand, of those in Israel who, in obedience to the Gospel, became the nucleus of the nascent Church (note the absence of Pharisees in the trial of Jesus, and the many converts, including priests and Pharisees in Acts 2:41, 47; 4:4; 5:14; 6:7; 15:5). Like the Jews of Beroea in contrast to those of Thessalonica (Acts 17:10ff.), the people of Capernaum "were more noble" than those of

Nazareth. The lesson from Isaiah (61:1–2) which Jesus read is a definition of his messiahship (cf. Jesus' opening comment applying the reading to himself with his answer to the disciples of John the Baptizer, 7:22f.), and his homily is an argument for the mission to the gentiles. The attempt on his life connects this story with the expulsion and martyrdom of Stephen which bring an end to the Temple scenes in the early part of Acts.

As in Mark and Matthew, Jesus' teaching and healing are closely related manifestations of the same divine power and bear the same messianic meaning. By several means Luke establishes this relationship: the teaching in the first synagogue and healing in the second; the repetition, in the second scene, of the word ""authority" (Greek: *exousia*) in reference to Jesus' teaching, verse 32, and his healing of the demoniac, verse 36; and the two succeeding pericopae on healings followed by his pronouncement on preaching and the editorial summary (cf. Matthew's summaries of Jesus' ministry, 4:23 and 9:35–36). With this definition of Jesus' ministry Luke has prepared his readers for the introduction of the disciples.

The Preparation of Disciples, Lk. 5:1–9:50   An extended editorial passage beginning with a travel note, "Soon afterward he went on through cities and villages preaching" (8:1), and a reference to the twelve and several women divides this section into two parts. The effect of the travel note, apparently intentional, is to give Jesus' ministry in the second part of this section a wider itinerary in anticipation of the long section on the journey to Jerusalem which follows. That this pattern is deliberately, though artificially, imposed on the material seems evident from the way Luke has omitted two references to Jesus going to the sea (cf. Lk. 5:27 with Mk. 2:13, and Lk. 6:17 with Mk. 3:7) and a reference to Capernaum (cf. Lk. 5:17 with Mk. 2:1). These changes, and the one reference to Capernaum in 7:1, create the impression that, except for the one unavoidable reference to Lake Gennesaret in 5:1–11 and the city of Nain (7:11–17), Jesus' ministry prior to 8:1 took place in the immediate vicinity of Capernaum. The effect of the travel note is reinforced by references to Gerazene (8:22–40) and Bethsaida (9:10ff.). Nor does the editorial remark in 4:44 about his "preaching in the synagogues of Judea" (if this is the correct reading) contradict this impression. Because that verse, which is a conclusion to Jesus' announcement of his purpose to preach in "the other cities also," is in no way connected with what follows, it must be taken as a generalization on the entire story.

Three pericopae in the first part of this section concerning calling and appointing disciples, correspond to three significant episodes involving the twelve disciples in the second part. The role of the twelve in the beginnings of the Church, one of Luke's major themes, is established by the opening story of the miraculous catch of fish (5:1–11) which resulted in the call of Peter, James, and John. Followed by the calling of Levi (5:27ff.), the theme is completed in the appointment of the twelve in 6:12–16 (cf. Acts 1:13). In the second part of this section the three episodes, the stilling of the storm (8:22–25), the mission of the twelve (9:1–10), and the feeding of the five thousand (9:11–17), as in Mark, are a commentary on the meaning of discipleship. That the first of the three episodes in each of these series takes place on Lake Gennesaret, indicates the meaning of the lake in his Gospel. It represents the divine call and providential care of the disciples and therefore the Church (cf. 10:19).

Ten pericopae on healings, including one resuscitation, 5:12–15, 17–26; 6:6–11, 17–19; 7:1–10, 11–17; 8:26–39, 40–42 and 49–56, 43–48; 9:37–43, scattered through this section represent not only the healing aspect of Jesus' ministry but also that of the disciples (cf. 9:1ff.), and therefore anticipate and explain the apostolic healings in Acts. The three discourses, which occupy prominent positions in the section, are clearly distinguished by preceding editorial material, appropriate settings, and changes of locale at their conclusions. By placing the first of these, the Sermon on the Plain (6:17–49), on a "level place" in contrast to Matthew's mountain and by reference to the crowds, Luke has made his sermon a public teaching rather than private instruction of the disciples. The reference in verse 10 to disciples suggests that here, too, as in Matthew, traditions of private instruction and public teaching are being combined, and that the beatitudes belong to the former.[104] Except for the four beatitudes, however, which here have a more literal meaning than their Matthean parallels, Luke's version of the Sermon consists largely of the Q materials, including a short homily on loving one's enemies, which Matthew used in expanding the first part of his Sermon, and about half of the final chapter (ch. 7) of Matthew's Sermon, along with other short sayings from Q scattered in Matthew through chapters 10, 12, and 15. Noteworthy in Luke's Sermon are the four woes, verses 24–26, which, by complementing the four beatitudes, complete the motif of the reversal of fortunes (cf. the Magnificat, esp. 1:51–53), and his substitution of "merciful" for "perfect" (cf. Mt. 5:48) in verse 36. In this discourse are represented the teachings which it is the office of the apostolic mission to hand on, and by which the developing Church is to be governed.

The second discourse, 7:22–35, on John the Baptizer, is paralleled very closely and almost completely by Matthew 11:4–19. In the only two changes of any importance, Luke has removed to a later section

104. See pp. 117–118.

(16:16) the sayings on violence and the Kingdom, and the Law and the Prophets and John (Mt. 11:12–13), omitting altogether the equation of John with Elijah (Mt. 11:14), and inserted in its place a comment on the contrasting responses of the people and tax collectors versus Pharisees and lawyers, to Jesus' statements about John (cf. Mt. 21:32). The discourse on John serves here not only to emphasize the parallel prophetic roles of John and Jesus, but also to interpret the apostolic mission for which the disciples are being prepared.

With the third discourse, 8:4–21, Luke resumes his use of Mark which he has followed quite consistently with some additions from the beginning of John's ministry to the introduction of the first of the three discourses, 3:3–6:19. By omitting Mark's parable of mysterious growth of seed (Mk. 4:26–29), transferring his parable of the mustard seed (Mk. 4:30–32) to the thirteenth chapter, and inserting the pericope on Jesus' true family from Mark 3:31–35 as a conclusion, Luke has condensed and intensified Mark's discourse of parables of seed. He has also rewritten the concluding saying on Jesus' true family, verse 21, to correspond with the conclusion of the interpretation of the parable of the sower, verse 15. These conclusions underscore the purpose of the discourse to define discipleship as "those who hear the word of God and do it." As the first part of this section (chs. 5–7) is concerned with the call to discipleship, the second part, which the third discourse opens, is concerned with its meaning and mission.

Although mountains do not play the prominent role in Luke that they do in Matthew, the three mountain scenes—Nazareth where Jesus is threatened with death (4:29), the appointing of the twelve (6:12ff.), and the Mount of Transfiguration (9:28ff.)—lend emphasis to and indicate a connection between these significant episodes and anticipate the three scenes on the Mount of Olives: the entry (19:28ff.), Jesus' lodging (21:37), and his prayer of agony (22:39–46), in the Passion narrative. The significance of these parallels can be seen in the reference to the Passion and the presence of heavenly persons in the third, climactic scene in each series. Four of the seven scenes of Jesus at prayer occur also in this section. The first scene, at the conclusion of the editorial summary on Jesus' spreading fame and the growing demands of the multitude (5:16, cf. prayer for laborers, 10:2, and in Matthew's mission of the twelve, 9:37–38) anticipates the other three, all of which introduce episodes involving disciples: (1) the appointment of the twelve, 6:12; (2) Peter's confession, 9:18; (3) the Transfiguration, 9:28.

Three scenes of Jesus at meals occur in each of the two main parts of Luke's Gospel. In each division also the first two meals lead to a third which is of Eucharistic significance. Thus in this division the meals with Levi, the tax collector (5:29–39), and with the Pharisee (7:36–50) anticipate Jesus' feeding of the five thousand (9:12–17), as the two meals with Pharisees (11:37–52 and 14:1–24) in the second division anticipate the Last Supper. The breadth of Luke's concern for all classes of people, so prominent in Acts, is reflected in the types of persons included in these scenes. The meaning of these meals is further developed by the discussions for which they are the setting. At Levi's table the discussion concerns Jesus' eating with tax collectors and sinners and his disciples failure to observe the fasts. The answer is that a new age has dawned and the innovations of which they complain define its character, as do the two stories concerning the Sabbath which follow (6:1–11).

These latter stories anticipate two similar Sabbath controversies in the next section (13:10–17; 14:2–6). All four of these stories are closely related in pattern, if not in origin. The conclusions, however, indicate an interesting development of thought. The first of these, 6:5, speaks to the controversy itself, whereas the second, 6:11, uses the controversy to explain the opposition to Jesus which led to the Passion. In the conclusions to two Sabbath stories in the section on the journey to Jerusalem (13:17; 14:6), on the other hand, Jesus' discomfiture of his critics is the main interest.

The sinful woman anointing Jesus' feet while he is at the Pharisee's table (7:36–50) again raises the issue of Jesus' association with sinners, but this time the discussion focuses on his authority to forgive sins, a subject with which Luke has already dealt in a context of a dispute with Pharisees in the story of the Healing of the Paralytic (5:18–26). These controversies, anticipating the increasing tension with Judaism in the later sections of the Gospel and in Acts, allow Luke to argue the Church's side of the issues and at the same time to define the character and mission of discipleship.

By omitting Mark 6:45–8:26, Luke brings Peter's confession, Jesus' first prediction of his Passion, and call of the cross (9:18–27) to a position immediately following the feeding of the five thousand, where they perform an interpretive function, as do the discussions associated with the other two meals. In order to make this function clearer, he has also omitted Peter's rebuke (cf. vss. 22–23 with Mark 8:31–34). The significance of the pattern, anticipating the Last Supper, Trial, Crucifixion, and post-resurrection commission of the disciples, is obvious.

That Luke introduces the desert setting for the feeding (vs. 12), in spite of the setting in the city of Bethsaida that he has already provided (vs. 10), calls attention to his symbolic use of deserts which in this division are also the scenes of Jesus' temptation (4:1), retreat (4:42), and prayer (5:16). John the Baptizer's association with the desert (1:80, 3:2) is a part of this motif and represents another parallel between his ministry and that of Jesus. The background for this desert symbol is to be found in such Old Testament stories as Israel's wilderness journey to the Promised Land and Elijah's prophecy (cf. Isa. 40:3–5, quoted by Lk. 3:4–6).

Intensified by omissions and abbreviations, the important central section of Mark retains in Luke's setting here essentially its original meaning for discipleship and the mission of the Church. An instructive example of Luke's method of interpreting his sources both literally and symbolically is the way in which the story of the stilling of the storm (8:22–25) anticipates in the stories of Acts not only divine deliverance in the persecutions and dangers of the apostolic mission but also the climactic storm story, the shipwreck from which Paul was delivered to witness before Caesar (Acts 27). Luke's addition to the story of the Transfiguration concerning Jesus' "departure, which he was to accomplish at Jerusalem," not only defines the meaning of Jerusalem in the Gospel, but gives the Transfiguration even more pointed reference to the Passion and Resurrection. The healing of the demoniac son (9:37–43a), the second prediction of the Passion (9:43b–45), and a dispute which leads to the definition of true greatness (9:46–48), all of which interpret the meaning of discipleship, culminate in the brief story of the strange exorcist (9:49–50), in whom all of the faithful missioners of the advancing Church are foreshadowed. With this story the section on the dangers, responsibilities, and resources of the apostolic mission for preaching, teaching, and healing closes and the journey to Jerusalem is introduced.

The Journey to Jerusalem, 9:51–19:27   The central section of Luke, amounting to slightly more than one third of the Gospel, begins with the dramatic statement, "When the days drew near for him to be received up, he set his face to go to Jerusalem" (9:51a). These words, along with a series of references to his journey and the fact that the section leads to the story of Jesus' entry (19:28–44), justify its customary designation as the journey to Jerusalem. Yet closer analysis will show that the journey motif is superficially imposed on the material. Aside from the scattered editorial notes and a few comparatively brief narratives, the section consists almost completely of teaching material.

The mission of the seventy (some manuscripts have seventy-two), for example, is introduced with the words, "After this the Lord appointed seventy others, and sent them on ahead of him, two by two, into every town and place where he himself was about to come" (10:1), which sounds as though the mission was to continue to Jesus' arrival at Jerusalem, but in verse 17 they return to Jesus at the conclusion of the mission as though he had not left their point of departure. Similarly, the journey begins with an attempt to enter a Samaritan village (9:51b–56), yet eight chapters later Jesus "was passing along between Samaria and Galilee" (17:11). Except for his story of the Samaritan village, Luke gives us in nine chapters no more information on Jesus' movement to Judea than does Mark in one verse (Mk. 10:1).

Luke's motif of the journey to Jerusalem is therefore not to be taken literally. Yet, on the other hand, it is not merely an appropriation of a popular literary device. It is rather his way of dramatizing the divinely ordained progress of the Gospel in ever widening areas until it should encompass the world. What this progress meant for Luke's theology and purpose we shall observe in more detail in another chapter, but here we should note that the journey motif anticipates and prepares for the story of that progress in Acts.

The story of the Samaritan village and the reference in 17:11 to Jesus passing between Samaria and Galilee raise the question of Jesus' route. Opinion among interpreters of Luke is divided. A number of them speak of this section of Luke as Jesus' Perean ministry, while others conclude that, in spite of Jewish prejudice, Jesus must have gone through Samaria (cf. Jn. 4:4ff.). Against the former, it must be pointed out that Luke nowhere mentions Perea or "beyond the Jordan" (cf. Mk. 10:1), and for the latter the reference, so late in the story, to the border between Samaria and Galilee becomes a problem. Hans Conzelmann is probably correct in stating that Luke is working on a misconception of Palestine geography in which he conceives the borders of Galilee and Judea to join, with the Jordan on the east, Samaria lying between them, and the Mediterranean coast on the west. Conzelmann calls attention to similar misconceptions of Palestinean geography in Pliny and Strabo.[105] Perhaps Luke simply shared a common Graeco-Roman misconception of the geography of the East.

For interpreting Luke, however, it is the symbolic meaning rather than the literal geography that is important. We have already seen how Luke, in omitting a considerable part of Mark's central section, eliminated Jesus' travels through Phoenicia, the Decapolis, and Caesarea Philippi. Thus, in Luke, Jesus leaves Jewish territory only once when he crosses the Lake of Gennesaret to Gerazene (8:22–40). Jesus' ministry is therefore confined to Israel. His rejection by the Samaritan village makes it clear that the evangelization of the world beyond Israel remains the task of the post-Resurrection Church according to a plan and itinerary in which it would be guided by the Spirit (cf. the way in which the Holy Spirit prevented Paul and his company from going into Bithynia, Acts 16:7).

As we have already observed,[106] this section opens with a parallel to

105. *The Theology of St. Luke,* pp. 68ff. See Pliny, *Natural History,* V, pp. 68–70 and Strabo, *Georgraphy,* XVI, p. 760.
106. See p. 168.

the beginning of Jesus' ministry consisting of a rejection, departure, and a pericope on becoming disciples (9:51–62), which introduces the controlling item in this section, the mission of the seventy (10:1–17). That Luke drops the second feeding story in his source and adds instead a second mission, unique to him, is significant of his purpose and emphasis. In several ways Luke has reinforced his emphasis upon this story. The very position of the mission of the seventy as well as its greater length give it a prominence for which the mission of the twelve in the previous section was a preparation. Along with transferring to this story the sending of the disciples "two by two," which stood in his source for the earlier mission (cf. Mk. 6:7), he has reserved to this mission the material from Q with which Matthew supplements Mark's story of the mission of the twelve. The story of the mission of seventy, as a result, is more than twice as long as the earlier one.

The prior position of the mission of the twelve, on the other hand, means more than simply a preparation for the seventy. For one thing, the numbers twelve and seventy, as in the twin stories of feeding the multitude in Mark and Matthew, symbolize the Jewish and gentile missions. The sequence represents and anticipates, therefore, Luke's constant theme in Acts of the movement of the Gospel from the Jews to the gentiles. By his reference to Herod's execution of John the Baptizer in the earlier mission and by omitting, in contrast to the conclusion of the story of the seventy, any reference to its success (cf. 9:10 with 10:17–20), Luke has suggested the Jewish rejection of the Gospel which, in Acts, in each case turned the mission to the gentiles. While emphasizing the possibility of rejection in both missions, Luke has, especially when compared to Matthew, surprisingly little suggestion of persecution. This is in keeping with his general plan. The theme of persecution Luke reserves for passages dealing with apocalyptic Jewish rejection of the Gospel (especially in Acts), or for developing his apologetic motif.[107] Something of his attitude may be seen by comparing his version of Paul's experiences with the latter's own list of his troubles and persecutions in II Corinthians 11:23–29. Luke's concern is to show the dramatic progress of the Gospel rather than the difficulties its bearers encountered.

Finally, the positions of the two missions represent Luke's concept of the position of the twelve in the developing Church. At their number suggests, they represent the continuity of the church with historic Israel, and it is therefore appropriate that they remain associated with the Mother Church in Jerusalem. Although he follows Mark in using the word "apostles" in the story of the return of the twelve, Luke carefully

---

107. See below, pp. 188, 291–307. This fact forms part of the basis for Conzelmann's theory that the ministry of Jesus was a special period in the middle of time in which satanic power was curtailed, *The Theology of St. Luke*, pp. 50–51, 82.

avoids applying the term to the "seventy others." That the distinction is not accidental is evident from the way he uses the word with reference to Jesus' followers. With very few exceptions it always refers to the twelve. It occurs only twice in the other Gospels (Mk. 6:30, Mt. 10:2), but occurs in this sense five times in Luke's Gospel and twenty-eight times in Acts.

How he understands the role of the apostles can be seen in the important story in Acts 8:1–4 of the persecution which scattered the Church: those who "went about preaching" did not include the apostles, who remained in Jerusalem. Later when Paul and Barnabas were sent to Jerusalem over the question of circumcision, it was the "apostles and elders" there who arbitrated the dispute. Paul and Barnabas, on the other hand, are only spoken of as apostles twice in Acts (14:4, 14), and both instances, in the same story of the journey through the Galatian Province, are so out of keeping with the remaining uses in Acts of the term that one wonders if these are glosses. As we shall see in a later chapter, Luke systematically disassociates Paul from the apostles and their witness to the Resurrection. Significantly, the last occurrence of the term in Acts is in 16:4.

In the Gospel the two missions anticipate and symbolize the two-stage scheme in Acts by which Luke represents the purpose and growth of the Church. Contrary to the etymology of the word (meaning delegate or messenger), Luke understands the apostles as the essential link between Jesus and the growing Church and as a college seated in the Mother Church at Jerusalem for governing the Church and giving unity and direction to its mission as it carried their witness across the world. The mission of the twelve (Lk. 9:1–10), therefore, represents the apostolic witness in the environs of Jerusalem in the early chapters of Acts, while the journeys of Paul have their precedent in the mission of the seventy. Something of this meaning adheres to the entire journey section.

The remainder of the journey becomes therefore, in the broadest sense, a commentary on the mission. As a part of that commentary, several recurring themes, often in alternating sequence and highlighted by contrasts, run through the subsequent chapters in a way reminiscent of Mark. These themes represent important items in Luke's understanding of the Church of his own time and its mission. His sympathy and concern for the poor, the tax collectors and sinners, the social outcasts, and gentiles, which have already been established at the beginning of the Gospel, appear repeatedly in the way he places them in contrast to the rich and the hypocritical who put their greed and pride ahead of the demands of the Kingdom. The common people who hear and obey the Word are contrasted with the leaders who refuse to enter and "hindered those who were entering." Disciples are set over against those who reject the Kingdom; the anxious are contrasted with those who heed the teaching of Jesus and seek the Kingdom; the faithful servants who obediently do their master's will and expectantly watch for his return are contrasted with the wicked servants who are caught unprepared; the gift of the Holy Spirit stands in contrast to possession by evil spirits.

There are two pericopae on prayer, two on the controversial subject of the Sabbath. That the special hour for repentance has come, and judgment awaits those who fail to heed it, is either explicit or implicit all through the section. That the motif of reversal of fortunes, introduced in the Magnificat (1:46–55) and repeated in the earlier sections, reappears here in several forms indicates something of its importance for Luke's thought. One half of the material in the journey section is exclusively Luke's, approximately three fourths of the remainder is from Q, and the rest from Mark. Except for chapters 15 and 16, where occur the largest blocks of material peculiar to Luke, the Markan and Q materials are distributed fairly evenly throughout the section, but under the control of Luke's own plan. The story of the Pharisees' warning to Jesus that Herod is plotting to kill him divides the section into two major parts. Several other vignettes serve as transitions and introduce new themes. Frequently, catchwords, associations of ideas, and the like form the bond holding Luke's groupings of materials together.

Immediately following the mission of the seventy is a series of materials (10:18–37) which, by placing it in the setting of the return of the missioners, Luke has arranged as a first step in his interpretation of the mission. That he intends this material as a connected series relating to the return of the seventy is established by the editorial connections: "The seventy returned . . . ," verse 17; "In that same hour . . . ," verse 21 (cf. Mt. 11:25); "Then turning to the disciples . . . ," verse 23; "And behold, a lawyer stood up . . . ," verse 25. Word associations tie the first three of the four pericopae together Two Greek words, translated "rejoice," form the link between the first and second, and the words "reveal" and "see" join the second and third. The four are arranged in a chiasm: (a) "your names are written in heaven"; (b) "and revealed them to babes"; (b) "blessed are the eyes which see what you see"; (a) "what shall I do to inherit eternal life." The new situation, which prophets and kings had longed to see, is heralded by the mission and has resulted in contrasts between those who, even though they represent the wise and understanding of the religious establishment, have rejected the Kingdom, and the disciples, babes, and Samaritans who have responded to its call.

By a vignette (10:38–42) picturing the contrast between Martha's anxiety and Mary's listening to the words of Jesus, Luke marks the transition to a triad of themes: *prayer,* the *Holy Spirit,* and the *Kingdom of God.* The sixth of the seven scenes of Jesus at prayer—the only one in this section—introduces the Lord's Prayer (cf. Mt. 6:9–13), the parable of the friend at midnight, and the saying on asking and receiving (cf. Mt. 7:7–11). The Holy Spirit, the ultimate answer to prayer and the sign of the Kingdom, is by the Beelzebub controversy contrasted with the Satanic spirits whose dominion are now being overthrown. A pathetic picture of a man who, lacking the Holy Spirit, falls victim to repossession by demons and is therefore in a worse condition than before climaxes the passage and leads to the vignette of the woman blessing Jesus' mother.

Jesus' response to this blessing provides the third of three occurrences of the saying on hearing and doing the word of God (cf. 8:15, 21), which in turn introduces another triad: *hearing, seeing,* and *doing.* Again the proclamation of the Kingdom produces contrasts. Ninevah heeded Jonah and the queen of the South came to hear Solomon's wisdom, but though "something greater than Solomon is here," this evil generation does not listen. The contrast between the darkness and light produced by the unsound and sound eye follows immediately and provides the warning which summarizes the meaning of this triad: "Therefore be careful lest the light in you be darkness" (vs. 35). The meaning of this metaphor is further indicated by the simile of the lamp repeated from the previous section (8:16–18) where seeing and hearing are joined to interpret the interpretation of the parable of the sower. In the mission the seed of the word has been sown, the lamp has been placed on the stand, woes to those, therefore, who fail to hear and see. The first of two meals with Pharisees in this section provides the setting for the woes which present by negative contrast the theme of doing (11:37–52). Constructed from Q materials used by Matthew for the first part of his fifth discourse (ch. 23), which Luke has arranged in two groups of three woes against Pharisees and three against lawyers, the woes spell out what is meant by "keeping" the word of God (vs. 28). A change of locale and plotting by the Pharisees to trap Jesus provide the transition to the next triad of themes (12:1–59).

With a picture of a vast multitude trampling one another and the sayings about the leaven of the Pharisees and the hidden being revealed, Luke introduces the third triad: *fear God, be not anxious, and watch.* Again the themes are presented by contrasts. Fear of men is placed in contrast with fear of God whose providential care removes all anxiety and, through the Holy Spirit, extends to those endangered by their acknowledgment of the Son of Man. A request for Jesus to arbitrate an inheritance introduces the parable of the rich fool, which in turn introduces the homily on anxiety from Q (vss. 22–31, cf. Mt. 6:25–33), and the saying on treasures in heaven (vss. 32–34, cf. Mt. 6:19–21). Like Martha's distraction by "many things" (10:41), covetousness is a basic cause of anxiety which a confident trust that seeks first the Kingdom can dispel. With the saying, "Let your loins be girded and your lamps burning" (vs. 35), Luke introduces the first of a series of passages anticipating and leading to his version of the Little Apocalypse (ch. 21). By their emphasis on watching and judgment these passages indicate how he understands the meaning and significance of eschatology for his own time. The phrase "and your lamps burning" recalls Matthew's parable of the wise and foolish virgins indicating that this passage may be related to it. In the paradox of the master seating his servants at the table and serving them, the theme of service as the mark of true leadership is presented in a way remarkably similar to John's story of Jesus washing the disciple's feet. The saying may also have Eucharistic reference. By means of Peter's question, whether that parable is for the disciples "or for all," which recalls the puzzling references to the multitude and the disciples in 12:1, Luke appears to repudiate any idea of an esoteric teaching. At the same time, there may be in the figure of the steward in the following parable (vss. 41–48), a suggestion of the special apostolic responsibilities for faithful leadership. The contrast here is between the watchful and unfaithful servants. In the closing verses of this theme Luke provides another definition of Jesus' ministry. The fire of judgment and divisions are the setting within which his Passion (baptism) is to be understood. His hearers are called upon, therefore, to discern the meaning of "the present time." This generation is being led to the Judge and had better settle with the accuser "on the way" (vss. 37–50).

The grisly report of the Galileans slaughtered by Pilate and the eighteen people killed by the fall of the tower of Siloam introduce the final triad of the series (13:1–30): *repentance, growth,* and *decision.* Reinforced by the parable of the barren fig tree, the ominous warning, "unless you repent you will all likewise perish," sums up the meaning both of Jesus' mission and that of his disciples.

By way of transition to the second theme Luke introduced the first of the two pericopae in this section on the Sabbath controversy, the healing of the woman with the infirmity (vss. 10–17). This story and the healing of the man with dropsy in the next chapter (14:2–6), which are tied together by a doublet of the parable on the care of animals on the Sabbath, balance the two Sabbath pericopae in the previous section (6:1–11). Both stories are used here to show, by the way Jesus silenced his critics, the truth and power of the Gospel. By reference to the rejoicing of the people (vs. 17), Luke once more underscores his distinction between the leaders and the people. Bit by bit he is building his case against the Jewish leadership as the real culprits in the death of Jesus, while at the same time anchoring the beginnings of the Church in the faithful multitudes of Israel who heeded the Gospel and repented. Luke is careful, in picturing the rising opposition to the Gospel, always to keep the reader's attention on the growing numbers of those who became obedient to the Gospel. To this intent he follows immediately the reference to the rejoicing people with two similes of the growth of the Kingdom of God: the mustard seed and the leaven in the meal.

Separated by the editorial note on the journey, the theme of decision (vss. 23–30) forms a climax to the first half of the section. The motif of the closed door, like the lamps at the beginning of the theme of watching (12:35), echoes Matthew's parable of the wise and foolish virgins (25:1–13). Picking up the note of urgency in the concluding pericope of the previous triad, on interpreting the present time (12:54–59), this passage makes clear not only the eschatological meaning of the mission but its universality as well: "Men will come from east and west, and from north and south, and sit at table in the kingdom of God" (vs. 29). By interpreting the eschatology and universality of the mission with the "reversal of fortunes" motif (vs. 30), Luke takes one more step in developing the significance of this motif so basic to his Christology and understanding of sacred history.

The way in which Luke resumes the journey theme (13:31–35) as a transition to the second part of this section has suggested to some interpreters that he intended this passage to be the actual beginning of the journey to Jerusalem. Such an interpretation, however, ignores the preceding travel notes in 10:1, 38, and especially 13:22, as well as the natural sense of the passage, 9:51–56, introducing this section. Nor are we to suppose that, because Herod's territory included Perea, this scene is to be located there. The travel note that follows in 17:11 excludes such a supposition. As we observed earlier, Luke is not concerned with literal geographical data. This passage not only serves as a division in the section, but also allows Luke to interpret further the journey to Jerusalem.

That the Passion must be and that it must take place in Jerusalem are matters of divine necessity. The reference to the prophets, by picking up the theme in the third woe to the lawyers earlier in the section (11:47–52), sets the Passion in the context of the sufferings of Israel's ancient prophets and interprets it as the final rejection by a corrupt official leadership of God's salvation by which the rejections of the Gospel in the Temple and synagogues are to be understood. For this reason the Passion must be in Jerusalem, Israel's ancient capital. Whatever else Jesus' messiahship means, it does not mean a restoration of Israel's political fortunes.

Herod's desire to kill Jesus explains his desire, in the previous section (9:7–9), to see him. As in the phrase, "my hour has not yet come," in the fourth Gospel, Jesus' response to Herod's threat makes the point that the time as well as the place is a matter of divine necessity—Herod's is an empty threat. By these two vignettes the realer is prepared to understand Herod's role in the trial of Jesus. The phrase, "the third day," which Luke prefers to Mark's "after three days" (cf. Mk. 8:31; 9:31; 10:34), belongs to the Resurrection. Its use here is obviously not to be taken literally, but

Jerusalem today, looking across the Kidron Valley. The "Dome of the Rock" at the right of the picture stands on the site of the ancient Temple. (Courtesy of Dr. Richard Schiemann.)

symbolically places the ministry in the same divine timetable as the Resurrection. As a climax to this interpretation of the journey, as well as to the first part of the section, Luke includes the lament over Jerusalem which Matthew uses later in his final discourse just before the Passion (cf. Mt. 23:37–39). Although the cry of blessing did occur in the entry to Jerusalem (19:39), that cry was not the fulfillment of Jesus' words, "I tell you will not see me until you say 'Blessed be he who comes in the name of the Lord!'" (13:35b). Both references are eschatological and point forward to the parousia.

The second half of the section on the journey to Jerusalem manifests a definite change in structure. The majority of Luke's longer, narrative parables occur in it and control its organization. In the opening series (14:1–24) the pericopae, for example, are connected by the theme of meals which leads to a climax in the parable from Q of the unwilling guests (cf. Mt. 22:1–10). The first of these pericopae, the healing of the man with dropsy, repeats the silencing of Jesus' opponents on the question of the Sabbath from the previous chapter, 13:10–17. The second, on seeking seats of honor (vss. 7–11), may be an expansion of Mark 12:39. By itself it is a typical piece of prudential wisdom. As the concluding saying (vs. 11) shows, however, Luke is interested in it because of the way it exemplifies the motif of reversal of fortunes (cf. 1:52). The saying on inviting the poor (vss. 12–14), manifesting again Luke's concern for them, also by its reference to invitations, introduces the Q parable of the unwilling guests. In Matthew this parable emphasizes judgment, but Luke focuses attention on the different responses to the invitation. By placing the parable as a response to one of the guest's pious remarks about the Kingdom of God, Luke raises the question whether the man would really enter the Kingdom when it comes. In contrast to Matthew's version, in which the house was filled, Luke adds, "and still there was room" (vs. 22), which with the addition of verse 23 introduces once more the idea of the mission: "Compel people to come in." A series of sayings and short parables on the cost of discipleship furnishes an appropriate conclusion and transition to the next series.

There follows another series (15:1–17:10) consisting of five major narrative parables interspersed with shorter parabolic sayings, aphorisms, and the like. The first three, the familiar parables of the lost sheep, the lost coin, and the prodigal son, form a trilogy connected by the theme of joy over recovering that which was lost. These parables are not only an effective answer to the objection by Jesus' opponents to his association with tax collectors and sinners but also a vivid expression of Luke's theology of the mission. The parable of the dishonest steward, 16:1–9, the fourth in this series and the first of two parables, peculiar to Luke, in this section which feature unethical persons (cf. the unrighteous judge, 18:1–8), has because of its difficulties generated a variety of interpretations. The two conclusions to the parable, "for the sons of this world are wiser in their own generation than the sons of light," verse 8, and, "make friends for yourselves by means of unrighteous mammon, so that when it fails they may receive you into the eternal habitations," verse 9, suggest that it had been subjected to various interpretations before Luke's use of it.

It may be helpful in understanding this parable to observe that several of its characteristics appear in other parables. There is a similarity between it and Matthew's twin parables of the treasure in the field and the pearl of great price (13:44, 45) in that morally questionable actions are used to illustrate a point concerning the Kingdom. A parallel to the characteristically rabbinic argument from the lesser to the greater suggested in verse 8 can be found not only in the parable of the unrighteous judge, but also in the saying about giving a serpent for a fish or a scorpion for an egg: "If you, then, who are evil, know how to give good gifts to your children, how much more will the heavenly Father give . . ." (11:11–13, cf. Mt. 7:9–11).

Luke's own understanding of the parable is provided in the four short sayings and conclusion which follow (vss. 10–15). The contrasts in the conclusions to the parable between the "sons of this world" and the "sons of light" (vs. 8), and "unrighteous mammon" and "the eternal habitations" (vs. 9) are extended in those between the faithful and dishonest in little and much (vs. 10), the "unrighteous mammon" and "true riches" (vs. 11), "that which is another's" and "that which is your own" (vs. 12), and God and mammon (vs. 13). The point is not unlike that in Matthew's twin parables of the treasure in the field and the pearl of great price: Since this is the way men behave toward the material values they treasure most, how much more seriously ought one to behave toward the eternal value of the Kingdom. In verses 14 and 15 Luke draws his conclusion. The Pharisees, who at the beginning of chapter 15 objected to Jesus' association with the tax collectors and sinners, are now branded as "lovers of money." Although they justify themselves before men, they are "an abomination in the sight of God." With the coming of John the Baptizer the era of the Law and the Prophets has come to a close and now the good news of the Kingdom of God has precipitated a crisis calling for a radical choice, but this does not invalidate the true meaning of the Law. It is rather the true continuity of the Law.

The final parable in the series is the well-known parable of the rich man and Lazarus (16:19–31). Its inclusion here was probably suggested by the reference to the "Pharisees who were lovers of money" (vs. 14). The rich man, therefore, represents a warning to Israel's wealthy leadership, while Lazarus corresponds to the concern for the poor which runs through Luke's Gospel. In this parable the motif of reversal of fortunes comes to dramatic expression (cf. especially 1:53 and 6:20, 24–25). The concluding verse, "If they do not hear Moses and the prophets, neither will they be convinced if someone should rise from the dead," makes it clear that what the Gospel demands is a decision of faith which is willing to renounce all for the sake of the Kingdom. That Luke's two great evidences for the truth of the Gospel, the Scriptures and the Resurrection, cannot compel repentance in those who will not believe, the book of Acts abundantly illustrates.

Another group of four short sayings concludes this series. The ways in which the disciples are addressed here and at the beginning of chapter 16 have the effect of making the obstinacy of the wealthy Pharisees an object lesson for discipleship. The brief parable of the servant doing his duty (17:7–10) forms an effective climax. Unlike Jesus' proud opponents the true disciple can only assume the posture of humble servitude: "When you have done all that is commanded you, say, 'We are unworthy servants; we have only done what was our duty.' "

Each of the last two series of pericopae in this section begins with a healing. By means of the travel note placing Jesus on the border between Galilee and Samaria, Luke establishes the background for the healing of the ten lepers. The function of the story here is revealed in the Samaritan who returned to thank Jesus for his cleansing and is underscored by the question, the homiletical value of which is obvious, "Where are the nine?". Like the parable of the good Samaritan in 10:29–37, this story is an extension of Jesus' condemnation of Jewish exclusivism in his sermon in the synagogue of Nazareth (4:21–27, note especially the reference to Naaman the Syrian leper in vs. 27).

There follows in the remainder of chapter 17, a miniature apocalypse. Anticipating Luke's version (ch. 21) of Mark's Apocalypse (Mk. 13), this passage is comprised mostly (except for one verse, from Mt. 10:39, and two verses from Mk. 13: 15–16) of materials from Q with which Matthew in his Apocalypse has supplemented Mark. Beginning with a variation on the request for a sign of the coming Kingdom (cf. 11:29–30; 21:7, also Mk. 8:11–12 *passim*), and including one of Luke's additional predictions of the Passion, the passage makes two basic points: beware of false signs and be watchful. Both points, the latter of which has received special emphasis twice earlier, 12:35–59 and 13:23–30, anticipate and are repeated in Luke's Apocalypse, 21:5–36. While Luke has deemphasized the immediacy of the parousia, he nevertheless still takes it very seriously and is at pains to prevent it from becoming merely a formal article of faith as it has in some of the later epistles.[108]

That the delay of the parousia has become a problem, however, is evident in the way Luke follows the exhortation to watchfulness with the parable of the unrighteous judge and the persistent widow (18:1–8). The basic point of the parable is identical with that of the friend at midnight in the first half of this section (11:5–8), and probably its original intent was nothing more, but the reference to not losing heart, in Luke's introduction, which is connected in thought with the concluding question, "When the Son of man comes, will he find faith on earth?", and the saying in verses 7 and 8 that God will "vindicate his elect, who cry to him day and night," make it into a lesson in faithful watching in which prayer plays an important part.

The subject of prayer has led to the inclusion of the parable of the Pharisee and the tax collector (vss. 9–14). in which the recurring themes of judgment upon the self-righteous Pharisees and sympathy for the social outcasts reappear. The concluding saying (vs. 14b), which reemphasizes the important motif of the eschatological reversal of fortunes, is a doublet of the conclusion to the parable on seeking seats of honor (14:11). The

---

108. For a significant analysis of this passage with special reference to the question of Luke's eschatology, see Richard H. Hiers, "Why Will They Not Say, 'Lo, Here!' or 'There?'," *JAAR*, Vol. XXXV, No. 4, Dec. 1967, p. 379–384.

parable also states the conditions for entering the Kingdom, as do the two following pericopae on the blessing of the children (vss. 15–17) and the rich ruler (vss. 18–30). Jesus' answer to the ruler's question (vs. 22b) is a repetition of the saying on selling one's possessions and giving alms which occurs in his discourse on anxiety in the first half of this section (12:13–34, see vs. 33a). With the story of the blessing of the children, Luke resumes the thread of Mark's narrative which he follows more or less consistently to the end of Mark.

The conclusion to this series of pericopae (vss. 31–34) forms a minor climax to the section. With this pericope Luke has used all three of Mark's predictions of the Passion (9:22, 44; cf. Mk. 8:31; 9:31–32; 10:32–34), but he has added three of his own: one in the story of the Transfiguration, 9:31; one in response to Herod's threat, 13:32–33; and one in the discussion of signs of the parousia, 17:25. In three terse statements, the conclusion Luke has supplied to this prediction emphasizes the disciples' utter failure to grasp its meaning. Since the remainder of this section functions as a transition to the final sections of the Gospel, this pericope, which points forward to the Passion itself, provides an appropriate climax to the section and introduction to the last series in it. Like a litany the three cries for mercy in the healing of the blind man of Jericho (18:35–43) correspond to the three statements of the disciples' misunderstanding in verse 34. The healing, as in its Markan version (Mk. 10:46–52), is a paradigm of conversion.[109] In the faith of the blind man lies the solution to the blindness of the twelve.

As the journey section closes, three short travel notes, picturing Jesus' approach to and entrance into Jericho and approach to Jerusalem, quicken the pace and introduce each of the three items in this final series. Following the first of these items, the healing of the blind man of Jericho, and standing in the place of Mark's story of James and John seeking the highest seats, is a second paradigm of conversion, the familiar story of Zacchaeus (19:1–10). As saving faith is illustrated in the blind man, so in Zacchaeus are exemplified the renunciation of wealth and concern for the poor appropriate to such faith. Zacchaeus stands in the sharpest possible contrast to the rich ruler in the previous series (18:18–30); indeed the two characters form a striking parallel to those in the parable of the Pharisee and the publican (18:9–14).

The long central section of Luke's Gospel closes with the parable of the pounds, which is probably a variant of Matthew's parable of the talents. A number of differences, not the least of which is the monetary difference between pounds and talents (the latter, estimated to be worth approximately a thousand dollars, is of fifty times greater value than the pound

109. See p. 102.

[Greek *mina*]), have caused some interpreters to question that these parables are from a common source. Because they determine the meaning of the parable in Luke's setting, two of these differences must be noted. In the first of these, Matthew has placed the parable between that of the wise and foolish virgins and the great assize, thereby making it a parable of judgment,[110] while Luke, by connecting it with his journey motif and addressing it to those who "supposed that the kingdom of God was to appear immediately" (vs. 11), has made it a commentary on the delay of the parousia. The second difference consists in Luke's addition in two places of a secondary plot concerning the king's rejection by his citizens. (Is Herod the Great the original of this story? Cf. Mt. 22:6–7.) Thus the parable in Matthew concludes with the punishment of the wicked servant, whereas in Luke it is the rebellious citizens who are punished. The function of the parable here is to counsel faithfulness and patience while waiting for the parousia and to warn of the judgment awaiting those who reject the Kingdom.

The Temple, Passion, and Resurrection, 19:28–24:53   For the story leading up to the Passion Luke follows Mark relatively closely. Among the more obvious changes he has made we may note the omission of the cursing of the fig tree; the question of the greatest commandment, which he has already used in chapter 10; the warning against false Christs, a variant of which appears in chapter 17; and the parable of the absent master, a variant form of which he has used in chapter 12. Luke has added, on the other hand, a lament over Jerusalem (different from the one Matthew has inserted immediately before the Apocalypse, 23:37–39, which Luke has already used in chapter 13) at the end of the story of the entry (19:41–44), and a warning against dissipation and exhortation to watchfulness (21:34–36) which takes the place of Mark's parable of the absent master as the conclusion of the Apocalypse. In a number of details Luke has edited Mark's material to conform to his own purposes and point of view.

In one of the more important of these editorial changes, he has excised the references to Jerusalem and added references to the Temple so as to locate Jesus' ministry, including the apocalyptic discourse, exclusively there (cf. Mk. 11:11, 15, 27; 13:1–3 with Lk. 19:45, 47; 20:1; 21:1–5, 37–38). As we have already noted, Luke distinguishes between Jerusalem and the Temple as though Jesus entered the latter without going through Jerusalem.[111] Jesus' presence in Jerusalem itself is reserved for the Passion. Luke has altered the story of the entry by identifying the shouting multitudes as disciples and by omitting any reference to David. He has made

110. See p. 144.
111. See p. 152.

this procession a climax of his entire story thus far by changing the object of the crowd's praise from the procession itself to "all the mighty works that they had seen" (vs. 37), and by adding to their cry the words, "Peace in heaven and glory in the highest" (vs. 38b). What the angels sang at Jesus' birth has become the cry of the disciples, with the one exception that the promised peace has not yet descended upon earth. The royal messianic symbolism is thus reduced in favor of the response of the people to Jesus' ministry.

By omitting all of the details possible and adding a reference to Jesus "teaching daily in the temple" (vs. 47a), Luke has similarly altered the story of the cleansing of the Temple (vss. 45–48). According to Luke's version of the story, it is at least as much Jesus' teaching as his cleansing of the Temple that provoked the chief priests and scribes to plot his destruction. The point is important to Luke because according to his interpretation the time for the separation of the movement from the Temple had not yet arrived.[112] Not until the martyrdom of Stephan (Acts 7:54–60) was the breach between the Temple and the Church complete.

With the exception of the question of the greatest commandment which he has already used in 10:25–28, Luke follows Mark very consistently in the controversies that intervene between the cleansing of the Temple and the Apocalypse (20:1–21:4). Only a few editorial changes need to be noted. To the conclusion of the parable of the wicked tenants he has added the saying, based on Daniel 2:31–35, "Every one who falls on that stone will be broken to pieces; but when it falls on any one it will crush him" (vs. 18), which gives a hortatory thrust to the parable's emphases on Christology and on the judgment of Israel's leaders (cf. Mk. 12:12). In anticipation of their deliberate misrepresentation of Jesus' answer at the trial before Pilate (23:2), Luke stresses the malice of the scribes and chief priests in asking the question of paying tribute to Caesar (vss. 20–26).

Like the controversies which precede it, the Apocalypse remains quite faithful to its Markan source. Yet several minor changes produce significant differences in meaning. To the saying about relying on the Holy Spirit when answering authorities Luke adds, "for I will give you a mouth and wisdom, which none of your adversaries will be able to withstand or contradict" (vs. 15b). This addition recalls not only the astonishing wisdom of the boy Jesus in the Temple (2:47) but also the way in which Jesus' teaching could silence his opposition (cf. 13:17a; 14:6; 20:26, 40). Thus the reader is prepared for the invincible march of the Gospel in Acts, wherein the hearers confronted by the unassailable truth must either submit in penitent obedience or strike out in angry persecution.

112. Contrast Mark's interpretation, pp. 104–105.

A Gospel for Theophilus

The implied eschatological timetable in Mark 13:10, "And the gospel must first be preached to all nations," Luke has removed. As the conclusion of the Apocalypse shows, Luke's eschatology is no less realistic than the other Synoptists, but he has moved it farther into the future. He also has more interest in the success of the world mission for its own sake and for its apologetic significance.

In a third change Luke has substituted the siege of Jerusalem for Mark's "desolating sacrilege" as the signal for flight from the city (cf. vs. 20 with Mk. 13:14) and substitutes for Mark's shortening of the days the ominous words, "Jerusalem will be trodden down by the Gentiles, until the times of the Gentiles are filled" (cf. vs. 24b with Mk. 13:20). This change corresponds to the lament over Jerusalem (19:41–44). Both passages apparently reflect Luke's knowledge of Titus' conquest of Jerusalem.

"Sheckel of Israel" coined by the revolutionaries during the revolt of A.D. 66–70, which ended in the destruction of Jerusalem. (Courtesy of the Money Museum, National Bank of Detroit.)

That this identification of Mark's warning with what for Luke was a past event removes it from the realm of eschatological signs and turns the entire paragraph into a prediction of judgment on the city (cf. vs. 20b) may be another example of his concern to draw attention away from too much preoccupation with the parousia and focus it instead upon the advancing mission of the Church.[113] The destruction of the city, then, represents divine judgment upon it because of its role in the Passion.

Luke has omitted Mark's warning against false Christs, because he has already included a similar passage in 17:20–24. Similarly, because in the parable of the pounds (19:11–27) and earlier in the watchful servants and the faithful and wise Steward (12:36–46) he has already included parables essentially the same as the conclusion to Mark's Apocalypse, he

113. See Conzelmann, *The Theology of St. Luke,* pp. 134–135.

substitutes a warning against dissipation, drunkenness, and other preoccupations which can distract the believer from faithful watchfulness (cf. vss. 34–35 with Mk. 13:33–37).

Although Luke has been following Mark closely up to this point, when he comes to the Passion story he manifests such independence as to suggest that he has used another source of his own which he has correlated with Mark. The freedom with which he has modified his sources throughout the Gospel makes such a supposition unnecessary. As elsewhere in his Gospel, the changes here reveal Luke's own emphases and concerns. We must therefore observe some of the more important of these changes.

We have already seen that Luke has removed to an earlier chapter (7:36–50) the story of the anointing of Jesus, and conversely he has inserted into the story of the Last Supper the dispute over greatness which in a fuller form Mark used in his version of the journey to Jerusalem (cf. 22:24–27 with Mk. 10:35–44). The flight of the disciples (Mk. 14:26–31) has been omitted, and in its place as an introduction to the prediction of Peter's denial are a saying concerning Satan's designs on Peter and Jesus' admonition which seems to assume the story of the restoration of Peter in John 21:15–17, "When you have turned again, strengthen your brethren." This entire pericope has been moved back from the scene on the Mount of Olives to the end of the Supper and followed immediately with another addition having to do with new preparations for the mission (22:35–38). The Passion is the dividing line between Jesus' mission and that of the Church which is to reach to "the end of the earth" (Acts 1:8b). The disciples are therefore to equip themselves for the long journey.[114] What role the swords play in this saying is impossible now to tell. That two swords are said to be enough indicates that they are not to be taken literally.

In the story of the Supper itself (vss. 14–20) there is the well-known difficult problem of the longer and shorter texts.[115] Neither version corresponds satisfactorily with Mark; the shorter version has the cup-bread sequence found nowhere else, and the longer version simply adds a second cup. What is important to notice is that for Luke the cup is secondary. For him the "breaking of bread" represents the essence of the Eucharist. Thus the feeding of the multitude and the meal at Emmaus become more obvious in Luke's Gospel as antecedents of the Eucharist parallel with the Last Supper. There is no mention of the Garden of Gethsemane, and the exhortation to "Pray that you may not enter into temptation" is repeated at the beginning and end. All these changes place additional emphasis on the

---

114. For a different interpretation, see Conzelmann, *The Theology of St. Luke*, pp. 80–82.

115. On this problem see Joachim Jeremias, *The Eucharistic Words of Jesus*, pp. 87–106.

A Gospel for Theophilus

disciples and point forward to the world mission they are to lead. The Prayer of Agony, however, has an additional emphasis. This is the seventh and final scene of Jesus at prayer. Part of the reason, therefore, for Luke's changes is to strengthen the parallel with the other six scenes. Jesus' prayers serve as preludes to underscore the key events in the story. The Prayer of Agony, then, introduces the climax of the Gospel, the arrest, trial, and Crucifixion. The strengthening angel, which echoes the story of Elijah's flight to Horeb (I Kg. 19:4ff.), as an additional accent on the prayer scene, may have been suggested by the angels in Mark's story of the temptation (Mk. 1:13). The angel and the temptation theme emphasize the significant connection between these two events at the beginning and end of Jesus' ministry.

Perhaps because of the historical difficulties in Mark's account of the night session of the Sanhedrin Luke has omitted it, leaving only Peter's

Inscription bearing the names of Pilate and the Emperor Tiberius, seen here at the door of the museum at Caesarea. It was discovered in 1961 in a theater nearby. (Courtesy of Dr. Richard Schiemann.)

denial and a heightened story of the taunting of Jesus in the high priest's house. His regard for Roman authorities and his apologetic motives may account for the way he has transferred the mocking of Jesus from Pilate's soldiers to those of Herod (cf. 23:11 with Mk. 15:16–20). The trial before Herod, unique to Luke, ends with an acknowledgment of Jesus' innocence (23:15), and Jesus is remanded to Pilate. The reader will recall this story with new perspective when he comes to Paul's hearing before Herod Agrippa II during his trial under a successor of Pilate (Acts 25:13–26:32). In three solemn pronouncements, significantly more em-

The Via Dolorosa (the Way of Sorrow), according to tradition the street along which Jesus was taken to be crucified. (Courtesy of the Israel Government Tourist Office.)

phatic than Mark (cf. 23:14–15 with Mk. 15:5), Pilate declares the innocence of Jesus. The point is clear. In the interest of his apologetic purpose, Luke turns Pilate's hesitation into an evidence of Jesus' innocence. Although Jesus was executed on Roman charges, Luke, like Matthew and Mark, insists that his condemnation was the result of pressure from the high priest and his associates. John concurs and supplies a motive for their action, as we shall see (Jn. 11:47–53), and leaves the reader to recognize the awful irony that the very destruction, for fear of which they demanded Jesus' death, came upon them. In the rebellion of A.D. 66–70 their office, and the Sadducean party which controlled it, disappeared from history.

Once more, in 23:27–31, Luke introduces his apocalyptic theme. The address to the weeping women, closely parallel to 21:23–24, interprets the Crucifixion by setting it in the context of the apocalyptic woes. Jesus' prayer for his executioners, anticipating that of Stephen (Acts 7:60), the story of the penitent thief, and Jesus' confident prayer, "Father, into thy hands I commit my spirit!" replace the cry of dereliction in Mark's version. Along with Luke's omission of the confirmation of Jesus' death (cf. 23:52–53 with Mk. 15:44–45), these changes profoundly alter the mood of the Crucifixion. Luke's apologetic interest is again apparent in the change of the centurion's cry from "Truly this man was a son of God!" to "Certainly this man was innocent!". His interest in the Temple and Jewish institutions reappears in the tearing of the curtain (23:45) and the observance of the Sabbath (23:56b).

Luke stands apart from the other Synoptic writers in locating the entire story of the Resurrection in the area of Jerusalem. After some minor editing of Mark's story, including a full repetition of the prediction of the Passion and the report of the women which anticipate items later in the chapter, he builds his chapter around the journey to Emmaus (24:13–35). This "journey into faith" bears an interesting, and undoubtedly intentional, resemblance to the journey of Saul of Tarsus to Damascus (Acts 9:1–31). The breaking of bread at Emmaus and the eating of fish in the assembly at Jerusalem replace the feeding of the four thousand, which Luke has omitted, and associate the Eucharist with the Resurrection as well as with the Passion. Jesus' homily which follows, "everything written about me . . . must be fulfilled," complements his homily in the Nazareth synagogue with which the story opened, "Today this scripture has been fulfilled in your hearing" (4:21). The function of the homily here is to establish the authority of the Risen Lord for the content of the apostolic sermons in Acts. Similarly, by the command to wait for the "power from on high," the Ascension, and the concluding words, "And they . . . were continually in the temple blessing God," Luke prepares the reader for his second volume, which we know as The Acts of the Apostles.

We have come to the end of our study of the Synoptic Gospels and have seen how each writer in his own way has sought to relate the story of Jesus to the needs of his own church and time. Mark's kaleidoscope, in a rapidly changing series of scenes of Jesus and his disciples, presents a paradigm of discipleship whose essential meaning can be summarized in the words of I Peter 2:21: "For to this you have been called, because Christ also suffered for you, leaving you an example, that you should follow in his steps." The five great discourses of Matthew, like the columns of a synagogue, invite the reader to enter and learn the ultimate Torah from him who is the Ultimate Teacher, Prophet, and Deliverer. Luke has taken up the historian's pen to picture, by means of the popular motif of the travelogue, the triumphant march of the Gospel across the land of Israel and from Jerusalem to Rome, the capital of the world. The first half of his story we have surveyed, but before we examine the second volume we must turn our attention to another, strikingly different Gospel, written by a profound and dramatic theologian who has attempted to penetrate beneath the surface of events to expose the meaning of Jesus for eternal life.

The Structure of Luke

PREFACE—PROLOGUE, 1:1–4:13
Birth of John the Baptizer and Jesus
The baptism and temptation

BEGINNING OF JESUS' MINISTRY, 4:14–44
Rejection in Nazareth—healings in Capernaum

THE PREPARATION OF DISCIPLES, 5:1–9:50
The region of Capernaum—travels in Galilee
The mission of the twelve

THE JOURNEY TO JERUSALEM, 9:51–19:27
The mission of the seventy and teaching
Herod's threat—lament over Jerusalem

THE TEMPLE, PASSION, AND RESURRECTION, 19:28–24:53
The entry and cleansing of the Temple
Controversies and Apocalypse
The Passion and Resurrection

Selected Readings

MARK

Best, Ernest, *The Temptation and the Passion in Mark* (Cambridge: Cambridge University Press, 1965).
Grant, F. C., *The Earliest Gospel* (New York: Abingdon Press, 1943).

Lightfoot, R. M., *The Gospel Message of Mark* (Oxford: At the Clarendon Press, 1952).

Marxsen, Willi, *Mark The Evangelist,* tr. Roy A. Harrisville (New York: Abingdon Press, 1969).

Robinson, J. M., *The Problem of History in Mark* (Naperville, Ill.: Alec R. Allenson, Inc., 1957).

Slusser, Dorothy M. and Gerald H., *The Jesus of Mark's Gospel* (Philadelphia: The Westminster Press, 1967).

COMMENTARIES

Johnson, Sherman, *The Gospel According to St. Mark* (New York: Harper & Row, 1960).

Taylor, Vincent, *The Gospel According to St. Mark* (London: Macmillan and Co., Ltd., 1952).

MATTHEW

Bacon, B. W., *Studies in St. Matthew* (Henry Holt and Co., 1930). An older work which was ahead of its time.

Bornkamm, Günther, Barth, Gerhard, and Held, Heinz Joachim, *Tradition and Interpretation in Matthew* (Philadelphia: The Westminster Press, 1963).

Davies, W. D., *The Setting of the Sermon on the Mount* (Cambridge: At the University Press, 1964).

————, *The Sermon on the Mount* (Cambridge: At the University Press, 1966). An abridgement of the above book.

Kilpatrick, G. D., *The Origin of the Gospel According to St. Matthew* (Oxford: At the Clarendon Press, 1946).

Stendahl, Krister, *The School of St. Matthew* (Philadelphia: Fortress Press, 1968).

LUKE

Cadbury, Henry J., *The Making of Luke-Acts* (New York: The Macmillan Company, 1927).

Conzelmann, Hans, *The Theology of St. Luke,* tr. Geofrey Buswell (New York: Harper & Row, 1960).

Keck, Leander E., Martyn, J. Louis, *Studies in Luke-Acts* (Nashville: Abingdon Press, 1966).

See also the books listed at the end of chapter 4.

THE LIFE OF JESUS

The volumes written on the life of Jesus are virtually innumerable. The following are among the best known and represent some of the most important among the various methods used and conclusions reached, indicating the difficulty of the undertaking.

Bornkamm, Günther, *Jesus of Nazareth,* tr. Irene and Frazer McLuskey with J. M. Robinson (New York: Harper & Row, 1960).

Bultmann, Rudolph, *Jesus and the Word,* tr. L. P. Smith and E. H. Lantero (New York: Charles Scribner's Sons, 1958).

Dibelius, Martin, *Jesus,* tr. C. B. Hedrick and F. C. Grant (Philadelphia: The Westminster Press, 1949).

Enslin, Morton Scott, *The Prophet from Nazareth* (New York: Schoken Books, 1968) .

Goguel, Maurice, *The Life of Jesus,* tr. O. Wyon (New York: The Macmillan Company, 1933; Harper Torchbook, 2 vols., 1960).

Guignebert, Charles, *Jesus,* tr. S. H. Hooke (London: Kegan Paul, Trench, Trubner & Co., 1935).

Saunders, Ernest W., *Jesus in the Gospels* (Englewood Cliffs, N.J.: Prentice-Hall, Inc., 1967).

Stauffer, Ethelbert, *Jesus and His Story,* tr. Richard and Clara Winston (New York: Alfred A. Knopf, 1960).

Taylor, Vincent, *The Life and Ministry of Jesus* (New York: Abingdon Press, 1955).

THE TEACHING OF JESUS AND OTHER SPECIAL SUBJECTS

Branscomb, B. Harvie, *The Teaching of Jesus* (New York: Abingdon Press, 1931).

Boslooper, Thomas, *The Virgin Birth* (Philadelphia: The Westminster Press, 1962).

Dodd, C. H., *The Parables of the Kingdom* (New York: Charles Scribner's Sons, 1961).

Jeremias, Joachim, *The Parables of Jesus,* tr. S. H. Hooke (New York: Charles Scribner's Sons, 1963).

―――, *The Eucharistic Words of Jesus,* tr. A. Ehrhardt (Oxford: Basil Blackwell, 1955).

Manson, T. W., *The Teaching of Jesus* (Cambridge: At the University Press, 1963).

Rowlingson, Donald T., *Jesus, The Religious Ultimate* (New York: The Macmillan Company, 1961).

―――, *The Gospel-Perspective on Jesus Christ* (Philadelphia: The Westminster Press, 1968).

Chapter Three

That You May Have Life
The Fourth Gospel

Now Jesus did many other signs in the presence of the disciples, which are not written in this book; but these are written that you may believe that Jesus is the Christ, the Son of God, and that believing you may have life in his name. . . . John 20:30-31.

The Gospel of John presents us with some of the most difficult problems to be found in the New Testament. Because of its position among the documents of the New Testament, questions of its origins, its relationship, on the one hand, to the Synoptic Gospels, and, on the other, to the burgeoning Christian movement become the more pressing. One of the most explicitly theological works and the fourth longest book in the New Testament, it stands at the end of the four Gospels as a climax and conclusion. The ancient Fathers of the Church, as we have seen,[1] were well aware of John's uniqueness, and, placing the highest value upon it, regarded it as the summation of the truth about Jesus. Its fascination for modern scholars is indicated by the voluminous literature its study over the last century and more has produced.

1. A Spiritual Gospel

We have already noted some of the striking differences in order and

1. See pp. 40–43.

content between John and the Synoptics.[2] There are others no less important which we must now consider.

JOHN AND THE SYNOPTIC GOSPELS

In the teaching of Jesus the parables have given way to a few complex allegories, and the short pungent aphorisms have become extended and involved discourses. The patterns of the discourses are formed by the moral dualism between good and evil, life and death, light and darkness, and the like, familiar to us from the Wisdom Literature. Even where a short saying, whether actually parallel to Synoptic material or of a similar type, does occur in John it becomes a text for an expanded homiletical treatment. The person of Jesus and his relation to the Father completely dominate the teaching. There are no beatitudes, no commands to love our enemies, turn the other cheek, no exhortations to deeds of mercy. Love within the fellowship takes the place of love of neighbor. The dialogues between Jesus and his opponents are sharpened and interlocked with the discourses. Although less easily catalogued, there are also wide and important differences in the themes and content of Jesus' teaching.

Although fewer in number, the miracles in John are more prominent and impressive than in the Synoptics. This prominence is due in part to the way in which the miracles provide the setting, occasions, and subject matter for the long discourses which follow. Although several of them have sufficient points of contact with the Synoptic accounts to warrant the assumption that they are variants of the same stories (cf. 4:46–54 with Lk. 7:2–10; Mt. 8:5–13), others, such as the turning water into wine at the wedding at Cana, are not only unique to John but are of a different caliber. Whereas in the Synoptics the emphasis falls on the compassion displayed in the act of healing and on the one healed, in John the glorification of the healer comes to the fore.

It is impossible for us, of course, to conceive what our picture of Jesus would be like if we had only the fourth Gospel as our source. Our knowledge of the other Gospels inevitably colors our reading of John more than we can appreciate. Undoubtedly, also, the author expected some knowledge of the tradition, whether of our Synoptic Gospels or other sources, on the part of his readers.[3] It will be profitable, nevertheless, to attempt some comparisons between the picture of Jesus in John and in the other Gospels. For one thing, there would be a question whether Jesus was a native of Judea, if not Jerusalem, or of Galilee. Of the 866 verses in John at least 661 of them have their setting in Judea or Trans-Jordan, leaving only slightly more than one fourth of the Gospel concerned with Galilee and

2. See pp. 43–45. For a valuable comparison see Donald T. Rowlingson, *Introduction to New Testament Study,* pp. 73–78.
3. Cf. Morton Scott Enslin, *Christian Beginnings,* p. 447.

Samaria. Several passages seem to imply that Jesus was a native of Judea. The familiar saying about a prophet having no honor in his own country, for example, is used by John to explain Jesus' move to Galilee (4:43–45, cf. vs. 54). Jesus' baptizing activity took place "in the land of Judea" (3:22, cf. 10:40 ;11:54), and his departure to Galilee in verse 4:3 hardly sounds as though he were returning home (cf. 7:1). Yet in several other verses Jesus is explicitly identified with Galilee. He is called "Jesus of Nazareth" in 1:45–46; 18:5, 7. Except, of course, at the Crucifixion it is in Galilee that his family meets him (2:1, 12; 6:42; 7:3–10). That he was a Galilean is indicated in the question, "Is the Christ to come from Galilee?" (7:41, cf. vs. 27 and 52). From 7:42 the reader would conclude that Jesus was definitely not born in Bethlehem.

If we had only the fourth Gospel, furthermore, our picture of the disciples and their role in the story of Jesus would be quite vague. Although the word "disciple" occurs more often in John than in any of the Synoptics (seventy-nine times compared with seventy-three times in Matthew, forty-seven times in Mark, and thirty-eight times in Luke), only six of the names familiar to us from the other Gospels appear in this one: Simon (Peter), Andrew, Philip, Thomas, Judas (not Iscariot), and Judas the betrayer. The phrase "the sons of Zebedee" occurs in 21:2, but although interpreters have often supposed that the elusive "beloved disciple" (13:23, *passim*), was one of them, their names are not given. Only in the post-Resurrection story of the miraculous catch of fish, 21:1–8, is there an indication that any of them were fishermen. As we shall see, this chapter is probably a later addition.

"The Twelve" are mentioned only in two places: in connection with Peter's confession, 6:66–71, and the post-Resurrection scene in 20:24ff., but they are not sent out on a mission, nor are there any scenes with Jesus instructing them. Jesus is found either in discussion with an individual, such as Nicodemus or the woman at the well in Samaria, or addressing the crowds of the Jews. We hear, on the other hand, of other names peculiar to John, such as Nathanael and Nicodemus. Lazarus, instead of being a character in a parable (Lk. 16:19–31), is here a particularly close friend of Jesus. We hear, too, of secret disciples who include Nicodemus and Joseph of Arimathea (12:42–43; 19:38–42; cf. 3:1ff., 7:50ff.). While chapter 6 reads as though the disciples are at home in the Galilean scenes, 7:3 implies that they were Judeans and had remained there while Jesus was in Galilee. Except for the post-Resurrection scene in 21:1ff., there are only two brief notices in one sequence of the Sea of Galilee (6:1, 15–25, eleven verses in all).

Although we learn of Joseph in 6:42 and read of Jesus' mother in three settings (2:1–12; 6:42; 19:25–27), were John our only Gospel we would not know her name. There are, however, three other women in the

Gospel who bear the name of Mary (11:1; 19:25).[4] Although the phrase "We were not born of fornication" (8:41) may be an oblique reference to the calumny occasioned by the Christian doctrine of the Virgin Birth, we would not suspect it, nor would we have the wonderful stories of Jesus' birth, nor the article in the Apostles' Creed, "conceived by the Holy Ghost and born of the Virgin Mary." Instead, we would have only the grand poem of the divine preexistent Logos, who is the light and life of the world and who "became flesh and dwelt among us."

There would also be some question whether Jesus was a Jew. The sustained polemic against "the Jews" throughout the Gospel have led some interpreters to call John the most anti-Semitic book in the New Testament. This polemic, furthermore, is not simply against perverse Jewish leaders but has the effect of a blanket indictment of the nation. Certainly such remarks as "Is it not written in your law" (10:34; cf. "Your father Abraham," 8:56; and "Their law," 15:25) would appear to place Jesus outside of Judaism. Yet his name is a Greek transliteration of the great Hebrew name Joshua. At the opening of the Gospel he is identified as the Jewish Messiah (1:41, cf. 4:25; 7:31, 41f.; 10:24–25), the "Son of Man" (1:51; cf. 3:13f.; 5:27; 6:27, 53, 62; 8:28; 9:35; 12:23, 34; 13:31), and associated with Moses (1:17, 45; 5:39–47). His attention to the Jewish feasts is one of the distinctive characteristics of this Gospel's picture of him. He was called a Jew by the woman of Samaria (4:9) and could declare to her that "salvation is of the Jews" (4:22b). The statement occurs, however, in a context that goes beyond both Judaism and the Samaritans: "neither on this mountain nor in Jerusalem will you worship the Father." Finally, in the bitter irony of Pilate's question, "Your own nation and the chief priests have handed you over to me; what have you done?" (18:35), Jesus is explicitly identified as a Jew (cf. 19:19).

Instead of the preaching, teaching, healing ministry of Jesus, familiar to us from the Synoptics, if John were our only Gospel we would have a few spectacular signs, John's announcement of "the Lamb of God, who takes away the sin of the world" (1:29), a few conversations with individuals, largely concerned with the necessity of faith in him, and a running polemic with his Jewish opponents over their diabolical rejection of him. The proclamation of the Kingdom of God would give place to having eternal life; the call to repentance and believing the Gospel would become believing in him. Instead of the compelling mood of compassion, which in the Synoptics furnishes the motive for the healings, we would have only the picture of the mighty wonder-worker who explains, in answer to his

---

4. It is barely possible to make 19:25 yield the name Mary for Jesus' mother and to leave her sister nameless. But would it occur to the interpreter to do so if the other Gospels had not supplied that information? See C. K. Barrett, *The Gospel According to St. John*, p. 458.

disciples' question, that the blind man whom he is about to heal was not born that way because of sin "but that the works of God might be manifest in him" (9:3). Tender scenes such as the blessing of the children (Mk. 10:13–16) would be out of place in a Gospel in which Jesus deliberately delays his arrival to make certain that his friend Lazarus will be dead in order that he might show by raising Lazarus from the dead that he is "the resurrection and the life" (11:25; cf. vss. 4, 6; 14:15). Rather than rebuking the crowds for seeking signs from him (cf. Mk. 8:11ff.), Jesus complains that in their interest in food they ignore the signs (6:2, 6 but cf. 4:48). Far from being "sent only to the lost sheep of the house of Israel" (Mt. 15:24), the Johannine Christ addresses himself to the world (the word occurs in John more than eighty times).

Were we dependent upon John for our information, our picture of Jesus' ministry would be even more sketchy than it is. Although six Jewish feasts are mentioned, including three Passovers requiring a ministry of more than two years (2:13; 5:1; 6:4; 7:2; 10:22; 11:55, *passim*), there are fewer actual episodes. There is, in fact, little real development of the narrative in John. Rather, the Gospel appears to be constructed around a series of themes, more or less self-contained, for which the narratives provide the setting and starting point. There is, on the other hand, more emphasis on the violence of Jesus' opposition. Twice they attempt to stone him (8:59; 10:31); and in a dozen other passages plots to do away with Jesus are kept before the reader (5:18; 7:1, 19, 25, 30, 32, 44; 8:37, 40; 10:39; 11:53, 57).

In spite of the heavy emphasis on the Eucharist especially in the sixth chapter, if we had only John's Gospel we would learn of the institution of the Lord's Supper only from Paul (I Cor. 11:23–26). Whether the parenthetical explanation in 4:2, that only Jesus' disciples did the baptizing, be regarded as original or a gloss, we would probably assume without much question what the Synoptic Gospels ignore if not virtually deny (cf. Mk. 1:8, parallels): that Jesus included as a part of his ministry a baptism similar to that of John the Baptizer (3:22, 4:1). A number of commentators discuss the possibility that Jesus collaborated with John the Baptizer at an early time in his ministry. That they inevitably limit this activity to a period before the story begins in the Synoptics is an example of the influence of the latter on the interpretation of the fourth Gospel.[5]

Beyond these contrasts in order and content between John and the Synoptics is a difference in the character of the Gospel, which, although less easy to describe or illustrate, is even more important. John stands among the Gospels at the opposite end of the continuum from Mark. If Mark is preoccupied with the activities of Jesus, mentioning his teachings

5. Cf. Eusebius' theory that John was writing about an earlier period than the other Gospels, pp. 40–41.

but seldom pausing to include them, John reverses the matter. By several references to "many signs" and "works" John calls attention to Jesus' activities (2:23; 3:2; 5:20, 36; 6:1; 7:3ff., 31; 9:16; 10:25, 38, 41; 11:47; 12:37; 14:12; 15:24; 20:30), but he recounts only three healings. The whole structure of the Gospel, on the other hand, is controlled by the discourses and dialogues which give it the character of a theological treatise. It is this quality which led Clement of Alexandria to call it a "spiritual Gospel."[6] It is this quality, too, with which the modern interpreter must deal if he is to make any progress in understanding it. The nature of the relation of the discourses to the slender thread of narrative indicates clearly that it was written for the sake of the discourses. It is an interpretive document written for those who are presumed to be already familiar with the external facts about Jesus.

THE BACKGROUND OF THE GOSPEL

Such observations as those we have made concerning the uniqueness of John among the Gospels raise the question of the milieu out of which it came. The question is difficult and has no certain answer. There are, in fact, at this point two related questions: the conceptual world of the author himself and that of his anticipated readers.

When the debate over the authorship of the fourth Gospel, which had absorbed so much scholarly energies during the nineteenth century and early years of this century, had subsided,[7] and the attempt to identify the author as the son of Zebedee was generally abandoned, scholars began to reexamine the Hellenistic elements. The word *Logos* in the opening line has long intrigued interpreters of John. The term, usually translated "Word," has a complex history and is capable of many subtle shades of meaning. It was used in early Greek philosophy of the rational process, and thus Plato used it to mean reason. The Stoics were fond of the term and in their usage it referred, in a way similar to the word "wisdom" in the late Hebrew Wisdom Literature, to the rational order behind the phenomenal world which sustains it and directs the course of its history.[8]

It was the Alexandrian Jewish philosopher Philo, however, who provided the most promising source for the term as it appears in John. In his attempt to wed Greek philosophy and Mosaic religion, Philo made extensive use of the term *logos* which for him represented a personification of divine wisdom and the "word of Yahweh." This personification became the intermediary between God and his world. The affinity between this concept and the creative logos in the Gospel is apparent. When further character-

---

6. See p. 42.
7. For a particularly important account of that debate see B. W. Bacon, *The Fourth Gospel in Research and Debate*. Also William Sanday, *The Criticism of the Fourth Gospel* (New York: Charles Scribner's Sons, 1905).
8. See pp. 273–274.

istics of the Gospel congenial to Philonic thought, such as allegorizations, a pervading dualism, numerous other terms in common, and the like, were considered John's origins in a Hellenistic Christian environment seemed established.[9] Whether directly or through the influence of Philo's writings, Platonic and Stoic terms and categories had through the fourth Gospel found entrance into the new Faith to further the Hellenization of Christianity. That the Gospel was presumed to have been written in Ephesus, where Apollos of Alexandria is first introduced (Acts 18:24ff.), seemed to add weight to this conclusion. Literary analysis of the prologue, furthermore, revealed fragments of a poem which the author used as the starting point of his Gospel. Whether this "Logos Hymn" was originally Christian or pre-Christian, it was saturated with Greek ideas and established the Greek character of the Gospel.

Further research into the religions of the Levant, however, soon revealed that Hellenism had a far larger component of oriental elements than had been supposed.[10] Particularly from Iranian sources the philosophical thought of the first century had become modified until it was more religious than philosophical. The discovery in the early years of this century of several ancient texts has thrown considerable light on the character of the religious environment of John's world. A group of ancient Christian hymns known as the *Odes of Solomon,* a collection of pagan religious literature assembled around the prophetic figure of one known as the Thrice Greatest Hermes and therefore known as the Hermetic literature, and a body of sacred writings of an obscure ancient sect still surviving in Iraq, known as the Mandaeans who claim John the Baptizer as their founder, have especially attracted the attention of Johannine scholars.[11] Although the dates of these documents and the antiquity of the traditions back of some of them are problematical, they do represent parallel developments of ancient traditions which provide important insights into the diversity of religious ideas in the Levant in the first century. Significant similarities between these documents and second-century Gnosticism, on the one hand, and the fourth Gospel, on the other, turned the search for the milieu of the latter in the direction of Gnostic influences.[12] Bultmann,

9. See James Moffatt, *Introduction to the Literature of the New Testament,* pp. 522–530.
10. See p. 271. See Benjamin W. Bacon, *The Gospel of the Hellenists* (New York: Henry Holt and Company, 1933), pp. 74–110.
11. On the Odes of Solomon see the article by J. Rendel Harris, who discovered and published them, in Schaff-Herzog, *Encyclopedia of Religious Knowledge* (New York: Funk and Wagnalls Company, 1908), Vol. X, pp. 497–498. On the Hermetic literature and the Mandaean texts see C. H. Dodd, *The Interpretation of the Fourth Gospel* (Cambridge: At the University Press, 1965), pp. 10–53 and 115–130. Also on the latter see F. C. Burkitt's important review of S. A. Pallis, *Mandaean Studies* (Milford, London, 1916) in JTS, April, 1928, pp. 226–235.
12. On Gnosticism see pp. 271–272.

in particular, believes that a pre-Christian oriental Gnosticism is disclosed by these materials whose influence is to be found in Judaism, especially the Wisdom Literature, in the Dead Sea documents, and which continued in the sectarian followers of John the Baptizer who eventually became the Mandaeans.

Working from this premise, Bultmann has reconstructed a Gnostic Redeemer Myth which he believes John appropriated, with suitable modifications, as the framework of his own Christology. It is this working hypothesis which underlies his massive commentary on John.[13] The myth consists in a preexistent divine being who enters the evil world to reveal to men their true heavenly origins and thus to bring them redemption. The evidence of this myth in a pre-Christian form is slender and highly subjective. Consequently, the hypothesis has not found wide acceptance. That the Gnosticism known to us from second-century Christian heresies had its roots in oriental as well as Greek ideas which were mingled in the syncretism of the first century is beyond question. To push a definite, identifiable movement back that far, however, requires such modifications of the definition of Gnosticism as to make the term relatively useless. Many scholars prefer, therefore, to speak of these syncretisms as pre-Gnostic. The metaphysical dualism, for example, which is so essential to the Gnostic system, is absent not only in John but in the literature of Judaism supposedly influenced by oriental Gnosticism. In several instances where similarities do appear, furthermore, the probabilities are at least as great that the influence has moved in the other direction. That John was aware of prophetic and baptizing cults which had grown up in the East, and that he deliberately chose his language at times to refute them is, on the other hand, very likely.[14]

In contrast to Bultmann, who found the most important clues to the background of the Gospel in the Mandaean texts and the *Odes of Solomon,* C. H. Dodd has given more attention to the Hermetic literature and to Philo. Although the Hermetic documents are admittedly not as old as John, they represent a high level of Greek philosophical religion which, as Dodd demonstrates at length, has many significant similarities to the fourth Gospel, and are therefore parallel developments from a common background. John, then, is to be read against a background made up of components of rabbinic Judaism and "the higher religion of Hellenism."[15] With some modifications, Dodd's position represents a return to older

---

13. *Das Evangelium des Johannes* (Göttingen: Vandenhoeck, [1941], 1959). See also *Theology of the New Testament,* tr. Kendrick Grobel (New York: Charles Scribner's Sons, 1965), I, pp. 164–183, II, 3–92.
14. For an excellent review of the modern history of Johannine studies see Reginald H. Fuller, *The New Testament in Current Study,* pp. 101–132; also Raymond E. Brown, S.S., *The Gospel According to John* (i-xii), *The Anchor Bible* (Garden City, N.Y.: Doubleday & Company, Inc., 1966), pp. LII–LXX.
15. *The Interpretation of the Fourth Gospel,* pp. 10–130.

interpretations based on the assumption that Platonism and Stoicism provide the background for Johannine language and thought-forms. Bultmann and Dodd represent two polarities in the interpretation of John, and their comprehensive works on the Gospel still dominate its study.[16]

More recently, studies in the Dead Sea documents have broadened dramatically our knowledge of Palestinian Judaism. Terms and ideas once supposed to be peculiar to Hellenistic thought are found in the vocabulary of the Scrolls. Because of this discovery and the numerous Jewish elements in the Gospel—elements which in the concern with Hellenism are sometimes overlooked—some interpreters place John in a clearly Jewish setting. J. A. T. Robinson, for example, believes it to be "an appeal to those *outside* the Church, to win to the faith that Greek-speaking Diaspora Judaism to which the author now finds himself belonging as a result (we may surmise) of the greatest dispersion of all, which has swept from Judea Church and Synagogue alike."[17]

Although not many scholars would narrow the scope and purpose of John quite so much—his explanations of Jewish feasts and customs seem to anticipate gentile readers—the suggestion does call for a reconsideration of the question. Discussions of the purpose of the author have usually begun with the closing words of the body of the Gospel, "but these are written that you may have life in his name" (20:31). Whether, on the basis of the language and background of the Gospel, it is assumed to be addressed to Jewish or pagan readers, these closing words seem clearly to show the purpose to be the winning of converts. When the several features of the book, including the sustained polemic which runs through its central chapters, are taken into account, however, the words "that you may believe" can hardly have so simple a meaning. The word "believe" in the New Testament generally has a more complex meaning than intellectual assent to a body of ideas. It carried with it a strong element of existential commitment, and especially in the later books of the New Testament (Hebrews, for example), it involves faithful endurance and perseverance in the face of the pressures of heresies, ostracism, and persecution. Jesus' question to the twelve, "Will you also go away?" in 6:67 and Peter's response, for instance, exemplify this meaning of the term, and suggest that at least one important purpose of John was, by defining and clarifying the challenge of the Faith, to forestall defections from the Church. The material in the farewell discourse, chapters 14–16, are manifestly more edifactory than evangelical. Whether to Diaspora Judaism,[18] gentiles

16. For an illuminating discussion of these alternatives in the interpretation of John see Rudolf Bultmann's review of C. H. Dodd's work, *The Interpretation of the Fourth Gospel*, in New Testament Studies 1 (1954–55), pp. 77–91, translated by W. B. Robinson and reprinted in HDB, Jan. 1963, pp. 9–22.

17. *Twelve New Testament Studies*, p. 125. See pp. 107–125 also ch. VII, pp. 94–106.

18. On the diaspora, see pp. 274–275.

in the Hellenistic world, or those under the influence of competing and heretical movements such as incipient Gnosticism or followers of John the Baptizer, John's Gospel was addressed to Christians.

Ernst Käsemann has attempted to identify the purpose of John by locating its author in a more or less remote area out of touch with the mainstream of the Church's developing institutionalism (i.e., "early catholicism").[19] The Gospel, on this account, is a protest against the sterility of the developing orthodoxy, and the danger of setting the institutional Church in the place of the true Shepherd and his fellowship. In doing this, however, the author's reinterpretation of the Gospel carries him to the borders of heresy, into a "naive docetism," which explains the appeal his work had for the later Gnostics.

In a strikingly different approach to the Gospel, J. Louis Martyn has attempted to locate its milieu in the antagonism that developed between Synagogue and Church.[20] Beginning with the story in chapter 9 of the healing of the man born blind, he finds that the emphasis, unlike that in the miracle stories in the Synoptic Gospels, falls on the one healed rather than on the healer. This emphasis, furthermore, takes the form of a struggle with the Jewish authorities which reaches its climax in the former blind man's excommunication. The story, Martyn concludes, is a drama on two levels: (1) an episode in Jesus' earthly ministry and (2) an experience in John's own city (Alexandria?).[21] This feature of the Gospel is not unlike the paradigmatic use of the tradition which we observed already developing in Mark. The precipitating cause of the crisis Martyn finds in the twelfth benediction, which was rewritten by the Jamnia scholars under the leadership of Rabban Gamaliel II to include a curse upon the Christians (Nazarenes) and delivered to the local synagogue by a representative. By requiring a member of the synagogue suspected of being a secret Christian to "stand before the ark" to lead the congregation in the benedictions, the leaders could make him expose himself. Since he would be calling a curse upon himself if he were guilty, the new prayer would betray him. Martyn finds the problems arising from this crisis in John's Church to lie back of the entire Gospel.

If the fourth Gospel is to be associated with the reworded twelfth benediction, the question of its date can be fixed with some confidence within Gamaliel's term of office (80–115).[22] Although, as we have observed, the Dead Sea Scrolls have shown that the language and terminology of John are not so alien to Palestinian Judaism as was once supposed and therefore

19. *The Testament of Jesus,* tr. Gerhard Krodel (Philadelphia: Fortress Press, 1968), see especially pp. 39ff.
20. *History and Theology in the Fourth Gospel* (New York: Harper & Row, 1968).
21. *History and Theology in the Fourth Gospel,* p. 58, n. 94.
22. On the date of John see p. 79. See Martyn, *History and Theology in the Fourth Gospel,* pp. 34–36.

are no barrier to an early date, several further considerations make the location of the Gospel in this later period most likely. Whereas in Acts, for example, the dispute with the Synagogue and Judaism, although intense, is open to such a degree that debate is still worthwhile, in John the break between the two is complete. Similarly, the question of the believer's relationship to the Law, which so concerned Paul and was still an issue for Matthew and Luke, has now become a matter external to Christianity (e.g., the phrase, "your law" in Jn. 10:34). The gentile mission, which in the Synoptics is justified from a Jewish perspective and from Israel's Scriptures, is in John no longer an issue.[23] Although the expectation of the eschaton still occupies a place in the thought of the fourth Gospel, it has receded to the periphery as a formal concept not unlike that found in the Pastoral Epistles.[24] Along with references to such phenomena as secret disciples, these observations present a picture of the Church altogether plausible at the end of the first century but hard to imagine much earlier.

It should be apparent by now that the quest for the milieu of John is full of difficulties. In the various theories that have sought to solve the problem, the starting point within the Gospel has exercised a determining influence. For those who have started their search with the prologue, the Logos has usually led to a Hellenistic background of one sort or another. Some investigators, moving farther into the prologue to the words, "the Word (Logos) became flesh and dwelt among us" (1:14a), have found the key to John in an anti-Gnostic Christology. Ernst Käsemann, as we have seen, begins with the great prayer in chapter 17, which he regards as a farewell address.[25] J. Louis Martyn takes his departure from the healing of the blind man in chapter 9. In a very valuable study of the rabbinic elements in the Gospel, Peder Borgen begins with the homily on the bread from heaven in 6:31–58.[26] B. W. Bacon, a generation earlier, found the story of the Samaritan woman in 4:4–42 directing his attention to the history of the Church in Samaria within which he found his answer to the question of the background of the Gospel.[27]

The persistent difficulties in the study of John are revealed by the way in which each of these approaches, after solving the problems in the area with which they begin, runs into difficulty when it is carried out in the remainder of the Gospel. Often the hypothesis has to be imposed upon the material in a manifest *tour de force,* and some principle has to be devised

---

23. Martyn, *History and Theology in the Fourth Gospel*, p. 46, n. 77.
24. See pp. 408–411.
25. *The Testament of Jesus*, p. 4. For a good statement of the difficulties encountered by various approaches to the "Johannine Problem" see James L. Price, "The Search for the Theology of the Fourth Evangelist," *JAAR*, Vol. XXXV, March, 1967, pp. 3–15.
26. *Bread from Heaven.* Cf. Sydney Temple, "A Key to the Composition of the Fourth Gospel," *JBL*, Vol. LXXX, Sept. 1961, pp. 220–232.
27. *The Gospel of the Hellenists*, chs. VIII–XI.

for excluding troublesome exceptions as later redactions. At times the difficulties have been simply ignored, or at least minimized. Probably we shall never know many elements of the complex history of the process which brought this intriguing work into being. The very complexity of the problem should, perhaps, warn us against attempting to locate John in any one setting. Yet we must not reduce the Gospel to a melange of disparate materials. There is a lofty unity about it which, like the seamless robe of Jesus (19:23–24), is not to be torn asunder. The theological quest which the Gospel pursues is likewise profound. Not without reason its portrait of Jesus has been called a painting in oils. Since our interest in the fourth Gospel is primarily in its position in the literature that makes up the Canon, the historical difficulties it presents are not fatal to our purpose. It is instructive to observe the way in which Christians of many ages, in many and varied circumstances, have turned to this Gospel to find a portrait of Christ which, however it may differ from that in the mind of the author, nevertheless carries with it its own validation. Not alone for its emphasis on the Spirit is it justly called "a Spiritual Gospel."

2. Sources, Transpositions, and Redactions

If John's Gospel was written as late as we have suggested, and the author cannot have been an eyewitness to the life of Jesus, the question of his sources of information demands our special attention. The problem becomes more acute because of wide differences between John and the Synoptic Gospels of a kind that will not permit John's material to be dovetailed into the Synoptic framework or vice versa. Although, as in the Synoptics, religious and theological interests have controlled its composition so that matters of chronology and the like are secondary, the fourth Gospel differs from the others at several points in such a way as to suggest that it contains historical information which may be more accurate than the corresponding material in the Synoptics.[28]

THE QUEST FOR SOURCES

The comparison of John with the Synoptic Gospels sends the quest for sources in two directions: first, the possibility that one or more of them may have served as a source for John; and second, the possibility of detecting sources independent of those used by the Synoptic authors. The obvious place to begin is with the Synoptic sources.

Did John Know the Synoptic Gospels?   Points of similarity between John and material peculiar to Matthew are so few and ambiguous that it is gen-

28. See Wilbert F. Howard, *The Fourth Gospel in Recent Criticism* (London: The Epworth Press, 1945), pp. 146–157.

erally assumed that John did not know Matthew (but cf. Jn. 4:46–54 with Mt. 8:5–13 and Lk. 7:1–10, where the word "servant," Greek: *pais,* is capable of meaning "son" as in John whereas Luke's word "slave" is not). The question of John's use of the Synoptics, therefore, usually focuses on Mark and Luke. Insofar as source theories are concerned, these contacts with Luke consist mostly in a few items such as coincidences of names.[29] The question, therefore, reduces itself principally to the relationship between John and Mark. The relevant passages occur in three sections of both Gospels: events surrounding the beginning of Jesus' ministry, a cluster of four episodes in the middle, and events associated with the Passion and Resurrection. The following table gives the points of similarity in question:

Pericopae Common to John and the Synoptics

I. John the Baptizer as the precursor of Jesus	John 1:19–34	Mark 1:2–11 (cf. 8:27–29)
Cleansing of the Temple	John 2:13–21	————
* (Healing of centurion's son)	(John 4:46–54	(Luke 7:2–10)
II. Feeding the 5,000	John 6:1–14	Mark 6:30–31, 35–44
Walking on the water	John 6:16–21	Mark 6:45–53
Peter's confession	John 6:66–71	Mark 8:27–33
Healing of the blind man	John 9:1–7	Mark 8:22–26
III. Anointing at Bethany	John 12:1–8	Mark 14:1–9
Triumphal entry	John 12:12–19	Mark 11:1–10
Cleansing of the Temple	————	Mark 11:11, 15–19
The Last Supper	John 13:1–4 18, 21–30, 36–38	Mark 14:12, 17–21, 27–31
The Passion and Resurrection	John 18–1–13, 15–19:30, 38–42, 20:1–10	Mark 14:43–54 60–63, 66–72; 15:1–46; 16:1–8
(The miraculous catch of fish)	John 21:1–8	(Luke 5:1–11)
(The restoration of Peter)	(John 21:15– 19	(Luke 22:31–32)

* Lukan parallels are enclosed in parentheses. Lines indicate important transpositions of order. There are several minor transpositions in details of the Passion story. Some scholars would also include the healing of the impotent man, John 5:2–9; Mark 2:1–12.

29. On similarities between Luke and John beyond the question of literary dependence, see pp. 157–159.

Within these parallels there are several shorter phrases in common between Mark and John whose verbal correspondence appears to reinforce the impression that John is using Mark as a source. There are, in addition, several sayings familiar to us from the Synoptics which are found also in John but in different settings. "That a prophet has no honor in his own country" occurs, for example, in John 4:44 and Mark 6:4; the saying about losing and saving one's life in Mark 8:35 occurs with some variations in John 12:25; a variant of the saying about a disciple being above his teacher in Matthew 10:24 and Luke 6:40 appears twice in John 13:16 and 15:20; and the saying, "he who receives any one whom I send receives me" in John 13:20 and Mark 9:37b. From this data the older scholars concluded that John's principal, if not his only, sources were Mark and Luke.[30]

The several episodes unique to John, the major differences between it and the Synoptics not only in chronology but in its entire outlook, and with a few notable exceptions, the insignificant amount of verbal agreements within the parallels, nevertheless, leave the theory of John's dependence on any of the Synoptics insecure. It is not surprising, then, that a small book published by P. Gardner-Smith in 1938, which challenged the thesis that John had any acquaintance with the other Gospels, has exerted an increasing influence on the discussion of Johannine sources to the present time.[31] There are, of course, explanations for a number of the divergencies in John. The long discourses, like the speeches in Acts,[32] are interpretive. Their homiletical quality may, in fact, suggest their origin in early Christian sermons and identify the author as a prophet. In this respect John might be regarded a commentary on the Synoptics.[33] At several points the fourth Gospel appears deliberately to be correcting the Synoptic tradition. Jesus' rebuke of "sign seekers" in Mark 8:11, for instance, is reversed in John 6:26. Some interpreters see in John's reference to Jesus as Joseph's son, 6:42 (1:45), an attempt to avoid the slander which Mark had invited by referring only to Jesus' mother (3:33, cf. Mt. 13:55; Lk. 4:22). In John's version of Peter's confession, 6:66–71, Judas Iscariot is called a devil, which may be a correction of Mark's version in which Peter is called Satan (8:33). Similarly, the prayer in Gethsemane, Mark 14:35–36, appears to be corrected in Jesus' announced readiness to accept his Passion in 12:27 and 18:11; as Mark's story of Simon of Cyrene, 15:21, seems to be contradicted in 19:17.

30. B. H. Streeter, *The Four Gospels,* pp. 395–426; and W. F. Howard, *The Fourth Gospel in Recent Criticism,* pp. 218, 267–268.
31. *Saint John and the Synoptic Gospels* (Cambridge: At the University Press, 1938).
32. See pp. 286–287.
33. Cf. R. H. Lightfoot, *St. John's Gospel* (Oxford: At the Clarendon Press, 1957), pp. 26–42. Cf. B. H Streeter, *The Four Gospels,* pp. 365–392.

Gardner-Smith has called attention, however, to a number of divergencies from the Synoptic tradition, such as the identification of Peter and Andrew with Bethsaida rather than Capernaum (cf. Jn. 1:44 with Mk. 1:21–29) for which there appears to be no reason other than the likelihood that John had a different tradition. This argument is weighty and at least reinforces the impression left by literary analyses that John was not dependent upon the Synoptics sources in the way that Matthew and Luke are dependent upon Mark and Q. B. H. Streeter, in developing his theory that John used Mark and Luke as sources, had anticipated these objections and suggested that John had come upon information, perhaps from a Jerusalem tradition, with which he presumed to correct his sources.[34] His argument is not completely convincing and leaves several difficulties still standing.

There are, on the other hand, several places in which, if he used Mark and Luke as sources, John appears to have conflated his materials. The story of the healing at the pool of Bethzatha, in 5:1–18, for example, contains elements from both the healing of the paralytic in Mark 2:1–22 and the healing of the man with the withered hand in Mark 3:1–6. Several items appear in John's story of the feeding of the five thousand—one of the clearest examples of correspondence between John and Mark outside the Passion—which are found in Mark in other settings. That he locates the episode on the east side of the Sea of Galilee in contrast to Mark 6:35–45 may be the result of the influence of Mark's story of the feeding of the four thousand (8:1–10, cf. 6:31ff.). John's setting in the hills, 6:3, may have come from Mark's story of the appointment of the twelve, 3:13. It is interesting that, except for one reference in 20:24, only in this chapter (cf. vss. 67, 70–71) does John refer to the twelve. The word "thanks" (Greek: *eucharistesas*) in verse 11 is not found in Mark's parallel but comes from the feeding of the four thousand (Mk. 8:6). The blind man in 9:1–7 is healed with spittle as in Mark's story in 8:22–26. To complete the healing, however, he is sent to wash in the pool of Siloam, which recalls Jesus' command to the leper in Mark 1:44, but even more the ten lepers in Luke 17:14. We have already observed how John's story of the anointing at Bethany, 12:1–8, combines elements of Mark 14:1–9, Luke 7:36–50, and 10:38–42. Similar evidences of conflation may be detected in the Passion story. In view of these observations the possibility of other conflations which we can no longer detect, perhaps incorporating sources unknown to us, cannot be overlooked in dealing with the contrasts in parallel passages between John and the Synoptics.

These observations become more significant in the light of a study made by Charles Goodwin of John's way of handling his sources as

---

34. *The Four Gospels,* pp. 417–418.

exemplified in his use of the Old Testament.[35] His conclusion is worth quoting:

> If John did use the Synoptics, we shall expect to find many important passages ignored, and to find that Synoptic material and especially traces of Synoptic wording appear but rarely. Where Synoptic material does appear, we shall expect to find that sometimes the original is followed with surprising fidelity, but that more often it is reproduced very loosely. Often details of one story or passage will appear in another. The whole point and lesson of a passage is likely to be radically altered. We suspect that alien elements may be introduced.

The question of John's relationship to the other Gospels is far from settled. As with the question of the milieu, the evidence is ambiguous. Yet if John did not know our documents, he does show clear knowledge of traditions found in them, and he has used those traditions with a great deal of creative freedom. This freedom and the high degree of selectivity which he must have used—it is hard to imagine that, knowing the segments of the tradition which he used as well as he did, he was unaware of much more of it—suggest that he had no intention of supplying a Gospel to a Church which had none, or replacing other Gospels with his work. If John is not a commentary on the Synoptic Gospels, it is a commentary on a tradition very like them.

One indication of the interpretative role of this Gospel is the way at a number of points it seems to assume the readers' prior knowledge of the tradition found in the other Gospels. In 3:25–30, for example, the reader finds it difficult to see the connection between the dispute over purifying and the discussion of John's relation to Jesus that follows unless he recalls the story of the argument over fasting in Mark 2:18–20 (cf. 7:1ff.). John's puzzlingly ambiguous treatment of Jesus' origins and homeland, in 1:45–46; 4:43–45; 6:42; 7:27–28, 41–42, 52; 8:41; 9:29, can be understood without the radical surgery of redactional theories only by assuming that, presupposing the readers' knowledge of such traditions as those contained in Mark 6:3 and Luke 1–2, he has made skillful use of irony.[36] When in 5:14 Jesus commands the formerly sick man, "Sin no more," the connection is hard to see unless the reader recalls Mark's story of the healing of the paralytic, 2:5–12. The reference in 6:70 to the choosing of the twelve disciples assumes the reader's familiarity with a tradition such as Mark 3:14–19, as the references to the Last Supper, 13:1–4, 21–30, 36–38, require a knowledge of the tradition preserved in Mark 14:12–27 and

---

35. "How Did John Treat His Sources?," *JBL,* LXXIII, June, 1954, pp. 61–75.
36. See Streeter's comment on 7:41–42 in *The Four Gospels,* p. 407.

parallels. So also the highly compressed story of Barabbus in 18:39–40, the reference to the "two others" crucified with Jesus, and the statement that "the stone had been taken away from the tomb" (20:1f) when no mention has been made of the stone in the account of the burial in 19:38–42 (but cf. 11:38ff.), seem to reflect the almost unconscious assumption of the Synoptic tradition. John's "corrections" of the tradition we observed earlier are, of course, to the same effect.

Whatever solution we choose in order to account for the uniqueness of John's Gospel, it cannot include any assumption that he was ignorant of the tradition represented in the other Gospels. The fourth Gospel, however, does contain materials which can scarcely be accounted for by the traditions from which the other Gospels came, or by expansions and interpretations of them.[37] It is the question raised by these materials which warrants the quest for other sources in John.

Did John Have Sources Peculiar to Him? Whether the Synoptic Gospels or a tradition lying back of them was used by the author of the fourth Gospel, a significant body of material remains to be accounted for which has no parallels. That much of this material is related to Judea and Jerusalem suggests the possibility of a separate body of tradition from that area, whether oral or written, available to the author.[38] The existence of a collection of traditions of Jesus in the Jerusalem area is quite likely. There are indications in the Synoptic tradition that the Galilean ministry was preceded by something like the Judean period pictured in John. Certainly Mark's dating of Jesus' return to Galilee by John's incarceration leaves open the possibility of an undetermined amount of time between it and his baptism. Luke's reference to Judea in 4:44, as we have already observed, seems to call for such a period. The story of the call of the fishing disciples in Mark and Matthew seems to require some such prior acquaintance with Jesus as is described in the opening of John. To this extent the Ancient Church historian Eusebius offered a valid suggestion when he explained the difference between John and the Synoptics by an earlier Judean ministry.[39] To proceed from such generalizations to the reconstruction of a southern source, however, is another matter.

One of the best-known and most thorough-going attempts at source

37. See Streeter, *The Four Gospels,* pp. 416–427.
38. See, for example, J. A. T. Robinson, *Twelve New Testament Studies,* pp. 105–106; C. H. Dodd, *Historical Tradition in the Fourth Gospel* (Cambridge: At the University Press, 1963), pp. 233–247; 423–432; *The Interpretation of the Fourth Gospel,* pp. 449–453. D. Moody Smith, "John 12¹²ff. and the Question of John's use of the Synoptics," *JBL,* LXXXII, March 1963, pp. 58–64; C. K. Barrett, *The Gospel According to St. John,* pp. 17–18.
39. See p. 41.

analysis of the fourth Gospel is that of Bultmann, which underlies his commentary.[40] Partly by style criticism, partly by an analysis based on the theological point-of-view which he has established through a consideration of the book as a whole, and partly by comparison with other literature, such as the *Odes of Solomon,* which he believes to represent the same milieu of oriental Gnosticism, Bultmann identifies three principal sources: a source for the discourses which he calls "revelation discourses," a "signs source" which lies back of the miracles, and a "Passion story." Beside these Bultmann detects five possible minor sources and traditions scattered through the Gospel. The author, he believes, came into Christianity from a circle of followers of John the Baptizer which eventually became identified with the Mandaeans. This Evangelist drastically rewrote his sources, "demythologizing" the miracles in the signs source, revamping the Gnosticism of the revelation discourses to conform to his own theology, and leaving upon all the material the stamp of his own genius.

The great skill and labor evident in Bultmann's work have evoked considerable admiration, but not many scholars have accepted his results. Critics of his source theory have included his own former students.[41] Beyond the problem we have already discussed of finding convincing evidence for the Gnostic groups and the mythology which it assumes, this theory has the further difficulty of explaining the manifest unity of style in John. That Bultmann believes the Evangelist to have deliberately imitated the style of his revelation source is a concession to that difficulty. His critics are fond of quoting quips such as that of Pierson Parker, "It looks as though, if the author of the Fourth Gospel used documentary sources, he wrote them all himself."[42] Perhaps the most significant contribution Bultmann's source study has made is the way in which it reveals the difficulty, if not impossibility, of source analysis in John. Not that such attempts have been—or should be—abandoned, but until new evidence is uncovered they will remain highly conjectural and the interpretation of the Gospel must take that into account.[43] We cannot suppose that John did

40. *Das Evangelium des Johannes.* For a summary of his theory of authorship and sources of John see his *Theology of the New Testament,* Vol. II, pp. 3–14.
41. For a very valuable analysis of Bultmann's theory and method, the text of his reconstructed sources, and a summary of the criticisms by other scholars along with his own see Dwight Moody Smith, Jr., *The Composition and Order of the Fourth Gospel* (New Haven: Yale University Press, 1965), pp. 1–115. See also R. E. Brown, *The Gospel According to John,* I–XII, pp. XXVIII–XXXII; and Reginald Fuller, *The New Testament in Current Study,* pp. 111–115.
42. "Two Editions of John," *JBL,* LXXV, Dec. 1956, p. 304. Cf. the words of P. H. Menoud, "La tradition, c'est moi!" quoted among others, by J. A. T. Robinson in *Twelve New Testament Studies,* pp. 98 and 106.
43. See the important summary and critique of two more recent attempts to retrace the history of the fourth Gospel by Wilhelm Wilkens and Siegfried Schulz, in James M. Robinson "Recent Research in the Fourth Gospel," *JBL,* LXXXIII, Sept. 1959, pp. 242–252.

not use sources, but he has so thoroughly assimilated his materials and made them serve his own purpose as to make the recovery of their sources virtually impossible.

THEORIES OF DISPLACEMENT

There are in the Gospel several disjunctures, which have stimulated numerous attempts to restore the text to its presumed original order. The most striking of these disjunctures occurs at the end of chapter 14 where the words, "Rise, let us go hence," are followed by three more chapters before Jesus and his disciples actually depart. A similar problem occurs at the beginning of chapter 6. Although chapter 5 (cf. vs. 1) leaves Jesus in Jerusalem, he crosses the sea in 6:1 as though he is still in Galilee (cf. 4:43, 54). Again, in 7:21–23, Jesus refers to his healing of the impotent man on the Sabbath (5:2ff.) as though he is still engaged in the debate which follows in the rest of chapter 5. Once the reader's eye has been caught by these more glaring disjunctures, others less obvious begin to appear. The final paragraph of chapter 3, for example, reads more like the conclusion to Jesus' discourse with Nicodemus (vss. 1–21) than, as it now stands, the words of John the Baptizer; 7:25 would appear to connect more naturally with verse 14 than it does with verse 24, as 10:1ff. would fit more meaningfully after 10:29 than after 9:41. Some scholars rearrange chapter 12 so that the editorial material in verses 36b–43 follows rather than interrupts Jesus' discourse. Also, Jesus' trial under Annas rather than the high priest Caiaphas in 18:13–24 is a little surprising (cf. vs. 19 with 24).

A number of scholars have attempted to rearrange the text of John to restore what they assume to be the original order. One of the best known of these rearrangements is that of James Moffatt which he used in his justly famous translation of the Bible. J. H. Bernard, G. H. C. Macgregor, and Rudolph Bultmann organized their commentaries around their respective reconstructions.[44] Of these, Bultmann's is by far the more complex and is further complicated by his elaborate theory of redactions. D. M. Smith, Jr., has subjected Bultmann's reconstruction to rigorous critical examination and finds its complexity self-defeating. He finds it impossible to imagine how a text could have become so mutilated and survive to be restored, edited, and interpolated yet leaving the disjunctures we now have. In fairness to Bultmann, however, we should note that very complex dislocations were not unknown in antiquity. B. H. Streeter, in commenting on the frequency of such accidents to ancient manuscripts, calls attention

44. *The Gospel According to St. John* (ICC) 2 vols.; *The Gospel of John* (MNTC) (New York: Harper & Brothers, 1928); *Das Evangelium des Johannes.* Except Bultmann's, these and two others are given by reference in W. F. Howard, *The Fourth Gospel in Recent Criticism,* Appendix D, p. 264, also pp. 125–141.

to such an instance, which can be demonstrated by comparison with the original order in a Ciceronian text.[45] Smith's criticism has considerable validity, nevertheless, and applies in varying degrees to all other reconstructions as well. Reconstructions run the risk, furthermore, of importing into the text the interpreter's own preconceptions. The fourth Gospel is not primarily a narrative, and the discourses which control its structure do not move in a straight line but revolve around a series of themes for which the narratives provide the base. More recent interpreters, therefore, are disinclined to attempt rearrangements.[46]

One difficulty in the way of supposing these disjunctures to be the result of accidents to the text is that, except for the last one we noted, in chapter 18, there is no textual evidence for a different order. An ancient Syriac translation places verse 24, "Annas then sent him bound to Caiaphas the high priest," immediately after verse 13, so that the trial which follows in verses 19–23 takes place before Caiaphas. If the other difficulties we have noted are the result of accidental displacements, those displacements must have happened early enough to have affected the parent to all the manuscripts known to us.

Another difficulty is that rearrangements do not completely solve the problems, nor as the variety of reconstructions show, is it clear in which direction the materials should be transposed. Moffatt, for example, moves the reference in 7:15–24 to the healing of the impotent man back to the end of chapter 5, but by leaving chapter 6 where it is fails to account for Jesus' appearance in Galilee. Those, on the other hand, who transpose chapters 5 and 6 have to interpret 7:1, "After this Jesus went about in Galilee," to mean that he was returning from Jerusalem. The problem is that there are only two explicit trips to Galilee in the Gospel, 1:43 and 4:3, 43–45, but three to Judea, 2:13; 5:1, and 7:1–14, leaving Jesus' presence in Galilee in 7:1 (or 6:1) unaccounted for.

It is possible, of course, by identifying the trip to Jerusalem in 5:1 with that in 7:1–14 and placing the rest of chapter 5 (assuming 5:1 to be a gloss required by the dislocation) between 7:14 and 15, and identifying the trip to Galilee in 1:43 with that in 4:3, 43–45, placing the material in 1:43b–2:12 after 4:45 (omitting 2:13b and 4:46a), to place all of the Galilean material in one section. This rearrangement would in some respects simplify the problem of harmonizing John with the Synoptics. A rearrangement of this sort can appeal to the words at the conclusion of the healing of the officer's son, "this was now the second sign that Jesus did when he had come from Judea to Galilee" (4:54, cf. vs. 46), which imply that both miracles at Cana occurred during the same tour of Gali-

45. *The Four Gospels,* p. 380, n. 1.
46. For example, C. H. Dodd, *The Interpretation of the Fourth Gospel,* pp. 289–290; R. E. Brown, *The Gospel According to John* (i–xii), pp. xxvi–xxviii.

lee.[47] But it would do such manifest violence to the structure of the Gospel, leaving other problems such as the position of the cleansing of the Temple, 2:14–22, even more insoluble, that it cannot be taken seriously. The experiment does, however, help to illustrate the problems encountered in attempting to remove the disjunctures in John. In a study of this problem by B. W. Bacon, published early in this century, the summary of the history of this enterprise, including reconstructions made by nineteenth-century scholars but actually going all the way back to Tatian's *Diatessaron,* illustrates the point.[48] The way in which, especially in comparing Tatian's rearrangement with modern ones, transpositions can be made in different directions, each of which solves the immediate problem surprisingly well but leaves others or creates new ones, should indicate that the problem of the Johannine text involves more than simply dislocations.

THE QUESTION OF REDACTIONS

That in several notable instances the proposed rearrangements of John delete some material as editorial additions required by the dislocations points to the related problem of redactions. At the end of his chapter on dislocations, Bacon contends that at each of the displacements material is to be found which on other grounds must be regarded as later editorial additions.[49] Bultmann explicitly credits the author of these additions with restoring the badly mangled text to its present order. According to Bultmann, however, the redactor did not confine himself to harmonizing the disjunctures which his restoration failed to eliminate, but made other additions which helped to adjust John to the Synoptics, accentuate its apostolic authority, and bring it more into line with the practice and theology of developing catholicism of the Church.[50]

The question of redactions has more behind it, therefore, than the editorial seams connecting the disjunctures. Two textual problems clearly indicate that the text has been amplified at some point in its history. In the story of the healing of the invalid in chapter 5 the last phrase of verse 3 and all of verse 4, explaining the healing powers of the pool, are missing in several of the most important of the ancient Greek manuscripts. Whether the passage was dropped, as some interpreters think, because of

47. Cf. Sidney Temple, "The Two Signs in the Fourth Gospel," *JBL,* LXXXI, June, 1962, 169–174, who finds this point a clue to a separate source.
48. "Dislocations of Material and Tatian's Order," *The Fourth Gospel in Research and Debate,* ch. XIX, pp. 497–527. On Tatian's *Diatessaron,* see above, p. 41.
49. *The Fourth Gospel in Research and Debate,* pp. 523–527.
50. For the text of the redactional material according to Bultmann's theory, and a critical analysis of his criteria for distinguishing it, see D. M. Smith, Jr., *The Composition and Order of the Fourth Gospel,* pp. 213–226. See also the brief but perceptive treatment by R. E. Brown, *The Gospel According to John* (i–xii), pp. xxx–xxxii.

the paganism implicit in it, or was added in later manuscripts because the context, especially verse 7, demands some such explanation, the textual problem presents unmistakable evidence of editorial work on the Gospel. The second problem concerns the familiar story of the woman caught in adultery, 7:53–8:11.[51] Not only is the textual evidence against its inclusion here even more decisive than in the case of 5:3b–4, but unlike the latter which fills a need in its context, the *Pericope Adulterae,* as it is called, actually interrupts the continuity between 7:52 and 8:12. In various manuscripts it has, in fact, been found in two places earlier in chapter 7, at the end of the Gospel, and following Luke 21:38. Although it may well be a piece of authentic Gospel tradition, it certainly is no part of the original text here, nor, for that matter, elsewhere in the fourth Gospel.

The existence of editorial material in the Gospel, which these two instances establish, warrants the search for further instances of redaction. The most important of such instances is the twenty-first chapter. Several evidences combine to show that this chapter, too, was a later addition. Chapter 20 which reaches its climax in the confession of Thomas, "My Lord and my God" (vs. 28), so fits the style and pattern of the Gospel that the closing paragraph, verses 30–31, manifestly belongs where it is. The words, "After this Jesus revealed himself again . . ." (21:1), therefore, introduce an appendix which was not a part of the original plan of the Gospel. Considerations of vocabulary, style, and content reinforce this conclusion. Whether from another hand or added by the author himself, this appendix witnesses to the complex history of the Gospel.[52] Several other short passages, such as the explanation in 4:2 that Jesus himself did not baptize, and the "eyewitness" in 19:35 (cf. 21:24–25), can with some confidence be identified as redactional.

When, however, we take the whole series of problems of sources, relations to the Synoptics, disjunctures, and redactions into account, the question arises whether we should think of the origins of this Gospel simply in terms of an author and his sources, and a few editorial additions. Admittedly, the overarching unity in style and conception of the book which moves, or perhaps better, revolves in grand monotony around a handful of major themes, bears the impress of one powerful, profoundly theological mind. When we view them from the perspective of the discourses which are central to the purpose of the Gospel, rather than that of a biography of Jesus, even the disjunctures become less troublesome. Yet they are real, and so are the tensions created by the other problems we

51. For a full discussion of this pericope and its history see Sir Edwyn Hoskyns, ed. Francis Noel Davey, rev., *The Fourth Gospel* (London: Faber and Faber, Ltd., 1947), pp. 563–572.

52. See C. K. Barrett, *The Gospel According to St. John,* pp. 479–490.

have surveyed. That the fourth Gospel is the direct product of the pen of a single author is therefore improbable.

R. E. Brown has outlined a five-stage theory of the origin and development of John which, not unlike Krister Stendahl's theory of the origin of Matthew, attributes it to a school of Christian preachers and teachers gathered around the powerful figure whose preaching and teaching first shaped the discourses and narratives from tradition materials. Perhaps it was he who also wrote the first edition of the Gospel, and in doing so gave it the structure and outline which it still retains. With this beginning it was subjected to a process of editing, perhaps partly by the author himself, and finally by a friend and disciple who left it much as we now have it.[53] This worthwhile suggestion is made more probable, at least in principle, when we consider the Epistles and Apocalypse which bear the name of John but which, while sharing with the Gospel and each other a number of significant characteristics, are presumed by a number of scholars to be from different authors. The Apocalypse certainly was written by a different hand from any of the others. These writings, too, can be accounted for by "the School of St. John."

3. Characteristics and Structure

There are in the fourth Gospel several characteristics reminiscent of the drama. Louis Martyn, for example, has called attention to the way John is careful to obey the rule not to permit more than two speakers on the stage at a time.[54] The Gospel moves in well-defined scenes, each of which is brought to an appropriate climax. At several points editorial comments, like an off-stage voice, help keep the reader abreast of the movement. The discourses are broken into by interlocutors whose questions serve much the same purpose as the rhetorical questions in a diatribe.[55] As the drama, also, the Gospel contains elements which perform symbolic roles or otherwise function in a consistent way throughout the work to further its meaning and sustain the continuity. Before we examine the structure of John, therefore, it will be helpful for us to notice a few of the characteristics.

SOME CHARACTERISTICS OF THE GOSPEL

The first twelve chapters of John which carry the story of Jesus' ministry up to the Last Supper are organized around two kinds of material:

53. *The Gospel According to John* (i–xii), pp. xxiv–xxxix.
54. *History and Theology in the Fourth Gospel,* p. 6.
55. See p. 274.

signs and discourses. In several instances the discourses have a sign as their starting point. At other times editorial comments call attention to the signs and the responses in belief or disbelief elicited by them. The word "sign" occurs sixteen times in these chapters and only once, in a concluding statement (20:30), after that. It is not surprising that commentators frequently treat this part of the Gospel as the "Book of the Signs." An understanding of the role of the signs in John is therefore among the most important requisites to its interpretation.

Signs, Works, and Miracles   Especially from its use in the two miracle stories of Cana in Galilee, 2:1–11 and 4:46–54, the word "sign" in John is taken to be equivalent to "miracle" (cf. "the signs which he did on those who were diseased," 6:2). Some interpreters have counted seven such miracles which, along with a series of discourses by way of commentary on several of them, provide the structure of the first twelve chapters. Admittedly, the enumeration of the "first" and "second" signs at Cana invites such a scheme. There are, nevertheless, several difficulties in the way of this interpretation. John's enumeration is, in the first place, confined to these two miracles. Second, John in his use of the plural, "signs," in the editorial note, 2:23–25, probably intended the reader to understand it as a generalization which includes more than he has recorded. This note, therefore, and the similar ones that follow have the effect of directing attention away from the number of miracles recounted. Beside these two miracles at Cana only one other, the feeding of the five thousand, in the third place, is explicitly designated as a sign. The author's later reference to the raising of Lazarus (12:18) as a sign, and the phrase, "such signs," in 9:16, which clearly alludes to the healing of the man blind from birth, show that the word has not become for John a technical term. Elsewhere he refers to them as "works" (e.g., 5:20, 36; 7:3, 21; 9:3–4; 10:25ff., *passim*).

There are other episodes, furthermore, which John probably intended to be manifestations of divine power in the same category. Nathanael's response when Jesus told him that he had seen him under the fig tree (1:48–51), for example, is remarkably similar to that of Thomas upon seeing the Risen Lord (20:28). So, too, the exclamation of the woman at the well, "Come, see a man who told me all that I ever did. Can this be the Christ?" (4:29), serves as an example of superhuman insight which became a convincing sign for the Samaritans. The story of Jesus walking on the sea (6:16–21), on the other hand, should probably not be counted. It is in John a private experience of the disciples which apparently remained unknown to the people. John's version of the story when compared to that of Mark also shows a surprising deemphasis of the miraculous element; and John seems deliberately to avoid any reference to it later. For these reasons several interpreters have, by excluding this story, reduced the traditional list of miracles or signs to six.[56]

More important than the number of miracles is John's intended meaning of the word "signs." It is worthy of note that only once, in 4:43, does the word "wonders" which frequently accompanies this term in the Old Testament (and in Acts) occur. John's use of the word "works," for a synonym, however, indicates a breadth of meaning which points back to the Old Testament. Signs in the fourth Gospel are by no means an appeal to popular credulity, an attempt, in other words, to startle or frighten the mind into assent to the claims for Jesus by means of the miraculous. No less than the Synoptists, John is aware that the supernatural might as easily be attributed to demonic as to divine forces (cf. Jn. 8:48ff. with Mk. 3:22–30; also the law concerning the test for evil signs in Deut. 13:1–5). Like the terms which the Septuagint translates with the same Greek word, John's signs are evidences of God's benevolent activity in the world. Thus John quotes Jesus: "If I am not doing the works of my Father, then do not believe me, but if I do them, even though you do not believe me, believe the works" (10:37–38a). For him who has the eyes of faith to see, they define God's purpose in history and point the direction in which he is moving. Signs may be a symbol of God's presence in the form of a supernatural act, as Moses' rod (Ex. 4:1ff.). The deliverance itself may be regarded as a sign, as Israel's escape from Egypt (Deut. 11:3ff.), or the arrival of the ideal age (Isa. 55:13). The sign is not always miraculous, nor an event or action. Thus over against the chirping mediums and wizards Isaiah places himself and his children as "signs and wonders . . . from the Lord" (Isa. 8:18–19). It may be a past event, such as the crossing of the Jordan (Josh. 4:6–7), or future as in God's words to Moses, "This shall be the sign for you, that I have sent you; when you have brought forth the people out of Egypt, you shall serve God upon this mountain" (Ex. 3:12).

There is no good reason, therefore, to limit the meaning of the word "signs" in the fourth Gospel to miracles. In a sense all the actions of Jesus are bearers of his meaning and therefore signs. If we recognize the cleansing of the Temple (2:13–20) as a sign, the irony in the question which

56. See J. H. Bernard, *The Gospel According to St. John,* I, pp. clxxvi–clxxxvi; J. N. Sanders in *IDB,* III, pp. 933–934. On the meaning of signs see also Eric L. Titus, *The Message of the Fourth Gospel* (New York: Abingdon Press, 1957), pp. 31–32; Rudolf Bultmann, *Theology of the New Testament,* II, pp. 44ff.; *IDB,* IV, pp. 346–347, 348–351. On the number and John's designation of "signs" see Sidney Temple, "The Two Signs in the Fourth Gospel," *JBL,* Vol. LXXXI, June, 1962, pp. 169–174. C. H. Dodd manages to retain the scheme of the ideal number seven while avoiding the problem of the number of signs by dividing the "Book of Signs," chs. 2–12, into seven periods according to the alternation of narrative and discourse material. See *The Interpretation of the Fourth Gospel,* pp. 289–389.

the Jews, who had just witnessed the sign, ask of Jesus, "What sign have you to show us for doing this?" is patent, and is amplified in the scene following the feeding of the five thousand in which those who had eaten reveal by their question, "What sign do you do, that we may see, and believe you?" (6:30) their failure to perceive the sign. In the first instance Jesus responds to the request by pointing forward to his Resurrection; in the second instance the manna in the wilderness becomes a sign and symbol of him who is "the Bread of Life." This latter sign recalls the thrice-repeated figure of the "lifting up" of Jesus which is prefigured by Moses' lifting up the serpent in the wilderness (3:14, 8:28; 12:32). The character and quality of the signs or works are important also to their meaning. When the Jews, in 10:31ff., attempt to stone Jesus he responds, "I have shown you many good works from the Father; for which of these do you stone me?". The blasphemy in charging Jesus' signs to demonic powers is that good and evil have become so confused in their minds that works which can only come from God are credited to the devil. Signs are not, therefore, automatically convincing. Yet John is willing to appeal for belief on whatever level is necessary. It is in the intimacy of the circle of disciples at the Supper that Jesus says, "Believe me that I am in the Father and the Father in me; or else believe me for the sake of the works themselves" (14:11). For those open to truth the signs become valid guides into faith, but those perversely set against the truth remain unbelieving (12:37).

Beyond Signs   At the end of the farewell discourse at the Last Supper (16:31), Jesus asks of the disciples the rather surprising question, "Do you now believe?". When taken with the statement "his disciples believed in him," in 2:11, and Peter's confession in 6:68, this question suggests a progress in believing. In several ways, in fact, John points beyond the signs to a belief no longer sustained by them. In so doing he indicates that he is by no means so far from the Synoptic attitude toward signs as is sometimes assumed. Jesus' complaining, in 4:48, "Unless you see signs and wonders you will not believe" is in the same mood as his condemnation of the evil generation which seeks a sign, in Luke 11:29. At times even the signs are of no interest as signs. Thus Jesus can say to the crowd following him after the feeding of the multitude, "You seek me, not because you saw signs, but because you ate your fill of the loaves" (6:26), or to Nicodemus, "If I have told you earthly things and you do not believe, how can you believe if I tell you heavenly things?". Signs as "earthly things" are of no use unless they point beyond themselves to "heavenly things." So, too, belief must move beyond its dependence upon signs, or it will fail. This "beyondness" in belief is the point of the surprising development in the passage, 8:31–44, which begins, "Jesus then said to the Jews who had believed in him, 'If you continue in my word, you are truly my disciples,' " and ends with the awful words, "You are of your father the devil." The two crucial passages which carry this theme to its conclusion, and in doing so come close to the major purpose of the Gospel, are 4:39–42 in which the Samaritans move from belief based on the woman's testimony that Jesus had told her "all that I ever did," to a belief "because of his (Jesus') word"; and 20:26–29 wherein doubting Thomas, upon seeing the wounds of the Risen Lord, falls to his knees crying, "My Lord and my God!". Jesus' response, comprising the very last words of the body of the Gospel, "Have you believed because you have seen me? Blessed are those who have not seen and yet believe" is as much an expression of its purpose and conclusion as the postscript which follows.

The Two Ways: Antitheses and Word Plays Among the literary patterns that John employs are two which appear so prominently in the Gospel as to deserve special notice. One of these patterns appears in a series of antitheses presenting the basic alternatives of belief and unbelief in a manner closely allied to the doctrine of the two ways in the Wisdom Literature.[57] A number of these antitheses involve on the positive side the principal terms used to convey the thought of the Gospel.[58] In the opening section of the prologue, for instance, the reader is introduced to the antithesis of light versus darkness (1:5). Light becomes in the body of the Gospel a key figure for expressing the meaning and significance of Jesus. At the conclusion of the prologue occurs the antithesis of Law versus Grace (1:17) introducing the important contrast between the Church and Israel which the reader encounters in the controversies (cf. 7:19, 23, 49, 51 *passim*). The Spirit is contrasted with water in the account of John the Baptizer (1:26, 33), and with flesh in the dialogue with Nicodemus (3:6). The antithesis between "earthly things" versus "heavenly things" (3:12) adds further definition to the contrast between Spirit and flesh. Life is contrasted with the wrath of God (3:36) and with judgment and death (5:24), as truth is contrasted with evil (3:20–21) and with falsehood and lies (7:18; 8:44–46). Significantly, it is in the context of truth and falsehood that John places the antithesis between one's own glory versus the "glory of him who sent him" (7:18). These and other antitheses to the same effect form a connected series which depicts the consequences of the alternative responses to Jesus. Abiding belief possesses eternal life; rejection brings judgment and perishing.

In several places John makes interesting use of plays on words, a device which appears not infrequently in the Old Testament and other Hebrew

---

57. West, *Introduction to the Old Testament*, pp. 390–391.
58. For a valuable study of several of the most significant terms and concepts see C. H. Dodd, *The Interpretation of the Fourth Gospel*, pp. 133–285.

works.[59] The most prominent of these word plays is the pun, in 3:5–8, on the word "spirit" which in Greek (*pneuma*) means both wind and spirit. Later, in the story of the raising of Lazarus, there is a similar play on the word "sleep" (*koimaomai*, 11:11–13). In the first paragraph of the prologue (1:5), the word translated "overcome" (*katalambano*) can mean to grasp or understand, to accept or receive, or, in a hostile sense, to seize or overcome. Probably the ambiguity is intentional and represents another type of play on words. Some advocates of the theory that John was originally written in Aramaic call attention to a possible pun, lying back of this sentence, on the Aramaic words for "darkness" and "receive."[60] Another word play of this type may be seen in the statement to Nicodemus, "unless one is born anew, he cannot see the kingdom of God" (3:3). The word "anew" (Greek, *anothen*) can mean either "from above" or "again." In this instance the double meaning is underscored by Nicodemus' dull-witted misunderstanding of the metaphor.

Misunderstanding and Irony   Throughout the Gospel John uses two literary devices to underscore the main themes of his work, to extend the dialogues and further explicate his propositions, and to intensify the drama. Although both elements are familiar to us from the Synoptics, John gives them a prominence in the structure of his Gospel which merits special attention. By means of a dull-witted interlocutor, the dialogue is extended to include a belabored exposition of the truth under discussion. This exposition, which often concludes in a monologue, reaches its climax by contrasting the merely earthly meaning with the "true," i.e., eternal, spiritual meaning. At times the stupidity of the interlocutor seems to be a willful resistance to the truth; at other times it seems to imply that the ability to understand Jesus' truth is a gift of God reserved for the elect.

Nicodemus, by taking Jesus' statement about the new birth literally (3:4ff.), for example, reduces it to an absurdity which provides the setting for Jesus' exposition of the contrast between the "earthly" and "heavenly" things which becomes a monologue. As Jesus describes the "living water" to the woman at the well in Samaria, her response, "Sir, give me this water, that I may not thirst, nor come here to draw" (4:14), shows that she, too, is thinking of "earthly things." Jesus leads the conversation finally to the issue of true worship. Similarly, the persistent misunderstanding of Jesus' statements concerning his coming from above and his going away (6:35ff. *passim*; 7:34ff. *passim*) lead to expositions of his relation to the Father and to his glorification on the cross and its meaning for the future of the believers. John's interpretation of the Res-

59. See West, *Introduction to the Old Testament*, pp. 247–249, 273.
60. See R. E. Brown, *The Gospel According to John* (i–xii), p. 8.

urrection is developed around the misunderstanding of Jesus' words in reference to the death of Lazarus (11:11f., 23–25), and the misunderstandings in the Resurrection story (20:1–2, 11–16). In an especially clear use of this device, John comes close to Mark's use of the motif of dull-witted disciples. Probably in the allegory of the shepherd (10:1–5) John comes nearer than anywhere else to the parables in the Synoptics. It is interesting, therefore, to observe how similar to Mark's link between the parable of the sower and its interpretation (Mk. 4:10–13) is the way the failure of Jesus' hearers to understand this allegory (vs. 6) leads to the extended interpretation which follows (vss. 7–18).

Another example of this device, Pilate's failure to understand the nature of Jesus' kingship (18:33ff.; 19:19ff.), also recalls Mark's use of irony.[61] Whereas in Mark only occasional touches of irony in the body of the Gospel anticipate the strain of irony in the Passion story, John uses it throughout his Gospel, beginning with the words in the prologue, "He came to his own home, and his own people received him not" (1:11), to Pilate's title, "Jesus of Nazareth, the King of the Jews" (19:19). These two devices overlap at a number of points. Nicodemus' misunderstanding of the new birth, for instance, leads to Jesus' ironic question, "Are you a teacher of Israel, and yet you do not understand this?" (3:9–10). Some of the Gospel's main themes are developed or reinforced by means of irony. The paradox of the incarnation, for instance, is developed by a series of questions and statements that when taken together appear contradictory. Nathanael's question, "Can anything good come out of Nazareth?" (1:46, cf. 7:52), identifies Jesus as a Nazarene. This identification is confirmed, when taken with the references to Jesus' family in Galilee in 2:12 and 7:2–5, by the question in 6:42, "Is not this Jesus, the son of Joseph, whose father and mother we know?" The curious fact, then, which Matthew and Luke take to be a matter of fulfillment of prophecy, that although Jesus was reared in Galilee and was known as a Nazarene he was born in Bethlehem makes an irony of the people's question, "Is the Christ to come from Galilee? Has not the scripture said that the Christ is descended from David, and comes from Bethlehem, the village where David was?" (7:41–42). The irony of their reference to a prophetic condition which, unknown to them, was met in Jesus is matched by the contradictory statements in 7:27, "Yet we know where this man comes from; and when the Christ appears, no one will know where he comes from" and in 9:29, "We know that God has spoken to Moses, but as for this man, we do not know where he comes from." This contradiction brackets one of the crucial arguments of the Gospel in which Jesus' claim to be the Son of God and to have

---

61. For Mark's use of these terms see above, pp. 101–107.

descended from the Father is set in contrast to the claim of the Jews to be descendants of Abraham and disciples of Moses. The argument reaches its climax when Jesus brands the Jews as descendants of the devil (8:42–47), and the Jews in turn call him a demon-possessed Samaritan (8:48–52). Their failure to understand the preexistence of the Son (8:53–59) leads to the irony in chapter 9 of accusing one who does the works of God of being a sinner. Closely akin to this is the irony of Jesus' kingship. In 6:15 the people mistakenly seek to make Jesus an earthly king, which anticipates Pilate's question, "Are you the king of the Jews?" (18:33). Against this background the irony of the mockery (19:2–3) and the title on the cross (19:19–22) done to one whose "kingship is not of this world" (18:36a) becomes clear.

That Jesus' works are signs of his divine mission and authority is ironically misunderstood or ignored by the Jews. At the cleansing of the Temple (2:18) and again after the feeding of the multitude (6:30), the demands for a sign ignore the fact that they have just witnessed the true signs (cf. 9:16, 25–34 and Mk. 8:11ff., parallels). The point is underscored by the question, "Can a demon open the eyes of the blind?" (10:21b), and reaches its climax in the contrast between the confession of the healed blind man, "Lord, I believe" (9:38a), and the Pharisee's question, "Are we also blind?" (9:40), to which Jesus replies, "If you were blind, you would have no guilt; but now that you say, 'we see,' your guilt remains" (9:41).

The irony becomes intense in John's treatment of the Passion. Because the reader has already been informed (7:1, cf. vss. 25–26) of the Jews' intention to kill Jesus, the irony in the people's denial of such an intent becomes vividly apparent. So also the claim of the Jews to be descendants of Abraham is, in the light of their attempts to kill him who came from Abraham's God, ironic (8:33–47, cf. 56). The stories of the anointing at Bethany (12:1–8) and the entry (12:12–15) retain, of course, much the same irony that they have in Mark, but to these John has added three scenes which bring this element in the Passion story to a climax. Following the raising of Lazarus the chief priests and Pharisees convened the Sanhedrin, according to 11:45–53, because of their fear that the Romans would "come and destroy both our holy place and our nation." John undoubtedly assumes the reader's knowledge that, although they had executed Jesus according to plan, within forty years the Romans did come to accomplish the fall of Jerusalem under the leadership of Titus, and that in the process the Temple was destroyed (cf. Lk. 19:42–44). The final irony lies in Caiaphas' proposal to solve the problem: "it is expedient for you that one man should die for the people, and that the whole nation should not perish." John is at pains to point out that this expression of the theology of the Passion was an unwitting exercise of the high priestly office by Caiaphas (11:49–52).

That Pilate, too, is an unwitting agent of the divine purpose is made clear as Jesus replied in response to his warning, "You would have no power over me unless it had been given you from above" (19:11). Perhaps the bitterest irony of all is the chief priests' cry "We have no king but Caesar" (19:15c). The small, unpopular Sadducean clique, which held office at the pleasure of the Roman overlords, had everything to lose and nothing to gain in the realization of the popular Jewish hope of freedom and independence. There is a double irony here, for those who would have made Jesus king by force (6:15) and the shouting crowds at the entry crying "Blessed be he who comes in the name of the Lord, even the King of Israel!" (12:13 cf. 1:49) are also wrong. Jesus' kingship is to be manifested in the very death which would seem to deny it (cf. 12:20–26).

The Role of Scripture   The role of Scripture in the fourth Gospel presents a puzzling ambiguity. There are some seventy passages which either quote or paraphrase the Old Testament, utilize Old Testament themes and motifs, or refer to Jewish customs and history which are explained in the Old Testament. Although the Old Testament, as we should expect from the difference in form and character, appears somewhat less prominently in John than in the Synoptics, the ways in which it appears are essentially the same. There are, for example, fourteen formula quotations compared to seventeen in the much longer Gospel of Luke. The ambiguity appears at exactly the same point at which, as we have already seen, John tends to disassociate Jesus from Judaism. The second-person pronouns in the argument at the Temple, 7:19ff., for instance, in Jesus' question, "Did not Moses give you the law?" and his parallel statement, "Moses gave you circumcision," place Jesus outside scriptural authority. At the same time the whole argument over healing on the Sabbath, including the clause "so that the law of Moses may not be broken" (vs. 23) assumes a common acceptance of responsibility to the Law. An identical argument appears in 10:34–36, and the second- or third-person pronoun to the same effect in reference to the Scriptures appears in 8:17 and 15:25. On the other side of the argument, the Jews exclude Jesus by the remark, "We know that God has spoken to Moses, but as for this man, we do not know where he comes from" (9:29).

At a number of points, on the other hand, John appears to take the authority of Scripture for granted. So Philip describes Jesus as "him of whom Moses in the law and also the prophets wrote" (1:45). The Biblical story of Moses' brass serpent in the wilderness (Num. 21:6–9) becomes a prophecy of Jesus' Passion (3:14). The formula quotations, too, represent the same assumption of the predictive authority of Scripture as their Synoptic counterparts.[62]

The clue to this enigma is to be found in three passages in which the comparison is made directly. In the Eucharistic discourse on the bread from heaven, Jesus responds to the peoples' reference to the manna in the wilderness with the statement, "It was not Moses who gave you the bread from heaven; my Father gives you the true bread from heaven" (6:31–32). The Scriptures are neither wrong nor irrelevant; rather they point forward for their true meaning to Jesus. This point is made in so many words in the controversy in 5:39–47, "You search the scriptures, because you think that in them you have eternal life; and it is they that bear witness to me; yet you refuse to come to me that you may have life" (vss. 39–40). It is not the Scriptures that are at issue, but the misuse of the Scriptures by the failure to recognize their witness to the action of God—action which is only completed in Jesus. Jesus and the Scriptures stand therefore in the closest possible relationship. Only when the Jews fail to recognize this relationship do the Scriptures become "their law." "If you believed Moses, you would believe me, for he wrote of me. But if you do not believe his writings, how will you believe my words?" (vss. 46–47). This passage provides the perspective from which the words at the end of the prologue, "For the law was given through Moses; grace and truth came through Jesus Christ" (1:17), are to be understood. When the believer, understanding this witnessing role of Scripture, has received the grace of the "fulness" of Jesus (1:16) he must confess with Peter, "Lord, to whom shall we go? You have the words of eternal life" (6:68).

The Jews, People, Disciples, and Secret Disciples   The main drama of the fourth Gospel is acted out between Jesus and two groups. On the one hand are the Jews and the crowds, and on the other the disciples. In general, the Jews are the unalterable opponents of Jesus. As in Luke, these include the Pharisees (mentioned twenty-one times in John) as the leaders whose culpability is therefore greater. The people (Greek: *ochlos*, crowds) serve as the audience which is divided in its opinion of Jesus (cf. 7:12, 40–41, 43; 11:42; 12:9, 12ff., 17f., 29), and the disciples represent, of course, those who have become believers. John does not, however, adhere strictly to this terminology. Although in several places in the Gospel the word "Jew" merely serves to identify feasts and customs, and in a few others, such as the two occurrences in the story of the Samaritan woman at the well (4:9, 22) and Jesus' trial under Pilate (e.g., 18:33,

62. See 1:23; 2:17; 6:31, 45; 7:38; 10:34; 12:15, 38, 40; 13:18; 15:25; 19:24; 36, 37.

39; 19:3, 19, 21), it is incidental to the story, most of the nearly seventy occurrences refer to Jesus' opponents. It may not be carelessness on John's part that at three significant points the crowds and the Jews exchange roles. In 7:20 and 12:34 the crowds play the role usually assigned to the "Jews," whereas in 11:45; 12:9–11 and 42, "Many of the Jews (even of the authorities)" believed.

Among the disciples there is a similar division. There are, for example, secret disciples who lack the courage to identify themselves publicly as Jesus' followers. Nicodemus is the prototype of these. In chapter 3 he comes to Jesus "by night"; in 7:45ff. as a member of the ruling Pharisees he plays a role, although with less success, remarkably similar to that of Gamaliel in Acts 5:34ff.; in 19:38ff. he is linked with Joseph of Arimathea, another secret disciple, in the burial of Jesus. These scenes undoubtedly afford the reader a glimpse into the precarious life of the Early Church in which the efforts of sympathetic friends among the authorities were not always successful. John, nevertheless, views these secret disciples with something less than approval. His description of them ends with the sad comment: "For they loved the praise of men more than the praise of God" (12:42–43).

There is a distinction, too, between those who believe and "true" disciples. The reader is surprised, for instance, by the way in which Jesus' address to "the Jews who had believed in him," in 8:31–59, develops into one of the bitterest controversies in the entire Gospel. It ends with an attempted stoning reminiscent of the conclusion to Luke's story of Jesus in the synagogue at Nazareth (Lk. 4:16–30). In the opening words "If you continue in my word, you are truly my disciples" John indicates that this passage is a definition of belief. As in the crucial scene, in 6:66–71, in which "Many of his disciples drew back and no longer went about with him," true belief involves "continuing" (the Greek word, *meno*, here is more often translated "abide," "remain," or "stay"); and continuing, more than simple constancy, means acceptance of the unfolding truth of his "words" including those which Jesus speaks in later times through the Spirit (cf. 8:26; 14:25–26; 16:12–13). Peter's confession (6:68) and that of Thomas (20:28), therefore, become models of that belief which constitutes true discipleship.

There is a significant fluidity in the roles which these groups play. Many from among Jesus' Jewish opponents, including the authorities and Pharisees (e.g., Nicodemus), believe. The crowds at times unite in opposition, and believers depart or follow only in secret. In observing this fluidity we are undoubtedly looking into the state of affairs in the church of John's time and are very close to his main concern and purpose in writing the Gospel. In contrast to this fluidity, however, stand such statements as the one in Jesus' prayer of intercession, "I kept them in thy name which thou has given me . . . and none of them is lost but the son of perdition" (17:12). This concept of election running through the Gospel, for which the traitorous act of Judas provides a foil, is prevented by the way John holds it in tension with the challenge to belief from becoming deterministic. Almost every reference to election is placed in a context which appeals to the human will to believe as a free agent (cf. 6:35–71; 7:17). At the very least this paradox of belief as a free act, and yet at the same time one which is made possible by a divine choice (15:16), means that the ability to abide in the truth is available to every believer who desires it (10:26–29).

THE STRUCTURE OF THE GOSPEL

Something of the complexity of the fourth Gospel can be seen in the variety of outlines interpreters have made of it. A large part of the difficulty one encounters in attempting to outline John is due to the author's involved literary habits. Series appear in numerous places which are broken off incomplete or, more often, interlocked with others. The author in the course of treating one theme will return to an earlier one, and by placing it in the new context will develop it in another direction. As he allows his terms to bear more than one meaning, so his symbols and episodes can lead to a complex of interrelated themes. Probably some of the difficulty, on the other hand, reflects the literary history of the Gospel itself and the tradition which lies back of it. At several points, for example, the purpose for which an episode is included in the Gospel appears in the story itself to be secondary or even tacked on as an afterthought. The problem of displacements, which we discussed earlier, is another example of complexity which may be the result of editing and expansion.[63] Yet the Gospel cannot be said to be unstructured or in basic disarray. There is a clear line of development running through the Gospel as a whole, and the main divisions are well defined. In the following analysis we will attempt to understand the structure of the Gospel as it now stands in its final edition.

The fourth Gospel falls into five distinct parts: the prologue, 1:1–18; the public ministry of Jesus, 1:19–12:50; the Last Supper, 13–17; the Passion and Resurrection, 18–20; and the appendix, 21, which as the Gospel now stands serves as an epilogue. Of these the public ministry, comprising nearly two thirds of the Gospel (555 vss. of a total of 866 vss.), is characterized throughout by dialogues with Jesus which in most instances develop into monologues. Considerably more than half (over 300 vss.) of the first main division consists of such material. The second division, except for the dialogues accompanying the washing of the dis-

63. See pp. 215–217.

ciple's feet and the defection of Judas, is entirely discourse (counting the intercessory prayer as discourse). Even the Passion and Resurrection are expanded from the Synoptic version by dialogue. A dozen major scenes or episodes provide the background for the dialogues and discourses in the first division, while editorial comments and explanations, like a voice

Site of the Pool of Bethesda (Jn. 5:2ff.) at St. Anne's Church in Jerusalem. Excavations by French archaeologists have penetrated to the level of the pool which existed in the time of Jesus. (Courtesy of the Jordan Ministry of Information.)

A page of the great third-century manuscript Codex Vaticanus, known to have been in the Vatican Library since the fifteenth century. The first two columns contain the conclusion of Luke's Gospel beginning with the last two words of 24:32. The third column contains most of the prologue of John's Gospel, 1:1–14a, ending with the word "beheld. . . ." (Courtesy of the Vatican Library.)

off-stage, serve to accent important points and help the reader to understand their deeper meaning.

The Prologue, 1:1–18 The opening of John's Gospel stands in a decided contrast to the others. Mark plunges immediately into the story of John the Baptizer, while Matthew and Luke carry the story back to the birth of Jesus which Matthew introduces with a genealogy, and Luke (after the preface) with the birth of John the Baptizer. Except for the brief phrase, "the Word became flesh and dwelt among us," John bypasses Jesus' earthly origins to concentrate on the preexistent Logos (Word) as the true and ultimate statement of Jesus' origin. This highly theological introduction of major themes of the Gospel does, however, have parallels in the prologues to two books later in the New Testament, I John and Hebrews. Although I John originated in the same Johannine circle, if not from the same author, and manifests a direct relationship to the Gospel, the prologue of Hebrews is closer in thought and form to that of John. Yet neither of these stands as distinctly apart from the material which follows, or reaches the extended grandeur of poetic expression.

The opening lines manifest a rhythmic structure and progressive parallelism so reminiscent of Hebrew poetry as to suggest to a number of interpreters that the prologue is an expansion of an ancient hymn. Some have concluded that it is a fragment of an ancient Judaic or pagan (Stoic?) poem which John adapted to his own purposes. Comparison with such poetic passages as Philippians 2:5–11 and Colossians 1:15–20 suggests that it is more likely an early Christian hymn, possibly originating within the Johannine circle itself, which was expanded by prose interpolations to make an appropriate introduction to the Gospel. While the theory of a Logos hymn underlying the prologue is quite widely accepted, there is little agreement as to how much of it belongs to the original hymn. Certainly the references to John's witness, verses 6–8, 15, and the explanatory verse 13 are prose additions.[64]

The sonorous opening phrase, "In the beginning," is the same as the opening of Genesis, and probably is deliberately intended to associate the hymn with the great story of creation in Genesis 1:1–2:3 as the Logos is associated with the role of the Creator. The prologue as a whole has four parts: (1) the preexistent Logos whose meaning is described in the four words, God, Creation, Life, and Light (1:1–5); (2) John the witness to the Light (6–8); (3) the Light enters the world, his rejection and reception (9–13); (4) the Incarnation of the Logos who "dwelt among us" as the "only Son" and has become the revelation of the glory, grace, and truth of God (14–18).

That several terms, such as "Logos," "fulness," (Greek: *pleroma,* 1:16), and "dwelt" (Greek: *skenoö,* 1:14), do not appear at least with the same meaning in the remainder of the Gospel has led some scholars to suppose that the entire prologue is a later addition by another hand. The differences are far outweighed, however, by the connection. Although Logos does not appear again as an hypostatic term, the idea is developed and interpreted extensively throughout the Gospel. The prologue, in fact, like an operatic overture, is made up of major themes which reappear for full development in later sections. The witness of John (1:6–8, 15), for

---

64. For a good survey of the various possibilities on the composition of the prologue see R. E. Brown, *The Gospel According to John* (i–xii), pp. 18–23. C. K. Barrett, however, believes the entire prologue to be a unity composed as it now stands. See his, *The Gospel According to St. John,* pp. 125–127.

example, follows immediately in 1:19–37 and appears again in 3:25–30 (–36? cf. 5:33–36). The theme of "light" is developed in a series of short passages, 3:19–21; 8:12; 9:4–5; 11:9–10; 12:35–36a, 46, which interpret the figure by placing it in the context of judgment, witness, the healing of blindness, Resurrection and life, and the Passion. The term "life," frequently coupled with the word "eternal," receives extensive development especially in 5:25–29; 6:27–71; and in terms of the Resurrection, 11:1–44; and 20. In the opening dialogue with Nicodemus, 3:3–8, the idea of being born of God (1:13) receives its interpretation. The glory of the Son (1:14), evident in his works, becomes finally manifested in his Passion, 12:28; 17:1–5, *passim*. The first half of the overarching concept of the Son coming into the world from the Father and returning to him again, which becomes more and more explicit as the Gospel progresses, constitutes the basic motif by which the prologue introduces the Gospel.

The Son's Witness in the World, 1:19–12:50   The first division of the body of the Gospel, after an introduction involving the witness of John the Baptizer and the call of disciples, unfolds in a series of episodes alternating with dialogues and discourses in which the latter become more and more extended until they dominate the division. The first four chapters emphasize the manifestation of Jesus as the Son come from God, but beginning with chapter 5 the hostility of Jesus' opponents increases until the polemic reaches a climax in the ironic quotation from Isaiah 6:10 on hardened hearts and Jesus' ominous words on judgment. Suspense is built up as five times (2:4; 7:6, 8, 30, 33; and 8:20) we are told that Jesus' "hour" or "time" has not yet come. Those who refuse to believe are left without excuse because John the Baptizer, Jesus' own works and words, the Scriptures, the Spirit, and the Father have borne witness to him (the verb and noun of "witness" occur some forty-five times in the Gospel). Although the scenes transpire in Judea, Samaria, and Galilee, the actual setting is the world, for it is the world (mentioned thirty-three times in the first twelve chapters) that he came to save. Jews, Samaritans, "the people," and Greeks all appear on stage in their turn and are confronted by the Son's witness in the world.

Two items comprise the introduction to this division of the fourth Gospel: the witness of John the Baptizer and the call of four disciples. In both respects it parallels the opening sections of Mark and Matthew. The author has significantly modified the material on John the Baptizer. He is no longer Elijah who "must come," but only a "voice of one crying in the wilderness"; he no longer baptizes for repentance and forgiveness of sins, but "that he (Jesus) might be revealed to Israel" (cf. 1:31 with Mk. 1:4). Instead of the call to repent assigned to him by Matthew and Luke he simply witnesses to the descent of the Spirit on the Son of God who is "the

Lamb of God who takes away the sin of the world!" (cf. 1:29–36 with Mt. 3:7–10; Lk. 3:7–14). In abbreviated form the quotation from Isaiah 4.0:3 is retained together with the saying about the coming one who will baptize with the Spirit (cf. 1:26–27, 33 with Mk. 1:7–8, para.). John's interview with the delegation from Jerusalem which opens the section, appears to be modeled on the story of Peter's confession (cf. 1:19–23 with Mk. 8:27–29). John's function is no longer a precursor to "prepare the way of the Lord," but a "witness to the light" (1:7) by identifying Jesus as the Son of God. Although the author may be presuming the reader's knowledge of Jesus' baptism, by omitting any mention of it he shifts the emphasis to John's witness and avoids the difficult question of its meaning for which Matthew wrote an apology and which Luke softened by removing it as far as he could from John's story.[65]

The second part of the introduction likewise represents a considerable modification of the Synoptic material. Although, as in the Synoptics, Simon and Andrew are the first disciples to be named, the circumstances of their call is totally different. They are in the vicinity of "Bethany beyond the Jordan" (1:28) rather than by the Sea of Galilee. Andrew, at least, is a disciple of John. There may be some historical reminiscence, missing in the Synoptics, back of this story. If Simon and Andrew were disciples of John and had become acquainted with Jesus then, their readiness precipitately to abandon their fishing business to follow Jesus becomes more understandable. The tradition of the Galilean ministry is not lost sight of and is reflected in the story of Jesus' move to Galilee and the calling of Philip and Nathanael.

As with the treatment of John the Baptizer, the essential point in the call of these disciples is the witness to the true identity of Jesus. So Andrew, after hearing John's announcement, "Behold, the Lamb of God!" went to his brother Simon with the news, "We have found the Messiah." Similarly, Philip summoned Nathanael with the words, "We have found him of whom Moses in the law and also the prophets wrote, Jesus of Nazareth, the son of Joseph." Nathanael's cynical response, "Can anything good come out of Nazareth?" sets the stage for Jesus' own encounter with Nathanael. That these scenes are also models of discipleship is clear from such elements as the twice-repeated "Come and see" (vss. 39 and 46b). Nathanael represents in some way, furthermore, the ideal Israelite, and Jesus' reference to having seen him under the fig tree represents a supernatural insight, eliciting a confession of faith from the astonished Nathanael which reverses his cynical question. But beyond that point the allusions in this final scene in the introduction are not clear. Commentators have offered a variety of suggestions as to the meaning of the phrase "under the fig tree"

65. See pp. 123, 167.

(vss. 48, 50). Perhaps the suggestion that this is a rabbinic picture of a faithful Jew studying Torah is the most likely. Most obscure is the meaning of Jesus' promise of the vision of "Angels of God ascending and descending upon the Son of Man" (vs. 51). The repetition of a verb of saying, and the change to the plural in the main verb, "you will see," have suggested to some interpreters that this verse is out of place.[66] That angels are involved in the stories of the temptation in Matthew (4:11) and Mark (1:13), and the prayer of agony in Luke (22:43), both of which are omitted in John, suggests that this promise may be a vestige of those traditions. The similarity of this saying to Jesus' reply to Caiaphas in Matthew 26:64, on the other hand, suggests that it may be a cryptic allusion to the Passion, or, perhaps, a deliberate modification of the apocalyptic eschatology expressed in the Matthean tradition (cf. Mk. 8:38, Lk. 9:26). Since the time of St. Augustine, commentators have noted the similarity between this saying and Jacob's vision at Bethel (Gen. 28:12), but attempts to discover the meaning of the saying on that basis become too fanciful to be convincing. The meaning of the figure was undoubtedly clear to the author's original audience, but beyond the fact that it promises to reward Nathanael's faith with a confirmation by "greater things," and that it in some way defines his confession, its meaning is no longer available to us.

Chapters 2 through 4, which comprise the first major section of this division of the Gospel begin and end with miracles at Cana in Galilee. There is a chiasm formed by the four episodes which surround the discourse with Nicodemus: (a) the miracle of the wine at the wedding of Cana (2:1–11); (b) the cleansing of the Temple at Jerusalem (2:13–22); (b) Jesus' encounter with the woman of Sychar, at the foot of the Samaritan shrine of Mt. Gerizem (4:7–42); (a) the healing of the officer's son at Cana (4:46–54). The two sides of the chiasm are separated by chapter 3 containing the discourse with Nicodemus and the second witness of John the Baptizer.

In a manner similar to the incredible harvest in the parable of the sower (Mk. 4:8, para.) the enormous amount of wine (approximately one hundred and fifty gallons) in the story of the miracle of Cana (2:1–11) alerts the reader's attention to its symbolic intent. Several items in the story, which have parallels in the Synoptics, function to carry out its symbolic meaning. The setting of a wedding banquet was a popular symbol for the Messianic Age (cf. Mt. 22:1–14, Lk. 14:16–24, and the "marriage supper of the Lamb," Rev. 19:9); the explanation for the six stone jars places Jesus' action in the context of Jewish cleanliness rituals (cf. Mk. 7:1–23), hence the "good wine" stands in some kind of contrast with

---

66. See R. E. Brown, *The Gospel According to John* (i–xii), pp. 88–91. Also J. H. Bernard, *The Gospel According to St. John*, I, pp. 70–72.

Jewish worship; Jesus' protest that his "hour has not yet come" calls attention to the Passion. It may be worth noting that Jesus' mother is mentioned in this Gospel only here (including vs. 12), in the dialogue following the feeding of the multitude (6:42), and at the Crucifixion (19:25–27). That there are difficulties in the continuity of the dialogue, such as Jesus' apparent rebuke of his mother after which he proceeds to fulfill her implied request, suggests the presence of cryptic meanings. The mention of the first of three Passovers in the Gospel following this story (vss. 13, 23) connects it with the feeding of the multitude (6:4) and the Last Supper and Passion (11:55; 12:1; 13:1). The nature of the miracle, furthermore, has a parallel in the Gospels only in the multiplication of the loaves in the feeding of the multitude, and both miracles are significantly similar to stories of Elijah and Elisha (cf. I Kings 17:8–16; II Kings 2:19–22; 3:20–23; 4:1–7, 42–44).

The structure of the Cana story is remarkably like that of the pericope on fasting in Luke 5:33–39 (cf. Mk. 2:18–22, Mt. 9:14–17), which concludes with the parable of the wine and wineskins:

Luke 5:33–39	John 2:1–10
1. The disciples of Jesus are the occasion for the discussion.	The disciples of Jesus are the guests and their belief provides the conclusion.
2. The setting of a marriage feast.	The setting of a marriage feast.
3. The issue is the Jewish ritual of fasting.	The Jewish ritual of purification is involved.
4. "My hour has not yet come."	"The days will come."
5. The jars are filled with water which becomes wine.	"New wine must be put into new wineskins."
6. A concluding comment on the quality of the wine.	A concluding comment on the quality of the wine.

Whatever other meanings each of the pericopae may have, the essential meaning is the same: With the coming of Jesus something new has entered history which replaces the cultus of Judaism. The meaning of the wine is not yet clear to the reader. As is true of a number of items John introduces in these early chapters, the wine will receive further treatment later. Eric Titus has called attention to the fact that the Jews are absent in this story.[67] Like the story of Jesus' walking on the water (6:16–21), the miracle is a private experience of the disciples and does not become a subject of debate between Jesus and his opponents. In this regard its setting is similar to that of the Supper in chapters 13–17.

After a brief reference to Capernaum, the scene is changed to the

67. *The Message of the Fourth Gospel*, pp. 88–89.

Temple in Jerusalem at the Passover. Placing the cleansing of the Temple here, which in the Synoptics following the entry sets the stage for the Passion story, has the effect of placing the body of the Gospel in a Passion setting. The effect is further enhanced by the interpretation which John gives it. Instead of a judgment upon the Temple cultus and an eschatological announcement of its end, John sees Jesus' action as a sign of his Passion and Resurrection. Here we have an example of John's reinterpretation of the eschatology of Gospel tradition. In the reference to the disciples' post-Resurrection recollection and understanding (2:22) John is describing the perspective from which his own interpretation arises.

Between the two sides of the chiasm appear two scenes: Nicodemus' clandestine meeting with Jesus and the second witness to Jesus by John the Baptizer. Jesus' conversation with Nicodemus begins with a development of the idea in the prologue (1:13) of being born of God, which now becomes a rebirth from above by "water and the Spirit" (3:5). This birth, a manifestation of "heavenly things" in contrast to "that which is born of the flesh" (earthly things), is made possible by the Son of Man's descent from heaven to be "lifted up." In the descending, "lifting up" (i.e., Crucifixion), and ascending (i.e., Resurrection) of the Son we are given a precis of the basic motif of the Gospel. Beginning with the sixteenth verse, surely one of the most familiar in the Bible, the conversation, in a manner that is characteristic of the dialogues throughout this division, gives way to a general address to the world. The determinism implicit in the analogy of the wind (vs. 8) is here countered by the universal appeal to belief; a further modification of traditional eschatology appears in the redefinition of divine judgment as the will to disbelief.

A brief note concerning their parallel activities provides the transition to John the Baptizer's second witness to Jesus. In this arrangement the author is not concerned with chronology. R. E. Brown's suggestion that this material really belongs with the first witness of John in 1:19–36 is quite plausible,[68] but its position here serves to advance the developing witness to the coming of the Light into the world (1:5–9). As the wedding at Cana, this scene has manifest connections with the pericope on fasting (Mk. 2:18–20; Lk. 5:33–39). It opens with a dispute with John's disciples, the opponents in this scene are not Jesus' disciples but "a Jew" (some texts make this plural), and the issue is not fasting but purifying, which associates this scene with the wedding at Cana (cf. 2:6). That the dispute bears little relationship to the report brought to John and his reply which follows indicates the influence of the Synoptic pattern. John's reply to the reporters, as that of Jesus in the Synoptic model, takes the

68. On the several problems raised by this section, including the location of Aenon, see his *The Gospel According to John* (i–xii), pp. 150–156.

form of an analogy of a bridegroom. Here, however, the point of the analogy is found in the "friend of the bridegroom" (the best man) John the Baptizer, rather than the wedding guests, who represent Jesus' disciples. The relationship between John and Jesus, first indicated in the prologue (1:6–8, and 15), and restated in John's first witness (1:23, 26, 29–36), comes now into full view. John's parallel ministry in 3:22–23 is to give way before that of Jesus. "All are going to him" (vs. 26), therefore "he must increase, but I must decrease" (vs. 30). The climax of John's witness is a reinforcement of Jesus' own testimony to Nicodemus (3:11–21) concerning the descent of the Son into the world and the judgment based on one's response in belief or disbelief.

Chapter 4 presents the second half of the chiasm: the scene at the foot of the Samaritan shrine Mount Gerizem and the second miracle at Cana. The first of these is introduced by a rumor of Jesus' success in making and baptizing more disciples than John which occasioned his departure for Galilee. This statement appears to be a correction of Mark 1:14 which dates the beginning of the Galilean ministry by John's imprisonment. That this note does not in fact introduce the Galilean ministry—there is, strictly speaking, no such ministry in John comparable to the Synoptics—and that the parenthesis in 3:24 seems to assume the Markan account suggest the complex history of these traditions which lies beyond our recovery. Some of these modifications may be due to literary accident. The introduction does, on the other hand, perform a significant function here. Beyond confirming John's statement that Jesus must increase, it sets the dialogue at Jacob's well in the context of baptism in a way that not only makes the discussion a commentary on John's baptism but a cryptic interpretation of the Christian sacrament.

Jesus' dialogue with the woman of Samaria over the water from Jacob's well versus the "living water" completes the series on the theme of water which begins with John the Baptizer's thrice-repeated reference to his own baptizing with water (1:26, 31, 33, cf. 3:23), appears again in the miracle of turning water into wine at Cana (2:7–9), and in the reference to being "born of water and the Spirit in dialogue with Nicodemus (3:5). In the first of these the water of John's baptism gives way to Jesus' baptism with the Holy Spirit, and in the second the water of the purification rites of Judaism are miraculously changed into the good wine of the wedding feast, but in the third water and Spirit are conjoined in the rebirth into the Kingdom of God. In Jesus' dialogue here the apparent discrepancy is explained by the contrast between the two kinds of water. The water from Jacob's well which needs constantly to be replenished is contrasted with the once-for-all given "living water" for eternal life. The symbolism here is complex. Whereas the water of baptism is certainly in the author's mind, by means of the figure of the spring he carries the meaning further to include the inner resources of the Spirit for the believer (cf. I Cor. 12:13). The thought here is not unlike the treatment of wisdom in the Wisdom Literature (Ecclus. 24:24–31, cf. Isa. 58:11).

This story is for John a model of conversion. Jesus elicits from the woman an unwitting confession of sin (vss. 16–19), to which she responds by confessing him to be a prophet. He then instructs her in the matter of true worship in Spirit in which both the Jewish and Samaritan shrines are set aside (vss. 20–24), completing John's interpretation of the cleansing of the Temple and discloses to her his true identity as the Messiah (vss. 25–26). The disciples are introduced at this point as an audience which will provide the basis for the brief dialogue and discourse to follow. With the woman's witness to Jesus' messiahship in her own city (vss. 28–30), the picture is complete.

The dialogue and discourse which follow develop the theme, introduced by the contrast—paralleling the contrast between the two kinds of water—between the food brought by the disciples and Jesus' food which "is to do the will of him who sent" him. There is undoubtedly in the background an Eucharistic reference here, but the main thrust is the mission of the Church. The harvest which, although said to be four months in the future, is already white and ready (vs. 35), like the hour which "is coming and now is" (vs. 23), represents the two stages in John's drama. His readers are in the "hour" to which Jesus is referring. As an epilogue to the story, the many Samaritans whose faith no longer rests on the woman's testimony because they "have heard for themselves" (vss. 39–42) anticipate Jesus' words to Thomas which conclude the body of the Gospel, "Blessed are those who have not seen and yet have believed" (20:29b) and serve as a foil for the second miracle at Cana.

The point of the story of the healing of the officer's son, which completes the chiasm and concludes the first part of this division, lies in Jesus' complaint, "Unless you see signs and wonders you will not believe" (4:48). That Jesus' response to the officer's request is, if anything, more jarring and incongruous than his response to his mother in the first Cana story, suggests that it is not integral to the story, but represents in some way the author's comment on the role of the story in the plan of the Gospel. The plural of the pronoun confirms the suggestion. The statement is really addressed to the readers rather than the officer and belongs with the series of John's comments on belief which we noted earlier.[69] As at the wedding at Cana there is no audience of Jews and no subsequent dialogue or discourse. Although this story is manifestly a parallel to the healing of the centurion's servant in Luke 7:2–10 (cf. Mt. 8:5–13), it is not clear that John intends it to involve a gentile. The officer by his title is not Roman

69. See pp. 220–230.

(Greek: *basilikos,* the word itself means of or belonging to the king), but is apparently a member of Herod's family or staff. John is at pains both at the beginning and end of the story (vss. 46 and 54) to connect the two Cana stories. A further clue to its meaning here is to be seen in its contrast with the raising of Lazarus (11:1–44). In both stories Jesus is asked to come to the aid of a dying person; in both stories the person is restored to health and others respond in belief. Here, however, Jesus acts immediately to heal at a distance, while in Lazarus' story he deliberately delays until death has taken place "so that you (the disciples) may believe." The story therefore begins John's preparation for his interpretation of the Resurrection and indicates his preoccupation with its evidential value for the beginning of belief in Jesus.

Four episodes provide the framework for the second part of this division of the Gospel: The healing of the sick man (5:2–9); the feeding of the multitude (6:3–14); the healing of the blind (9:1–7); and the raising of Lazarus (11:1–44). In several respects the pattern is different in the second part. Instead of a chiasm divided by one principal discourse, the episodes follow in linear sequence and alternate with dialogues and discourses relating to each. In each of the four episodes there is an audience of Jews and "people" which becomes involved in the subsequent dialogue and discourse. Four secondary episodes, Jesus' walking on the water (6:15–25), his debate with his brothers over attending the Feast of Tabernacles (7:2–14), his anointing at Bethany (12:1–11), and the triumphal entry (12:12–19), are included having to do with the movements of Jesus and efforts of the Jews to find him, but which, like the two Cana stories, are private affairs and are not involved in the dialogues and discourses. In one way or another, however, they are related to two of the main episodes: Jesus' walking on the water and debate with his brothers follow and refer to the feeding of the multitude (cf. 6:22–23; 7:3); The anointing and entry follow and are associated with the raising of Lazarus (cf. 12:1, 17). In addition to these, several brief notes, such as the attempted arrest of Jesus (7:32, 45–52) and attempted stoning (8:50), retreat across Jordan (10:40–42) to Ephraem (11:54), his hiding himself (12:36b), help to heighten the drama and anticipate the Passion. Jewish feasts also play a significant role in this part of the Gospel.[70] An unnamed feast introduces the story of the healing of the sick man at Bethesda (5:1); the feeding of the multitude has its setting in the Passover (6:4); and a note at the end of the story of the raising of Lazarus suggests that it also occurred at the approach of the Passover season (11:55); the Feast of the Tabernacles introduces the discourses of chapters 7 and 8; in the discourse following the healing of the blind man we are told incidentally that it was the Feast

70. See R. E. Brown, *The Gospel According to John* (i–xii), pp. CXLIV, 199ff.

of the Dedication (10:22). In addition to the feasts, the Sabbath controversy also plays a part in the healings of the sick man (5:9bff.) and the
blind man (9:14). Although these references to the festivals explain Jesus'
presence in Jerusalem, they were probably intended to convey more subtle
meanings. The sacramental implications of the association of the feeding
with the Passover, for instance, are obvious, as are the connections between
the raising of Lazarus and Jesus' Passion and Resurrection which are dated
by a Passover. Possibly John here reflects the tendency of the Ancient
Church to reorient the Jewish feasts to its own history and theology.

One of the most important changes in this part of the Gospel is the
appearance of the motif of opposition which was anticipated in the
prologue (1:5, 10–12), hinted at in the cleansing of the Temple (2:18–
25), and in Jesus' move to Galilee (4:43–45). Three consequences follow
from this opposition: the determination of the Jews to kill Jesus builds
until it results in the plot that effected his Crucifixion (11:45–47); many
disciples find the threat too great and either remain disciples secretly or
abandon the movement (6:66; 8:31ff.; 12:42–43); and those who persist
in remaining faithful are harassed and expelled from the synagogue
(9:13–34; 10:10–12; 12:10–11). Against this background of opposition
John is able to develop his theme of witnesses to the Son and his doctrine
of true, enduring belief.

The first of the four controlling episodes, the healing at Bethesda
(5:1–9), although brief presents several problems.[71] We have already
observed that verses 3b and 4 are not included in the best manuscripts. Yet
the complaint of the sick man that he had no one to put him in the water
when it was troubled demands some such explanation. In the light of the
specific identifications of the feasts mentioned elsewhere, the indefinite
reference to "a feast" in the introduction (5:1) is puzzling. The conjecture, based on the discussion of Moses' writings in verses 39–47, that the
feast may have been Pentecost which celebrates the Torah may be true, but
while it completes John's references to the major feasts of Judaism it makes
even more difficult the question why he leaves it unidentified. More important is the fact that the item of the story which John develops in the discourse material, Jesus' authority over the Sabbath, is not integral but
attached as an afterthought. It may be significant of the literary history of
the Gospel that the story itself (vss. 1–9) is in the characteristic form
of a miracle story, while the dialogue which leads into the discourse is
characteristically Johannine.

Although Jesus' admonition "Sin no more" (vs. 14), and the command, "Rise, take up your pallet and walk" (vs. 8), associate this story

71. The ancient texts vary on the name of this place. On the problem and the likelihood
that Bethesda is correct see Brown, *The Gospel According to John* (i–xii), pp.
206–207.

with the healing of the paralytic in Mark 2:1–12, in which the emphasis is on forgiveness of sins, the point John draws from it is expressed in the editorial transition from the dialogue to the discourse: "This was why the Jews sought all the more to kill him, because he not only broke the sabbath but also called God his Father, making himself equal with God" (vs. 18). The Sabbath issue is not, however, John's real concern. It merely provides an instance of Jesus' exercise of his divine authority which is in turn based on his origin as the Son in the Father. Since he is totally and obediently dependent upon the Father, his actions are the actions of God (vs. 30). What follows, then, in the remainder of the chapter concerns this relationship and its meaning for judgment and eternal life. Something of the importance of the Resurrection for John's thought is indicated by the way in which the brief section on the Resurrection (vss. 25–29), like the healing of the officer's son, points forward to the story of Lazarus which in turn interprets Jesus' own Resurrection. The discourse concludes with an argument from the "witnesses" to Jesus. The witnesses are John the Baptizer, the "works" which the Father has granted him to perform, the "voice" of the Father himself (1:32–33; 12:28?), and Scripture.

By placing the second major episode, the feeding of the multitude

An ancient mosaic of the loaves and fishes, now preserved in a Benedictine monastery on the shore of the Sea of Galilee. (Courtesy of the Israel Government Tourist Office.)

(6:1–14), at the Passover, John relates it closely to the Last Supper which it anticipates and interprets. Like the Samaritan woman and the sick man of Bethesda, the people recognize Jesus as a prophet and therefore have yet to learn his true identity. This question is set in sharper relief by their misguided attempt, anticipating Jesus' dialogue with Pilate (18:33–38) and the title over the cross (19:19–22), to make him an earthly king (vs. 15). Separating the feeding of the multitude and the discourse based on it are the story of Jesus walking on the sea and the effort of the people to find him (vss. 16–24). As in Mark this story represents the presence of the Risen Lord in the Church and thus indicates again the two levels of John's drama.

Three distinct discourses separated by changes of scenes follow, only the first of which is based on the feeding of the multitude. The development of thought in the first discourse has several contacts with earlier material. The dialogue begins by placing mundane bread which, like the water from Jacob's well (4:7–15), does not endure in contrast to "the food which endures to eternal life" (vs. 27). This theme is then developed by a homily on "bread from heaven," the text for which is furnished not by Jesus but by his opponents (vs. 31). As the witnesses to Jesus' cleansing of the Temple, the witnesses to the feeding of the multitude, in the face of the sign they have just witnessed, perversely ask for a sign (vs. 30). As the homily begins they, like the Samaritan woman (4:15), still not comprehending ask "Lord give us this bread always." The development moves from a contrast between mundane loaves and food of eternal life to a contrast between the manna in the wilderness and the true bread from heaven which is Jesus, and to the paradox that the earthly Jesus "the son of Joseph" (vs. 42; cf. Mk. 6:1–6, Lk. 4:16–22) is the one who came down from heaven. In the statement, "I am the living bread," which occurs four times in this discourse (vss. 35, 41, 48, and 51) we meet one of John's key phrases in this delineation of Jesus: the "I am" passages (cf. 4:26 and 6:20). In the Eucharistic statement, "He who eats my flesh and drinks my blood has eternal life, and I will raise him up at the last day," (vs. 54) the wine of Cana, the healing of the officer's son and of the sick man of Bethesda (perhaps also the "living water" in 4:10–15) along with the loaves in the feeding of the multitude find their meaning. The note at the end locating the discourse in the synagogue at Capernaum reminds the reader of the opening scene in Jesus' ministry in Mark 1:21–22 and the astonishing authority with which Jesus taught, and thus provides a transition to the epilogue on the offense which this teaching gave.

The following scene (vss. 66–71) in which many of the disciples abandon Jesus, Jesus' challenge to the twelve, and John's version of Peter's confession is crucial to the purpose of the Gospel. The meaning and consequences of belief and unbelief have now been made clear, and the reader is called upon to follow the example of Peter because only in such an enduring belief is eternal life. In a sense this discourse forms a secondary climax to the Gospel. The themes developed in the early chapters are brought together and interpreted in the Eucharistic setting provided by the feeding of the multitude and the homily on the bread from heaven, whereas the epilogue (vss. 66–71), concluding in Peter's confession, anticipates and is closely related to that of Thomas at the end of the body of the Gospel (20:26–29). What follows in the remainder of this division is an extension and development of these themes along two parallel lines: One is the increasing tension between Jesus and the Jews and their determination to kill him, and the other is the hostility encountered by those who persist in believing in him.

Separating the first and second discourses is a brief scene in which Jesus' brothers urge him to go to Judea for the Feast of Tabernacles (7:1–9). The story provides a further explication of the meaning of belief for John. That "even his brothers did not believe in him" and yet they presumed to advise Jesus on how to conduct his ministry presents a bitterly ironic commentary on the failure of his "works" to produce true belief. By the twice-repeated statement, "my time has not yet come" (vss. 6, 8), the story points forward to the true sign, the Passion and Resurrection, to be displayed in Judea. There is a striking parallel between the brothers' suggestion that Jesus make a crass display of his miraculous power and his temptation, in Matthew 4:5–7, Luke 4:9–12, to leap from the Temple. Ironically, the brothers here play the role of Satan.[72] As in the crossing of the Sea of Galilee in 6:16–24, Jesus' secret return to Judea and the search for him set the stage for the next discourse.

John has given this discourse (7:14–44), which takes the form of teaching in the Temple, a strikingly different structure. Only once, in the charge that he has a demon and the ironic question, "Who is seeking to kill you?" is Jesus addressed directly; the dialogue otherwise takes the form of a series of asides and off-stage discussions to which Jesus speaks as though overhearing them. The first of these, strongly reminiscent of Acts 4:13, questions Jesus' learning, hence his authority (vs. 15). His answer, based on his unique relation to God, raises again the issue of blasphemy (cf. 5:17–18), and the resulting discussion closely parallels that of 5:19–47. The parallel is made explicit by the reference in verses 21–24 to the healing in 5:2–9. A new argument is added, justifying healing on the Sabbath; and the issue of Jewish reliance on the Mosaic Torah (7:19) is treated from a different angle. Whereas in 5:39–47 they fail to recognize that the true function of Scripture is to witness to Jesus, here their determination to kill him deliberately violates the law and therefore proves

---

72. Raymond Brown finds parallels to all three temptations in 6:15, 30–31, and 7:2–9, *The Gospel According to John* (i–xii), p. 308.

their inability to keep it. In terms of their own assumptions they have lost the argument. To the earlier discussion of Jesus' claim that he was sent from heaven (5:24, 30–37; 6:38–65) is added in two places, verses 25–29 and 40–43, the paradox of his divine and human origins. The theme of his return to the Father, verses 33–36 (cf. 6:62), which complements it is introduced by the attempt, reminiscent of Acts 4:1ff. and 5:17ff., to arrest him, and is developed in a way which anticipates his reply to the Greeks in 12:20–26 and the major theme of the discourse at the Supper (chs. 14–17).

Commentators have called attention to probable allusions to the rituals of the Feast of Tabernacles in Jesus' proclamation of the "rivers of living water" on the "last day of the feast, the great day" (7:37), and in his declaration at the opening of the third discourse in this series, 8:12, "I am the light of the world, he who follows me will not walk in darkness, but will have the light of life." Both of these seem to echo Zechariah 14 which was read at this feast (cf. vss. 7–8).[73] The proclamation on living water picks up this theme from the scene at Jacob's well in 4:5–15, and extends the definition of this water to include the gift of the Spirit (cf. 3:5–8). The second and third discourses are separated by the conclusion to the story of the attempt to arrest Jesus (vss. 45–52). That the story bears a significant resemblance to Acts 5:17–26, as does the role of Nicodemus (vss. 50–51) to that of Gamaliel in Acts 5:34–39, represents again the two levels on which John's drama takes place. The arrests and harassment of the church leaders are here placed in significant parallel to the opposition which finally accomplished Jesus' Crucifixion.

Beginning with another of the familiar "I am" passages, "I am the light of the world," the third discourse (8:12–59), as the second, moves quickly to resume a theme in the discourse in chapter 5. This time the issue concerns the "witnesses" to Jesus (cf. 5:31–47 with 8:13–30) to which is added the witness of the Passion: "When you have lifted up the Son of man, then you will know that I am he" (vs. 28). The new witness is introduced by another reference to his return to the Father (vss. 21–22, cf. 7:33–36) which elicits an ironic allusion to the Passion in the form of a ridiculous question, "Will he kill himself?" (vs. 22, cf. 5:18; 7:1, 19–20, 25).

Introduced by the statement that "many believed in him" (vs. 30), the final section moves in an atmosphere of increasing conflict to a climax in the attempt to stone him (8:59; cf. the story of Jesus in the synagogue at Nazareth, Lk. 4:16–30, and the stoning of Stephen after his sermon at the Temple, Acts 6:12–7:60). It is, on the one hand, a commentary on Jewish

73. See R. H. Lightfoot, *St. John's Gospel*, pp. 181–184. Also C. H. Dodd, *The Interpretation of the Fourth Gospel*, pp. 347–352.

believers who no longer believe and therefore a definition of the belief of true disciples as continuing "in my word" (vs. 31), and, on the other, a bitter commentary on the hostility of unbelief which brought about the Passion. The argument begins with Jesus' pronouncement: "You will know the truth, and the truth will make you free" (vs. 32) and continues with a series of statements and counterstatements in response:

Jews	Jesus
vs. 33 We are descendants of Abraham (and have never been in bondage).	vs. 34 You are slaves of sin. (You seek to kill me.)
vs. 39 Abraham is our Father.	vs. 40 You seek to kill me. (Abraham would not have done so.)
vs. 41 We have one Father, even God. (We were not born of fornication.)	vs. 44 You are of your father the devil. (He was a murderer.)
vs. 48 You are a Samaritan and have a demon.	vs. 51 Whoever keeps my word will never die.
vs. 53 Are you greater than Abraham? (who died).	vs. 58 Before Abraham was, I am.

The last two stages of the argument reflect the influence of Synoptic materials. The charge that Jesus has a demon is found in Mark 3:22–30 and parallels; and the argument concluding with the play on the tenses of the verb "to be" in verse 58 is modeled on Jesus' dispute with the Sadducees over the resurrection in Mark 12:18–27.

Several characteristics indicate that the third sign in this series (9:1–41) occupies a place of particular importance in the Gospel.[74] The story of the healing of the blind man is interrupted as are the healing of the officer's son, in 4:48, and the raising of Lazarus, 11:14–15, with a comment by Jesus, "it was not that this man sinned, or his parents, but that the works of God might be made manifest in him," which underscores its intended meaning. Jesus' method of healing by the use of spittle appears elsewhere only in Mark 7:33 and 8:23.[75] Sending the man to "wash in the pool of Siloam" (vs. 7) recalls Jesus' sending of the lepers to the priests in Mark 1:44 and Luke 17:14, but it reflects even more closely the healing of Naaman, in II Kings 5:10ff. Quite possibly John intends a veiled allusion to baptism here. That the water for the ritual on the last day of the Feast of Tabernacles (cf. 7:37) was drawn from this pool recalls Jesus' use of Jewish ritual water in the miracle at the wedding of Cana (2:6ff.). The pool also recalls Jacob's well in 4:6ff. and the pool of

74. Cf. Louis J. Martyn, *History and Theology in the Fourth Gospel,* whose interpretation of the Gospel begins with this story.
75. See pp. 100, 135.

Bethesda in 5:2ff. and thus extends once more the meaning of water in the Gospel.[76]

Two parallel motives control John's use of this story. It is in the first place a model of conversion. As the Samaritan woman in chapter 4, the former blind man begins by acknowledging Jesus to be a prophet (vs. 17), but finally responds to Jesus' announcement that he is the Son of Man with the words, "Lord, I believe" (vss. 35–38, cf. 4:26–29; 6:14, 62, 68; 7:40–41; 20:28). This movement is a definition of what it means to "continue in my word" (8:31) and therefore truly to believe. As in Mark's use of the stories of the blind man of Bethsaida (8:22–26) and Bartimaeus (10:46–52), this restoration of physical sight symbolizes the gift of spiritual vision and supplies the meaning of Jesus' claim, "I am the light of the world" (vs. 5).

The main thrust of the story, on the other hand, concerns the opposition and recriminations which the convert encounters as a result of his identification with Jesus. The dialogue which makes this point involves Jesus even less directly than that in 7:14–44. Only at the conclusion, after the former blind man is expelled from the synagogue, does Jesus reenter the picture (vss. 35–41). Nowhere in the Gospel are the two stages on which John's drama takes place more clearly visible. John's contemporaries would have little difficulty recognizing in this story the experiences of Jewish converts of their own time. The dialogue is divided into four scenes: the first interrogation of the former blind man as to his own identity and the identity of the one who had healed him; the interrogation of his parents who identify their son but disclaim any knowledge of the healing; the second interrogation of the former blind man which results in his excommunication; and finally Jesus' conversation first with him and then with the Pharisees, in which he confesses his faith while the Pharisees are condemned.

The discourse which follows in chapter 10 begins with the allegory of the shepherd (vss. 1–6). This analogy, one of John's nearest approaches to the Synoptic parables (cf. Mk. 6:34, Lk. 15:3–7), is followed, as is the Synoptic parable of the sower, with an interpretation (vss. 7–18). The point of the allegory, the contrast between the false leadership of the Pharisees and Jesus the true shepherd, who gives his life for the sheep, affords John the opportunity for another step in his interpretation of the Passion and the definitive Christological statement, "I and the Father are one" (vs. 30 cf. 17:20–23). Two more of John's "I am" passages are added here: "I am the door" (vss. 7, 9) and "I am the Good Shepherd" (vss. 11, 14). The third charge that Jesus has a demon (vss. 19–21, cf.

76. On the use of the stories of the Samaritan woman, the sick man at the pool of Bethesda, and this story in connection with baptism in ancient lectionaries, see Sir Edwin Hoskyns, *The Fourth Gospel*, pp. 363–365.

A present-day bedouin shepherd in Israel carrying on the age-old occupation. (Courtesy of the Israel Government Tourist Office.)

7:20, 8:48–49) and a brief note which locates the discourse at the Feast of the Dedication separate the allegory and its interpretation from the dialogue on belief which follows. A second attempt to stone Jesus and a second attempted arrest (vss. 31 and 39, cf. 7:32, 45–52; 8:59) intensify the drama. The levels of belief beginning with belief in the "works" (vs. 38) and concluding that Jesus is "the Son of God" (vs. 36) are made to stand out in sharp relief. Jesus' retreat across the Jordan and a note that "many believed in him there" (vss. 40–42) close the discourse.

In the raising of Lazarus (11:1–44), the fourth and climactic sign in this division, John departs from his usual pattern in that the dialogue directly relating to it precedes rather than follows the sign itself. We have already noted the ways in which early in this division the author, to better prepare the reader to catch its significance, began to anticipate it (4:46–54 and 5:25–29).[77] In it also the meaning of the "living water" (4:10–15) and the "bread of life" (6:35–58) is disclosed. By his reference in verse 2 connecting this story with the anointing of Jesus at Bethany, John indicates its importance for what follows. The basic function of the story, in fact, as the dialogue and the elaborate structure indicate, is to interpret the Resurrection. The dialogue which gives the story its structure is in three parts: Jesus and the disciples (vss. 7–16), Jesus and Martha (vss. 21–27), Jesus and Mary (vss. 32–34). Three times Jesus' words point up the meaning for the Gospel of this episode (vss. 4, 15, 42). Three times also Jesus' deliberate delay until Lazarus had died is lamented (vss. 21, 32, 37). The disciples' apprehension of returning to Judea where the Jews had recently attempted to kill Jesus points forward to and associates Lazarus' death with the Passion, as the removal of the stone from Lazarus'

Tomb at Bethany traditionally said to be the one from which Lazarus was raised (Jn. 11:43–44). (Courtesy of Dr. Richard Schiemann.)

77. See pp. 241, 243.

tomb associates his resurrection with that of Jesus (vss. 38–41, cf. 20:1). In the act itself of raising Lazarus the first step occurs in the fulfillment of Jesus' words in 5:25–29: "Truly, truly, I say to you, the hour is coming, and now is, when the dead will hear the voice of the Son of God, and those who hear will live."

In the mixed reaction which follows (11:45–57) the significance of the story becomes clear. Many believed, but others reported the affair to the Pharisees (cf. 7:32, 45–52) who with chief priests began the plotting which accomplished the Passion. In this story it has proved true that as Jesus had said, when in the parable of Lazarus the beggar (Lk. 16:19–31) the rich man asked that Lazarus be sent back to the world of the living to warn his brothers, "If they do not hear Moses and the prophets, neither will they be convinced if someone should rise from the dead" (vs. 31). The difference between acknowledging the miracle and saving faith is now abundantly clear. The astonishing irony of Caiaphas' inadvertent prophecy that "one man should die for the people" (vs. 50), Jesus' retreat with his disciples to Ephraim (cf. the withdrawal to Caesarea Philippi in Mk. 8:27ff.), and the announcement of the Passover prepare the reader for the movement toward the Passion which follows.

In chapter 12 the events appear which in the Synoptics begin the Passion story. This point in John therefore affords a good opportunity for observing the differences in structure between it and the Synoptics. In the Synoptic tradition the events leading to the Crucifixion follow a consistent pattern beginning with the triumphal entry and the cleansing of the Temple and followed by a series of controversies, the Little Apocalypse, the anointing at Bethany (Luke omits the anointing), the Last Supper, the arrest and trials. John's rearrangement of these items involves the structure of his entire Gospel. As we have already seen, he has moved the cleansing of the Temple to the end of chapter 2 which has the effect of including nearly the entire Gospel as a prelude to the Passion. The controversies in the Synoptics have their counterpart, as we have observed, in most of the material from the fifth chapter on. In the Synoptics these controversial dialogues are explicitly associated with Jerusalem. It is interesting therefore to observe that, with exception of 6:1–7:9, all of this material has in John a Jerusalem setting. One of the key items in the controversies, furthermore, is the dispute over the resurrection (Mk. 12:18–27, para.) whose function is performed in John by the raising of Lazarus.

John has reversed the order of the entry and the anointing, but in this he had a precedent in Luke who, as we have seen, moved the anointing out of its Passion context altogether. By this rearrangement, it may be worth noting, John has avoided the necessity of returning Jesus to Bethany. The place of the Little Apocalypse is in John taken by the farewell discourse at the Supper. The emphasis in this discourse on Jesus' departure and the coming of the Holy Spirit along with its detachment from the Temple represent John's extensive reinterpretation of Synoptic eschatology.

The twelfth chapter, then, forms a transition which moves the drama toward the Passion and is related more closely to what follows than to the division which it closes. That the raising of Lazarus also plays this transitional role is made clear by the two references to it, especially the plot to kill Lazarus along with Jesus, before and after the entry (12:9–11, and 17–18). In the story of the Greeks wishing to see Jesus, the ironic allusion to Jesus going to teach the Greeks in 7:35 is picked up to add another dimension to the meaning of the Passion. That Philip and Andrew in this story play similar roles to those in the first chapter, in reverse order, represents again the two stages of the drama and the mission of the Apostolic Church. The prayer of agony in Gethsemane (Mk. 14:32–41, para.) and the Transfiguration (Mk. 9:2–8, para.) are combined in verses 27–36a and reinterpreted in terms of the glorification of the Father by the "lifting up" of the Son (cf. also 18:11). An extended editorial note (vss. 36b–43) including quotations from Isaiah 53:1 and 6:10 raises again the issue of belief, concluding with a bitter comment on secret believers. With a brief discourse on belief and judgment, significantly parallel to one near the beginning of this division (3:16–21), the division comes to a close.[78]

The Son's Presence in the Church, 13–17   The second division, comprising nearly one fifth (155 out of 866 vss.) of the Gospel, transpires entirely at the Last Supper wherein Jesus is alone with his disciples. The elaborate dismissal of Judas to perform his traitorous mission (13:18–31) emphasizes this new orientation of the final discourse. What follows is therefore addressed not to the "people" or the Jews but to disciples. The statement in the opening verse "that his hour had come to depart out of this world to the Father" fixes this division within the framework of the Passion. That John dates the Supper "before the Passover" (13:1) and places the Crucifixion on the Day of Preparation, i.e., the afternoon of the night the Passover was observed, seems to suggest his intention in contrast with the Synoptics to disassociate it, and therefore its meaning, from the Passover meal. John is fond of making his material bear multiple meaning, as we have observed, however, and is quite capable of bending the literal chronology to his symbolic purposes. Jesus' death at the same time the Paschal lambs were being slain at the Temple accords well with John the Baptizer's twice-repeated announcement, "Behold, the Lamb of God!" (1:29, 36). Thus Jesus himself becomes the food of the new Passover (cf. 6:50–58, I Cor. 5:7, I Pet. 1:19. That he uses a different word for

78. See p. 239.

lamb from that used of the Passover offering in the LXX and assigns to it a sin-bearing function not usually associated with the latter, as C. H. Dodd has pointed out, only indicates how John can gather the various cultic elements into his interpretation of Jesus. John's failure to call attention to this meaning of his arrangement, which Dodd thinks disproves it, is entirely consistent with his use of cryptic allusions throughout the Gospel.) [79]

This division plays a dual role in the structure of the Gospel as a whole by gathering up in summary, on the one hand, the essential points of the previous division, and by its emphasis on Jesus' return to the Father, on the other hand, interpreting what is to follow. It falls into three parts: actions at the Supper (ch. 13); the farewell discourse (chs. 14–16); and the prayer of intercession (ch. 17). Three items, the washing of the disciples' feet, Judas' dismissal, and the prediction of Peter's denial, control the first section.

That there is no "narrative of institution" is undoubtedly, as Joachim Jeremias has shown, an instance of the *disciplina arcanorum* (secret instructions) to protect the Eucharistic words from pagan profanation.[80] The story of the washing of the disciples' feet is told in elaborate detail and probably contains more than one cryptic meaning (e.g., the prominence of Peter here and at the end of the chapter). Its position here has a basis in Luke 22:24–27 (cf. Mk. 10:35–45) and is virtually in fact a dramatization of verse 27. That John prefers Luke's version of the anointing of Jesus' feet rather than his head as in Mark and Matthew (cf. Jn. 12:1–8 with Lk. 7:37–46 and Mk. 14:1–9; Mt. 26:6–13. But note how John retains the reference to Jesus' burial, applying it, however, to the ointment, not to the anointing) makes this story a complement to the anointing at Bethany. As Mary anointed Jesus' feet, so he anoints the feet of his disciples as an example for their service to one another. As in the Synoptic Gospels the stories of Judas' betrayal and Peter's denial serve as ominous commentaries on the problems of traitors and defectors in the Church. The role of Judas here, however, serves also to underscore the divine determination which the Passion was to fulfill. Thus the betrayal itself becomes a sign (vss. 18–19). The glorifying of the Son of Man and the "new commandment" to "love one another; even as I have loved you" (vss. 31–35) present themes which are to be developed at length in the discourse which follows.

The farewell discourse is itself divided into two parts between chapters

79. Cf. C. K. Barrett, *The Gospel According to St. John*, pp. 39–42, 364; C. H. Dodd, *The Interpretation of the Fourth Gospel*, pp. 233–238, with Jeremias, *The Eucharistic Words of Jesus*, pp. 142–146.
80. *The Eucharistic Words of Jesus*, pp. 72–87. Also C. K. Barrett, *The Gospel According to St. John*, 71, 364; and C. H. Dodd, *The Interpretation of the Fourth Gospel*, pp. 393, n. 1.

14 and 15 by the puzzling command, "Rise, let us go hence" (14:31b, cf. Mk. 14:42). Because of this sentence several commentators have rearranged the discourse, as we have seen, placing chapter 14 at the end. The problem is that chapter 14, although it has some subjects in common (cf. vss. 25–27 with 16:7–15), is actually a separate discourse with no apparent connection with either the beginning or the end of the following two chapters. That two independent discourses have been thrown together here is, of course, possible, but it is hard to believe that a redactor would be so clumsy as to leave this awkward sentence standing where it is.[81]

Several elements in the discourse alert the reader to the presence of cryptic meanings (the word "mystical" sometimes used of this element is hardly appropriate). In 16:25, for example, Jesus promises, "the hour is coming when I shall no longer speak to you in figures but tell you plainly of the Father." Although nothing is said that has not been said the same way before, four verses later his disciples respond, "Ah, now you are speaking plainly, not in any figure!" A few verses earlier, when the disciples ask the meaning of the phrase "a little while" (vss. 18–24), they are answered only indirectly by the figure of the woman in travail. Other veiled references to future knowledge to be conveyed by the Spirit (e.g., 14:7, 25–31a, 16:12–15, 23a) are to the same effect. The possibility that 14:31b is not a literary accident but was intended as a division in the content must not be ruled out. It is interesting that it comes at about the point, in terms of length, at which the dismissal of the catechumens occurs in the later ancient liturgies. Perhaps the giving of "the Peace" just preceding it, although they come in reverse order (vs. 27) is to be associated with the kiss of peace. The Eastern rites still retain at about the same point this ancient dismissal. Such a meaning would be altogether consistent with the *disciplina arcanorum* which, as we have seen, probably accounts for John's omission of the narrative of institution.[82]

Such an interpretation of 14:31b would suggest that, in contrast to chapter 14, chapters 15 and 16 should represent a more esoteric teaching to the faithful, and there is some evidence in that direction. That the very general answer to Judas' question (14:22–23) finds its true exposition in the allegory of the vine (15:1–11) becomes significant when we recall that the vine serves in Luke as a synonym for the wine of the Last Supper (cf. "the fruit of the vine" in the Jewish benediction over the cup. *Mishnah, Ber.*, 6, 1). Only in the cup in the "Liturgy of the Faithful," in other words, after the catechumens have gone can Judas' question truly

81. C. K. Barrett believes these to have been two independent Eucharistic sermons which were brought together here. He has no satisfactory explanation, however, for 14:31b. *The Gospel According to St. John,* pp. 378–380, 392.

82. There is evidence that in some places the worshippers actually moved to another location for the Eucharist proper. See J. H. Srawley, *The Early History of the Liturgy* (Cambridge: At the University Press [1913], 1957), pp. 74–75, 134.

be answered (cf. 6:53–57). The all-important term "believe" occurs in chapter 14 with the same contingency and challenge, appropriate to an address to catechumens, which it has had throughout the preceding division. With exception of the judgment on the unbelieving world in 16:9, on the other hand, it occurs in the second part of the discourse only at the end (16:27, 30–31), where it takes the form of a confession and confirmation of the disciples' faith. Along with the hint of an esoteric teaching in such passages as 15:3 and 13–17, these observations suggest a change of audience similar to that in John's version of Peter's confession in 6:60–69, and that the entire section may reflect elements of, if not the shape of, the Eucharistic celebration in John's day.

There are also in this section some possible reflections of the Passover celebration. The four questions asked by Thomas, Philip, Judas, and "some of his disciples," in 14:5, 8, 22, and 16:17–18, may reflect the four questions of the Passover, as the vine in 15:1–6 can represent both the Paschal cups and the cup of the Eucharist.[83] It is interesting to compare the way Jesus prompts the question in 16:5 (in apparent contradiction to 14:5) with the Father's responsibility to guide the questions at the Passover (*Mishnah, Pes.,* 10, 4). The figure of the vine here in fact carries several meanings. As the parable of the wicked husbandmen in Mark 12:1–9, it may go back to the song of the vineyard in Isaiah 5:1–7. Some interpreters find a connection between it and "the vine (brought) out of Egypt" in Psalms 80:8–16. It represents, therefore, the new people of God constituted by their abiding union with the Son, a union which is expressed in the Eucharistic cup (cf. 6:57). The words, "I am the true vine" (15:1, 5), incidentally, complete the list of Johannine analogies of Jesus introduced by the words, "I am." The list includes "I am the Bread of Life" (6:35–51); "I am the light of the world" (8:12); "I am the door" (10:7, 9); "I am the good shepherd" (10:11, 14); "I am the resurrection and the life" (11:25); "I am the way and the truth, and the life" (14:6).

There is possibly also a play on the word "prepare" in 14:2. It is the same word (Greek: *hetoimadzo*) as the key term in the story of the mission of the disciples to prepare for Jesus' Passover with his disciples which introduces Mark's version of the Last Supper. The preparation, especially cleansing the premises of leaven, is an important feature of the Passover (cf. 15:3; I Cor. 5:7).[84] Here John reverses the roles—Jesus goes to prepare a place for the disciples—and thus dramatizes the eschatological dimension of the Supper.

The first three of the four questions in this section, with Jesus' answers, control the first part of it, chapter 14:

83. *Mishnah, Pes.,* p. 10.
84. *Mishnah, Pes.,* pp. 1–3.

Question	Jesus' Answer
Thomas: How can we know the way? (vs. 5)	I am the way, and the truth, and the life. (vs. 6)
Philip: Show us the Father. (vs. 8)	He who has seen me has seen the Father. (vs. 9b)
Judas: How is it that you will manifest yourself to us, and not to the world? (vs. 22)	If a man loves me, he will keep my word, and my Father will love him, and we will come to him and make our home with him. (vs. 23)

The fourth question, "What does he mean by 'a little while'?" asked by "some of his disciples" at the end of the section (16:16–19), raises the eschatological question with which the Synoptic Little Apocalypse begins (cf. Mk. 13:4, Mt. 24:3, Lk. 21:7). That it is repeated three times indicates its climactic importance for the discourse. The analogy, a woman in travail (16:21), with which Jesus answers the question comes the nearest of any in John to the form of the Synoptic parables. In both form and point it is especially reminiscent of those in Luke 15. Although its most obvious application is to the Passion and Resurrection, it bears also a double reference to the eschatological dimension of the Gospel following as it does the final treatise on the coming of the Spirit (16:7–15). The answer to the final question draws together three items, the Resurrection, the gift of the Spirit, and the eschaton, in such a way that, without eliminating any of them or blurring the distinctions among them, the attention and emphasis fall on the present age of the Spirit in which John's readers live. Both the Resurrection and the eschaton define, therefore, the meaning of the believer's present life in the world. As in the Synoptic Little Apocalypse, though more prominently, the Spirit, the Advocate or Counselor (Greek: *Paraklatos* meaning the lawyer for the defense) will defend them (16:7–11 with Mk. 13:11). John, however, carries the role of the Spirit much farther to include their whole life: "He will guide you into all the truth."

Two contrasting movements of Jesus control this section as a whole and tie it to what precedes and follows. The first movement is from the Father into the world and back again to the Father (16:28). This movement describes the largest pattern of the Gospel, the first division of which describes Jesus' coming into the world as the latter two describe his return. In the contrasting movement Jesus leaves the disciples to return in "a little while" (14:2–3, 18–24, 28; 16:16–22). That this movement describes the Passion is made clear in the reference to one laying "down his life for his friends" (15:13). The conjunction of these two movements is both soteriological and eschatological. As is made more clear in the great prayer which follows, this conjunction results in the believer's union with the

Father who will "keep them from the evil one" and make it possible for them to be with the Son to behold his glory (17:15, 24). This is the meaning of eternal life.

On the disciples' part their response to these movements is to keep his "new commandment" (cf. I Jn. 3:23), to "love one another; even as I have loved you" (13:34; 14:15, 21, 23; 15:10–17), to remember what he has told them (14:26; 15:20; 16:4), and to "abide" as fruit bearing branches in him (15:1–11, 16; 16:1). In contrast stands the world's disbelief, hatred, and consequent judgment (14:27; 15:18–16:4). The two levels on which, as we have observed, the whole Gospel moves are evident in the world's hatred and persecution, described here in terms very similar to those in the Synoptic Little Apocalypse (cf. Mk. 13:9–10, Lk. 21:12–19): "If the world hates you, know that it hated me before it hated you" (15:18). The two levels appear also in a passage which probably refers both to the flight of the disciples at Jesus' arrest (cf. Mk. 14:27, 50) and harassments of the Church of John's time: "The hour is coming, indeed it has come, when you will be scattered . . ." (16:32, cf. "And now I am no more in the world, but they are in the world," 17:11).

As the climax and conclusion both to this division and the Johannine discourses as a whole, Jesus' great prayer (ch. 17) follows. In comparison to the Synoptics it replaces the prayer of agony (Mk. 14:32–41, para.); from the standpoint of the Eucharist it anticipates the intercession or prayers of the faithful in the ancient liturgies.[85] There may be, on the other hand, a veiled allusion to the consecration of the Eucharist, perhaps including the narrative of institution, in the words, "And for their sake I consecrate myself" (vs. 19). The prayer falls into three petitions: "Glorify thy Son that the Son may glorify thee" (vss. 1–5), "I am praying for . . . those whom thou hast given me" (vss. 6–19), and "That they may all be one" (vss. 20–26).

The Son's Glorification in the Passion and Resurrection, 18–20   In the discourses throughout the Gospel John has supplied a careful and profound interpretation of the events of the Passion and Resurrection of Jesus. There is therefore no need for interrupting the story by inserting extended interpretive materials. John's Passion narrative, consequently, follows more closely the Synoptic pattern than any other part of his Gospel. He has, nevertheless, shaped his material to make as clear as possible its connections with the discourses which precede it. Not all of the contrasts between John and the Synoptics here appear to reflect his interpretive modifications. While Matthew twice mentions Caiaphas in connection with the trial and Luke refers to Annas and Caiaphas at the opening of his Gospel (3:2), only John has trials before both. That Jesus' taunt of the soldiers has been

85. Cf. Justin Martyr, *First Apology,* LXVII.

Looking southward down the Kidron Valley between Jerusalem and the Mount of Olives. Jesus crossed this valley after leaving the Last Supper (Jn. 18:1). (Courtesy of Dr. Richard Schiemann.)

moved to the trial before Pilate and made to refer to the content of his teaching (cf. 18:20–21 with Mk. 14:49) probably represents, on the other hand, his interpretive modification. The Scriptures which John cites as having been fulfilled in the Passion are unique to this Gospel.[86] Although there are good reasons for supposing that he may have had a parallel but independent source, the modifications which reflect John's interpretations are the ones which are important to us.

As in the Synoptics the narrative falls into four parts: the arrest (18:1–14), the trials (18:15–19:16), the execution (19:17–30), and

86. C. H. Dodd, *The Interpretation of the Fourth Gospel*, pp. 427–428.

the burial (19:31–42). Perhaps the most noticeable contrast in John's version is the absence of elements of pathos. There is no agony in the garden, no outcry from the cross, no weeping women, no penitent thief nor confessing centurion, no taunts while he is on the cross, no darkness or earthquakes. That Simon of Cyrene bore his cross for him is flatly denied (19:17). The only emotions expressed are the hatred of the Jews and the fear of Pilate. The story moves on a predetermined timetable. At the arrest Jesus steps forward majestically to announce, "I am he" (18:6), whereupon the soldiers fall to the ground in involuntary obeisance. Instead of the flight of the disciples, Jesus, in fulfillment to his own words, orders their release. In place of the Synoptic prayer of agony are Jesus' words, "shall I not drink the cup which the Father has given me?" (18:11, cf. 12:27–28, 17:1). Instead of the silence emphasized in the Synoptics (Mk. 14:61, 15:5, para.), Jesus' retort to the high priest brings on an altercation reminiscent of Paul's trial before the Sanhedrin (Acts 23:2–5). That the Jews lacked the authority to execute is cited as a sign of the divinely predetermined mode of Jesus' death (18:31–32). Although he refuses to make any comments before the high priest, referring them only to his previous teaching, Jesus makes two short speeches to Pilate the first of which (18:36–37) is a definition of his kingship (cf. 6:15 and 19:19–22) important to John's Christology. The second (19:11) is a clear statement of the divine power in control of the Passion. Jesus' last words from the cross are likewise unique to this Gospel. The first of these, in which Jesus commits his mother to the "beloved disciple" (19:26–27) is another instance of a cryptic passage whose meaning can only be surmised.[87] Each of the persons mentioned here appears three times at significant points in the Gospel (excluding the appendix). As we have noted, Jesus' mother appears in connection with the wedding at Cana (2:1–5, 12) and is referred to in the dialogue following the feeding of the multitude (6:42); the "beloved disciple" appears also at the Last Supper (13:23) and at the empty tomb (20:2); the word for "loved," however, is different here. That he appears twice also in the appendix (21:7, 20) does not affect the original intention of these three instances. Probably the second word, "I thirst," is an amplification of the Synoptic story of giving Jesus vinegar to drink (Mk. 15:36, para.), but its effect is to accent the introduction of the hyssop with its obvious connections with the Passover.[88] With the same dignity with which he had conducted his ministry he died. The theological meaning of the final word, "it is finished" (19:30), is patent.

---

87. Cf. R. H. Lightfoot, *St. John's Gospel*, pp. 317–318; C. K. Barrett, *The Gospel According to St. John*, pp. 455, 459; *et al.* with C. H. Dodd, *The Interpretation of the Fourth Gospel*, p. 428 and n. 2.
88. See pp. 252–253.

Jesus' words in the great prayer are now fully true, "I glorified thee on earth, having accomplished the work which thou gavest me to do" (17:4).

In the burial scene the soldiers' failure to break Jesus' legs provides another instance of fulfilled prophecy (19:31–33). The water and blood issuing from the spear wound bear obvious sacramental significance and complete the references to water which run throughout the Gospel. That Jesus' body is properly prepared for burial removes the Synoptic motive for the women's visit to the tomb (cf. Mk. 16:1). Although John is highly critical of the secret disciples (cf. 12:42–43), his inclusion of Nicodemus (cf. 3:1ff.; 7:50–52) with Joseph of Arimathea here shows that he has not entirely excluded them.

John's story of the Resurrection follows more closely but is hardly dependent on that of Luke. The twice-repeated cry of the women, "They have taken away my Lord, and I do not know where they have laid him" (20:2, 13) may have polemical overtones. Its main purpose here, however, is to shift the accent from the empty tomb to the appearances of the Risen Lord. Jesus' appearance to Mary Magdalene (vss. 11–18) replaces Luke's story of the journey to Emmaus (Lk. 24:13–35). Jesus' command to Mary not to hold him because he had "not yet ascended to the Father" is, especially in the light of his invitation to Thomas to touch him (vs. 27), most puzzling. Undoubtedly cryptic meanings, clear enough to his first readers but lost to us, are present here also.

Within this last item, however, along with the first appearance of Jesus to the disciples, John has gathered together the three basic elements of Luke's introduction to Acts (ch. 1): the commission, "As the Father has sent me, even so I send you" (vs. 21); the gift of the Holy Spirit so emphatically promised in the farewell discourse, "Receive the Holy Spirit" (vs. 22); and the Ascension. In the bestowal of the Holy Spirit, John uses a term which occurs in the LXX in the story of the creation of man (Gen. 2:7). As man came to his physical life because "God breathed into his nostrils the breath of life," so now through the infusion (Greek: *emphusao* is the word for breathed in both passages) of the Spirit the believer comes to life eternal. The association of the Logos with God's creative activity which opens the Gospel is in this act of Jesus brought to completion. The power given to the disciples to forgive sins is one of the few contacts of this Gospel with material exclusive to Matthew (cf. vs. 23 with Mt. 16:19 and 18:18).

The "eight days" of verse 26 may have some connection with the length of the Feast of Unleavened Bread which the Passover introduces and, consequently, some influence on the octaves of later Christian festivals. The story of Thomas is John's final commentary on the problem of believing. Without the final step of believing the witness of the Church to the Risen Lord (vs. 25) and the confession, "My Lord and my God!" (vs. 28), all belief becomes faithless. Like Thomas every believer must make the journey from believing him because of the "works" (14:11) to Thomas' confession. With the blessing on "those who have not seen and yet believe" (vs. 29, cf. 17:20–21), which comprehends the Church of John's age and every age, and the editorial postscript, the body of the Gospel comes to a close.

The Epilogue, 21 Whatever may have been the editorial process by which this material became attached to the Gospel, it functions as an epilogue on the mission of the disciples, and therefore, the Church. The story of the miraculous catch of fish, which in Luke is the story of the call of the disciples (cf. Lk. 5:1–11 with 21:2–11), becomes here their recall. The Eucharistic reference in the breakfast is obvious (vss. 9–14, cf. Lk. 24:30–31, 41–43. Note how John reverses the latter; here Jesus prepares the food for the disciples), the significance of the one hundred and fifty-three fish is not so clear. The restoration of Peter (vss. 15–19), which appears to have some connection with Jesus' words in Luke 22:32, "When you have turned again, strengthen your brethren," has the appearance also of a version of his confession (cf. Mk. 8:27–29, para.; Jn. 6:67–69). It is here, at any rate, a story of Peter's restoration, commission, and prediction of his martyrdom. Like a number of elements in this chapter, the meaning of the final paragraph on the "beloved disciple" is no longer available except possibly that it is an attempt to correct the eschatological saying, "Truly, I say to you, there are some standing here who will not taste death before they see the kingdom of God come with power" in Mk. 9:1. An editorial note claiming that the author was an eyewitness "to these things" (vs. 24, cf. 19:35) and a further comment on the failure of the book to include all that Jesus did (cf. 20:30) conclude the Gospel of John as it now stands.

We have now come to the end of our study of the development, preservation, collection, and interpreting of the tradition of Jesus which resulted in our four Canonical Gospels. While this process was going on the Church which started as a small group of "people of the way" in Jerusalem was spreading across the Mediterranean world and elsewhere to become a world Church. A key figure in the first great surge of this movement, the Apostle Paul, was also the author of a number of letters which were preserved to be read and reread in the recipient churches and finally collected to become the foundation of the Epistle side of the developing New Testament. Before we turn to these Letters, however, we must return to Luke, the author of the third Gospel who in the second volume of his history of Christian beginnings has provided us with invaluable background material.

The Structure of John

THE PROLOGUE; 1:1–18
The Logos Hymn—John as a witness—the Incarnation
THE SON'S WITNESS IN THE WORLD; 1:19–12:55
Introduction: The witness of John and call of disciples, 1:19–5
1. The wedding at Cana—cleansing of the Temple, ch. 2
    Discourse to Nicodemus—second witness of John, ch. 3
    The woman at the well—healing at Cana, ch. 4
2. Healing at Bethesda and discourse, ch. 5
    Feeding of the multitude and discourse, chs. 6–8
    Healing of blind man and discourse, chs. 9–10
    Dialogue, raising of Lazarus and transitional discourse, chs. 11–12

THE SON'S PRESENCE IN THE CHURCH, 13–17
Washing of the disciples' feet, dismissal of Judas, prediction of Peter's denial, ch. 13
The Supper discourse and intercessory prayer, 14–17

THE SON'S GLORIFICATION ON THE CROSS, 18–24
The arrest, trials, and Crucifixion, 18–19
The Resurrection, appearances in Jerusalem, 20
The appearance in Galilee and recall of the disciples, 21

Selected Readings

CRITICAL PROBLEMS

Bacon, B. W., *The Fourth Gospel in Research and Debate* (New York: Moffatt, Yard and Company, 1910).
———, *The Gospel of the Hellenists* (New York: Henry Holt and Company, 1933).
Gardner-Smith, Percy, *Saint John and the Synoptic Gospels* (Cambridge: At the University Press, 1938).
Howard, Wilbert F., *The Fourth Gospel in Recent Criticism* (London: The Epworth Press, 1945).

INTERPRETATION

Dodd, C. H., *The Interpretation of the Fourth Gospel* (Cambridge: At the University Press, 1965).
———, *Historical Tradition in the Fourth Gospel* (Cambridge: At the University Press, 1963).
Käsemann, Ernst, *The Testament of Jesus,* tr. Gerhard Krodel (Philadelphia: Fortress Press, 1968).
Martyn, J. Louis, *History and Theology in the Fourth Gospel* (New York: Harper & Row, 1968).

COMMENTARIES

Barrett, C. K., *The Gospel According to St. John* (New York: The Macmillan Company, 1955).

Bernard, J. H., *The Gospel According to St. John* (*ICC*).

Brown, Raymond E., S.S., *The Gospel According to John* (2 vols.), *The Anchor Bible* (Garden City, N.Y.: Doubleday & Co., Inc., 1966).

Hoskyns, Sir Edwin, ed. Francis Noel Davey, rev., *The Fourth Gospel* (London: Faber and Faber, Ltd., 1947).

Lightfoot, Robert H., *St. John's Gospel* (Oxford: At the Clarendon Press, 1957).

Titus, Eric Lane, *The Message of the Fourth Gospel* (New York. Abingdon Press, 1957).

Part II

That Together We May Share in a Common Life

What we have seen and heard we declare to you,
so that you and we together may share in a
common life, that life which we share with the
Father and his Son Jesus Christ.
... I John 1:3

Chapter Four

To the End of the Earth
The Graeco-Roman World;
The Book of Acts;
The Story of Paul

But you shall receive power when the Holy Spirit has come upon you; and you shall be my witnesses in Jerusalem and in all Judea and Samaria and to the end of the earth.... Acts I:8.

The Acts of the Apostles, the second volume in Luke's two-volume story of the beginnings and progress of Christianity, provides a valuable bridge from the Gospel side to the Epistle side of the New Testament. Although not an Epistle, it is, nevertheless, as the only explicit source we have for the earliest period in the life of the Church including an account of Paul's life and mission, an indispensable background to the Epistles. When we cross this bridge, however, we move out of the small strip of land which has been the setting for most of our study thus far into the larger Western world of the Roman Empire. Before proceeding to our study of Acts, therefore, we must survey briefly some of the significant characteristics of that world.[1]

1. Among the Gentiles

As a broad generalization we may describe the Graeco-Roman world into which the Book of Acts carries us as culturally Greek and politically

1. For a more detailed history and description of the Graeco-Roman world see Donald J. Selby, *Toward the Understanding of St. Paul,* ch. 4.

Roman. In the introduction we observed the way in which the successors of Alexander had reduced his conquests to small warring kingdoms each of whose rulers victimized the native populace while maneuvering to restore under his own aegis the whole Empire of Alexander.[2] In reaction to the increasingly intolerable situation thus created, a recrudescence of orientalism challenged the rule of the Greek dynasties. Mesopotamia was lost to the West, and, as a result, the upper Euphrates became the eastern boundary of the Hellenistic world. In the chaos of ensuing invasions and native uprisings that followed, Rome was drawn into an involvement with the East from which it could not withdraw. By conquest or legacy piece after piece of territory in the East came into the burgeoning empire. To preserve its own peace and protect its commerce, Rome found it necessary to extend its control farther East and West until the Mediterranean became a Roman lake (*Mare Nostrum*).

THE ROMAN EMPIRE

Unresolved internal problems and the difficulty of ruling so heterogeneous an empire with a city government precipitated in Rome itself the series of civil uprisings and political wars that ushered in the Augustan Age. With the Empire organized by Augustus a new unity and political stability came to the Mediterranean world. Commerce flourished, pirates were suppressed, and the famous Roman roads made travel easier and safer. Thanks to Alexander and his successors Greek language and culture were to be found throughout the Empire. Although Latin was the language of government and politics, Greek was the international language of literature and culture of the Mediterranean world which made travel and cultural exchanges possible on a wide scale. That the New Testament was written in Greek is not accidental but indicative of the world from which it came. The bearers of the Christian message, therefore, not only found the way open for them to travel in comparative safety across the Empire (although such travel was still not without its dangers as Paul observed in II Cor. 11:26), but they also could communicate their message in a common language.

Although the power and organization of Augustus' Empire brought much needed peace and unity, particularly to the Levant, it was not without its drawbacks and its detractors. The Greek culture of the Alexandrian successors was never more than a veneer. Native languages persisted alongside Greek, so too did local loyalties and religions. Aramaic, for example, continued to be the common language of the Jews. That the superscription above the cross was, according to John 19:22, written in Greek, Latin, and Hebrew (i.e., Aramaic) provides a significant commentary on the linguistic

2. See pp. 4ff.

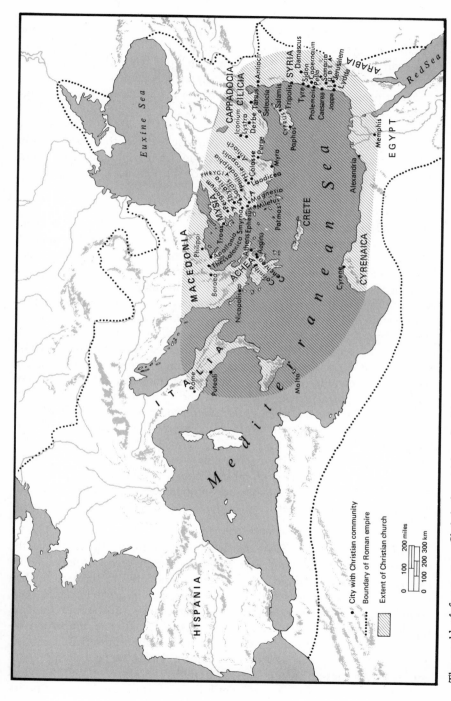

The world of first-century Christianity. (Adapted with permission of The Macmillan Company from *Macmillan Bible Atlas* by Y. Aharoni and Michael Avi-Yonah. Copyright © 1964 by Carta, Jerusalem. © Copyright 1966 by Carta, Jerusalem.)

situation in much of the Roman world. In the famous story of Paul and Barnabas at Lystra not only did the people hail them in their native Lycaonian tongue, but identified them with gods who, although bearing Greek names, were nevertheless native Lycaonian deities.

Many peoples felt that their freedom and independence were too high a price to pay for the new unity and peace of Roman rule. We have already noted the restless antagonism of the Jews which came to its most violent expression in the Zealots. The contrast between the latter and the Sadducees may be taken as a fair and not uncommon picture of the situation in the eastern districts and provinces of the Empire.

RELIGIONS IN THE EMPIRE

Several factors contributed to this feeling. The sight of Roman soldiers, an ever-present reminder of foreign rule was a bitter blow to national pride, but even more, the tax system—often unfairly administered—money lenders, and other economic abuses created abrasive situations which tended to offset the advantages of membership in the Empire. Less obvious but more profound and far-reaching consequences followed the historic changes which resulted in the Empire. As the smaller kingdoms were swallowed up in the larger provinces of the Roman world, and as the population became more mobile, people found themselves disoriented. Without the frame-of-reference and self-understanding provided by their former national religions and cultures, many were lost in the vast sea of humanity that was the new world. Philosophical skepticism, one of the gifts of the Greeks, further eroded the old national religions and left the common people little to cling to in the great impersonal world into which they had been thrown. Emperor worship which was designed to provide the much needed social cohesion was of little help. Among the masses of the people personal circumstances were often deplorable. Slavery was widespread. Grinding poverty and interminable indebtedness among the lower classes left little room for hope. Fatalism settled over the people like a cloud and inevitably became a kind of religion.

The Mystery Religions Since the beginning of the Hellenistic Age the increasing contacts between East and West stimulated considerable religious syncretism. At times this syncretism amounted to little more than renaming the local deities with Greek names, but in other instances composite religions began to appear. The irrelevance of the old national religions in the new world and the manifest artificiality of Emperor worship left a vacuum into which several of these composite religions flowed. These mystery religions, as they were known, had a particularly powerful appeal to the masses because they addressed themselves to the individual and his needs. Free from any responsibility to furnish sanctions for political authority, social structures, or national identity, the mysteries created cultic fellowships within which the individual could find acceptance, meaning, and identity. In these sacred fraternities, moreover, the devotee was given secret knowledge of the divine forces behind the universe by which he might in the course of his mortal existence outwit the fates and finally win a safe passage to a blessed immortality.

The background of the mysteries is the variety of fertility cults of the ancient Orient. The myths which gave the ancient cults their structure were concerned with the meaning of the rotation of seasons and the problem of fertility. The key to these myths was the death, or absence, of a deity whose loss brought paralysis on the fecundity of nature. Eventually, as the drama unfolded, the god was restored and the earth became fertile again. No longer concerned with the agricultural basis of the myths, the mysteries fastened attention upon the death and resurrection of the deity which now represented the solution to two problems, the triumph over an evil fate and the achievement of a divine immortality. The basic myth was elaborated with ideas borrowed from astrology and the popular philosophies as well as the various ethnic religions of the Levant. By participating in a secret rite which with appropriate mystery and fascinating and colorful pageantry dramatized the mythical story, sharing a sacred meal, and receiving of secret knowledge, passwords and the like, the initiate was united in a saving identification with the victory of his god.

Astrology and Magic   Alongside the mystery cults astrology offered its way of salvation to the tortured souls of the masses. Having made its way from the Mesopotamian world where it had enjoyed a long and venerable history, astrology offered the believer a geography of outer space and the aid of the astral deities in predicting the future, in averting a disastrous fate, and finally in breaking free from the prison of this physical existence to the peace of reunion with the divine abode beyond the stars. For the problems of many of the less sophisticated, a simpler and cruder answer was found in magic. Across the land exorcists and miracle workers were to be found who, armed with books of magic formulae, claimed to be able to expel demons, cure ills, and ameliorate the sundry troubles of those who would pay for their services (cf. Acts 8:4–25; 19:13–19).[3]

Gnosticism   In the fluidity of the times these competing religions and philosophies could hardly be expected to remain in neat categories. Out of the syncretism of the Imperial Age, consequently, grew a pattern of ideas which, because of its claim to impart secret, divinely revealed knowledge for the deliverance of the soul from the temporal miseries of its material

3. For examples of these formulae see Adolph Deissmann, *Light From the Ancient East,* tr. Lionel R. Strachen (London: Hodder and Stoughton, 1927), pp. 255–263.

existence, was known as Gnosticism (from *gnosis,* the Greek word for knowledge). Because of the lateness of our sources, and the fact that it embraced a bewildering variety of theories, many of the features of Gnosticism, and indeed its history, are not entirely clear. Like much of the thought of the time it was sharply dualistic, believing the material world to be the creation of an inferior deity and essentially evil. In contrast to the incorruptible spirit of man, his body and soul share the origins and nature of the cosmos in which he is imprisoned. Man's spirit, on the other hand, having "fallen" from its proper element of divine light with the true transcendant God beyond the seven planets, lies dormant within created man, pathetically ignorant of its true nature and origins. By the divine revelation which Gnosticism presumes to provide, the spirit is enabled to find its way back at death to its own element. The debt of Gnosticism to the mysteries, astrology, and popular Greek philosophies is obvious. The ethical consequences of the Gnostic movements ranged all the way from extreme asceticism to unabashed libertinism.[4]

Our interest in these movements lies in the fact that the later writings of the New Testament reflect the presence of their influence. How early they began to appear and how widespread they were at the beginning of Christianity are impossible to know. The great heresies of the second and succeeding centuries, which evoked from the Church Fathers an extensive literature on which we are dependent for much of our knowledge, were Gnostic. That docetism, which turned the humanity of Jesus into an illusion or separated him from the divine Christ in order to preserve its strict dualism, was a standard feature of these heresies suggests that Christianity may have been a catalyst in the process of their development. The anti-Judaic and Old Testament bias and the depreciation of creation, which characterize the Gnostic systems, stand in such contrast to the perspective of the New Testament that it is risky, at any rate, to treat the Gnostic movements as sources of Christian ideas, especially within the New Testament itself.

PHILOSOPHIES

For more sophisticated and doughty souls, of course, there remained the Greeks' greatest gift to mankind, philosophy. Although the great universal systems of Plato and Aristotle had given way to philosophies of more modest and practical sorts, philosophy itself was still very much alive.

Two philosophical schools, Epicureanism and Stoicism (cf. Acts 17:18), merit our attention here. Both of these schools share with Plato

---

4. For a valuable study of Gnosticism see Hans Jonas, *The Gnostic Religion,* 2nd ed. rev. (Boston: Beacon Press, 1963). Also Rudolf Bultmann, *Primitive Christianity,* tr. R. H. Fuller (New York: Meridian Books, 1957), pp. 162–171.

and Aristotle the legacy of the Socratic tradition, although they draw on different facets of that tradition. Rejecting Platonic dualism, they based their systems on a monistic materialism which set the individual over against an impersonal and essentially unfriendly world.

Epicureanism   The founder of the first of these philosophies, Epicurus (341–270 B.C.), based his system on the assumption, taken from the teaching of Aristippus, a disciple of Socrates a century earlier, that pleasure is the basic good. But since many, especially the more intense and sensual, pleasures are fleeting and leave painful aftereffects, the nobler pleasures of the mind, such as virtue, beauty, and wisdom, are the true values. These pleasures are more passive, and therefore Epicurus advocated withdrawing from public life with a few faithful friends to lead a life of quiet contemplation.

Perhaps even more than pain, fear, in Epicurus' view, is the great destroyer of values. By teaching that the gods, although they exist, have nothing to do with human affairs, he sought to free man from fear of their vengeance; and by teaching that at death man, soul and body, simply dissolves into the atoms of which he is composed, he sought to allay man's fear of death.

As the ancient motto, "eat, drink, and be merry," attributed to them shows, the later Epicureans did not always enjoy a reputation for the high-minded contemplative life advocated by their founder. Epictetus (b. A.D. 50), the famous Stoic teacher, although not altogether unbiased, spoke of Epicurus in a scathing criticism as little more than an out-and-out hedonist.[5] The kind of retirement from the world that Epicurus advocated demanded resources of both wealth and temperament that only a minority could afford. Epicureanism, consequently, never gained the popular influence which its rival, Stoicism, enjoyed.

Stoicism   Perhaps because it took the turmoil and problems of life more seriously, Stoicism was far more popular and influential. Zeno (ca. 340–265 B.C.), a Phoenician from Cyprus who founded the school, took as his starting point the Cynic tradition which goes back to Antisthenes, another disciple of Socrates, whose chief concern was to cultivate the ability to live the simple life, being content with poverty and finding one's pleasure in hard work and self-sufficiency. Zeno's school acquired its name from the porch (*stoa*) in Athens where he taught. Essentially fatalistic, it identified virtue as the highest good. By virtue the Stoics meant a kind of personal integrity which accepts its fate and refuses to be perturbed or broken by it. Epictetus, one of the school's best exponents, wrote, "Seek not that the things which happen should happen as you wish; but wish the things

5. *Discourses*, II, 20.

which happen to be as they are, and you will have a tranquil flow of life."[6]

In an essentially pantheistic way Stoicism identified God as the governing reason behind nature which has predetermined in advance its entire course. Since only man's will is in his own power, it is his only freedom. He must therefore exercise that freedom by bringing his will into harmony with the divine predetermination of his life and circumstances or his virtue and happiness will be broken by the inexorable wheel of fate. The way of the Stoic was lonely and essentially self-centered, but the sheer courage it evoked was not without its appeal.

One by-product of Stoicism is of interest because of its influence on the style of some parts of the New Testament. No longer content to convey their teaching to the privileged circle of their own disciples these philosophers, following the example of the Cynics earlier, abandoned the formal schools and as mendicant lecturers carried their message to the streets and marketplaces of the cities. For this activity the formal lectures were ill-suited. Consequently, they developed instead a form of popular hortatory discourse known as the diatribe. Concerned with practical ethics rather than metaphysical speculation the diatribe moved from one theme to another by a chain of association rather than by logical outline. The themes were developed dramatically by anecdotes, rhetorical questions, proverbs, and the like which had strong popular appeal. Paul occasionally shows the influence of the diatribe, and the Epistle of James is a notable example.

THE DIASPORA

Among the heterogeneous peoples in the cities throughout the Empire were Jewish communities known as the Diaspora (from the Greek word for sowing or scattering as of seeds. The term is not used in this sense in the New Testament except possibly in Jn. 7:35), which are of interest to us because of their importance to the spread of Christianity. From the time of the Babylonian Exile significant communities of Jews were to be found outside Palestine. After Alexander the Great Jews in greater numbers migrated to Egypt, Syria, and cities of Asia Minor. By the time of Augustus, Strabo could write: "Now these Jews have already gotten into all cities; and it is hard to find a place in the habitable earth that hath not admitted this tribe of men, and is not possessed by them."[7]

The Character of Diaspora Judaism   Several factors enabled these communities to maintain their identity with Judaism in the homeland. By means of the annual half-shekel Temple tax every loyal male Jew had a

---

6. *Encheiridion*, 8. Quoted from *Discourses of Epictetus*, tr. George Long (London: The Chesterfield Society, n.d.), p. 425.
7. Quoted by Josephus, *Ant.*, XIV, ch. 7 (Whiston's translation).

share in the services in the Temple at Jerusalem, and each day as he turned his face toward the Holy City to say his prayers he could do so knowing that the sacrifices were being offered there for him. Although most Jews of the Diaspora had little knowledge of, or contact with, the vast body of interpretation that was the Oral Torah,[8] they had the Scripture, their "portable fatherland," and in the Exile long before, they had learned to offer "the sacrifice of the lips" in prayers and study of Torah. There was also the possibility of realizing, as many of them did, the dream of making a festal pilgrimage to Jerusalem. The many "devout men from every nation under heaven" to whom Peter preached at Pentecost (Acts 2:5) were probably pilgrims who for one reason or another had not returned home.[9]

Many Diaspora Jews probably had little if any knowledge of Hebrew or Aramaic. For them the Septuagint was the Scripture, or at least served as the Targum for the liturgical readings in the synagogues. Through the Greek Scriptures, and the subtle but pervasive influences of having Greek as their mother tongue, the Jews of the Diaspora were open to gentile influences to a greater degree than their brothers in the homeland. Philo may be an extreme example, but he nevertheless represents the way in which a sophisticated Jewish scholar could interpret his faith by means of Greek ideas. As real as these influences on Diaspora Judaism were, they were far outweighed by the influence of the synagogue, which served not only as a place of worship in lieu of the Temple but as a school and community center. Since the synagogue was essentially a Pharisaic institution, the Diaspora Jews may be classed, in a general way at least, with the Pharisees. Their kosher laws and religious exclusivism kept them from melting into the general population and disappearing. Because of the assistance which the Jews had given him, Julius Caesar had granted them certain privileges which protected their religious scruples and traditions not only in Palestine but throughout the Empire.[10] These privileges were generally respected down to the time of Hadrian and left the Jews, wherever they were, free to maintain their exclusive communities intact. In its earliest period the Church was essentially a Jewish sect and consequently enjoyed the protection of these privileges.[11]

Proselytes The Diaspora in the first century has been estimated to be far larger than the Jewish population of Palestine.[12] Since many of these were more than likely proselytes, they call our attention to a factor of

8. See Selby, *Toward the Understanding of St. Paul*, pp. 35–39.
9. Henry J. Cadbury, however, regards these men as gentiles. See *The Beginnings of Christianity*, V, pp. 67–68 and 113–114.
10. Josephus records documents to this effect in *Ant.*, XIV, ch. 10.
11. For later developments see pp. 406–407.
12. Charles Guignebert, *The Jewish World in the Time of Jesus*, tr. S. H. Hooke (New York: E. P. Dutton & Company, 1939), pp. 214–215.

importance for the spread of Christianity in the gentile world, namely, the prior influence of Judaism upon the gentiles which helped immeasurably to prepare the way for the Church. How much deliberate effort was expended in winning proselytes to Judaism is hard to say.[13] Jesus' well-known remark concerning the zeal of the Pharisees for proselyting (Mt. 23:15) indicates that such efforts were not unknown. Along with the exotic appeal that oriental religions seem to have had, the high ethical monotheism of Judaism held a strong appeal for those in the Roman world who had had enough of the decadence and libertinism of the old polytheisms and the fantastic mythologies of the newer faiths.

The God-Fearers   Not all of those attracted to Judaism, however, were willing to undergo circumcision. As a result there was on the fringes of the synagogues of the Diaspora a number of people known as God-fearers (Acts 10:2). Attending the synagogue and obeying the so-called Noachian Laws,[14] they provided a fertile soil for the seed of the Christian Gospel. The extent of Jewish influence, of course, went beyond the proselytes and God-fearers. Latin writers such as Juvenal bitterly complained of it; and the Jewish historian Josephus could boast of it to his Greek opponent.[15] It is hard to overestimate the importance of this influence for the beginnings of Christianity.

It was a bewildering variety of peoples, cultures, and ideas, held together by the authority of Rome and the language of the Greeks, into which Christianity entered as it began its journey across the Empire. The Greek language was not an unmixed blessing. Required to express its Gospel in Greek the Church inevitably found that language, which it shared in common with many other religions and philosophies, a two-way street. For that language was destined to carry into Christianity many shades of meaning, many ideas which in other contexts had attached themselves to the terms the Church was obliged to use. The gentile converts, moreover, were bound to find their understanding colored by their backgrounds in that variegated world. Before the New Testament was finished, controversies had already begun which were to rock the Church for the next several centuries. The ideas which generated those controversies were awaiting the first missionaries as they set out across the gentile world. For that story we return to the book of Acts.

13. For a valuable study of Jewish proselyting see F. M. Derwacter, *Preparing the Way for Paul* (New York: The Macmillan Co., 1930), esp. ch. III, pp. 41–60, also 86–94.
14. See pp. 299–300. Also Selby, *Toward the Understanding of St. Paul*, pp. 56–57.
15. Juvenal, *Satirea*, 14, 96, and Josephus, *Against Apion*, II, 39. Also *Ant.*, XIV, 7, 2. Cf. Plutarch, *Superstition.*

2. A Second Volume for Theophilus: Acts

Because of the close connection of the two volumes, we may expect to find the same basic characteristics of method, themes, and purpose in Acts which we have already observed in Luke's Gospel. For the same reason questions of date, authorship, and the like, to the extent to which they are answered for the Gospel, are answered also for Acts. In several ways, therefore, Luke's Gospel has prepared us to understand his second volume. This preparation extends beyond the introductory matters to those involving the content and purpose of the work.

THE GOSPEL AND ACTS

Not only the final words (24:53), but the treatment of the Temple throughout the Gospel, for example, lead us to expect a continuation of the Temple theme which concludes in a separation of the Christian community therefrom (cf. Lk. 13:35). The essential content of the Church's message in its "witness" to the world has been given in words of the Risen Lord (24:45–49). From the concluding words of the same passage, we should expect something like the outpouring of the Spirit at Pentecost and the world mission which occupies the major part of Acts. That the mission should be directed toward the gentiles is a theme developed in the Gospel with increasing clarity from Simeon's prophecy in the opening section (2:32) to the phrase "to all nations" in this passage (24:47. Cf. 4:23–27; 7:2–10; 8:26–34; 13:29; 17:18; *passim*). From the role of the twelve in the Gospel we should expect to find them, in Acts, in charge of the Church and its mission; and the defection of Judas together with the emphasis on the number twelve should almost lead us to expect such a story as the election of Matthias in Acts 1:15–26. Similarly, the mission of the seventy (10:1–7) and the strange exorcist (9:49–50) point forward to all those outside the circle of the twelve who carried the Gospel to Samaria, Antioch, and beyond, especially Paul whose office it was to carry the Church's witness to Caesar himself (Acts 27:24).

Not only the demands of the commission (Lk. 24:47) but the prominence of journeys in the Gospel should lead us to expect the journey motif to be in control of the story in Acts. By such contrasts as those between the synagogues of Nazareth and Capernaum (Lk. 4:16–37), between the common people and Jewish leadership (Lk. 7:29, *passim*), and Jesus' trials before the Sanhedrin and before Herod and Pilate (Lk. 22:66–23:25), we can anticipate the arrests and trials of the Apostles by the Sanhedrin and the stoning of Stephen in contrast to the vindication of the Christian witnesses before every Roman magistrate before whom they were brought. We should expect also to find in Acts the fulfillment of

Scripture and the Resurrection to be the two evidences of the truth of Christian claims for Jesus and the answers to the problem of the Crucifixion of him who was presumed to be the Messiah (Lk. 24:19–31, 45–46).

THE PROBLEM OF THE TEXT

The Book of Acts presents problems, on the other hand, which are different from those found in the Gospel. The text of Acts, for example, is more problematical than that of any other book in the New Testament. The difficulty is not so much in the number and extent of variant readings as in the fact that the variant manuscripts fall into two distinct groups in such a way as to present us with two editions of Acts. From the families of texts they represent, the two groups are usually designated as the Neutral and Western texts. The Western Text, being the longer, is regarded by most scholars as a later expansion of the original which therefore is more accurately represented by the briefer Neutral Text. This does not mean that the Neutral Text is to be preferred in every instance. The text underlying the Revised Standard Version, for example, basically follows the Neutral Text; but in a number of passages, in which the Western reading contrary to its general character is shorter, and intrinsically more probable, the latter is preferred.

The problem of the original text of Acts is far from solved. Some earlier scholars argued that both text traditions are from Luke who revised and enlarged his own work. Others have argued for the priority of the Western Text.[16] The prevailing opinion now favors an eclectic text, such as that of the RSV, which gives precedent to the so-called Neutral Text but weighs each variant on its own merits. It is not difficult to see how the problems of the interpreter are compounded when in numerous places he cannot be sure what are the author's actual words. Perhaps it is not a great exaggeration to say that in the Western Text we have in hand the first interpreter of Acts.[17] Martin Dibelius has called attention to the way in which this text smooths over the seams between the narratives in the early part of Acts. Since such a process would hardly work in reverse, the Western text must be the latter.[18] These seams, as we shall see, have important implications for the question of the sources of Acts.

16. For a leading proponent of this view see A. C. Clark, *The Acts of the Apostles.* For an extensive and thorough treatment of this problem including an answer to Clark's theory and other important theories, with conclusions which are followed essentially by most interpreters today, see James Hardy Ropes, "The Text of Acts," Foakes Jackson and Lake, *The Beginnings of Christianity,* Vol. III.

17. That textual criticism may have given too much attention to the "original author" and too little to the Church's growing tradition has been suggested in a provocative article by Harold H. Oliver, "Implications of *Redaktionsgeschichte* for the Textual Criticism of the New Testament," *JAAR,* Vol. XXXVI, Mar., 1968, p. 41ff.

18. "The Text of Acts: An Urgent Critical Task," *Studies in the Acts of the Apostles,* pp. 84–87.

One conclusion that can be drawn from the peculiar problem of the text of Acts is that Luke's two volumes were separated early and came into the Canon by different routes. In spite of the fact that the oldest tradition we have on such matters, the Muratorian Fragment,[19] explicitly affirms their common authorship, no manuscript or Canonical list known to us places Luke's two volumes together. When in the middle of the second century the heretic Marcion created his new canon to replace the Hebrew Scriptures—an action which was to shape and give impetus to the formation of the orthodox Canon—he used a mutilated version of Luke's Gospel and ten of Paul's letters but not Acts. As Luke's Gospel, along with the other Synoptics, began to make its way into the liturgical readings of the Church as an alternate to the Prophets, Acts was left behind. The text of Acts was not, in consequence, afforded the protection which the Church's concern for the traditions of Jesus would naturally provide for the Gospel. Until Paul's collected Letters, and probably some of the Catholic Epistles, began to appear in the liturgical readings, and a new interest in the Apostles made Acts important to the Church, its text "was exposed to the typically varied fate of a literary text."[20] Thus, contrary to the Gospel, Acts is a comparative latecomer to the Canon, and its various positions before and after Paul's Letters in the ancient texts are explained by its use as a background for the Epistles. Whatever else the textual history of Acts may indicate, it means at least that the Church's interest in it was different from Luke's purpose in writing it.

THE SOURCES OF ACTS

A second problem arises from the fact that, unlike Luke's Gospel, there are no parallel works with which Acts shares common sources. Whereas we know from the study of his Gospel how Luke tended to handle his sources, the subject matter and character of Acts are so different that such knowledge is of comparatively little help. We must keep in mind that even after the first fervent expectations of the parousia had waned the interests of the Church centered in Jesus rather than her own history. The accumulation of sources for the latter would be meager and of a different character than for the Gospels. We cannot suppose, of course, with the author of the Muratorian Fragment that Luke was a witness to all he wrote in Acts, but neither can we reduce the question of sources to the first few chapters by assuming on the basis of the "we sections," that Luke accumulated his information for Paul's career as a companion. It is significant that even Martin Dibelius, who unlike many scholars has

---

19. See pp. 74–75.
20. Martin Dibelius, *Studies in the Acts of the Apostles*, p. 89. On Luke's intended audience and the literary character of Acts, see p. 147.

defended the traditional identification of the author of Acts with the Luke of Paul's letters, could make no use of this theory in answering the problem of sources.[21]

The Early Period Source analyses have, of course, been attempted in the study of Acts. Such phenomena as the markedly larger number of Semitisms in early chapters have encouraged such attempts. Perhaps the best known of these theories is the work of Adolph Harnack who identified no fewer than five sources in the first fifteen chapters of Acts.[22] The suspicion, nevertheless, can never be removed that, in part at least, the material in the early chapters came into Acts directly from oral traditions. It was just this suspicion which led Martin Dibelius to the publication in 1923 of an essay which has become a landmark in the study of Acts. By application of the insights of form criticism he developed a method of literary analysis of the stories of Acts which he called style criticism.[23] Most of the stories in the early chapters of Acts, when separated from the editorial cement which binds them together, Dibelius found to be legends (i.e., edifying stories of holy men). None of these stories by itself shows any interest in the history or development of the community. The continuity and generalizations which give these chapters the character of a history of the beginnings of the Church are therefore the work of the author and may often have back of them little more than his inferences from the stories themselves.

There are a few sentences in these stories which as they stand are confused and rather meaningless, but when translated into Aramaic become convincingly meaningful. This fact does suggest, for some of them at least, written Aramaic sources.[24] Such evidence, however, can hardly be stretched to indicate extended documents back of these chapters. Whether these stories came to Luke in written or oral form makes little difference to the main question. Their brief scenes, like windows, allow us glimpses into the life of the beginning Church, but little more. The question is not so much, are they historical? as what sort of history do they convey? Source analysis, in other words, can do little to take us back of Luke's understanding of the history of the beginnings of the Church.

21. *Studies in the Acts of the Apostles,* pp. 5f. *passim.*
22. For an excellent survey of this and other source theories of Acts see Foakes Jackson and Lake, *The Beginnings of Christianity,* Vol. II, pp. 121ff., and 363–433.
23. "Style Criticism of the Books of Acts" reprinted in *Studies in the Acts of the Apostles,* pp. 1–25. This entire book, consisting of a number of articles on the study of Acts written by Dibelius from 1923 to the end of his life, is an invaluable contribution to scholarship.
24. See Wilfred L. Knox, *The Acts of the Apostles* (Cambridge: At the University Press, 1948), pp. 19–21.

Paul's Itinerary For the journeys of Paul, on the other hand, Dibelius believes that Luke had a series of travel notes.[25] Perhaps, as he suggests, Paul or one of his company kept a log for future reference on a return trip. As evidence for this assumption, Dibelius calls attention to the unimportant stations and similar details of the journey (e.g., Acts 20:13–14) mentioned in the course of Luke's narrative, which serve no apparent purpose nor contribute to the development of his theme. Certainly the notable change in the character of the narrative between the early chapters and the journeys of Paul makes such a theory plausible. It is worth noting that where in the letters of Paul we have references to his movements which allow a comparison with Acts Luke's general knowledge of Paul's itinerary seems vindicated. Yet, as we shall see, there are differences at these same points which indicate that at best Luke's knowledge was second hand. The episodes, on the other hand, with which Luke rounds out his narrative came to Luke, like the stories in the early chapters, as independent traditions and likely in oral form. Probably many of them came from the local traditions of the churches involved.

The Voyage and Shipwreck of Paul The story of the voyage and shipwreck of Paul in Acts 27 is a different matter. The vivid realism of this story has often been commented upon[26] and assumed to show that it comes from an eyewitness who, if not the author of Acts, was the author of the diary which Luke used as a source. Dibelius disagrees with this assumption and has revived a theory, advanced by Julius Wellhausen, that the story of Paul's shipwreck was derived from popular secular literature. Observing that only nineteen of the forty-one verses, 27:4–44, which comprise the story of the voyage have anything to do with Paul (i.e., 27:9–11, 21–26, 30–38, 43) and that these could be excised without interrupting or damaging the story, Dibelius concludes that Luke has in this chapter utilized a piece of conventional Greek literature. He cites the evidence for this kind of literature collected by Edward Norden[27] and points out that a story of such obviously literary character—it is one of the most literary passages in Acts—would hardly come from the diary of a traveling companion of Paul. The first-person pronouns in this chapter are not therefore, according to Dibelius, to be related to the earlier "we sections" which came from actual travel notes. That Luke may have

25. *Studies in Acts*, pp. 104–105, 126, 197ff.
26. See Foakes Jackson and Lake, *The Beginnings of Christianity*, IV, pp. 324–325; *IB*, IX, pp. 331–332; W. M. Ramsay, *St. Paul the Traveller and the Roman Citizen* (Grand Rapids, Mich.: Baker Book House [1897], 1960), pp. 336ff.
27. *Agnostos Theos* (B. G. Teubner, Leipzig-Berlin, 1913). It should be noted that Lake and Cadbury allow the possibility that "the narrative has been coloured in a few details by traditional accounts of shipwrecks." Foakes Jackson and Lake, *The Beginnings of Christianity*, IV, p. 324.

elaborated the story, especially in verses 21–26 and 30–38, has been suggested by a number of scholars,[28] but not many would contend that the entire story has such a secular origin. The theory, however, is at least possible, but in the absence of more concrete evidence must remain no more than a plausible guess.

To summarize, Luke's sources for Acts probably consisted in a series of individual traditions from the Jerusalem church and other churches in the surrounding area as far north as Antioch, together with travel notes from a companion of Paul, isolated traditions from the churches founded by or visited by Paul, and possibly a conventional story of a voyage and shipwreck.

THE SPEECHES

The speeches that punctuate the narrative throughout Acts are a special case, and the question of their sources and relation to their contexts must be examined apart from the other materials. The following table lists the speeches which, more than simply extended dialogue, are long enough to have significance of their own.

The Principal Speeches in Acts

Peter	Church's Prayer	Paul
1:16–22	1:24–25	13:16–41
2:14–40	4:24–30	14:15–17
3:11–26	**Gamaliel**	17:22–31
4:8–12	5:35–39	20:18–35
5:29–32	**Stephen**	22:1–21
10:34–43	7:2–53	24:10–21
11:5–17	**James**	26:2–23
15:7–11	15:13–21	27:21–26
	21:20–25	28:17–20
	Ephesian Town Clerk	28:25–28
	19:35–40	
	Tertullus	
	24:2–8	
	Festus	
	25:14–21	
	25:24–27	
	Letters	
	15:23–29	
	23:26–30	

28. For example, Ernst Haenchen, "The Book of Acts as Source Material for the History of Early Christianity," in Keck and Martyn, *Studies in Luke-Acts,* pp. 275–278.

These speeches, which constitute nearly one third of the book, are scattered throughout Acts and reflect a familiar and important characteristic of ancient historiography. The question is whether they represent the actual words of the speakers to whom they are attributed or are later compositions. Even if we assume Luke to have been Paul's traveling companion, we cannot suppose him to have been present on the occasions of the speeches in the early chapters of Acts. If, as some of the older scholars maintained, Luke composed these early chapters from written sources, the question is only pushed back one step by attributing the speeches to the author of Luke's sources. That the community in those first few years, waiting almost daily for the return of Jesus and the end of the age, would keep records of such speeches is most improbable. The Aramaic flavor of the speeches in the environs of Jerusalem, which is sometimes urged as evidence of their authenticity, probably reflects nothing more than Luke's sense of appropriateness.

Common Style of the Speeches   Two observations may serve both to indicate Luke's authorship of the speeches and his purpose in including them. First, their style, regardless of the speaker to whom they are assigned, has a uniformity that not only identifies them with one another but also with the author of the narratives in which they are embedded. Attempts have occasionally been made to compare the speeches of Peter and Paul with their respective letters in the New Testament in order to discover characteristics which might indicate that however much Luke may have modified their style in harmony with his work they do rest ultimately on authentic speeches of the Apostles. Aside from the fact that some of them have become self-defeating by including with equal success works such as II Peter, which cannot have been written by Peter, and the Pastoral Epistles which were probably not the work of Paul,[29] these studies have been effectively countered by comparisons of the same speeches with other New Testament writers which produced similar results.[30]

Interdependence of the Speeches   A second indication of Lukan authorship of the speeches is their interdependence. The way in which they supplement one another by supplying steps in the argument, and the like, needed to complete the thought otherwise incomplete in each creates

29. See pp. 410–412, 451–452.
30. See Henry J. Cadbury, "The Speeches in Acts," Foakes Jackson and Lake, *The Beginnings of Christianity*, V, pp. 413–415. This entire article, pp. 402–427, is most important. See also by the same author *The Making of Luke-Acts*, pp. 184–193. Two other important studies are Dibelius, "The Speeches in Acts and Ancient Historiography," in his *Studies in Acts*, pp. 138–185 and Edward Schweitzer, "Concerning the Speeches in Acts," in Keck and Martyn, *Studies in Luke-Acts*, pp. 208–214.

an interlocking effect that ties the speeches together as a distinct element of the book. The reader scarcely notices this characteristic because of the way the arguments unfold as he progresses from one speech to another. Cadbury has called attention to several clear examples of this interdependence.[31] One of these will illustrate the point.

In Peter's speech at Pentecost he includes a quotation from Psalm 16:8–11 (Acts 2:25–28; cf. 13:34ff.) the key words of which are, "For thou wilt not abandon my soul to Hades, nor let thy Holy One see corruption." The argument which is developed in the speech following this quotation is that this statement must either apply to the Psalmist David or to someone else at a later time. Since it obviously cannot apply to David whose "tomb is with us to this day," it must apply to Jesus whom "God raised up." David is therefore a prophet of the Resurrection of Christ. The proposition that the statement must either apply to the writer or to another is not explicit, but in the story of Philip and the eunuch the proposition appears in the eunuch's question, "About whom, pray, does the prophet say this, about himself or about someone else?" (Acts 8:34). In this latter passage, in contrast, the remainder of the argument although basically the same is only implied.

Another characteristic of the speeches, which not only shows the way they interlock, but in the way they connect Acts to Luke's Gospel indicates their interpretive role in the over-all plan of Luke-Acts, is their relation to certain passages in the Gospel. We observed several times in the Gospel that events in the life of Jesus, especially his Passion and Resurrection, were divinely ordained and anticipated by Israel's prophets, but with one or two minor exceptions the actual prophecies are not given. The "necessity" of the Passion in Jesus' announcements, Luke 9:22, 44 (cf. vs. 51); 13:33; 17:25; and 22:22, becomes explicitly associated with Scriptural predictions in 18:31 (cf. 10:24) and 22:37, but only in the latter passage is a Scripture cited. Even here, although the informed reader recalling the remainder of that chapter might recognize the connection, the words, "And he was reckoned with transgressors," quoted from Isaiah 53:12, by themselves hardly support Luke's claims of Biblical authority for the Passion. Appropriately, this motif reaches its climax in the final chapter of the Gospel where in two passages, 24:26–27, and 44:47, both the Passion and Resurrection are said to have been plainly predicted of the Christ, but again no hint is given as to what these Scriptures are.

In the last of these passages, however, standing at the very end of the Gospel, the reader is given the necessary clue for finding the prophe-

31. Foakes Jackson and Lake, *The Beginnings of Christianity,* V, pp. 407–410.

cies. This passage, as we observed in a previous chapter,[32] is the model for the apostolic proclamation of the Gospel (which is thereby given the weight of Jesus' own authority) and consequently points directly to the sermons in Acts. When we turn to these speeches we find the answer to our question in an impressive array of Scriptural texts with appropriate exegesis. The following table will show how thoroughly Luke has documented his claim.

Fulfillment of Scripture in the Speeches in Acts

Acts	Prophecy Cited	Event Predicted
3:25	Gen. 12:1ff.; 22:18	Christ's coming
13:33	*Ps. 2:7	Christ's coming
3:22–23; 7:37	Deut. 18:15–19	Jesus the prophet
4:25–26	Ps. 2:1–2	Rejection and opposition
4:11	*Ps. 118:22	Rejection and opposition
1:20	Ps. 69:25	Judas' betrayal
7:49–50	Isa. 66:1–2	Judgment on the Temple
8:32–33	Isa. 53:7–8	Crucifixion
2:25–28; 13:35	Ps. 16:8–11	Resurrection
2:34–35	Ps. 110:1	Ascension (cf. Lk. 24:50)
2:17–21	Joel 2:28–32	Outpouring of Holy Spirit (cf. Lk. 24:49 also 3:22, 4:1)
13:47	Isa. 49:6	Gentile mission (cf. Lk. 2:22; 13:29; 24:47)
15:16–18	Amos 9:11–12	
13:41	Hab. 1:5	Coming judgment (cf. Lk. 21:10–11, 25–26)

* These two texts are also cited in the Gospel.

The Speeches and Contemporary Literature   Discussions of the speeches in Acts usually include a well-known quotation from the Preface of Thucydides, *The Peloponnesian War*, in which he explains his practice in including speeches in his story:

> With reference to the speeches in this history, some were delivered before the war began, others while it was going on; some I heard myself, others I got from various quarters; it was in all cases difficult to carry them word for word in one's memory so my habit has been to make the speakers say what was in my opinion demanded of them by the various occasions,

32. See p. 193.

of course adhering as closely as possible to the general sense of what they really said.[33]

Since for other reasons we may conclude that Luke was influenced by the practices of Greek writers of history, it is reasonable to assume that his use of speeches in Acts is also similar to theirs. Inasmuch as Thucydidean scholars differ considerably on how much literal accuracy he is actually claiming for the speeches in his history, however, the passage is not as decisive as one could wish in determining that practice. Certainly, as is clear in such writers as Xenophon and Herodotus whose works contain speeches which are obviously not authentic, composing speeches for important junctures in the story was a common and accepted means by which the author heightened the drama and interpreted the events for his readers. Often such speeches also afforded the author an opportunity to display his own rhetorical skill.

That some of the speeches in Acts are of a different character and function does not, as is sometimes suggested, argue against the conclusion that Luke was following Greek literary conventions.[34] For these speeches differ from conventional Greek literature in the same way and degree as do the subject and purpose of Acts. Similarly, the correspondence of the consistent outline of the missionary sermons with the kerygma proves nothing more than Luke's familiarity with the tradition. It would be surprising indeed if Luke had not acquired a good knowledge of the themes and patterns of Christian preaching which had been developed in the first-century Church. The sermons therefore represent "what seemed to a well-informed Christian of the next generation the main outline of the Christian message as first presented by Jesus' followers in Palestine and in the cities of the Mediterranean world."[35]

The Interpretative Role of the Speeches The comparison of Acts with Thucydides, however, calls attention to another and important aspect of the speeches. Far more than dramatic effect and literary interest, the speeches afford Luke an opportunity to interpret his material. In this interpretation at least three points are prominent: (1) the proclamation of the Gospel for which Luke's examples are both models and apology, (2) defense of Christianity before Roman authorities, (3) an explanation of the significance of the separation of the Church from the synagogues and Temple. It is instructive to observe when the Gospel and Acts are

---

33. Quoted from *The Complete Writings of Thucydides.* The unabridged Crawley translation with an introduction by John H. Findley, Jr. (New York: The Modern Library. 1951), p. 14.
34. C. S. C. Williams, *The Acts of the Apostles* (New York: Harper & Row, 1957), pp. 40ff.
35. Cadbury in Foakes Jackson and Lake, *The Beginnings of Christianity,* V, p. 427.

taken together how wide is the range of this element in Luke's work. The worship of the Church in Luke's time is reflected, for example, in the hymns of the birth stories, Luke 1–2, and the prayers of the Church in Acts 1:24–25 and 4:24–30. Similarly, the Christian version of the homilies of the synagogues is represented in Luke 4:21–27 and Acts 13:16–41. Paul's speech to the presbyters of Ephesus is both an answer and extension to the charge to the missioners in Luke 10:2–16; as the kerygma speeches in Acts answer to the post-Resurrection commission in Luke 24:44–49. Special models for the mission to the gentiles are provided in Paul's addresses to the Lycaonians, 14:15–17, and to the Athenians, 17:22–31. In Jesus' controversies with the scribes and Pharisees and in such speeches as that of Stephen, Acts 7:2–53, and the speeches of Paul in 13:46–47; 22:3–21; and 28:25–28, Luke presents his polemic against the Jewish Establishment because of its rejection and opposition to the Christian movement. Likewise Paul's defense before Felix, Festus, and Agrippa II (Acts 24:10–21 and 26:2–23) conveys Luke's apologetic in defense of the innocence of Christianity with respect to the law and well-being of the Empire.

SOME STRUCTURAL PATTERNS OF ACTS

We have already observed in his Gospel a number of the literary habits and patterns by which Luke interprets his material.[36] It will be useful for us to note how these appear in his second volume. Some of them, such as the journey motif, of course, are simply carried through both volumes, giving them unity and continuity. Several others, however, because of the way in which they reveal Luke's emphases and interests in Acts, deserve special attention.

Anticipations All through the Gospel Luke has guided the attention of the reader by briefly mentioning items which become important in later developments. At the end of the Gospel four such anticipations, the kerygma (Lk. 24:46–47), the commission (vss. 47–48), the promise of the Holy Spirit (vs. 49), and the Ascension (vs. 51), lead the reader directly to the opening chapters of Acts and to one of the main themes of the entire book. Similarly, in Acts such anticipations help to maintain the thread of the narrative, to sustain the reader's interest, and to direct attention to those items which Luke wants to emphasize.

The reference, in 2:44, to the community of goods in the church at Jerusalem, for example, anticipates the story of Barnabas' generosity (4:32–37), the duplicity of Ananias and Sapphira (5:1–11), and the introduction for Stephen's sermon and martyrdom (6:1–8). At the same

36. See pp. 149–162.

time the mention of Barnabas anticipates his role in establishing the important church at Antioch and the career of Paul (9:27; 11:25–30; 12:25–15:40). The story of Paul's conversion and his mission which dominates the book is anticipated in the two brief references to him at Stephen's martyrdom (7:58, 8:1). In the founding of the church in Antioch, during which the Gospel was first preached to the Greeks (11:19–26), the commissioning of Paul and Barnabas (13:1–3) to the gentile mission is anticipated. That Peter baptized Cornelius, an uncircumcised gentile, anticipates Paul's abandonment of circumcision, as Peter's defense of his action before the Jerusalem apostles (11:1–18) anticipates the similar defense by Paul and Barnabas (15:1–31) of theirs. The arrests and trials of the apostles anticipate those of Paul, as the accusation that Stephen had spoken against the Temple anticipates the charge that Paul had profaned it.

Restatements Perhaps the most striking device for underscoring and interpreting the key episodes in his narrative is the retelling of the story in a later speech. Thus Paul's conversion is twice retold in his defense before the mob in Jerusalem (22:1–21) and before Agrippa (26:2–23), and Peter restates the story of the conversion of Cornelius before the Apostles in Jerusalem (11:5–17) and makes a less specific allusion to it again at the Council in Jerusalem (15:7–9). (Cf. 15:19–22 with 15:23–29 and 21:25; ch. 19 with 20:18–23; 21:27–23:22 with 23:26–30; 21:16–23:10 with 24:10–21; 25:1–12 with 25:13–21 and 24–27; 21:16–25:12 with 28:17–19.[37])

Doubles or Pairs Luke's fondness for the number two seems in many instances to have gone beyond a conscious literary device to a mental habit. Examples of duality either of pairs or doubles in the Gospel and Acts are too numerous to list. Yet a number of them not only reflect the way in which Luke's mind worked, but are deliberate devices for interpreting items and for maintaining meaningful continuities by setting them in parallels.

The two volumes, the Gospel and Acts, are themselves the most obvious pair, which in a number of ways set the pattern for many of the others, especially those which tie the two volumes together. The Passion and Resurrection form the dividing line between the story of Jesus and the disciples and that of the Church under the leadership of the apostles and the guidance of the Holy Spirit.

Prominent among the pairs in Acts are the two heroes of the story, Peter and Paul. Among the duplicated items which make their stories

37. See Henry J. Cadbury, "The Speeches in Acts," Foakes Jackson and Lake, *The Beginnings of Christianity,* Vol. V, pp. 422–423.

parallel are: Each of them was delivered from prison (cf. 12:2–11 with 16:19–34); each of them healed a man lame from birth (cf. 3:1–10 with 14:8–10); each of them performed many indirect healings, Peter with his shadow and Paul with handkerchiefs (cf. 5:15–16 with 19:11–12); each of them raised a dead person (cf. 9:36–42 with 20:7–12); each of them offered his defense before an assembly of the apostles for baptizing uncircumcised gentiles (cf. 11:1–18 with 15:1–29); each of them rebuked an evil magician (cf. 8:18–24 with 13:7–12); although they share this characteristic with Stephen, their initial sermons are similar extended summaries of Israel's history. The similarities of several of these parallels to stories in the Gospel (cf. Lk. 4:40; 5:15, 17–26; 7:11–17; 8:41–42, 49–56, *passim*) help to establish the continuity between the ministry of Jesus and the Apostolic Church, as the parallels themselves express the continuity between that Church and Paul's gentile mission.

Other parallels serve to delineate connections or add emphasis to important elements of Luke's story. The stoning of Stephen and that of Paul, for example, make a connection between them which has a number of ramifications (cf. I Thess. 2:14–16). Peter's question, "Whether it is right in the sight of God to listen to you rather than to God, you must judge" (4:19), becomes a stated principle in 5:29. The parallel stories of the economic threat of the Gospel in the healing of the clairvoyant slave girl in Philippi (16:16–21) and the declining sale of idols in Ephesus (19:24–27) express one of Luke's interpretations of the gentile opposition. By means of a second filling of the Holy Spirit (cf. 2:1–4 with 4:31), Luke underscores the basic role of the Spirit in his second volume. The two arrests of Apostles which dominate the first section of Acts (4:1ff. and 5:17ff.) introduce and emphasize the violent opposition the mission encounters wherever it goes. Agabus' prediction of the famine (11:27–28) anticipates and intensifies his ominous warning to Paul in 21:10–11. The two occasions on which pagans mistake Paul for a god (14:8–13 and 28:3–6) underscore his miraculous power, as his two recitals of the story of his conversion (22:1–21 and 26:4–23) add emphasis to the importance to Luke's purpose of that event. The break between the Synagogue and Church is dramatized by the two occasions on which Paul moved his teaching from a synagogue to private or gentile quarters (cf. 18:6–7 and 19:9–10).

That some of these doubles and pairs, such as Agabus' prophetic warning standing before each of Paul's two journeys to Jerusalem with alms (11:28; 21:10–11), the two trips through Galatia (13:13–25 and 15:40–16:6), the two plots against Paul's life (20:3 and 23:12ff.), the two stories of Paul and the Nazarite vow (18:18 and 21:23ff.), and his being rescued from the Jews twice by the tribune (21:31ff. and 23:10), may actually be doublets of the same incidents should not keep us from observing the use to which Luke puts this device. His use of parallels, in other words, reflects not so much his inability to control his sources as the patterns and stereotypes in his own mind as he interprets the meaning and growth of the Church.

Models By means of highly dramatic situations, extended treatment, repetitions, and the like Luke calls attention to several key characters in his story who serve as models for his controlling interests. There are, for instance, three models of Christian conversion: the Ethiopian eunuch (8:26–39) whose story is told once; the gentile centurion, Cornelius (10:1–48 and 11:1–18) whose story is told twice; and Paul (9:1–31, 22:1–21, and 26:4–23) whose story is related three times. Paul, of course, becomes an even more important model of a Christian missionary in chapters 13–23. A picture of the ideal martyr is provided in the story of Stephen (6:1–8:1), just as the ideal leadership of the Church is depicted in the roles of Peter and James. To a lesser degree several other persons set examples for the benefit of Luke's readers. Gamaliel, whose advice to the Jewish Council becomes a proposition on the basis of which Luke proposes to demonstrate the validity of Christianity (5:33–39), is an example of the wise open-mindedness which Judaism should exercise toward the Church. Gallio and Festus furnish similar examples for gentiles (18:12–17, 25:1ff.).

Echoes of the Passion At a number of crucial points in Acts, a saying or description occurs which contains a striking echo of the Passion theme in the Gospel. There are four of these, for instance, in the story of Stephen's martyrdom. At the beginning of his sermon before the Sanhedrin the members "saw that his face was like the face of an angel" (6:15), which echoes the altered countenance of Jesus at the Transfiguration (Lk. 9:29). His vision of "Jesus standing at the right hand of God" (7:55–56) recalls Jesus' words at his trial, "But from now on the Son of man shall be seated at the right hand of the power of God" (Lk. 23:69). Two of the three "Last Words" of Jesus, occurring only in Luke, are reflected in Stephen's dying words, "Lord Jesus, receive my spirit", and "Lord, do not hold this sin against them" (cf. 7:59–60 with Lk. 23:34, 46).

In the story of Peter's arrest Herod intended "after the Passover to bring him out to the people" (12:4c) which recalls the attempt of chief priests and scribes, which Luke omits in his Gospel, to arrest Jesus secretly, "for they said, 'not during the feast, lest there be a tumult of the people.' " (Mk. 14:2).

Similarly, in the story of Paul, beginning with his final journey to Jerusalem, echoes of the Passion appear. Paul's apprehension of trouble in Jerusalem expressed in his speech at Miletus (20:22–25) and the warnings he received at Tyre and Caesarea (21:4, 10–12) are strongly reminiscent of the three predictions of the Passion which Luke's Gospel has in common with the other two Synoptic Gospels (Lk. 9:22, 44; 18:31–33). His declaration of readiness to be imprisoned or even to die for the name of Jesus, in 21:13, recalls Peter's similar words in Luke 22:33, as the words of his friends, "The will of the Lord be done," verse 14, recall Jesus' prayer of agony, Luke 22:42. The cries of the mob in 21:36 and 22:22 correspond with those against Jesus in Luke 23:18, 21. (Cf. Paul's rebuke of the high priest, 23:2–5, with John 18:20–23.) Paul's trial before Herod Agrippa II, included with the trials before two Roman governors (25:13–26:32), which concludes with the declaration of Paul's innocence, recalls Jesus' similar trial before an earlier Herod between two hearings before Pilate and the latter's attempt to acquit him (Lk. 23:6–23). Thus in the stories of Peter, Stephen, and Paul Luke dramatizes the meaning of Jesus' command to take up the cross and follow him (Lk. 9:23–26).

THE OUTLINE OF ACTS

It is significant of Luke's way of thinking that the Book of Acts can be divided into two parts between chapters 12 and 13, or into three divisions, 1:1–8:1, 8:2–15:35, and 15:36–28:31 with equal justification. The two-part structure reflects Luke's interest in his two heroes, Peter and Paul, whereas the three-part outline is concerned with the journeys which carried the Gospel from Jerusalem to Rome. There is no need to attribute either of these structures to his sources. Luke has shown in handling his material in his first volume a complexity of mind sufficient to account for this organization of Acts. That the three-part structure is important to his purpose Luke has shown by the way in which the commission in the prologue, 1:8, much as a table of contents, provides an outline for it: (1) Jerusalem (1:1–8:1a), (2) Judea and Samaria (8:1b–15:35), (3) the end of the earth (15:36–28:31). At least part of that purpose can be seen in the way Gamaliel's advice to the Sanhedrin (5:34–39) furnishes the proposition by which Luke intends to prove Christianity to be the true religion: "If this plan or this undertaking is of men, it will fail; but if it is of God, you will not be able to overthrow them. You might even be found opposing God!"

Preface and Prologue, 1:1–26 Characteristically the brief preface to this second volume connects itself by a reference to Theophilus, the patron, with the main preface that opens the first volume, offers the briefest possible summary of what has gone before, and leads almost imperceptibly into the prologue to follow. The prologue itself, except for the final item, is in essence a review of the last chapter of the Gospel. It consists of four items which are (1) the appearances of the Risen Lord "during forty days" which complement the forty days of the temptation in the wilderness (Lk. 4:1ff.); (2) the promise of the Holy Spirit and the commission to be witnesses "to the end of the earth" (1:8); (3) the Ascension of Jesus and the promise of his return; (4) the restoration of the twelve—made necessary by the treachery and suicide of Judas—in the election of Matthias. With this restoration the stage is set for the opening episode on the day of Pentecost.

In Jerusalem, 2:1–8:1a The body of the book opens with the story of the descent of the Holy Spirit upon the believers. This story is basic to the entire work, for the Holy Spirit supplies the power and direction for the Church's mission at every point in the story. There are, in fact, two sources of divine power in Acts, the Holy Spirit and the name of Jesus. As the quotation from Joel indicates, the Holy Spirit is associated with prophecy, hence with the proclamation of the Gospel, while by the name of Jesus his "signs and wonders" (i.e., healings) continue through the Church.

Three events follow the outpouring of the Spirit: the gift of other languages, Peter's sermon, and the baptizing of three thousand believers. The whole passage functions as a proleptic statement of a dominant theme of Acts, the inspiration of the Spirit for the world mission of the Church. That the "one place" is left so indefinite and that the "multitude" could hardly have gathered at the "house where they were sitting" may indicate the symbolic character of the story. In the "tongues as of fire" in verse 3 and the "other tongues" of verse 4 there appears a play on words which connects the gift of the Holy Spirit directly with the proclamation of the Gospel to the nations. The nations are, of course, represented in the "devout men from every nation under heaven" (vs. 5). That there is some question whether Luke means the multitude to be Jews (the word is absent in vs. 5 in some manuscripts) or to include gentiles (cf. vss. 10b and 11a) may be the result of his deliberate ambiguity. Perhaps he is attempting to dramatize the connection between the Spirit and the gentile mission by including symbolically in this opening scene the nations of the world.[38]

By means of the diversity of languages Luke carries out his definition of the promised "power" (cf. Lk. 24:29; Acts 1:8) and the divine nature of the Church's witness. In the fact that the "other tongues" were intelligible languages so that "each one heard them speaking in his own language" there may be a subtle repudiation of the ecstatic gibberish which

38. See Foakes Jackson and Lake, *The Beginnings of Christianity,* Vol. V, pp. 67–68, 113–114.

already in Paul's time had become a problem (cf. I Cor. 12–14). The cynical charge that the apostles were drunk may reflect an earlier tradition of such an ecstatic experience, but it is more likely that Luke is here representing again the ludicrous lengths to which those will go who are determined not to believe. The charge of drunkenness is therefore set over against the prophecy of Joel.

Although Peter's sermon begins with the quotation from Joel 2:28–32, it consists in an expansion of the post-Resurrection saying in Luke 24:44–49 (cf. Acts 2:22–24, 38–39) with an exegesis of Psalm 16:8–11 as a proof text of Jesus' Resurrection and Ascension. This sermon sets the pattern for those that follow. The interlocution in verse 37 separates and accents the concluding call to repentance, a device which Luke uses several times throughout the book. The story concludes with a summary, which expands the picture of the apostles in the "upper room" in the Prologue (1:12, 14) by describing the life of the new community and

Archaeological excavations of the southwest corner of the Temple area in Jerusalem, uncovering the stonework of Herod's building. (Courtesy of Dr. Richard Schiemann.)

introducing several items to be developed later such as the community of goods and their distribution, "signs and wonders," prayer, and the Temple.

The remainder of this section moves along two complementary lines: the proclamation of the Gospel and the opposition and response to it; and the inner life of the community. The first of these is developed by three stories of arrests, trials, and finally martyrdom; the second is carried through by means of the editorial summaries and three stories concerning the community of goods. The healing of a lame man by Peter and John provides the occasion for Peter's second sermon which in turn provokes their arrest and trial. Peter's third speech, the first of several defenses of Christianity in Acts, concludes after another interlocution with the question of obedience to man or to God (4:19) by which this story is related to the second story of Apostolic arrests (cf. 5:29).

By an extended editorial summary on healings (5:12–16), which provides the setting for the second arrest as the healing of the lame man and Peter's sermon (3:1–26) did for the first, Luke reaffirms the connection, established in the Gospels, between preaching and healing (cf. 4:15–17). That those arrested are designated by the indefinite phrase "the apostles" suggests that this story may actually be a doublet of the first. Luke uses it, however, to restate the principle "We must obey God rather than men" (5:29) which in turn leads logically to Gamaliel's advice so important to the purpose of Acts. The release of the apostles by an angel keeps the reader reminded that, in spite of the rearrest and trial before the Sanhedrin, God is still in control of the situation (cf. Lk. 21:12–19). Both "signs and wonders" and a dispute with the synagogue of the freedmen (anticipating Paul's experiences in synagogues later) set the stage for Stephen's sermon and martyrdom. In this ultimate "witness" (the English word "martyr" comes from the Greek *martyreo,* I witness) the motif of the proclamation of the Gospel and its opposition is brought to a climax.

The thread of continuity for the complementary motif on the inner life of the Church is carried by the theme of community of goods. Thus in the scene separating the two stories of the arrests and trials of the apostles, the Church's prayer (4:23–30; cf. 1:14; 2:42) which interprets them and the second filling with the Holy Spirit (4:31) introduce an elaboration of this theme. The elaboration serves to introduce Barnabas, who becomes important to the story later, and whose generous spirit in his participation in the community of goods is set in bold relief by the deception of Ananias and Sapphira. This motif concludes with the story in 6:1–6 of the dissension between the Hellenist and Hebrew widows that occasioned the appointment of the seven administrators. That the first two of these, Stephen and Philip, become important in the story not as administrators of the distribution of food but as proclaimers of the gospel indicates another meaning to this story.

It is noteworthy that except for the story of Peter and Cornelius, which plays a special role in Acts, the movement of the Church beyond Jerusalem is carried out by others than the twelve apostles (note that in the "scattering" of the Church the apostles remained in Jerusalem, 8:1; cf. The mission of the seventy, Lk. 10:1ff.). The seven administrators represent for Luke a second level in the leadership of the Church, in which he includes Paul, that bears the real burden of its world mission. It is interesting that while Luke honors the apostles his real heroes, except for Peter, are found among these "apostolic men." Threaded through this section as a theme which ties together the two motifs is a series of notes on the astonishing numbers of converts received by the Church (2:41, 47; 4:4; 5:14[39]; 6:7). Like the later success of Paul's mission, this theme is an answer to Gamaliel's proposition (5:38–39).

The Beginnings of the Mission, 8:1b–15:35　In the conclusion to the story of Stephen's martyrdom two items appear which lead into the next section: the outbreak of persecution in consequence of the animosity aroused by Stephen (8:1b.) and the introduction of "a young man named Saul" (7:58b). These items comprise the two divisions of the second section: the scattering (8:1b–12:25) and the mission of Paul and Barnabas (13:1–15:35).

The first division takes its departure from the believers scattered by the outbreak of persecution who "went about preaching the word" (8:4a). Philip, whose story typifies the witnessing in Judea and Samaria, opens the section with the establishment of a church in an unnamed Samaritan city. Peter and John reappear in the story in a comparatively passive role by confirming Philip's work and bestowing the gift of the Holy Spirit. Peter's rebuke of Simon the magician sets the gift of the Spirit in the sharpest contrast to the claims of pagan magic. In the conversion of the Ethiopian eunuch, the first of the three models of conversion which dominate the first half of the section, Philip's story reaches its climax. Perhaps in giving this story the emphasis he has, Luke had in mind the passage on the acceptance of foreigners and eunuchs in Isaiah 56:1–8 which concludes with the words, "Thus says the Lord God, who gathers the outcasts of Israel, I will gather yet others to him beside those already gathered." Philip is left in Caesarea where we hear of him only once more in a brief scene in Paul's final journey to Jerusalem (21:8–9).

39. As a solution to the puzzling contradiction to this statement in the preceding verse Dibelius suggests that we should read "rulers" for "rest," indicating a distinction between the leaders and the people similar to that in the Gospel (7:29–30, *passim*). See *Studies in the Acts of the Apostles,* p. 91.

In the second and most prominent of the three conversions, the story of Saul, who is to become Paul the key figure in the latter half of Acts, begins and the ground is laid for the second part of this section. The part Barnabas is to play in that story is also anticipated as he vouches for Saul to the apostles in Jerusalem (9:27).

Like a number of the stories in Acts the account of the third conversion, that of the Roman centurion Cornelius (10:1–11:18), is prefaced by a miracle. The story of Peter's raising of Dorcas places him in Joppa where Cornelius' messengers find him and bring him to Caesarea to preach to their master. By the elaborate accounts and repetitions of the visions of both Peter and Cornelius and by the repetition of the story in Peter's speech before the church in Jerusalem (11:1–17), Luke underscores the importance of this event. What it means is indicated first by Peter's vision which, as he makes clear in his speech to Cornelius, does not concern dietary laws but the Church's relationship to the gentiles. As Peter explains in the climax of his speech in Jerusalem, the filling of the Holy Spirit which only here in Acts has preceded baptism makes mandatory the baptizing of uncircumcised gentiles. Finally, of course, by the success of Peter's apology (11:18) which led his opponents to the conclusion that "to the gentiles also God has granted repentance unto life," Luke has taken care that the reader not miss the meaning of this story for the gentile mission.

The meaning of the three conversions in this section is now apparent. More than an account of the churches in the area of Judea and Samaria, these stories are a preparation for the world mission which begins with Paul and Barnabas in the second half of the section. In the baptism of the Ethiopian eunuch the acceptance of the foreigner and eunuch points forward to the "others" yet to be gathered (Isa. 56:8). Saul's conversion provides the "chosen instrument" to carry the Gospel to gentiles "and kings and the sons of Israel" (9:15). With the baptism of Cornelius by Peter, the head of the apostolic college, the great barrier of exclusivism represented in circumcision has been removed. The way is now open for an overt appeal to the gentile world.

As a final step in this preparation Luke recounts the founding of the church at Antioch of Syria (11:19–26). In designating Antioch as the place at which, in contrast to the previous practice of the "scattered" preachers (vs. 19b), the first deliberate appeal to the Greeks was made (vs. 20), Luke has established the character of the church there. It was the place where the confrontation between Jewish and gentile Christianity first occurred. (Cf. Paul's picture of Antioch in Gal. 2:11ff.) Perhaps in saying that the term "Christian" arose here (vs. 26b) Luke is indicating that out of this confrontation came the Church's self-understanding. It is appropriate, therefore, that the church in Antioch should be the one to launch the mission to the Roman world. The story of the relief sent to Jerusalem by the church in Antioch (11:27–30; 12:25) places the two churches in a relationship interestingly similar to that between the "seven," especially Stephen and Philip, and the twelve apostles 6:1ff.). With the coming of Barnabas to assume leadership and his presentation of Paul to the church there, as he had to the church in Jerusalem once before, the stage is set for the mission.

Before beginning the story of the mission, however, Luke inserts a series of stories of Herod (Agrippa I). The martyrdom of James (son of Zebedee) and the arrest of Peter resume the motifs of martyrdom and persecution as ominous reminders that they are inevitably a part of the price of the mission. Peter's release by an angel and Herod's revolting death, on the other hand, keep the reader aware that God is in control.[40] Along with the deaths of Ananias and Sapphira (5:1–11), Peter's warning to Simon the magician (8:20–24), and Paul's cursing of Elymas the magician (13:8–12), Herod's death illustrates the danger of "opposing God" against which Gamaliel warned (5:39).

With the commissioning and sending off of Barnabas and Saul in chapter 13 a basic change in the narrative of Acts takes place. For the first time a deliberate mission is undertaken beyond the general environs of Palestine, and, more important to Luke's story, it is the beginning of Paul's great mission to the Roman world. From this standpoint chapter 13 begins the second main division of the book. Yet in several ways the series of episodes in 13:1–15:35 belong more closely with the five preceding chapters than with those that follow. Antioch is still the home base of the missioners; Jerusalem is still prominent in the story; and the mission is still in the eastern world, getting no farther west than Antioch of Pisidia (named for the Syrian ruler, Antiochus the Great). Although as the narrative progresses Paul's name appears before that of Barnabas with increasing frequency, it is still not his mission. The real dividing line for Luke is the basically important council in Jerusalem in 15:1–35 in which the gentile mission was accepted in principle and the effective removal of the barrier of circumcision was fully established. As the change of name from the Hebrew Saul to the Latin Paul suggests, this first mission was a transition from the haphazard founding of churches by those "scattered" by the persecutions to a calculated program for evangelizing the Empire.

The conversion of Sergius Paulus is the first of a series of encounters between Paul and Roman officials in which the officials are favorably

---

40. Cf. Josephus, *Ant.*, XIX, 8. Such stories of horrible deaths of evil persons were common in antiquity. Beside this one and the suicide of Judas (Mt. 27: 3–10; Acts 1:18–19) see the death of Antiochus Epiphanes (I Mac. 6:5–17; II Mac. 9:5–29; Josephus, *Ant.* XI, 9, 1).

Bull's head at Antioch of Pisidia. These were frequently carved on tombs in this area, apparently to ward off evil spirits. (The Roderick Slide Collection, courtesy of Catawba College.)

disposed and serves Luke's apologetic purpose. Paul's sermon in the synagogue of Antioch of Pisidia, which is an interesting parallel to the beginning of Jesus' ministry in Luke's Gospel (4:16ff.), and has affinities in substance with Peter's sermon on Pentecost, establishes the pattern of this mission maintained to the end of Acts of beginning with the Jewish community and upon its rejection turning to the gentiles (13:14b–48). When the pagan Lycaonians, after the healing of a man crippled from birth, attempted to worship Paul and Barnabas as gods, Paul responded with a speech which is the first of two models (cf. 17:22–31) Luke has provided for sermons to gentiles.[41] Luke's martyr motif reappears as the stoning, which Paul escaped in Iconium, met him in Lystra. He who had consented to the stoning of Stephen has himself become a victim of stoning for the same cause. The irony of the people, under the instigation of Jews from Antioch and Iconium, stoning one who moments before they were ready to worship becomes a bitter commentary on the malevo-

41. See Dibelius, *Studies in the Acts of the Apostles*, pp. 26–77, *passim*.

lence of the opposition to Christianity. With that near-martyrdom Luke concludes his story of the first "missionary journey" and brings the team back to Antioch for the journey to Jerusalem for the council.

In the council on circumcision and the gentile mission the story of the growth of the church in Jerusalem and its environs reaches its conclusion. This council is for Luke a pivotal event and, as is apparent by a comparison of this story with Paul's version (Galatians 2:1–10), he has exercised editorial license in shaping it to his purposes. Whereas in Paul's description the meeting is private (Gal. 2:2), Luke makes it a major assembly of the Church (15:4, 22), and he omits completely the issue of Titus' circumcision. That the question of circumcision arose both in Antioch and Jerusalem (15:1, 5) indicates how basic it was to the whole mission of the Church and how intimately it was connected with the Jewish roots of Christianity. The meeting itself is divided into three speeches, in the first of which Peter recalls his baptism of Cornelius and indicates how decisive that event was for the future direction of the Church. Paul and Barnabas then respond with a recital of the "signs and wonders God had done through them among the Gentiles" (vs. 12), which indicates the divine approbation of their mission. Finally James concludes the debate with the recommendation that the gentile converts be required only to abstain from idols, unchastity, what is strangled, and blood. That this conclusion and the letter to the gentiles which follows are absent from Paul's account represents in part the different solutions to the problem of circumcision offered by Luke and Paul.

As we shall see, Paul found it necessary to justify the abandonment of circumcision by a profound theological argument built around the provisional role of the Law itself in the history of salvation. Luke's understanding of the matter, like his interpretation of the Passion and Resurrection, is based primarily on the "necessity" of prophetic fulfillment. As the allusions and proof texts throughout both volumes show, Luke included the gentile mission in the messianic program. Since circumcision was a serious practical barrier to the gentiles, and since the Holy Spirit had shown both in the conversion of Cornelius and in the success of the mission of Paul and Barnabas that this barrier was to be set aside, Luke needed no further justification. Insofar as the continuity of the Church with Israel was concerned, the simple strictures proposed by James against idolatry and immorality and rudimentary dietary regulations in recognition of Jewish abhorrence of eating blood appeared sufficient.

These apostolic decrees have frequently been compared to the so-called Noachian Laws, a set of seven commandments said to have been given by Noah and binding on all mankind (cf. the regulations binding on the heathen "sojourners" in Lev. 17:7–10; 18:6–26; Exod. 12:18f.; 20:10f.), which would secure the obedient God-fearing gentile a place in the Age-to-Come.[42] That the tradition of these seven laws goes back as far as Luke's time is by no means certain, but it is likely that these decrees reflect at least Luke's knowledge of the rabbinic thinking that led to it.

In his account of the apostolic letter, Luke creates some historical difficulties. The natural inference from Paul's conversation with James and the elders in 21:25 is that the letter had been sent in his absence and Paul was hearing of it for the first time. In his own letters, furthermore, Paul says nothing about it.[43] That a letter containing such decrees issued from Jerusalem sometime after the council is altogether possible, but Luke's placing it here was motivated not so much by his understanding of the history as his desire to complete his treatment of the issue in preparation for Paul's great westward trek to follow. With the conclusion of the council all things are ready for the final and climactic section of Acts. The principle of the mission to the gentiles has been established, the barriers have been removed, and the divinely appointed leader has been commissioned.

To the Aegean Provinces and Rome, 15:36–28:31 The final section of Acts falls into two divisions: Paul's missions in Macedonia, Achaia, and Asia; and the series of events, beginning with his final journey to Jerusalem, which brought him to Rome. Paul's change of partners from Barnabas to Silas dramatizes the new stage in the story. Paul is now definitely in charge. Silas clearly plays a more subordinate role than did Barnabas. That Silas, like Paul, is a Roman citizen (16:37) is highly appropriate for the new mission westward into the Roman world. Barnabas, like Peter, belongs to the East. The courage and perseverance demanded by this bold new venture are underscored by the replacement of "John called Mark," over whom Paul and Barnabas separated (13:5b, 13b; 15:37–40), with Timothy as the new assistant. The reader is reminded by this change of Jesus' saying (occurring only in Lk. 9:62), "No one who puts his hand to the plow and looks back is fit for the kingdom of God." That, according to Luke, Paul circumcised Timothy indicates once more Luke's understanding that the suspension of circumcision was an expedient for the gentile mission. He seeks, on the other hand, to avoid any unnecessary widening of the gap between Church and synagogue, or any

---

42. *Sanhedrin,* 56a. See also Foakes Jackson and Lake, *The Beginnings of Christianity,* Vol. V, pp. 207–212.
43. John C. Hurd, Jr., thinks, however, that although he does not explicitly cite the decree, Paul's argument with the Corinthians is the result of his attempt to enforce it as a result of a compromise made with the church at Jerusalem subsequent to his initial work in Corinth. *The Origin of 1 Corinthians* (New York: Seabury Press, 1965), pp. 253–270, *passim.*

action that might provide the Jewish opponents with a valid charge against the Church.

With the brief visit to the church in southern Galatia completed, Paul and his company started westward. Prevented by the Holy Spirit from turning aside to Asia or Bithynia, they came directly to the Aegean port city of Troas where Paul experienced the vision of the Macedonian call which complements Peter's vision at Joppa and anticipates those which guided him to Rome. In the Macedonian's plaintive call for help the reader hears the cry of the gentile world (cf. Rom. 11:12, 32). So Paul crossed the Hellespont into Europe—a crossing that was to have a greater impact on the history of man than the famous crossing of Alexander the Great some three centuries before.

The story of Paul's Aegean mission, which forms the first half of this section, is divided according to provinces into three parts, Macedonia, Achaia, and Asia (the coastal province in western Asia Minor). In each city, except Philippi, the pattern is maintained of beginning with the local synagogue until opposition forced them to turn to the gentiles. The story of the healing in Philippi of the girl with a clairvoyant demon is Luke's commentary on the impact of the Gospel on the gentile world and the unworthy motives of those gentiles who oppose it. Just so a little later the reader knows that the cry of the Thessalonian rabble, "These men who have turned the world upside down have come here also," is wrong. They are really turning it rightside up. Following the miraculous release of Paul and Silas from jail, the third such deliverance in Acts (cf. 5:19–21, 12:6–11), the baptism of the Philippian jailer has provided Luke with another model of conversion. At the same time the apologetic magistrates furnish another example of Paul's encounter with Roman authorities who can find nothing illegal in his mission. Several difficulties in the story such as the failure of Paul and Silas to plead their Roman citizenship until the next day, after they had been beaten (cf. 22:25ff.), suggest that Luke may have conflated two different traditions here. He would not, at any rate, be so concerned with historical consistency as with the dramatization of the mission and its significance.

As the outbreak of persecution in Jerusalem, scattering the believers to preach the Gospel in the surrounding districts, set the Church on its mission, so now persecution pushes Paul from place to place leaving behind churches to continue the work as he goes. Thus the very opposition which the Gospel encounters becomes under the Holy Spirit a force for propagating it. The "more noble" Beroeans, on the other hand, provide Luke with an edifying example of wise and appropriate response to the mission (17:10–12), as well as another opportunity to stress the importance of Scriptural proof of the Gospel.

The Theater of Dionysius at Athens. The cult of the god of the vine developed the comedies which were performed in theaters such as this throughout the Hellenistic world. (The Roderick Slide Collection, courtesy of Catawba College.)

By the elaborate dialogue introducing it, Luke indicates the importance of Paul's visit to Athens, the ancient home of Greek philosophy (17:16–34). In Paul's speech on the Areopagus Luke presents his masterpiece of Christian apologetic.[44] The entire scene appropriately symbolizes Christianity's confrontation with Greek culture and thought. Luke's contempt for the philosophers who "spent their time in nothing except telling or hearing something new" (vs. 21) matches their contempt for the Christian preacher (vs. 18). The reader is made to feel the poignant irony in their rejection of the one thing truly new and valid that had come their way.

44. The inscription which furnishes the starting point for the speech must have read "to unknown gods" (plural rather than singular). On this, the sources of the quotations, and other matters see Foakes Jackson and Lake, *The Beginnings of Christianity,* Vol. V, pp. 240–251; Dibelius, *Studies in the Acts of the Apostles,* pp. 26–83; Conzelmann, "The Address of Paul on the Areopagus" in Keck and Martyn, *Studies in Luke-Acts,* pp. 217–230.

The year and a half that Paul spent in Corinth suggests something of the importance which that church assumed in early Christian history (cf. 18:10) and allows Luke more elaborately to picture Paul's method of establishing churches. In the story of his working as a tentmaker with Aquila and Priscilla, Luke acquaints the reader with Paul's means of support. Here and in Ephesus, as he is compelled to leave the synagogue, Paul has established a gentile location for his lectures (18:7; 19:9). Paul's arrest and appearance before Gallio, brother of Seneca the famous Stoic tutor of Nero, bring him for the first time into contact with a prominent Roman official. Gallio's disdain for those pressing the charges serves Luke's apologetic interests well.

That Luke is following an itinerary of Paul's travels, as Martin Dibelius has suggested,[45] seems evident from the brevity of the account of Paul's hurried trip to Caesarea (Jerusalem?)[46] and Antioch (18:18–19:1) for which no reason is given and which apparently contributes nothing to Luke's purpose. The trip does, however, furnish an incidental occasion for two items of significance. Paul's vow (18:18; cf. 21:23ff.) reaffirms his loyalty to Judaism and underscores again Luke's contention that the Jewish leaders are without justification for their opposition to Christianity. Apollos of Alexandria, who arrived in Ephesus and crossed to Corinth in Paul's absence, represents the Church's contact with that other great ancient center of Greek learning and culture in Egypt.

That Paul, upon his return from the East, spent more than two years in Ephesus indicates the importance of that church, and in fact the whole province of Asia of which it was the capital, in later Christian history (cf. the seven letters in Rev. 1:4–3:22). Several problems appear in the account of Paul's stay in Ephesus. His arrival there in 19:1 seems to ignore completely both his previous visit (18:19) and the presence of Aquila and Priscilla. Why, for example, was it necessary for him to instruct and baptize the believers whom he had "found" there after his own preaching earlier and the presence of Aquila and Priscilla who had instructed Apollos "more accurately" in the "way of God"? That the reference to Paul in the Ephesian synagogue in 18:19 is simply an editorial stereotype is likely, but this only partly solves the problem. It is possible also that Luke has combined here several traditions, some of which actually do not belong to Ephesus. Luke's insertion of the story of the Ephesian riot (19:23–41) after the beginning of the account of Paul's departure from Ephesus is obviously awkward and requires another version of his departure in 20:1–2.

Whatever the difficulties in the way of recovering the history of Paul

45. See p. 281.
46. On the question whether Luke intended the "church" in vs. 22 to mean Jerusalem see Foakes Jackson and Lake, *The Beginnings of Christianity*, Vol. IV, pp. 230–231.

The Arcadian Way in Ephesus leading to the baths and ancient harbor which is now completely filled with silt. Even before Paul's time the harbor could not be used by the larger Mediterranean ships. The Way begins at the theater which was the scene of the riot described in Acts 19:28–41. (The Roderick Slide Collection, courtesy of Catawba College.)

and the Ephesian church from this material, it does allow Luke to make several points. The story of Paul's rebaptizing the believers in 19:1–7, for example, expresses Luke's understanding of Christian baptism and its relationship to the gift of the Holy Spirit, and also brings Paul into as close connection as possible with the founding of the Ephesian church. In the story of the itinerant exorcists, the power of the name of Jesus is contrasted with pagan incantations in a way strikingly similar to the contrast between magic and the Holy Spirit in the story of Simon of Samaria (8:9–24). With the account of the Ephesian riot Luke brings the narrative of Paul's Aegean ministry and the first half of the final section of Acts to its conclusion. In this vivid story, the disturbing impact on idolatrous pagan society and great success of the Gospel are dramatically portrayed, and a suitable climax to the story of Paul's mission is provided. By Gamaliel's test the Gospel is indeed "of God."

The final chapters of Acts are organized around a series of speeches by Paul most of which are addresses in his own defense. As the speeches in the early chapters represent the kerygma used in the propagation of the Gospel, and those in the middle of the work are more concerned with such matters as the problem of circumcision and Christianity versus paganism, these speeches are apologies seeking to make it clear that Christianity is neither heretical from the standpoint of Judaism nor inimical to the best interests of the Empire.

Beginning with the plot against his life in Corinth (20:3), the story of Paul's final journey to Jerusalem has a mood of apprehension that gives it the quality of a passion story. Perhaps the story of the raising of Eutychus "on the first day of the week" (20:7–12) is intended as a relief to the foreboding by its correspondence to the references to the Resurrection in Jesus' predictions of his Passion. In this regard the journey is significantly similar to the story of Jesus' journey to Jerusalem in the Gospel. Paul's speech at Miletus to the Ephesian elders (20:18–35) provides not only an excellent summary of Paul's missionary work, but also, like Jesus' charge to the mission of the seventy (Lk. 10:1–17), a charge to the Church for its own mission and future. Paul's example becomes an inspiration and example for the later Church.

There is a significant irony in the fact that in the course of his participation in the Temple ritual by way of helping four believers to complete their vows, which he undertook on the advice of James to demonstrate his unswerving loyalty to Judaism, he was arrested and began the chain of events that brought him finally to Rome.

The arrest, of course, sets the stage for the speeches which control this part of the book. Twice the story of Paul's conversion is recounted (22:1–21; 26:2–29), and twice his innocence of any violation of Judaism and his belief in the Resurrection are the subjects of his defense (23:1–10; 24:10–21). Only by his transfer to Caesarea and finally by his appeal to Caesar did Paul escape death at the hands of his fellow countrymen. It may be symbolic that on both his journey to Caesarea and his voyage to Rome Paul's transportation is furnished by the Empire. Paul's innocence is stated throughout this material in the strongest possible terms. Only the vain hope of a bribe and his desire to placate the Jews cause Felix to leave Paul in custody. As Pilate had declared the innocence of Jesus, so both Festus and Agrippa find no valid charge against Paul. Indeed, Luke pleads Paul's case so eloquently that some interpreters have supposed Luke-Acts to have been an actual trial brief prepared for his trial before Caesar.[47]

With Paul's appeal to Caesar the dark foreboding is gone. Twice Paul is assured in visions (23:11 and 27:23–24) that he will reach Rome in

47. For a discussion of this theory see Cadbury, *The Making of Luke-Acts*, pp. 314–316.

Mediterranean ship as represented on an ancient sarcophagus. (Reprinted with permission of The Macmillan Company from *Macmillan Bible Atlas* by Y. Aharoni and Michael Avi-Yonah. Copyright © 1968 Carta, Jerusalem. © Copyright 1964 by Carta, Jerusalem. © Copyright 1966 by Carta, Jerusalem.)

safety. Even the violence and danger of the voyage are offset by the divine assurance given to Paul. In the ordeal of the storm, so skillfully and vividly narrated, the reader catches the symbol, reminiscent of the storm in the Gospel (Lk. 8:22–25), of the Church's ordeal in its mission to the world. Perhaps, too, there is significance in the fact that the safety of all those aboard was at least influenced by Paul's presence on the ship (vs. 24b).

That the two references to brethren in Puteoli and Rome (28:14–15) are the only notice Luke gives to the existence of churches in Italy may be an attempt, like his treatment of Paul's relationship to the church at Ephesus, to relate Paul as closely as possible to the beginnings of the Church in Rome. One further suggestion that the case against Paul was invalid appears when Paul asked to see the leaders of the Jewish community in Rome. In all probability if Paul's Jerusalem opponents were to prosecute their case against him they would do it through the Jewish officials resident in Rome. That the latter had heard nothing of Paul's case suggests that it was being dropped.[48] As the synagogues everywhere Paul had been, however, the Jews of Rome were divided in their reaction

48. See Selby, *Toward the Understanding of St. Paul*, p. 232.

to Paul's Gospel, and once more in the closing scene of the book Paul turns to the gentiles.

Did Luke intend to write a third volume? It has frequently been suggested that he did. Certainly the modern reader finds the ending of Acts unsatisfying. We should remember, however, that Luke was not writing a biography of Paul. With the arrival of Paul in Rome his purpose was accomplished. True the Gospel had not yet reached "the end of the earth," but it had reached the imperial capital. It had shown itself in its overcoming of obstacles, in "signs and wonders," in impressive conversions and gifts of the Holy Spirit, in fulfillment of the Scriptures to be of God. As his first volume had "dealt with all that Jesus began to do and teach," so this one has related the beginnings of the mission of the Church. With Paul in his own hired dwelling "preaching the kingdom of God and teaching about the Lord Jesus Christ quite openly and unhindered," Luke's narrative is finished.

3. The Apostle to the Gentiles: Paul

Although, as we have seen, Acts has no parallel documents with which it might be critically compared, we are not entirely without alternate sources of information for part of the period it covers. In the course of his letters Paul incidentally alludes to events in his life and work which at several points may be compared with his story in Acts. A survey of these comparisons will be useful for our evaluation of Acts as a source for the life of Paul and the history of the Primitive Church, and will afford us a brief account of Paul's life and career in preparation for our consideration of his letters.

ORIGINS AND EARLY LIFE

In the account of Paul's conversion, Acts 9:1–31, and Paul's speeches in his own defense, 22:1–21; 24:10b-21; 26:2–23, Luke provides a number of details of Paul's early life, some of which may be compared with statements in Paul's own letters.[49] Luke identifies Paul as a Pharisee, for example, when, according to the speech in Acts 23:6, he told the Sanhedrin, "Brethren, I am a Pharisee, a son of Pharisees," and in 26:5 he "lived as a Pharisee, . . . the strictest party of our religion." In his letter to the Philippians 3:5, Paul confirms this fact saying that he was "circumcised on the eighth day, of the people of Israel, of the tribe of Benjamin, a Hebrew born of Hebrews; as to the law a Pharisee" (cf. Rom. 11:1). In

49. For reasons which will appear in another chapter, we will not include Ephesians or the Pastoral Epistles.

his argument with the Corinthians, Paul cries out, "Are they Hebrews? So am I. Are they Israelites? So am I. Are they descendants of Abraham: So am I" (II Cor. 11:22).

That Paul had been circumcised Luke could take for granted, but Paul's letters do supply us with the information, which Luke omits, that he was a Benjamite. Yet only Luke informs us that Paul's Hebrew name was Saul. Since the name goes back to Israel's first king who was a Benjamite, this information may be an incidental correspondence between Acts and Paul's letters. That all of those letters are addressed to churches in the gentile milieu of the provinces may explain Paul's exclusive use of his Latin name.

Luke provides us, on the other hand, with three important items of information which are absent from the letters. In Acts 21:39 and 22:3 we are told that Paul was born a citizen of Tarsus in Cilicia, that he was also born to Roman citizenship, and that he was brought up a disciple of Gamaliel. While none of these statements is intrinsically improbable, we have little more than Luke's story for evidence. Some interpreters have inferred from the way Paul speaks of going up to Jerusalem and of returning to Damascus, in Galatians 1:17–18, that he was actually a native of Damascus. The phrase, "returned to Damascus" does appear to suggest that he was returning home, but it is more likely that Paul presupposes his readers' knowledge that his revelation had occurred in the region of Damascus. Because of Luke's preoccupation with Jerusalem as the center and starting point of the Church, we may assume that his association of Paul with a city as distant as Tarsus rather than Jerusalem was based on firm knowledge. Similarly, Paul's possession of a Latin name (*Paulus* means small) is consistent with the claim that he was a Roman citizen but by no means confirms it. Falsely claiming the prerogatives of Roman citizenship was serious enough, however, that we may doubt that Luke would do such a thing for his hero unless it was based on what seemed to him at least to be reliable information.[50]

Some interpreters detect in Paul's statement, "I advanced in Judaism beyond many of my own age among my people, so extremely zealous was I for the traditions of my fathers" (Gal. 1:14) an oblique reference to his training under Gamaliel. His failure to mention his teacher may have been due to his realization that the name would mean little or nothing to his readers. Certainly attempts to disprove Luke's claim for Paul on the basis of Paul's divergence from rabbinic theology and affinity for ideas from the mystery religions are unconvincing. Paul's theology was a new departure precisely because he was convinced by his revelation that something new

50. See Selby, *Toward the Understanding of St. Paul,* pp. 130–132, and works there cited. For opposite view see E. R. Goodenough, "The Perspective of Acts," in Keck and Martyn, *Studies in Luke-Acts,* pp. 55–56.

had entered history in Christ. His skill with rabbinic methods of exegesis, his carefulness to graft the "new" onto the stalk of Judaic tradition so that even the terms coinciding with terminology from the Hellenistic mysteries, upon closer examination, prove to be rooted in Jewish presuppositions, all show Paul to be a knowledgeable Jew. His letters, in other words, while they do not confirm the statement in Acts that he was "brought up at the feet of Gamaliel," are nevertheless consistent with it.

The argument, occasionally advanced on the basis of Paul's words in Galatians 1:17, "nor did I go up to Jerusalem," and 1:22, "And I was still not known by sight to the churches of Christ in Judea," that Paul had not been in Jerusalem before his "conversion" and therefore could not have been a disciple of Gamaliel overlooks the words "Judea" (rather than Jerusalem) and "by sight" (lit. by face) in verse 22, and the reference to his persecution of the Church in verse 23. A program of persecution that significant to the Church so early in its development must have included the environs of Jerusalem.

PERSECUTION AND CONVERSION

Along with his background as a Pharisee, Paul's role as a persecutor of the Church provides a point of correspondence between his letters and Acts. His own expressions of poignant remorse matches remarkably closely Luke's references to his persecutions (cf. 8:3; 9:1–2; 22:4–5; 26:9–12 with Gal. 1:13, 23–24; I Cor. 15:9; Phil. 3:6).

It is when we come to Paul's conversion that we encounter a significant comparison between Acts and the letters. In contrast to the agreements in the general outline of events, there is a clear and basic difference of interpretation.[51] That the experience took place near Damascus is stated in all three versions of the story in Acts (9:3; 22:6; 26:12–13) and implied in Galatians 1:15–17. Paul's escape from Damascus by being let down over the wall is told, with only one difference worth noting, both in Acts 9:23–25 and in II Corinthians 11:32–33. In Luke's version it is the Jews who are in pursuit, whereas Paul tells us that it was the governor under King Aretas from whom he escaped. Luke, on the other hand, knows nothing of Paul's retreat into Arabia, which may account for his misunderstanding of Paul's opponents in Damascus. Probably Luke's "When many days had passed" (9:23) can be stretched to agree with the "after three years" of Galatians 1:18 for Paul's first visit to Jerusalem after his revelation. All three accounts in Acts agree, at any rate, with the outline in Galatians of Paul's movements from Damascus to Jerusalem; and Acts 9:30 accords with Galatians 1:21 on his retreat to Cilicia. It is significant of Luke's method and interests that his three versions of Paul's "conversion" vary

51. See Selby, *Toward the Understanding of St. Paul,* pp. 161–179.

among themselves in detail about as much as they differ from Paul's version. His "preaching boldly [in Jerusalem] in the name of the Lord" (Acts 9:28), for example, fits the divine command "make haste and get quickly out of Jerusalem" (Acts 22:18) no more closely than it does the statements in Galatians (1:18–19) that he stayed with Cephas fifteen days and that of the other apostles he saw only James.

When we come, however, to the nature of the revelation to Paul at the center of this story serious differences appear. One of the more subtle of these is that Luke treats the experience as a model of conversion of which he has several in Acts, while Paul regards it as a call and revelation. He would certainly not agree that he had been "converted" from one religion to another. Paul insists that what happened to him was an appearance of the Risen Lord of the same order as the appearances to the original apostles (Gal. 1:15–16; I Cor. 9:1; 15:4–8). This difference is an example of the change of perspective between Paul and Luke which was produced, among other things, by the separation of the Church and the Synagogue.

According to Acts Paul had experienced a vision not unlike the theophanies of the Old Testament. Even less specific than the dying vision of Stephen, it consisted only in an ineffable light and a voice. The words "to see the Just One" in 22:14 and "I have appeared to you" in 26:16 do not contradict this statement. That according to Acts Paul needed to be told what he had seen, that he was promised further appearances, in 26:16b, and that he calls the experience a "heavenly vision," 26:19, show how Luke intended these phrases to be understood. In the prologue of Acts, Luke has already precluded an interpretation of Paul's experience as a Resurrection appearance, by limiting Jesus' appearances to the forty days which ended with the Ascension. Stephen's vision of the "Son of man standing at the right hand of God" (Acts 7:5, 6; cf. Ps. 110:1; Lk. 22:69) follows logically and represents the interim between the Ascension and the eschaton.

Luke's difference from Paul, however, is not simply a matter of eschatological programs. Paul's concern in insisting on identifying his revelation as a Resurrection appearance was to defend his authority as an apostle "not of men nor through men" (Gal. 1:1). Although he could not agree with Luke's limiting the apostles to a college of the twelve, nor to the insistence that they must have accompanied Jesus from his baptism, he did agree that apostles in this primary sense must have witnessed an appearance of the Risen Lord (cf. Acts 1:15–26 with Gal. 1:1, 15–17; I Cor. 9:1; 15:4–10; II Cor. 12:11–12). According to Paul, therefore, his experience on the Damascus road was just such an appearance and constituted not only his apostolic qualification but his appointment as well.

Luke could agree, of course, that Paul was thus appointed to a special mission to the gentiles (cf. Acts 9:15; 22:10, 14–15; 26:15–18 with Gal. 1:16; 2:9), but as we have already observed, he deliberately avoids identifying Paul with the apostles.[52] That Paul's own statements of the matter are in contexts of controversy indicates that his claim to the apostolate was a bone of contention. There is an almost plaintive note in his words to the Corinthians, "If to others I am not an apostle, at least I am to you; for you are the seal of my apostleship in the Lord" (I Cor. 9:2). His very success in the gentile mission was, in other words, proof that Jesus had indeed called him as the twelve had been called!

We may surmise that there was more at stake in the argument than Paul's status in the leadership of the Church. Luke is probably correct in saying that gentiles had been admitted to the Church without the rite of circumcision (i.e., initiation into Judaism) before Paul, but as he indicates in the story of Cornelius' conversion (Acts 10:1–48) and in his version of the Jerusalem council (Acts 15:7–11, 13–21), he understood the action simply as a new step in the divine program and a matter of reducing the Law to its essentials. To Paul the matter was not so simple. In his view dropping the requirement of circumcision in the gentile mission called into question the fundamental position of Torah in the life of the People of God. So he set about with rabbinic thoroughness to establish a solid theological basis for his policy toward the gentiles.[53] Especially among conservative Jewish members of the Church this action raised serious questions about Paul's authority which Luke from his later perspective could not appreciate. Probably Paul is responsible for establishing as a policy for the gentile mission this practice which had been heretofore merely an occasional practical concession. For that he needed apostolic authority, and he claimed it by equating his experience on the Damascus road with the call and appointment by Jesus and witness to the Risen Lord that constituted the authority of the Jerusalem apostles. Perhaps here better than anywhere else we can see the contrast between the minds of Luke and Paul.

VISITS TO JERUSALEM

Paul's references to his itinerary are for the most part fragmentary and therefore difficult to compare with Acts. In one area, however, such a comparison is not only significant and necessary to the study of both Acts and Paul, but also presents us with a notorious problem. Acts 9:26; 11:27–30; 12:25; and 15:1–35, on the one hand, and Galatians 1:18–2:10, on the other, represent Paul's movements with respect to Jerusalem from the time of his conversion to the convening in Jerusalem of the council on the issue of circumcision. On his first visit to Jerusalem and his

52. Above, pp. 176–177. On this see also H. J. Schoeps, *Paul,* tr. Harold Knight (Philadelphia: The Westminster Press, 1961), pp. 70–74.
53. Below, pp. 327–337, 396–400.

journey to Cilicia, Paul and Acts agree, as they appear to on the visit for the council and return to Antioch, but Galatians makes no mention of the so-called "famine visit" to Jerusalem mentioned in Acts 11:27–30 and 12:25.

Although the immediate question is the relation of the three trips to Jerusalem in Acts to the two mentioned in Galatians, it will be useful for us to examine it in the larger setting of all of his visits to the Mother Church.[54] There are in Acts five occasions upon which Paul journeyed to Jerusalem which we may designate as (1) the conversion visit, 9:26ff; (2) the famine visit, 11:27–30 and 12:25; (3) the council visit, 15:1–35; (4) the visit from Achaia, 18:18–19:1; (5) the final visit, 20:3–5, 13–16; 21:1–15; 24:17. In contrast Paul's letters only mention three such visits which we may list as (A) the conversion visit, Gal. 1:18ff.; (B) the council visit, Gal. 2:1ff.; (C) the contribution visit, Rom. 15:25–31; I Cor. 16:1–4; II Cor. 7–8. The following table will help us visualize the comparison

Acts	Paul's Letters
1. The conversion visit.	A. The conversion visit.
2. The famine visit.	
3. The council visit.	B. The council visit.
4. The visit from Achaia.	
5. The final visit.	C. The contribution visit.

One apparent solution to the question is to assume that visits number 1, 3, and 5 equal visits A, B, and C, respectively, and that Paul simply omitted to mention visits 2 and 4. Traditionally scholars have rejected this solution on the ground that in Galatians 1–2 Paul is arguing his independence of the apostles at Jerusalem and is stressing, therefore, in 1:18 and 2:1, that from his conversion to the time of his writing Galatians he had only been in Jerusalem twice. For him to have omitted any mention of the intervening famine visit if he had made it would, consequently, have been a serious misrepresentation.

Assuming on this basis that the famine visit in Acts is out of place, several solutions have been offered. Some have suggested that 2 equals B and that 3 constitutes a second council which was convened some time after Paul had written Galatians. That both Acts 15:1–35 and Galatians 2:1–10 clearly assume that the issue of circumcision is being debated for the first time, that the same key persons are involved in both, and that both accounts reach the same general resolution of the problem, renders this solution unsatisfactory.

Somewhat simpler is the suggestion that Paul never actually made the

54. For a fuller discussion of this question see Selby, *Toward the Understanding of St. Paul,* pp. 196–204, and works there cited.

trip in number 2.[55] Still other scholars, noting that Luke has two tours of the four cities in southern Galatia each of which follows a visit to Jerusalem, have supposed that both the tours of Galatia and visits 2 and 3 are doublets of the same series of events, and equal B, one of them having come to Luke from an Antiochian source and the other from a source originating in Jerusalem.[56] Although the comparatively barren account of the second tour suggests that it may well be a doublet of the first, this solution rests on a theory of sources which, as we have seen, is for other reasons questionable.

Much of the problem rests on the assumption that Paul in Galatians 1–2 is trying to prove his independence of the apostles in Jerusalem. When we observe that by his admission to a fifteen-day visit with Peter Paul has hopelessly compromised such an argument, we must question this assumption.[57] Other elements of the problem, however, are not relieved by returning to the first suggestion (of equating 1, 3, and 5 with A, B, and C). First, if the famine referred to in Acts 11:27 as the occasion of the second visit is the same as the one mentioned by Josephus, as is probable, it occurred after the death of Herod Agrippa (A.D. 44, cf. Acts 12:20–23) and therefore is out of sequence in Acts. Since Luke has elsewhere exercised considerable license in subordinating chronology to the development of his themes, we cannot rely on his order of events here. Second, if visit 3 equals B, the fourteen years in Galatians 2:1 must be inserted into the chronology of Acts before Paul's journey to Macedonia which leaves him in the region Cilicia for eleven or fourteen years (depending on whether we include the three years in Gal. 1:18). Not only is there no hint of such a stay in his letters, but it is also difficult to understand why we hear nothing of churches in an area in which he had invested so much time. Third, although visits 1, 2, and 3, have clear purposes in Acts, the purpose of visit 5 is only mentioned incidentally in 24:17, and that of visit 4 is completely omitted.

In view of questions such as these a more recent hypothesis, proposed by Professor John Knox, has suggested a rearrangement of the whole chronology of Paul in Acts which may most easily be presented by repeating the table on page 312 with arrows as follows:[58]

55. See Edgar J. Goodspeed, *Paul* (New York: Abingdon Press, 1947), p. 35 and note, pp. 226–227.
56. See M. S. Enslin, *Christian Beginnings,* pp. 226–230.
57. On the difficult question of the relation of Gal. 1–2 to Acts 11–15 see Jack T. Sanders "Paul's 'Autobiographical' Statements in Galatians 1–2," *JBL* LXXXV, Pt. III, Sept. 1966, pp. 335–343.
58. *Chapters in a Life of Paul* (New York: Abingdon Press, 1950), pp. 47–88. Donald T. Rowlingson has given this hypothesis an interesting support by comparing Luke's literary method here with his treatment of Markan material in his Gospel, 4:16–30. See "The Jerusalem Conference and Jesus' Nazareth Visit," *JBL,* LXXI, Pt. II, June 1952, pp. 69–74.

Acts	Paul's Letters
1. The conversion visit ⟶	A. The conversion visit
2. The famine visit	
3. The council visit	
4. The visit from Achaia ⟶	B. The council visit
5. The final visit ⟶	C. The contribution visit

Therefore:

1 = A

3 and 4 = B

2 and 5 = C

This arrangement means that the council visit did not occur until after Paul's ministry in Macedonia and Corinth. Probably Paul's progress from Antioch to the west was slower than Luke's dramatic compression suggests, so that on this theory it may account for a considerable part of the fourteen years of Galatians 2:1. Clearly, then, this rearrangement eases the problems of Pauline chronology, It also supplies a motive for visit 4; since the purposes of visits 2, 5, and C are basically the same, it helps to explain Luke's vagueness on the motive of visit 5. Although this hypothesis is not without its difficulties, it solves more of the problems and is based on a sound appreciation of Luke's method and interests in writing Acts.

THE AEGEAN MINISTRY AND AFTERWARD

It is interesting to note that, especially if we assume his letter to the Galatians to have been written to the cities of the southern region of that province, Paul's letters provide a remarkable confirmation of the itinerary of Acts. With the unimportant exception of places like Beroea (which may be included in his references to Macedonia) and Miletus and his failure to mention specific cities in Galatia, Paul indicates in his letters his presence in every place mentioned in Luke's account (Rome, of course, is indicated only in anticipation). Conversely, Acts fails to mention any journey of Paul up the Lycus Valley to the triangle of cities, Laodicea, Hierapolis, and Colossae, and his letter to the Colossians indicates that, although he has friends and co-workers in all three of them, Paul had never been there (Col. 2:2, 4:13).

There is wide agreement, too, in the names of Paul's companions and co-workers. No fewer than eleven names appear in both. With exception of three of those who accompanied him on his final journey to Jerusalem, all the names of those associated with Paul in Acts reappear in one or more of the letters. It is all the more surprising, then, to discover in Acts no mention of Titus (unless Titius Justus be he, which is unlikely).

In several of these references, moreover, Acts and the letters supplement one another in interesting and valuable ways. We learn only from Colossians 4:10, for example, that Mark, who is also called John in Acts, was a cousin of Barnabas, a bit of information which helps considerably in understanding the quarrel over him between Paul and Barnabas (Acts 15:37–40). The especially warm greetings Paul, writing from Ephesus, conveyed to the Corinthians (I Cor. 16:8, 19) from Aquila and Prisca (Priscilla in Acts) become more significant when we recall from Acts 18:2 and 18–19 that he had stayed with them in Corinth and had taken them with him to Ephesus on his way to the East. So, too, considerable light is thrown on the strange role of Apollos in the troubles at Corinth (I Cor. 1:12; 3:4–22; 4:6; 16:12) by the information in Acts 18:24–19:1 that Apollos was an eloquent (i.e., well-educated) Alexandrian Jew who had crossed from Ephesus to Corinth shortly after Paul had left there for the East. The Corinthian references associate him in some way with wisdom and eloquence, but only when we learn that Apollos was from Philo's city, the great seat of learning and Jewish center which gave the world the Septuagint, does the significance of Paul's argument appear.

If Acts succeeds in throwing light on some of the obscure allusions in Paul's letters, the latter also supply information which supplements and corrects the story in Acts. Paul's descriptions, for example, of the "foolish Galatians," the factious Corinthians, and the sometimes lazy and excitable Thessalonians help to correct Luke's idealized pictures of the harmonious little communities that were the earliest Christian churches. In other ways, too, the letters supply useful details omitted in Acts. A personal note in Galatians 4:13, for instance, reads: "You know that it was because of a bodily ailment that I preached the gospel to you at first," which indicates that Paul's work was not always so much the unfolding of a master strategy as Acts seems to imply.

We may, for geographical reasons, assume that Luke is correct in placing the founding of the churches in Galatia before Paul's mission to Macedonia, but there is little or nothing in the letters to help us reconstruct Paul's itinerary until his arrival in Philippi. From Philippi to the projected journey to Jerusalem, Rome, and Spain, however, the letters contain a number of allusions which confirm the general pattern in Acts of Paul's movements. In I Thessalonians 2:2, Paul indicates not only that he had evangelized Philippi before coming to Thessalonica, as in Acts, but had "suffered and been shamefully treated" while there, which the story in Acts 16:19–40 confirms. His letter to the Philippians, furthermore, adds the information that they had more than once supplied material assistance to him during his stay at Thessalonica. (This statement may be taken to imply that his stay in Thessalonica was longer than Acts allows.) It is possible, too, that the "security" taken from Jason at Thessalonica when Paul left was the Satanic hindrance to his return he refers to in I Thessalonians 2:18. As much as he was willing to put himself in jeopardy, he would not make further trouble for a member of the Thessalonian church.

Although Boroea, mentioned in Acts 17:10–13, does not appear in the letters, Paul's movement from Macedonia to Athens and Corinth, according to Acts 17:14ff., is confirmed, with one interesting difference, in I Thessalonians 3:1–6 and II Corinthians 11:9 (cf. Phil. 4:15). According to Acts Timothy remained at Beroea until he and Silas rejoined Paul in Corinth, but according to I Thessalonians Timothy had accompanied him to Athens and, having been sent back to Thessalonica, rejoined Paul at the time of the writing of the letter. This is the sort of difference we should expect from a first-hand account and one generally well-informed at second hand. In Luke's account of Paul's stay in Corinth one other point of contact with Paul's letters appears. His work as a tentmaker with Aquila and Priscilla recalls his words, "working with our own hands," in I Corinthians 4:12.

That Paul went from Corinth to Ephesus (Acts 18:18–19:10) is attested by the fact the I Corinthians was written from Ephesus (I Cor. 16:8). Something of the trouble there described in Acts 19:23–41 may be reflected in his words "I fought with wild beasts at Ephesus" (I Cor. 15:32). If the Sosthenes of I Corinthians 1:1 is the same as the one in Acts 18:17, Paul here supplies an interesting sequal to Luke's story of his troubles at Corinth. His trip to Jerusalem and back through Galatia, which according to Acts preceded his stay in Ephesus is suggested by the fact that the phrase, "as I directed the churches of Galatia, so you also are to do" (I Cor. 16:1),[59] implies that Paul had been in Galatia since being in Corinth. While it is impossible to determine all that he is referring to in II Corinthians 1:15–2:13 (cf. 7:5–6, 8:1ff., 9:3–5), it seems clear that he was returning to Corinth by way of Macedonia, and that he intended to go from there with the contributions for the church at Jerusalem (cf. Rom. 15:25–26) and on to Spain (II Cor. 10:16; Rom. 15:24). Probably Luke's own interests in Paul's story are reflected in his failure to mention the projected Spanish mission. It may be, on the other hand, that Luke omits any reference to Spain because to his knowledge the Spanish mission was never accomplished.

With the projected journey to Jerusalem, at any rate, the evidence in Paul's letters for his travels comes to an end. Only in Acts do we learn of his final visit to Jerusalem, his arrest and trials, and his voyage to Rome. For what happened after that neither the letters nor Acts gives us a hint. It is possible, as we shall see, that there are fragments of Paul's letters from a Roman prison in II Timothy 4 (according to the traditional interpretation, of course, Paul's prison letters were written there). If so, we

---

59. For the possibility that this may have been the council visit see pp. 312–314.

are afforded brief glimpses into a crisis which may well have been the end of his life. Beyond this possibility we are dependent on later tradition for the conclusion to the story of the Apostle to the Gentiles.[60]

From this survey it is clear that, although Luke did not derive his information from Paul's letters, he was in possession of a significant body of generally reliable information about Paul. It is apparent also that Luke's use of his material, as we should expect from his treatment of his sources in the Gospel, was controlled by his own purposes and interests. We may discern three principal interests which govern Luke's use of the story of Paul. (1) For him, Paul is a model of conversion to the Christian faith, along with the Ethiopian eunuch and Cornelius, and for faithfulness in the face of opposition and persecution. (2) Paul's story is an exposition and vindication of the gentile mission. In this regard it affords Luke a polemic against an obstinate Judaism which would not accept the Church's claims for Jesus (we should note that the two strongest statements in Acts on the theme of turning from the Jews to the gentiles are in 13:46–49 and 28:25–29, the beginning and the end of the story of Paul's mission), and especially in the way Paul's speeches in his own defense argue the innocence before Roman authority of his Gospel, an apologetic to Rome. (3) Paul dramatically personifies the triumphant march of the Church from Jerusalem, the capital of Judaism, to Rome, the capital of Luke's world. Unlike Luke we find our interest in Paul drawn largely to his letters; and we read Luke's portrait of him principally 'for the light it sheds on that correspondence which began and remains the heart of the Epistle side of the New Testament. To the letters of Paul we must now turn.

The Structure of Acts
The Jewish Mission and Peter 1–12
WITNESS IN JERUSALEM, 1–7
Pentecost
  Peter and John before the council
  The apostles before the council
  Stephen's martyrdom
WITNESS IN JUDEA, SAMARIA, SYRIA, AND GALATIA, 8–15:35
The scattering
  Philip in Samaria and conversion of Ethiopian eunuch
  Saul's conversion
  Peter and Cornelius

The Gentile Mission and Paul 13–28
The church at Antioch and the mission of Barnabas and Saul
The council in Jerusalem

60. See Selby, *Toward the Understanding of St. Paul*, pp. 230–232.

WITNESS IN ASIA, GREECE, AND ROME, 15:36–28:31
Paul's westward mission
Through Galatia to Macedonia
Achaia
Return to Antioch and in Asia
Return to Jerusalem arrest and trials
Appeal to Caesar and to Rome

Selected Readings

THE GRAECO-ROMAN WORLD

Bultmann, Rudolf, *Primitive Christianity,* tr. R. H. Fuller (New York: Meridian Books, 1957).

Cullmann, *The State in the New Testament,* rev. ed. (London: SCM Press, 1963).

Glover, T. R., *The Conflict of Religions in the Early Roman Empire* (Boston: Beacon Press, 1960).

Goguel, Maurice, *The Birth of Christianity* (New York: The Macmillan Company, 1954).

Grant, F. C., *Roman Hellenism and the New Testament* (New York: Charles Scribner's Sons, 1962).

————, ed., *Hellenistic Religions* (New York: The Bobbs-Merrill Company, Inc., 1953).

Grant, Robert M., *The Sword and the Cross* (New York: The Macmillan Company, 1955).

Hatch, Edwin, *The Influence of Greek Ideas on Christianity* (New York: Harper Torchbook, 1957). A classic study originally published at the end of the last century.

Jonas, Hans, *The Gnostic Religion* (Boston: Beacon Press, 1963).

Lietzmann, Hans, *A History of the Early Church,* Vol. 1, tr. Bertram Lee Woolf (New York: Meridian Books, 1953).

Nock, Arthur Darby, *Early Gentile Christianity* (New York: Harper Torchbook, 1964).

ACTS

Cadbury, Henry J., *The Book of Acts in History* (New York: Harper & Row, 1955).

Dibelius, Martin, *Studies in the Acts of the Apostles,* ed. H. Greeven, tr. M. Ling (New York: Charles Scribner's Sons, 1956).

Foakes Jackson, F. J., and Lake, Kirsopp, *The Beginnings of Christianity,* 5 vols. (London: Macmillan & Co., 1933). The most extensive study of Acts in English and still indispensable.

Knox, Wilfred L., *The Acts of the Apostles* (Cambridge: At the University Press, 1948).

Williams, C. S. C., *A Commentary on the Acts of the Apostles* (New York: Harper & Row, 1957).
See also *Luke* in books listed at the end of chapter 2.

THE LIFE OF PAUL

Bacon, Benjamin W., *The Story of St. Paul* (Boston: Houghton, Mifflin and Company, 1904).

Coneybeare, W. J., and Howson, J. S., *The Life and Epistles of St. Paul* (New York: Charles Scribner's Sons, 1892). A classic in Pauline studies which provides a good picture of the results of the more conservative scholarship of the nineteenth century.

Deissmann, Adolph, *Paul,* tr. W. E. Wilson (New York: Harper Torchbook, 1957). Another deservedly famous study of Paul's life and times written at the beginning of this century by a man whose studies in Greek papyri and inscriptions created a minor revolution in New Testament lexicography.

Dibelius, Martin, and Kümmel, Warner Georg, *Paul,* tr. Frank Clarke (Philadelphia: The Westminster Press, 1957).

Duncan, George S., *St. Paul's Ephesian Ministry* (New York: Charles Scribner's Sons, 1930).

Goodspeed, Edgar J., *Paul* (New York: Abingdon Press, 1947).

Klausner, Joseph, *From Jesus to Paul,* tr. William F. Stinespring (Boston: Beacon Press, 1961).

Knox, John, *Chapters in a Life of Paul* (New York: Abingdon Press, 1950). This book is important for the radically new solution it offered to the solution of the problem of the relationship between Acts and Paul's Letters.

Nock, Arthur Darby, *St. Paul* (New York: Harper & Row, 1937).

Quimby, Chester Warren, *Paul for Everyone* (New York: The Macmillan Company, 1946).

Ramsay, Sir William M., *St. Paul the Traveller* (Grand Rapids, Mich.: Baker Book House, 1960). A reprint of a famous study of Paul's mission against its background, written at the end of the nineteenth century by a pioneer in the archaeology of Asia Minor whose contributions are still indispensable.

Robinson, B. W., *The Life of Paul* (Chicago: University of Chicago Press, 1918).

Selby, Donald J., *Toward the Understanding of St. Paul* (Englewood Cliffs, N.J.: Prentice-Hall, Inc., 1962).

Schoeps, H. J., *St. Paul,* tr. H. Knight (Philadelphia: The Westminster Press, 1961).

Chapter Five

In Every Letter of Mine
The Pauline Epistles

I, Paul, write this greeting with my own hand.
This is the mark in every letter of mine; it is the
way I write. . . . II Thess. 3:17.

That Paul's mission to the gentiles was neither haphazard nor superficial is evident from the "anxiety for all the churches" (II Cor. 11:28) which prompted his letters. These letters, written over a period of a decade or more around the middle of the first century and therefore the earliest books to be written in the New Testament, provide for us our most direct access to the first period of the nascent Church. Neither the reminiscences of a later historian nor the theoretical generalizations of a contemporary interpreter, they deal with immediate problems of newly formed communities under pressures from traditional Judaism, on the one hand, and the paganism of the Graeco-Roman world, on the other.

In time the churches, having preserved Paul's letters to be reread again and again, began to exchange them with one another and to share them with other churches until, finally, they were gathered into the collection which established the Epistles in the New Testament. The importance of this *corpus Paulinarum* is indicated by the epistolary form of subsequent additions to the Canon of New Testament Epistles, and by the presence in the Canon of Epistles which, although actually anonymous, bear the name of Paul. Second only to Luke in the amount of material contributed to the New Testament, Paul through his letters has become the father of the ethical and theological development of Christianity.

320

1. *The Way I Write*

The first thing to remember in studying Paul's letters is that, unlike the formal epistles which are literary creations, they are genuine *ad hoc* letters. We are concerned in this chapter, therefore, with a very different kind of material, which will require different methods of study from any that we have used so far. Instead of questions of sources, editors, and the like, we will be concerned, for the most part, with attempts to reconstruct the problems and circumstances which occasioned each of the letters. Only when the background and purpose of a letter are understood—insofar as that is possible—can we gain a perspective from which to understand Paul and the meaning of his interpretation of the Gospel.

THIS IS THE MARK

The verse which stands at the head of this chapter is a subscription to II Thessalonians indicating that the body of the letter was penned by an amanuensis or secretary to which Paul had added these closing words. Similar subscriptions are found in several of his other letters (cf. I Cor. 16:21; Gal. 6:11; Col. 4:18; Philemon 19). In Romans 16:22 the amanuensis, Tertius by name, actually identifies himself and adds his own greetings. Probably all of Paul's letters were dictated in this way, a fact which will become important for us at several points later in this chapter. Although Latin writers had a system of shorthand and a method of brief writing was not unknown among the Greeks, it is doubtful that Paul's assistants possessed such skill. Even where shorthand writers were available, letters in antiquity were often composed by the amanuensis from general instructions by the author with a subscription added for authentication.[1] There were available, in fact, formula letters suitable for various occasions to which one only needed to add the appropriate details.

We may therefore visualize Paul in the home of his host standing or pacing the floor with his amanuensis seated before him, a wax tablet on his lap on which he takes notes as Paul dictates. Later the amanuensis presents to Paul what he has drafted on papyrus. Paul reads it and taking the reed pen from his assistant adds the final words in his own hand. The letter is folded and tied, the binding sealed with wax, and directions for its delivery written on the outside. A copy of it would be retained on a copy scroll for future reference. The salutation, opening greetings, and the like would be abbreviated on the copy if not omitted. Official government posts were not available for private use so Paul's letters had to be carried by private arrangement. Epaphroditus would naturally be the bearer of

---

1. See Adolph Deissmann, *Light from the Ancient East*, pp. 166, n. 7, 171–172. More recently Gordon J. Bahr, "The Subscriptions in the Pauline Letters," *JBL*, Vol. LXXXVII, Pt. I, March, 1968, pp. 27–41.

the letter to Philippi which concerned his return to the church there. Colossians 4:7–9 indicates that Tychicus and Onesimus were bringing with them that letter, and perhaps the letter to Philemon as well. From II Corinthians 7:6–8 and 8:17–18 we may infer that Titus was responsible for delivering at least some of the Corinthian correspondence. In several of these instances, of course, Paul's companions for one reason or another had to make the trips anyway. Other letters such as Romans probably were sent through the courtesy of a trader or shipmaster.

TIMOTHY HAS BROUGHT US THE GOOD NEWS

In a number of places Paul refers incidentally to the sources of the information to which he is responding in the letter at hand. I Corinthians, for instance, was written in response to disturbing news brought by "Chloe's People" (I Cor. 1:11) and to several questions raised in a letter the Corinthians had written him (I Cor. 7:1, 25; 8:1; 12:1; 16:1, 12). According to II Corinthians 2:12–13; 7:5–7, 13–16, Titus was the messenger for the church at Corinth. The return of Timothy brought the news to which Paul was responding in I Thessalonians (cf. 3:1–6). These references underscore the intimate connection between the content of the letters and the life of particular local churches. For the student of these letters this means that he must attempt insofar as possible to reconstruct the information which came to Paul and prompted them. All such information, of course, has a background. Any knowledge that can be had of the character, thinking, and circumstances of the churches to which Paul wrote is of importance for interpreting them.

Interpreting Paul's letters and therefore understanding Paul and his contributions to Christian life and thought become a matter of reconstructing their story by the inferences they allow us to make and balancing these inferences with the best knowledge we can obtain of the background of the people who made up his churches, on the one hand, and Paul's own background on the other.[2] Yet when our best efforts have been made we will have to admit, in the words of II Peter 3:16, that "there are some things in them hard to understand." A considerable part of the difficulty is, of course, that many details of Paul's relation to his churches are lost beyond recovery. Perhaps the modern interpreter can take some comfort from the fact that although Paul claimed "We write you nothing but what you can read and understand" (II Cor. 1:13), he himself found it necessary to correct misunderstandings of his letters by the original recipients (cf. I Cor. 5:9–13; II Thess. 2:1–2).

2. An older but still important study of this kind is Adolph Deissmann, *Paul* (New York: Harper & Brothers, 1957).

WHAT WE SAY IN THIS LETTER

If we could know more about how Paul wrote his letters, especially how much of a part his amanuensis had in their composition, it would be of considerable help in interpreting them. The possibilities, as we have seen, range all the way from a word-by-word recording of Paul's dictation to a free composition based on his general directions as to what to say. Undoubtedly, Paul's practice varied with the circumstances both of the urgency of the situation to which he was writing and the abilities of his assistant.

Several factors contribute to variations of style and character one finds in Paul's letters. One of them is, of course, the circumstances to which he speaks. His impatience with the "foolish Galatians" and his anger with the arrogant Corinthians stand in understandable contrast to the warmth of his gratitude for the generosity the Philippians had shown him. The appearance of other names with his in the salutation of several letters (I and II Cor., Phil., Col., I and II Thess., and Philemon) may be only a courtesy, but it is at least equally possible that these co-workers had some influence on the content of the letters.

Probably also, as time went on, Paul tended to allow his amanuenses, who were also his fellow workers and traveling companions, more and more freedom in composing the letters. Their involvement in the adminis-tration of the churches and their increasing familiarity with Paul's teach-ing would make such sharing in the composition of the letters not only feasible but inevitable. The fate of the letters after they had been written and sent is a factor which needs also to be kept in mind. With the wear and tear of repeated readings the papyrus scrolls would become worn and at times come unglued. The churches as time went on would have less and less interest in their chronological sequence and, in the churches which possessed more than one, even their separate identity. In the version of the letters which we now possess, therefore, some of them may have come from the copy scrolls rather than the letters actually sent; pages may have been lost or, more probably, rearranged, separate letters combined, and damaged or blurred places would require the collector to amend the text as best he could. At all events, the words of the apostle, which had become by this time virtual Scripture (cf. II Pet. 5:15–16), were the paramount concern of the editors. We have, for example, a list of the books of the New Testament from the end of the second century which groups Paul's letters according to the churches addressed into the perfect number of seven. According to the author of the list this number, like the seven letters in Revelation, shows the universality of the letters.[3] The local

3. The Muratorian Canon, 3.

communities and specific situations to which these letters were actually written had become irrelevant. Paul's letters had already by this time become Epistles.

The reader of Paul's letters encounters numerous characteristics which reflect the influence of these factors. The oral style, the digressions, the breaks in sentence structure (*anacoluthon*), the impassioned outbursts all reflect the spontaneity of Paul's dictation.[4] That some of his letters may represent quite closely his own wording can be seen in instances such as the way he parenthetically corrects himself in I Corinthians 1:14–17. Phrases, passages, and ideas which appear repeatedly in the several letters echo the ideas and emphases in Paul's teaching. Some of the differences in vocabulary and more orderly literary styles, on the other hand, in some of the letters which have caused scholars to question their authenticity may more likely be due to different amanuenses and differences in the extent of their participation in the composition. The line between Paul's authentic letters and Deutero-Pauline documents composed by his assistants and followers is by no means absolute. Discontinuities such as the one created by the brief passage in II Corinthians 6:14–7:1 are probably due to manuscript accidents which occurred before the *Corpus Paulinarum* was collected and published. Hymns, liturgical materials, and repeated use of key Scriptural passages appearing here and there in the letters reflect the life of the early Christian communities and refer Paul's original and intended readers to the instructions which he had imparted while he was with them (cf. the explicit reference to such instruction in I Thess. 4:1–2, 9; 5:1–2). Among these instructions, also, were the traditions of the ministry, teaching, and Passion of Jesus which Paul shared with the rest of the Church of his time. Paul's allusions to these traditions and echoes of the teaching afford us a glimpse of the growth of those oral traditions which later became the sources of our Gospels.[5] Running through all of the letters is a certain greatness of spirit, a bold vigorous genius that marks them, however much of a share others may have had in their compositions, as products of the mind of Paul.

BE READ TO ALL THE BRETHREN

Although these are real letters written to specific people and dealing with specific issues, they are not private letters. Paul intended for them to be read before the congregations (cf. I Thess. 5:27). In Colossians 4:16 he actually asks that that church and the Laodiceans exchange letters. They

4. On Paul's style and the characteristics of his letters see Johannes Weiss, *Earliest Christianity*, Vol. II, pp. 399–421; Deissmann, *Light from the Ancient East*, pp. 233–242, and *Paul*, pp. 8–26; Arthur Darby Nock, *St. Paul* (New York: Harper & Brothers, 1937), pp. 233–237.
5. Selby, *Toward the Understanding of St. Paul, pp.* 299–311, 339–345.

are therefore more literary than private letters; in them Paul has created his own literary genre. Although he used the common language of his time, he skillfully moulded it into a flexible vehicle for the broad range of his thought. One can still hear in the letters echoes of the homilies and the teaching and admonitions with which Paul had nurtured his churches while he was with them. From this standpoint, the letters are an extension of his personal ministry and provide us therefore with a first-hand, if not always clear, picture of this complex man at work.

In studying Paul's letters it is necessary to arrange them in some sort of order. For this purpose the Canonical order based essentially on length is hardly meaningful. Arranging them in chronological order would be useful, but too much uncertainty remains concerning the dates, places of origin, and sequence of several of the letters for this system to be practical. Some scholars have arranged them in two groups: letters written during Paul's travels and letters from prison. Such an arrangement is too general. In view of their character as *ad hoc* letters, the most helpful classification is according to the areas to which they were written. At least such an arrangement will accent the particular characteristics of the several areas in which Paul's churches were planted. For the sequence of the provinces themselves, we will in this chapter follow the general pattern of the itinerary in Acts of Paul's mission westward.

2. *To the Churches of Galatia*

Although among the shorter letters of Paul (less than one third the length of Romans) and concerned primarily with an issue which faded within a comparatively short time, Galatians is one of the most influential Epistles in the New Testament. At the same time it contains some problems which are not only among the most difficult but most crucial for understanding Paul. The first two chapters also give us some of the most important data on his own life with which Paul supplies us. Written in the heat of controversy, this letter, along with the Corinthian correspondence, reveals an impassioned man vigorously contending for the validity of his gospel and the integrity of his churches.

O FOOLISH GALATIANS

This letter is the only one among Paul's letters, at least as they now stand, which was addressed to more than one church. When we recall the account in Acts of Paul's mission to Antioch, Iconium, Lystra, and Derbe in the southern part of the Roman province of Galatia, it seems only natural to assume that the churches being addressed are in these cities. The traditional opinion, which was seldom challenged until the close of the nineteenth century, however, located the recipients of this letter in the old Galatian kingdom to the north. With Sir William M. Ramsay, whose archaeological studies in Asia Minor have been of great help in Pauline studies, the traditional view came under heavy attack. As a result, a number of scholars have adopted the "South Galatian hypothesis." The background to the issue is that, following the death of the client-King Amyntas in 25 B.C., whose will had donated the territory to Rome, until the reorganization of the Asian provinces in the second century A.D., a considerable extent of Phrygian and Lycaonian territory in the middle of Asia Minor as far south as the Taurus mountains was joined to the old Galatian kingdom and identified as the Province of Galatia. The question is whether Paul would have addressed people who were ethnically Phrygians and Lycaonians as "Galatians" merely because they happened to be in the comparatively recently created Roman province of that name.

Apart from the fact that Paul generally preferred the Roman geographical terms, and that he could hardly have used any other term to include the people of all four of these cities, the argument hinges principally on the question whether Paul had ever been in the old Galatian kingdom or had founded churches there. The debate on this question over the years has been too long and involved for us to enter into here.[6] Perhaps a few general observations will suffice for our purposes. Our study in chapter 4 concerning the sources and character of Acts has shown that in spite of the general reliability of its outline of Paul's itinerary it will not support the weight of the kind of detailed arguments which seek to prove that Paul did travel in the old kingdom. To establish that Paul went through north Galatia furthermore, does not prove that he founded churches there. We should note also that, in view of Luke's interest in the progress of Christianity westward, it is hard to understand why he would omit the founding of churches in north Galatia important enough to Paul to occasion the writing of this letter, unless to his knowledge there were no such churches. Finally, if the four churches in south Galatia are the ones intended, Paul's indication in I Corinthians 16:1 that the "Churches of Galatia" are participating in the contribution to the church at Jerusalem accords well with the story in Acts, especially the list in 20:4 of those who accompanied Paul on its delivery. Since the terms in Galatians 1:2 and I Corinthians 16:1 are exactly the same, the presumption is that they refer to the same churches. Although the issue is not settled, the probabilities are that this letter was addressed to the four churches in Pisidian, Antioch, Iconium, Lystra, and Derbe.

6. For excellent summaries of this debate see Ernest DeWitt Burton, *The Epistle to the Galatians* (ICC), pp. xxi–liii; and Enslin, *Christian Beginnings,* pp. 224–226. For Ramsay's own summary of his contribution to the debate see his articles under Galatia and Galatians in Hastings' *Dictionary of the Bible.*

WHO HAS BEWITCHED YOU?

Equally difficult and more important than the location of the Galatian churches is the question of the problems which necessitated this letter. That unlike any of his other letters this one plunges without any amenities or felicitations immediately into the controversy suggests something of seriousness of the crisis. There are, as we shall see, indications that Paul is speaking to more than one issue, but in one way or another they all revolve around the question of the Christian's relation to the Law, hence to Judaism. In the word "Law" (Greek: *nomos*) Paul is following the LXX which uses it to translate the word "Torah." This translation is unfortunate and undoubtedly exercised a subtle influence on Paul's thinking. Torah, more than simply laws and commandments, means teaching or instruction, doctrinal as well as ethical. The term occurs some thirty-two times in the six chapters of this letter. Because the question of the Law involves the whole issue of the Church's relationship to Judaism it will be well for us to examine that issue briefly.[7]

The Christian movement began, of course, as a sect within the commonwealth of Israel. It understood itself in terms of the eschatological hopes and expectations which flourished in bewildering variety in late Judaism. Convinced that in Jesus the promised Messiah had come, it saw itself standing at the climax of Israel's history. Therefore, on strictly Jewish premises, it stood in an oblique but not always clearly understood relationship to Torah. Matthew, as we have seen, writing a generation after Paul believed Torah to be still in force but only in terms of the new interpretation Christ had given it. John, on the other hand, could speak of the Law as something alien and put in its place Jesus' "New Commandment." Both ideas have their roots in Jewish concepts of the messianic age.

With respect to contemporary Judaism, the beginning Church interpreted itself in terms of Isaiah's doctrine of the righteous remnant.[8] Its first task, therefore, was calling Israel in the name of Jesus the Messiah to repentance and preparation for the coming eschaton. That in this task it was far less successful than expected created new problems which eventually turned its energies, as Luke is at pains to show, in another direction. We must not suppose, however, that the gentile mission developed simply as an alternative to the mission to Israel. As the numerous Old Testament quotations in the New regarding the gentiles show, the Church could use the Scriptures in support of its belief that the conversion

---

7. For further on this highly important issue see H. J. Schoeps, *Paul,* tr. Harold Knight (Philadelphia: The Westminster Press, 1961); W. D. Davies, *Paul and Rabbinic Judaism* (London: S.P.C.K., 1958); Johannes Munck, tr. Frank Clarke, *Paul and the Salvation of Mankind* (Richmond, Va.: John Knox Press, 1959).
8. See p. 19.

of the gentiles would be a part of the events of the final age in which it believed itself to be living.

The moment the Church deliberately addressed itself to the nations, however, it found itself confronted by the same problem which Judaism had already faced: Under what terms may a gentile be admitted into the commonwealth of Israel?[9] That the God-fearing gentile who observed the Noachian Laws would find a place in the Age-to-Come was conceded, but this left him essentially an outsider. While the debate between Rabbi Eleazer and Rabbi Joshua over the necessity of circumcision along with baptism, often cited in this connection, was more academic than a reflection of actual practice, it does indicate the problem and at least some of the thinking about it that was taking place within Judaism.[10] Josephus' story of the proselyte Izates, king of Adiabene, who finally found it necessary to be circumcised probably represents the characteristic Jewish solution to the problem.[11] Primitive Christianity, convinced that in Jesus the messianic age was at hand, could see the matter from a different perspective. Scriptures were not lacking to show that a wide-spread conversion of gentiles would be a sign of the eschaton. To reason from this conviction to a modification of the requirements for admitting gentiles was not a long step. Probably Luke is reflecting a genuinely primitive tradition in his picture of Peter setting aside circumcision purely on the basis of a revelation.[12] Such a change, it could be argued, was part of the messianic reinterpretation of Torah.

Very early in the Church's struggle with these issues, Paul appeared and began his mission to the gentiles which brought matters to a head and precipitated decisions of far-reaching consequences for the future of the Church. The following series of diagrams will help to illustrate the development which took place. In the first stage the Church is within Judaism in such a way that a gentile must enter through Judaism into the Church:

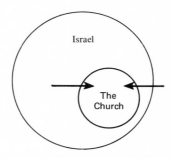

9. On Jewish missionary activity see F. M. Derwacter, *Preparing the Way for Paul.*
10. See Selby, *Toward the Understanding of St. Paul,* pp. 52–58, and works there cited.
11. *Ant.,* XX, ch. 2.
12. See pp. 296–299.

Very soon, however, gentiles were occasionally being admitted on a more "liberal" policy which was partly pragmatic and partly based on an interpretation of the new situation created by the coming of Christ.

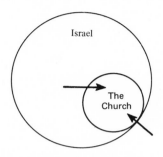

As we shall see, Paul's solution was at the same time more systematic and more radically eschatological. He saw his mission being carried out in a brief interval between Christ's first coming and his final appearance to usher in the Kingdom of God. With this interval the Law had fulfilled its function and come to an end; Israel, likewise, was for the most part being temporarily set aside for the sake of the gentiles. The Church—or perhaps more accurately, Christ—consequently has superseded the old commonwealth as a new entity into which both Jews and gentiles are being called. Paul speaks at times as though each of them retains his own identity within the new body, hence the broken line in Diagram C. At other times he declares that those baptized into Christ are no longer either Jew or gentile but "one in Christ" (Gal. 3:28, cf. Eph. 2:14–16).

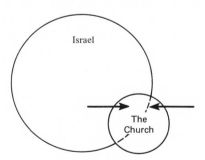

By the time of the fourth Gospel the separation between Church and Synagogue was regrettably but irrevocably complete.[13] The Church now regarded itself not only as the remnant, the new Israel, but because of Judaism's apostasy in refusing to recognize its Messiah, also as the only true Israel.

13. See, for example, the expulsion of the former blind man from the synagogue in chapter 9. See pp. 247–248.

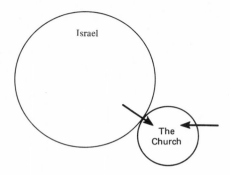

Within another half century the rift was to become so wide that the famous heretic Marcion would, in the name of Christianity, reject both Israel's God and Scriptures. Marcion had, of course, carried the matter to an extreme. The Church refused to go so far, but his movement was the final result of the bitter controversies between Church and Synagogue which this issue engendered.

The letter to the Galatians belongs in the early part of this development. Paul's position (Diagram C) as argued in the letter was manifestly in advance of that of the apostles in Jerusalem (Diagram B), whereas both Acts 15 and Galatians show that there was still a significant group in the Church which insisted on circumcision (Diagram A) for gentile converts. Yet because this group had no direct relationship to the churches in Galatia, the Galatian situation cannot simply be placed between these two positions. A long tradition in Pauline scholarship accounted for the major troubles in his churches by a task force sent out by the Mother Church in Jerusalem to correct Paul's antinomian errors and bring his churches into line with the modified Judaic legalism prevalent there. This theory developed by F. C. Baur, of Tübingen University (Germany), around the middle of the last century resulted from an application of Hegel's doctrine that history moves in a three-stage pattern which he called thesis, antithesis, and synthesis. Accordingly, Peter and the conservative, Judaistic, Jerusalem church provided the thesis; Paul became the champion and hero of the liberal and progressive Hellenists who represented the antithesis; while Luke in his irenic picture of Christian origins became the spokesman for the later synthesis in the ancient Catholic Church. The story of the first period of Christianity is therefore reduced essentially to a running battle between Paul and Jerusalem in which circumcision was a key issue. Although the theory itself has been abandoned, unfortunately by no means all of its ideas, including these troublers of Paul, have disappeared.[14] That the apostles approved of Paul's

14. For example, the notion that Paul's collection for the Jerusalem church was the

missionary policy is as clearly stated in Galatians 2 as it is in Acts 15, and the notion of agents from Jerusalem pursuing Paul's churches is purely gratuitous. The group from Jerusalem which caused the trouble in Antioch cannot be cited as evidence of such agents; Paul's troubles in Galatia were from another source. Paul knew well enough who the "certain men from James" at Antioch (2:12) were, but he did not know the identity of the troublemaker in Galatia (cf. 5:10).

The problem in Galatia was as complex as it was inevitable. The local synagogues could provide all the influence necessary to account for the legalistic reaction in Paul's churches. It would be surprising indeed if within the Christian movement, still an essentially Jewish movement and using Israel's Sacred Writings as its Scriptures, there had not been such a reaction. In the statement, "For even those who receive circumcision do not themselves keep the law" (6:13, cf. 5:3) and references to pagan "elemental spirits" (Greek: *stoichia*) there are indications, furthermore, that those promoting circumcision in Galatia were not Jews at all but gentiles who somehow had become convinced that its omission was a bad compromise. Some interpreters have detected a veiled reference to the rites of the Cybele mysteries in Paul's astonishing wish that the trouble-makers "would mutilate themselves" (5:12). Along with Paul's implication that the promoters of circumcision were not interested in the other aspects of the Law (5:3; 6:12–13), this interpretation suggests the possibility that the problem arose among pagan converts who saw in circumcision a less dramatic equivalent to the emasculation of the priests of Cybele and therefore a way of achieving a higher status in their newfound faith and supposed that they would have the approbation of Jerusalem in doing so. It also explains why Paul could speak of their movement as a return to paganism (4:8–10).

Although much of Galatians is occupied with the issue of circumcision, the problem of the letter cannot be reduced to a simple argument against it. Paul's puzzling question "But if I, brethren, still preach circumcision, why am I still persecuted?" (5:11) hints that the problem is more complex. That there were serious divisions among the Galatians themselves is indicated by his warning against their "biting and devouring one another" (5:15). The Jews who in joining the Galatian churches had conceded at considerable personal difficulty Paul's position must have been placed in a very awkward position by the sudden demand for circumcision. Some of them probably would welcome this return to what was for them a traditional position; others would remain faithful to Paul.

---

result of a bargain by terms of which he obtained agreement with the apostles at the council. See John Knox, *Chapters in a Life of Paul*, pp. 53–59; and J. C. Hurd, Jr., *The Origin of I Corinthians*, pp. 262–269, *passim*.

On the other side, to the gentile converts Paul would appear to be still well within traditional Judaism. His abolition of the requirements of proselytes in admitting gentiles into his churches would hardly offset his rabbinic use of the Scriptures of Judaism or his preaching of a Jewish ethic. They would hardly understand his distinction between being under the Law and walking by the Spirit. The rigorous ethical admonitions in 5:13–6:10, therefore, are probably not merely an anticipation of possible excesses resulting from his doctrine of freedom from the Law. Along with those who desired "to be under law" (4:21), therefore, it appears likely that Paul had to contend with a second group consisting of those "who are spiritual" (6:1). His admonitions against the "desires of the flesh" (5:16–21) provide a picture of their libertinism. The alarming news of the turbulence in the Galatian churches left Paul puzzled and concerned, "I could wish to be present with you now and to change my tone, for I am perplexed about you" (4:20).

THE GOSPEL WHICH I PREACH

How deeply Paul is disturbed by the troubles in Galatia is evident in the language of the letter. Probably not all of our difficulty in understanding it arises from our lack of knowledge of the background. The agitation under which Paul wrote has played havoc with the syntax in some places and obscured the connections in his thought in others. The general pattern, nevertheless, is clear. He addresses himself to three major issues: (1) his authority as an apostle (chs. 1–2); (2) the question of circumcision and other requirements of the Law (3:1–5:12); (3) the ethics of freedom in the Spirit (5:13–6:10).

An Apostle Not from Men, 1–2   In the very opening words of the salutation Paul begins his debate, "an apostle—not from men or through man, but through Jesus Christ and God the Father, who raised him from the dead." What follows in verses 6–12 establishes the basis of his argument. The developments in Galatia amount to an abandonment of the gospel. Twice Paul pronounces a solemn anathema upon any who would so fatally mislead them. The criterion of the true Gospel is what Paul had originally preached to them, which rests his argument squarely on his authority as an apostle.[15] When taken with the question of pleasing men (vs. 10), the phrase "even we, or an angel from heaven" (vs. 8) may be more than a rhetorical expression of an improbable condition. Although some of the agitators may have claimed angelic visions for their authority, others quite possibly were claiming that Paul in the interest of attracting more gentile converts by abandoning circumcision had actually exceeded

15. On Paul's apostleship see pp. 310–311.

his authority and subsequently had been required to retreat to a more conservative position (cf. his strange words, "But if I, brethren, still preach circumcision, why am I still persecuted." 5:11). Paul is now reaffirming his original Gospel unchanged. Is he, then, in spite of the Jerusalem leaders still "watering down" the demands of the Gospel? No, because he "did not receive it from men" but from Christ himself (vs. 12).

In what follows Paul recites the story of his call. Like the ancient prophets (cf. vs. 15 with Jer. 1:15 and Isa. 49:1) God had destined him from birth to this ministry and in due time had called him from his misguided zeal as a persecutor of the Church to the gentile mission. Paul's apostolic authority rested on this revelation of the Risen Lord (cf. I Cor. 9:1) who appointed him, belatedly, to that office (cf. "those who were apostles before me," vs. 17, with "last of all, as to one untimely born, he appeared also to me" I Cor. 15:8). When three years later he went to Jerusalem, therefore, he was already an apostle; he did not go to be made one! With a solemn oath Paul swore that he saw only Peter (Cephas) and James the Lord's brother. The natural interpretation of this sentence is that some in the Galatian churches were associating him with others in the church in Jerusalem, perhaps to explain the alleged change in his Gospel. The issue here is not the number of visits to Jerusalem or their brevity, but the people with whom Paul had associated. To make his words in 1:22, "I was not known by sight to the churches of Judea," mean, in contradiction to Acts, that he was a stranger to Jerusalem is, in view of his reference in the very next sentence to his persecution, to make his whole statement self-contradictory. Although he appears anxious to disassociate himself from some person or group in Jerusalem (cf. 2:2), Paul is not claiming independence from the apostles themselves; he is claiming equality with them.

In the next stage of his argument Paul relates his version of the council in Jerusalem (2:1–10, cf. Acts 15:1–35), the point of which is that he and the "pillar" apostles found themselves in agreement on the Gospel, and they affirmed his mission to the gentiles as parallel to theirs among the circumcised. Significantly, the same two apostles, Peter and James, with whom he had met on the first visit are involved along with John. The troublesome part of this passage, however, is the reference to Titus. There is a textual variant which omits "to whom" and "not" which makes verses 4 and 5 read: "But because of false brethren . . . we did even yield submission for a moment, that the truth. . . ." That such a change does improve the otherwise hopeless syntax is to be admitted, but it also means that in apparent contradiction to verse 3 Paul had permitted the circumcision of Titus. Whereas some interpreters have adopted this conclusion, it is more likely that the variant resulted from an attempt to make sense of the grammar and, therefore, that Titus was not circumcised. Johannes Munck lifts the entire statement from its context in Jerusalem and makes it refer to an episode in one of Paul's churches.[16] The necessary clues for the solution to this problem have been lost beyond recovery. Whatever actually happened, however, Paul's language indicates that the affair over Titus was disturbing to him. It is interesting in that connection to compare this passage with Acts 21:27–36 and 24:17–20 where another Greek, Trophimus, precipitated a crisis for Paul and where, according to Luke, he stumbles into another anacoluthon.

There are two points of difference between the story of the council in Acts 15 and Paul's account here which are worth noting. According to Acts Paul and Barnabas went to the council because of the arrival in Antioch of a group of proponents of circumcision (Acts 15:1–2). In contrast Paul makes that event the occasion for his argument with Peter (Gal. 2:11–12); his trip to Jerusalem was "by revelation" (Gal. 2:2). Paul's attitude toward his relationship to Jerusalem is to be judged by this statement. Although he could, by way of maintaining the authority of his own apostleship, say of those "of repute," "what they were makes no difference to me; God shows no partiality" (vs. 6), he initiated the meeting to win approval for his Gospel lest he was "running or had run in vain" (vs. 2). His gentile Christians must be accepted; the Church cannot be divided (cf. I Cor. 1:13a: "Is Christ divided?"). Paul stoutly maintains his equality with "the pillars" but not his independence from them. The council in Acts also is an open meeting involving the whole church there, whereas Paul emphasizes that it was a private meeting with the leaders (cf. Acts 15:4, 12, 22 with Gal. 2:2). Along with his concern to establish the approval of his Gospel by the leaders, he appears equally anxious to disassociate himself from some others (false brethren?) at Jerusalem. As for the leaders, so far from disapproving of Paul's mission they could do no more than exhort him to something for which he had already manifested a deep concern: "Remember the poor" (vs. 10).

Although primarily intended to provide the setting for the speech with which he sums up his argument and makes his transition to his next approach to the question, Paul's argument with Peter (2:11–21) underscores two important points: First, Peter's initial behavior and the weight of Paul's rebuke rested on and therefore confirmed the principles enunciated in Jerusalem: "If you, though a Jew, live like a Gentile and not like a Jew, how can you compel the Gentiles to live like Jews?" (vs. 14).

16. Cf. George S. Duncan, *The Epistle of Paul to the Galatians* (*MNTC*) (New York: Harper & Brothers, 1934), pp. 41–45; Ernest DeWitt Burton, *The Epistle to the Galatians* (ICC), pp. 84–86; Munck, *Paul and the Salvation of Mankind*, pp. 95–98.

Second, abolishing circumcision must include the admission of the gentiles to full fellowship, including eating together with the Jewish members. Otherwise the gentiles are simply put in the position in which traditional Judaism had placed the "God-fearers," and the new community, being placed back in the age of the Law, loses its eschatological significance. The essence of the whole argument of the letter is expressed in Paul's speech to Peter: "By works of the law (including circumcision) shall no one be justified" (vs. 16), "for if justification were through the law, then Christ died to no purpose" (vs. 21). The very fact that Christ's death was necessary shows the inadequacy of the Law. The believer, therefore, participates in Christ's death in order to possess the new life in him. In other letters Paul develops this point more fully, but here he turns his attention to the inadequacy of the Law.

By Works of the Law, or by Hearing with Faith? 3:1–5:12 Beginning with a direct appeal to their original religious experience, which because it was not based on the Law proved the Law unnecessary, Paul in rabbinic fashion presents a series of arguments from Scripture, especially Torah itself, to show that it was not intended as a means of salvation. Abraham whose faith "was reckoned to him as righteousness," through the promise that he would be a blessing to all nations, has become the father of all men of faith. Therefore the true children of Abraham, i.e., the true people of God, become so by faith (3:6–9). Because of its absolute demands (Deut. 27:26), furthermore, the Law can only curse man, hence "He who through faith is righteous shall live" (Hab. 2:4); but this statement, because it indicates faith as the true source of righteousness, excludes the law (Lev. 18:5). The meaning of the death of Christ now becomes clear: On behalf of sinful man, he who obviously cannot be cursed, came under the curse upon "everyone who hangs on a tree" (Deut. 21:33), bringing the Law to an end, and he therefore becomes the vehicle through faith of the blessing of Abraham to the gentiles (vss. 10–14).

Paul now returns to the theme of the promise to Abraham in order to take another approach. On the principle that a will once established cannot be altered or qualified, the Law which was given four hundred and thirty years later cannot be made a condition to the promise made to Abraham and his offspring. The term "offspring," being singular, means Christ. The promise therefore comes to the believer directly from Abraham through Christ. The subordinate position of the Law is further shown by its having been mediated, unlike the promise which came directly from God, through angels. The Law was therefore an interim provision as a custodian to hold man in check and finally to expose his sinfulness until Christ came in whom the believers become sons of God (3:15–26). In moving eloquence Paul reaches his conclusion:

> For as many of you as were baptized into Christ have put
> on Christ. There is neither Jew nor Greek, there is neither
> slave nor free, there is neither male nor female; for you are all
> one in Christ Jesus. And if you are Christ's, then you are
> Abraham's offspring, heirs according to promise.   3:27–29

Using the word "heirs" as a catchword, Paul proceeds to illustrate his point by the analogy of the contrast between the slave who always remains a slave and the heir who upon reaching his majority becomes the owner of the estate. Christ the Son and heir came to that time by his incarnation. Born under the Law, therefore "no better than a slave" (4:1), he has become the heir through whom the believers by adoption also become sons and heirs (4:1–7).

By using the first-person plural with the words "elemental spirits" (vs. 3) in the analogy and the same word with the second person in his application of the analogy to the Galatian gentiles (vss. 8–9), Paul has drawn a rather surprising parallel between being under the Jewish Law and paganism. This radical application of the doctrine of the new oneness in Christ (3:28) has the effect of invalidating circumcision for the Jewish believers as well as the gentiles. It also suggests that what was taking place in the Galatian churches was a syncretism of the sort that was rife in that part of the world.

Paul returns abruptly to the theme of the change that has taken place among the Galatians with which he began this section. Recalling that their sympathy for his illness was so great that they would have given him their own eyes, he asks, "Have I then become your enemy by telling you the truth?". The words, "they make much of you . . . that you may make much of them" suggest that the Galatian problem involved a power struggle not unlike that in Corinth.[17] Paul is perturbed and perplexed (4:11–20).

Just as abruptly Paul comes back to the main argument, this time to develop an allegory on Abraham's two sons by Sarah and Hagar. Hagar's son, born to a slave, represents the bondage of the present Judaism under the Law. The believers, "like Isaac, are children of promise"; the slave and her son are therefore disinherited and cast out (4:21–31, Gen. 21:10). The reference to the slave persecuting the free son in verse 29 and references to persecution in 1:23 and 5:11 reinforce Paul's statement in 6:12 that those who are promoting circumcision are doing so "only in order that they may not be persecuted for the cross of Christ." It is interesting to note that the quotation from Isaiah 54:1, in verse 27, belongs to the Haftarah appointed in the ancient three-year cycle of synagogue lections

---

17. See pp. 351–353, passim.

to be read with Genesis 21 from which Paul has taken the story of Hagar. With the forceful admonition not to return to the slavery of the Law because to do so places one under the responsibility to keep the whole Law and severs his connection with Christ, Paul concludes his argument (5:1–12).

If You Are Led by the Spirit, 5:12–6:10   That their new-found freedom in the Spirit provides to the libertines no license for immorality Paul spells out in a brief homily on the meaning of life in the Spirit. Since "the whole law is fulfilled in one word, 'you shall love your neighbor as yourself,'" they are "through love to be servants of one another." Following the admonition not to "gratify the desires of the flesh," Paul gives one of his familiar parallel lists of vices and virtues which in the contrast between flesh and Spirit (5:13–26) define his meaning.

Paul becomes more specific. Being "spiritual" means in humility and gentleness to restore those who fall into sin, to assist one another, and do good to all men. He adds the somber note of the eschatological Judgment: What one sows that he will reap; to sow to the flesh is death, to sow to the Spirit is eternal life (6:1–10). In a brief postscript in his own handwriting Paul recapitulates: "For neither circumcision counts for anything, nor uncircumcision, but a new creation (6:11–16). Almost fiercely he adds, "Henceforth let no man trouble me; for I bear on my body the marks of Jesus" (vs. 17), and closes the letter. We will meet much of the line of thought in this letter again in another one written under different circumstances and for a different purpose, but for now we turn to a group of letters written in a very different mood.

3. To All the Believers in Macedonia: I and II Thessalonians and Philippians

Although Acts lists three churches in Macedonia founded by Paul at Philippi, Thessalonica, and Beroea, we have letters from Paul to only the first two of them. These letters are marked by their lack of controversy and warmth of affection. Elsewhere Paul speaks with feeling of the loyalty and support the Macedonians had shown him (cf. II Cor. 8:1–5; 11:8–9); the irenic mood of these letters, therefore, should not surprise us. It is interesting that only to these churches does Paul write to continue doing what they are doing "more and more" (I Thess. 4:1, 10; Phil. 1:9). Although they come from different times and circumstances in Paul's life, their common mood even more than the similarity of the character and circumstances of the people to whom they were written justify their being treated together here.

TO THE CHURCH OF THE THESSALONIANS

In all probability the two letters to Thessalonica are the earliest that we have from Paul. From both Acts (17:10–18:5) and I Thessalonians 2:1, 15, 17–3:6 we learn the circumstances behind the letters. After having been driven out of Thessalonica Paul and his company had gone first to Beroea and then to Athens. Perhaps it was the bond under which his host, Jason, had been placed that was Satan's hindrance to Paul's return to Thessalonica (cf. Acts 17:5–9 with I Thess. 2:17–18). Still deeply concerned for the well-being of the Thessalonians, he sent Timothy back to them from Athens (Acts mistakenly has Silas and Timothy remain behind at Beroea), while he went on to Corinth. When Timothy rejoined Paul at Corinth with his report from Thessalonica Paul responded with the first letter.

A Letter Purporting to Be from Us   Two characteristics of the second letter in comparison with I Thessalonians has in the minds of some scholars raised questions of its authenticity. Similarities of outline and content between the two letters combined with a lack of warmth and more impersonal atmosphere, on the one hand, and serious differences in the eschatological ideas at the heart of each of them, on the other, make it appear that the second letter was forged to "correct" the eschatology Paul expressed in the first. The loud insistence on the authenticating mark of Paul at the end, and the warning in 2:2 not to be misled "by letter purporting to be from us" seem to reinforce the suspicion.[18] In order for the letters to bear such close resemblance, so it is argued, the second one must have been written shortly after the first. How then could Paul have so quickly revised his concepts on eschatology?

For several reasons these objections to the authenticity of II Thessalonians have not won wide support among the scholars. One reason is that the literary similarities and differences are easily exaggerated and probably due to role of amanuensis and the closeness in the time of their writing. The alleged differences in eschatological ideas, in the second place, are better understood from the standpoint of the nature of the apocalyptic language and thought forms being used, and the fact that Paul is speaking in the two letters to different situations. In the first letter he is reassuring the Thessalonians that the believers who had died would not be left out in the Day of the Lord; in the second he is reassuring those who had heard the rumor that the eschatological day had already come that it cannot come without their knowing it. However suddenly, "like a thief in the night" (I Thess. 5:2) the Lord's coming will be, there are recognizable preconditions, such as the great rebellion and the ap-

18. See Enslin, *Christian Beginnings,* pp. 241–244; James Everett Frame, *The Epistles of St. Paul to the Thessalonians* (ICC), pp. 39–54.

pearance of a "lawless one" (II Thess. 2:3–12), by which the informed believer will recognize the event when it happens. The suggestion of a forged letter, furthermore, is not as clear in II Thessalonians 2:2 as it appears in translation. Spirit, word, and letter are correlatives, all of them belonging with "purporting to be from us." It seems more likely that Paul is assuming that they have misunderstood him.

We Would Not Have You Ignorant, I Thessalonians   The first letter falls into two main parts. The first, chapters 1 through 3, is concerned with the faithfulness and progress of the Thessalonian Christians; the second, chapters 4 and 5, contains admonitions and instructions which comprise the real purpose of the letter. An interesting literary habit appears in the number of triads which occur throughout the letter. Four of these occur in the opening section: faith, love, hope (1:3; cf. I Cor. 13:13); word, power, Holy Spirit (1:5); affliction, joy, Holy Spirit (1:6); and welcome, serve, wait (1:9–10). In the later chapters at least four more triads appear: faith, love, remember (3:6); live quietly, mind your own affairs, work (4:11); admonish the idle, encourage the fainthearted, help the weak (5:14); rejoice, pray, give thanks (5:16–18a). That they occur mostly among the gratulations and general admonitions suggests that they represent stock items and patterns in Paul's teaching and homilies. This suggestion is reinforced by several allusions to Paul's teaching while he was with them in Thessalonica (e.g., 3:4; 4:1–2, 6, 9; 5:1–2).

Four items comprise the first part of the letter: two thanksgivings (1:2–10 and 2:13–16), separated by a review of Paul's ministry among the Thessalonians (2:1–12), and an explanation of the circumstances of the letter (2:17–3:13). Paul begins by thanking God for the piety and influence of the Thessalonians (1:2–10). They had been chosen by God, and in imitating Paul and the Lord they had become an example to the believers in Macedonia, Achaia, and everywhere. He then turns to a recitation of his experiences in establishing their church (2:1–12). Beginning with his troubles at Philippi and the opposition he encountered in Thessalonica, he recalls without false modesty the purity of his motives, which without guile or greed were only to please God, and his gentle care for them, "like a nurse" with children. He recalls also his labor "day and night" to support himself, his blameless behavior, and his fatherly exhortations.

Once more Paul thanks God for them (2:13–16). This time for receiving the word for "what it really is, the word of God," and for imitating the churches in Judea by steadfastly enduring persecution at the hands of their own countrymen. In a brief but bitter sentence he recalls how the Jews had crucified Jesus and having driven him out continued to harass Paul's mission to the gentiles.

Paul comes now to the circumstances which have caused him to write. Although he had hoped more than once to return to Thessalonica, Satan had hindered him. When, therefore, he "could bear it no longer" he sent Timothy to aid and encourage them and to bring him news of them. Timothy had returned with the welcome news of their faithfulness. So now he is writing in response to Timothy's report. With a short benedictory prayer (3:11–13) the first part of the letter closes.

Preceded and followed by a series of moral admonitions, the principal substance of the second part of the letter (chs. 4–5) consists of eschatological instructions (4:13–5:11) which reflect concerns of the Thessalonians reported by Timothy and, therefore, comprise the real purpose of the letter. In the opening exhortation (4:1–12) Paul admonishes them to abstain from immorality, lust, and dishonesty, and increasing more and more their love of the breathren, to live quietly, mind their own affairs, and work with their hands.

In his discussion of eschatology Paul deals with two questions, the first and most important of which is in response to the concern of the Thessalonians for those of their number who had died. Beginning with the words, "We would not have you ignorant, brethren," Paul reassures them that "the dead in Christ will rise first" and all believers therefore will share equally in the eschaton and will "always be with the Lord" (4:13–17). Paul follows this reassurance with a warning of the sudden and unexpected way in which the day will come. Let them remain sober and awake as children of the day, armed and ready for Christ's return (5:1–10; cf. Rom. 13:11–14). In 5:8 there is a brief form of the figure of the panoply which is expanded in Ephesians 6:11–17. Each of the two sections closes with an admonition: "Therefore comfort one another with these words" (4:18); "Therefore encourage one another and build one another up just as you are doing" (5:11). After a brief series of exhortations to respect their leaders, be at peace among themselves, to help and admonish one another, and not to quench the Spirit but test everything (5:12–22), Paul closes the letter with another benedictory prayer.

Let No One Deceive You, II Thessalonians   Paul's second letter to the Thessalonians falls into three parts: (1) prolegomena, (2) on the parousia, (3) on idleness. The concerns which dominate the letter are, therefore, to correct a misconception concerning eschatology (2:1–12) and to rebuke members of the church who were living in idleness and becoming busybodies (3:6–15). Neither of these topics is new. Eschatology was, as we have seen, the primary reason for the first letter, which also included two brief exhortations against idleness (4:11; 5:14). Nearly all of the topics in the second letter are found also in the first. Some of them are in condensed form, whereas others are expansions of items only briefly mentioned in the earlier letter. The opening thanksgiving (1:3–4, cf. I Thess. 1:2–10, 2:13–16) for their faith and endurance, for example, is a condensation of the two thanksgivings in the first half of I Thessalonians. The following section (1:5–10) on the eschatological Judgment is likewise an expansion of the words, "But God's wrath has come upon them at last!" (I Thess. 2:16b).

Separated by a brief benedictory prayer (1:11–12) similar to the one in I Thessalonians 3:11–13 which closes the prolegomena and precedes the main issues of that letter, the correction of the eschatological misunderstanding (2:1–12) begins the body of the second letter. Somehow the Thessalonians had gotten the idea that the Day of the Lord had already arrived. Perhaps, as in I Thessalonians, they were apprehensive lest the believers who had died be left out, they were now concerned that they themselves had missed the eschaton. What the source of their misinformation was is impossible to say; apparently Paul himself did not know (cf. 2:2–3). Admittedly, Paul's description of the parousia as "a thief in the night" (I Thess. 5:2) and the believers being "caught up together . . . in the clouds to meet the Lord in the air" (4:17) would leave him open to some such misunderstandings.

To allay their fears Paul supplies further details which demonstrate the impossibility of the eschaton's arrival without being known. First there must come the apocalyptic rebellion and a mysterious "man of lawlessness" (2:3). Because Paul is reiterating teaching he had given them in person, much of what he has written here is no longer clear to us. Even more obscure is the identity of "he who now restrains it" (2:7). Johannes Munck, following a suggestion by Oscar Cullmann, suggests that the restraining element (the word is neuter in vs. 6 but masculine in vs. 7) is the incompleteness of the world mission and therefore, since he is the apostle to the gentiles, Paul himself.[19] The statement in the Little Apocalypse (Mk. 13:10; cf. Mt. 24:14), "And the gospel must first be preached to all nations," would certainly support such an interpretation. A second thanksgiving (2:13–15) follows which expands the theme in I Thessalonians 1:4 of the divine election of the Thessalonian believers. A second benedictory prayer (2:16–17; cf. I Thess. 5:23–24) closes the section.

In a brief passage Paul asks the prayers of the Thessalonians and expresses his confidence in their continued obedience (3:1–5). That the themes in this passage correspond to those in Paul's review of his mission in Thessalonica (I Thess. 2:1–12) makes this passage a complementary of the latter. Its real function is, however, to introduce the

19. *Paul and the Salvation of Mankind*, pp. 36–42.

second of the two main issues of the letter, the problem of idleness (3:6–15). In its appeal to Paul's own example which the idle are called upon to imitate (3:7, 9; cf. I Thess. 1:6), this passage also picks up a theme from his mission (I Thess. 2:9–12). The weight of his emphasis here falls on how the community is to treat the idle busybodies: "If any one refuses to obey . . . have nothing to do with him, that he may be ashamed" (vs. 14). For "if anyone will not work, let him not eat" (vs. 10). Here as in the previous section (2:5, 15), Paul twice appeals to the instructions he had given while with them (3:6, 10; cf. I Thess. 3:4; 4:1–2, 9). With a prayer for their peace he brings the letter to a close.

TO ALL THE SAINTS AT PHILIPPI

It is interesting that Paul's letter to the Philippians, which was written neither to resolve a controversy nor to solve a problem but to respond to a very gracious gift, contains also his most intimate and profound statement of his spiritual autobiography. Significant, too, is the fact that in this letter in which he speaks at greater length and more apprehensively than in any others except, possibly, the fragments in II Tim. 4 of his imprisonment and possible execution, he uses the word "rejoice" more than twice as often as in any material of equal length in all of his other letters. The warmth and graciousness which emerge here make us realize how one-sided and distorted would be our picture of Paul if we did not have his Macedonian correspondence. Before we examine the content, two problems, the provenance and integrity of Philippians, require our attention.

My Imprisonment That Paul wrote this letter from prison is clearly stated in the opening chapter (1:7, 12–14, 16–17, 19–26, 29–30). There appears also to be a real possibility that he might be executed. For several reasons the location of this imprisonment has traditionally been placed in Rome. In the Book of Acts, first of all, Paul was in prison in only two places, Caesarea and Rome, long enough to have written anything (the episode in the Philippian jail was in the city to which this letter was sent and lasted only until midnight). Second, the circumstances pictured in 1:19–26 appear similar enough to have obtained shortly before his situation in II Timothy 4:6–18, which because it corresponds so well with the tradition of Paul's execution has been identified with it. The third and most important reason for locating this imprisonment in Rome is Paul's reference to "the whole praetorian guard" (1:13) and "those of Caesar's household" (4:22).

From two directions has come evidence to make a reassessment of the tradition necessary. First is the observation that on the basis of Paul's own letters the account in Acts of his imprisonments is incomplete. In the account in II Corinthians 11:23–29 of the troubles he endured for the Gospel he begins with the statement "far more imprisonments." Since that letter was written before his final trip to Jerusalem the "imprisonments" could not have included either Caesarea or Rome. Paul was in prison, therefore, more than once during his ministry in Galatia and the Aegean area. There are references in his letters, furthermore, that point to Ephesus as the place for at least one of them. He refers in I Corinthians 15:32 to having "fought with wild beasts at Ephesus." Although there are difficulties in the way of taking this statement literally, since he makes it in connection with the Resurrection, it surely refers to physical danger.[20] Later in the same letter, written too early to have referred to the riot described in Acts 19:23–41 (16:8–9), he talks about

Prison at Ephesus said to be the one in which Saint Paul was imprisoned. (Courtesy of Don R. Smith.)

20. For a summary of these difficulties see Selby, *Toward the Understanding of St. Paul*, pp. 218–219.

"many adversaries in Ephesus." Of his experience in Asia (of which Ephesus was the capital) he writes, in II Corinthians 1:8–9, "we felt that we had received the sentence of death." If Romans 16 is a separate letter addressed to Ephesus, which as we shall see is probable, Paul's reference to his fellow prisoners, Andronicus and Junias (vs. 7), makes an Ephesian imprisonment definite and helps to explain his allusion to Prisca and Aquila (who worked with him in Corinth and later moved to Ephesus cf. Acts 18:1–3, 18–19, 26; I Cor. 16:19) his "fellow workers . . . who risked their necks for my life" (vs. 3).[21] This conclusion is important because it affects not only the possibilities for the provenance of Philippians but also that of the other prison letters.

To show that Paul was in prison in Ephesus does not, however, establish that Philippians was written there. The second line of evidence, therefore, concerns the letter itself. In the first place, the praetorian guard and Caesar's household (Phil. 1:13; 4:22), which would appear to be decisive in placing Paul in Rome, have been shown upon archaeological evidence to be found in important cities of the Empire including Ephesus.[22] There remains, therefore, no definite reason to associate Philippians with Rome. There is evidence in the circumstances of the letter, on the other hand, which points away from Rome to another location for the provenance of the letter. We may outline those circumstances as follows:

1. News of Paul's imprisonment reached the Philippians.
2. They responded by sending Epaphroditus with assistance.
3. Epaphroditus became seriously ill, and news of his illness reached the Philippians.
4. News of the Philippians' concern for Epaphroditus reached Paul.
5. When Epaphroditus had recovered sufficiently to travel, Paul sent him home bearing the letter.
6. In the letter Paul promised to send Timothy to the Philippians.
7. And, pending his release, hoped to follow with a personal visit.

Each of these items involves a trip, or projected trip, by someone between Paul, prison, and Philippi. Items 1, 3, and 4, furthermore, were not messages deliberately sent, but simply rumors which traveled incidentally from one to the other. The problem here is that at the point of the writing of the letter four communications had already been made and one was to follow immediately. Since Rome was more than seven hundred land miles and across the Adriatic Sea from Philippi, not only would these trips require considerable time but the incidental rumors

---

21. The classic statement of the case for an Ephesian imprisonment is George S. Duncan, *St. Paul's Ephesian Ministry* (New York: Charles Scribner's Sons, 1930).
22. Deissmann, *Light from the Ancient East*, pp. 237–238.

would be rather surprising. If, however, Paul was imprisoned in Ephesus, the distance would pose no problem, and the small Aegean vessels plying up and down the coast would explain the rumors that traveled back and forth.

More important is Paul's reference to his own plan to visit the Philippians (2:23–24; cf. 1:24–26). Both Acts 20 and Romans 15:14–24 make it clear that when he set out for Jerusalem and Rome Paul was permanently leaving the Aegean world. When he left Ephesus, however, he went by way of Troas to Macedonia (II Cor. 2:12; 7:5ff.; 8:1ff.; 9:2ff.) before paying his final visit to Corinth. Finally, it should be noted that the apprehension in Philippians 1:19–24, which appears to fit the circumstances of the end of Paul's life, accords equally well with his descriptions of his troubles in Ephesus (cf. I Cor. 15:32, 16:8–9, II Cor. 1:8–9). We are probably warranted, therefore, in assuming that Paul wrote this letter from a prison in Ephesus.

To Write the Same Things   Writing shortly after the beginning of the second century to the church at Philippi, Polycarp, Bishop of Smyrna, exhorted them to study the letters which Paul had written them.[23] Although it is possible that he was referring to the collected letters, yet Polycarp's use of the plural, along with some characteristics of Philippians itself, has raised the question whether it may not contain more than one letter. Because Paul's explanation for sending Epaphroditus back to them suggests that some time has elapsed since he had received their gift, it would seem only proper that he had in the meantime written the Philippians some note of acknowledgment and thanks. There is a sharp break in the letter, furthermore, between the first two verses of chapter 3; and his words in verse 1, "To write the same things to you is not irksome to me," can be taken to refer to a previous letter.

The curious structure of this letter also points in the same direction. As in the Thessalonian letters, Paul by placing his thanks for their gift in 4:14–19 leaves the essential matter in this letter until the last. The equally important matter of the return of Epaphroditus, however, comes neither at the end or the beginning but at the end of the first division (2:25–30) just before the break following 3:1. The two parts of this letter, therefore, resemble each other in much the same way that the two letters to Thessalonica do. There are gracious admonitions (cf. 1:27–2:18 with 3:15–4:9), comments on Paul's opponents (cf. 1:15–18, 28–30 with 3:2, 18–19), descriptions of his circumstances (cf. 1:12–14, 19–26; 2:19–24 with 4:10–13), and, at the close of each, references to their assistance to him through Epaphroditus (cf. 2:25–30 with 4:14–19).

23. *To the Philippians*, 3, 2.

It is strange, moreover, that in his final thanksgivings to the Philippians in 4:14–19 he says nothing at all about either Epaphroditus' work with him or his illness, whereas in 2:25–30 he says nothing of the gift. Although some scholars, believing the section in 3:2–4:1 to be alien to the letter, have assigned it to a letter addressed to another church, it is more likely that if Philippians is not a single letter chapters 3 and 4 comprise the major part of an earlier letter which Paul wrote upon the arrival of Epaphroditus, and the first two chapters a letter written sometime later. Although this theory is plausible, and perhaps probable, it cannot be proved. Since in either event the same circumstances and purposes are involved, a decision on this question is not essential to understanding the content of Philippians.

To Send You Epaphroditus   The letter, as we have seen, falls into two main divisions (or letters): 1:1–3:1 and 3:2–4:23. Paul begins as he usually does with a prayer of thanks for those to whom he is writing (1:3–11). In one of the warmest expressions of appreciation found in any of his letters, Paul thanks God for the partnership of the Philippians in the work of the Gospel and prays that their love will increase more and more to the glory of God. By his reference to their being partakers in his imprisonment (1:7), he anticipates the purpose of his letter, the help they have sent him.

Paul takes up first his circumstances (1:12–26). His imprisonment has "served to advance the gospel" (1:12). The praetorium "and all the rest" have now heard of Christ and most of the brethren have found new courage from it. In his comment on those who preach out of partisanship "thinking to afflict me in my imprisonment" (1:15–18), Paul makes the first of several references to his opposition. Unlike those in his later references, however, these opponents are within the Christian community (but cf. 2:20–21). Perhaps he is thinking of the rivals who, as we shall see in the next section, gave him so much trouble in Corinth. How serious the circumstances of his imprisonment are is revealed in his debate whether "to remain in the flesh" or to "be with Christ" (1:19–26). The suggestion that he has a choice in the matter is probably a reflection of his confidence in divine providence. If he is needed by his churches and for his mission God will not permit him to be executed.

There follows a long section of general exhortations (1:27–2:18). As gracious and noble as the Philippians were they were not without their faults. Paul calls on them to work in unity with courage, in the face of their opponents, for the Gospel, following his example. His fondness for triads appears again in 2:1–2 (cf. I Thess. 1:2–10, 3:6, 4:11, 5:14–18): encouragement in Christ, incentive of love, participation in the Spirit, and affection, sympathy, joy. As an example for their own humility, Paul recites the well-known description of the humility of Christ's incarnation which because of its poetic quality and creedlike content appears to be a piece of Christian liturgical material. This impression is reinforced by the reappearance of this same theme in an abbreviated form in II Corinthians 8:9, where it is introduced as something the Corinthians know. The well-known difficulties, particularly in the word "grasped" in verse 6, which this passage presents furnish another example of the gaps in our knowledge of the beginnings of Christianity. The doctrine of Christ's preexistence both here and in II Corinthians 8:9 shows that the essentials of John's Logos theme (Jn. 1:1f.) belong to a very early period in the development of Christian thought. Paul brings his exhortations to a close with a general admonition. In his absence the Philippians are obediently to work out their own salvation as God works in them and continue to shine as lights in the world so that his sacrifice will have been worth it.

Briefly Paul recites his plans and states the main purpose of the letter. As soon as he sees the outcome of his own trial, he will send Timothy, as he had to Thessalonica, in order to bring him news. After commenting warmly on Timothy's faithfulness in contrast to others who look after their own interests, he expresses the hope to visit them shortly in person (2:19–24). Because they have been disturbed over Epaphroditus' illness and near death and to ease his own anxiety, Paul is sending Epaphroditus home. They are to receive him with joy and honor (2:25–30).

If chapters 3 and 4 are an earlier letter, the opening and probably a considerable part of the opening section have been lost, including the context for the startling warning, "Look out for the dogs" (3:2a, cf. Gal. 6:13). Whether this verse originally had a context different from the present one, there is no warrant for assuming here any more than in Galatians that it refers to Judaising emissaries who have come from Jerusalem to alienate Paul's Church. The local synagogue would see in the church an aberrent form of Judaism which they must correct. With the comment, "For we are the true circumcision," Paul begins his *confessio fidei,* one of the deservedly best-known and most richly rewarding passages in all his letters (3:3–16). His credentials in Judaism are impressive: A Benjamite born and circumcised as a Hebrew, he grew up a blameless Pharisee and proved his zeal by persecuting the Church. Yet all of this he has laid aside and counted as refuse for "the surpassing worth of knowing Christ Jesus" and having a righteousness "that depends on faith." Consequently Paul seeks to share Christ's sufferings (cf. Col. 1:24) and participate in his death in order that he might also attain the resurrection. He has not yet attained his goal, but he writes, "forgetting what lies behind and straining forward to what lies ahead,

I press on toward the goal for the prize of the upward call of God in Christ Jesus" (3:13). Boldly he calls the Philippians, in the midst of enemies of the cross, to imitate him as they await the parousia (3:17–4:1).

After a brief plea for two women to "agree in the Lord" and a request that Synzygus (the name means yokefellow) help them (4:2–3), Paul calls once again for them to rejoice and have no anxiety (4:4–7). In an inspiring poetic passage he invites the Philippians to think on the noble and excellent things (4:8–9). He returns finally to the coming of Epaphroditus and the gracious gift he brought. More for their love and concern than the gift, Paul is deeply moved and, remarking on their previous generosity, accepts it as "a fragrant offering, a sacrifice acceptable and pleasing to God" (4:18). God, he assures them, will supply all their needs. On this high note of gratitude and affection the letter ends.

4. In the Whole of Achaia: I and II Corinthians

Paul's Corinthian correspondence, comprising more than a third of the entire collection, is in several ways the most important. Although Romans, his longest single letter, is of greater theological interest because of its comprehensive statement of his understanding of the Faith, and his other shorter letters allow us a glimpse into now one and then another of the many facets of Paul's complex personality, the Corinthian letters give us the full range of his mind and soul. Two of the best-known and treasured passages in the New Testament, the hymn to love and the essay on the Resurrection, for example, are found in I Corinthians 13 and 15. Practical piety and abstruse reasoning appear side by side with vigorous argument in defense of his leadership, stinging rebuke of the wayward and arrogant troublemakers, and generous forgiveness of the penitent. There is no organized theology in these letters but few ideas found in any of Paul's letters fail to be reflected here. Partly because they extend over a period of time and encompass considerable intercommunication and partly because of the variety of problems which arose in this troubled church, the Corinthian letters provide for us an unparalleled view into the everyday life of an early first-century church.

Although in the salutation of II Corinthians Paul addresses "all the saints who are in the whole of Achaia," the only church in Achaia that we know of other than Corinth was in Cenchraea the harbor city seven miles east of Corinth. Both Acts and I Thessalonians mention Paul's visit to Athens, and Acts lists a few believers (17:34), but there is no suggestion of a church there. Although there may have been scattered believers elsewhere in Achaia, as in Athens, and the influence of the Corinthian church may have begun to reach beyond the city, this part of Paul's salutation was still probably more of a hope than a reality. Corinth, therefore, represented Christianity in Achaia in Paul's time. Because of the peculiar intensity and character of the problems there, and because circumstances made it necessary for Paul to deal with them by letter, we have Paul's side, or at least part of it, of this invaluable correspondence.

I WROTE YOU AS I DID

In both letters there are references to previous letters, which indicate that the correspondence as it now stands is either incomplete or out of order. Along with other indications of disarrangement, these references require us to examine the possibility of recovering as much as can be had of the original order. The first of these references is in I Corinthians 5:9–12, and in it Paul describes the earlier letter as concerned with associating with immoral men. In II Corinthians 2:3–9 and 7:12 he refers to a prior letter which he had written "out of much affliction and anguish of heart and with many tears." From the context it clearly caused the Corinthians considerable pain. This "severe letter," as scholars usually designate it, can scarcely be identified with I Corinthians. There were, therefore, on the evidence of the letters themselves, at least four letters from Paul to Corinth, one prior to I Corinthians and one between it and II Corinthians.

In II Corinthians, on the other hand, there are two places in which the continuity is manifestly disturbed. The brief section in 6:14–7:1 is completely out of context and goes with nothing before or after it, but breaks into what is, if not a single sentence, at least a single thought. When this section is removed, the thought flows smoothly from 6:13 to 7:2: "In return—I speak as to children—widen your hearts also. Open your hearts to us; we have wronged no one. . . ." Between chapters 9 and 10 the break is equally obvious. Throughout the first nine chapters Paul is manifestly making up after a quarrel. The whole mood of the letter is conciliatory. It is astonishing, therefore, to find in the next three chapters Paul lashing out in sharp rebuke and bitter sarcasm against disobedient persons in Corinth. When the two parts of the letter are compared, furthermore, a number of cross references appear in which the passages in the first nine chapters apparently refer back to matters which in the last three chapters are referred to as in the future (e.g., II Cor. 10:6 and 2:9, 13:2 and 1:23, 13:10 and 2:3). That chapters 10–13 were written, as was I Corinthians (cf. 16:8, 19), from Ephesus appears likely from Paul's reference to preaching in "lands beyond you." From Romans 15:28 we can infer that he meant Italy and Spain which would hardly be beyond Corinth from Macedonia. Chapters 1–9, on the other hand, were clearly written from Macedonia (cf. 7:5, 8:1, 9:2).

When these data are taken together it appears likely that at least parts of the two missing letters are these sections of II Corinthians which so ill fit their contexts. The exhortation in 6:14–7:1 not to be "mismated with unbelievers" sounds very much like the warning against associating with immoral men referred to in I Corinthians 5:9–12, and the severity of chapters 10–13 accords well with the letter Paul refers to in II Corinthians 2:3–9. There is more to the prior letter, of course, than we have in II Corinthians 6:14–7:1; how much more is impossible to say. How much more than the opening is missing from the intervening letter is likewise unknown.

There were also communications coming to Paul from Corinth, some of which are indicated in the letters. In I Corinthians 1:11 he indicates that he is responding to a report brought by "Chloe's people." He refers in I Corinthians 7:1 to a letter from the Corinthians which may have been carried by the three men, Stephanas, Fortunatus, and Achaicus, mentioned in 16:17; and the phrase "now concerning" which occurs in 7:25; 8:1; 12:1; 16:1, 12 (the translation in the RSV unfortunately obscures the last of these) probably indicates the questions in their letter which he is taking up. Titus was the bearer of the welcome news (cf. 7:6, 13–15) to which Paul is responding in II Corinthians 1–9. Perhaps it was Paul's own unpleasant encounter with the church on a return visit (cf. II Cor. 1:15–2:1ff.) that occasioned the intervening letter. We may therefore reconstruct Paul's communications with Corinth as follows:

1. Paul's initial stay in Corinth, founding the church.
2. Later, probably in Ephesus, he receives word of problems of immorality in Corinth.
3. Paul responds with the first letter, a fragment of which is contained in II Corinthians 6:14–7:1.
4. Chloe's people and a letter from Corinth bring Paul word of further problems and questions.
5. Paul answers from Ephesus with I Corinthians.
6. Apparently an attempted visit to Corinth by Paul, and perhaps a report from Timothy (cf. I Cor. 16:10–11) or Titus (cf. II Cor. 7:13–15), bring news of increasing trouble.
7. Paul responds with the "severe letter," part of which is contained in II Corinthians 10–13.
8. Paul moves to Macedonia where Titus meets him with welcome news that the conflict has been resolved.
9. Paul writes from Macedonia the "conciliatory letter," which consists of II Corinthians 1:1–6:13; 7:2–9:15.

10. Paul comes to Corinth, and after spending the winter, leaves by way of Macedonia and Troas for his final trip to Jerusalem (cf. Acts 20:1ff.).[24]

THIS IS WHY I WROTE

The city of Corinth, situated on the northwest of the Peloponnesus near the southern end of the Isthmus which joined it to the mainland of Greece to the north, was one of the famous and important cities of the Graeco-Roman world. The original city, capital of the Achaian League and notorious for its licentiousness, had been destroyed in 146 B.C. by the Roman general Lucius Mummius and lay in ruins for a century. By the time of Paul Corinth had regained its political importance by becoming the seat of the Roman provincial government for Achaia, and its commercial importance by its own industries and its role in commerce with the East. It had also regained, unfortunately, much of its reputation for licentiousness. From the letters we can discern both Jewish and gentile members in the church there, but from scattered remarks it is clear also that they came largely from the lower classes (cf. I Cor. 1:26, 6:11, 7:21). From the character of the city the troubles Paul had with the Corinthian church are not surprising. Indeed, the ultimate success of Christianity in Corinth is a tribute to the power of Paul's gospel.

As one would expect, prominent among the problems Paul has to deal with is immorality. The entire fragment, II Corinthians 6:14–7:1, is concerned with this issue, and Paul becomes more specific in I Corinthians 5:1–13 (cf. II Cor. 12:21). There are, at the same time, other difficulties. A serious tendency to factiousness shows itself in quarrels and divided loyalties, in childish pride over their new-found "wisdom," in vying with one another over glossolalia, and selfishly disregarding one another at the Lord's Supper. Some scholars have suggested that Paul's ode to love in I Corinthians 13 was a veiled criticism of the Corinthians; they are the obverse of his description of love (cf. II Cor. 12:20b). Some of the questions the Corinthians had raised in their letter, on the other hand, would be natural to a new congregation of Jews and gentiles.

Running through the letters, however, are references to a person or persons who seem to be at the bottom of the troubles in Corinth. In I Corinthians 5 it is an incestuous member. Paul alternates between the

24. Because II Corinthians 8 and 9 appear to have no connection with what precedes and seem to be separate notes on the collection for Jerusalem, some scholars regard them as two separate letters following the conciliatory letters. See B. W. Robinson, *The Life of Paul* (Chicago: University of Chicago Press, 1918), pp. 164–174. Other scholars are unconvinced by such restorations. See James L. Price, *Interpreting the New Testament* (New York: Holt, Rinehart and Winston, 1961), pp. 370–372 and works cited; Alfred Plummer, *The Second Epistle of St. Paul to the Corinthians* (ICC), pp. xxi–xxxvi. For further discussion of the problem see Selby, *Toward the Understanding of St. Paul*, pp. 258–263.

The Temple to Aphrodite, the goddess of love and patron deity of the city, on the hill above Corinth. Strabo the ancient geographer wrote that the original temple (before 146 B.C.) had a thousand temple prostitutes in its service. (The Roderick Slide Collection, courtesy of Catawba College.)

singular and plural in speaking of his opponents in the third letter (II Cor. 10–13, cf. 10:2, 6, 7, 10–13; 11:4, 11–15, 20, 21–23; 12:11; 13:2); but in the fourth letter the resolution of the problems in the church seems to have resulted from the punishment of one person (2:5–11). Although the reference to "a different gospel" in II Corinthians 11:4 is reminiscent of Galatians 1:6–9, there is little warrant for associating the problems in Corinths with those in Galatia; still less is there reason to take this verse as a reference to traveling emissaries from the conservative wing in Jerusalem who were subverting Paul's churches. The Corinthian correspondence reflects none of the concerns over circumcision or other aspects of the Jewish Law which such a supposition would require. When Paul's references to the troubles in Corinth are taken as a whole there are no definite indications that they had—or needed—outside help in creating them.[25]

Who the troublemaker or troublemakers were in Corinth is no longer possible for us to know. Apollos and Peter are both mentioned in connection with the factions in I Corinthians 1:12, but Peter is mentioned again only in passing (3:22; 9:5; 15:5), and in later references to Apollos Paul is at pains to show that there is no disagreement between them (cf. 3:4–9, 22; 4:6; 16:12). More than in any of his other letters Paul alludes to persons and matters that are lost to us (e.g., the elusive "brother" in II Cor. 8:18; and 12:18). Although even to the Corinthians he found it necessary to protest that "we write you nothing but what you can read and understand" (II Cor. 1:13), these allusions were intended for them and would be understood by them far better than by us.

DO NOT BE MISMATED WITH UNBELIEVERS: II CORINTHIANS (6:14–7:1)

Whether the material in II Corinthians 6:14–7:1 comprises all or most of the body of a brief first letter or is only a fragment of a longer one, it is for its brevity remarkably self-contained and complete. Although Paul's reference to it in I Corinthians 5:9ff. shows that he was writing to a specific problem, it has the appearance of a homily on sanctity which might have been delivered out of general edifactory concern. It consists in three parts: a series of five rhetorical questions, a catena of Scriptural quotations, and a summary conclusion.

The five rhetorical questions, each expecting a negative answer, represent in a manner reminiscent of the Wisdom Literature the contrast between good and evil. The terms of relationship, "partnership," "fellowship," "accord," "in common," and "agreement," indicate more permanent and profound involvement than casual or mundane relationships with society in general. They describe, rather, the ideal relationships of a cultic community. These relationships of the community must not be extended to those who by their evil conduct show themselves to be

---

25. John C. Hurd, Jr., has advanced the thesis that between Paul's initial stay while founding the Corinthian church and writing I Corinthians he had attempted to impose on them the Apostolic Decrees (Acts 15:22–29), and that it was their refusal to accept them which caused the trouble. Although it ignores important questions concerning the Corinthian letters and goes beyond the evidence concerning the Decrees, Hurd's book offers a number of significant insights and is very valuable for its comprehensive surveys of scholarly studies in Corinthians. See *The Origin of I Corinthians*. On the problems in Corinth see also Johannes Munck, *Paul and the Salvation of Mankind,* pp. 135–195. For an attempt, from a somewhat different approach, to interpret the correspondence, see Charles Buck and Greer Taylor, *St. Paul* (New York: Charles Scribner's Sons, 1969).

unbelievers. It is this point which Paul underscores in his reference to this letter in I Corinthians 5:9–13. The contrasts provide significant definitions of the believer and the unbeliever:

Righteousness	Iniquity
Light	Darkness
Christ	Belial
Believer	Unbeliever
Temple of God	Idols

The catena of scriptural quotations consists of three verses which are rather free paraphrases, probably influenced by the recollection of other passages, and distinguished from one another by the phrases "As God said," "says the Lord," and "says the Lord Almighty" at the beginning of the first, middle of the second, and end of the last verse. The sources are

Verse 16b, Leviticus 26:11a, 12 (cf. Ezek. 37:27)
Verse 17, Isaiah 52:11
Verse 18, II Samuel 7:14

As the five questions serve to support the exhortation not to "be mismated with unbelievers," so the three Scriptures, suggested by the proposition, "we are the temple of the living God," give it Scriptural sanction, and prepare for the conclusion: "Since we have these promises, beloved, let us cleanse ourselves from every defilement of body and spirit, and make holiness perfect in the fear of God" (7:1).

THERE IS QUARRELING AMONG YOU:
I CORINTHIANS

Paul's second letter to the church at Corinth, Canonical I Corinthians, is by far the longest, incorporating three fifths of the Corinthian correspondence as we have it. In it Paul is responding, as we have seen, to information which came to him from Chloe's people and a letter to him from Corinth. Since the letter from Corinth is first mentioned in 7:1, and the allusions to it (i.e., "now concerning") are scattered through the remaining chapters, it is natural to divide the letter at that point into two parts, the first six chapters dealing with the oral report by Chloe's people and the remainder dealing with the letter. Several factors indicate, however, that the matter is not so simple.

With regard to the material associated with the oral reports, for example, we should observe that the last of Paul's three allusions to these reports occurs not in the first part of the letter but in 11:18, after the first three references to the questions in the Corinthians' letter. The topics in chapter 6, which is still in the first part of the letter, on the other hand, are not identified with the oral reports. Although the discussion on immorality in 6:9–20 may have suggested itself to Paul from his exhortations concerning the incestuous man rather than being a response to news from Corinth, the issue of believers taking one another to pagan courts is obviously dealing with another actual issue in the Corinthian church. If in the slogans in verses 12 and 13 Paul is quoting pet sayings of the Corinthians, as a number of interpreters believe, the entire chapter is a response to information whose source we can no longer determine.

Several discussions in the second part of the letter, likewise, have no explicit connection with either the letter from Corinth or the report from Chloe's people. Paul's discussion of his rights as an apostle in chapter 9 and warning against idol worship in chapter 11 may have developed from his discussion of eating meat offered to idols; but the instructions concerning women in 11:2–16 and the argument for the resurrection in chapter 15, although they are based on Paul's knowledge of Corinthian affairs (note 11:16 and 15:12), could be based on information either in the report or the letter, or perhaps on an otherwise unknown communication.

We cannot be certain, furthermore, that the report from Chloe's people included anything more than the divisions under discussion in the first four chapters. Unlike the consistency of his "now concerning" in reference to the questions in their letter, the language in 5:1 and 11:18 (the Greek word *akouo* for "reported" and "I hear" in these verses is different from *deloo,* "reported" in 1:11) is less definite. It is possible, although to the minds of most interpreters not likely, that Timothy's mission to Corinth mentioned in 4:17 had been completed and he had reported these matters to Paul. More significant is the fact that Corinth is only a short sail across the Aegean Sea from Ephesus where Paul was writing, and news would likely come to Paul from there with a fair degree of regularity.[26] Although it is useful in interpreting the letter to be able to sort the materials into groups according the sources of information to which Paul is responding, it is equally important to recognize those places in which that cannot, at least with any certainty, be done. Since the problem reported by Chloe's people dominates the first six chapters as does the letter from Corinth the last ten, however, it will be useful to divide I Corinthians into two divisions between chapters 6 and 7, recognizing at the same time the strong possibility that in places Paul may be commenting on other information which the Corinthians would recognize but whose sources and nature are no longer discernible.

26. For an attempted reconstruction of the Corinthian letter to Paul as well as his first letter to them see J. C. Hurd, Jr., *The Origin of I Corinthians,* pp. 238–239, 290–293.

It Has Been Reported to Me Not unlike the opening of Galatians, the salutation of I Corinthians in the words, "with all those who in every place" (1:2), contains a hint of the concern of the letter. The overarching problem in Corinth was the inability of the believers to forget their self-centeredness in the interests of their larger identity in the body of Christ. After a brief thanksgiving (1:4–9), which because of terms such as "all speech," "all knowledge," and "spiritual gift" that figure prominently later in the letter may contain more than a touch of sarcasm, Paul comes directly to the matter of divisiveness.

In verse 12 Paul appears to be identifying four groups who by their contentious loyalty to one leader have created the divisions. Of the four only the first two seem to be important to the problem. Unless as some scholars have suggested the references to those who claim to be Christ's in II Corinthians 10:7; 11:13, 23 are to such a group, those who "belong to Christ" are never mentioned again. Although Paul and Apollos are mentioned again in this connection three times, 3:4–9, 21; and 4:6, Cephas (Peter) is referred to again only once in 3:21 (but cf. 9:5 in another connection). The only clearly identifiable characteristics of any of these groups, furthermore, attach to the partisans of Paul and Apollos. The numerous attempts which have been made to detect the nature of the problem in Corinth from this list of partisans, especially those which relate it to the "circumcision party" in Galatians (cf. 2:12) and Acts 15, have not, because of the absence of references in the Corinthian letters to such issues, proved convincing. It is quite possible, as some have suggested, that the phrase "I belong to Christ" is a gloss from a marginal note by a pious copyist, or that Paul intended it as his own slogan which should replace the others. The real issue is the contentiousness of the Corinthians rather than the merits or lack of them among the contending groups. Paul may therefore have intended nothing more than a list of names by way of illustrating the problem.

Beginning with those who were using his name for their partisan loyalties, Paul plunges into the issue by means of a series of sharp rhetorical questions: "Is Christ divided? Was Paul crucified for you? Or were you baptized in the name of Paul?" (vs. 13). He is grateful that he had baptized only a few in Corinth, for Christ had sent him not "to baptize but to preach the gospel" (vs. 17). With the words, "not with eloquent wisdom, lest the cross of Christ be emptied of its power," he establishes the underlying premise of this entire section, that God has deliberately chosen the weak, the humble, the foolish, and unlikely as the vehicles of his purpose in order that the beneficent wisdom and power of God's redemptive action may stand out in bold relief unobscured by any objects of human pride. Over against the Jewish quest for signs of God's mighty saving acts and the Greeks' quest for "wisdom," Paul places the paradox of the Crucifixion of Christ, "For the foolishness of God is wiser than men, and the weakness of God is stronger than men" (1:25). The humble station of the Corinthians whom God has chosen as the vehicle of his Gospel in Achaia (1:26–31) and the lack of eloquence and "wisdom" in Paul's own preaching (2:1–5) are examples of this paradox.

There is, on the other hand, a true wisdom which Paul conveys to the spiritually mature; but far from a wisdom of human discovery, it is a secret wisdom which can only be conveyed by the Spirit of God (2:5–16). The problem is that the contentious Corinthians, "behaving like ordinary men," have not matured as they should have and, therefore, are not ready for such wisdom. As proof of their immaturity Paul returns to their partisan loyalties. Their failure to grasp the true role of human leadership in the divine plan left them unprepared to understand the more profound aspects of the "wisdom" of God's program for the climax of history and the coming eschaton. The Corinthians were regarding Paul and Apollos as teachers of wisdom like the itinerant sophists and mendicant philosophers familiar to the Hellenistic world. Thus they became arrogant and competitive.[27]

With two analogies Paul attempts to set matters straight. "I planted, Apollos watered, but God gave the growth." Since the Gospel is not of human discovery but divinely disclosed through God's chosen human agents, the human agents are unimportant (3:5–9). Paul has, therefore, laid the foundation which is Christ, and each of the Corinthians is responsible for the way he builds thereon. Instead of quarreling over who is better because he has the wisest and most eloquent teacher, they should be concerned whether their "building" will withstand the judgment of the apocalyptic fires. Not human wisdom but only Godly holiness can pass this test (3:10–23). Their quarreling has led them, furthermore, to make invidious comparisons between Paul and Apollos. Comparative eloquence is irrelevant; only faithfulness to their divinely assigned task is required of the servants of Christ. The Corinthians cannot, therefore, sit in judgment on Paul, indeed he does not even judge himself. Evaluation as well as wisdom and power is the prerogative of God alone (4:1–7). In a paragraph of biting sarcasm Paul taunts the vain Corinthians who have become so self-important while the leaders over whom they are arguing are enduring all manner of deprivation and abuse for the cause of the Gospel (4:8–13). In a more dispassionate tone Paul continues: "I do not write this to make you ashamed, but to admonish you as my beloved children . . . I urge you, then, be imitators of me" (4:14–16). After a note about the purpose of Timothy's visit to Corinth, and a stern warning, "Shall I come to you with a rod, or with love in a spirit of

27. For a good treatment of this material see Johannes Munck, *Paul and the Salvation of Mankind*, pp. 148–167.

gentleness?" (4:18–21), Paul turns to a different but not unrelated matter.

Probably cases of incest were not so unheard of as Paul suggests, but the case of the "man living with his father's wife" (5:1) was shocking enough in a Christian community. The phrase Paul uses suggests that the rumor, rather than being communicated directly to Paul, may have circulated generally. Apparently Paul's information included the knowledge that the Corinthians were refusing, on the ground that the culprit was not an unbeliever, to apply the instructions concerning immoral men in his previous letter (5:9–13). He orders the church, at any rate, to "drive out the wicked person from among you" (5:13b). Just what delivering him "to Satan" (vs. 5) meant is no longer clear, but it is worthy of note that in his disgust Paul did not lose his concern for the culprit's salvation. Nor has he forgotten, on the other hand, the original problem of the arrogance and contentiousness of the Corinthians. If they were as wise as they claim to be, they would have known how intolerable is such an evil and how to deal with it (5:6–8).

How Paul learned of it and what connection, if any, it had with the case of incest we can no longer tell, but he turns abruptly to the issue of believers taking their internal grievances into the courts of the very pagans before whom they are supposed to be witness of righteousness (6:1–8). For all their boasted wisdom they cannot govern their own affairs: "And if the world is to be judged by you, are you incompetent to try trivial cases?" (vs. 2b). It would be better to be defrauded and suffer wrong!

Perhaps because he has the case of incest still in mind Paul returns to the subject of immorality (6:9–20). After one of his typical lists of vices, he calls upon the Corinthians, in an ethical appeal particularly characteristic of his thinking, to be what they are. This idea underlies all of his ethical thinking. The believer being now "in Christ" he has become, in spite of outward appearances and circumstances, "a new creation"; he is therefore to "realize" this spiritual newness increasingly in the brief course of this life until the arrival of the eschaton makes all things new. As the quotation marks in the RSV indicate, the two sayings, "All things are lawful for me" and "Food is meant for the stomach and the stomach for food" are probably popular slogans which were being quoted by the Corinthians. Paul may have had more reason than the case of incest for this section on immorality. What follows in his answer to their use of these slogans is a statement of the morality of Christian freedom quite similar to that in Galatians 5:14–6:10. As in connection with their divisiveness he reminded them that they as a community of believers are the Temple of God, so now he points out that each of them must keep in mind that his body is a Temple of the Holy Spirit (vs. 19, cf. II Cor. 6:16b); they are therefore to glorify God in their body (vs. 20).

The Matters About Which You Wrote   The questions in the Corinthian's letter to Paul, as indicated by the phrase, "now concerning" are

1. Marriage and divorce, 7:1b–24
2. Celibacy, 7:25–40
3. Food offered to idols, 8:1–13, (chs. 9–10?)
4. Spiritual gifts, 12–14
5. The contribution for the saints, 16:1–4
6. The possibility of a visit by Apollos, 16:12

At least three important topics appear which are not identified with the letter: the status of women (11:1–16); abuses at the Lord's Supper (11:17–34); and the Resurrection (ch. 15). The second of these, abuses at the Lord's Supper, is explicitly associated with an oral report. Whether the material in chapters 9 and 10 is simply Paul's development of the issue of eating meat offered to idols in chapter 8, or is separate material in response to further news from Corinth, the sections on the status of women and the Resurrection are almost certainly responding to current issues in Corinth.

The first two topics, on marriage and divorce and celibacy, are closely related, and, partly because the questions to which Paul is speaking are so uncertain, they offer some of the most difficult problems for the interpreter of Paul. As a result scholarly opinions have differed widely on the interpretation of chapter 7.[28] Of major importance is the question whether the asceticism reflected here originated with Paul or the Corinthians. That it came quite early to be attributed to Paul is shown by the preoccupation with celibacy of the fictitious *Acts of Paul* which appeared shortly after the middle of the second century. Although Tertullian tells us that the presbyter who wrote it was deposed for the forgery, its survival and influence show that on this point its estimate of Paul was widely accepted.[29]

In interpreting this chapter several factors in its background need to be kept in mind: First, although in rare instances rabbis were known to remain single, Judaism regarded marriage as not only normal but a duty.[30] Paul's own vigorous insistence on his identification as a Jew and a Pharisee would identify him with this viewpoint on marriage (Phil. 3:5; II Cor. 11:22). That the Essenes appear to have practiced celibacy has led some scholars to regard Paul's preference for celibacy here as evidence of the

28. For a valuable survey of these opinions see J. C. Hurd, Jr., *The Origin of I Corinthians*, pp 163–182.
29. For an English translation of the extant portions of this work, especially *Paul and Thecla*, see M. R. James, *The Apocryphal New Testament* (Oxford: At the Clarendon Press, 1955), pp. 270–299. On the author see Tertullian, *On Baptism*, XVII.
30. See *Yebamoth*, 6, 6.

influence of the Qumran sect on Christianity.[31] If the issue of celibacy here originated with Paul and therefore represents his theological conviction, it is strange indeed that, unlike his other theological ideas which appear in one form or another repeatedly in his letters, there is no hint of this idea elsewhere. That his own unmarried state was no more than a matter of personal preference is clearly implied in his reference to the "right" of other apostles to be accompanied by their wives (I Cor. 9:3–7). The metaphor of marriage which he uses of the Corinthians themselves in II Corinthians 11:2 is based on a typically Jewish view of marriage (cf. Rom. 7:1–3; Eph. 5:21–32).

Second, the extremes of both asceticism and libertinism were common ingredients of the Hellenistic paganism of the time. We have already found Paul dealing with the influences of libertinism in his churches, we should therefore not be surprised to come upon this instance of ascetic reaction to the widespread immorality, especially in a city like Corinth. We may assume, then, that the slogan, "It is well for a man not to touch a woman" (7:1b), came from the Corinthians. In the context of the licentiousness of Corinth, and especially the background of some of the believers themselves (6:9–11), Paul can hardly repudiate the slogan. Yet he can easily foresee disastrous consequences in an unqualified approval of it. This chapter provides an example of what Paul means by becoming "all things to all men" (9:22).

Third, the points in this chapter at which Paul does reflect ideas familiar to us from his other letters happen, significantly, to be by his own statement (vs. 29) the real basis of his argument here. His intention is to maintain, wherever practicable and morally acceptable, the status quo (7:17–24, 26; Phil. 4:11). "This," Paul says, "is my rule in all the churches" (vs. 17b). The reason, however, for everyone remaining "in the state in which he was called" (vs. 20) is that "the appointed time has grown very short" (vs. 29) and, since "the form of this world is passing away" (31b), there is little use in pursuing in it what would otherwise be commendable goals. Even slaves should no longer be concerned with manumission. Because his is the final generation of world history the normal obligations of man "to be fruitful and multiply" (Gen. 1:28) are no longer relevant. Paul can therefore confine his treatment of the Corinthian question to problems of temptations to immorality, the threat of "the impending distress" (vs. 26), and the importance of "undivided devotion to the Lord" (vs. 35). (It is interesting to note, in connection with the possibility of Essene influence here, that the thinking of the Qumran community was likewise controlled by vivid eschatological ex-

---

31. See Frank M. Cross, Jr., *The Ancient Library of Qumran and Modern Biblical Studies,* pp. 71–74. But see O. J. Baab, in the article on "Marriage," *IDB,* Vol. III, p. 286.

pectations which called for suspension of what would otherwise be normal and proper modes of life.)

Finally, we should notice how careful Paul is to maintain a clear distinction between the tradition of the teaching of the Lord and his own advice (cf. vss. 6, 10, 12, 25, 40b). The only point at which he appeals to any authority other than his own best judgment (enlightened, presumably, by the Holy Spirit) is in his use of Jesus' stricture against divorce (Mk. 10:2–9, para.). His reticence is remarkable and suggests the delicacy with which Paul found it necessary to steer the Corinthians into a morally safer path without destroying their enthusiasm.

Paul begins his response to the Corinthian slogan by counseling marriage "because of the temptation to immorality" (vs. 2), and within marriage the conjugal rights of both husband and wife are to be fully respected. Even seasons of abstention for devotional purposes are not to be overextended. Such abstentions for the sake of ritual purity were recognized both in Judaism and paganism. If the unmarried and widows can manage it without undue temptation, let them remain single. The married, on the other hand, are not to seek divorce even though the other partner is an unbeliever. As in their other circumstances, the Corinthians are to stay as they are unless an unbelieving partner demands separation or their situation is morally hazardous. "In whatever state each was called, there let him remain with God" (vs. 24).

Paul turns next to a related question concerning "the unmarried" (7:25–40). Just what this question involved is no longer possible to tell (the word translated "unmarried," *parthenos,* here is different from that in verse 8 *agamos*). Opinions differ as to whether he is speaking to fathers of daughters of marriageable age, or to engaged couples (cf. vss. 36–38). Others have supposed a special ascetic relationship which they describe as a "spiritual marriage." Paul continues this theme, at any rate, of remaining as one is. In the face of the impending apocalyptic tribulations marriage is ill-advised. The closing of the age has made marriage like other earthly concerns—mourning, rejoicing, business—irrelevant. The goal is therefore to be free of anxieties and preoccupied only with pleasing the Lord (cf. the story of Mary and Martha in Lk. 10:38–42). If those who are betrothed find the strain of their position too difficult, they should marry. Otherwise they will find refraining from marriage to their spiritual advantage.

The third question, concerning food offered to idols, involves a problem which in different ways would confront both Jewish and gentile Christians. For the gentile, accustomed to regard the eating of meat from animals which had been ritually slaughtered in offering to a pagan deity as a sacramental act, such an act would now be for him idolatry; for the Jew it would also raise the issue of the kosher laws. The availability of such meat in the marketplaces of cities of the Empire made this an important question. If, as the punctuation in the RSV suggests, the sayings, "all of us possess knowledge," "an idol has no real existence," and "there is no God but one," are quotations from the Corinthians' letter, the prevailing opinion in Corinth was that eating the sacred meat was a matter of indifference. As a result of this attitude those with more scruples were either scandalized or led to act against their own consciences. Thus the same self-centeredness and pride which caused the quarreling dealt with in chapters 1–4 appear again behind this problem. Without denying their principles, Paul is appealing for a more responsible use of their freedom by consideration for others who could not share their enlightened emancipation.

From the structure of chapter 8 it appears likely that verse 8, like the slogans in verses 1 and 4, is also a quotation from the Corinthian letter. If so, the pattern of the argument is quite regular:

The Corinthians' Slogans	Paul's Answers
1. All of us possess knowledge.	Knowledge puffs up, but love builds up.
2. An idol has no real existence; there is no God but one.	However, not all possess this knowledge.
3. Food will not commend us to God. We are no worse off if we do not eat, and no better off if we do.	Only take care lest this liberty of yours somehow become a stumbling block to the weak.

Conclusion

4. Therefore, if food is a cause of my brother's falling, I will never eat meat, lest I cause my brother to fall.

Probably these sayings, or at least the latter two, originated in Paul's own teaching. Certainly he could hardly take issue with them, but the one-sided application of them, unqualified by a charitable concern for its effect on others, distorted them into serious error.

Although the conclusion to this discussion occurs in 10:23–11:1, the two intervening sections, chapters 9 and 10:1–22, appear to be so remotely related to it that several earlier scholars regarded them as dislocations. Paul's vigorous defense of his apostleship in chapter 9 accords so well with II Corinthians 11–12 as to suggest that this is a fragment of the severe letter; similarly, his exhortations against immorality and idol worship make 10:1–22 look like it belongs with II Corinthians 6:14–7:1 as a fragment of the previous letter.[32] On closer examination, however, the likelihood of dislocations here is not so great. Not only is there no textual

32. See the discussion in McNeile, *An Introduction to the Study of the New Testament*, pp. 132–42; Weiss, *Earliest Christianity*, Vol. I, pp. 323–357.

evidence for it, but, more important, there is really no break in continuity between the end of these sections and the conclusion to the discussion on eating meat offered to idols (10:22 and 23; cf. 10:19 with 8:4, 7–11; and 10:23–29a). Nor is the continuity at this point improved when these sections are removed and 8:13 is joined to 10:23. Since the problem is created by the disjuncture between 8:13 and 9:1, the removal of chapter 9 would be the most satisfactory solution. Yet even here there is a logical progression of thought between the analogy of the race in 9:24–27 and the lesson drawn from the exodus and journey in the wilderness in 10:1–6.

There is a pattern which Paul uses in this letter quite consistently, furthermore, in which he interrupts his discussion of the problem with a subject usually involving his prior relations with the Corinthians but whose relationship to the problem becomes apparent only as he returns to the original discussion. His essay on human wisdom versus his original preaching in Corinth, 1:18–2:16, comes in the middle of his treatment of the problem of quarreling. He interrupts his discussion of the case of incest (5:1–13) to correct a misinterpretation of his previous letter on a point relevant to that case (5:9–13a). Chapter 6 seems to be an exception, yet the essay on immorality serves in a similar manner to conclude the first division of the letter and to anticipate the second. In chapter 7 the excursus on remaining in the state in which one is called (vss. 17–24) and the references to the nearness of the eschaton (vss. 26–31) supply the explanations for his treatment of marriage and celibacy; as his essay on love in chapter 13 supplies the true solution to the problem of spiritual gifts. From the way these sections lead from one to the other and then back into the original discussion, therefore, we should probably regard them as examples of the same pattern rather than dislocations. In chapter 9 Paul is using his own willingness to forego his right for the higher goal of the Gospel as an example of the kind of consideration he is asking for from the "knowledgeable" Corinthians, whereas in 10:1–22 he is pointing out the real danger that lurks behind their supposed knowledge (cf. 10:12 with 8:2).

That Paul suddenly becomes defensive in chapter 9 is puzzling. It is interesting that his sudden emotionalism has nothing to do with idol meat, the subject at hand, but the question of his rights as an apostle. In some way these had been called into question by his refusal to accept support from the Corinthians. Since this point becomes a key issue in the severe letter (II Cor. 11–12), we should probably assume that from the time that the Corinthians had had an opportunity to learn of the practice of other apostles, Paul's refusal of such support had been a source of misunderstanding. By way of an aside to rectify this misunderstanding, he uses it as an illustration of the attitude which they should adopt in the issue of idol meat.

After a vigorous affirmation of his apostleship Paul's argument runs in a pattern similar to the fragment in II Corinthians 6:14–7:1 of the previous letter: a series of five rhetorical questions, a Scriptural proof text, and an analogy from the Temple. Like the soldier, the vineyard keeper, and the herdsman, he and Barnabas have the same rights as other apostles to "food and drink," i.e., sustenance, and the maintenance of families. As the ox must be allowed to eat from the grain it threshes so they have a right to "material benefits." Yet to avoid any obstacle to the Gospel they have foregone those rights. The priests at the Temple share in the sacrifices, but that Paul has declined and still insists on declining such rights is his only boast. To preach the Gospel is his obligation; to do it "free of charge" is his freedom. The point is that the key to true Christian freedom lies not in insisting on one's rights but in willingness to subordinate them to the higher goal of the Gospel. "For though I am free from all men, I have made myself a slave to all, that I might win the more" (9:19). As the athlete by rigorous self-discipline directs all his energies to winning the race, so Paul places his body fully at the service of his mission. Freedom without this dedication and discipline becomes pointless and even dangerous.

The last clause of chapter 9, "lest after preaching to others I myself should be disqualified," provides the transition to another aspect of the matter. Beginning with an analogy drawn from the Exodus (10:1–5) in which he reminds the Corinthians that although all Israel participated sacramentally in the Exodus deliverance most of them were subsequently "overthrown in the wilderness," he makes the point that belonging to the People of God does not make one immune to God's judgment. They are warned, therefore, not to "desire evil," to "be idolaters," to "indulge in immorality," or to "grumble" as some of the followers of Moses had done (vss. 6–10). Since these stories were recorded for the instruction of the believers "upon whom the end of the age has come," "therefore let anyone who thinks that he stands take heed lest he fall" (vss. 11–12). God has provided that the believer can "escape" the temptations; let him see that he does (vs. 13). The point of his analogy is that the danger of idol worship is more real and subtle than they had imagined. They had claimed that food had nothing to do with their relationship to God, but what of the Lord's Supper? Is it not a participation in Christ? Idols and the food offered to them may be nothing, but idol worship is demonic. To share in the food of idol worship runs the risk of approving, and even participating in, a demonic kind of worship (vss. 14–22).

Paul now returns to the discussion of idol meat which he left at the end of chapter 8. Picking up a slogan he had quoted in his discussion of immorality at the end of the first division of the letter (6:12), he lays down a practical guiding principle, "let no one seek his own good, but the good of his neighbor" (vs. 24). By all means, "eat whatever is set before you." Do not raise the issue, but if someone else does, then abstain from eating for the sake of his conscience (vss. 25–29a). Perhaps the following questions are again quoting the Corinthians: "For why should my liberty be determined by another man's scruples? If I partake with thankfulness, why am I denounced because of that for which I give thanks?" (vss. 29b–30). If so, Paul's answer is in the command to "do all to the glory of God," and "give no offense to Jews or to Greeks or to the church of God" (vss. 31–32). As Paul does not seek his own advantage, neither should they (vss. 33–11:1).

The next three topics treated in the letter concern practices in public worship: (1) women veiling their heads (11:2–16), (2) abuses at the Lord's Supper (11:17–34), (3) spiritual gifts (12–14). The first two of these topics, dealt with in chapter 11, are introduced with the word "commend." There may be a touch of sarcasm in the first of these, "I commend you because you . . . maintain the traditions even as I have delivered them to you" (11:2), which adds force to the second, concerning abuses at the Lord's Supper, "But in the following instructions I do not commend you because . . ." (vs. 17, the word "following" is not in the original). There were, apparently, a few things still amiss in their adherence to the traditions. What social customs and issues lay back of Paul's insistence on women veiling their heads in church is no longer clear. Apparently, however, some women were abandoning the symbols of their subordination to men which, although he qualifies it (vs. 11), Paul is unwilling to surrender altogether. It was another instance of reckless use of their new-found freedom. Paul argues from custom, from the Scriptural tradition of creation, from nature, and from the prevailing custom in the churches. Although flouting established social customs would undoubtedly affect the reputation of Christianity and create unnecessary handicaps, the modern reader cannot help suspecting that here the social customs in Paul's background are showing through his theology.

The second problem, abuses at the Lord's Supper (11:17–34), is far more serious and more revealing of the character of the Corinthians. Again there are divisions among them, but this time the divisions are between the rich and the poor: "Each one goes ahead with his own meal, and one is hungry and another is drunk" (vs. 21). It is likely that Paul is being sarcastic when he says that factions are necessary among the Corinthians in order that those who are esteemed (the word *dokimos,* translated "genuine" in the RSV, can also mean esteemed or respected) may be recognized (vs. 19). At the very point in their worship at which the unity of the Body of Christ finds its most profound expression, their self-seeking pride and lack of concern for one another show up most glaringly!

Paul's answer to this problem was to clarify the sacramental character of the Supper, and therefore the danger in unworthy or sacrilegious participation. Indeed, some of them have already been "chastened" for so doing. His final comment, "If any one is hungry, let him eat at home— lest you come together to be condemned" (vs. 34), in effect distinguishes the sacrament from the meal of which it was then a part. It may be that this verse was a precipitating cause of the removal of the rite from the meal which persisted thereafter as a "love feast." We owe to this problem in Corinth, at any rate, the oldest narrative of the Last Supper (vss. 23–26 cf. Mk. 14:22–24).

The third and, from the space Paul allots to it (chs. 12–14), the most serious problem in the Corinthian worship has to do with "spiritual gifts," more specifically, glossolalia (ecstatic gibberish). The words "now concerning" indicate that he is responding to a question in the letter from Corinth, but exactly what that question asked is impossible to tell. That Paul's information from other sources on the Corinthians' behavior at worship included their abuses of glossolalia is likely. Possibly one of the motives for their letter to Paul was the knowledge that he was receiving information about them from other less-favorable sources. Paul's treatment of this problem brings to a climax the thesis, which runs all through the letter, that the governing principle of true spiritual behavior is a love for one another which seeks the common good.

Significantly, Paul begins with a reference to their pagan background which undoubtedly was a source of their fondness for such ecstatic outbreaks (12:2). Their glossolalia, rather than a sign of the Holy Spirit, in other words, may have had demonic roots. The test he proposes, that no one by the Spirit curses Jesus and only by the Holy Spirit can one confess "Jesus is Lord," states the matter in extremes bordering on the sarcastic. Yet it makes the important point that any genuinely Spirit-inspired action will be consistent with the confession of the Lordship of Jesus. From this point he proceeds to deal with the issue in three stages.

In the first stage (12:4–31a) Paul argues that two aspects are necessary to the life of the church: "varieties of gifts" all of which are necessary "for the common good," and "the same Spirit," "the same Lord," "the same God" (vss. 4–7). He lists examples of the gifts: wisdom, knowledge, faith, healing, working of miracles, prophecy, ability to distinguish between spirits, various kinds of tongues, emphasizing the one and same Spirit behind each. Five times he intersperses the word "Spirit" in the list (vss. 8–11). The long and detailed analogy of the human body makes clear the significant distinction between unity and uniformity, on the one hand, and between diversity and divisions, on the other (vss. 12–26). The Corinthians are "the body of Christ" and therefore must develop the variety of gifts necessary to that body, while at the same time maintaining "the same care for one another" that maintains the unity of the body: "If one member suffers, all suffer together" (vss. 25b–26a). Paul names eight offices corresponding to his list of "gifts" in verses 8–11 and representing the different parts of the body: apostles, prophets, teachers, workers of miracles, healers, helpers, administrators, speakers in various kinds of tongues. Looking forward to the next stage of his argument, he concludes, "But earnestly desire the higher gifts" (vss. 27–31a).

In one of the best-known and most popular passages in the New Testament Paul describes the highest gift of all, agape (ch. 13). Because the chapter divisions separate the introductory words, "And I will show you a still more excellent way" (12:31b), and the conclusion, "Make love your aim" (14:1a), the connection between this "hymn to love" and Paul's treatment of the problem of glossolalia is easily overlooked. The point is, of course, that this spiritual gift of selfless good will and concern for others is the essential ingredient in every gift that makes the life and unity of the Body of Christ possible. The lyric quality of this passage has the appearance of an independent composition which Paul is quoting, but the obvious connections with the problems in Corinth, such as jealousy, boastfulness, arrogance, and the like, which run all through it show that it is an integral part of the letter. It falls into three parts: (1) the emptiness of all religious achievements without love (13:1–3), (2) the magnanimity of love (vss. 4–7), (3) the endurance of love (vss. 8–13). With the triad familiar to us from other letters (Rom. 5:1–5; Col. 1:4–5; I Thess. 1:3; 5:8), Paul concludes his eloquent argument: "So faith, hope, love abide, these three; but the greatest of these is love" (13:13).

The essential argument in the third stage (ch. 14) is that the gift of prophecy is more beneficial, and therefore more important, than glossolalia. "He who speaks in a tongue edifies himself, but he who prophesies edifies the church" (vs. 4). If glossolalia is used, there must be an interpreter to convey the speaker's meaning to the church. If the prayers are said in glossolalia how can the people say the amen? (vss. 13–17). With perhaps more than a touch of sarcasm Paul boasts that he speaks in glossolalia more than any of them, but "in church" he would rather say five intelligible words than any number in glossolalia (vss. 18–19). By a tortured exegesis of Isaiah 28:11–12 he concludes that glossolalia is supposed to be a sign for unbelievers: but since a church full of people speaking gibberish would hardly convert an unbeliever, prophecy is to be preferred (vss. 20–25). Paul therefore lays down a rule which should probably put an end to the practice: They are to confine glossolalia to groups of not more than three, including an interpreter, and speak one at a time (vss. 26–33a). Although there were in the comparatively low station of women in the time some practical reasons for it, probably Paul's Jewish background is showing in his command that "women should keep silence in the churches" (vss. 33b–36; cf. 11:2–16). In order not to "quench the spirit" (I Thess. 5:19) and yet to wean the Corinthians from their preoccupation with self-centered, immature, and essentially pagan practices in worship, Paul has proceeded with cautious steps, and so he concludes: "Earnestly desire to prophesy, and do not forbid speaking in tongues; but all things should be done decently and in order" (vss. 39–40).

The opening words of chapter 15, along with the entire first paragraph, suggest that this chapter on the resurrection may not have been in response to any issue in Corinth, but Paul's way of drawing the letter to a conclusion by means of an exposition of the hope promised in the Gospel which he had delivered to them initially. The question, "how can some of you say that there is no resurrection of the dead?" (15:12) and the sustained argument which follows, however, indicate that probably this question also was at issue in Corinth. Whether the question came to Paul in the letter or from an oral report we cannot tell, but the absence of the introduction "now concerning" suggests the latter.

One of the half-dozen most important chapters in the New Testament, it contains along with the earliest account of Jesus' Resurrection appearances several theological ideas which have become basic to the development of Christian theology. The first instance we have of the statement "that Christ died for our sins" occurs, for example, in verse 3; the contrast between Adam and Christ as representing the contrasts of death and life, beginning and conclusion of history, sin and redemption appears here also (vss. 22, 45, cf. Rom. 5:14–19),[33] and with it the concept of Christ's Resurrection as the precursor (the first-fruits), which exemplifies, promises, and makes possible the resurrection of the believer. The question to which Paul is speaking is not whether there is life beyond death; the logic of the argument in verses 16–19 rests on the assumption that there is. Nor does the direction of the argument support the suggestion sometimes made that the Corinthians believed that the resurrection had already taken place, they were now in a resurrected state of existence and therefore immortal. The three stages of the argument, the tradition of Christ's Resurrection, the reality of the believers' resurrection, and the bodily changes involved, indicate that the Corinthians were contending for the Greek notion of the immortality of the incorporeal soul which upon death is released from its prison in the material body. This dichotomy between soul and body often led to libertinism on the ground that sensual indulgence attaches only to the body which will disintegrate at death anyway. At death the soul uncontaminated is free to return to its own element. Probably this danger explains why Paul concludes his treatment of the first question on a moral note (vss. 33–34). Here, then, is another instance of the continuing influence of the pagan background out of which most of the Corinthians had come.

33. Cf. C. K. Barrett, *From First Adam to Last* (London: Adam & Charles Black, 1962).

In this earliest account of the tradition of the Resurrection Paul lists six appearances of the Risen Lord: three to individuals, Cephas, James, and himself; and three to groups, the twelve, "more than five hundred," and "all the apostles." Although he says nothing of the locations or circumstances of these appearances, and omits many items, such as the empty tomb, familiar to us from the Gospels, it is possible that the appearances to Cephas and the twelve reflect the Galilean tradition of Mark, Matthew, and John 21; the others reflect the Jerusalem tradition found in Luke and John 20. That Paul includes among the appearances his own experience on the Damascus road explains both his claim to having "seen Jesus our Lord" (9:1), and the basis of his claim to be an apostle (cf. Gal. 1–2, I Cor. 9; II Cor. 11–12). His claim to be an apostle brings to mind, however, his prior activity. What had been the proud mark of his zeal in Judaism is now a matter for humility: "For I am the least of the apostles, unfit to be called an apostle, because I persecuted the church of God" (vs. 9).

Paul's answer to those who say there is no resurrection moves in three steps. The first is based on the tradition he just recalled to them. If there is no resurrection, either the tradition of Christ's Resurrection becomes inexplicable or he was not raised and his redemption has failed (vss. 12–17). In the second step Paul implicitly denies the possibility of life after death without a resurrection: "Then those who have fallen asleep in Christ have perished." The benefits of Christ being confined therefore to this life becomes meaningless (vss. 18–19). The hope of the Gospel, on the contrary, lies in the fact that Christ's Resurrection has made resurrection a reality for man. It is the beginning of the apocalyptic program in which Christ will destroy all of God's enemies, including death, and all will finally be subjected to God. That there can be no life after death without a resurrection Paul assumes also in the third step, in which he appeals to their practices and his. Why do the Corinthians baptize vicariously for the dead or why does Paul "die every day" if there is no resurrection and therefore no life after death? Why not join the hedonists? (vss. 29–32). The questions answer themselves. Brusquely Paul brushes them aside, "Do not be deceived: Bad company ruins good morals." In succession Paul quotes two popular Greek sayings (but cf. Isa. 22:13) to underscore his point. The Corinthians are to come to their senses and abandon the company of pagan ideas before they are ruined by hedonistic morality.

Paul appears in the final section of the chapter to be addressing a rhetorical question suggested by the previous argument: "With what kind of body do they come?" His discussion would have particular pertinence to the Greek mind which tended to disdain the material world. Beginning with two analogies from nature, the seed versus the plant (reminiscent of

John 12:24), and terrestrial versus celestial bodies, he develops his theory of an imperishable "spiritual body" which will be raised from the death of the physical body (vss. 35–44). As usual he turns to Scripture for confirmation which he finds in the contrast between Adam and Christ that he introduced earlier in the chapter (vs. 22); one was the source of the physical, the other of the spiritual existence. Thus he sets his whole argument in the framework of sacred history (vss. 45–50). Finally, he turns to a question which, since he expected many if not most of his generation to live to see the eschaton completed, must have occurred to his readers: How will this change from the physical to the spiritual body be accomplished for those who do not die? His answer is an instant transformation which accomplishes the same effect as death (vss. 51–53). In an exultant mood Paul brings the discussion to a sublime climax with a paraphrase of Hosea 13:14 and the words, "Thanks be to God, who gives us the victory through our Lord Jesus Christ" (vss. 54–57).

Briefly Paul takes up several matters concerning his future plans. The Corinthians had asked about the proposed collection for the saints at Jerusalem. He informs them that it has begun; Galatia has already been informed and they are to begin gathering their contributions in preparation for his arrival. It is not yet clear whether he will need to accompany those taking the gifts to Jerusalem. This is the first mention of a project which assumed increasing importance as time went on (cf. II Cor. 8–9, Rom. 15:25–31). Jerusalem had for a long while its quota of poverty, and now with the political situation rapidly deteriorating a crisis was developing which must have left the church there in dire circumstances. Christian love and the oneness of the Body of Christ, therefore, demanded this assistance as an expression of concern.[34]

Instead of an unsatisfactorily brief visit now Paul plans, after a visit to Macedonia, to come to Corinth for the winter. There were, apparently, some changes in plans in this regard, as we learn from II Corinthians 1:15–2:3, which offended the Corinthians. Timothy is coming to them in the meantime, but Apollos finds it impossible at this time to return to them. It may have been good pastoral judgment from the standpoint of the troubles there that kept Apollos from responding to their request. An appreciative mention of the three brethren from Corinth, greetings from "the churches of Asia," and the closing in Paul's own hand bring the second letter to a close.

TO PUNISH EVERY DISOBEDIENCE:
II CORINTHIANS (10–13)

The third, severe letter—or what we have of it (II Cor. 10–13)—apparently followed a highly unpleasant visit during which Paul's author-

34. See Robinson and Plummer, *I Corinthians* (ICC), pp. 381–383.

ity and leadership were questioned if not rejected outright. In 12:14 and 13:1 he announces that he is coming to Corinth for "the third time," suggesting that he had been in Corinth after writing I Corinthians. Later, in his fourth letter (II Cor. 1:15–2:1), his reference to a "painful visit" preceding the severe letter (II Cor. 2:1) confirms this suggestion.

I Am Not the Least Inferior   The issues and circumstances are far from clear. Three parties are involved: Paul, the Corinthians, and some elusive "apostles." The letter, however, addresses the Corinthians; the "apostles" are off-stage. The issues seem to be more psychological than theological. Although Paul refers to them in the bitterest of terms, sarcastically calling them "superlative apostles" (11:5; 12:11b), false and deceitful (11:13), and even servants of Satan (11:14), he makes no attempt to correct the errors in what they taught. Who they were and where they came from elude us. Probably the reference in the fourth letter (II Cor. 3:1) to some who required letters of recommendation to and from the Corinthians is to these same persons. That they were emissaries from Jerusalem, as some scholars have suggested, is quite unlikely. Not only is there no hint of such a connection, but in the next letter (II Cor. 9:1, 12), in which he is still promoting the collection for Jerusalem, and in Romans 15:25–28, referring to the same project, Paul can speak of the church in Jerusalem with respect and concern and even affection.[35] All that we can say, then, is that they were probably itinerant preachers, not unlike the wandering philosophers and lecturers who were a familiar sight in the marketplaces of the ancient world. They boasted that they were Israelites and "servants of Christ" and, while taking advantage (financially?) of the gullible Corinthians, claimed to work on the same terms as Paul (11:12–13, 20–23).

Although he speaks of them angrily, Paul is not writing to the so-called apostles but to the Corinthians. They have been so taken in by the interlopers that they have repudiated Paul. Not only have they refused to obey him (10:6), but are in grave danger of being "led astray from a sincere and pure devotion to Christ" (11:3). Paul fears that when he comes to them again he may find quarreling, jealousy, anger, selfishness, and the like, not to mention licentiousness and immoralities of the sort the Corinthians were accustomed to in their pagan days (12:20–21). Probably, it is to the Corinthians rather than the so-called apostles, that Paul refers in such phrases as, "If any one is confident that he is Christ's" and "when they measure themselves by one another," in 10:7 and 12. Inspired by their new teachers they have become independent. Except that in the situation in I Corinthians 1–4 Paul could continue to have full confidence in Apollos, who was the unwitting party to the Corinthians'

35. See Johannes Munck, *Paul and the Salvation of Mankind.* pp. 177–179.

disaffection, the situation here in the third letter is little more than an intensification of the earlier problem.

On Paul's part, the Corinthians apparently have accused him of being no genuine apostle. Although he writes impressive letters (10:1, 10), in person he is so ineffective that he cannot compete with self-assured eloquence of their new-found apostolic teachers.[36] Paul had committed the unforgiveable offense of preaching the Gospel to them without charge (11:7–12; cf. I Cor. 9:1–18). From their experience with the practitioners of other religions, the Corinthians could only regard such a practice as self-demeaning (11:7). If, therefore, Paul had so little self-regard how could they have confidence in him? Some of them, on the other hand, seemed to suspect (10:2–3; 12:14–18) that his refusal of support was a ruse to acquire even more money from them (by means of the collection for Jerusalem?). Perhaps, too, the almost constant troubles that Paul found himself in made it hard for the Corinthians to believe that he was favored of God. Nothing in their background would make it easy for them to believe that persecutions and hardships are a mark of divine approbation.

I Am Ready to Come to You   Paul's answer to the Corinthians is two-pronged. On the one hand, he attacks the problem directly, threatening, apparently, some sort of supernatural punishment (10:4–5). They have misread him! He will show them that he can be as bold as his letters (10:9–12). His authority is not based on the impression he makes but on his divinely appointed relationship (10:8) to them as the one who brought them the Gospel and "betrothed" them to "Christ" (10:13–11:2). There may be a touch of sarcasm in Paul's reference to his unwillingness to boast "in other men's labors" (10:15–16), for that was precisely what the so-called apostles were doing in Corinth.

Paul, at the same time, decides that he will match boasts with the interlopers. His boast, however, is in his weakness, "that the power of Christ may rest upon me" (11:30; 12:9b; cf. 10:17–18). The whole passage is heavy with sarcasm; repeatedly he speaks of his "boasting" as foolishness (11:1, 16–17, 19, 21b; 12:11), implying that theirs is also. He proceeds, however, to boast of the very things of which they have accused him. Along with his divinely given authority over them, which is the question at issue, and his founding of the church there, he boasts that he preached to them free of charge. The claim of these so-called apostles to be working on the same terms as he are thus undermined. He boasts also of the troubles he has endured for the Gospel (11:23–33). Imprisonments, beatings, shipwrecks, stoning, hardships of every sort have been his lot. Apparently he regarded these troubles as his share in the

36. See Johannes Munck, *Paul and the Salvation of Mankind,* pp. 157–158.

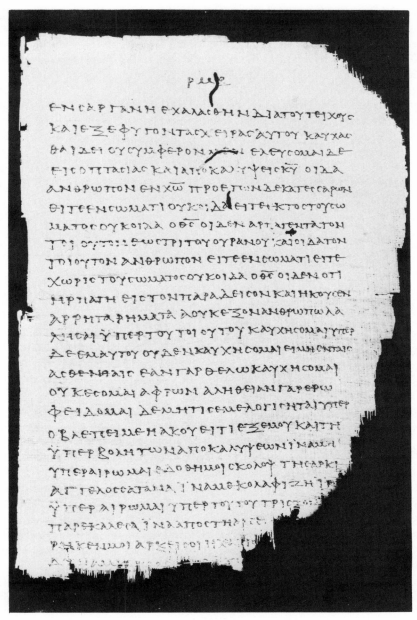

A leaf of the Chester Beatty Papyri (P⁴⁶) found in Egypt during the first half of this century and dating from the third century A.D. It includes II Corinthians 11:33–12:9. (Courtesy of the University of Michigan Library.)

messianic woes that signal the coming eschaton (cf. II Cor. 1:5; Phil. 3:10–11; Col. 1:24). They are, therefore, more appropriate marks of true apostleship than the proud eloquence of the so-called apostles. It is this kind of participation in the messianic age, rather than pagan wisdom, that the Corinthians should emulate. Paul has another boast: visions and revelations (12:1–9). What the thorn in the flesh was (vs. 7) that was given to keep him from being too elated we can only guess. The mention of Satan points up the typically Jewish apocalyptic background to Paul's boast. Because he is Christ's emissary he finds himself caught in the conflict between the Satanic powers of this present evil age and the invading forces of the Messiah ushering in the age to come. The combination of troubles and revelations is therefore the best authentication Paul could desire for his apostleship: "For the sake of Christ then, I am content with weaknesses, insults, hardships, persecutions, and calamities; for when I am weak, then I am strong" (vs. 10). After again apologizing for his boast, he lists "signs and wonders and mighty works" as other marks of his apostleship (12:11–13).

Paul again addresses himself directly to the issue. Have those who suppose that he had refused their support in order to get "the better of them by guile" seen any evidence that either he or Titus and "the brother" had done so? Paul is coming to them for the third time; let them examine themselves and rectify their errors lest he come and find it necessary to deal severely with them (12:14–13:10). The closing of the letter is the source of the familiar liturgical grace (13:14).

WIDEN YOUR HEARTS ALSO:
II CORINTHIANS 1:1–6:13, 7:2–9:15

The storm is over. The severe letter and, doubtless, the good offices of Titus who carried it to Corinth had accomplished what Paul's own "painful visit" could not do, and the repentant Corinthians are now ready to welcome Paul on what turned out to be his final visit. In grateful response to the news Titus brought him of their change in heart he writes a fourth letter. Paul has in the meantime left Ephesus and is now writing from Macedonia. There are still some misunderstandings to be cleared, some admonitions, and the collection must be completed in preparation for the trip to Jerusalem.

The Ministry of Reconciliation, 1:1–6:13; 7:2–16   The first part of the letter responding to the welcome news of the Corinthians' repentance follows the general pattern of the third letter. At the beginning and end (1:3–2:13 and 6:11–13, 7:2–16) Paul speaks directly to specific matters concerning their reconciliation, whereas in the central section (2:14–6:10) he discusses the meaning of his ministry and Gospel. He begins, after the opening salutation, with profound gratitude for the comfort God has given him and which the Corinthians now share: "Our hope in you is unshaken" (1:7a). Some interpreters believe the "afflictions" he had "experienced in Asia" (1:8–10) to be his anxiety over the behavior of the Corinthians (cf. 11:28–29). Although we know from other sources[37] that Paul had other troubles in Ephesus, certainly the Corinthian problem added heavily to them. He now calls upon them to join in thanksgiving for his deliverance (1:11). To his boasts in the third letter he adds this, which in the prior letter had been a matter of protest, that his behavior was not worldly but in "holiness and Godly sincerity" (1:12–14 cf. 17).

There had been some misunderstanding concerning his plans to visit Corinth (1:15–23). At the end of the second letter (I Cor. 16:5–7) he explained why he did not intend to visit them until after his trip to Macedonia. Here he apologizes for not having visited them on his way to Macedonia. From the fact that the third letter was written from Ephesus we must assume either that Paul, having changed his plans after sending the second letter, had made an attempt to visit Corinth on his way to Macedonia, with such bad results that he returned to Ephesus (cf. 2:1), or that their complaint was made after the third letter, and that they felt he should have come to them rather than going to Troas and Macedonia in search of Titus (cf. 2:12–13). Whatever the circumstances, he explains, "It was to spare you that I refrained from coming to Corinth" (1:23).

He turns next to the "severe letter" which he had written "not to cause you pain but to let you know the abundant love that I have for you" (2:4b). The one who has caused the trouble (the indefinite here, esp. vss. 5, 10, may be taken to mean there were possibly more than one culprit, and may explain why Paul is so unspecific) has been punished enough (2:5–11). Let them reaffirm their love for him. Anyone they forgive, he forgives. He then recalls his anxiety over the Corinthians which was so great that he could not remain in the promising work in Troas but went on to Macedonia. Once more he thanks God for the victory in Corinth (2:14–17).

After an allusion to his boasts in the third letter and paying them the high compliment of calling them his letter of recommendation (3:1–3), Paul turns to an exposition of his Gospel and ministry. God has qualified him as a minister of a new covenant, "not in a written code but in the Spirit" (3:4–6). The mention of the new covenant leads to a comparison with the Mosaic covenant by means of the story in Exodus 34:29–35 of the shining of Moses' face. How much greater must be the splendor of the new covenant which gives life than the old one which, although it required Moses to veil his radiant face, can only condemn. This veil

37. See pp. 341–344.

becomes a symbol. It was used to obscure the disappearing splendor, and it remains over the minds of Israel to prevent their understanding Moses. Only through Christ can the veil be lifted and Moses be truly understood (3:7–18).

It is Paul's ministry to proclaim the Gospel of this new covenant, which requires no clever promotions but only frank appeal to every man's conscience with the truth. If there is any veiling of this Gospel (like that of Moses), it is done by the "god of this world" to prevent "those who are perishing" "from seeing the light of the Gospel of the glory of Christ, who is the likeness of God" (4:1–6). "But," Paul continues, "we have this treasure in earthen vessels, to show that the transcendent power belongs to God and not to us." Therefore the troubles and persecutions he endures are part of the process of death by which he must carry out this ministry after which he will share with all believers in Christ's Resurrection (into an eternal "glory beyond all comparison") (4:7–18). The mention of the Resurrection leads to a discussion of eternal life and his longing for it (cf. I Corinthians 15 and Philippians 1:19–26), which he carries through by an analogy comparing the tent of our earthly body with the house of our eternal one (5:1–10; I Cor. 15:35–50). Scattered throughout this section are expressions of the courage which this Gospel and hope inspire: "Such is the confidence that we have" (3:4); "Since we have such a hope, we are very bold" (3:12); "we do not lose heart" (4:1b, 16a); "So we are always of good courage" (5:6). This hope in the invincible Gospel, therefore, not only sustains him, but is also the strength and courage he is seeking to impart to the Corinthians. Paul is not commending himself to them again (5:14; cf. 3:1), but trying to clarify the difference between the "human point of view" and the "new creation" in Christ. "This ministry" which Paul refers to in 4:1 is therefore "the ministry of reconciliation" (5:18), bringing men to that reconciliation to God by which the new creation takes place (5:11–6:3).

In another sense Paul does commend himself. He is a servant of God. Against the background of this hope of eternal life and in a passage which both recalls and interprets his boast in his hardships in the third letter (11:23–29), Paul sets forth his commendation through the paradox of his afflictions which go hand in hand with the "weapons of righteousness." His troubles which from the worldly point of view would be proof of his failure are actually badges of his divine commission (cf. the paradox of wisdom in I Cor. 1:25 *passim*). He is "in honor and dishonor," dying and yet alive, "having nothing yet possessing everything" (6:4–10).

Paul therefore calls on the Corinthians to open their hearts to him in unrestricted affection (6:11–13; 7:2–4). Returning to the recent events of the painful letter and Titus' welcome news, he describes his comfort by their repentance (7:5–13a). The reference in 7:12 to "the one who did the wrong" and "the one who suffered the wrong" adds to the mystery of the troubles in Corinth. Paul has been too frank in reference to his own relationships to the Corinthians for us to suppose, as some commentators do, that he himself is the injured one here. Yet the mention of an injured party and the definite reference to the one who wronged makes unlikely any connection between this verse and the indefinite reference to anyone "who has caused pain" in 2:5–11. Even more improbable is any connection with the case of incest in I Corinthians 5:1–13. The most plausible connection is with the instance, in 6:1–8, of one taking a fellow believer into a pagan court. This allusion, at any rate, is another indication of the complexity of the problems in Corinth, problems which, in view of the pagan background of the Corinthian church, should not surprise us. With a final note of appreciation for the way in which they have also rejoiced the heart of Titus and vindicated Paul's boast of them to him, Paul closes the matter: "I rejoice, because I have perfect confidence in you" (7:13b–16).

In the Relief of the Saints, chs. 8–9   Much as in the second letter, Paul turns to matters concerning the plans in the immediate future which in this instance are exclusively concerned with the collection for Jerusalem. With pride he tells them of the astonishing liberality of the poverty-ridden Macedonians, and exhorts the Corinthians to follow their example (8:1–7). No fewer than three times he stresses that their gift is not of compulsion but voluntary (8:8; 9:5, 7). In a brief passage remarkably similar in thought to Philippians 2:5–11, he sets the incarnation of the preexistent Christ before them as an example for their giving (8:9, cf. I Cor. 8:6). As they had begun with enthusiasm a year ago, they must now complete their collection. The idea of equality, or perhaps better, mutuality according to which the Corinthians are to supply the wants of Jerusalem so that Jerusalem may supply theirs becomes more clear in Romans 15:17, written shortly afterward: "For if the Gentiles have to share in their (Jerusalem's) spiritual blessings, they ought also to be of service to them in material blessings."

Paul gives some details of his plans. He is sending with Titus two brethren whom he commends to them (8:16–24). They are called only "the brother" and "our brother" (8:18, 22). Although "the brother" (the phrase sounds almost like a title) is well known to "all the churches," we have no clue to the identity of either of these men. Paul seems, incidentally, to be protecting himself and Titus by means of these brethren from any accusation of mishandling the funds (cf. 12:16–18) which they had initiated (cf. I Cor. 16:1–4 and II Cor. 8:6).

Chapter 9 sounds at first reading like a separate note which followed the fourth letter, but the theme follows that of chapter 8 well enough to make such an assumption unnecessary.[38] As Paul had earlier boasted to the Macedonians of the Corinthians' enthusiasm for the collection (cf. his boast to them of the Macedonians in 8:1–5), he is sending the brethren now to see that they are ready lest when he arrives with the delegation from Macedonia he be embarrassed. "God loves a cheerful giver," so let them give liberally, that God may be able to bless them liberally (9:6–15). On this note ends what we have at least of Paul's correspondence with the Corinthians. With reconciliation and hope the drama of the Corinthian crises has ended: "Thanks be to God for his inexpressible gift!"

5. The Churches of Asia:
Philemon, Colossians, Ephesians, Romans 16

According to Acts 19:8–10, 21ff., Paul's stay in Ephesus, the capital of the Roman Province of Asia, lasted for something over two years. This estimate accords well with the hints in the Corinthian letters, the first three of which were probably written in Ephesus. The collection for Jerusalem, which was started after the second letter, had been in process for a year by the time Paul wrote the last letter. Whether Paul had personally traveled in Asia to any extent beyond Ephesus, his influence was felt widely throughout the province (cf. Acts 19:26). Four churches in the province are listed in Paul's letters: Ephesus and three others in a triangle of cities, Laodicea, Hierapolis, and Colossae, in the Lycus Valley on the eastern side of the province. In the list of seven churches in Asia to which the collection of letters in Revelation 1–3 are addressed (1:11), two of these churches, Ephesus and Laodicea, reappear. Probably most of the other five churches were founded under Paul's direction.[39] We should note also that in the letters to Asian churches more names of Paul's fellow workers begin to appear. Paul's stay in the environs of Ephesus must, then, have been a time of intense and productive activity in which more and more of the burden was assumed by the able associates he continued to gather about him.

One reason for his use of associates was undoubtedly his confinement in prison during a part of this time. The probability of Paul's Ephesian imprisonment we have already discussed in connection with the provenance of Philippians.[40] It is interesting in this connection to observe that all three of the letters which bear Asian names indicate that they were written from prison (cf. Philemon 9b, 10, 13, 23; Col. 4:10a, 18b; Eph.

38. See B. W. Robinson, *The Life of Paul* (Chicago: University of Chicago Press, 1918), pp. 164–174.
39. See Duncan, *St. Paul's Ephesian Ministry.* Polycarp in his *Letter to the Philippians* (11:3), however, seems to exclude his church at Smyrna from those that had known Paul.
40. See pp. 341–344.

3:1; 4:1). Although tradition has assigned the provenance of these letters, like that of Philippians, to a Roman prison, it is more likely that Philemon and Colossians were from Ephesus. The letter called Ephesians, if it is by Paul, cannot have been addressed to Ephesus, but would more likely have been written there. There is another letter, now attached as the sixteenth chapter to Paul's letter to the Romans, which, as we shall see, was probably addressed to Ephesus. This letter was written from Corinth and is therefore the only part of the Asian correspondence not written from prison.

I APPEAL TO YOU FOR ONESIMUS:
PHILEMON

Although the Pauline authorship of this brief note to Philemon and company on behalf of Onesimus has never been seriously questioned, it was for a long while regarded by the Early Church as too personal and of too little consequence to be in the Canon. The Muratorian Canon, for example, distinguishes it as a private letter, along with the Pastoral Epistles, from Paul's Epistles to the seven churches. One of four books of the New Testament—five in the entire Bible (Obadiah; II and III John, and Jude)—having only one chapter, its brevity seems to have contributed to its early neglect. Yet its address includes a church (vs. 2), and its content is no more personal or any less concerned with the business of Paul's mission than his other letters.

Probably because Paul is returning the slave Onesimus and refers to his former uselessness, his absence "for a while," and the possibility that he has wronged or owes his owner, it has been traditional to assume that Onesimus was a runaway slave. Somehow he came into contact with Paul, so the interpretation runs, and having been converted was now returning to his master armed by this letter asking Philemon to forgive him and accept him back into the household. The careful reader is, therefore, surprised to discover that the letter nowhere says that Onesimus had run away. Although Paul does ask Philemon to "receive him as you would receive me" (a phrase not uncommon in ancient letters of introduction), the emphasis of his letter falls not on Onesimus' return to his owner but on Paul's need and affection for him. That the slave was formerly useless is stated in the context of his conversion and probably refers to his behavior as a slave rather than his absence. As for his wronging Philemon, a slave would not necessarily wait until his escape to steal from his owner. Paul mentions it, at any rate, only as a possibility to remove any impediment to his request.[41]

41. See the classic study of Philemon by John Knox, *Philemon Among the Letters of Paul* (New York: Abingdon Press, 1959), in which he provides the full text of a letter by Pliny in behalf of a runaway slave (*Epistolae* ix. 21) for comparison. Also *IB*, Vol. 11, pp. 555–560; and C. F. D. Moule, *The Epistles of Paul the*

Quite possibly Onesimus had been sent on an errand to Paul who was at the time imprisoned in Ephesus, and some of his co-workers were detained with him (vs. 23; Col. 4:10–13). Onesimus became a Christian under Paul's influence and showed promise as a valuable assistant. Perhaps Epaphroditus had recently been sent home, and Paul was in serious need of an attendant. So he dutifully sent Onesimus back to Colossae with this letter containing one of the broadest hints in history, hoping for Onesimus to be returned to him. Years later Ignatius, the early second-century Bishop of Antioch, in his letter to Ephesus (esp. chs. 1–6), written while he was on his way to martyrdom in Rome, refers to an Onesimus as the bishop there. Tradition has it that the bishop was Philemon's former slave. Jon Knox takes this tradition seriously and further suggests that this same Onesimus was responsible for the collection of Paul's letters.[42]

The letter is written with marvelous care and skill. After the usual opening thanksgiving Paul states that, although he could use his authority to command, he prefers to appeal to Philemon for Onesimus who has become his child in the Faith. Playfully he puns on the name which means "useful." He subtly suggests that Onesimus will be useful to Philemon by his service, as Philemon's gift, to Paul. He also reminds Philemon that, although he is returning Onesimus, he could have kept him, "but I preferred to do nothing without your consent in order that your goodness might not be by compulsion but of your own free will" (vs. 14). Perhaps Onesimus' coming to Paul was providential in order that Philemon along with Paul may have him eternally as a brother rather than as a slave (vss. 15–16). If there are any financial impediments Paul will pay them—of course, he would not mention what Philemon owes him! In another pun Paul writes, "I want some benefit (*onaimen,* a verb related to the noun Onesimus) from you in the Lord." "Confident of your obedience," he continues, "I write to you, knowing that you will do even more than I say" (vss. 20–21). With a brief remark about his own hope to visit Philemon, and greetings from several companions, he closes. Because of the coincidence of some of these names, including that of Onesimus himself, we may assume that this letter is in some way related to, and addressed to the same church as, the letter to the Colossians to which we now turn.

CHRIST IS ALL, AND IN ALL:
COLOSSIANS

Whereas the letter to the Colossians is, by the coincidence of names, at least, related to Philemon, it is also, by a considerable body of similar

---

Apostle to Colossians and to Philemon (Cambridge: At the University Press, 1962), pp. 34–37, for two other ancient documents on the subject.

42. *Philemon Among the Letters of Paul,* pp. 71–108, especially 107–108.

material, ideas, and literary characteristics, closely related to the letter called Ephesians. There are differences at the same time between Colossians and Ephesians, on the one hand, and the rest of Paul's letters, on the other, which have caused many scholars to question Paul's authorship of one or both of them.[43] The argument with regard to Colossians rests on three points: (1) the style and vocabulary, (2) the errors being combatted, (3) the highly developed Christology.

The question is much too complex for more than a brief summary here. That there are differences in style and vocabulary can be observed even in translation. Long and complex sentences have taken the place of the exclamatory sentences, rhetorical questions, antitheses, and vigorous if sometimes broken sentence structures. Some of Paul's favorite terms are absent, and a number of new ones appear. Perhaps most surprising is the absence, except in one possible reference (1:8), of any mention of the Holy Spirit. There are, however, important considerations on the other side of the issue. The number of new terms encountered here is no greater than in some of the undisputed letters; the new terms, on the other hand, are for the most part required by the new subject matter. Similarly, the absence of Pauline terms corresponds to the absence of the themes and arguments that require them. Two factors help to account for the involved and dispassionate style. First, we are dealing here for the first time in our study with a letter addressed to a church Paul had never seen (2:1). Philemon, although its address included the church in the house of Archippus, was actually addressed to Philemon whom Paul apparently had known (vss. 7, 19). Founded by Epaphras, one of Paul's co-workers (1:7) and now a fellow prisoner (4:12; Philemon 23), this church along with the other Asian churches, came under Paul's oversight. Epaphras has reported to him on the conditions there, and Paul is responding to them on behalf of Epaphras as well as himself. He is responding, therefore, to no urgent crisis in which he is personally involved and which would call forth the agitated rhetoric of such letters as Galatians. Second, we have already noted some of the ways in which Paul's use of an amanuensis would affect the style and color of his letters.[44] How large a part Timothy, whose name appears with Paul's in the opening greeting, and Epaphras may have had in the composition we can only surmise from the alternate plural and singular first-person pronouns.

Because of our increased knowledge of the bewildering variety of

43. For useful surveys of the question as it applies to Colossians see F. W. Beare, "Introduction," *IB,* Vol. 11, pp. 142–145, and George Johnston, "Colossians," *IDB,* Vol. I, pp. 658–659, and works there cited. Statistics on the vocabularies of Colossians and Ephesians as well as a table of comparison of the two letters are given in T. K. Abbott, *The Epistles to the Ephesians and to the Colossians* (ICC), pp. xiv–xix, xxiii, xxxi–xxxii, lii–lx.
44. See pp. 321–324.

syncretisms in the first-century Graeco-Roman world, arguments based on the errors against which Paul is contending have in recent years been largely abandoned.[45] The question of the comparatively highly developed cosmic Christology remains and is, perhaps, the most serious argument against Pauline authorship. Paul's thought of Christ, as we have thus far encountered it, is more functional than here in Colossians. The emphasis falls on his being sent into the world, his Crucifixion, Resurrection, and return to judge the world. Yet the elements of the Colossian Christology (1:15–20; 2:8–15) are not absent from the other letters. His preexistence and share in creation are affirmed in Philippians 2:5–8; I Corinthians 8:6; II Corinthians 4:4; and 8:9, whereas his victory over the cosmic forces of this present age is affirmed in such passages as I Corinthians 15:20–28, Philippians 2:9–11, and Romans 8:37–39.

Much depends upon one's preconceptions as to the flexibility of Paul's style and thought. Because of the Canonical position of the letters, it is easy for us to overlook the variety of situations and circumstances under which and to which they were written. Not only were the letters *ad hoc,* but to a considerable degree so were the theological arguments. Paul had a basic body of concepts concerning God's actions in and through Israel in fulfillment of his redemptive purpose in history. He saw the advent of Christ as the climax and promise of the soon-to-be-realized culmination of that purpose, and therefore, of history itself. Beginning always with these concepts, he reasoned in good rabbinic fashion to apply his Gospel to the problems at hand. He was not building a theological system, but responding to an historical situation by seeking to prepare the world for the final moment in history in which God's redemptive purpose would be completed. In contrast to our Western tradition, steeped as it is in Greek categorical thinking, Paul's emphasis fell rather on orthopraxy than on orthodoxy.

Finally, there is to be considered the connections between this letter and the one to Philemon. It is hard to imagine why anyone writing at a later time in Paul's name would so obviously associate his work with the shortest and least regarded of Paul's own letters. This connection can be seen chiefly in the coincidence of names. Of the eleven names appearing in Colossians and the ten found in Philemon, eight are the same. Timothy's name appears with Paul's in the salutations of both letters. Epaphras, Paul's "fellow prisoner" who is listed first among those sending greetings in Philemon 23, is mentioned twice in Colossians. In 1:7 he appears as the founder of the Colossian church who has reported to Paul on conditions there, and in 4:12 his greetings are included in a way that implies the imprisonment stated in Philemon. Perhaps the most important of these

45. Cf. W. M. Ramsey, *The Church in the Roman Empire* (New York: G. P. Putnam's Sons, 1893), pp. 465–480.

names is Onesimus, the subject of Philemon and in Colossians 4:9 the bearer along with Tychicus of the letter. From this reference it is generally assumed that both letters were written and delivered together.

From the discussion in the letter, we may assume the Epaphras had "made known" to Paul more than the Colossians' "love in the Spirit" (1:8). How critical the problem was is difficult to tell from the tone of the letter, but it involved some form of syncretism with the popular pagan religions of the area. From the hints in Paul's discussion and what is known of the cults of that area, it appears to have placed Christ alongside other angelic beings, "elemental spirits" (Greek: *Stoichia*, 2:8, 20) in a hierarchy which mediated between man and the highest god, and in its totality was known as the "fullness" (Greek: *pleroma*, a favorite term of later Gnosticism). Terms and allusions appear which reflect a range of influences from the mystery religions and astrologies, on the one hand, to an aberrant form of Judaism on the other. Ethically, the general trend seems to have been toward asceticism rather than libertinism. The natural phenomena of the area lent themselves to the development of such religions. Strabo, the ancient geographer was intrigued, for example, by the Plutonion, a cave emitting poisonous gas which was supposed to be the entrance for Pluto the god of the nether world.[46] The Colossians—and Laodiceans—had brought their variegated religious background with them into the church. It would be too much to expect them to understand the exclusive claims of the Christian faith anymore than they had understood those of Judaism. Rather than a later development the syncretism in Colossae was probably there from the start.

If You Have Been Raised with Christ, chs. 1–2   The body of the letter falls into two parts. In chapters 1 and 2 Paul is concerned with the "philosophy and empty deceit" which threatens to distort the faith, whereas chapters 3 and 4 contain moral exhortations based on a true knowledge of Christ. After the opening thanksgiving for their faith in Christ, love of the saints, and hope in heaven, a brief mention of Epaphras, and a prayer that they may increase in spiritual knowledge, lead worthy and fruitful lives, and be strengthened "for all endurance and patience with joy" (1:3–11), Paul opens his discussion by a brief recitation of the terms of the Gospel. God "has qualified us to share in the inheritance of the saints" by delivering us into the "kingdom of his beloved Son" from the "dominion of darkness." He immediately focuses attention on the Son, "in whom we have redemption, the forgiveness of sins" (1:12–14).

Anticipating the discussion to follow, he defines the Son: first as the image of God preexistent co-creator and sustainer of "all things," and

---

46. *Geography*, XIII, 4, 14. See Abbott, *Ephesians and Colossians*, p. xlix; and Selby, *Toward the Understanding of St. Paul*, pp. 222–224.

then as the head of the Church and the beginning of the resurrection. For emphasis he reiterates: The fullness (*pleroma*) of God dwells in him, and by his Crucifixion he has reconciled "all things" to himself (1:15–20). The Colossians have themselves experienced this reconciliation in order to be presented blameless "before him" provided they do not deviate from the Gospel of which he is a minister. Thus he has carefully laid the foundation for his argument (1:21–23).

With the reference to his ministry he turns to the reason for his concern and the basis of his right to admonish them. As in his letters to the Corinthians (cf. II Cor. 1:5; 4:7–12; 6:4–10; 11:23–33) he cites his sufferings as a badge of his ministry which is to make the Word of God fully known. Hidden for ages, the mystery of that word is now revealed to be the presence of Christ in the gentiles. (Significantly, Paul is using terms characteristic of the mystery religions here.) This is Paul's gentile mission: to "present every man mature in Christ" (1:24–29). The gentile mission is his responsibility; the Colossians are a part of that mission, therefore, he is responsible to admonish them. He is, then, greatly concerned for the Colossians, and the Laodiceans, as well as all who have not seen him, that they be united in love and understanding of this mystery so that no one may delude them. Unknown to them in person, he is with them in spirit and admonishes them to be established in the faith as they were taught (2:1–7).

With the definition of the Gospel and his own responsibility to it and to the Colossians established, Paul now turns to the issue at hand. "See that no one makes a prey of you by philosophy and empty deceit, according to human tradition" (2:8). Paul has already shown by the doctrine of Christ's preexistence and possession of the fullness of God, and, by their experience of redemption in him, that Christ is preeminent in everything (1:15–23). There is no room, therefore, for including the demons of the area in their worship. Christ contains the fullness of deity, and in him they have come to the fullness of life. We should note the juxtaposition of pagan (Gnostic?) and Jewish terms as he moves from repeated use of the word "fullness" (*pleroma*) to speak of their "spiritual" circumcision and participation in the death and Resurrection of Christ by baptism. Thus they have been "made alive," their trespasses forgiven, and the legal demands (of Torah) nullified by the cross (cf. Rom. 7:1–6, Gal. 3:10–14). He returns to pagan concepts to point out that "principalities and powers" were disarmed by the cross along with the Law (2:9–15).

It follows, therefore, that the ascetic and ritual practices which have evolve from the syncretism are likewise excluded. They are only a shadow; "the substance belongs to Christ." Again we encounter a melange of Jewish and pagan terms. "Food" in verse 16 may refer to the kosher laws, but "drink" would not. Self-abasement, angels, visions, and the like reflect a diversity of pagan religions in the background. Christ, who is the head, holds together the Church and gives it its true nourishment and godly growth (2:16–19). If the Colossians are in Christ, they are dead to these "elemental spirits" and, therefore, have no business submitting to the regulations that apply to them (2:20–23), however pious they may appear.

Seek the Things That Are Above, chs. 3–4   As we have learned to expect from Paul, he turns to the moral issues which follow from being "raised with Christ." Since they have died to earthly things they are, in anticipation of Christ's appearance in glory, to set their minds on "things that are above" (3:1–4). In a comparison reminiscent of Galatians 5:19–24 (cf. Rom. 1:29–32, I Cor. 6:9–19, Eph. 4:31–32), he lists the earthly behavior to be put to death and the heavenly attitudes to be "put on." They have "put off the old nature" and "put on the new" in which all human distinctions are excluded and "Christ is all, and in all" (cf. Gal. 3:27–28). Above all they are to "put on love," be ruled by the "peace of Christ," and be thankful. Teaching and admonishing one another, and singing with thankfulness to God, they are to do everything "in the name of the Lord Jesus" (3:5–17).

Paul concludes the ethical section with instructions to specific groups: Wives are to be subject to their husbands; husbands are to love their wives. Children are to obey their parents; but fathers are not to "provoke" their children. Slaves are to obey their masters, remembering that their true servitude is to Christ; masters are to treat their slaves "justly and fairly," for they, too, "have a Master in heaven." In sum, the Colossians should "continue steadfast" in prayer, watchfulness, and thanksgiving, praying also that Paul, who is now in prison, may have opportunity clearly to "declare the mystery of Christ." With the admonition to behave wisely and graciously toward outsiders, he closes the body of the letter (3:18–4:6).

In his closing notes Paul introduces Tychicus and commends Onesimus, the bearers of the letter, and adds a long list of greetings. He extends greetings to Laodicea and to "Nympha and the church in her house," and asks that, having read this letter in the church, they exchange letters with Laodicea. An enigmatic exhortation to Archippus closes the letter.

ONE NEW MAN:

EPHESIANS

Whatever else we may conclude about Ephesians, we can be sure that it was not written to Ephesus. In the first place, like Colossians it indicates that it was written to a church which Paul did not personally know (1:15; 3:1–4). Absent also are the greetings and personal notes which in other letters reflect Paul's knowledge of and relationships with the church to which he is writing, all of which would be inexplicable in a letter to a church in which he had spent more than two years. Second, several of the best ancient manuscripts omit the words "in Ephesus" from the salutation (1:1). Their omission from the RSV indicates how well established is the evidence against them. Yet without some such words the grammar is awkward and incomplete. From these data some earlier scholars surmised that Ephesians was actually a circular letter, copies of which contained blanks to be filled in by Tychicus, the bearer, upon delivery.[47] Because of the lack of evidence for any such practice in antiquity, and the failure of any other names, with one possible exception, to appear in this place, the circular letter theory has generally been abandoned. That according to Tertullian the second-century heretic, Marcion, entitled the letter "To the Laodiceans" has led some scholars to suppose that Ephesians was "the letter from Laodicea" referred to in Colossians 4:16.[48] More recently Richard Batey has suggested that, since in Greek uncial (capital) letters the words "saints" and "Asians" could be confused, some scribe had made that mistake and therefore the address should read: "To the Asians, faithful in Christ Jesus."[49] How the name Ephesus came to be attached to it we cannot tell.

A second and more serious problem concerns the question of Paul's authorship. We have already observed that there are similarities between Colossians and Ephesians in thought, structure, and literary style which distinguish them from Paul's other letters and have caused scholars to raise questions about the authorship of Colossians. Not only the fact that these characteristics are more pronounced in Ephesians, but the lack of personal references and a specific situation along with subtle differences in thought from Colossians suggest that this letter may have been written by a disciple of Paul using Colossians as a model. There are more words unusual to Paul; the sentences are even longer and more redundant and cumbersome; and in a few places there are suggestions of theological development and perspective appropriate to a time later than that of Paul. Eschatology, for example, has been formalized and deemphasized; references to the Holy Spirit, virtually absent in Colossians, become in Ephesians comparatively prominent; and Paul is made to speak of himself and of the apostles with a veneration more appropriate for a disciple at a later time (2:20; 3:1–6). With the exception of these subtle, perhaps unconscious developments, on the other hand, there is virtually nothing

47. See W. J. Conybeare and J. S. Howson, *The Life and Epistles of St. Paul* (New York: Charles Scribner's Sons, 1892), pp. 396–398.
48. *Against Marcion*, V. 11, 17. For the modern theory, and a defense of Pauline authorship, see Benjamin W. Bacon, *An Introduction to the New Testament* (New York: The Macmillan Company, 1902), pp. 116–121.
49. Critical Note, "The Destination of Ephesians," *JBL,* LXXXII, Pt. I, March, 1963, p. 101.

original in the letter. Not only does the letter echo much of the content of Colossians, but parallels appear from all of Paul's other letters.

On the basis of such difficulties many scholars have concluded that Ephesians was compiled at a later time by an ardent Paulinist. Edgar J. Goodspeed has offered the suggestion, which has interested a number of scholars, that Ephesians was written by the collector of Paul's letters and attached as an introduction to the published collection.[50] Of particular interest is the way in which Goodspeed's theory deals seriously with one of the chief difficulties of those who deny Paul's authorship of this letter, namely, the fact that by external evidence it is one of the best attested of all his letters. Because it appeared at the head of the initial publication, Paul's published letters were, on this theory, never known without Ephesians. The evidence is, nevertheless, far from conclusive, and a number of scholars still reserve judgment. As in the question of Colossians, much depends on one's preconceptions. If Ephesians was not by Paul, it came from the circle of his disciples and co-workers; if it was not written during his lifetime, it was written shortly afterward. Considering such matters as the varying degrees of participation by the amanuenses in the letter-writing process, it is not impossible that it was written from Paul's Ephesian prison to the churches founded by Paul's lieutenants throughout the Province of Asia, much as Galatians was addressed to all the churches in that province, and therefore may be, after all, the "letter from Laodicea" mentioned in Colossians 4:16. Such a letter would be of necessity general in tone, yet sensitive to the particular angelologies and syncretisms for which the Asian peoples were noted. Such a letter would also invite greater participation in its composition by Paul's co-workers. Whether written in his lifetime or later, Ephesians is from the "school of St. Paul" and offers a remarkable compendium of his teaching. The form may be from the hand of a disciple but like other ancient digests such as the *Manual* of Epictetus the material is from the mind of Paul.

The Unity of the Spirit, chs. 1–3   Not only in specific materials, but also in outline and shape, Ephesians follows the pattern of Colossians. It also falls into two parts: chapters 1–3 develop the theological theme of the new unity between Jew and gentile in Christ; chapters 4–6 exhort the reader to the kind of life appropriate to that unity as the body of Christ.

50. See his *The Key to Ephesians* (Chicago: The University of Chicago Press, 1956) for his last writing on the subject in which he lists twenty arguments against Pauline authorship, followed by parallels between Ephesians, Colossians, and the other letters of Paul. Also C. L. Mitton, *The Epistle to the Ephesians* (Oxford: At the Clarendon Press, 1951), offers a definitive study of the problem, prompted by Goodspeed's theory, in which he also finds Ephesians to be Deutero-Pauline. See F. W. Beare, "Ephesians," in *IB*, Vol. X, p. 603, for a criticism of Goodspeed's theory. Also Selby, *Toward the Understanding of St. Paul*, pp. 278–283, and works there cited.

Almost the entire first division is cast in the form of prayers, and the second division consists of a series of homiletical exhortations, so that it might almost be described as a liturgical interpretation of Colossians.

After the salutation, the first division begins with a blessing of God for blessing us in Christ, for choosing us "before the foundation of the world," for destining us to be his sons, and bestowing upon us his grace, in that "in the Beloved we have redemption." He has revealed to us the mystery of his purpose in "the fullness of time to unite all things in" Christ. In Christ we "have been destined to live for the praise of his glory" (1:1–14). For these blessings Paul is offering thanks and prays for the readers that God may give them knowledge of him, that they may know the hope to which they have been called and his power in the believer which was manifested in the Resurrection and exaltation and will culminate in the eschaton. The prayer ends in a doxology to the exalted Christ (1:15–23).

Almost without a break the passage continues with a recital, reminiscent of the prefaces in the ancient liturgies, of the believers' redemption. Although once subject to the spiritual and fleshly powers and passions of this present evil age, and therefore dead, they have been "made alive" as God in his love has raised them up with Christ in order to display in the coming ages the immeasurable riches of his grace. It is this grace, not their own doing, that has saved them, so that created in Christ Jesus they may walk in good works (2:1–10). The uncircumcised gentiles are to remember that they were once outside Israel's commonwealth, covenant, and hope, but have been brought in by the blood of Christ (2:11–13).

Christ has brought peace by bringing together both Jews and gentile into "one new man" in Christ. The reference to the breaking down of the "dividing wall" of hostility may refer to the wall in the Temple area in Jerusalem separating the court of the gentiles beyond which on pain of death they may not go.[51] This emphasis on the new unity of Jew and gentile, the logical conclusion to the emphasis on the gentile mission both in Paul's letters and the Gospels, forms the climax for the first division of Ephesians. The theme of unity developed here differs significantly from that in the fourth Gospel (cf. 9:24–41; 15:18–25 with 10:16; 15:4–6; 17:20–23) in that here as in Romans (cf. chs. 9–11) Israel as a people is still expected to participate in the new "people of God"; whereas in John the "Jews" have already become hopelessly apostate, and a Jew becoming a believer is expelled from the synagogue. John's concern for unity within the Church belongs to a later period in the history of the Church than the concern for unity between Jew and gentile expressed here.

51. See Deissmann, *Light from the Ancient East*, pp. 79–80, for a translation of the inscription containing the warning to the gentiles.

Following the pattern of Colossians, the prayer is interrupted by an interpretation of Paul's ministry within this theological setting. In an obvious reference to Galatians 1:11–17, he recounts how he was given the stewardship of the mystery which had been withheld from previous generations but now was revealed to him as it was to the holy apostles and prophets. Thus Paul was "made a minister" to the gentiles (cf. II Cor. 4:1) of this Gospel even though he is "the very least of all the saints" (cf. I Cor. 15:9), in order that through the Church the wisdom of God might be disclosed to the cosmic powers. As in Colossians 1:24 and II Corinthians 1:5, *passim,* Paul's suffering is the badge of his ministry (3:1–13). There follows a concluding intercessory prayer that the readers might be given inner strength through the Spirit, that Christ may dwell within them through faith, that "grounded in love" they may be able to comprehend the dimensions of the love of Christ and be filled with "the fullness of God" (3:14–19). An ascription (3:20–21) concludes the prayer and the first division of the letter.

A Life Worthy of the Calling, chs. 4–6   The second division of the letter consists of a series of hortatory homilies which probably characterize Christian preaching in that period. Such homiletical characteristics as proof texts, chiasms, and triads appear, along with lists of vices and virtues, rules of household relationships, and analogies. The theme of the first homily is leading a life worthy of the new man in Christ. This life calls for lowliness, meekness, patience (cf. I Cor. 13:4–7), love, unity, and peace in order to exemplify the unity of body, Spirit, and hope into which the believer has come through "one Lord, one faith, one baptism." Over all is the "one God and Father of us all." But each member has his own gift of grace. The quotation from Psalm 68:18 is introduced in connection with the gifts, but its applicability is demonstrated in midrashic fashion by relating the word "ascended" to the Ascension of Christ. The reference to his descent into the nether world (note the chiasm: ascended-descended, descended-ascended) is paralleled, as are several passages in this part of Ephesians, in I Peter (3:19; 4:6; cf. Acts 2:27) where an explanation of its significance is offered.[52] The gifts are the five offices in the Church: apostles, prophets, evangelists, pastors, teachers, whose task it is to build up the Church in unity, knowledge, and maturity. No longer children, the members then, avoiding the winds of conflicting doctrine, may grow up in the unity and love of Christ (4:1–16).

To approach the matter from another angle (a second homily?) the readers must no longer live as the gentiles with darkened understanding, alienated from God, callous, and licentious, but leaving the "old nature" with its lusts behind, they are instead to put on the new nature of true

52. See p. 443.

righteousness. They are to be truthful, kind, and forgiving; they are to live by honest labor (cf. II Thess. 3:6–13) and avoid grieving the Holy Spirit (cf. I Thess. 5:19) by evil and malicious talk (4:17–32).

The theme of the next homily is, "be imitators of God." Living by the example of the love demonstrated in Christ's sacrificial death, the believers are to avoid immorality, covetousness, unsavory talk. The points which have been picked up from the previous homily are reemphasized. No such evil persons will inherit the Kingdom of God. The believer has left the shameful darkness of such evils, which incite the wrath of God, for the light of Christ. Where the quotation in verse 14 originated is impossible to tell (cf. Isa. 60:1); some have conjectured that it is from an ancient baptismal hymn. If so, this way of reminding the readers of their baptism interprets also the whole preceding passage on light (vss. 8–13, esp. vs. 8) and bases the ethical appeal on their baptismal vows. They are to be wise, not foolish, not drunk with wine (the allusion may be to pagan rites) but filled with the Spirit, singing hymns, and offering thanksgiving (5:1–20).

There follows an expanded version of the admonitions to wives, husbands, children, slaves, and masters in Colossians 3:18–4:1 in which, by using the analogy of marriage including the proof text, Genesis 2:24, to apply to the relationship between Christ and the Church, the mundane relationships themselves are set within the larger context of their relationships in the Church (5:21–6:9). Concluding the whole series of exhortations is the familiar analogy of the panoply. The believers are involved in a cosmic war with the forces of the present evil age, they must therefore be armed with "the whole armor of God." They are also to pray for all the saints and for Paul. A brief commendation of Tychicus, the bearer of the letter (cf. Col. 4:7–8), and the peace and grace close the letter.

I COMMEND TO YOU PHOEBE:
ROMANS 16

One more brief note belongs among the letters addressed to the Province of Asia. The sixteenth chapter of Romans both by the evidence of the text and contents cannot be a part of that letter nor can it be intended for the Christians at Rome. The brief exhortation in verses 17–20 is completely out of keeping with the content of Romans, but more important, the extensive list of greetings, including twenty-six names along with references to relatives, is inexplicable in a letter to a church which Paul had never visited and for which neither he nor his co-workers had any responsibility. These names, on the other hand, insofar as they can be identified, all point to Ephesus. The last we knew of Priscilla and Aquila, for instance, they were in Ephesus (I Cor. 16:19; Acts 18:18ff.). Epaenetus is said to have been "the first convert in Asia"; Andronicus and Junias were fellow prisoners with Paul. That all of these people, probably more than thirty, had migrated to Rome is incredible.

There is textual evidence also pointing in the same direction. The Chester Beatty papyrus (P^{46}), the oldest extant manuscript of Romans, distinctly separates chapter 16 from the body of Romans, placing the doxology in 16:25–27 at the end of chapter 15. Since this doxology, which as we shall see in the next section is found in different positions or not at all in various manuscripts, was in all probability intended to conclude the letter to the Romans, if not the whole collection, this papyrus is good evidence that chapter 16 was a separate letter which became attached later to Romans.[53] It is safe to conclude, therefore, that this chapter is

The coastline at Ephesus, looking south into the Aegean Sea. (Courtesy of Don R. Smith.)

53. Johannes Munck, following T. W. Manson, believes that Paul himself added this note to a copy of Romans which he sent to Ephesus after the original had been sent to Rome. *Paul and the Salvation of Mankind,* pp. 197–198.

actually a short letter of recommendation (cf. II Cor. 3:1–3) for Phoebe, a deaconess who was going from Cenchrea to Ephesus. It is also likely that Paul wrote it while he was in Corinth, perhaps at the same time he wrote Romans.

The letter consists simply of a request for a favorable reception and whatever assistance she may require for Phoebe, a long list of greetings, and a brief paragraph exhorting the Ephesians to be wary of self-seeking troublemakers (vss. 17–20). The list of greetings by name is so unusual to Paul—the only other instance is that of Nympha in Colossians 4:15 —that some commentators have regarded this chapter to be spurious. Such greetings were customary, however, in letters of recommendation.[54]

6. *To All God's Beloved in Rome:* *Romans 1–15*

One letter of Paul's remains which was written to a church in the capital of the Graeco-Roman world. Since he had never visited this church nor had any jurisdiction over it, he writes in a different, more carefully reasoned style. That he wrote this letter to the Romans (probably in Corinth) shortly before embarking on his final trip to Jerusalem "with aid for the saints" Paul tells us himself at the end of the letter (15:23–32). If his prison letters were written, as appears likely, from Ephesus, this becomes the last letter we have, in its original form at least, from the hand of Paul. There is evidence that copies of this letter once circulated which ended with chapter 14. Tertullian and Origen indicate that Marcion's edition of Romans, for example, did not include the last two chapters, and several of the ancient capitulations, or tables of contents, also stop at the same point. The doxology in 16:25–27, which as we have already seen appears in the Chester Beatty papyrus at the end of chapter 15, is found in some manuscripts at the end of chapter 14, in others at the end of chapter 16 as it is in the RSV, and in a few in both places. That some manuscripts omit it altogether adds weight to the suggestion of a number of scholars that this doxology is not a part of Paul's writing, but since in the Muratorian Canon, and therefore probably in the earlier collections, Romans stood at the end of the list of Paul's letters, the doxology was added to it as a suitable conclusion to the collection. Because there is slight evidence of an edition which lacked the words "in Rome" in 1:7 and 15, some interpreters have supposed that the shorter edition and the edition without the address to Rome both go back to an abbreviated edition which Paul himself had prepared as a circular letter for all his churches. The evidence, however, is not convincing. Because the

---

54. See John Knox, "Romans," in *IB*, Vol. 9, pp. 366–368. Contra. Adolph Deissmann, *Light from the Ancient East*, pp. 197, 234–236.

continuity of thought in chapter 14 remains unbroken through at least most of chapter 15, and there is no evidence connecting the shorter edition with one which omits the address, we may conclude that these variants were probably nothing more than accidents to some of the manuscripts.[55]

From the opening and closing of the letter we learn Paul's purpose in writing. He has long entertained the hope of visiting the Roman Christians in order to impart to them "some spiritual gift" for their strengthening and for mutual encouragement, and in order that he might "reap some harvest" among them "as well as among the rest of the gentiles" (1:9–15). Because of his occupation with preaching the Gospel from Jerusalem "as far round as Illyricum," he has been hindered thus far from realizing this hope. Now that he has concluded his work in the East, however, he is free to realize his ambition of many years to visit them. He must first go to Jerusalem "with aid for the saints," but after that he hopes, having visited with them for a time, to be helped by them on his way to Spain (15:18–29).

Such a simple and obvious intention would at first thought hardly require the longest of Paul's letters. There is more to his purpose, then, than a courteous request for hospitality. What Paul is asking for is significant support and endorsement, probably personal assistance as well. For the Romans to comply with Paul's request as he hoped would mean their own wholehearted commitment to the world mission to the gentiles. As the digressions and excursuses in his own letters show, Paul was never content simply to settle the immediate point at issue. He must always place the issue in the larger framework of the new situation created by the coming of Christ to bring into reality Israel's hope for the new age. With Christ's Resurrection the atmospheric pressure of the eschaton began already to be felt, and now it only awaited the proclamation throughout the world of that "good news" and the call to repentance in preparation (cf. Mark 13:10). The whole purpose and meaning of the Church are comprehended in that task. When Paul called the Roman Christians to understand his mission, therefore, he was calling them to understand and fulfill the meaning of their own existence. Paul's way of reasoning was not yet systematic theology, the abstractions of philosophical reasoning of that sort were foreign to the rabbinic mind, but in his habit of reasoning always from the same controlling idea he planted the seed—to use his own metaphor—out of which it grew. The Fathers of the next century transplanted the tender shoots of Paul's interpretation of Christ into Greek soil where they grew into the towering systems of theology that have controlled the history of the Church ever since. Because of its full

55. For more complete statements of these problems see William Sanday and A. C. Headlam, *Romans* (ICC), pp. lxxxv–xcviii; Enslin, *Christian Beginnings,* pp. 264–268; McNeile, *An Introduction to the New Testament,* pp. 154–158.

and comparatively orderly statement of Paul's Gospel, Romans has been a particularly important source for theology. The modern reader needs to keep in mind, nevertheless, that Paul's interest was not theological, nor is Romans a considered summary of his thought. Too many of his basic ideas, important to his other letters, are missing or are simply alluded to in passing. Romans is a full and considered argument, based on his understanding of God's ultimate purpose, for the gentile mission. The similarity between sections of Romans and Galatians, especially with regard to the Law and salvation by faith, along with the coincidence of Scriptures which are used in the supporting argument, have led many interpreters to describe Romans as a more dispassionate form of the letter to Galatia. The differences in purpose and much larger amount of dissimilarity, however, make these similarities incidental overlapping in his treatment of two different questions.

I AM NOT ASHAMED OF THE GOSPEL, CHS. 1–8

The letter falls into three distinct parts. In chapters 1–8 Paul argues the need and nature of the salvation proclaimed in his Gospel. In order to show the place of Israel in this understanding of God's plan he places this salvation, in chapters 9–11, in the setting of the history of God's people. From this line of reasoning he draws, in chapters 12–15, the practical conclusions as they apply to the moral life of the believer and finally as they apply to his own future plans.

Called to Be an Apostle, 1:1–17 As we have learned to expect, Paul anticipates in his salutation the main thrust of his letter. Perhaps it is appropriate that this his longest letter should also have the longest salutation. He introduces himself as an apostle whose commission from Jesus Christ is to "bring about obedience to the faith . . . among all nations." The Gospel concerning this faith he outlines in what approaches a creedal formula. What was promised beforehand through the Biblical prophets God has realized in his Son, Jesus Christ, "descended from David" and "designated Son of God . . . according to the Spirit . . . by his resurrection."

In moving terms Paul describes his thanksgiving and prayers for the Romans, and his longing for many years to see them, both for their mutual spiritual benefit and to further the cause of the Gospel. The word "gospel" leads to a concise statement of the thesis of the letter. We may, as the Moffatt translation does, convert the litotes, which begins verse 16, to read "For I am proud of the gospel" (cf. his "boast" in II Cor. 11–12; also Rom. 15:17). The point is that this Gospel presents God's power to save all who have faith, the Jew first and the Greek, i.e., the gentile, as well (note the pattern, a basic motif in Acts: Jew-gentile).[56] As in Galatians 3:11, Paul cites the proof text so basic to his thought: "He who through faith is righteous shall live" (Hab. 2:4). Much of Romans is a midrash on a combination of texts for which this is the key.

The Wrath of God Is Revealed, 1:18–3:20   Paul begins his argument for the necessity of the Gospel by showing that the gentiles do not stand outside God's interest and concern. The Old Testament prophets characteristically pictured the active judgment of God as falling on the pagans only when they violated his people Israel. Otherwise, although their idolatry and immorality were held up as negative examples to Israel, they were left like brute beasts to the self-destruction of their own ignorance. On the principle which Paul himself accepted, "sin is not counted where there is no law" (5:13b, cf. vs. 20; 3:20; 7:7–13), the gentile would therefore be free of the judgment which God would mete out to his own people who had broken the Law. But for the same reason, the gentile was excluded from Israel's hope in the age to come. One might argue, therefore, that since the gentiles are outside of God's plan, except for those, of course, who on their contacts with Israel seek admission, they should be left there.

Paul's argument is that the gentiles are not without the Law. "What can be known about God is plain to them, because God has shown it to them" (1:19, 32; cf. 2:14–16), but "they exchanged the truth about God for a lie" (1:25a) and turned deliberately to idolatry. "Therefore God gave them up" to unspeakable immoralities. Three times Paul uses this ominous phrase (1:24, 26, 28); it is God's judgment on the gentiles. Paul finds added proof in the pagan moralists who show their awareness of God's moral demand by passing judgment on others. Yet they, too, are without excuse and stand condemned for doing the same things (2:1–11). Three times he emphasizes their presumption: "Do you suppose" (2:3); "do you presume"; "do you not know"? (2:4). The gentiles' apparent immunity to God's judgment is really God's kind patience (cf. 3:25); they are therefore "storing up wrath" for themselves in the coming eschaton. Paul now draws the first major conclusion: "To those who in well-doing seek for glory and honor and immortality, he will give eternal life," but "for those . . . who do not obey the truth . . . there will be wrath" (2:7–8). Twice he repeats the formula from 1:16, "to the Jew first and also to the Greek," as he emphasizes the point that, whether they have sinned "without the law" or "under the law" judgment awaits "every human being who does evil" and glory, honor, and peace await those who do good, "for God shows no partiality" (2:9–12).

56. See p. 298ff.

Paul turns now to the position of Judaism with respect to the Gospel. If the pagan moralist is condemned or exonerated according to whether he practices the morality he knows, it follows that the Jew who possesses the Law but does not obey it is equally condemned. Indeed, he is less excusable. To illustrate, Paul considers the hypothetical gentile who keeps the precepts of the law. Although he is physically uncircumcised, he is "a real Jew" (2:13–29). "Then what advantage has the Jew?" (3:1a), Paul raises the obvious question and answers it with the paradox that although they have every advantage they are no better off (cf. 3:1 with 9). The Jews have every advantage because they have the privilege of being the vehicles of God's revelation. That they were unfaithful to it does not discredit the revelation. Indeed God's judgments on their unfaithfulness confirm his justice, but since God's use of their unfaithfulness does not thereby excuse it (there is a missing step in Paul's logic here), they are from the standpoint of divine judgment no better off than the gentiles. All "are under the power of sin." In proof of this conclusion he cites a catena of Scriptures from Psalms 14:1–2; 53:1–2; 5:9; 140:3; 10:7, and Isaiah 59:7–8 (3:1–19). By way of transition to the next major point of his argument he summarizes his conclusion: For no human being will be justified in his sight by works of the law since through the law comes knowledge of sin (3:20).

The Righteousness of God Has Been Manifested, 3:21–5:21 If, then, we conclude that gentiles and Jews are on the same footing in regard to their culpability, the gentile by his conscience and the Jew under the Law, two conclusions follow: First, they stand in the same need of salvation ("there is no distinction," 3:22b). The gentile is no longer to be regarded as a mere brute outside the sphere of God's demands and judgment. Second, the Law which can only condemn leaves both Jew and gentile hopeless. If there is to be salvation it must come from elsewhere. With great care Paul proceeds to show that as the Law has revealed God's wrath, so faith discloses his righteousness.

The argument which follows through chapter 4 is familiar to us from Galatians. Although the Law condemns, at the same time the Law and the prophets, i.e., all Scripture, reveal "the righteousness of God through faith in Jesus Christ for all who believe" (3:22). "All have sinned" and therefore can only be justified by "grace as a gift." Expiation by the blood of Christ has made redemption available "to be received by faith." Man is thereby left with no room for boasting of his own achievements in righteousness. This principle of faith applies equally to Jew and gentile; God is therefore the God of the gentile as well as the Jew (3:21–30).

That salvation is a gift received by faith does not discredit the Law. For the Law by exposing sin has made righteousness through faith necessary, and at the same time, in the story of Abraham (Gen. 15:6), whose faith "was reckoned to him as righteousness," has established it. In further support of the point he quotes also from Psalm 32:1–2 the blessing on those who are forgiven, which he understands to refer to those whose "faith is reckoned as righteousness." Since this salvific event in Abraham's life occurred before he was circumcised, Paul uses it to prove his point that the blessing of salvation by faith applies equally to gentiles as to Jews. The modern reader may feel that Paul is stretching his exegesis a bit far when he says that Abraham's circumcision was a sign of righteousness already received by faith, and was "to make him the father of all who believe without being circumcised" i.e., the gentiles, as well as the circumcised who follow his example of faith (3:31–4:12). With elaborate argument Paul sets out to prove that the great "promise to Abraham and his descendants, that they should inherit the world" is addressed to faith as a gift of grace and is not conveyed by the Law. The birth of Isaac, the first step in the fulfillment of the promise, to the barren and aged couple exemplified that grace and rewarded Abraham's faith. Jesus, "who was put to death for our trespasses and raised for our justification" becomes the final step which brings the promise to its consummation (4:13–25).

With profound feeling Paul celebrates this grace. Through Christ by faith we are justified and have "peace with God." We rejoice in our hope, and rejoice even in our sufferings which through God's love conveyed to us by the Holy Spirit condition us for the hope. What is astonishing about God's love is that "while we were yet helpless," "while we were yet sinners," "while we were enemies," Christ died to reconcile us to God so that we might "be saved by his life" (5:1–11). Taking up a theme he had introduced in I Corinthians 15:21–22, 45, Paul develops the typology between Adam and Christ who stand, as he viewed it, at the beginning and end of history. "As one man's trespass led to condemnation for all men, so one man's act of righteousness leads to acquittal and life for all men" (5:12–19). In one contrast he summarizes the essence of his argument thus far. The Law was introduced to increase the sin, i.e., the culpability, but at the same time grace increased. So that the problem of sin, being now exposed, might be solved by that grace which through Jesus Christ bestows eternal life (5:20–21).

Are We to Continue in Sin? chs. 6–8   This doctrine of salvation by faith apart from the Law would seem on the face of it to cut the nerve of moral effort. Paul is aware of the objection, and with a concept of re-creation remarkably similar to that of Ezekiel (cf. Ezek. 36:25–27) he sets about to answer it. What has actually happened to the believer is that by his identity with Christ in baptism he has participated in Christ's death and Resurrection, and therefore lives now a new life freed by death from sin. Paul is careful to maintain that the believers' actual resurrection lies still in the future; he is living now in an interim. Paul calls him, therefore, to be what he is and is to become. Avoiding sin from whose slavery he has been freed, he is to be instead a "slave of righteousness" as is appropriate to those who are "alive to God" (6:1–23).

As Paul had discovered in the Law a confirmation of his doctrine of righteousness by faith (3:21; 4:1–25), so now he turns to the Law for proof of the new freedom which the believer enjoys from sin and the Law that reveals it. As a woman is freed from her marriage vows by the death of her husband, so the believer's death in Christ has freed him from "sinful passions, aroused by the law" (7:1–6). The analogy from the Law leads him to parallel his treatment of the Law in connection with the culpability of gentile and Jew, by a discussion of the Law in relation to the new moral situation. Because he has been speaking of freedom from both sin and the Law, the reader is not to suppose that the Law and sin are identical. Rather since the Law reveals sin and "revives it," i.e., makes it sinful, the bondage of the Law is sin. It follows, then, that the Law is no longer a bondage to one who has been freed from sin. In his eagerness to make this point, Paul comes very close to contradicting his opening argument that all men have what the Law requires "written on their hearts" (2:15, cf. 1:18–2:12): "Apart from the Law sin lies dead. I once was alive apart from the Law, but when the commandment came, sin revived and I died" (7:8b–9). It is sin, not the Law, that is the problem. The Law is therefore holy, just, and good (7:7–12).

The remainder of chapter 7 has been the subject of much discussion. The question is whether the section is to be regarded as autobiographical, and Paul is here describing his own subjective experience before his conversion,[57] or is it simply a further extension of the analogy in 7:1–3? The debate has often either ignored or misunderstood the sequence of the argument in the letter. Paul is still dealing with the question, "Are we to continue in sin?" (6:1a), and therefore with the believer's relationship to the Law. It is to be granted that one's own experiences are bound to be reflected in his thought, and that Paul's letters give ample evidence of his profound knowledge of the inner contradiction one encounters in trying by his own efforts to earn God's approval under the Law. Paul is speaking here, nevertheless, of the "body of death" which characterizes the believer's life in the interim before the eschaton. His death and resurrection with Christ, as Paul has already indicated (6:5), are not yet complete; the believer consequently finds the struggle of the ages (the present evil age and the age to come) struggling within his own life while he

---

57. For example, C. H. Dodd, *The Epistle of Paul to the Romans* (MNTC) (London: Hodder & Stoughton, 1932), pp. 123–126. Cf. Sanday and Headlam, *Romans,* pp. 184–186.

awaits to be delivered, "thanks be to God, through Jesus Christ our Lord!" (vs. 25a). Paul is not really the antinomian that many interpreters, ancient and modern, have supposed. His concern throughout Romans is to describe the role of the Law in the history of salvation. He finds that role in the way the Law by exposing man's helpless slavery to sin makes way for God's grace made available to all men through faith by his final act of deliverance in Christ. Once the sin, which makes the Law a dreadful pronouncement of condemnation, is removed, Paul in true rabbinic spirit can "delight in the law of God" (7:22, cf. vs. 12; 8:4, and Ps. 1:2; 119:12–20, *passim*).

In one of the greatest lyric passages in all his letters, Paul summarizes his conclusions: "There is therefore now no condemnation for those who are in Christ Jesus." With this statement and its amplification in the next two paragraphs he summarizes the first five chapters. A new Law, the Law of the Spirit of life in Christ Jesus, has taken over from the Law of sin and death. By "sending his own Son in the likeness of sinful flesh" God condemned sin and set the believers free so that "the just requirements of the law might be fulfilled" in those "who walk not according to the flesh but according to the Spirit." Those who have their minds set on the flesh cannot please God, but the believer has "the Spirit of Christ"; although his body is dead because of sin (cf. 7:23–24), his spirit is alive because of righteousness. "He who raised Christ Jesus from the dead" will therefore raise the believer (8:1–11).

Summarizing chapters 6 and 7 he turns to the moral response called for by this deliverance: "If by the Spirit you put to death the deeds of the body you will live." Those "led by the Spirit" and suffering with Christ are sons of God and "fellow heirs with Christ of his glory" (8:12–17). The mention of suffering turns Paul's thought to the future. The redemption Christ has brought is not yet complete but awaits the eschaton, for "hope that is seen is not hope." The believer therefore patiently awaits its realization. In an extraordinarily inspiring passage he envisions, in contrast to "the sufferings of this present time," the "glory that is to be revealed." All creation, including nature itself, which is groaning under its "bondage to decay" awaits its release in the revelation of the glory of the sons of God (cf. Isa. 65:17–25). In the meantime the Spirit intercedes for the saints who in this waiting period do not know even how to pray as they should (8:18–27).

The conclusion of the matter is that "in everything God works for good with those who love him." He has foreknown, predestined, called, and justified them and will glorify them. Therefore who can be against them? If God gave his Son for man's salvation, would he withhold anything else? Who can condemn the believer when Christ died and was raised again to intercede for him? Not all the sufferings in the world nor all the forces of the cosmos can separate him from "the love of Christ" (8:28–29). Nowhere else are we afforded such a view of the panorama of Paul's Gospel. It was this grand vision of a universe restored in Christ that had captured his imagination, and for the rest of his days he spent every ounce of his energies to carry it around the world in preparation for its consummation. It was this vision, too, which he was seeking to share with the Roman Christians, in order that they might also share the task of its proclamation.

MY HEART'S DESIRE FOR ISRAEL, CHS. 9–11

Because of his essentially negative treatment of the Law, his placing the gentiles on the same footing with Jews, and his emphasis on the gentile mission, Paul appears to have set Israel aside as the People of God. Jewish opposition to the Gospel, furthermore, reinforces the impression that, although individual Jews like gentiles may find their way into the new community of faith, Israel as a people having served its purpose as a vehicle of God's revelation has been thrust aside (cf. 11:1). In the next three chapters, which have often been regarded as a parenthesis or digression, Paul not only answers this question by placing his Gospel in relation to Israel in the perspective of the history of salvation, but he also uses the question to state his understanding of God's plan for both Israel and the gentiles in calling the world to repentance in preparation for the eschaton. Nowhere in his letters does Paul's rabbinic method of exegesis show more clearly than here in the unusually large number of Scriptural quotations he uses.

The Elder Will Serve the Younger, 9:1–10:4 Paul begins by placing himself, as he repeatedly does (9:3; 11:1, 14), among the people of Israel and speaking with profound appreciation of their role in God's actions in history. In an astonishing spirit of self-offering he confesses that he could wish to be accursed for the salvation of his people. Sonship, glory, covenant, Law, worship, promises, and the patriarchs belong to Israel, and finally Christ himself "according to the flesh" is of Israel. In the first step of his argument Paul makes two important points: The first is that "not all who are descended from Israel belong to Israel" (9:6b). By means of the stories of Abraham's two sons (cf. Gal. 3:16, 29; 4:22–31) and of Jacob and Esau he establishes the point that God selects his own as he wills from among the physical descendants of Abraham. Borrowing from the Wisdom of Solomon (15:8, cf. Jer. 18:1–6), the analogy of the potter who makes from clay vessels both for beauty and for menial use as he wills, Paul makes the second point that God can for his benevolent purpose use his creatures as he chooses. He quotes and interprets out of context Hosea 1:10, 2:23 in further support of the point that if God chooses to harden Israel's heart in order to make the gentiles become the sons of the living God he is acting in a way consistent with his own purpose and character. By an appeal to the doctrine of the remnant, in Isaiah 10:22–23, 1:9, and 28:16, he adds further that God's treatment of Israel has not been arbitrary.[58] Rather, the Israelites, by faithless misuse of the Law and in spite of their unenlightened "zeal for God," deserve to be set aside.

Christ Is the End of the Law, 10:5–21 This last point and the inseparable link between Israel and the Law lead Paul for the third time in this letter (cf. 2:12–4:25 and 7:1–25) to take up the issue of the Law to show that on its own terms the Law was never intended to be Israel's salvation. The Law demands, on the one hand, total obedience which Israel has not and cannot give (10:5; 9:31). It speaks, on the other hand, of the word which "is near you, on your lips and in your heart" (Deut. 30:11–14). This word, he argues is the Gospel which Paul himself preaches. Since, as Isaiah 28:16 says, "No one who believes in him will be put to shame," the Gospel is for Jew and gentile alike. Quoting Joel 2:32 as further proof of the universal address of the Gospel, Paul draws from this argument a major conclusion of the letter. How can people believe and call upon "him of whom they have never heard"? They cannot hear without a proclaimer and the proclaimer must be sent. With a chain of Scriptures from Isaiah 52:7, 53:1, Psalm 19:4, Deuteronomy 32:21, and Isaiah 65:21, he supports his point, which is basic to the whole purpose of the letter, but for the time being he carries it no farther.

Until the Gentiles Come, ch. 11 Paul comes back to the basic question of this section, "Has God rejected his people?" By an analogy drawn from Elijah's flight to Horeb in I Kings 19:1–18, along with a catena of quotations from Isaiah 29:10, Deuteronomy 29:4, and Psalm 69:22–23, he again appeals to the concept of the remnant (cf. 9:27–29) in order to answer the question with a resounding "no." Rather they have been temporarily set aside in order that the Gospel may be addressed to the gentiles. When "the full number of the Gentiles come in," all Israel will become jealous and thus will return and also be saved (11:25–26). Once more, from Isaiah 59:20–21, Jeremiah 31:33, and Isaiah 27:9, he supports his point with Scripture. After calling attention to his own apostleship to the gentiles by which he hopes, having provoked them to jealousy, to save some of his fellow Jews, Paul addresses a warning to his gentile readers. Using a horticulturally unsound analogy of grafting on olive trees (11:17–24), he warns that if God can set Israel aside, he can do the same to the gentiles; they are therefore not to "become

58. On the remnant, see West, *Introduction to the Old Testament*, p. 279.

proud, but stand in awe," especially since God will regraft the natural branches into their own tree. "For God has consigned all men to disobedience, that he may have mercy upon all" (11:32). With a grand doxology, including quotations from Isaiah 40:13–14 and Job 41:11, Paul celebrates the wonder of God's program for the salvation of mankind.

Many of the Scriptures Paul has used have been loosely quoted, their combinations have been made gratuitously, and the exegesis at times is, to say the least, arbitrary. The modern reader may object, but only a brief reading in the *Mishnah* will show that, if his theology was strange and radical, Paul's methods of handling Scripture in its support were not. The idea of election which becomes comparatively prominent in this section, also, many readers will find uncongenial. It should be remembered, however, that Paul is speaking not of persons as individuals, but of Israel and the gentiles as the two classes into which the Jew divided all of humanity. All through the discussion, it should be noted, Paul has left open the possibility of individuals, regardless of the election or rejection of the class, finding their salvation through faith (cf. 9:6ff., 27; 10:11–13, 16; 11:5, 14). Finally, we should observe how carefully Paul, by this outline of the program for the salvation of the gentiles and Israel, has laid the foundation for his request in chapter 15 for assistance from the church at Rome for his own mission to the gentiles.

I APPEAL TO YOU THEREFORE, CHS. 12–15

As we have learned to expect from him, Paul turns in the closing section of his letter to practical exhortations based on the moral consequences of the Gospel he has outlined. The "therefore" in the opening sentence applies to all of the previous eleven chapters. Much of the material is familiar to us from his other letters, especially I Corinthians, and two or three passages reflect the Sermon on the Mount. The whole section follows from his appeal, in the familiar verses with which the section opens, for the readers "to present your bodies as a living sacrifice" and to be transformed rather than "conformed to this world."

Let Love Be Genuine, ch. 12 In a passage which closely parallels I Corinthians 12:4–30, Paul calls upon each of the Roman Christians in humility to exercise his own gifts as one of the members of the body of Christ. The gifts he lists are prophecy, service, teaching, exhortation, contributions, and acts of mercy. It is interesting, in view of his request in connection with the journey to Spain and mention of the contribution for the saints at Jerusalem at the end of the section, that he should place contributions and acts of mercy in the climactic position at the end of the list. The essence of the chapter is to "let love be genuine" (vs. 9a).

He concludes a long list of Christian virtues with an exhortation to kindness to one's enemies reminiscent of Proverbs 25:21–22 and Matthew 5:44.

Be Subject to the Governing Authorities, ch. 13 In his exhortation to respect the officers of civil government as authorities "instituted by God" (13:1–7), Paul displays an attitude toward the local and imperial powers that later Christians found increasingly hard to maintain. Prior to the Neronian persecution the Christians, including Paul, found their opposition stemming from Judaism and other local religions. The governors and magistrates tended to function as neutral arbiters when outbreaks of violence against the Church were brought before them. So Paul could exhort his readers to civil obedience, paying taxes, revenues, respect and honor to the authorities as "ministers of God" (cf. I Tim. 2:1ff.). Returning to the subject of love (13:8–10), he follows the discussion of civil authority with a treatment of the commandment to love your neighbor as yourself which appears as a combination of Matthew 22:21 and 5:21–48. The passage ends with an eschatological warning reminiscent of I Thessalonians 5:1–11. The "night is far gone, the day is at hand," therefore in sobriety and well armed they are to keep themselves ready (13:11–14).

As for the Man Who Is Weak, 14:1–15:13 Although in broader and more general terms, this extended passage dealing with one's responsibility toward those whose religious scruples are more conservative is closely similar to I Corinthians 8:1–10:33. There is to be mutual respect between the vegetarians and those who are not, as well as between the man who observes a religious calendar and those who do not. For all of these are valid acts to the Lord. "None of us lives to himself, and none of us dies to himself . . . whether we live or whether we die, we are the Lord's" (14:7–8). It follows, then, that they are not to judge one another (14:13; cf. Mt. 7:1–5). More important, they are to respect one another's scruples lest they cause a brother to violate his own conscience. What he is led to do may not be wrong, but if it is against his conscience it is to him a sin. "It is wrong for anyone to make others fall by what he eats" (14:20b). The strong ought, furthermore "to bear with the failings of the weak." Following the example of Christ, "Let each of us please his neighbor for his good, to edify him" (15:1–2). Finally, the readers are to live in harmony, "welcome one another" as Christ has welcomed them. By almost a *tour de force* Paul manages a final reference to the gentile mission that concludes with catena of quotations from Psalm 18:49, II Samuel 22:50, Deuteronomy 32:43, Psalm 117:1, and Isaiah 11:10, and a blessing.

To Win Obedience from the Gentiles, 15:14–33   With the high compliment that the Roman Christians are already "full of goodness" and
knowledge, Paul turns back to the immediate point of the letter. He has
written to remind them of certain points because of his own apostleship
to the gentiles, which is his priestly service to God, he has finished his
work as far as Illyricum and, after his trip to Jerusalem, hopes now to
be aided by them in his Spanish mission. In the meantime they are to
pray for the success of his trip to Jerusalem that this expression of the
love and unity of the Church may succeed. With a brief blessing this
epistle, Paul's longest and one of the most influential letters in history,
ends.

Thus ends also our survey of the collection of Paul's letters. More
voluminous, and more literarily elegant, collections of ancient letters
have survived to us, but none of these has wielded a fraction of the influence of these letters in shaping subsequent Western history. Paul's
influence after his death continued and grew until his name stood second
only to that of Jesus in importance for the beginnings of Christianity.[59]
To some of the early effects of that influence we must now turn.

Selected Readings

PAUL'S THOUGHT

Barrett, C. K., *From First Adam to Last* (London: Adam & Charles
Black, 1962).

Davies, W. D., *Paul and Rabbinic Judaism* (London: S.P.C.K., 1958).

Dodd, C. H., *The Meaning of Paul for Today* (New York: Meridian
Books, 1957).

Ellis, E. Earle, *Paul's Use of the Old Testament* (Grand Rapids, Mich.:
Wm. B. Eerdmans, 1957).

Enslin, Morton Scott, *The Ethics of Paul* (New York: Abingdon Press,
1957).

Gale, Herbert M., *The Use of Analogy in the Letters of Paul* (Philadelphia: The Westminster Press, 1964).

Hunter, A. M., *Interpreting Paul's Gospel* (Philadelphia: The Westminster Press, 1954).

Munck, Johannes, *Paul and the Salvation of Mankind,* tr. Frank Clarke,
(Richmond, Va.: John Knox Press, 1959).

Prat, Fernand, *The Theology of Saint Paul,* 2 vols. (Westminster, Md.:
The Newman Press, 1946).

Schweitzer, Albert, *Paul and His Interpreters,* tr. W. Montgomery (New
York: The Macmillan Company, 1948). Like his *Quest of the*

59. Adolph Deissmann, *Paul,* p. 3.

Historical Jesus, this is a survey of the history of modern scholarship in the field of Pauline studies.

————, *The Mysticism of Paul the Apostle,* tr. W. Montgomery (New York: The Macmillan Company, 1960). An interpretation of Paul from the perspective of "thoroughgoing eschatology," similar to his interpretation of Jesus.

SPECIAL TOPICS

Goodspeed, Edgar J., *The Key to Ephesians* (Chicago: The University of Chicago Press, 1956).

Hurd, John C., Jr., *The Origin of I Corinthians* (New York: Seabury Press, 1965).

Knox, John, *Philemon Among the Letters of Paul* (New York: Abingdon Press, 1959).

Mitton, C. L., *The Epistle to the Ephesians* (Oxford: At the Clarendon Press, 1951).

See also *The Life of Paul* at the end of chapter 4.

COMMENTARIES

Barth, Karl, *The Epistle to the Romans,* tr. Sir Edwyn C. Hoskins (Oxford: University Press, 1933). The appearance of this now famous commentary marked the beginning of the Barthian theological movement which has exerted such a profound influence upon twentieth-century systematic theology.

Dodd, C. H., *The Epistle of Paul to the Romans* (MNTC).

Chapter Six

In Imitation of Paul

The Pastoral Epistles, Hebrews, Catholic Epistles, Revelation

And you became imitators of us and of the Lord, for you received the word in much affliction, with joy inspired by the Holy Spirit.... I Thess. 1:6

The death of Paul and the Neronian persecution mark a major transition in the history of the Early Church. It was, to begin with, the end of a generation. The original apostles and witnesses to the Resurrection were disappearing and the leadership of the Church was passing into the hands of a new generation of leaders whose lack of association with the origins of the movement left them dependent upon the deposit of tradition left behind by those who had been the original followers of Jesus.

1. Times of Stress

Before entering upon the literature from this later period, we must look briefly at some of the changes which had taken place. Because of the persistent opposition from the synagogues everywhere the Christians appeared and the increasing percentage of gentiles in the churches, the Roman officials apparently became convinced that Christianity was not a Jewish sect and therefore not entitled to the recognition and rights afforded Judaism. This situation was, of course, complicated by the revolt and fall of Jerusalem (A.D. 66–70) which seriously strained the relations between Rome and Judaism itself. Although the Neronian outbreak was confined to the city of Rome and we do not hear of another official persecution of the sort until the reign of Domitian at the end of the first century and his persecution may have been a local affair, local harassments and executions of Christians on trumped-up charges seem to have become increasingly common. As we learned from such passages as I Thessalonians 2:13–16, persecutions were present in the Church's life from the beginning, but after Nero they took on a new and ominous dimension. Rome seems to have been deathly afraid of any assembly over which it did not have direct control.

Gold coin (*aureus*) of Nero. In an attempt to improve his economic plight Nero reduced the size of the Aureus, which later produced serious economic reactions. (Courtesy of the Money Museum, National Bank of Detroit.)

As the churches became more and more gentile, not only in constituency but in character, new problems arose. The traditional Hebraic background of the Church's thought and teaching began to be submerged in Hellenistic thought forms. The dynamic understanding of existence which resulted from Israel's preoccupation with history and eschatology was gradually overlaid with the more static concepts of Greek categorical thought. Although these Greek concepts aided the Church in its adjustments to the delay of the eschaton, their characteristic division of the human person into soul (*psyche*) and body (*soma*), as we have already seen, led to the extremes of asceticism and libertinism and therefore created serious ethical problems for the Church. Innumerable possibilities for syncretistic combinations from ubiquitous Eastern religions were brought into the Church almost from the beginning by gentile converts throughout the Levant. The mystery religions, astrology, and the local religions of the Eastern cities combined with Greek speculation to develop philosophical systems which in combinations with Christianity during the second century produced the great Gnostic heresies of that and following centuries. It was the appearance of these heresies which by reaction crystallized Christian thought into a system of orthodoxy and the collection of Paul's letters and the four Gospels into a Canon of Scriptures attached to what then became known as the Old Testament.

Since the word "heresy" (Greek: *hairesis*) originally referred to a sect or cult, these syncretisms with Christianity cannot, strictly speaking, yet be called heresies. Their deviations from Judaic assumptions and teaching as well as from the received traditions concerning Jesus were, at the same time, obvious enough; and the pleas for unity in Ephesians and John, for example, show that the heretical divisions that later became so prominent in the history of the Church were already, during the last half of the first century, in the making.

Finally, the changes in its eschatological expectations, made necessary by the delay of the parousia, not only aggravated the problems which the Church encountered, but also produced significant modifications in its life and structure. So long as the Church, under the conviction that it was living at the end of history, understood itself as the remnant of Israel, the waiting community prepared to receive the coming Kingdom of God, divisions were unthinkable. As years stretched into decades and the ardent hope became more and more a formal doctrine, however, the emphasis, aided by Hellenistic ideas, began to shift from the eschaton to individual immortality, and the necessity for the unity of the People of God had to be supported from other premises. The early enthusiasm began to wane and personal ambitions and other differences began to assert themselves until the Church found itself facing dangers from within almost as great as those from without.

Because the Church had not reckoned with a future beyond the generation of the original apostles, it had preserved its traditions only in the forms it needed for propagating the Gospel and establishing churches. In the latter part of the century, therefore, tradition took on a new importance. Paul's letters, the only significant body of writing from the early period, very soon became important to the whole Church. The Gospels, which had heretofore existed only as oral tradition or as brief collections to be used by evangelists and teachers, were written along with the Book of Acts during this period. These documents, Paul's Letters, the Gospels, and Acts, gave the Church a much needed, though not always undisputed, foundation of tradition for its continued growth.

Church leadership, also, took on new importance. In the earlier period charismatic leaders under the direction of the apostles arose to assume, as the lists we have observed in Paul's letters show, a variety of functions in the local churches. Although they sometimes got out of hand, and the motives of some of them were not above question so that Paul found it necessary at times to defend his authority over the churches founded under his leadership, their leadership was not so serious a problem as long as the parousia was imminent. In the later period, when the apostles were no longer present to represent the tradition or to give direction and stability, and the fortuities of charismatic leadership were too precarious and even divisive, more orderly successions of authority were needed. Thus arose the three orders of the ministry of the Church—the bishops, presbyters (elders or priests), and deacons—which we find in the Pastoral Epistles. We are not to assume that these were the only offices in the churches of the time, nor were the titles unknown in the earlier period, but now the structure of the churches begins a process of standardization which led to the monarchical episcopacy which obtained in the Church during the following centuries.[1]

Among the responsibilities of these leaders was the guarding of the traditions of the Faith both as to doctrine and morals, as well as the unity and peace of the Church. Out of this new circumstance of the Church came a number of documents which gradually came to take their places in the developing New Testament Canon after the Gospels and "the Apostle" in a position not unlike that which the Writings occupy after the Torah and the Prophets in the Canon of the Old Testament.

In at least three ways the influence of Paul shows itself in these documents. The first and most obvious is the use in most of them of the literary form of the epistle. Although this device of putting short tracts in the form of letters was popular, its predominance in this last division of the New Testament is unquestionably due to the influence of Paul's correspondence (cf. II Pet. 3:15–16). The seven letters to Asian churches in Revelation 1–3 are undoubtedly in imitation of the collection of Paul's letters and show that the sevenfold shape of the collection given in the Muratorian Canon was early, if not original. The second mark of Pauline influence consists in the number of echoes in this material of the content of his correspondence. This point can, of course, be easily overemphasized. Many ideas once credited to Paul have been found to be part of the common tradition of the beginning Church in which Paul shared. Knowledge of Paul's letters is evident, nevertheless, in the content of these later writings. A third evidence of the influence Paul's letters exerted on the subsequent development of the New Testament is the appearance of his name as the author of several of these documents. The book known as the Epistle to the Hebrews, for instance, is, as we shall see, anonymous, but by the time it secured a place in the Canon it carried the name of Paul. If, as many scholars believe, Ephesians was written after the death of Paul, it also belongs among this literature as an example of Paul's influence. The three tracts addressed as Epistles to Timothy and Titus are, however, the clearest and most important evidence of the way Paul's letters have influenced the shape of the remainder of the Canon. Although they probably contain fragments of his otherwise unpublished correspondence, these documents came from the circle of

1. For the history of the ancient church orders see B. H. Streeter, *The Primitive Church* (New York: The Macmillan Company, 1929).

Paul's disciples—"the School of St. Paul." Not only because his letters were the earliest of the Epistles and comprise at least half of them, but also because his influence did so much to shape the rest of it, Paul's name rightly dominates this half of the New Testament. The documents in this division, which comprises about one fifth of the New Testament, can be divided into four groups: (1) the Pastoral Epistles, (2) Hebrews, (3) the Catholic Epistles, (4) the Apocalypse.

2. *Guard What Has Been Entrusted to You: The Pastoral Epistles*

Because they are ostensibly addressed to individual persons rather than churches, the Muratorian Canon distinguished the three Epistles to Timothy and Titus, along with Philemon, from the collection of Paul's letters to seven churches. From their concern with pastors and pastoral problems they have, since the eighteenth century, been called the "Pastoral Epistles." Although they bear the name of Paul in their salutations the evidence that as we have them they come from a later period and another hand is so strong that scholarly opinion is virtually unanimous in regarding them as Deutero-Pauline. We may summarize this evidence in the following four arguments:

1. The differences in vocabulary and style, especially vocabulary, between the Pastorals and the ten letters of Paul are more than twice as great as the widest differences among the others. As we have already seen, many factors affect the vocabulary of such documents, and therefore linguistic arguments should be used with considerable reserve. In this instance, however, the linguistic differences are not only greater, but the peculiarities in the vocabulary, particularly, are more characteristic of the second century than of the first.

2. There is also a significant development of ideas beyond the letters of Paul. Key words have developed in meaning in the direction of the apostolic fathers. The word "faith," for instance, which for Paul denoted the act of believing or putting one's trust in something or someone, in the Pastorals represents in the doctrinal sense the deposit of tradition. Although there are apparent similarities between the heresies dealt with here and in Colossians, the method of dealing with them is markedly different. In Colossians Paul reasons carefully from his claims for Christ to show that the pagan elements must be laid aside. Paul's patience reflects his sensitivity to the newly converted Colossians' difficulty in disengaging themselves from their pagan background. The errors opposed in the Pastorals have no such excuse. With bitter invective the writer lashes out against those who deliberately set themselves to distort the teachings of the Church.

Guard What Has Been Entrusted to You

3. The organization and problems in the Church, as the Pastorals picture them, belong to a later period than that of Paul. Maintaining the Church in purity and unity has taken the place of the enthusiasm for the world mission. As the parousia recedes into the future, eschatology has become a formal doctrine rather than a fervent hope. Although the organization of the earliest churches must not be underestimated, and bishops, presbyters, and deacons have been mentioned in connection with some of the earliest churches of which we have record, the functions of church officers in the Pastorals have changed, and the changes reflect the differences in the Church's life, problems, and self-understanding between Paul's time and the succeeding generations.

4. When the personal references in the Pastorals are compared with one another and with what we know of Paul's life from his other letters and Acts, contradictions appear which make it impossible for these letters to have come from him as they now stand. While it is possible, for example, that altered circumstances required Paul to change his mind between the two letters and ask Timothy, after having commanded him to stay in Ephesus, to come to him in Rome (cf. I Tim. 1:3 and II Tim. 4:9), it is unlikely. Also, although the mention of Illyricum in Romans 15:19 shows that our knowledge of his itinerary is incomplete, nevertheless, the extensive Cretan ministry (note the phrase, "in every town") implied in Titus 1:5 is impossible to fit into his Aegean ministry or the known movements of Timothy and Titus (e.g., in the Corinthian correspondence). In II Timothy 4:11 he writes, "Luke alone is with me," but ten verses later he sends greetings from four persons by name and "all the brethren." These problems cannot be answered, as has sometimes been suggested, by supposing that Paul was freed from his first imprisonment in Rome and, having returned for awhile to the Aegean world, is now enduring a second imprisonment in Rome. In Acts 20:17–38 Luke, who was surely writing after the death of Paul, makes it clear that he was then leaving the Aegean world for the last time. If these letters are from a later Aegean ministry, furthermore, it is impossible to see how Paul could have written to Timothy who had been with him for so many years, "Let no one despise your youth" (I Tim. 4:12; cf. 5:1–2; II Tim. 2:22).

The cumulative weight of these arguments is too great to be ignored. We must conclude that the documents in their present form are from a later hand.[2] P. N. Harrison, who has made a definitive study of this question, has called attention, however, to a number of passages which stand out from their contexts by reason of their similarity in style and vocabulary

---

2. For a defense of the Pauline authorship of the Pastorals see Walter Lock, *The Pastoral Epistles* (ICC), pp. xxix–xxxi.

to Paul's other letters. These passages, he believes, are fragments of letters, otherwise lost to us, which Paul had written to his two assistants, and which the author of the Pastorals had embedded in the present Epistles.[3] The idea of fragments of genuine letters being incorporated in the Pastorals has involved other scholars in attempts to identify them. While opinions differ on the identity of the fragments, and some scholars remain unconvinced of their existence, the likelihood remains that such fragments were used, and it may well be that their discovery provided the incentive for writing the Pastorals.

We should remember that literary conventions and concepts of authorship in antiquity, like methods of writing and publishing, were far different from ours. Footnotes, quotation marks, and the like to indicate the sources used were unknown. Although for one to have attempted to alter the tradition or foist onto a succeeding generation a new teaching would have incurred justifiable rejection—witness the treatment of the author of *The Acts of Paul*[4]—for a loyal disciple to seek to perpetuate by appropriate literary devices the teaching of his master (e.g., Socrates, Plato, and Epictetus) was proper and commendable. In a manner not unlike posthumous publications of compendia and anthologies of modern times, our author, appropriately choosing the popular literary form of the Epistle, has placed in circulation fragments of Paul's notes to Timothy and Titus, and with material from his other letters has applied the teaching and authority of Paul to the problems of a later time. Paul's name belongs to these documents not as the writer in the immediate sense, except for the fragments, but as the author of the teaching and tradition out of which they came. Two purposes are evident throughout the three documents: good order and qualified leadership for the life of the Church, and the safeguarding of the faithful from erroneous doctrine and immoral practice. With justice they have been called "Pastoral Handbooks." Attempts to date the publication of these works closer than some time between the end of the first century and the middle of the second have not been convincing. Probably they were published together and should be regarded, in spite of some repetitions, as a single work in three parts. The Canonical sequence, a number of interpreters believe, is incorrect. Although some scholars, on the basis of the increasing emphasis on opposition to the errorists which results, reverse the order, the most convincing dramatic progress results from simply placing Titus between I and II Timothy, leaving the dramatic fourth chapter of II Timothy with its gripping picture of the close of Paul's life as the conclusion. Our analysis will follow this order.

---

3. *The Problem of the Pastoral Epistles* (Oxford University Press, Humphrey Milford, 1921), Part III, pp. 87–135. Essentials of Harrison's statistical arguments are summarized by Fred D. Gealy, *IB*, Vol. 11, pp. 360ff.

4. See p. 359.

HOW TO BEHAVE IN THE HOUSEHOLD OF GOD:
I TIMOTHY

The structure of I Timothy consists in a preamble (ch. 1), instructions on Church order (chs. 2–3), and instructions on Church discipline (chs. 4–6). The reference in 1:3 to Timothy's remaining at Ephesus, along with references to Asia and Ephesus in II Timothy 1:15, 18, and Crete in Titus 1:5, may be a cryptic indication of the area in which the Epistles were published. In three short paragraphs the preamble sets the tone for the epistle. Timothy is urged to put a stop to the teaching of "any different doctrine" including speculations generated by "myths" and "endless geneologies" in order that the "divine training" in faith may produce the "love that issues from a pure heart and a good conscience and sincere faith" (1:5). Misguided persons must therefore be prevented from becoming "teachers of the Law."

The author's understanding of the Law in the next paragraph differs significantly from that of Paul. In this context it can hardly refer, as it does in his writing, to Torah; nor would Paul speak of using it "lawfully." The author seems sensitive to Paul's insistence that the Christian is no longer under the Law (1:9a), but since for him the word apparently means a code of morals in keeping with "sound doctrine" rather than Torah, he uses it, as the list of immoralities in 1:9b–10 shows, to refer to Paul's distinction between "the works of the flesh" and "the fruit of the Spirit" (cf. Gal. 5:17–23).

The two emphases of sound doctrine and pure morals which run throughout these documents are in the next paragraph established by an appeal to the authority of Paul. The "sound doctrine" for which the writer appeals is "in accordance with the glorious gospel" entrusted to Paul (1:11). In a passage reminiscent of I Corinthians 15:9 and Philippians 3:6 the writer depicts Paul as the one who, although the foremost of sinners and misguided persecutor and blasphemer, became an example of Christ's salvation and was appointed to his service. The preamble reaches a climax in the doxology in 1:17. By way of transition to the first main division, "Timothy" is charged in faith and a good conscience to "wage the good warfare" (1:18–19a). As a grim warning, "certain persons" are recalled who by rejecting conscience had fallen into disaster (1:19b–20).

Care for God's Church, chs. 2–3 Although there is some overlapping between the two divisions of this Epistle, the first is concerned with matters of public worship and leadership. The Church's prayers (ch. 2) are to be offered for all men, including "kings and all who are in high position" for the sake of "a quiet and peaceable" and godly life, and for the salvation of all men (2:1–4; cf. Rom. 13:1–7). The creedal formula depicting Christ as the mediator between God and man, in 2:5–6, is identified in the next two verses as a summary of Paul's teaching. While the women in modest dress and virtuous behavior remain silent (cf. I Cor. 11:3–16, 14:33b–36), the men are to pray. Interestingly, he extends Paul's argument for the subordinate place of women from the order of creation to include Eve's role in the fall of Adam (2:14).

The qualifications for the offices of bishop and deacon are considered next (ch. 3). Each is to have only one wife, to live sober, gentle, exemplary, lives, and to show by the management of their own families their ability to govern the Church. Not prone to avarice or gossip, they are to be able teachers well grounded in the faith. To avoid the temptation of the novice to conceit, the bishop must not be a recent convert. Similarly, the deacons are to be subjected to a period of testing. It is not clear whether the reference in verse 11 is to the wives of the clergy or to deaconesses. Nothing specific is said, unfortunately, of the duties and functions of these offices. Later in 4:13 "Timothy" himself is exhorted to "attend to the public reading of scripture, to preaching, to teaching." In 5:17 a distinction is made among the elders (presbyters), whose qualifications are not discussed until Titus 1:5–6, by attaching special importance to those who preach and teach. The underlying assumption, of course, in all three of these Epistles is that the officers being addressed have the authority and responsibility to govern the churches in their care (cf. 5:19), but the relationships and specific responsibilties of the several ministers remain obscure. Beyond the phrase addressed to "Timothy" himself, "when the elders laid their hands upon you" (4:14b), and the exhortation not to "be hasty in the laying on of hands" (5:22a), we are given no information as to how they were selected and set in office. Although this passage and the one in the first chapter of Titus provide us a glimpse into the emerging orders of clergy that were to become standard in Church, they leave open questions which have been the subjects of endless debate, and which lie beyond our purpose here.[5] After a personal note, the author concludes this division with a confession which probably functioned as a creed (or hymn?) in the worship of the churches involved. In two other places in this Epistle, 1:15a and 4:9–10, sayings are introduced by the formulae, "The saying is sure" (cf. 2:5–6 and 3:1). These tantalizingly brief glimpses into the worship in this period afford us some idea of the theology which controlled the developing liturgies of the Church.

Aim at Righteousness, chs. 4–6 The remainder of I Timothy consists in instructions regulating the life and teaching of the Church. Ascetic prac-

5. For a good discussion of these problems see Fred D. Gealy, "I and II Timothy, Titus," *IB*, Vol. 11, pp. 344–347.

tices are strongly condemned (4:1–5). Good doctrine and godly living are opposed to "silly myths" (cf. 1:4) and mere physical discipline; "Timothy" is in every way to reinforce his prophetic gift by an example "in speech and conduct, in love, in faith, in purity" (4:6–16). A brief bit of advice on diplomacy in dealing with older men emphasizes again the comparative youth of "Timothy" (5:1–2; cf. 4:12). There follows a long section on the care and discipline of widows. Where possible they are to be cared for by relatives; young widows should remarry. Widows, by the time of these Epistles, constituted an organized religious order (cf. Acts 6:1ff.) which occupied itself with prayers and good deeds. To prevent members from leaving the order to marry, indulging in reprehensible conduct, or otherwise breaking their commitment, the author places a minimum age limit of sixty years (5:3–16). There follows a paragraph on remuneration (cf. I Cor. 9:14), discipline, and caution in ordaining presbyters, a bit of advice on using wine for stomach ailments, and a saying reminiscent of Mark 4:22, para., on the impossibility of hiding anything either good or evil (5:17–24).

In rapid succession the writer takes up several further matters. The exhortation to slaves in 6:1–2 is virtually a copy of that in Colossians 4:1–6 (cf. Eph. 6:5–9). Teachers are warned against conceit, contentiousness, and simony. The latter is expanded into a warning to "those who desire to be rich" that includes the well-known saying, "the love of money is the root of all evils" (6:3–10). In contrast "Timothy" is called upon to "aim at righteousness," which is described by a characteristic list of virtues, in order to conform to the "good confession" which they publicly made. The exhortation ends with a reference to the coming of the parousia which concludes with an ascription and is phrased in such liturgical language that its character as a formal doctrine stands in sharp contrast to the fervent hope of Paul (6:11–16). With a brief warning to the rich not to trust in their riches but to use them for charitable deeds (cf. Mt. 5:19–21, 33, *passim*), and a parting warning against contentious errors, the Epistle ends.

AMEND WHAT IS DEFECTIVE:
TITUS

With exception of the last paragraph, the Epistle to Titus is almost completely a restatement and condensation of I Timothy. Beginning with a salutation based on the triad, faith, knowledge, and hope (1:1–4), the writer, in a condensed version of I Timothy 3:1–13, outlines the qualifications of elders (presbyters) and bishops. By way of contrast to these qualifications, he describes "many insubordinate men" who are guilty of deception and simony and therefore "must be silenced." The mention of "the circumcision party" (cf. Gal. 2:12) and "Jewish myths" coupled with the proverb from the legendary pagan poet Epimenides that Cretans are liars[6] suggests the presence in the Church of this period of a syncretistic movement, not unlike the one we encountered in Galatians, which was enamored of Jewish practices. The phrases can hardly refer to a remnant of conservative Jewish Christianity. The author's condemnation of asceticism is parallel to that in I Timothy 4:7–8.

The remainder of Titus is concerned with the teaching of sound doctrine and Christian virtue. Paralleling his discussion of older men, widows, and younger widows in I Timothy 5:1–16, the author presents exhortations, which incorporate a typical list of virtues of love, sobriety, gentleness, and chastity in the form of a chiasm for older men, older women, young women, and younger men (2:1–8). A condensed version of the admonition, in I Timothy 6:1–2, to slaves (2:9–10) leads to another formal statement of eschatology (2:11–15), cf. I Timothy 6:14–16). In a passage which begins with an echo of Paul's exhortation to civil obedience in Romans 13:1–7 (cf. I Tim. 2:1–2) the writer calls the Christians to industrious, courteous, and peaceful living in contrast to their former evil ways (3:1–3; cf. I Tim. 1:9–10) from which they have been saved by the appearance of "God our Savior." That this last phrase occurs in a passage which by the words, "The saying is sure," in verse 8a is shown to be a liturgical (baptismal?) formula is important for the light it sheds on the development of Christology in this period. With further exhortations to avoid foolish controversies and to expel any who persist in factiousness the section ends (3:8b–11; cf. I Tim. 1:3–5; 5:20–21; 6:18–19). The brief personal note in 3:12–15 is one of the passages which P. N. Harrison believes to be a fragment of Paul's otherwise unknown letters. The remaining fragments he so identifies are in II Timothy.[7]

TAKE YOUR SHARE OF SUFFERING:

II TIMOTHY

II Timothy is more personal and dramatic than either I Timothy or Titus. The dominant theme is the call to follow Paul's example in "suffering as a good soldier of Christ Jesus" (2:3). Three times this point is dramatically made. The words, "Take your share of suffering," in 1:18b and 2:3, are followed first by, "I suffer as I do," in 1:12a, and by "I am suffering and wearing fetters," in 2:9a. The order is reversed in the third instance as the reference in 3:11 to "my sufferings" is followed in 4:5 with the exhortation to "endure suffering." The theme reaches its climax in the dramatic picture, with which the Epistle ends, of Paul's last im-

---

6. On Pagan quotations in the New Testament including this one see Foakes Jackson and Lake, *The Beginnings of Christianity,* Vol. V, pp. 246–251.
7. See *The Problem of the Pastoral Epistles,* p. 115.

prisonment and his farewell in 4:6–22. Parallel to this theme is the exhortation to "Timothy" not to "be ashamed of testifying to our Lord, nor of me his prisoner," in 1:8, which is followed in 1:12b by Paul's example, "I am not ashamed," and in 1:16 by the example of Onesiphorus, who "was not ashamed of my chains." These patterns are interwoven with recitations of the Gospel, moral exhortations, warnings of the evils of the "last days," and personal notes. Along with the last paragraph of Titus, according to Harrison's estimation, almost one third of this Epistle is made up of fragments from otherwise unknown letters of Paul.[8]

A thanksgiving and prayer follow the salutation which are much more in the pattern of Paul's letters than the openings of I Timothy and Titus. The references to the mother and grandmother of Timothy may be based on actual knowledge of his background. Harrison believes these references and the salutation, 1:1–2, 5, to be fragments from Paul. Surprisingly, in 1:6, Timothy's ordination is by the hands of Paul rather than the elders (cf. I Tim. 4:14). In the remainder of the chapter Timothy is exhorted to "rekindle the gifts of God," and unashamedly testify to the Lord, taking his "share of suffering for the gospel in the power of God." The recital of the Gospel which follows in verses 9 and 10 is a compendium of characteristically Pauline statements, but the description of him as a preacher and apostle and teacher (vss. 11–12) is less so. Still less characteristic of Paul are the formal reference to "that Day" and the exhortation to "follow the pattern of sound words which you have heard from me" and to "guard the truth" which follow (vss. 12–14). Who the faithless men in verse 15 were is impossible to tell. They are named here as a foil for the courage and kindness of Onesiphorus. Verses 16–18, Harrison believes, are also a fragment of a Pauline letter.

In the first part of chapter 2 the pattern is repeated. "Timothy" is again exhorted to be strong and bear suffering. This time, however, he is advised in addition to entrust the tradition he received from Paul to "faithful men" who will in turn hand it on to still others (2:1–2). Instead of a recitation of the Gospel, furthermore, the reference to suffering is followed by the figures of the good soldier who remains unencumbered with mundane affairs, the athlete who plays by the rules, and the farmer who has the first share of the crops (2:3–7). The reference to Paul's suffering in the next verse, on the other hand, is embedded in a liturgical recital of the Gospel (vs. 8) and another "saying" on endurance which may be a fragment of a hymn (vss. 11–13).

There follows in the remainder of the chapter a series of exhortations characteristic of the Pastorals. The seriousness of doctrinal controversies

8. *The Problem of the Pastoral Epistles*, pp. 115–127.

in the Church in this period is indicated by the frequent exhortations such as this one against them (2:14–19, and 22–26). Although the apostate Hymenaeus (2:17b) is mentioned along with an Alexander (cf. the "coppersmith" in 4:14) in I Timothy 1:20, these men, like Phygelus and Hermogenes in 1:15b, are otherwise unknown. Their notion that the resurrection had already passed recalls the misunderstanding which had so disturbed the Thessalonians (cf. II Thess. 2:1–12). The analogy which stands in the middle of these exhortations (vss. 20–21) is a strange combination of Paul's analogy of the buildings in I Corinthians 3:12–15 and his figure of the potter in Romans 9:20–21. Not only are the figures here unrealistic, but Paul's point that God had the right to determine what is to be noble and what is to be menial is completely lost in the exhortation, by cleansing one's self from the ignoble, to become noble.

After a grim picture of the apostasies and immoralities, like those that plagued Moses, which will characterize "the last days," the author returns once more to the theme of suffering. In a reference to Paul's persecutions in the Galatian cities, which Harrison believes to be another fragment, Paul's sufferings are recalled in order to state the point which has been implied all through the Pastorals—indeed throughout the New Testament —that persecution is a mark of faithfulness to Christ. An exhortation to study the Scriptures, all of which are "inspired by God" and equip the "man of God" for "every good work," leads to the solemn "charge" to "Timothy" to "preach the word," and patiently to rebuke, exhort, and teach. The section closes as it opens with a warning of the coming apostasy, and the pattern of following Paul's example of suffering, which controls this Epistle, is completed for the third time (1:8–2:3; 3:11 and 4:5) with the closing words calling for "Timothy" to "endure suffering" and "fulfill your ministry" (3:1–4:5).

The rest of the Epistle (4:6–22), which may be, as Harrison believes, made up entirely of fragments from letters from Paul, is a picture of Paul's final days in a Roman prison, saddened by the desertion of Demas, harassed by the opposition of "Alexander the coppersmith," but still full of courage in the Lord. Whether they actually come from his pen or were supplied by this admiring author, the words which open this picture are a worthy tribute to Paul:

> For I am already on the point of being sacrificed; the time of my departure has come. I have fought the good fight, I have finished the race, I have kept the faith. Henceforth there is laid up for me the crown of righteousness, which the Lord, the righteous judge, will award to me on that Day, and not only to me but also to all who have loved his appearing. (II Tim. 4:6–8)

3. *The Mediator of a New Covenant: Hebrews*

The traditional title of this work, The Epistle of St. Paul to the Hebrews, is virtually a complete misnomer. So little is known of its origins and original destination that the scholarly speculations have from the earliest times run the gamut of possibilities. Although, as modern interpreters often lament, it is one of the most neglected and least understood of the books in the New Testament, it is a remarkable document. The clearest example in the New Testament of self-conscious literature, it is also one of the most deliberately theological treatises. Yet its manifest purpose is the totally practical one of meeting a crisis in the Church of its time. As we should expect from a problem so enigmatic as this one, modern opinions vary widely and the literature on the debate is large.[9] For our purposes a brief discussion of the most probable conclusions will suffice.

The document is, to begin with, neither a letter nor an epistle. Although the author has in mind a specific problem and concrete circumstances, he is not writing an *ad hoc* letter to specific persons and has not chosen to use the popular epistolary form. The document begins with a prologue remarkably similar to that of the Gospel of John. That in its present form the book closes with personal notes, greetings, and a grace, which as we shall see can hardly have been original, cannot offset the lack of address and salutation in the opening. Like Acts and I John this document is a book and can only be called an epistle for convenience because of its place in the collection of letters and epistles which comprises most of the second half of the New Testament.

In style the book represents the best literary Greek in the New Testament and indicates the work of an author possessed of a very good Greek education. This observation alone is sufficient to rule out Pauline authorship. Other evidence within the document leads, however, to the same conclusion. The underlying dualism, the interest in Israel's cultus, the absence of the issues and concerns which most characterized Paul, and the author's deliberate identification, in 2:3b, with the second generation of Christians all locate the author in a later period than that of Paul. Even those references that have occasionally been cited as representing Pauline influence more probably represent the common tradition of the Early Church.

9. For a good survey of the debate and literature see James Price, *Interpreting the New Testament*, pp. 493–502, and notes. See also Morton S. Enslin, *Christian Beginnings*, pp. 308–316. Alexander Purdy provides a helpful selection of extracts from Patristic sources in his "Introduction," *IB*, Vol. 11, pp. 581–583. An excellent analysis of the literary style is provided in James Moffatt, *The Epistle to the Hebrews* (ICC), pp. lvi–lxiv.

That the document itself does not identify the author in any way makes the tradition of Pauline authorship all the more surprising. But for the insistence of the Alexandrian Fathers, Clement and Origen, it probably would have remained anonymous. Their curious reasoning, which, while frankly acknowledging that the style was unlike Paul's writing, insisted that the content in some way went back to him, suggests that they were more anxious to use Paul's name to gain Canonical acceptance than to discover the true author of the book. Origen's statement, regularly quoted in this connection, that only God knows who wrote it, was meant to refer only to the actual composition rather than the ideas, but is true in a way he did not intend.

Probably this misinterpretation was fortunate. For without it the book might well have been lost. The use of Paul's name succeeded, and before the end of the fourth century Hebrews was accepted into the Canon in the West as well as the East. It is ironic that the Western Church, which was reluctant to accept its alleged Pauline authorship and canonicity, has in the use of it in I Clement (ca. A.D. 95) provided us with the earliest external notice in its existence. The attitude of the Western Church is probably well represented in the statements of Jerome who, while gladly welcoming Hebrews to the Canon, had serious misgivings about Paul's connection with it. In his sketch of the life of Paul he wrote:

> The epistle which is called the *Epistle to the Hebrews* is not considered his (Paul's), on account of its difference from the others in style and language, but it is reckoned, either according to Tertullian to be the work of Barnabas, or according to others, to be by Luke the Evangelist or Clement afterwards bishop of the church at Rome, who, they say, arranged and adorned the ideas of Paul in his own language, though to be sure, since Paul was writing to Hebrews and was in disrepute among them he may have omitted his name from the salutation on this account. He being a Hebrew wrote Hebrew, that is his own tongue and most fluently while the things which were eloquently written in Hebrew were more eloquently turned into Greek and this is the reason why it seems to differ from other epistles of Paul.[10]

That this book was written for Jewish Christians, as the term "Hebrews" is intended to imply, is also no more than an inference from its preoccupation with the cultus of the ancient Tabernacle. Not all scholars have been as ready to give up this part of the traditional title as they have Paul's authorship. Some have contended that the purpose of Hebrews

10. *Lives of Illustrious Men,* Ch. V, "Paul." Philip Schaff and Henry Wace, *Nicene and Post-Nicene Fathers,* tr. Ernest Cushing Richardson, 2nd series, Vol. III, p. 363.

is to prevent Jewish Christians from lapsing back into Judaism.[11] The evidence is, however, against this part of the title as well. One of the striking characteristics of Hebrews, for example, is its failure to mention the Temple in Jerusalem anywhere in its treatment of the Jewish cultus. Attempts to find in Hebrews some evidence either that the Temple was still standing at the time of writing or had been destroyed by Titus (A.D. 70) have not succeeded simply because the Temple had no relation to the author's purpose. Such issues as circumcision and the gentile mission, and the place of the Law in the life of the Church, which would be essential to such a purpose, are absent. The author in his treatment of Israel's cultus confines himself to the Torah itself.

There are, on the other hand, clear indications of other interests and purposes. The reader of Hebrews must be struck immediately by the author's extensive use of Scripture and the care with which he depicts the sacrificial cultus only to show how it has been superseded by the true sacrifice in the Crucifixion of Jesus. In developing this theme he has assumed the reader's knowledge of the Old Testament but not necessarily of contemporary Judaism.

We have seen in the documents we have examined thus far how the Christians' use of Israel's Scriptures presented problems and required their reinterpretation. From this standpoint Hebrews is an approach from another angle, dealing with another aspect of a problem with which each in his own way, Paul, John, and the authors of the Synoptic Gospels have wrestled. To say that Jesus is the "mediator of a new covenant" (12:24) would make no sense without a clear understanding of the old covenant, and it is this understanding that the author has attempted to supply. His success can be seen in the way his idea of the typological role of the Torah has been used in Christian treatments of the Old Testament since.

A careful reading of Hebrews will show, however, that its author had a more immediate and pressing problem in mind. The primary purpose of the book is best seen by noting the way in which the author has developed the argument. Two words, "better" and "therefore," are the key terms that control the structure of Hebrews and represent in turn its two parallel lines of argument. The entire book consists, in other words, in a series of theological statements about Jesus, each of which is followed by a practical exhortation based thereon. The pattern can be stated in a formula: "Jesus is better than ———, therefore let us ———." Obviously, then, the real concern of the author is to be found in the consequent exhortations. When we examine the sections introduced by the word "therefore," we discover that the first several of them are quite

---

11. One of the most recent arguments for this interpretation is that of William Manson, *The Epistle to the Hebrews* (London: Hodder and Stoughton, Ltd., 1951).

general, but as the argument progresses, they become more specific until they reach a climax in chapter 12. In the first of these (2:1–4) the readers are exhorted simply to pay closer attention lest they "drift away" from the salvation of which they have heard. Later, in chapter 6, however, we are told that those who have once been enlightened by the Gospel, should they "commit apostasy," can never be restored to the faith. Although we are not yet told what this danger of apostasy is, the intensity of the warning and length of the passage indicate that the warning is close to the heart of the author's purpose. When he comes again, in 10:19–39, to his exhortation, after an extended exposition of the high priesthood of Christ, this warning is repeated and coupled with an exhortation to greater zeal, on the one hand, and a renewal of their former courage on the other hand, in the face of suffering and abuse. The climax of the argument is reached in the exhortations of chapter 12. Here Jesus is set before the readers as a model of endurance so that they will "not grow weary or fainthearted." "In your struggle against sin you have not yet resisted to the point of shedding your blood" (12:4). The implication is clear that other Christians have shed their blood and the possibilities are real that some of the readers may be called upon to do so. It is not accidental that, in the recital of the models of faith in chapter 11, faith is exemplified increasingly as the recital progresses by perseverance against obstacles and dangers until it ends in a list of martyrs.

A complex of problems had arisen in the Church in the author's time. With the delay of the parousia and the rise of a second generation of Christians, the original enthusiasm and fervor had begun to wane. At the same time, harassment and sporadic persecutions were increasing, with the result that many Christians were leaving the Church in disillusionment and fear. By a vigorous argument showing how essential for their salvation is an enduring faith in Jesus, and what are the resources for help in that faith, the author is attempting to stiffen the spines of his readers and restore to them the zeal of earlier days against the rising tide of persecution. The persecutions which occasioned Hebrews were destined to increase periodically until the Church, after the frightful attempt by Diocletian to stamp out Christianity, found relief in the Peace of Constantine in A.D. 317. The idea that lapsed Christians cannot be restored was also to play an important role in the Church's life. In the next century the shepherd of Hermas was to announce a special period of grace during which lapsed Christians would be admitted for one more chance, but the problem continued until it precipitated the well-known Donatist controversy in the fourth century.

The book of Hebrews stands near the beginning of that history. The identification of the author with the second generation of Christians in 2.3 (cf. the "former days" in 10:32–34) and the seriousness of the problem of persecution require a date sometime after Nero (A.D. 68). That Clement of Rome made use of it in his first Epistle (ca. A.D. 95) requires a date, on the other hand, not much later than A.D. 90. In his famous letter to Trajan concerning the Christians of Bithynia (ca. A.D. 114), Pliny the Younger claims to have examined a number of suspects who admitted to having been Christians but had left the Church some twenty-five years earlier.[12] This exodus from the Church would have occurred about A.D. 89. Probably it was in the same period and similar circumstances that Hebrews was written.

At several points there are similarities between Hebrews and the fourth Gospel. Attention is often called to the similarities in the prologues of the two works with their emphases on the Son's preexistence and role in creation and the new revelation which he brought into the world. Hebrews also shows a similar attitude to that of John toward Scripture. Hebrews may, in fact, be said to have carried out the program of demonstrating how the Scriptures testify of Jesus suggested in John 5:39–47. Both have elements which bear superficial resemblances to Alexandrian (Philonic) thought. More important is the emphasis in both on remaining in the faith (cf. Jn. 6:66–69; 15:1–10, *passim*, with Heb. 6:4–12; 10:35–39; 12:1–4, *passim*). In John's situation the harassments and opposition came from the synagogues; in Hebrews the persecutions were from the gentiles. The two sources of persecution, if we are to believe Acts (cf. 14:19; 17:5–9; 18:12–17, *passim*), were not unrelated.

One more matter requires our attention before we turn to the structure and content of Hebrews. In 10:1 the words, "For since the law has but a shadow of the good things to come instead of the true form of these realities . . ." succinctly state the thesis of the theological argument. This idea that the ceremonies prescribed by the Law are only a shadow of heavenly realities (see 8:1–2) sounds thoroughly Platonic. When coupled with the author's typological or symbolic treatment of Israel's history in the earlier part of the book, the idea appears to be very similar to those of Philo. A number of scholars have, in consequence, assumed that the author of Hebrews uses Philo's allegorical method based on a Platonic dualism, to solve the problem of eschatology created by the delay of the parousia. The realism of the historical eschatology is thereby dissolved into a symbolic expression of the relationship between this shadowy world of materiality and the spiritual eternal world which is truly real.[13]

That the theology of Hebrews is built on a dualism is obvious, but its resemblances to Alexandrian Platonism are of less significance than the

12. This letter has been reprinted in whole or in part many times. For convenient sources see Maurice Goguel, *The Birth of Christianity* (New York: The Macmillan company, 1954), pp. 537–539; Moses Hadas, *A History of Rome* (Garden City, N.J.: Doubleday and Company, Inc., 1956), pp. 129–131.
13. See Moffatt, *Hebrews* (ICC), pp. xxi-xxiv.

differences. The author of Hebrews does not, in the first place, allegorize Israel's history. His argument rests on the actual historicity and efficacy of the Torah's story and ritual (cf. 2:2–3, 10:28–29, 12:25–29) and moves in characteristically rabbinic fashion from the lesser to the greater. The author's basic assumption is the thoroughly Biblical one that since God acts in consistent patterns, his future actions are disclosed and anticipated in the past. The dualism of Hebrews, consequently, is a temporal dualism of time and eternity which takes seriously the Hebraic concept of linear time. It is significant that Jesus' great sacrifice, the eternal and final reality of which Israel's entire cultus was a "shadow," took place within earthly time and space. In the same way the author can take seriously and literally the eschatological hope of the parousia. Unlike the Alexandrian Platonists, he makes no metaphysical distinctions between the reality of time and eternity. Eternity is for him timeless, so that events which have eternal dimension stand equally related to every moment of time. Yet time is the theater of God's saving activity which, in the author's view, began with creation and has moved progressively toward its maturation in the final age which Jesus has ushered in. Beyond this age stands the eternity which brought time into being and has stood above it and interacted with it throughout human history. It was not the problem of eschatology which the author was trying to solve with this dualism, it was rather the problem of Christianity's relation to the Torah.

MUCH SUPERIOR TO ANGELS, CHS. 1–2

In the prologue (1:1–4) two points are established that are basic to both sides of the entire argument of the book. Like the Logos in the prologue of John's Gospel, the Son in the prologue of Hebrews is co-creator of the historical world "and bears the very stamp of his (God's) nature." As the Son preceded the created universe, he is therefore greater than anything in it, including the angels. As in John the Logos became flesh and, as the life which "was the light of men," entered the world, so in Hebrews God "has spoken unto us by a Son." It is the Son's priority over creation which stands back of the entire theological argument of Hebrews as his prophetic speech stands back of the hortatory argument. So also the contrast between God's message in various times and ways by the prophets of former days and his final speech "in these last days" by a Son provides the pattern of the argument as well as its eschatological setting.

The mention of the Son's superiority over the angels at the end of the prologue leads immediately to the first of his main theological points: Jesus is superior to the angels (1:5–2:18). In the brief hortatory section we learn the reason for this point. The Law was "declared by angels." Jesus' superiority over them establishes his priority over the Law. With a chain of quotations from the Psalms and one each from Deuteronomy and II Samuel, he argues that Jesus is not only God's son, but in contrast to the angels who are only created servants, he has been enthroned forever over the universe (1:5–14). It follows from this point that if the Law conveyed by angels had validity so that those who disobeyed were punished, how much more serious will be the consequences of failing to heed the salvation declared by the Lord himself and attested by miracles and "gifts of the Holy Spirit" (2:1–4).

Turning to the eschatological perspective, the author bases the final stage of his comparison of Jesus with angels on the eighth Psalm. The Psalm says that under man, who was for a short while made lower than the angels, everything has been placed in subjection. Two points follow from this statement: First, it is man rather than angels for whom God is concerned. Second, since the statement that all things have been subjected to man is manifestly not true, the statement must have another meaning. That meaning is Jesus, who in the incarnation "was made lower than the angels," but after his Crucifixion became the pioneer in fulfilling the psalm. In anticipation of a later point the author discusses the meaning of the Crucifixion. Because of his full identification with man, Jesus was able by sharing man's death to break its power, freeing man for his true destiny, and is now able as a merciful and understanding high priest "to help those who are tempted" (2:5–18).

MORE GLORY THAN MOSES, CHS. 3–4

Having established Jesus' superiority over the angelic bearers of Torah, both by the superiority of his message of salvation and his role as the pioneer of man's eschatological destiny, the writer turns now to the beginnings of the nation of Israel as God's house. It is interesting that, in contrast to Paul who symbolized the beginnings of the nation by Abraham and the Law by Moses, the author associates Moses only with the founding of the nation in terms of the Exodus and wilderness journey. This wilderness journey is the setting for the author's treatment of the Old Testament throughout the remainder of the book. Jesus is superior to Moses first because as co-creator he is the builder of the house, and second because, while Moses was a faithful servant in God's house, Christ as a Son was over the house (3:1–6). The story of Israel's rebellion in the wilderness affords the writer an excellent opportunity for his second exhortation. As those who faithlessly rebelled against God in the wilderness were condemned to die there without ever seeing the Promised Land, so, too, any readers who in unbelief "fall away from the living God" will be excluded from "his rest." "For we share in Christ, if only we hold our first confidence firm to the end" (3:14). That Psalm 95:7–11, on which his exhortation is based, really applies to the author's own time he shows by the fact that if the original arrival in Canaan under Joshua had been God's objective for his people, the psalmist would not afterward have used the term "today." Since nothing is hidden from God, the reader must strive to enter the true "rest" by avoiding the sort of disobedience from which the wanderers in the wilderness fell. Although the exhortations are still quite general, the direction in which the writer is moving, especially in the closing comment, becomes apparent. The Christians are here exhorted to "hold fast" their confession because Jesus the sympathetic high priest, through his own triumphant endurance, can make their endurance possible (3:7–4:16).

A PRIEST FOREVER, CHS. 5–7

At several points (2:17; 3:1; 4:14) the writer has already identified Jesus as the high priest of the believers. He comes now to develop that point on the basis of the words of Psalm 110:4: "Thou art a priest forever, after the order of Melchizedek," in order to show that Jesus is the reality toward which Israel's priestly cultus pointed. Beginning with three assumptions concerning priests: that the priest is chosen to function before God on behalf of men; that the priest being human and sinful, although he can for that reason "deal gently" with wayward humanity, has to offer sacrifices for himself as well as for others; and that the priest is not self-appointed but "called by God," the author measures the priesthood of Jesus by those assumptions. From a combination of Psalm 2:7 (cf. Heb. 1:5) and 110:4 he shows that Jesus was the divinely chosen Son whose obedient suffering made him the "source of eternal salvation to all who obey him" (5:1–10). All three of the author's assumptions relative to priests are briefly implied of Jesus here, but he postpones developing them until after his third and crucial exhortation.

By an almost contemptuous criticism of his readers' immaturity and a challenge to them to move on to maturity, the author indicates that he is stating something new, and underscoring the importance of what he is about to say, dares them to consider it. From his ominous warning that there can be no readmission and therefore no hope for those who leave the faith, he reveals the fact that his concern is not simply to reinvigorate the zeal of his readers but to prevent any from leaving the Church. Diplomatically, he expresses his confidence in them, hoping that they will maintain their earnestness "until the end" (5:11–6:12).

Returning to the matter of the priesthood of Jesus (6:13–7:28) the writer places the discussion in the framework of God's promise to "bless and multiply" Abraham. In that promise God disclosed "the unchanging character of his purpose" which is mediated to the believer by Jesus who is "a high priest forever after the order of Melchizedek." Since Jesus was of the tribe of Judah, he cannot be a priest in terms of Torah (7:14); he therefore must be a priest in a different order. In the enigmatic story in Genesis 14:17–20 of Abraham and Melchizedek,[14] the author finds the evidence that not only establishes Jesus' priesthood in spite of his Judean lineage but shows him also to be superior to the Levitical order. That Abraham paid homage to Melchizedek as the "king of Salem" and "priest of the most high God" acknowledged Melchizedek to be his superior. (With a fanciful exegesis and etymology he elaborates the parallels between Melchizedek and Jesus as the eternal king of righteousness and peace in 7:2b–3.) The Levitical priests were descendants of Abraham; therefore a priest after Melchizedek's order is superior to them as Melchizedek himself was superior to Abraham. Since Psalm 110:4 has declared Jesus to be "a priest after the order of Melchizedek" by a divine oath, he is superior to the Levitical priests. As the promise of another day in Psalm 95:7 proved that Canaan was only an anticipation of the true "rest" (4:6–10), so now the declaration in Psalm 110:4 of a priest after the order of Melchizedek shows the Levitical priesthood to be a shadow of the true one. Because Jesus' priesthood stands outside Israel's covenant Law, however, it requires a new one. In anticipation of the next step in his argument dealing with this point the writer simply asserts that God's oath in appointing Jesus a priest indicates that Jesus is "the surety of a better covenant." In summary he compares the two priesthoods:

Levitical Priesthood	Jesus' Priesthood
Many mortal	One eternal
Sinful, in need of atonement	Sinless, atonement only for others
Without an oath	By God's oath
Under the Law	Under a better covenant
Sons of Aaron	Son of God
In earthly sanctuaries	In heaven before the throne of Grace
Daily sacrifices	Once for all
Animal sacrifices	He offered himself

THE MORE PERFECT TENT, CHS. 8–10

Having shown Jesus, as the preexistent son of God and co-creator of the universe, to be superior to the angelic messengers who declared the Law to Israel, to have priority over Moses the founder of the nation, and to be a priest of a higher order than the Levitical priesthood, the author in the final stage of his argument brings all these claims for Jesus together in a climactic statement of the nature and function of the high priesthood of Jesus. He begins with a statement of his thesis: Jesus is our high priest in the heavenly sanctuary before the presence of God. Of this heavenly reality the earthly priesthood and tent under the Law are "a copy and shadow" (8:1–5). On the premise that the three essentials for a valid

14. On this story see Cuthbert A. Simpson, "Genesis," *IB,* Vol. 1, pp. 596–598.

sacrifice are a covenant, a sanctuary, and a gift, the author proceeds to compare Jesus' sacrifice with those of the Levitical priesthood on these points.

To show that Jesus mediates a better covenant (cf. 7:22), he argues, as in reference to the true rest (4:6–10) and the priesthood of Jesus (7:11), that if the first covenant, i.e., the Law, had been adequate there would have been no reason for a second one. In a lengthy quotation from Jeremiah 31:31–34 he shows that a new covenant has, in fact, been promised and the first one is therefore obsolete. By an elaborate description of the rituals of the tent in the wilderness, he makes the distinctions between the outer and inner sanctuaries, and the contrast between the daily sacrifices and the annual sacrifice on the Day of Atonement symbolizes the contrast between Israel's cultus and the true sacrifice of Christ. So the "shadow" itself indicates its typological relationship to the ultimate reality of Christ. For when Christ entered once for all into the heavenly sanctuary of the presence of God bearing his own Crucifixion as his sacrifice, the earthly shrine was superseded. In a passage reminiscent of Paul's argument for freedom from the Law in Romans 7:1–6, the writer reasons that as a will becomes effective only at the death of its maker, so the new covenant was brought into force by the death of Jesus. Both covenants were, in fact, ratified by blood—"without the shedding of blood there is no forgiveness of sins"—the first which was a "copy of the true one" by the blood of calves and goats, and the second by Christ's sacrifice "once for all at the end of the age." Christ, therefore, will appear a second time "to save those who are eagerly waiting for him" (8:6–9:28).

Once more, to emphasize the adequacy and finality of Christ's sacrifice, the priesthood after Melchizedek, and the new covenant, the writer argues that if the old animal sacrifices had been adequate they would not have been repeated. "Where there is forgiveness of these, there is no longer any offering for sin" (10:18). The Law was, therefore, only "a shadow of the good things to come," which have now come to reality in Christ. As the ultimate priest he has offered himself as the true sacrifice presented in the true sanctuary in heaven according to the terms of the new covenant based on better promises of an eternal inheritance. He now sits at the right hand of God awaiting the final vanquishing of his enemies (Ps. 110:1; cf. Heb. 1:13; 2:7–10).

The exhortation which follows calls first for a confident appropriation of the benefits of Christ's priesthood in faith, second for holding fast the confession of hope, and third for stirring "up one another to love and good works." As they see the "Day" approaching the believers are not to neglect the meetings. If one sins "deliberately after receiving the knowledge of the truth," he has no hope, but faces the awful prospects of judgment. In another instance of the argument from the lesser to the greater, the writer warns that if those violating the Law of Moses died without mercy, the punishment for spurning the Son of God will be much greater. The author becomes specific. Asking his readers to recall their zeal and faithfulness in former days, he pleads for endurance and confidence. They need only hold on "yet a little while."

FAITH IS THE ASSURANCE, CHS. 11–13

In chapter 11, one of the celebrated passages of the New Testament, the author reinforces his exhortations by another approach. By means of a list of the heroes of faith and endurance from the Old Testament, he seeks to inspire the reader to emulation. This faith which these stalwarts exemplified is the advance payment, the certification of the hope which the divine promise has inspired. Beginning with creation itself and in a remarkable survey of Old Testament history he displays the courage, trust, and endurance of the ancient heroes, none of whom had as yet received "what was promised, since God had foreseen something better for us, that apart from us they should not be made perfect (complete)" (11:40).

In the final exhortation which follows (ch. 12), the author pictures a stadium in which these heroes are seated witnessing the race which he and his readers in their turn must run. Strengthened by the example of Jesus who is the origin of their faith and who will bring it to the realization of its object, they are to persevere in running the course they are called upon to run. They have not yet been called upon to shed blood for the faith, let them not grow weary or fainthearted. Their persecution is a discipline of the Lord which they should regard as evidence of his loving concern for them. Warned by the example of Esau who sold his birthright and could afterward find no repentance, let them gather their strength and strive for peace and holiness. The awful terrors at Mount Sinai are nothing compared with those of the coming Day. "Therefore let us be grateful for receiving a kingdom that cannot be shaken, and thus let us offer to God acceptable worship, with reverence and awe; for our God is a consuming fire" (12:28–29).

How much if any of chapter 13 belongs to the original book is impossible to say. The climax in 12:28–29 makes a satisfactory ending well suited to the mood of the book. What follows in the first seventeen verses of chapter 13, furthermore, are traditional moral exhortations scarcely in keeping with the genius of the author of Hebrews. The passage exhorts the readers to brotherly love, charitable action, and morality. They are to follow the examples of their leaders, avoid heresies, and above all follow Jesus in enduring suffering and ostracism, and remain faithful in worship and obedience to their leaders. Several echoes of the body of Hebrews occur in ways which suggest that an editor has added this section to supply what he felt was a lack of emphasis on the traditional moral themes.

Verses 18–21 have the appearance of a fragment of a Pauline letter which became attached either accidentally, or perhaps to support the claims of Pauline authorship some were making for it. The benediction and doxology give the ending the appearance of an epistle, which may therefore be all the editor who added it intended. The second epistolary ending in verses 22–24 is surely an accident. Although it appears even more likely to be a fragment of one of Paul's letters, it adds nothing to the Pauline effect or to the book. The character of the book itself makes it highly unlikely that either of these endings belongs here. That both of them were included by the original author is impossible.[15]

4. *To the Twelve Tribes in the Dispersion: The Catholic Epistles*

The most immediately obvious characteristic of the seven brief Epistles which follow Hebrews is that they are named for their authors rather than for their destinations. This difference from the other New Testament Epistles explains, in part at least, their designation from earliest times as Catholic Epistles. In the truest sense of the term they are epistles rather than letters, i.e., brief pamphlets intended for a general reading rather than for specific addressees. One meaning of the term "catholic" as it is used of these documents is that they were addressed to the Church as a whole or to at least a significant area of the Church. The title can hardly have been a synonym for Canonical since several of them remained on the disputed list well into the fourth century. The term itself was used of the Church in connection with the struggle against erroneous teachings. The word "catholic" in that connection meant standard or orthodox; the traditional teaching, in other words, which is generally accepted and recognized throughout the Church. In that sense also the term is appropriate to these documents, for several of them are concerned with the problems of erroneous teachings and the immoralities which followed from them.

Other than their catholic character, brevity, and the fact that they stand outside the *Corpus Paulinarum*, there is little to bind them into a group. They come from several different authors, their subject matter varies widely, and each of them had to make its way into the Canon independently. I Peter, for example, seems to have been accepted from the first, whereas II Peter remained on the disputed list into the fourth century. Two significant groupings appear, on the other hand, among these Epistles. The three Epistles of John manifestly belong together, and, although I and II Peter are related in little more than name, II Peter and Jude coming from a similar, somewhat later, period reflect a similar concern

15. See Enslin, *Christian Beginnings,* pp. 314–316.

with problems of heresy and are related by a significant passage of material which they have in common. In the following survey, therefore, we shall depart from the Canonical order by examining II Peter along with Jude.

BE DOERS OF THE WORD:

JAMES

The author of the first of the Catholic Epistles calls himself simply "James, a servant of God and of the Lord Jesus Christ." If for no other reason than to aid in gaining Canonicity for the Epistle, attempts to identify him with an apostle were inevitable. Since James bar Zebedee was executed by Agrippa I in A.D. 44, and nothing beyond his place in lists of the disciples is known of James bar Alphaeus, tradition has fixed on the brother of Jesus (cf. Mk. 6:3; Act 15:13ff.; 21:18ff.; Gal. 2:9, 12; I Cor. 9:5; 15:7) as the author. According to a tradition preserved in divergent forms by Josephus and the Christian writer, Hegessipus, quoted by Eusebius, this James was killed in Jerusalem between A.D. 60 and 66.[16] Since there is very little to date the work either early or late, such an identification is on the face of it plausible. The difficulty is that the Epistle is written in the form of popular Hellenistic moral lectures. It is inconceivable that a Palestinian Jew could have been sufficiently familiar with Greek language and popular lecture forms to have written it. If the Epistle was known to have been by the brother of Jesus, furthermore, it is difficult to understand why it was so neglected in the first two centuries of its existence. Probably the wisest decision is to leave the author's identity as it stands and assume that it was written by a pious Christian leader who bore the common name Jacob, or in English, James.

In several ways James is a strange work. Its affinities with Jewish moralism and Wisdom Literature are sufficient to have given rise to serious studies claiming it to be a Christianized Jewish tract. Only three verses, in fact, specifically identify it as a Christian document: the mention of Jesus in 1:1 and 2:1 and the reference to the parousia in 5:28 (other passages, however, such as 2:14–26, would be hard to understand outside a Christian context). Because a Christianizer would hardly have been content with so few interpolations, however, we can assume that it was written originally as a Christian work. The affinities of James with Hellenistic writings, on the other hand, are equally obvious. Similes and metaphors from Greek moral lectures are numerous. The lecture on guarding the tongue, for example, the loose organization by means of catch-words and association of ideas, the extensive use of the rhetorical question, along with minor literary devices such as chiasms—all characteristics of the diatribe

16. *Ant.* XX, 9, 1; *Church History,* II, 23.

—show the author to be quite at home in the world of the late Hellenistic philosophers.[17]

Although there are several echoes of Gospel tradition (James H. Ropes cites six: Jas. 1:15—Mt. 7:7; Jas. 2:5—Mt. 5:3; Jas. 3:18—Mat. 5:9; Jas. 4:4—Mk. 8:38; Jas. 5:1–6—Lk. 6:24; Jas. 5:12—Mt. 5:34–37[18]), he is familiar with the Christian doctrine of salvation by faith (cf. 2:10–26), and he shares the eschatological hope of the Early Church (5:7–8), the pressing issues and dominant emphases of that period are surprisingly absent. There is nothing of the Crucifixion or Resurrection, or the issue of circumcision, or freedom from the Law. So little is said of suffering and trials (cf. 1:2–4; 5:10–11) as to suggest that he was writing at a time of comparative peace for the Church. The writer's whole concern is for a sincere moral rectitude. His theme can be summarized in two quotations: "Be doers of the word, and not hearers only, deceiving yourselves." (1:22), and "faith apart from works is dead" (2:26b).

Although James is not disorganized, its structure, as we have said, is formed by a chain of loosely connected ideas which are usually introduced by the word "brethren." An outline of the Epistle, therefore, amounts to little more than a list of topics. James begins with an exhortation on the benefit of enduring trials which echoes Paul's exhortation in Romans 5:3–5 (cf. Heb. 12:5–11; I Pet. 1:6–7). The trials here, however, may be nothing more than the ordinary adversities of life. The word "lacking" at the end of the exhortation leads to a discussion on the lack of wisdom which will be met if one asks without doubting. The word "doubting" leads in turn to a discussion of the instability of the doubter (1:2–8).

Abruptly James turns to the issue of the rich and the poor (cf. 2:2–7; 5:1–6). After a suggestion of the motif of reversal of fortunes of which Luke is so fond, he comments in stoic fashion on the fleeting nature of riches (cf. Mt. 6:19–21). Returning to the theme of trials, he adds to the promise of steadfastness and perfection, the assurance of "the crown of life," i.e., eternal life. The word "trial" leads to a discussion of temptations (both words, *peirasmos* and *peiradzo,* are in Greek from the same stem) which come not from God but from one's own evil desires. Good gifts, on the other hand, come from the unchangeable God who, in contrast to the death which sin "brings forth" (vs. 15), "brought forth" (note the catch-word) his people "to be a kind of first-fruits of his creatures" (1:9–18). The "word of truth" in verse 18 may have suggested the theme of doing and hearing the Word around which he develops a complex but imperfect chiasm beginning with the statement that every man should be "quick to hear, slow to speak, slow to anger." In the elaboration which

17. On the form and style of this Epistle see James Hardy Ropes, *The Epistle of St. James* (ICC), pp. 6–18, 24–27.
18. *The Epistle of St. James,* p. 38.

should deal with anger, bridling the tongue, and being doers of the Word as well as hearers, in that order, he spoils the structure by reversing the last two. His definition of religion in terms of charitable care of orphans and widows, and purity in relation to the world, forms a climax to the series of topics (1:19–27).

Along with the use of catch-words, another of James' favorite devices is reintroducing a theme from an earlier discussion, e.g., 1:2–4 and 12, for further development. In 2:1–7, therefore, he picks up the theme of the rich and the poor from 1:9–11 in order to warn, in an echo of Luke 14:7–14, against showing favoritism toward the rich. Harking back to the conclusion of his analogy of the mirror, in 1:23–25, he picks up the phrase "the law of liberty" to argue, on the premise familiar to us from Paul's argument to a different conclusion in Galatians 3:10ff; 5:13ff., that showing partiality is as much a breach of the "royal law" to "love your neighbor as yourself" as murder would constitute a breach of the Ten Commandments. The same principle applies to the "law of liberty" as was applied to the commandments (2:8–13).

This comparison raises the question of faith versus works. In an extended homily he argues that faith which does not result in corresponding moral conduct is as meaningless as charitable intentions which never produce any relief for their object (2:14–27). There are several echoes of Galatians in this chapter, one of which we have already observed (cf. 2:18–24 with Gal. 3:5–10, 16; 4:22–31), which makes it appear on the surface that James is deliberately correcting Paul's emphasis on faith. It was this aspect of the Epistle, particularly, that caused Luther to make his famous comment that it is "a right strawy epistle."[19] As commentators now generally agree, such an interpretation is a misunderstanding. Although James evidences little appreciation of the profundity of Paul's doctrine of faith, his plea for a morality consistent with faith is essentially the same as Paul's exhortation in Galatians 5:13–6:10. What James calls "faith apart from works," Paul would call no faith at all, and what James calls "faith completed by works," Paul would call "fruits of the Spirit." Abraham's "work" in offering Isaac and Rahab's "work" in harboring the spies Paul and others would regard as acts of faith (cf. Heb. 11:17, 31).

In the essay on the control of the tongue (3:1–13) James has returned to the theme of bridling the tongue in 1:26. Although the figures and style are characteristic of Stoic lectures, the thought would be equally at home in the Judaic Wisdom Literature. The essay is appropriately addressed to those who wish to become teachers and concludes with a reference to "works" which ties it to the previous homily on faith and works. The references to the "wise" and "the meekness of wisdom" (cf.

19. On Luther's attitude see Ropes, *The Epistle of St. James*, pp. 106–108.

1:5, 21) in turn lead to a brief contrast between the earthly wisdom of selfish ambition and jealousy and the pure, peaceable, and gentle wisdom from above (3:14–18).

The mention of peace in 3:17–18 suggests its opposite in the next passage which begins with the rhetorical question, "What causes wars, and what causes fightings among you?" The opening theme is a tirade against pleasure. (The Greek word translated "passions" is the original of the English "hedonism." The word means pleasure usually in the bad sense.) That the phrase "so you kill" in 4:2a can hardly be taken to apply literally to Christian communities has led a number of interpreters to attempt figurative interpretations or to amend the text to read "envy." It is more likely that James is quoting a Stoic moralist in 4:1–2ab, to which he adds his own application.[20]

James' method of attaching his material to the quotation can be seen in the way he repeats the parallelism of 4:2ab (concerning desiring and coveting) in 4:2c–3 (concerning asking and receiving, cf. Mt. 7:7–12). The connections of ideas here are made at three points: in the word "passion," i.e., pleasure, 4:1, 3; the words "desire" and "ask," 4:2, 3; and the words "do not have," 4:2ab, 2c. As the pagan's desire for pleasure leads to wars and murder, so similar desires in Christians lead to frustrated and unanswered prayers.

By means of a contrast between friendship with God and friendship with the world, closely paralleled with the two kinds of wisdom in 3:15–17, and a quotation from Proverbs 3:34, he develops the thought into a discussion of pride, which equals friendship with the world, and humility, which equals friendship with God (cf. 1:19–10). The source of the quotation in 4:5, which James apparently takes to be Scripture, is unknown. Suggested by his condemnation of the proud, the next topic, 4:11–12, on speaking against and judging one's brother (cf. Mt. 7:1–5), leads in turn to an exhortation against boasting about one's future plans. The connection is made by the word "judge" (Greek: *krino*), 4:11–12, which means also to decide. In humility the Christian must say, "If the Lord wills, we shall live and we shall do this or that." As a conclusion to the series of topics he adds, "whoever knows what is right to do and fails to do it, for him it is sin" (4:17).

Probably the mention of trading and getting gain (4:13) suggested the next topic. James returns, at any rate, to the subject of the rich which he has mentioned twice before in 1:9–11 and 2:1–7. With imagery reminiscent of Jesus' words in Matthew 6:19–21, he pronounces a wholesale condemnation upon the rich whose ill-gotten gains have been acquired by defrauding their laborers.[21] His picture of the loss of their wealth echoes the description of the brevity of life in 4:14 (5:1–6). The

20. Cf. Burton Scott Easton, "The Epistle of James," *IB*, Vol. 12, pp. 52–53.
21. Cf. Luke 16:19–31. On Luke's attitude toward the rich see p. 177.

picture of the eschatological judgment upon the rich and the mention of the righteous man in verse 6 lead to the exhortation to patient endurance (cf. 1:2–4) "until the coming of the Lord," which he elaborates with examples of the farmer, the prophets, and Job (5:7–11). After a brief exhortation against oaths (cf. Mt. 5:37), which had no apparent connection with what precedes or follows, James returns to the subject of suffering in order to introduce his concluding series of exhortations. Let the suffering pray, the cheerful sing praises, and the sick be anointed with oil by the presbyters. The prayer of faith will save him and sins will be forgiven. This verse is the earliest extant reference to the Christian rite of anointing the sick. Let the brethren confess their sins to one another and pray for each other; for like Elijah's prayer for the drought, a righteous man's prayers have great power. Anyone who brings back a sinner from his error should know that he has saved a "soul from death." Thus abruptly James ends this prime example of Christian Wisdom Literature.

WHEN YOU DO RIGHT AND SUFFER FOR IT:
I PETER

The quiet courage and noble vision of I Peter give it an importance all out of proportion to its length. Within its brief one hundred and five verses are brought together some of the most vivid expressions of Christian hope, ennobling ethical admonitions and challenges to courage in suffering to be found in the New Testament. Although the five major provinces "within the Taurus," comprising all of Asia Minor north and west of the Taurus Mountains, are named in the address they probably represent nothing more than the general area in which the Epistle was originally published. With the possible exception of 4:12–19, therefore, there is nothing in I Peter that suggests that it was written to meet any particular problems; its goal is to serve the needs of the Church generally and to strengthen it against the troubles which were increasingly becoming a part of its life.

Written in fluent Greek, I Peter has about it a homiletical or liturgical quality which has led recent interpreters to look for its setting in the cultic life of the Early Church. Some have gone so far as to contend that the Epistle is a baptismal liturgy with the actual rite being performed between 1:21 and 22. On the basis of a number of parallels with the *Apostolic Tradition* of Hippolytus and the frequency of the word "suffer," which occurs a dozen times in the Epistle, and therefore, he believes, is a play on the word "Paschal" (Greek: *pascho*-suffering; *pascha*-Passover, hence the Christian Easter), F. L. Cross has offered the hypothesis that I Peter is a liturgy for baptism and the Eucharist at the Easter Vigil.[22] That the exhortations are appropriate to the occasion of baptism

---

22. *I Peter: A Paschal Liturgy* (London: Mowbray, 1954). This monograph is virtually impossible to get hold of. For a summary of this and other similar

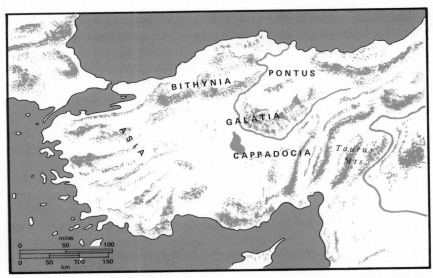

Provinces "within the Taurus" addressed in I Peter 1:1. (Adapted with permission of The Macmillan Company from *Macmillan Bible Atlas* by Y. Aharoni and Michael Avi-Yonah. Copyright © 1968 Carta, Jerusalem. © Copyright 1964 by Carta, Jerusalem. © Copyright 1966 by Carta, Jerusalem.)

(cf. 3:21ff.) is to be admitted, as well as the liturgical quality of both the language and structure, but the absence of rubrics of any kind and its epistolary form make it more likely that the author, as an appropriate basis for his admonitions, has chosen to model his Epistle on the liturgy.

Two passages in I Peter, because of their similarity to material otherwise unique to Ephesians and Colossians, invite further comparison between this Epistle and Paul's letters. In 2:18–3:7 a series of admonitions is addressed to servants, wives, and husbands in much the same form as the *haustafeln* which comprise one of the significant links between Colossians and Ephesians but occur nowhere else in the New Testament. Similarly, the descent of Christ to preach "to the spirits in prison" in 3:18–20 is paralleled in the New Testament, except for a possible allusion in John 5:25, only in Ephesians 4:8–10.[23] Since I Peter develops these points quite differently, the possibility of literary dependence which these

---

theories, including his own, see F. W. Beare, *The First Epistle of Peter* (Oxford: Basil Blackwell, 1958), pp. 6–9, 37–41, 52–54, 196–202.

23. Several translators, however, take this passage in I Peter to refer not to Christ but to Enoch. See *The Bible, A New Translation* (New York: Harper & Brothers, 1922) and E. J. Goodspeed, *The New Testament, An American Translation* (Chicago: The University of Chicago Press, 1923), and Goodspeed's defense of this conjecture in "Some Greek Notes," *JBL,* Vol. LXXIII, Pt. II, June, 1954. pp. 91–92.

passages imply requires examination. Several studies along this line have revealed a number of similarities between this Epistle and the Pauline writings, especially Romans and Ephesians. Echoes of material in the Gospels have also been found, which must be included in any discussion of the origin of I Peter. The following table, by no means exhaustive, attempts to give the more significant parallels in wording and ideas between this Epistle and other New Testament writings:

Comparison of Peter with Other New Testament Writings[24]

I Peter	Romans	Ephesians	The Gospels	Others
1:3–5		1:3; 2:4–61	Jn. 3:3	
1:7				I Cor. 3:11–15
1:10–12		3:2–6		
1:13–19	12:1–2	2:2–3	Lk. 11:2; Mt. 6:9	
1:20		1:4		
1:21	4:24			
1:22	12:9–10			I Cor. 13:13
1:23			Jn. 3:3	
1:24				James 1:10–11
2:2				Heb. 5:12–6:2
2:4–8	9:32–33 (12:1)	2:18–22	Mk. 12:10	II Cor. 6:16
2:9–10	9:25 (11:16–24)	2:11–17		
2:11		2:3		
2:12			Mt. 5:16	
2:13–15	13:1–7			
2:16				Gal. 5:13ff.
2:18–21		6:5–8		Col. 3:22–25
2:24	6:3, 11			
2:25			Mt. 18:12–14 Lk. 15:3–7 Jn. 10:14–15	
3:1–6	2:28–29; 4:1ff.	5:21–25 3:16		Col. 3:18 I Cor. 7:13–14; 11:2–16
3:7		5:25–33		Col. 3: 19
3:8–9	12:9, 14–21	4:32	Lk. 6:28 Mt. 5:38–42	Gal. 5:22–26
3:13–17	13:1–4		Mt. 5:10	
3:19–20		4:8–10	(Jn. 5:25)	
3:21–22	6:3–4, 7	1:20–22		Acts 1:9–11
4:5			Mt. 12:36	

24. For I Peter and Romans see Sanday and Headlam, *The Epistle to the Romans* (ICC), pp. xxiv–xxv; For I Peter and the Gospels see Archibald M. Hunter, "I Peter," *IB* Vol. 12, p. 83. Also C. L. Mitton, *The Epistle to the Ephesians*, Appendix I, pp. 280–315.

In Imitation of Paul

I Peter	Romans	Ephesians	The Gospels	Others
4:6				I Cor. 15:29
4:7–8	13:8–14			
4:9–11	12:3–8, 9, 13			
4:13				II Cor. 1:5; Col. 1:24
4:14			Mt. 5:11	
5:1	8:18			
5:2			Jn. 21:17	
5:5		5:21	Jn. 13:4–5	
5:6			Lk. 14:11	
5:7			Mt. 6:25–33	

Because of the difficulty of explaining how the apostle Peter could have known and used the Pauline letters, the manifest interrelation of I Peter with Romans and Ephesians, especially if the latter is assumed to be Deutero-Pauline, raises the question of authorship. The tradition is firm that Peter was executed in Rome at the same time as Paul under Nero (ca. A.D. 64). Whereas in the earliest reference, I Clement 5:2–7 (ca. A.D. 95), linking the deaths of the two apostles it is not explicitly said that they were martyred at the same time, Tertullian (Scorpiace 15) something over a century later repeats a similar tradition which specifically identifies both deaths with the action of Nero. Other characteristics of the Epistle reinforce the difficulty. The fluent literary Greek, the improbability that Christians were so early persecuted "for the name" (4:16), and the scarcity of reflections of first-hand knowledge of Jesus' teaching and ministry have been cited as reasons for doubting that this writing came from the apostle.

Certainly some of the similarities between I Peter and the other New Testament writings are simply the result of a common body of terms, ideas, and Old Testament proof texts. It is true also that some of the material common to I Peter and Ephesians is developed quite differently in each. But such similarities as those between the Epistle and Romans, especially chapters 12 and 13, are not so easily disposed of. Scholars are sharply divided on the question, and the recent commentaries on I Peter by F. W. Beare and E. G. Selwyn represent very well the opposing opinions. Selwyn, for example, has tried to explain the "Paulinisms" by means of small units of liturgical and catechetical material which he believes were very early in circulation among leaders of the Church and which both Peter and Paul used in their writing.[25]

25. For the development of this theory supported by elaborate tables of the evidence see his *The First Epistle of St. Peter* (London: Macmillan & Co., Ltd., 1961), Essay II, pp. 363–466; for opposite opinion see F. W. Beare, *The First Epistle of Peter,* Supplement, 1946–57, pp. 188–203.

To the Twelve Tribes in the Dispersion

Although Selwyn's argument shows that the question cannot be decided with certainty upon the basis of the "Paulinisms," he has not, in the judgment of many scholars, succeeded in answering some of the other difficulties. The references to Jesus and echoes of his teaching could easily have come from the Gospels, but since the Gospels are, on the other hand, our only way of testing such references it is impossible to decide, except by subjective impressions, whether the author had first-hand knowledge of Jesus.

On the question of style Selwyn follows a number of earlier scholars in crediting the style to Peter's amanuensis, Silvanus (Silas in Acts). Since Silvanus' name also appears with Paul's in the salutations in both letters to the Thessalonians, assuming that they are the same person, this theory would also account for some of the "Paulinisms." From what we know of him through Acts and Paul's letters, however, we have little reason to suppose that Silvanus was any more capable of writing the quality of literature exemplified in I Peter than the apostle himself. Certainly, there is little evidence in the style and vocabulary of the Thessalonian letters to support such a theory. It is possible, of course, that the name Silvanus is a mere coincidence and that Peter's amanuensis was an otherwise unknown, well-educated Greek, but this argument rests the matter upon sheer conjecture. Similarly, it is impossible to determine whether the reference to "my son, Mark" (5:13) reflects an authentic tradition of Mark's relation to Peter, which Papias was using in his famous account of the origins of Mark's Gospel, or whether it is actually the origin of Papias' conjecture.[26]

One of the most serious difficulties for Petrine authorship is identifying the persecutions to which the Epistle refers. It is clear from 1:6–7; 2:20–23; 3:14–18; 4:1–2, 12–19; and 5:8–10 that the author is writing at a time in which persecutions of the Christians were no longer incidental harassments, as in I Thessalonians 2:14–16, for example, instigated by the local synagogues, but were legal actions taken by Roman authorities. Such a situation can hardly have existed before Nero's time, and since in all probability Peter was executed during the Neronian persecution, it allows a very narrow margin of time for his writing of this Epistle. There is little evidence, furthermore, that Nero's persecution extended to the Asian provinces.

Because it reflects a situation remarkably similar to that in I Peter, Pliny's correspondence with Trajan (ca. A.D. 112) is often cited as evidence for dating the Epistle in the early years of the second century.[27] In both documents believers are liable simply for bearing "the name"

26. See pp. 70–74.
27. See p. 423.

of Christian, and yet there has been no consistent or well-known policy established.

Pliny's letter on the subject of the Christians, on the other hand, is itself evidence that sporadic persecutions had caused a number of people to renounce the faith as much as a quarter of a century earlier. Such a development was to be expected. As Christianity became more and more clearly separated from Judaism, it lost the protection and status afforded the latter and became a *religio illicita.* Being a religion unrecognized by Roman law would not in itself necessarily incur persecution, but in the context of the threat of provincial uprisings it would become suspect, and the believers' refusal to abandon their assemblies or to worship the Emperor's genius would be enough to bring action against it. Unless it can be shown, therefore, that Peter survived beyond the time of Nero, his direct responsibility for this document which bears his name is placed in serious question.

There is another problem requiring our attention which has some bearing on the question of the origins of the Epistle. The paragraph in 4:7–11 is manifestly a conclusion for all that has preceded it, and the doxology that closes it should logically mark the end of the Epistle. The reader is totally unprepared for the sudden outburst which follows: "Beloved, do not be surprised at the fiery ordeal which comes upon you to prove you, as though something strange were happening to you" (4:12). In the discussions of suffering earlier in the Epistle, persecution was spoken of as a distinct possibility, but here it has suddenly and unexpectedly come. In verses 12–19 the whole mood has changed. The writer is now speaking personally and urgently to a specific situation. Yet another change occurs in chapter 5. Unlike either the material in 1:3–4:11, or the impassioned exhortation on persecution in 4:12–19, this section, 5:1–11, consists in admonitions addressed to the leadership of the Church very much in the vein of the Pastoral Epistles. In contrast to these concluding sections, the material in the first four chapters appears much more like a sermon or discourse than either a letter or epistle. The epistolary salutation (1:1–2) and conclusion (5:12–14), therefore, fit more appropriately with either of these latter sections than with the discourse or the document as a whole. For this reason F. W. Beare has suggested that 1:1–2; 4:12–5:14 is the original letter into which a later editor has thrust the "Baptismal Discourse" in 1:3–4:11.[28]

It is possible, on the other hand, that the writer was interrupted at 4:11 by news of a sudden outbreak of persecution and added verses 12–19 in response. This suggestion, nevertheless, does not fully account for the admonitions to the elders in 5:1–11. Consequently, although it is the earliest and best attested by the Church Fathers of the Catholic

28. *The First Epistle of Peter,* pp. 6–9.

Epistles and shares with I John the distinction of never appearing in the lists of "disputed books" in the New Testament Canon, we must regard I Peter as almost certainly composite.[29] What its actual connections are with the great apostle we can no longer say, but its spirit and message are certainly worthy to bear the name of Peter. Although it was intended for the churches of Asia Minor, its echoes of the Hippolytan liturgy and the greetings from the church in "Babylon" (5:13), which surely means Rome (cf. Rev. 14:8, *passim*), suggest that it was written from Rome.[30]

As Newborn Babes, 1:1–210 In the opening phrase of the salutation the mood of the Epistle is established. The believers to whom it is addressed are "exiles of the dispersion," or more literally "chosen pilgrims," whose true home is in a future eternal world (cf. 1:17; 2:11). From this perspective they are to understand the duties and problems of this present life. The first section consists of a series of definitions of the Christian life interspersed with moral admonitions. These definitions are built around the idea of a new birth. Three times the author uses the term in this section: 1:3, 23; 2:2. In a series of three steps he develops the first definition. (1) A blessing is addressed to God (cf. II Cor. 1:3; Eph. 1:3) for the new birth of the believer to a living hope and imperishable inheritance, through Christ's Resurrection, which awaits the believer at the end of time. (2) Because of this inheritance the believer rejoices in the midst of suffering, knowing that the suffering is to refine his faith (cf. the analogy of the refiner's fire in Isa. 1:25; Zech. 13.9) in anticipation of his salvation. (3) The believers are in the enviable position of living in that final period toward which the prophets had pointed (1:3–12).

In a series of admonitions interspersed and concluded with further definitions, the writer draws out the moral implications of the believers' status. Setting their hope completely on the coming of Christ, and refusing any longer to be shaped by the paganism from which they had come, they must be holy even as God is holy (cf. Lev. 11:44–45, *passim;* Mt. 5:48). The blood of Christ, who was predestined "before the foundation of the world" and appeared "at the end of the times" has ransomed them from that paganism and given them faith and hope in God. Since they have purified their souls, they are to love one another. Having been reborn by the word of God which, unlike the withering grass, is imperishable, they are to be done with all malicious behavior. Like the newborn babes that they are, they must desire the "spiritual milk" for their growth to salvation. In a mixed metaphor, the writer calls upon the believers to become the stones of a temple and a holy priesthood in the service of

29. On the references to and use of I Peter in Patristic writings see Charles Bigg, *The Epistles of St. Peter and St. Jude* (ICC), pp. 7–15.
30. Cf. F. W. Beare, *The First Epistle of Peter,* p. 31, vs. 201–203.

God. Christ is to be at the same time the cornerstone of that temple and a stone of judgment for unbelievers (cf. Rom. 9:32–33 in which the same combination of proof texts from Isa. 8:14–15 and 28:16 occurs). The believers, who were once "no people," are now "a royal priesthood," the chosen nation of the People of God (1:13–2:10).

As Aliens and Exiles, 2:11–4:11 In the next section the writer turns to the pressing problem of their life in a hostile world. The first part of this section (2:11–3:12) is built around the household rules which we observed in Colossians 3:18–25 and Ephesians 5:21–6:9; the second (3:13–4:11) appeals to the Passion and Resurrection of Christ affirmed in their baptism as a model for their own courage in suffering. The basic theme of this section is that upright conduct, respect for civil authority, and internal solidarity based on Christian love are the only defenses against harassments and persecution. Christ has provided the model for the way in which the believer is to face the suffering he is called upon to endure.

Recalling the opening salutation, the writer calls the believers "as aliens and exiles" (lit.: strangers and pilgrims) to confute their accusers in the final Judgment by living exemplary lives (2:11–12). Because it stands much closer to Paul (Rom. 13:1–7) than to the bitter vindictiveness of the author of Revelation (cf. 6:10 and ch. 17), the next paragraph, on respectful obedience to all civil authority, provides some evidence that I Peter was written comparatively early, before the increasing persecutions had so embittered the Christians that they lost all confidence in the imperial government (2:11–17). In the instructions to servants (The Greek word, *oiketes,* here differs from *doulos* in Colossians and Ephesians. Occurring only four times in the New Testament, it usually means a household servant.), wives, and husbands, the opening statements are very close to the Pauline version, but the exhortations are developed independently along the lines of the main theme of the section. Servants are under obligation to obey the overbearing master as much as the kindly one. For accepting punishment for actual wrongdoing is no virtue, "but if when you do right and suffer for it you take it patiently, you have God's approval" (2:20). In his suffering Christ gave servants an example; since they have been healed by his wounds, they "should follow in his steps." Similarly, wives are to be submissive to unbelieving husbands, because through the inner adornment of a gentle spirit rather than the vanity of dress she may win him to the faith. Husbands, too, are to treat their wives considerately as "joint heirs of the grace of life." All believers are to live in unity and love, refusing to return evil for evil (2:18–3:12).

In the second part of the section he returns to the theme of the model of Christ's sufferings. Without fear the believers are to be prepared to defend their hope, and by virtuous living to shame their accusers. As Christ, though righteous, suffered for the unrighteous, as their baptism signified, and after his Resurrection ascended to the right hand of God, so they should accept suffering in the flesh as their break with a life governed by human passions. The enigmatic reference to Christ preaching in the interval between his death and Resurrection to those who died in the flood, in 3:19–20, is apparently introduced for the sake of a prototype for baptism, and the reference to it in 4:6 is apparently intended to use the conversion of those dead as a prototype of the transition of the believer to the spiritual life. The section, and apparently the original of this document, comes to a close with a series of practical exhortations based on the nearness of the end of the present age (3:13–4:11).

As You Share Christ's Sufferings, 4:12–19 Whether a postscript in response to news of a sudden outbreak of persecution, or a separate letter which became attached to the Epistle at a later time, this brief call to courage is a vivid picture of the precarious life the early Christians were called upon to live. The note simply tells the believers that they should expect such a "fiery ordeal" and rejoice in the opportunity to "share Christ's sufferings" (cf. Col. 1:24; II Cor. 1:5). Being sure that they do not suffer deservedly as wrongdoers, they must not be ashamed to suffer for the name of being Christians, by which they glorify God (cf. 2:12, 15, 20–23; 3:14–18). If believers are called upon to suffer thus, how much worse will be the punishment of unbelievers.

As a Fellow Elder, 5:1–14 This little tract to the presbyters, urging them to humility and faithful ministry, and warning them against simony and tyranny, is related to the rest of I Peter by the note on suffering in verse 9. The presbyters and their people are to be on their guard against the devil who is constantly looking for victims, knowing that they are simply experiencing the lot of their fellow believers around the world, and that in the end God will "restore, establish, and strengthen" them. With the closing greetings and peace, this courageous little document ends. Its emphasis on faithful witness in suffering matches closely the motif of martyrdom which we observed in the Gospels and may have come from the same general period.

IF GOD SO LOVED US:

THE JOHANNINE EPISTLES

Of the three Epistles which bear the name of John, only the first seems to have found, along with I Peter, an early and unchallenged place among the Catholic Epistles. Perhaps because of their brevity and relative unimportance, II John was often disputed and III John either ignored or disputed until the latter part of the fourth century.[31] Although the author identifies himself in the second and third Epistles simply as "The Elder" (cf. I Peter 5:1) and in the first Epistle not at all, he has from the earliest times, except where II and III John were rejected, been identified with the author of the fourth Gospel. We have already discussed the reasons for rejecting the corollary of this opinion, that the author was the son of Zebedee and disciple of Jesus.[32] In spite of the very many points of similarity between the Gospel and the first Epistle, however, modern scholars are divided on the question of common authorship. C. H. Dodd is convinced, for example, by the limited vocabulary and less skillful rhetoric, the absence of Old Testament quotations, and the more rudimentary theology, that the author of the Epistles was a later disciple of the author of the Gospel. A. E. Brooke, on the other hand, after listing more than fifty parallels in phraseology between the Gospel and first Epistle taken from H. Holtzmann's study of the question and several other studies of style and thought, concludes that they probably were by the same author.[33] If the Gospel, as is likely, developed in stages and came from a "Johannine school," the question is relatively unimportant.[34] The Gospel and the Epistles issue from the same circle of teachers and represent a common theological point of view.

The first Epistle, since it lacks an opening salutation and closing greetings, is, like Acts and Hebrews, more of a book—or more precisely, a homiletical tract in book form—than an epistle. If the address, "the elect lady and her children," be understood as an epithet for the Church and her members (cf. I Peter 5:13 where the word "chosen" is the same as "elect" here; the Greek word for church *ekklasia,* is in the feminine gender), II John is a brief tract in letter form and therefore an epistle in the strict sense of the word. III John, on the other hand, is written to what appears, at least, to be a specific situation, and therefore is probably, like Paul's correspondence, a genuine letter. It is interesting to note that, when Revelation is taken into account as the only apocalyptic book in the New Testament, the Johannine literature represents a kind of miniature canon; all five types of literature in the New Testament—Gospel, letter, epistle, book, and apocalypse—appear under the name of John.

Many Antichrists Have Come, I John   In two important passages the first Epistle refers to some who have separated from the community of

31. See A. E. Brooke, *The Johannine Epistles* (ICC), pp. lii–lxii; and C. H. Dodd, *The Johannine Epistles* (MNTC), pp. xi-xvi.
32. See pp. 77–79.
33. Cf. C. H. Dodd, *The Johannine Epistles,* pp. xlvii–lxvi, with A. E. Brooke, *The Johannine Epistles,* pp. i–xix. See also Brooke's discussion of the probability that the Gospel was written first, pp. xix–xxvii.
34. See pp. 218–219.

To the Twelve Tribes in the Dispersion

believers (2:18–27; 4:1–6). When taken with the emphasis in the prologue (1:1–4) these passages indicate one of the author's principal purposes. These antichrists and false prophets deny "that Jesus is the Christ" (2:22) and "that Jesus Christ has come in the flesh" (4:2–3). The emphasis in the opening verse on that "which we have heard, which we have seen with our eyes, which we have looked upon and touched with our hands, concerning the word of life," therefore, establishes the Epistle's opposition to those whose denial of the reality of the incarnation has led to a schism in the Church.

The syncretistic movements, which were to develop into the second-century Gnostic heresies and which were already making their influence felt in the Christianity of the latter part of the first century, incorporated as one of their basic tenets the Hellenistic dualism which regards the physical world as essentially evil and inferior. Consequently, there was a persistent tendency under their influence to distinguish the divine Christ from the human Jesus. Either there was only a temporary union between the two which involved neither Jesus' birth or Crucifixion, or Christ's real humanity was denied altogether by saying that he only seemed to be physical. This latter theory was known as docetism (from the Greek word *dokeo,* to seem or appear to be) and is the error with which I John is dealing. The false teachings whose shadowy forms we could barely make out behind the Pastoral Epistles have in this Epistle appeared in clearer definition, and their development into the great heresies of the second century is not difficult to trace.

Because of this Hellenistic contempt for the physical world, these errors often carried with them serious tendencies toward libertinism. In his emphasis on the believer's freedom from sin, therefore, John is speaking to the moral consequences of the doctrinal errors he is condemning (1:7–10; 2:1–6; 3:4–10; 5:16–18). To the despair of his interpreters John appears to contradict himself in these passages. In 1:8, for example, he says, "If we say we have no sin, we deceive ourselves, and the truth is not in us." At the same time, in 3:6, he writes, "No one who abides in him sins; no one who sins has either seen him or known him" (cf. vs. 9). Since the verbs in both of these sentences are in the same present tense, the grammatical distinctions between the tenses (the aorist, indicating a single act, and the present, indicating continuing action) to which interpreters sometimes appeal, and which in several instances in these passages could apply, cannot solve the problem, any more than subtle distinctions between the true character of the believer as one "born of God" and his actual predicament in this present evil world.[35] Nothing in the remainder of the Epistle warrants attributing such subtleties to

35. Cf. C. H. Dodd, *The Johannine Epistles,* (MNTC) pp. 78–81, with A. E. Brooke, *The Johannine Epistles,* (ICC) pp. 84–90.

this author. By means of the antinomy he has created, he is trying to increase the moral tension of his readers. He will allow them neither the false sense of security of supposing they are "good enough" nor the comfort of thinking that their sins do not matter.

The divisiveness which the errorists have introduced into the Church also concerns John. In the setting of the recent schisms, therefore, the "old commandment" to love God and one's brother, which has been in force "from the beginning" of the Christian movement, becomes a "new commandment" (2:3–11; cf. 3:11–18; 4:7–12, 19–21). John's approach to these problems is not an attack upon the errorists and schismatics but, as he explicitly indicates in 2:12–17, an exposition of Christian truth that will protect his readers from being deceived and confirm them in the faith. At the same time he does his best to arouse their moral energies and bind them together in a community of Christian love which cannot be torn apart by schism. The tests scattered all through the Epistle and introduced by such phrases as "By this we know. . . ," "If any one says. . . but. . . he is a liar" serve another of its important purposes to provide the means for testing the spirits as he exhorts the reader to do in 4:1.

I John is like James in the way it defies logical analysis. Although the rhetorical questions which James was fond of are absent, movement around a series of related ideas in I John and the affectionate terms of direct address remind the reader of the Epistle of James. James' use of "my brethren" or "beloved brethren" to mark transitions of thought correspond to John's "my little children" (Greek: *teknia,* the diminuitive, hence the affectionate familiar form, of the word "child") or "beloved" (4:1). The Epistle has affinities also with the Wisdom Literature of Judaism in its use of antitheses. From beginning to end the thought revolves around such opposites as light and darkness, truth and error or the lie, love and hate, God and the world or the devil, sin and righteousness, children of God and children of the devil. Although an outline of the Epistle is virtually impossible, it is not chaotic or without organization. Perhaps its structure can best be compared to a symphony. Between the prologue and the epilogue (1:1–4 and 5:13–21) the thought is developed in a series of movements by means of themes and counterthemes in such a way that the same themes reappear in new relationships and thus receive extended development.

THAT YOU MAY NOT SIN, 1:1–2:17 When we compare the prologue to this Epistle (1:1–4) with the other two prologues of this sort occurring in the New Testament, John 1:1–18 and Hebrews 1:1–4, one significant difference appears. Whereas the prologues of the Gospel and Hebrews place those works in relationship with antiquity, this one is concerned with the recent past. The opening of the fourth Gospel reaches back to creation and beyond: Hebrews begins with God's word through the ancient prophets; but the writer in I John takes the reader back to the foundation of Christian tradition, the ministry of Jesus. As the use of such words as "beginning," "logos," "life," and "testify" (Greek: *martureo*, witness) shows, this prologue is related to the one in the Gospel. That the author assumes rather than ignores the substance of the Gospel prologue he indicates by the skeletal summary of its content in verse 2. The "beginning" upon which he wishes to fasten the readers' attention, however, is that of Christian tradition in the life and ministry of Jesus. The Epistle is introduced, therefore, with the avowed purpose of witnessing to the physical reality of God's Son Jesus Christ, "the word of life," "so that you may have fellowship with us" and "our joy may be complete" (1:3–4).

The first movement is based on the contrast between light and darkness and is concerned with the believers' relationship to God. The light equals God, truth, righteousness, and love of the brethren, whereas darkness represents sin, lying, hating one's brother, and the world with its lust and pride. The movement begins with the matter of fellowship. Since fellowship with God and the Christian brotherhood is dependent upon walking in the light, it is made possible by the forgiveness and cleansing which Jesus has provided to those who confess their sins (1:5–2:2). John is writing so that the believers may not sin, but if they do they have an advocate, "Jesus Christ the righteous."

The movement continues with the question of knowing Jesus, the sign of which is keeping his commandments and walking "in the same way he walked." The commandment, which came "from the beginning" (i.e., from Jesus' teaching), is not new, and yet as the age of darkness moves to its close, it is new. John is restating it as a test for those who claim to be "in the light." Only those who love their brothers can make such a claim (2:3–11). In a series of six parallel sentences that are almost poetical addressed to children, fathers, and young men, John affirms that he is writing not to rebuke the errorists but to confirm the faith and strengthen the life of those who are already in the light (2:12–14). The movement concludes with the admonition to love the Father and not the world because the world is passing away, "but he who does the will of God abides forever" (2:15–17).

ABIDE IN HIM, 2:18–3:24 Beginning with a bitter comment on the "antichrists" (the term occurs in the New Testament only in I and II John) who had left the community, the second movement is concerned with the believers' relationship with one another. They did not remain (abide), but broke the fellowship because they denied "that Jesus is the Christ," in other words, because of their Hellenistic dualism the antichrists had rejected the incarnation and therefore the Sonship of Jesus

(2:18–23). The theme of this movement therefore is that if the true tradition about Jesus "from the beginning" abides in one, he abides in the Father and, consequently, in the Christian community (2:24–27). The movement is developed in three steps, the first of which is eschatological. Those who "abide in him" are "God's children now," and therefore will not "when he appears" "shrink from him in shame" but "will be like him" in his ineffable reality (2:28–3:3).

In the next two steps two themes, sin versus right and hate versus love, from the first movement are reintroduced. "No one who abides in him sins," therefore, the children of God can be distinguished from the children of the devil by whether they do right and love their brothers (3:4–10). Sin and hate are not unrelated. As the story of Cain and Abel (the only reference to the Old Testament in the Johannine Epistles) shows, sin creates envy which produces hate and murder. Love, on the contrary, is exemplified in Jesus' death for the believers, who should, consequently, be willing to lay down their lives for the brethren. Since this love must express itself in deeds, it is shown by the way one ministers to his brother's needs (3:11–18). With the reassurance that God "knows everything," and therefore those who keep his commandment to "believe in the name of his Son Jesus Christ and love one another" may be confident that they "abide in him, and he in them." The Spirit he has given them confirms this confidence (3:19–24).

DO NOT BELIEVE EVERY SPIRIT, 4:1–5:21 As the center of interest in the first movement is being in the light which involves freedom from sin, and the second movement is concerned with abiding in him which produces love and concern for one's brother, so the third movement is concerned with recognizing true and false spirits. As does the second movement, this one begins with a bitter comment on false prophets who have gone out into the world (cf. 4:1–6 with 2:18–27). The need to "test the spirits" to see whether they are of truth or error is therefore apparent (4:1). Again, themes from the earlier movements are reintroduced: love versus hate, the eschatological judgment, the reality of the incarnation, and Christ's expiation for our sins. The first test is the confession "that Jesus Christ has come in the flesh." Since "God is love" (4:8b and 16b), the second test is love. As God loved us and sent his Son for our sins, so we must love one another. By thus abiding in love, and therefore in God we can face with confidence the Day of Judgment. Repeatedly the author makes the point that "we love, because he first loved us." In loving our brother whom we can see, we express our love for God whom we cannot see. He who hates his brother, then, is in the spirit of error (4:1–21).

In the conclusion to the third movement John gathers these themes together to make the point that anyone claiming to love God must love those who believe "that Jesus is the Christ" (i.e., the incarnation) because such a believer is by definition a child of God. It is this faith, furthermore, by which the believer is "born of God" and which gives him victory over the world (5:1–5). Going back to an incidental remark in 4:14, John introduces a theme which he has otherwise not used after the prologue. In the prologue he witnessed to the truth of the tradition "from the beginning" concerning the incarnation; here he gives three further witnesses, Spirit, water, and blood, to which he adds the greater witness of God himself. Although, because we cannot be sure what idea he is conflating his point here is not altogether clear; this much is obvious that he is bringing together John the Baptizer's testimony on the descent of the Spirit upon Jesus in John 1:32 (cf. 3:5), and the witness to the story of the piercing of Jesus' side in John 19:34–35, to show that Jesus was both physically real and the Son of God. Probably, the "testimony that God has borne to his Son" (vs. 10b) is a reference to the voice in John 12:28. In summary: "He who has the Son has life; he who has not the Son has not life" (5:12).

In the epilogue John again reminds his readers that he is writing to those who are already true believers in order to reassure them, and to affirm that God will hear and answer their prayers. If anyone observes in a brother a sin which is not mortal, he will ask and God will forgive the brother. John's distinction between mortal sin and those which are not mortal, whatever his first readers may have understood by it, played its part in the long involved discussion in subsequent theological history over the problem of postbaptismal sins, and helped to shape the later theological distinction between mortal and venial sins. In spite of the distinction, however, he refuses to remove the antinomy earlier in the Epistle: "any one born of God does not sin" (vs. 18a), and therefore stands over against the world which "is in the power of the evil one" (vs. 19). The Epistle reaches its climax and conclusion in a series of affirmations of God's truth in Jesus Christ and eternal life. With the enigmatic exhortation "keep yourself from idols" the Epistle ends.

Do Not Receive a Deceiver, II John As we have already suggested, the "elect lady and her children" in the address of II John probably represent the Church at large, at least in John's area. If this suggestion is true, although it shares with III John the distinction of being the shortest "book" in the Bible, it is not a personal note but an Epistle. Until the end of the Epistle, the author is merely reinforcing two points in his first Epistle: The believers are to obey the commandment to follow love and to beware of deceivers who deny "the coming of Jesus Christ in the flesh." Otherwise, they may lose "the full reward" for which they have worked. In the last sentence the real purpose of this short note is revealed. No believer is to greet or receive into his house anyone who does not subscribe to this doctrine of the incarnation. To do so is to share the wickedness of the errorist. The closing comments suggest that the author may have sent this note ahead of him as he planned a tour of the churches. If this conjecture is correct, it may explain the significance of the next letter.

He Refuses to Welcome the Brethren, III John III John is addressed to Gaius who is probably an actual person and is therefore a letter in the true sense of the word. After a warm commendation of Gaius' faithfulness to the truth, reminiscent of Paul's letters, John commends him for his kind service to the itinerant brethren and urges him to continue supporting and assisting them. The problem is that a certain Diotrephes, who refuses to acknowledge the writer's authority, has not only been turning away the traveling brothers, but also refusing to allow the church to entertain them. Perhaps John expects Gaius to do something about the matter. Or it may be that Gaius is being asked, subtly, to take in those whom Diotrephes turns away. Who Demetrius is (vs. 12) John doesn't say. Perhaps he is the traveler on whose behalf the letter is being written.

As is to be expected of personal letters, too little of the circumstances is known for us to do more than guess at its meaning. Perhaps Diotrephes had seen the warning in II John (cf. vs. 9) against entertaining deceivers and was using it to avoid the obligation to entertain anyone. John intends, at any rate, to come to the church himself soon and set matters straight (vss. 10, 14). It is interesting to compare this little note with instructions on the same point in the Didache, a church manual written in roughly the same period:

> Let every apostle who comes to you be welcomed as the Lord. But he shall not stay more than one day, and if it is necessary, the next day also. But if he stays three days, he is a false prophet. And when an apostle leaves, let him take nothing except bread to last until he finds his next lodging. But if he asks for money, he is a false prophet.[36]

SCOFFERS WILL COME IN THE LAST DAYS, II PETER AND JUDE

Along with II and III John the two Epistles, II Peter and Jude, remained on the disputed list of the New Testament Canon well into the fourth century and were, therefore, among the last books to be admitted. Jude is mentioned earlier than II Peter by the Church Fathers and seems

36. From Edgar J. Goodspeed, *The Apostle Father, An American Translation* (New York: Harper & Brothers, 1950), p. 16.

to have encountered less opposition. Jerome says that Jude's reference to Enoch as Scripture caused it to be rejected by some.[37] Perhaps, also, like the latter two Epistles of John, its brevity contributed to its neglect. II Peter, on the other hand, was part of a cluster of Petrine writings, mostly of doubtful orthodoxy and value, vying for Canonicity which included, according to Jerome, an Acts, a Gospel, an Apocalypse, and two books known as Peter's Preaching, and his Judgment.[38] Eusebius (ca. A.D. 324) questioned the authenticity and Canonicity of all of the books bearing Peter's name except I Peter.[39]

The writer's claim in II Peter 1:16–19 to special knowledge concerning eschatology obtained during his experience—as Peter—on the Mount of Transfiguration (cf. Mk. 9:2–8, para.) parallels a similar claim by the author of the Apocalypse of Peter, and perhaps also the author of the Gospel of Peter.[40] The reference in II Peter 1:14–15 to Jesus' prediction of Peter's (the supposed author) death is likely based on John 21:18–19. There is also clearly a literary relationship between II Peter, especially chapter 2, and Jude. The editorial modifications and distribution of the common material in II Peter suggest, along with other borrowings found in that Epistle, that Jude is the original and therefore the earlier of the two documents.

When the circumstances of developed Gnostic heresies with their antinomianism and libertinism are taken into account, these two Epistles can hardly be dated much before the middle of the second century. The reference to I Peter in II Peter 3:1 followed by allusions to the "holy prophets," "the fathers" who have fallen asleep, and to the collected letters of Paul (3:15–16), show that the author is writing long after I Peter was in circulation and established alongside the *Corpus Paulinarum*.

II Peter, like the apocryphal Petrine books, is obviously pseudonymous. Unless we take Jude's reference to James in verse 1 to be intended as an allusion to "the Lord's brother" (cf. Mk. 6:3; Gal. 1:19; 2:1ff.; II Cor. 9:6), on the other hand, he is probably simply a second-century Christian writing under his own name. It seems doubtful, even though such an identification was ultimately responsible for getting the work into the Canon, that if Jude were trying to claim identity with the disciple (cf. Lk. 6:16; Acts 1:13) or "the Lord's brother" he would have left the matter so indefinite. The author's elaborate attempt to claim the authority of the great apostle and attach his work to I Peter in II Peter 1:1a, 13–19;

37. *Lives*, IV.
38. *Lives*, I.
39. *H.E.*, III, 1. For extant fragments of these documents see M. R. James, *The Apocryphal New Testament* (Oxford: At the Clarendon Press, 1955), pp. 13–14, 16–19, 90–94, 300–336, 474, 505–521.
40. See M. R. James, *The Apocryphal New Testament*, pp. 507–508.

3:1 places Jude's modest introduction in the sharpest contrast. The importance of these little documents lies in the picture they provide of the problems besetting the second-century Church.

Where Is the Promise of His Coming? II Peter   The purpose of II Peter is to restore to the Church the fervor of its original eschatological hope, and thereby to recover its original purity in doctrine and morals. As Paul did in his letters, the author establishes this purpose in the salutation. "A faith of equal standing with ours" means beliefs and fervent expectation of the parousia that match those of the apostle Peter. Not only are there several words in common, but the structure of this salutation is closer to that of Jude than to any of the other Catholic Epistles.

The introduction is in two parts: a brief exhortation, 1:3–11, and a statement of his purpose and authority in writing the Epistle, 1:12–21. The exhortation, based on God's gifts and promises, through the knowledge of Jesus Christ, of all that belongs to life and piety, calls the reader to add to his faith a list of virtues which will keep him from being ineffective and confirm his election and entrance "into the eternal kingdom." The list of virtues is reminiscent of Colossians 3:12–14 (cf. Gal. 5:22–24), whereas the form in which the ascending scale is arranged is found in Romans 5:3–5.

The statement of purpose and authority is in three parts. First, because he (Peter) is nearing the end of his earthly sojourn he wishes to stir up and prepare his readers for the problems they will face after he is gone (1:12–15). Placing it at the announced end of Peter's life (1:14; cf. Jn. 21:18–19) gives the Epistle the character of a farewell address in the tradition of Deuteronomy and Joshua 23 and 24. Second, the vision of Jesus' majesty and the divine announcement on the Mount of Transfiguration, of which Peter was a witness, removed from the realm of speculation and myth the apostolic proclamation of his parousia, and therefore confirmed the predictions of the ancient prophets (1:16–19). Since one meaning of the word "parousia" is the arrival of the king for a royal visit, the vision of his "majesty" in verse 16 is declared by a play on words to be a preview of the eschaton. In the third place, therefore, the readers must recognize this apostolic interpretation of the inspired prophetic Scriptures as the norm (1:20–21).

THERE WILL BE FALSE TEACHERS, 2:1–22   The first of the two parts into which the argument of the Epistle falls is a tirade against heretical teachers borrowing heavily from Jude. Through the first ten verses the author uses the future tense making it a prediction of a future crisis. Afterward this literary device is dropped and the author addresses himself directly to the situation. As false prophets appeared in antiquity (cf. Jude's reference in vs. 5 to unbelievers in Israel's wilderness journey), so heretical teachers will sneak into the Church to lead believers astray. The author accuses these heretics not only of "denying the Master" (cf. Jude 4), but of licentiousness and greed (2:1–3). Their judgment, however, is as certain as that which fell upon the fallen angels (cf. Jude 6, Gen. 6:1–4, the reference here is to apocalyptic speculations developed from this story, e.g., in I Enoch VI–XVI), the generation of Noah, and the cities of Sodom and Gomorrah (cf. Jude 7). As the Lord rescued Noah's family and Lot, on the other hand, so he will rescue the righteous from the punishment of these evildoers (2:4–10).

These brazen false prophets, presuming authority even angels do not possess (cf. Jude 8–10), like irrational animals will be caught and killed. The author piles invectives one upon another. They are blots and blemishes, carousing, full of adultery, enticing the unstable (cf. Jude 12a). Like Balaam who was rebuked by a dumb ass (Num. 22:5–35), they are inspired by greed (cf. Jude 11). Having no more substance than dry springs or wind-driven mists, they seduce others with high-sounding rhetoric into licentious passions (cf. Jude 12b–13, 16). Promising freedom, they themselves are imprisoned in their former worldliness and are therefore worse than before (cf. Mt. 12:43–45; Lk. 11:24–26); it would have been better for them never to have known "the way of righteousness" (cf. Heb. 6:4–8).

REMEMBER THE PREDICTIONS, 3:1–14   In the second part of the argument the author turns to the troublesome question of the delay of the parousia. Jude, in verses 17 and 18, had reminded his readers that the apostles had predicted the coming in "the last time" of unprincipled scoffers. The author of II Peter now supplies such a prediction and reinforces it by an allusion to the ancient prophets and a reference connecting this Epistle with I Peter (3:1–3). The appearance of such scoffers is itself therefore an evidence that the last time has come. These scoffers, who because everything appears to continue as it was from creation deny that the end of this world is coming, have forgotten that God once destroyed the world in the flood (3:4–6). Three times (3:7, 10, 12) he repeats the warning: He will destroy it again; this time by fire. The author appears to have in mind the promise in Genesis 8:20–22 that God would never repeat the devastation of the flood "while the earth remains." Since the earth itself will be consumed this time by fire, the promise will not have been broken. There may also be some influence here from Hellenistic cosmologies.[41] Quoting Psalm 90:4 he reminds the reader that God is not subject to our dimensions of time. He is therefore not tardy in his promises but mercifully delaying the end, "that all should reach repentance." The

41. Cf. Seneca, *De Consolatione Ad Marciam*, XXVI, 6; *The Apocalypse of Peter* (Ethiopic), M. R. James, *The Apocryphal New Testament*, p. 513, Cf. Heraclitus, *Fragment*, 22, 25.

readers should therefore live holy lives while they eagerly await the coming of the new heavens and new earth (3:8–13; cf. Rev. 21:1ff.). In the brief epilogue (3:14–18) he reiterates the last point while appealing to the authority of Paul's letters which these false teachers distort. With a final call for the reader to be on guard against the heretics, to grow in grace (cf. Jude 19–20), and a doxology he closes the Epistle.

These Who Set Up Divisions, Jude   This writer's announced purpose is an appeal to his readers "to contend for the faith which was once for all delivered to the saints" (vs. 3). Although most of the content of this short tract of 25 verses has been surveyed in our analysis of II Peter, this material needs to be seen in its own setting. Jude is not concerned to restore an earlier eschatological perspective but is writing in defense of orthodoxy and Christian morality. Without the literary device of prophetic warnings, he writes in the present tense to his own time (cf. vs. 17). Jude is also notable in that, whereas several other New Testament books reflect the influence of apocalypses such as I Enoch, it is alone in explicitly quoting I Enoch (vss. 14–15), and probably also a lost work known as *The Assumption of Moses* (vs. 9).[42]

Jude's appeal has been made necessary by certain impious persons who have sneaked into the Church to subvert morality and deny "our only Master and Lord." Let the reader recall how God destroyed the unbelievers in Israel after delivering them from Egypt, imprisoned the fallen angels, and punished Sodom and Gomorrah (vss. 4–7). Repeating the same sort of wickedness, these men "defile the flesh" and reject authority. Yet with an authority even Michael the archangel would not assume they revile "what they do not understand," and instead follow their disastrous course by animal instincts. They repeat the errors of Cain (Gen. 4:3–8) and Balaam, and duplicate Korah's rebellion (Num. 22–24). Blemishes on the Christian agape meals, waterless clouds, fruitless trees, wild waves, stars loosed from their orbits (cf. I Enoch 18:12–16), they will therefore also be punished as Enoch (I Enoch 1:9) has predicted when the Lord "with his holy myriads" comes to execute judgment (vss. 8–16).

The believers, on the other hand, should remember that the apostles had predicted the coming of such scoffers "in the last time" who will "set up divisions," and build themselves up in the faith, pray, and preserve themselves in the love of God, while they wait for the mercy of Christ and endeavor to rescue some who have been deceived (vss. 17–23). In one of the most beautiful ascriptions (vss. 24–25) in the New Testament, Jude commits his readers to the care and keeping of God through Christ.

42. *I Enoch* 1:9. On *The Assumption of Moses* see R. H. Charles, *The Apocrypha and Pseudepigrapha of the Old Testament* (Oxford: At the Clarendon Press, 1913), Vol. II, p. 407–413.

5. What Must Soon Take Place: Revelation

There is something appropriate in the way that the New Testament, and therefore the Bible, concludes with an apocalypse. From the earliest letters of Paul to II Peter—likely the last of the New Testament documents to be written—we have observed a preoccupation with the eschaton which concludes the present evil age and ushers in the new age of righteousness and eternal life. Within that setting the early Church understood Jesus' first coming and messiahship and expected his return. In this last book, therefore, the great hope of the believers' final salvation in the consummation of history and victory of Christ is summed up and dramatically portrayed with the language of apocalyptic imagery. Certainly this grand affirmation of faith in the final victory of God over all the forces of evil is a more appropriate conclusion to the Christian Scriptures than the tirade against heretics in the Epistle of Jude which precedes it.

The Apocalypse (Revelation) of John is a typical—some would say the best—example of this genre of literature.[43] A comparison of Revelation with such writings as Daniel, I Enoch, IV Ezra, and II Baruch will show a large number of bizarre symbols, largely standardized, in common. There are, for example, nearly forty such figures found in common between I Enoch and Revelation. The sharp division between God and his righteous ones, on the one hand, and Satan and his evil forces, on the other; the cataclysmic end of history and divine judgment followed by eternal blessedness; the tour of history and the future, seen from a heavenly perspective, and conducted by a heavenly being; the presumption that the reader stands at the beginning of this final age, all of these characteristics of apocalyptic are so fully represented in John's work that some earlier scholars believed it to be a Jewish apocalypse which had been interpolated with Christian elements to adapt it for use by the Church.

Of all the books in the New Testament that bear the name of John, the Apocalypse is the only one which itself claims John as its author (1:1, 4, 9; 22:8). Although the tradition which succeeded finally in getting this book in the Canon ascribed it along with the Gospel and Epistles to John the Apostle and son of Zebedee, the author himself makes no such claims. In 1:1 he calls himself a servant of Jesus Christ, and in 1:9 he is a brother of his readers in the Asian churches, otherwise he is simply John.

As is often pointed out, apocalypses are characteristically pseudonymous, borrowing great names from the past. This practice is, however, part of a larger scheme the other part of which is absent in John. In such apocalypses the name is borrowed, not only for prestige, but also to place

43. On the characteristics of apocalyptic, see West, *Introduction to the Old Testament*, pp. 417–419.

the writing in an ancient period so that the outline of history which the work contains will appear as the author's successful prediction, thus far, of the course of world events. That which remains, from the readers' point of view, still predictive of the future becomes thereby more convincing. To answer the obvious question, why such an ancient work had not been known before, the typical apocalypse was published as a providential "discovery" of a hidden ancient work.[44] Not only is this device absent in John's Apocalypse, but in 22:10, because this writer is himself writing at the end time and shares with his readers the beginning of the messianic woes, it is explicitly excluded (cf. 1:9f). That we may therefore assume the author's name to be John is, however, of little help. As Dionysius, the third-century bishop of Alexandria, has told us, there were many who bore that name, some of whom had assumed it in admiration of the apostle as a "Christian" name.

One important conclusion we can draw with confidence is that this John was not the author of the Gospels and the Epistles. In a study which anticipated remarkably the methods and conclusions of modern critical scholarship, Dionysius demonstrated that the differences in form, content, terminology, and style between the Gospel and the Epistles on the one hand, and the Apocalypse, on the other, are too great for them to have come from the same author. His description of the style of Revelation at the conclusion of his argument is worth quoting here:

> Moreover, it can also be shown that the diction of the Gospel and Epistle differs from that of the Apocalypse. For they were written not only without error as regards the Greek language, but also with elegance in their expression, in their reasonings, and in their entire structure. They are far indeed from betraying any barbarism or solecism, or any vulgarism whatever . . . I do not deny that the other writer saw a revelation and received knowledge and prophecy. I perceive, however, that his dialect and language are not accurate Greek, but that he uses barbarous idioms, and, in some places solecisms.[45]

Although no book in the New Testament manifests a literary style as appropriate to a Galilean fisherman as does Revelation, the late date, the postapostolic stance of the author (cf. 18:20; 21:14), and likelihood that John of Zedebee was an early martyr make his authorship of this book unlikely.

Modern students of Revelation will readily agree with Dionysius' description of its style and observe he might have added Hebraisms to his

---

44. See Daniel 12:9ff., and West, *Introduction to The Old Testament,* p. 419.
45. Eusebius, *H.E.,* VII, 25, 24–27. Quoted from *The Nicene and Post-Nicene Fathers,* tr. A. C. McGiffert, Vol. I, p. 311. The entire chapter is worth reading. On persons appropriating the name "John" see paragraphs 14–16. Also above, p. 78.

list. Because of its strange and difficult language, R. H. Charles, in his important commentary, supplies a grammar for the language of the Apocalypse along with his own translation.[46] John has developed, in other words, his own language. Dionysius' reason for discussing the question of authorship, however, was the widespread opposition, particularly in the East, which John's Apocalypse was encountering. Some opponents went so far as to credit it to the notorious heretic Cerinthus. While confessing his inability to understand it, Dionysius nevertheless refused to reject the book. One of the reasons for the opposition was the encouragement it gave to millennarians and other such enthusiasts, who like II Peter were trying to reverse the Church's modification of the primitive eschatological expectations. The mediating position of the Alexandrian scholars such as Dionysius was made possible by the allegorical interpretation, a penchant of that school, which under the influence of Dionysius' teacher, Origen, they applied to the Apocalypse. Undoubtedly, this Alexandrian influence played a large part in effecting its Canonization. Yet Jerome, a century and a half later, could still remark that as the Latins do not by usage accept Hebrews, so the Greeks do not accept Revelation. On the basis of ancient usage, however, Jerome accepted both, and in the end that position prevailed.[47]

The modern reader will readily agree with Dionysius that the Apocalypse is hard to understand. Although the Alexandrian teachers, as their allegorical treatment of Revelation shows, had little sympathy with or understanding of the apocalyptic mind, not all of their difficulty was on that account. Especially in the seven letters of the first three chapters there are references to local events, persons, and the like, which are lost to all but John's original readers. Who the Ephesian "false apostles" and Nicolaitans were (2:2, 6, 14–15) is as obscure as are the allusions to the "Synagogue of Satan," "Satan's throne," and "the deep things of Satan" at Smyrna, Pergamum, and Thyatira (2:9, 13, 24), and as the identity of the martyr Antipas, those who have not soiled their garments, and in contrast, the "woman Jezebel," in Pergamum, Thyatira, and Sardis (2:13, 20–23; 3:4).

There are allusions also to contemporary events and circumstances, some of which have not always been clear to later readers. Some interpreters think, for example, that the title "Lord God" especially "our Lord and God" in 4:11, is the author's deliberate response to Domitian's arrogation of that title to himself.[48] The suggestion is made more plausible

---

46. *The Revelation of St. John* (ICC), Vol, I, pp. cxvii–clix, and Vol. II, pp. 386–446.
47. See the translation of the relevant passage of Jerome's Epistle, *a Dardanum*, in Enslin's *Christian Beginnings*, p. 472. On the history of the Apocalypse's bid for Canonicity see Martin Rist, "Revelation, Introduction," *IB*, 12, pp. 351–354; and R. H. Charles, *The Revelation of St. John* (ICC), Vol. I, pp. xcvii–ciii.
48. Suetonius, *Domitian*, 13.

The great Hellenistic theater on the Acropolis at Pergamum. (The Roderick Slide Collection, courtesy of Catawba College.)

by two observations: (1) This term, although very common in the LXX, occurs elsewhere in the New Testament only in the Synoptics and Acts. (2). It occurs almost as often (eleven times) in the twenty-two chapters of Revelation as it does in the combined ninety-six chapters of the Synoptics and Acts (fourteen times). Possibly also the boast "I am rich" attributed to the church at Laodicea, in 3:17, may refer to that city's pride in recovering from a disastrous earthquake (A.D. 60–61) without imperial aid.[49] Probably, as some commentators suggest, the description of Laodicea as "poor, blind, and naked" and the counsel to buy from Christ gold, white garments, and salve to anoint their eyes are allusions to the banking business, woolen industries, and eye salve for which the city was famous. Some interpreters see in the reference to the high price of wheat and barley in contrast to the unharmed oil and wine, in 6:6, a reference to Domitian's rescinded order restricting the planting of vineyards.[50] That the edict was especially onerous to the provinces reinforces the impression made by the seven letters as a whole that the Apocalypse was probably written in Asia for circulation among all the churches of that province.

49. Tacitus, *Annals,* 14, 27. See the comments of R. H. Charles, *The Revelation of St. John* (ICC), I, pp. 93, 96–99.
50. Suetonius, *Domitian,* 7, 14.

Lower part of the theater on the Acropolis at Pergamum, showing the stage area along with the remains of shrines and other public buildings, and the long street descending to the lower part of the city. (The Roderick Slide Collection, courtesy of Catawba College.)

Difficulties in regard to the date of Revelation have arisen because of some of these allusions. The order to measure the Temple, in 11:1–2, for example, seems to imply a date before A.D. 70 when it was destroyed. Similarly, the puzzling count of kings—the reference to "seven hills" in verse 9 indicates that they are Roman emperors—in 17:9–11, would, unless we count the three unsuccessful pretenders between Nero and Vespasian, place the author in the reign of Vespasian (A.D. 69–79). The brief reign of Titus and coming of Domitian (the beast) would from this standpoint be the subjects of the author's predictions. John may have incorporated here some earlier material, but it is also possible that this is a minor instance of the apocalyptic device in which the author, who is actually writing in the reign of the "eighth king," describes historical events as though he were predicting them from a slightly earlier period. A number of interpreters regard, also, the mortal wound from which the beast in 13:1–3 recovers, and the king who "was and is not" but "is an eighth" which "belongs to the seven" in 17:8 and 11, as references to the myth, which circulated around the end of the first century, of a miraculous return of Nero from the dead. But who the ten uncrowned kings in verse 12 are, unless the conjecture that they are Parthian kings is correct, can no longer be determined. Undoubtedly, the mark or number of the beast, and the economic sanctions which enforce it are also allusions to events and circumstances which appear to place the author in the time of Domitian. The tradition that the Apocalypse was written during the latter part of Domitian's reign (ca. A.D. 92–96), which has persisted from earliest times, although not unchallenged, is still widely accepted among scholars and is probably correct.

Except for obscure local references such as we have noted, the difficulty in understanding Revelation for those familiar with apocalyptic language is not in the symbols so much as in the way John has used them. Going back at least as far as Zechariah—itself not an apocalypse—these symbols form a fairly standard vocabulary. Ferocious beasts, for example, represent enemy nations; horns and heads represent successions of monarchs; horses bear the divine messengers of judgment and deliverance; bowls or cups of wrath wreak the vengeance of God upon his enemies; and trumpets call the forces of God into the ultimate battle with evil. Each writer, however, uses these symbols according to his own circumstances and theory of eschatology. Along with allusions to the circumstances and problems of the Church around the end of the first century, Revelation, therefore, differs from the typical Jewish apocalypse by incorporating features and shaping its message according to its distinctly Christian orientation. In Jewish apocalypses the figure of the messiah was either absent or at best played a minor, comparatively passive role. In John's Apocalypse "the Lamb" is the key figure throughout, and the climax of the apocalyptic drama is the "Marriage Supper of the Lamb." The puzzling scene of the "great portent" in chapter 12 is also a distinctively Christian adaptation of ancient mythology which sets the persecution of the Church in the context of the incarnation.

Another source of difficulty in understanding Revelation is the number of apparent disjunctures and doublets in the text. The trumpets in chapter 8 and the bowls in chapter 14, for instance, are both based on the plagues in Egypt (Exodus 7–12) and appear to represent the same thing. At the same time the trumpets are so awkwardly interwoven with the three woes as to obscure if not dislocate them. The heavenly guide instructing John varies from Christ's angel to Christ himself, or one of the presbyters or angels out of the visions (cf. 1:1, 17–18; 4:1; 5:5; 7:13; 10:4–8ff.; 11:1–3; 14–13; 17:1, 7, 15; 19:9; 21:5–6, 9, 15; 22:1, 6, 8–10, 12–16). Although the alternate predictions and announcements of the fall of Babylon (Rome) in 14:8; 18:2, 21; 19:17–21 probably represent nothing more than the shifting perspectives characteristic of apocalypses, most interpreters will agree that chapters 20–22 are disarranged. These problems have led to attempts to reconstruct the original order, theories of redaction, and quests for sources.[51] R. H. Charles has provided the most noteworthy studies of this sort, Convinced that the original author intended the work to be a sketch of events of the future in a continuous order he has removed a number of passages as interpolations or glosses. Most conspicuous of these changes is the removal of the first four trumpets in chapter 8 as later interpolations, leaving the remaining three trumpets in chapters 9 and 10 as announcements of the three woes.[52]

Except for Charles' reconstruction of chapters 20–22, these attempts have not proved convincing to many scholars. Apocalypses are not noted for such orderly progressions of thought or theological consistency, nor has Charles succeeded in eliminating all of the discontinuities. That the author used earlier material is likely, but whether it was from another writer or his own is impossible to tell. Similarly, the attempts to isolate sources involve a kind of circular reasoning based on the interpreter's concept of John's theology which leaves them open to question. Whether John actually incorporated sources, he did make wide use of quotations, allusions, figures, and the like. Scholars have counted some five hundred such usages from the Old Testament alone, beside a considerable number from the new Testament. Notable among these passages are the plagues in Exodus 7–11, the symbols in Zechariah 1–6, the visions of Ezekiel, the

---

51. For a discussion of these attempts and of the problem of the structure, see McNeile, *An Introduction to the Study of the New Testament,* pp. 254–260. On the question of sources see also Moffatt, *Introduction to the Literature of the New Testament,* pp. 488–493.
52. See *The Revelation of St. John* (ICC), pp. xxii–xxvii, 1–lxi.

grapes of wrath in Isaiah 63, and the Little Apocalypse in Mark 13. As Daniel was produced to stiffen the spines of the Jews under the persecutions of Antiochus Epiphanes more than two centuries earlier, so Revelation is a typical apocalypse written to reassure the beleaguered Christians of Asia Minor in the uncertain days at the end of the first century of our era. It must, therefore, be so interpreted. Attempts, ancient or modern, to allegorize it, or to turn it into an outline of Church history do it even more violence than do those who in every troubled period in Christian history have supposed themselves to be living at the end of history and assumed the Apocalypse of John to have been written expressly for them.[53]

Although some of John's figures are probably nothing more than attempts to heighten the drama, others may have been deliberately designed to obscure the meaning to the uninitiated. In the nature of the circumstances under which these works were produced, they were a kind of underground literature, and it would not do to be too obvious with uncomplimentary pictures of the persecuting rulers. Although John's cries for vengeance upon the persecutors of the saints and his horrendous pictures of their punishments fall sadly short of the ideals of the Sermon on the Mount, his reaffirmation of God's righteous sovereignty over history and his beautiful pictures of a restored universe under God's own holy and peaceful reign add an important dimension to the definition of the New Testament term, the Kingdom of God.

Recently, attention has been directed to the liturgical elements in the Apocalypse as a clue to its meaning. Admittedly, the theme of worship is prominent: The large number of hymns, the scenes of angelic worship of God, the obvious Eucharistic reference of the "Marriage Supper of the Lamb," the liturgical reading of the scroll, and the like are manifest allusions to Christian worship. There are, in fact, nearly forty cultic items mentioned or depicted in the book. Yet the Apocalypse is not a liturgy, nor does it include a scene, strictly speaking, with a Eucharistic setting. Attempts to show that its structure follows the outline of the Paschal Liturgy are somewhat forced.[54] The cultic orientation of Revelation cannot, on the other hand, be minimized or overlooked. It can perhaps best be understood by observing the way in which the heavenly worship is placed in contrast to the demonic worship of the Emperor (the beast). The whole book is oriented to this contrast. Thus the scene for the apocalyptic visions is in a heavenly setting which is at the same time a royal

---

53. On the various methods of interpreting Revelation see Charles, *The Revelation of St. John* (ICC), pp. clxxxiii–clxxxvii; McNeile, *An Introduction to the Study of the New Testament*, pp. 251–254.

54. For example, Massey H. Shepherd, Jr., *The Pascal Liturgy and the Apocalypse* (Richmond, Va.: John Knox Press, 1960), pp. 77–97. See also Lucetta Mowry, "Revelation 4–5 and Early Christian Liturgical Usage," *JBL,* Vol. LXXI, Part II, June, 1952, pp. 75–84.

court and the heavenly Church at its Eucharist. The Lamb is the true ruler of the world and is, therefore, the proper object of worship.

John appears to be more concerned to expound the meaning of the liturgy, especially as it applies to the crisis of persecution, than to follow its pattern. The Christian Eucharist not only looks back, like the Jewish Passover, to God's past act of deliverance, but also looks forward to the consummation of that deliverance in the Eschaton. It is an anticipation of the messianic banquet. In the "Marriage Supper of the Lamb," consequently, he pictures the heavenly reality toward which the earthly Eucharist points. Other items in Revelation follow this perspective. If Edgar J. Goodspeed is correct in suggesting that the seven letters in chapters 1–3 reflect the influence of Paul's collected letters, this section becomes a heavenly counterpart to the practice of reading them in the worship of the churches of Asia.[55] Similarly, the scroll whose seven seals no one except the Lamb could open is probably the Torah—or perhaps the entire Old Testament—which cannot be properly understood except as Jesus Christ becomes the key to its meaning. Thus the Christian practice of interpreting the lessons from the Old Testament by means of the traditions of Jesus is confirmed, and at the same time the author's basis for his pictures, drawn from the Old Testament, of the punishment of the wicked and the resurrection and bliss of the faithful is established. So, too, the setting of the Apocalypse "on the Lord's Day" (1:10) probably has a three-way reference to Jesus' Resurrection, to Sunday as the Christians' day of worship, and to the Eschaton. The other cultic elements, the Trisagion (4:8), the numerous hymns, the prayers, incense, and the like fit into this pattern. It is interesting that although the "Marriage Supper of the Lamb" (19:9) with its obvious Eucharistic reference stands in the climactic position in the Apocalypse, as in the fourth Gospel's treatment of the Last Supper, there is no narrative concerning the Supper itself. References to the cup of blessing and the broken bread are completely absent. In contrast, the carrion birds are called to feast on slain armies of God's enemies in what is called "the supper of God" (19:17–18). Neither the readers of the fourth Gospel nor of the Apocalypse would need a description of the Eucharistic meal. Probably they would understand also from the way the gory meal of the birds is placed as the obverse of the marriage supper that the figures of the wine press, taken from Isaiah 63, and the cup and bowls of wrath are the obverse of the Eucharistic cup of salvation. That which becomes the sacrament of salvation to the believer becomes at the same time the instrument of divine punishment to the wicked (cf. II Cor. 2:14–16). The point is reinforced by the two resurrections in 20:4–6. Among the symbols John uses, numbers are prominent. A series of sevens, for example, control the structure of the first two divisions; the number

55. *An Introduction to the New Testament*, pp. 224–226, 234.

seven appears nearly fifty times in the book. There are seven letters to seven churches in chapters 2 and 3, seven seals in chapters 6–8, seven trumpets in chapters 8–11, seven thunders in chapter 10, six angels and the Son of Man in chapter 14, seven bowls in chapter 16, and seven kings in chapter 17. In the climax of the Apocalypse, chapter 21, as in the sealing of the saints in chapter 7, variations on the number twelve predominate.

The Apocalypse falls into three major divisions: (1) the letters to seven churches (1–3), (2) visions of Judgment (4–20), (3) the vision of the final restoration of all things (21–22). In contrast to Luke's prefaces, the preface to Revelation (1:1–3) functions more as a title and is modelled on the openings of the Prophetic books of the Old Testament rather than Greek literature. Especially when taken with the curse in the epilogue (22:18–19) upon those who would detract from or tamper with the content, the blessing in the preface (1:3) for the public reading (i.e., in the church's worship) of the Apocalypse and John's claim to be a witness (cf. John 19:35–36, 21:24) to Jesus Christ's revelation made through his angelic agent amount to a bid for Canonicity. This blessing upon the lector and hearers is the first of seven benedictions scattered throughout the book which express its purpose. In 14:13 the blessing is upon those "who die in the Lord"; in 16:15 he "who is awake, keeping his garments" is blessed; "those who are invited to the Marriage Supper of the Lamb" are blessed in 19:9; as are "he who keeps the words of the prophecy of this book" in 22:7, and in 22:14 "those who wash their robes."

WHAT THE SPIRIT SAYS TO THE CHURCHES, CHS. 1–3

Following the preface John introduces the Apocalypse by means of a letter "to the seven churches that are in Asia" (1:4–20). Since the seven letters in the next two chapters are not actually written, rather John is simply describing what, in the vision, he was told to write, they are placed in a position parallel to the apocalyptic visions in the remainder of the book, all of which are included in the command to write in 1:11 and 19. The material in 1:4–20, therefore, introduces not the seven letters but all the visions, and the epistolary conclusion in 22:20–21, which belongs with this opening, includes within the letter the entire Apocalypse, giving it the form of an epistle. Paul's influence can be seen in the way in which John has adopted the epistolary form which Christian prophetic writing, in imitation of the Apostle's letters, had taken.

After a doxology and an announcement of the parousia, which stand in a position similar to the opening thanksgivings in Paul's letters, John describes the circumstances of his writing and the source of his revelation. Exiled for the Faith on the island of Patmos, he was "in the Spirit on the Lord's day" when the voice and the vision appeared commanding him to write what he was about to see and hear. Although the preface describes the agent of the revelation as the angel of Jesus Christ, John clearly identifies the resplendent speaker standing among the seven lamp stands as Jesus himself. The seven lamp stands, although not a single seven-branched stand (menorah), probably go back to Zechariah 4:2ff. In Zechariah, however, the lamps represent the all-seeing eyes of God; here they represent the churches in their witness to the Faith. Something of the lineage of the apocalyptic tradition is reflected in the seven stars (planets) which are the guardian angels of the churches. This symbolism has its roots in Persian astrology.

In the vision of the seven letters the scene represents John in the role of an amanuensis as Christ dictates the letters. The position of these letters

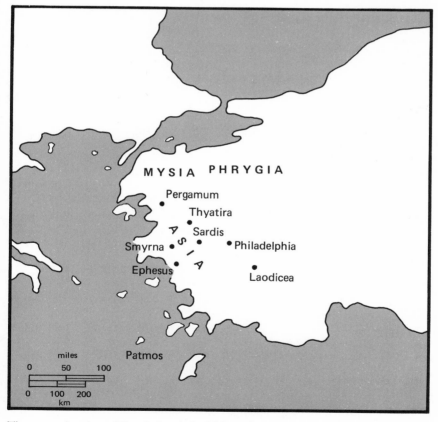

The seven churches of Revelation 1–3. (Adapted with permission of The Macmillan Company from *Macmillan Bible Atlas* by Y. Aharoni and Michael Avi-Yonah. Copyright © 1968 Carta, Jerusalem. © Copyright 1964 by Carta, Jerusalem. © Copyright 1966 by Carta, Jerusalem.)

The marketplace (Greek: *agora*) in Ephesus. Like the Roman Forum, this was the center of public life and activity. (Courtesy of Don R. Smith.)

at the beginning underscores the ethical thrust, a characteristic concern of apocalypses, which is basic to John's purpose.[56] With some slight variations the letters follow a consistent formula:

The Address. "To the angel of the church in ——————
write: The word of . . ." (followed by a characterization of Jesus Christ).

The Letter. (1) *Description,* "I know your works . . ." *or* "tribulation" *or* "where you dwell" (commendatory for Ephesus, Pergamum, Thyatira, Philadelphia; sympathetic for the plight of Smyrna; condemnatory for Sardis and Laodicea).

(2) *Reservations,* "But I have this against you . . ." *or* "a few things against you . . ." (only to Ephesus, Pergamum, and Thyatira).

(3) *Exceptions,* "Yet this you have . . ." *or* "But to the rest of you . . ." *or* "Yet you have still . . ." (only to Ephesus, Thyatira, and Sardis).

56. See R. H. Charles, *Religious Development Between the Old and the New Testaments* (New York: Henry Holt & Co., 1914), p. 19.

(4) *Admonitions,* "Repent" *or* "Do not fear" *or* "Hold fast" *or* "Awake."

The Conclusion. "He who has an ear, let him hear what the Spirit says to the churches" (cf. Mk. 4:9–12, 23, 33, and parallels; and Isa. 6:9–10), followed in the first three letters, and preceded in the rest, by "To him who conquers . . . *or* "He who conquers . . ." (followed by a promised benefit).

It is interesting that the second letter, to Smyrna, is only concerned with poverty and persecution, and in the last two, Philadelphia is commended without reservation, whereas Laodicea is condemned without exception. Although the connections in the last two are less direct, the descriptions of Jesus, the writer of the letters, in the addresses are taken from John's introduction to the vision of the letters (cf. 2:1 with 1:13, 16; 2:8 with 1:8, 17b–18; 2:12 with 1:16; 2:18 with 1:14b–15a; 3:1 with 1:4, 16, 20; 3:7 with 1:18b; and 3:14 with 1:5). Although some of the concluding promises to the victors are clear enough in meaning, others appear to have cryptic meanings which we can only surmise. The "tree of life" in 2:7b, for example, is an obvious reference to Genesis 2:9 and pictures the New Age in terms of a restoration of the originally perfect order of creation (cf. Rom. 8:22–25). The "second death," which in 2:11b has no effect on the victor, is explained later in the book, 20:6, 14; 21:8. The idea of the victor ruling over nations, in 2:26–27, and sharing Christ's throne, in 3:21, appears to go back to Psalm 2:8–9 and is similar to the position of believers in the New Age described in I Corinthians 6:2, Matthew 19:28 (cf. Jn. 14:2; 17:18; 20:21). So, too, the promise of white garments to the victor, along with having his name retained in the "book of life" and having Christ confess his name before the Father and his angels, in 3:5, recall Matthew 22:11–14, Malachi 3:16, Luke 10:20, and Matthew 10:32, as his being made a "pillar in the temple" recalls Ephesians 2:20–21. Although the "hidden manna" may refer to the Eucharistic bread (cf. Jn. 6:31–58), the "white stone" and "new name," in 2:17b and 3:12, and "the morning star," in 2:28, probably bear meanings which are lost to us (but cf. Phil. 2:9–11; Rev. 21:2, 10–21).

Whether the descriptions of the churches in the body of the letters correspond to the actual churches named is impossible to tell. The literary form of these letters and their position among the visions would suggest that they are a device for conveying John's pronouncements on the conditions he saw generally in the Church of his day. John commends the churches for their patient endurance and faithfulness in persecution, their resistance of "false apostles" and hatred of the Nicolaitans (whose identity, like that of those "who hold the teaching of Balaam," and "Jezebel," is no longer clear), their progress in love, faith, and service, and he sympathizes with their tribulation, poverty, and the slander to which they have been subjected by the "Synagogue of Satan." He rebukes them for abandoning the love they had at first, for allowing some to harbor those who "hold the teaching of Balaam," the Nicolaitans, and the woman Jezebel, for being dead, lukewarm, and self-satisfied in material prosperity. The invitation at the end of the last letter, 3:20, probably applies to all the letters; its Eucharistic reference is obvious.

IN HEAVEN AN OPEN DOOR, CHS. 4–19

The vision of the letters, being addressed to the immediate situation of the churches, occurred on earth; the visions which make up the main body of the Apocalypse concern "what is to take place hereafter" (1:19), and therefore John is for the remainder of the visions transported "in the Spirit" through an open door into the heavenly throne room. This throne room, which remains the reference point throughout the rest of the book, with the perpetual worship of God taking place in it stands in contrast to, and in judgment upon, the worship demanded by the beast and directed by the second beast in chapter 13. As chapter 1 served as an introduction to the vision of the letters, so chapters 4 and 5 set the stage and introduce the visions of the future which follow. Although for this introductory scene John borrows material from Isaiah 6, Ezekiel 1–2, and Daniel 7, along with secondary influence from other sources, particularly the Psalms, he reworks it into a form that is fully original. The scene of the throne of God surrounded by the worshipping throng is common to all three passages; the Trisagion is from Isaiah 6:3 and the hymn to the Lamb is reminiscent of that in Daniel 7:13–14; the four living creatures have features from both the seraphim of Isaiah 6 and those in Ezekiel; the scroll written on both sides is related to that in Ezekiel 2:9–10 (cf. Daniel 7:10c); and the Lamb occupies a position similar to the "one like a son of man" in Daniel 7:13.

The twenty-four presbyters around the throne are John's original addition. Their meaning is not entirely clear. That their number is the double of twelve points forward to chapters 7 and 21, in which the symbolism of that number is developed. Probably the symbolism, as others in Revelation, bears multiple meanings, but in light of its use in chapter 7 it at least represents the Jewish and gentile churches, and perhaps also, therefore, the Old and New Israel. That the scene is also reminiscent of the bishop surrounded by his presbyters at the Eucharist should not be overlooked.[57] We learn incidentally in 6:9 and 8:3 that there is an altar present (cf. Isa. 6:6). Such a combination of royal court, temple, and church is not at all incongruous, for Biblical worship is commonly ad-

57. See Massey H. Shepherd, Jr., *The Paschal Liturgy and the Eucharist,* pp. 87–88.

dressed to the majesty of God (cf. Heb. 4:16). John is sensitive also to the continuity between Israel's worship and that of the Church.

As Lucetta Mowry has convincingly argued,[58] the scroll written on both sides and sealed with seven seals which only the Lamb was worthy to open is the Torah, or perhaps, the entire Old Testament; the Scriptures, in other words, of both Israel and the Church. The scene is, therefore, the heavenly counterpart of the earthly worship of the People of God. Its essential point for the Apocalypse is the opening of the seals in order that the truth of the Scriptures might be revealed. That only the Lamb, who by virtue of his death had conquered and had ransomed men of all races and nations for God, was found worthy to open the seals dramatizes the point that Jesus is the key to the true and final meaning of Scripture (cf. II Cor. 3:12–18, Jn. 5:39–47). In a sense, then, the entire Apocalypse is the reading of the Scriptures by him who is at the same time the qualified lector and himself the embodiment of its meaning, which throws a new light on the title, "The Revelation of Jesus Christ." John's intention is not the promulgation of new truth but a new exegesis of the traditional and accepted Scriptures. Probably for him, as for Jude and other New Testament writers, these Scriptures included the Jewish Apocalypses and other writings which the rabbis finally rejected.

The Seven Seals, 6:1–8:4   As the Lamb opens the seals there unfolds a series of disasters of increasing intensity, in the midst of which appear, on the one hand, the Messiah and the faithful who follow him, and, on the other, the beast with his priest, and the hordes of wicked humanity who worship him, until the climactic battle brings defeat to the forces of the beast and ushers in the millennium. At the opening of the first four seals the well-known four horsemen appear. The white, red, black, and pale horses are familiar to us from Zechariah 6:1–8; the disasters which they bring are, however, from the little apocalypse in Mark 13:7–8 and parallels: wars, rumors of wars, famine, and pestilence (cf. Lk. 21:11).

As in Mark, these are merely the opening events of the final drama; "the end is not yet" (Mk. 13:7b). This point is made explicit as the opening of the sixth seal discloses a vision of the altar under which the souls of the martyrs cry out for vengeance. They are told to wait a little longer until all who are destined to be martyrs have been killed. With the opening of the sixth seal the list of preliminary catastrophes is completed by a series of monstrosities in nature which also come from the Gospel apocalypses (cf. Mk. 13:8, 24–25; Lk. 23:30–31).

At this point, chapter 7, the sequence is interrupted in order that the elect may be secured. Unlike the protection provided the Israelites during the plagues in Egypt, this "sealing" of the faithful is not to protect them

58. *JBL,* LXXI, Pt. II, June, 1952, pp. 75–84.

from physical danger in the midst of the disasters, but to guard them from being led astray by demonic pretenders (cf. Mk. 13:21–23). The interlude, therefore, corresponds to the shortening of the days and the angelic gathering of the elect in Mark 13:20, 27. The universal scope of the catastrophes is depicted by the four angels at "the four corners of the earth" who are restrained in order to produce the interlude of calm. The difficult question of the relationship between the 144,000 from the twelve tribes of Israel, in verses 4–9, and the innumerable multitude from every nation, in verses 9–17, has given rise to widely different interpretations of this chapter. Some interpreters have regarded one or the other of them as an interpolation, whereas others take the two passages to refer to the same group, verses 9–17 being a proleptic vision of their martyrdom.[59] Since John emphasizes the tribes of Israel in contrast to those "from every nation" and the number based on a series of twelves in contrast to the innumerable multitude, however, it is more likely that we should see here references to the Jewish and gentile churches. In view of John's emphasis, in verses 13–17, on the martyrdom which the multitude had suffered, it is possible that the second group includes the first; it is possible also that there is here a subtle allusion to the special religious privileges accorded the Jews which, with the separation of Church and Synagogue, gentile Christians no longer enjoyed.

With the opening of the seventh seal comes a period of silence for the reception of the prayers of the saints. The scene is reminiscent of and may have been shaped by Isaiah 6:4–7. At the same time, however, the seven angels of the trumpets are being readied for the next series of disasters. In effect, therefore, the remainder of the apocalypse unfolds from the opening of the seventh seal. Significantly, the same angel, the smoke from whose censor carried to God the prayers of the saints, now empties that censor upon the earth, as though in answer to the prayers (cf. 6:10), to initiate the new series.

The Seven Trumpets, 8:5–11:19 We have already noted the confusion in this section between the seven trumpets and the three woes, only the first two of which remain in the text (unless the entire climax in the great war and the fall of Rome is intended as the third woe, cf. 12:12; 18:10, 16, 19).[60] Whether the confusion is the result of the author's use of his sources, or was an intentional arrangement whose subtlety escapes us, or represents a later modification of the text can no longer be determined. As the text stands, the first woe consists of the disasters brought on by the first five trumpets. These catastrophes, like those in chapter 16, are modeled on the Plagues in Egypt: (1) hail and fire (cf. 8:7 with Exod.

59. Charles, *The Revelation of St. John* (ICC), Vol. I, pp. 188–203.
60. See, p. 461.

9:23–25, also Ps. 78:47–48), (2) sea turned to blood (cf. 8:8 with Exod. 7:20–21, also Ps. 78:44), (3) rivers become wormwood, (4) darkness (cf. 8:12 with Exod. 10:22–23), (5) locusts (cf. 9:1–11 with Exod. 10:13–15 and Joel 1:6–7; 2:1–11).

The second woe consists of the disasters resulting from the release of the four angels bound at the "great river Euphrates" (9:13–21). Whether these are related to the four angels who had been restrained at the corners of the earth in 7:1–3 is not clear. The differences in location and circumstances involve niceties of detail with which apocalyptic writers are seldom concerned. Their position in the series of disasters, at any rate, is analogous to that of the angel of death in Exodus 12:29–30.

As in the opening of the seals, the series is again interrupted before the seventh. This time four items intervene: First, the colossal angel astride land and sea utters a cry which is echoed by the seven thunders. Since the angel's oath involves the time of the eschaton, the command to John not to write down the message of the seven thunders amounts to a withholding of the date of the seventh trumpet and is therefore the equivalent of Mark 13:32, "But of that day or that hour no one knows. . . ." Second, John is commanded, in a passage obviously modelled on Ezekiel 2:8–3:7, to eat the little scroll in the angel's hand. His commission which follows is the reverse of that of Ezekiel; he is sent to prophecy, not to Israel, but "of many peoples and nations and tongues and kings." What this scroll represents we are not told, except that, as in Ezekiel, it involves the content of John's subsequent prophecies. If we take this episode to indicate the source of the remaining visions, however, we must conclude that with the colossal angel we have come to the end of the revelation from the scroll of the seven seals. Since the angel conveys the little scroll, it stands in some sort of relationship, on the other hand, to the former one.

It may not be too far-fetched to suggest, especially in view of the drama of the incarnation which follows in chapter 12 (note also the songs of Moses and the Lamb in 15:3–4, which may symbolize the two scrolls, cf. Jn. 1:17), that the little scroll in some way represents the Gospels. Certainly Mark and Matthew, and probably Luke, were in circulation by this time. If the vision of the seven letters reflects the influence of Paul's correspondence, and the scroll with seven seals represents the Old Testament (Moses and the Prophets) whose meaning can only be unlocked by Christ (the Lamb), to represent the Gospels, the tradition of the Lamb, by a little scroll would be a logical development. Such a representation would help to explain, at the same time, the extended interruption by chapters 12–15 of the series of sevens, as well as the shift of the scene from Asia and Rome (Babylon) to Jerusalem which follows in 11:7–8 (cf. the "new song," and "eternal gospel" in 14:3, 6).

The third intervening item (11:1–2) is the measuring of the Temple.

The word for temple (Greek: *naos*) here and throughout the book is the more restricted term usually indicating the sanctuary proper as distinguished from the Temple complex as a whole (Greek: *hieron,* in the Gospels, Acts, and I Corinthians). Since the announcement that the city and the outer court of the Temple will be overrun by pagans must be taken as a reference to the conquest of Jerusalem by Titus, these verses can hardly indicate that John was writing before that time. The measuring, i.e., the preservation, of the Temple, therefore, can hardly be taken literally. As the sealing of the saints in chapter 7, which did not prevent their martyrdom, so the destruction of the literal shrine does not destroy the worship of God. The point is reinforced in the fleeting scene of the open Temple and Ark of the Covenant, accompanied by the storm of Mount Sinai (cf. Exod. 19:16–25), which follows the hymn of the presbyters in 11:19. There is probably a dual reference here which includes the Church. Although overrun by persecution, it preserves in its worship the continuity of God's altar and sanctuary. The forty-two months (three and a half years) here and in varying forms throughout the remainder of the Apocalypse comes, of course, from Daniel (7:25 *passim*), and draws a parallel between the persecutions by Antiochus Epiphanes and by the Roman Empire.[61] Perhaps also Judas Maccabeas' restoration of the altar was in John's mind in this passage.

The fourth item (11:3–13) is the appearance of the two witnesses. An instance of that intricate complex of symbols and ideas growing out of Malachi 4:4–6, it serves a multiple role here. Although John does not identify them, more than likely he intends the reader to recognize the witnesses by the references to withholding the rain and turning the waters into blood to be Moses and Elijah. In the symbols of the olive trees and the lamp stands the reader will recognize the figures of Zerubbabel and Joshua, son of Jehozadak, the anointed king and priest promised in Zechariah 3–4 to the restored post-Exilic community. At this point the figure of the two witnesses stands in opposition to that of the two beasts in chapter 13. The connection with the transfiguration scene in Mark 9:2–13 is obvious (cf. II Pet. 1:16–19). Jesus' identification of John the Baptizer as Elijah and reference to John's execution at the hands of Herod (an appointee of the Roman emperor), which foreshadowed his own death, become part of the symbolism here (cf. 11:7–12 and 12:11 with the beheading of John and the Crucifixion in Mk. 6:14–29 and chs. 14–15). The word "witness," the use of which in reference to the role of John the Baptizer probably antedates the fourth Gospel, along with the obvious reference of these two figures to the Law and the Prophets, i.e., the Scriptures, explains the position of this item before the representation of the Incarnation in chapter 12. The reader, of course, will not forget the double

61. See pp. 4–6.

meaning of the word "witness" (Greek: *martus*) which includes martyrdom; nor will he forget, as he reads the allusion to the great city "where their Lord was crucified," that it was Pilate, a henchman of Rome, who sentenced Jesus to the cross. In the resurrection and ascension (cf. Acts 1:9) of the witnesses, 11:11–12, the assumption of Moses (an apocalyptic tradition which John is apparently following here transforms the death of Moses in Deut. 34:1–8 into an assumption) and Elijah (II Kings 2:9–12) are made to prefigure the resurrection and ascension of the saints, the "first-fruits" of which were the Resurrection and Ascension of Jesus. The earthquake completes the second woe brought on by the sixth trumpet (cf. Mt. 27:51–54). The partial and anticipatory nature of these disasters is indicated in the one tenth killed by the earthquake along with the one third (cf. Zech. 13:8) affected by the first four trumpets. Like the seventh seal, the seventh trumpet (11:15–19) is not a disaster but a scene of worship which anticipates the eschatological bliss that lies beyond all disasters and the Judgment (cf. chs. 21–22). Significantly the hymn of the presbyters is based on the coronation Psalm (Ps. 2:1) which was frequently applied to Christ. By placing the last trumpet after the little scroll and between the witnesses and the drama of the incarnation, John dovetails the visions of the two scrolls, and thereby emphasizes their relationship.

The Sign and the Beast, chs. 12–14 With the scene of the two witnesses in 11:3–13 and the new song of the angels in chapter 14, the drama of the Incarnation in chapter 12 forms an interpretation of the Gospels, the first advent, in other words, of Christ and its meaning for the end of time. The reader must not become bogged down in details, nor look for chronological order or accuracy in these scenes, many of which bear multiple reference. Apocalyptic literature is a kind of surrealistic art which requires of the reader a flexible imagination to understand it. Nowhere in this Apocalypse is this requirement more evident than in the twelfth chapter.

The scene is introduced as a "great portent" or sign (Greek: *semeion*). The word is the same as that in the message of the angel to the shepherds concerning the babe in the manger in Luke 2:12 (cf. the "signs" in the fourth Gospel). Here the sign is a woman giving birth to a male child who "is to rule all the nations," and the opposite sign, the dragon who seeks to devour the child, recalls the story of Herod's slaughter of the children of Bethlehem and the flight of the Holy Family into Egypt. That the child was caught up "to God and to his throne" at least represents Christ's divine origin and rule (cf. Jn. 1:1–18 and the theme of his descent from the Father throughout the Gospel). The victory of Michael over the dragon recalls the casting out of Satan in Luke 10:18 (cf. 12:10 with Job 1:9–11).

Attempts to locate the origins of the myth John has utilized here have not been successful, and if they were, they would be of little help in interpreting this scene. John has used it to place the Incarnation in a cosmic setting both in time and space (cf. Mt. 25:34, Jn. 17:24, Eph. 1:4, I Pet. 1:20), which in turn provides the foundation for the cosmic dimensions of the final battle and Judgment to follow. That the drama is paralleled in chapter 12 by the beasts, representing the Roman Emperors, requires that it represent the historical incarnation rather than an archetype. This parallel is made doubly clear by the seven heads on both the dragon and the beast. Although the woman primarily represents the Virgin Mary, as she is pursued by the dragon she represents in some sense also the Church, "the rest of her offspring" being that generation of the Church on which the great tribulation falls.

That this entire section, beginning with the colossal angel in chapter 10, is setting the stage for the final battle becomes evident in the way John has placed the rise of the beasts opposite the drama of the Incarnation. The repeated and varied use of Daniel's figure of three and a half years (11:2, 9, 11; 12:6, 14; 13:5) holds all this material from 10:1–20:3 together as a single sequence against the backdrop of the visions that unfolded from the seven seals.

Although the mortal wound which was healed suggests the myth of Nero *redivivis,* on the one hand, and the seven heads are, on the other hand, an obvious reference to the series of emperors (cf. 17:10–11), John's preoccupation with emperor worship, which is accented by the second beast acting as the high priest of the imperial cult, leaves little doubt that the vision was inspired by Domitian. Perhaps John regarded him as a reincarnation of Nero. That he has come to the heart of the crisis to which he is writing is indicated by the call, repeated from the vision of the seven letters, for him "who has an ear" to hear, and for faithful endurance (13:9–10). Perhaps John's original readers had the wisdom (13:18) to understand the clue to the beastly emperor contained in the number 666 (some texts have 616), but the innumerable mathematical manipulations performed on it since have been little more successful than those less worthy attempts by people who simply fastened that number on any political figure whom they happened not to like.

In chapter 14 the scene shifts back to the other side of the parallel and the continuation of the Gospel in the "new song" of the angels. That the scene is placed on Mount Zion rather than the throne room reflects the apocalyptic tradition that the Messiah will reign from there, and also ties this scene with the two witnesses in chapter 11 who died in Jerusalem. The presence of the twenty-four presbyters and four living creatures makes it an extension of the throne room. The hundred and forty-four thousand, who represent those sealed from the twelve tribes of Israel in chapter seven, are also, as those "who follow the Lamb wherever he goes," an extension of the twelve disciples. In the series of six "other angels" and the "one like a son of man" the content of the "new song" which only the hundred and forty-four thousand can sing is revealed.

The first three of these angels form a triad; the first flying in mid-heaven to announce "an eternal gospel," with the other two following with further definitions of that gospel. In the first angel's call to fear and worship the Creator God because "the hour of his judgment has come," the reader hears John's version of the preaching of Jesus, "The time is fulfilled, and the kingdom of God is at hand; repent, and believe in the gospel" (Mk. 1:15). The announcement of the fall of Babylon (Rome), anticipating chapters 18 and 19, defines that judgment; and the warning against worshipping "the beast and its image" represents the call to re-pentance. John's readers would recognize also in the cup of wrath the obverse of the Eucharist (cf. Obadiah 16). Separated by a call to en-durance and a blessing upon all those "who die in the Lord henceforth" (cf. I Thess. 4:13–18), there follows the vision of the harvest of wrath led by "one like a son of man" (cf. Dan. 7:13) and including another triad of angels. The references to the Temple, altar, and the wine press (cf. Isa. 63:3–6) again place the judgment as the obverse of worship.

The Seven Bowls, chs. 15–16 The opening verse of this section, by calling the vision "another sign in heaven,—great and wonderful," places it in sequence with the drama of the Incarnation in chapter 12. As the seventh seal extended to include the disasters of the seven trumpets, so the plague of the seventh bowl is carried forward by the assembly of the kings for battle at Armageddon and the guidance of one of the seven angels (17:1) to include the great battle and final judgment. They are, therefore, the last plagues, and with them "the wrath of God is ended" (i.e., has completed its function).

The seven bowls are prefaced, as were the seven seals and seven trumpets, by a scene of worship in which the completed number of martyrs are singing the songs of Moses and the Lamb. In these songs the Old Testament and the Gospels, and the deliverance from Egypt under Moses and the final deliverance by Christ are brought together, as the "sea of glass" ties this scene with that of the throne room (cf. 4:6), and the emergence of the seven angels from the "tent of witness" (probably the wilderness shrine) places this final act of judgment in the context of the whole continuity of the worship of the People of God. As the disasters of the seven trumpets, the plagues are modeled on the plagues in Egypt, but in contrast, these are total in effect. The sores in 16:2 recall Exodus

9:10; the sea and the rivers becoming blood in 16:3, 4 resembles Exodus 7:17 (the theological and liturgical parallel drawn by the song of the angel, 16:5–7, is obvious); the darkness in 16:10 repeats that in Exodus 10:21; the frogs in 16:13–14 echo the plague in Exodus 8:5–7; the drying up of the Euphrates recalls Moses' parting of the Red Sea in Exodus 14:21–29; and the lightning, thunder, and earthquakes in 16:18 remind the reader of the scene before Mount Sinai in Exodus 19:16–24.

The Fall of Babylon and the Supper, chs. 17–19 As a prelude to the final battle, one of the seven angels conducts John through a vision of the harlot and the beast. The harlot, as we learn from 17:5, 9, and 18, is Babylon (Rome) seated on the famous seven hills (note the requirement of a "mind for wisdom" in vs. 9 which parallels the requirement for understanding the number of the beast in 13:18), and drunk with the blood of martyrs. That the beast is red and has seven heads and ten horns associates it with the dragon in chapter 12 and identifies it as the first beast in chapter 13. Whatever the difficulties in identifying the seven kings in 17:10–11, the eighth, which is at the same time the beast and "belongs to the seven" and "who was and is not and is to come" (vss. 8, 11), is clearly Nero *redivivus*. John's use of this myth, popular at the end of the first century, makes it into a demonic parody on the Passion and Resurrection of Christ. The ten kings, represented by the beast's ten horns, are usually taken to be Parthian kings whose association with the beast leads to the surprising development of war being declared against the woman (Rome) by her mount (Nero *redivivus*). Suetonius tells of a man who, some twenty years after Nero's death, claimed to be Nero and enjoyed what support the Parthians were able to give him. John's explanation for Nero's war on Rome, aided by the Parthian kings, is the Old Testament idea of God's use of pagan kings to accomplish his purpose (17:17), but the historical basis for his idea is the fact that Nero died out of favor with the Empire, having committed suicide after the senate declared him a public enemy.[62]

Whereas the beast's devastation of the harlot (17:16) is described in terms reminiscent of Nahum's description of the fall of Nineveh (3:1–7), the battle with the Lamb is to come later. What follows is a series of taunt songs on the fall of Rome, introduced by "another angel," and "another voice" (from chapter 14?), balanced by laments by merchants and traders (18:1–19:3).

In 19:4 the scene changes, and once more the twenty-four presbyters and the four living creatures are at worship before the throne of God. That the antiphonal anthem which follows is constructed on phrases from the Hallel Psalms (cf. 19:5 with Pss. 113:1; 115:13 and 19:7 with

62. Suetonius, *Nero*, 49–57.

The Roman Forum, the historic center of Roman business, judicial, and political activities. (Courtesy of Don R. Smith.)

Ps. 118:24) associates this scene with the Passover and makes it therefore a celebration of God's final deliverance of his people.[63] Its reference to the Eucharist is obvious. By means of the command to "write this" (cf. 1:11, 19; 10:4; 14:13; 21:5) and the blessing (cf. 14:13; 16:15; 20:6; 22:7, 14), John underscores the focal position of the "Marriage Supper of the Lamb" (19:9). The marriage itself takes place later.

As a complement to the ultimate Eucharist the final battle now takes place (19:11–21). Riding a white horse, which makes this vision the completion of the meaning of the first seal in 6:1–2, the "Word of God" (i.e., Jesus Christ) leads the heavenly armies in total victory against the beast and the kings of the earth. Following the carnage of that war, the carion birds are assembled for a macabre meal on the flesh of the victims. Since the war of the beast and the harlot and the messianic war here are elaborations of the plague of the last of seven bowls which in turn are modeled on the plagues on Egypt, this war stands in the position of the death of the first-born in Exodus 12:29–32. The parallel between the Passover and the Marriage Supper is thus reinforced, and the final deliverance becomes a fulfillment of that ancient deliverance from Egypt which was so basic to Israel's faith.

63. Massey Shepherd therefore regards this as a representation of the Paschal Liturgy, see *The Paschal Liturgy and the Apocalypse*, pp. 96–97.

A NEW HEAVEN AND A NEW EARTH, CHS. 20–22

Although the material in the last three chapters is manifestly out of order, the general pattern is still discernible. According to John the consummation of history moves in two stages, the first of which is the millennium described in chapter 20. This period begins by the chaining of Satan. John by calling him the dragon identifies him as the genius of the dragon in the drama of the Incarnation in chapter 12 and, therefore, also of the beast. A resurrection of the Christian martyrs inaugurates the reign of Christ for a thousand years (hence, millennium, from Latin *mille,* one thousand, and *annus,* years). At the end of the millennium Satan is to be released for a brief period "to deceive the nations," following which another divine victory will conclude with the great Judgment and the "second death," i.e., the eternal "lake of fire" into which Satan and his followers will be cast (on the theme of the "second death" see 2:11; 20:6; 14; 21:8).

Interposing the millennium here is somewhat incongruous, detracting as it does from the Lamb's victory in chapter 19, and unnecessary as it is in view of the eternal new age which follows in chapters 21 and 22. The idea, found in several Jewish apocalypses, notably the Slavonic Enoch, 31–33, seems to have resulted from a combination of the militant messianism, which grew up around the figure of David, with the concept of the cataclysmic end of the world and the new age in a renovated universe which characterized the apocalypses. The model for it is the seven days of creation, which on the basis of Psalm 9:4 (cf. II Pet. 3:8) becomes a series of seven one-thousand-year periods. With some violence to the Hebrew calendar the theory divides history into six ages of evil followed by a millennium of "rest" (cf. Heb. 4:4–10) under the Davidic messiah. The eighth day becomes then the eternal resolution of creation and history. Although Paul makes no mention of millennialism, he does describe the pattern, the coming, victory, and messianic reign, after which all will be subjected to God, on which it is based (I Cor. 15:20–28).

In the last two chapters with the marriage of the Lamb and the bride, representing the New Jerusalem (i.e., the dwelling place of the Church), the new Israel is complete. The eternal bliss of the faithful is pictured in the figure of Jerusalem. The models for the description of the new city let down from heaven are Isaiah 65:17–25 and the Garden of Eden in Genesis 2:8–16. In it God will dwell with his people in full realization of that which his "glory" in the old Temple had foreshadowed. Through the new city will flow "the river of the water of life" (cf. Jn. 4:10–15; 7:37–39) nourishing the "tree of life." There can therefore be no death, or sorrow, or pain. The prominence of the number twelve draws together the destiny of Israel (cf. 7:4–8) and the Church, the "new Israel," in the new age. In the absence of a temple or a light of any kind is symbolized the direct and complete relationship of God with his people which will require no mediation. In the fantastic descriptions of the ornamentation of the city with gold and precious stones, the reader senses the difficulty the human mind experiences in trying to imagine absolute perfect existence. With certifications of the truth of the visions, a blessing on the reader who obeys, an assurance of the nearness of the second coming of Christ, a beautiful invitation to the reader to come to "the water of life," and a curse upon anyone who tampers with it John closes the Apocalypse. The prayer, "Come Lord Jesus!" and the grace connect the close with the opening (cf. 1:1, 4, 11) and give the entire work the character of a letter.

With this grand attempt to picture what the human mind by its very nature cannot conceive, the eternal age which lies beyond our tortured history, we come to the end of the Bible. It began with an equally great poem on the beginnings of things—and of man. Underlying both the poetic grasp for understanding of the eternity out of which history has come and the vision of the eternity toward which it moves is the assumption that all of it is in the hands of a perfectly righteous God. The universe began, therefore, in goodness and will end so. But between the third chapter of Genesis and the twentieth chapter of Revelation lie the stories of human sin and of a continuity of peoples, set in the larger context of history, who believed themselves to be the People of God, within whose story both the consequences of sin are to be seen and its solution is revealed.

Selected Readings

THE PASTORAL EPISTLES

Barrett, C. K., *The Pastoral Epistles in the New English Bible* (Oxford: At the Clarendon Press, 1963).

Harrison, P. N., *The Problem of the Pastoral Epistles* (Oxford: At the University Press, Humphrey Milford, 1921).

HEBREWS

Filson, F. V., *Yesterday, A Study of Hebrews in the Light of Chapter 13* (London: SCM Press, 1967).

Manson, W., *The Epistle to the Hebrews* (London: Hodder and Stoughton, Ltd., 1951).

COMMENTARIES

Bruce, F. F., *The Epistle to the Hebrews* (Grand Rapids, Mich.: Eerdmans, 1964).

Moffatt, James, *The Epistle to the Hebrews* (ICC).

Scott, E. F., *The Epistle to the Hebrews* (Edinburgh: T. & T. Clark, 1922).

THE CATHOLIC EPISTLES

Beare, F. W., *The First Epistle of Peter* (Oxford: Blackwell, 1947).

Dodd, C. H., *The Johannine Epistles* (MNTC).

Reicke, Bo, *The Epistles of James, Peter, and Jude, The Anchor Bible,* Vol. XXXVII (Garden City, N.Y.: Doubleday, 1964).

Ropes, James Hardy, *The Epistle of St. James* (ICC).

Selwyn, E. G., *The First Epistle of Peter* (London: Macmillan and Company, Ltd., 1961).

REVELATION

Charles, R. H., *The Revelation of St. John,* 2 vols. (ICC).

Shepherd, Massey H., Jr., *The Paschal Liturgy and the Apocalypse* (Richmond, Va.: John Knox Press, 1960).

Glossary

Allegory A more or less elaborate story in which the various elements bear symbolic meanings and often are included solely for the sake of such meanings. Not infrequently Old Testament stories have been given *allegorical* interpretations, i.e., treated as allegories. *See* Galatians 4:21–31.

Antichrist The arch-antagonist of Christ who, according to Christian apocalyptic thought, will appear at the end of time to bring about the great apostasy only to be defeated by Christ at his coming. He is mentioned by this title only in the first and second Epistles of John.

Antinomianism Literally, opponents of law, specifically, the belief that salvation by grace through Christ has relieved the believer of all obligation to the moral law. *See* Libertinism.

Aphorism A concise apt statement of a general principle or truth. A maxim.

Apocalypse, Apocalypticism A revelation or disclosure of a previously hidden truth. Specifically, a prophetic description of the events which lead up to and involve the cataclysmic end of history and the perfect New Age to follow. The system of beliefs fostered by such writings. Daniel and Revelation are two Canonical examples of this literature.

Apocrypha Literally "hidden" writings, either regarded as spurious or as too esoteric for general use. Protestants usually apply the term to the fourteen books in the Vulgate (Latin) Old Testament which are not in the Hebrew Canon. It is also used of extracanonical books paralleling both the Old and New Testaments. *See* Deuterocanon.

Apostasy The act of defecting from and ceasing to practice one's religious faith.

Apostle Literally, one who is sent forth as a messenger. Primarily the term applies to the twelve disciples who after the Resurrection assumed the leadership of the Church.

Apothegm (also spelled Apophthegm) A term used in form criticism to refer to short proverbs or apt statements of wisdom found in the Gospels. *See* Aphorism.

481

Baptism A rite of ritual cleansing with water which in Christianity is the sacrament of initiation into the Church. It is performed either by immersing the person in water or by applying water to the head.

Beatitudes The state of blessedness or happiness. Specifically the series of blessings that begin the Sermon on the Mount, Matthew 5:3–12.

Bishop A corruption of the Greek word *Episcopos* meaning overseer, hence, the presiding officer of a church. President and superintendent were used in the Ancient Church as synonyms. In time the bishops of important cities assumed leadership over churches in the surrounding territory, leading to the formation of the diocese. *See* Deacon; Presbyter.

Canon A standard or measure, hence, the list of those books that have been judged worthy to be included among the Holy Scriptures. In Christianity, the books worthy to be read in the liturgy, therefore, authoritative for doctrine and morals. *Extracanonical.* Books that have remained outside the Canon.

Catholic Epistles The collection of seven short Epistles at the end of the New Testament which were not addressed to any particular church, hence, were intended for general or catholic, i.e., universal use. The term probably also was intended to indicate that it represented teaching recognized as orthodox or correct by the Church generally.

Centurion A minor officer in the Roman army in charge of a division or century. The term means a unit of 100 men.

Christology The division of theology that deals with the nature of Jesus Christ, especially his divinity and role in the salvation of mankind.

Church The body of believers in Jesus Christ. The word, itself derived from a Greek word meaning "the Lord's house," translates the New Testament term *ecclesia,* meaning the assembly or the "called out ones."

Church Fathers The leading thinkers and writers of the early centuries of the Church, whose works not only helped to shape normative Christianity, but also are essential sources for our knowledge of the history of the Ancient Church.

Circumcision An operation performed in Judaism upon the male genital organ on the eighth day after birth, as a religious rite of initiation into the Commonwealth of Israel.

Codex See Scroll.

Composition Criticism A method of study of the Gospels which, by examining the editorial links, the rearrangements, omissions, additions, and the like, seeks to discover the purpose and theology of the final authors. Also known as redaction criticism.

Deacon One who serves or ministers. The lowest of the three orders of the ministry. In the early Church the deacon was particularly the assistant to the bishop.

Dead Sea Scrolls Documents recovered in a remarkable series of discoveries beginning in 1947 in the cliffs along the western side of the Dead Sea and belonging to a Jewish monastic community living in the area during the period of late Judaism. *See* Essenes.

Deuterocanon The fourteen books of the Vulgate not found in the Hebrew Bible. All but one are found in the Septuagint. The term is also used of the Catholic Epistles and Revelation in the New Testament. *See* Apocrypha.

Deutero-Pauline Books bearing Paul's name, included in the collection of his letters, and reflecting his influence and tradition, but not actually written by him.

Diaspora Literally a scattering, as of seed, hence, the Jewish communities located in cities throughout the world outside their own land. James and I Peter also use the term to refer to the Christian communities.

Disciple A student, hence, the followers and students of Jesus, especially the twelve.

Docetism The heretical doctrine that Jesus' humanity, including his Crucifixion and death, was illusory (from the Greek *dokeo* to seem or appear to be).

Doublet Two versions, from different sources, of the same story, both of which the author has included, apparently under the mistaken assumption that they are different stories.

Epistle A letter, hence, the documents in the Pauline collection and the Catholic Epistles. More technically, the term is used to distinguish the formal literary pamphlets such as the Catholic Epistles from the *ad hoc* letters that Paul addressed to particular churches to deal with particular situations.

Eschatology The division of theology dealing with "last things" (as the Greek, from which it comes, implies), i.e., the end of history and what lies beyond history and this mortal existence.

Essenes An ascetic sect within Judaism described by Josephus, Philo, and Pliny the Elder. Most scholars believe the community at Qumran, which produced the "Dead Sea Scrolls," to be of this sect.

Eucharist From the Greek word for thanksgiving. A name for the Christian sacrament of bread and wine derived from the prayer of thanks offered in the rite of consecration. *See* Lord's Supper.

Evangelist From the Greek for a good or welcome message, the bearer of good news. Primarily, the authors of the four Gospels. Also one who proclaims the Gospel. *See* Gospel.

Exegesis The technical analysis of a passage of Scripture to discover its meaning as precisely and fully as possible.

Expiation An offering intended to appease divine wrath against sin. An atonement or compensation for sin.

Feast of Dedication (Heb., *Hanukkah*) The eight-day festival commemorating the success of Judas Maccabeus against the armies of Antiochus Epiphanes in freeing Jerusalem and restoring the Temple, which was rededicated on the 25th of Kesliv (December), 165 B.C.

Feast of Passover Annual Jewish feast commemorating Israel's deliverance from Egypt. Specifically, it is a meal on the fourteenth day of Nisan (March–April) which includes roast lamb, unleavened bread, and bitter herbs and begins the eight-day feast of unleavened bread.

Feast of Pentecost So called because it occurs fifty days after the Feast of Passover, it is also known as the Feast of Weeks and celebrated the beginning of the presentation of the first-fruits of the harvest. The Christian observance is based on the account in Acts 2:1ff. of the descent of the Holy Spirit upon the Church.

Feast of Tabernacles The Jewish annual harvest festival. Also known as the Feast of Booths, from the practice of observing it by erecting booths of branches reminiscent of the wilderness journey from Egypt.

Form Criticism A method of study of the Gospels which, by examining the individual units of material for the characteristic "forms" of oral tradition, seeks to recover what can be known of the history of the tradition about Jesus which lies back of the written sources.

God-Fearers Gentile admirers of Judaism who attended the synagogues, observed the Sabbath, and other precepts of Jewish Law, but were unwilling to sever their own family and national ties and become proselytes.

Gospel Apparently from the Anglo-Saxon "God's Story," it translates the Greek word *evangelion* meaning a good or happy message. The term refers in the first place to Jesus' announcement of the Kingdom of God and, second, to the four books about his ministry, Passion, and Resurrection at the beginning of the New Testament.

Haftarah The Scripture lesson from the Prophets appointed to be read following the Sabbath reading of Torah. The Torah is read consecutively in an appointed cycle from Genesis to Deuteronomy, but the haftarah lessons are selected without regard to order to conform to the content of the Torah being read.

Hannukah See Feast of Dedication.

Hellenism The presence and influence of Greek language, culture, and thought. In the East and the Roman Empire Hellenism was widely disseminated by the successor of Alexander the Great and later by the conquest of the Greeks by the burgeoning Roman Empire.

Hermaneutics The process of translating and interpreting Scripture. The general principles of interpretation. *See* Exegesis.

Herodians Traditionally defined as a Jewish political party which favored and supported the Idumean dynasty of Herod, they remain something of a mystery.

Homily A discourse of exhortation and interpretation following and based upon the lessons read in the synagogue and church corresponding to the modern liturgical sermon. It is distinguished from the proclamation of the Gospel for the purpose of winning converts. *See* Kerygma.

Idumean The inhabitants of the Negeb—the former Edomites—during the late Persian period and afterward. The Herods were Idumeans.

Incarnation Literally to take on flesh, hence the doctrine of the divinity and humanity of Jesus.

Kerygma The act of making a public proclamation. Used in the New Testament with reference to the proclamation of the Gospel.

Law A literal translation of the Greek word *nomos* which is regularly used in the New Testament for Torah, the first five books of the Old Testament. "Law and Prophets" is the New Testament title for the Scriptures. *See* Torah.

Legend A story of a saint or holy person. In form criticism the term is used of stories in the Gospels which are intended to exemplify the greatness of Jesus.

Levant The countries of the eastern Mediterranean.

Libertinism Rejection of all moral restraints, hence licentiousness.

Logos A transliteration of the Greek term otherwise translated as word. It carries a more complex meaning, however, including rational thought, and the rational principle behind the universe. In the prologue of John's Gospel it refers to the creative power and activity of God.

Lord's Supper The ritual meal of bread and wine, which comprises the Christian's primary act of worship, perpetuating significant meals which the disciples ate with Jesus, i.e., the feeding of the multitude, the Last Supper, and the post-Resurrection meals recorded in Luke and John, and signifying the presence of Christ within his Church. *See* Eucharist.

Messiah A transliteration of the Hebrew word meaning anointed, referring to the rite of setting in office the king or priest. Prophets are sometimes spoken of as anointed. The rite symbolizes the divine endowment of the office. In New Testament usage it refers to the expected eschatological king who would bring deliverance to Israel, judgment on the wicked, and usher in the Kingdom of God. *See* Christology.

Midrash From the Hebrew word for explanation, hence, a commentary or exposition of Scripture.

Miracle An extraordinary or wonderful occurrence incapable of being explained by known natural causes and therefore presumed to be supernatural.

Miracle Story One of the forms of Gospel tradition, distinguished by form criticism, in which a story of a miracle is told with the primary interest in the miracle itself.

Mishnah From the Hebrew word meaning to repeat, hence, to teach or learn, it refers to the vast collection of rabbinic teaching and decisions, made by Judah ha Nasica, A.D. 200, which became the basis of the Talmud.

Myth A story in which the emphasis falls on the divine dimension of the event and its religious significance. In form criticism it designates those pericopae in the Gospels whose primary purpose is to reveal the divine nature of Christ.

Palestine Taken from the ancient Philistines who in the twelfth century B.C. settled on the maritime plain of Gaza, the name was used by outsiders to refer to the land of Israel and, especially after the disastrous rebellion of Bar Cochba, A.D. 132–135, became the established name for it.

Parable An item or story out of ordinary experience used to illustrate a point. It is to be distinguished from an allegory in which the symbolism is elaborate and often is artificially contrived. *See* Allegory.

Paradigm A model or pattern. In form criticism, a narrative which gives a setting for and helps to elucidate an edifying saying at its end.

Parousia From a Greek word meaning the coming, and sometimes used of the arrival of a king to assume his throne, it refers in the New Testament to the return of the Risen Christ to inaugurate the Kingdom of God.

Passion The suffering of Christ's Crucifixion. The term customarily is used, however, to include the ordeal of the entire series of events which led up to it.

Pastoral Epistles The three Epistles, I and II Timothy and Titus, ostensibly addressed by St. Paul to two of his pastors, hence, the term. Modern scholarship regards the address as a literary device used by a disciple of Paul to bring his teaching to bear on later pastoral problems. *See* Deutero-Pauline.

Pericope In form criticism, a section of Gospel material which is more or less complete in itself and connected to its context by secondary editorial links.

Pharisees The popular sect in Judaism as opposed to the Sadducees. Deeply concerned for the correct observance of the Law, and believing that it contained all that was necessary to know, they developed elaborate interpretations which were intended to make explicit what they believed was implicit in it.

Preexistence The belief in a person's existence in some way prior to his birth in his present human form. In the New Testament studies it refers to the belief that the Christ (Messiah) existed with God before his human advent.

Presbyter An elder. The term was used of the leaders of the synagogue and thus came to be used of the leadership of the Church, hence, one of the three orders of the Christian ministry. *See* Priest.

Priest A corruption of the word "presbyter." In English it is also used, however, to translate the Greek word *hiereus* and the Latin *sacerdos* which were used of the Temple priesthood in Judaism. Although, therefore, the Christian office apparently came primarily from the synagogue leadership, the Church soon came to compare its ministry with that of the Temple cultus. *See* Bishop; Deacon; Presbyter.

Procurator An administrator, usually a military officer of equestrian rank (knight), placed in charge of a minor province and subject only to the Roman Emperor. As a rule the presence of a procurator indicated the existence of a threat, either internal or external, to the peace of that area of the Empire.

Pronouncement Story A story in the Gospels which was told for the sake of the saying at its conclusion. *See* Paradigm.

Proselyte A convert to another religion. For the New Testament it refers to a gentile who has undergone the rites required to become a Jew. These include circumcision, baptism, and the offering of a special sacrifice.

Pseudepigrapha Literally "falsely ascribed," a document which pretends to be written by a venerable Biblical personality. The Jewish Apocalypses are an important example of this literature.

Rabbi A master or teacher. Specifically, the Jewish scholars and teachers of Torah.

Redaction Criticism See Composition criticism.

Sacraments Something sacred, or that which makes sacred, hence, a means of divine grace. In Christianity the rites stemming from Christ's commands in the Gospels which become sensible signs of his presence and grace upon the faithful. *See* Baptism; Eucharist.

Sacrifice Literally, to make sacred. An offering to God. In Christianity Christ's death is the sacrifice *par excellence,* which fulfills and replaces all the sacrifices of Judaism. The Eucharist, inasmuch as it is a representation of Christ's self-offering on the cross, can be called a sacrifice in Christian terminology.

Sadducees The sect in ancient Judaism representing the wealthy, landed aristocracy which controlled the priesthood of the Temple. As such, they represented the ruling class and were on comparatively good terms with the Roman overlords. Rejecting the interpretive work of the Pharisees, i.e., the oral Torah and such Pharisaic doctrines as the resurrection, they held exclusively to the written Torah. Although possessed of considerable power, they were not popular. *See* Essenes; Pharisees; Zealots.

Samaritans Inhabitants of the territory west of the Jordan River between Judea and Galilee, the old northern kingdom of Israel. They were despised by the Jews as descendants of foreigners who intermarried with the remnants of northern Israel after the fall of Samaria, 721 B.C. (II Kings 17). Their Scriptures consisted exclusively of their own version of the Pentateuch.

Scroll A book. Until the development of the codex, i.e., the hinged-leaf book developed in the second century A.D., books were made by gluing the leaves together in strips approximately 25 to 30 feet in length and rolled up on sticks.

Septuagint The Greek translation of the Hebrew Scriptures begun in Alexandria, Egypt, in the time of Ptolemy Philadelphus in the third century B.C. It came to include Jewish literature composed in Greek. Widely used in the synagogues of Hellenistic Judaism, it was traditionally supposed to have been translated by seventy Jewish scholars, hence, the symbol LXX customarily used to designate it.

Shema The "creed of Judaism," the highest confession of faith based on the words "Hear (Heb., *shema*), O Israel, the Lord our God, the Lord is One," Deuteronomy 6:4, and including Deuteronomy 6:4–9, 11:13–21, Numbers 15:37–41 (cf. Mk. 12:29–34).

Simile A brief analogy or figure, making a comparison for illustration or clarification.

Source Criticism The analysis of a document and, if possible, comparison with other similar documents to discover the written sources used by its author.

Synagogue Literally an assembly, it consisted of a congregation of not fewer than ten adult male Jews organized for worship, conducting a school for children, and regulating the affairs of the local Jewish community. Probably originating during the Babylonian Exile (586–538 B.C.) as a surrogate for the Temple, it became the effective center of Jewish life which enabled it to survive the destruction of the Temple. Its worship consisted of lessons from Torah and the Prophets (Haftarah), a homily, the Shema, Psalms, and eighteen prayers.

Syncretism From a Greek word for combination, it refers to the development of essentially new religions by borrowings and combinations of ideas and elements of different religions which are brought together by circumstances.

Synoptic Gospels The first three Gospels, so called because the very large amount of material in common—including identical wording in much of it—allows them to be compared extensively, or to be "viewed together" as the phrase implies.

Talmud The great collection of authoritative Jewish tradition dating from the fifth century A.D. It consists of two parts. In the center is the Mishnah surrounded by commentary known as *gemara* (Aramaic, learning), and exists in two forms. The Palestinian (sometimes wrongly called Jerusalem) Talmud is the shorter and is incomplete. The Babylonian Talmud is somewhat later and is complete. *See* Mishnah.

Textual Criticism The study of available ancient manuscripts for the purpose of detecting errors made by the copyists and restoring the true reading of the "autograph," i.e., the original copy of the document.

Theodicy A rational attempt to understand how a righteous God can permit evil to exist in his world.

Torah The Hebrew term for the Pentateuch. Although translated "law" in the New Testament, the word itself is broader, having the force of divine revelation or oracle.

Tradition A body of teaching recollections and interpretations which reflects the history and meaning of a people or community. In reference to the New Testament it refers to the oral material from and concerning Jesus which was handed down through the churches and finally recorded in writings that now make up the Gospels. *See* Form criticism.

Vulgate The Latin translation of the Bible which prevailed in the Western Church. Essentially, it is the translation made by St. Jerome in the fourth century A.D. The term means common or usual.

Writings The third division, after the Law (Torah) and the Prophets, of the Old Testament.

Zealots A militaristic patriotic party in Judaism, which was determined to free the land of foreign control by whatever means necessary. Several serious uprisings were generated by this party before the disastrous rebellion of A.D. 66–70 which brought about the fall of Jerusalem. They seem to have been a legacy of the Maccabean revolt.

Appendices

General Bibliography

RECENT TRANSLATIONS

The Anchor Bible (Garden City, N.Y.: Doubleday). Original translations with notes and commentary by a number of scholars. Still in process.

The Bible, A New Translation, tr. James Moffatt (New York: Harper & Row, 1935).

The Jerusalem Bible, ed. Alexander Jones (Garden City, N.Y.: Doubleday, 1966).

The New English Bible, New Testament (Oxford: Oxford University Press; Cambridge: At the University Press, 1961).

The New Testament, An American Translation, tr. Edgar J. Goodspeed (Chicago: The University of Chicago Press, 1923).

The New Testament, Translated into Modern English, tr. J. B. Phillips (New York: The Macmillan Company, 1961).

The Oxford Annotated Bible, Revised Standard Version, eds., Herbert G. May and Bruce M. Metzger (New York: Oxford University Press, 1962).

PARALLEL GOSPELS

Gospel Parallels, RSV, Burton H. Throckmorton, Jr. (New York: Thomas Nelson & Sons, 1949).

Records of the Life of Jesus, RV, H. B. Sharman (New York: Harper & Row, 1917).

Syllabus and Synopsis of the First Three Gospels, ASV, Walter Bundy (Indianapolis: Bobbs-Merrill Co., 1932).

CONCORDANCES

Cruden, Alexander, *Cruden's Complete Concordance* for the Authorized

Version of 1611, rev. ed. (Philadelphia: The John C. Winston
Company, 1949).

Ellison, J. W., ed., *Nelson's Complete Concordance of the Revised Standard Version of the Bible* (Camden, N.J.: Thomas Nelson & Sons,
1957).

Young, Robert, ed., *Young's Analytical Concordance to the Bible* for the
Authorized Version of 1611 (Grand Rapids, Mich.: Wm. B. Eerdmans, 1955).

DICTIONARIES

Buttrick, George A., ed., *The Interpreter's Dictionary of the Bible,* 4 vols.
(New York: Abingdon Press, 1962).

Hastings, James, ed., *A Dictionary of the Bible,* 4 vols. and supplement
(New York: Charles Scribner's Sons, 1902). An old but still very
useful classic.

————, *A Dictionary of the Bible,* rev. ed. F. C. Grant, H. H. Rowley,
1 vol. (New York: Charles Scribner's Sons, 1963).

ATLASES

Aharoni, Y., and Aui-Yonah, M., *The Macmillan Bible Atlas* (New York:
The Macmillan Company, 1968).

Kraeling, Emil, ed., *Rand-MacNally Historical Atlas of the Holy Lands*
(Chicago: Rand-MacNally, 1959).

May, H. G., and Hamilton, R. W., eds., *Oxford Bible Atlas* (New York:
Oxford University Press, 1962).

Wright, G. E., and Filson, F. V., *Westminster Historical Atlas to the Bible,*
rev. ed. (Philadelphia: The Westminster Press, 1956).

COMMENTARIES

Following are important sets of commentaries covering the entire
Bible or New Testament. Single commentaries on individual books and
commentaries of special importance in the following series are listed at the
end of the chapters.

Black, M., and Rowley, H. H., rev. ed., *Peake's Commentary on the Bible,*
1 vol. (New York: Thomas Nelson and Sons, 1962).

Briggs, C. A., Driver, S. R., and Plummer, Alfred, eds., *The International
Critical Commentary* (New York: Charles Scribner's Sons).

Buttrick, George A., ed., *The Interpreter's Bible* (New York: Abingdon
Press, 1951).

Moffatt, James, ed., *The Moffatt New Testament Commentary* (London:
Hodder & Stoughton). Based on Moffatt's translation of the New
Testament.

Neil, W., ed., *Harper's Bible Commentary* (New York: Harper & Row).

Sutcliffe, E. F., and Orchard, B., *A Catholic Commentary on the Holy Scriptures,* 1 vol. (New York: Thomas Nelson & Sons, 1953).

INTRODUCTIONS AND GENERAL STUDIES

Bultmann, Rudolph, *Theology of the New Testament,* 2 vols., tr. Kendrick Grobel (New York: Charles Scribner's Sons, 1951, 1955).

Crownfield, Frederick, *A Historical Approach to the New Testament* (New York: Harper & Row, 1960).

Enslin, Morton Scott, *Christian Beginnings* (New York: Harper & Row, 1938).

Fuller, R. H., *The New Testament in Current Study* (New York: Charles Scribner's Sons, 1962). An excellent survey of developments in scholarship through the middle of the twentieth century.

Goguel, Maurice, *The Birth of Christianity* (New York: The Macmillan Company, 1954).

Grant, R. M., *A Short History of the Interpretation of the Bible* (New York: The Macmillan Company, 1958).

————, *A Historical Introduction to the New Testament* (New York: Harper & Row, 1963).

Kittel, Gerhard, and Friedrich, G., eds., *Theological Dictionary of the New Testament,* tr. Geoffrey W. Bromiley (Grand Rapids, Mich.: Wm. B. Eerdmans, 1964–1969).

Kümmel, W. G., tr. A. J. Mattill, Jr., *Introduction to the New Testament* (New York: Abingdon Press, 1966). An extensive revision of the old Fiene-Behm *Introduction.*

Lietzmann, H., *The Beginnings of the Christian Church,* Vols. I and II, tr. B. L. Woolf (London: Lutterworth Press, 1953).

McNeile, A. H., rev. C. S. C. Williams, *An Introduction to the Study of the New Testament* (London: Oxford University Press, 1953).

Moffatt, James, *An Introduction to the Literature of the New Testament* (New York: Charles Scribner's Sons, 1911). Old but still useful, especially for the history of nineteenth-century scholarship.

Price, James, *Interpreting the New Testament* (New York: Holt, Rinehart & Winston, 1961).

Richardson, A., *Theological Word Book of the Bible* (New York: The Macmillan Company, 1951).

Stauffer, Ethelbert, *Theology of the New Testament,* tr. John Marsh (New York: The Macmillan Company, 1955).

Weiss, Johannes, *Earliest Christianity,* 2 vols., tr. F. C. Grant, *et al.* (New York: Harper Torchbook, 1959).

Wikenhauser, Alfred, *New Testament Introduction* (New York: Herder & Herder, 1963).

Parables and Parabolic Sayings in the Synoptic Gospels

In All Three

	Mark	Matthew	Luke
1. The well do not need a physician	2:17	9:12	5:31
2. Can the wedding guests fast?	2:19–20	9:15	5:34
3. New cloth / new wineskins (two)	2:21–22	9:16–17	5:36–39
4. Divided kingdom / and house (two)	3:24–25	12:25–26	11:17
5. Strong man overcome by stronger	3:27	12:29	11:18
6. The sower, and interpretation	4:3–9; 13–20	13:3–23	8:5–15
7. The lamp on a stand	4:21	5:15	8:16
8. Measure	4:24	7:2	6:38
9. Mustard seed	4:31–32	13:31–32	13:18–19
10. Leaven of Pharisees	8:15	16:6	12:1b
11. Salt	9:50	5:13	14:34–35
12. Camel through needle's eye	10:25	19:24	18:25
13. The wicked tenants	12:1–9	21:33–41	20:9–19
14. Sign of the fig tree	13:28	24:32	21:29–31

In Mark and Matthew

	Mark	Matthew
1. On defilement	7:15–20	15:11–20
2. Children's food not for dogs	7:27	15:26

None in Only Mark and Luke

In Matthew and Luke

	MATTHEW	LUKE
1. Eye is lamp of the body	6:22–23	11:34–36
2. Serving two masters	6:24	16:13
3. Speck and log in eye	7:3–5	6:41–42
4. Serpent for fish, etc.	7:9	11:11
5. Narrow door	7:13–14	13:23–24
6. Good and bad trees and fruit	7:16–17	6:43–44

494

Parables and Parabolic Sayings

7.	Houses on rock and sand	7:24–27	6:47–49
8.	As sheep among wolves	10:16	10:3
9.	Two sparrows for a farthing	10:29	12:6
10.	Children in the marketplace	11:16–19	7:31–35
11.	Animal in pit or well	12:11–12	14:5
12.	Good treasure from good heart	12:35	6:45
13.	The return of the evil spirits	12:43–45	11:24–26
14.	Leaven in the loaf	13:33	13:20–21
15.	Blind guides	15:14	6:39
16.	Predicting weather and times	16:2–3	12:54–56
17.	Faith as a mustard seed	17:20	17:6
18.	The lost sheep	18:12–13	15:4–7
19.	The wedding feast	22:1–10	14:16–24
20.	Heavy burdens on others	23:4	11:46
21.	Cleansing outside of cup	23:25	11:39–40
22.	Unseen graves	23:27	11:44
23.	Hen gathering her brood	23:37	13:34
24.	Where the body, there the eagles	24:28	17:37
25.	Householder and thief	24:43	12:39
26.	Faithful and wise servant	24:45–51	12:42–46
27.	Pounds or talents	25:14–30	19:11–27

In Mark Only

1.	Mysterious growth of seed	4:26–29
2.	Absent master and watchful servants	13:34

In Matthew Only

1.	Light	5:14a
2.	City on a hill	5:14b
3.	The holy to dogs, pearls to pigs	7:6
4.	Wolves in sheep's clothing	7:15
5.	Wheat and tares	13:24–30
6.	Treasure in field	13:44
7.	Pearl of great price	13:45
8.	The fish net	13:47–50
9.	Householder and things new and old	13:51–52
10.	Plants planted by the Father	15:13
11.	Tribute and the kings of earth	17:25–26
12.	Unforgiving debtor	18:23–35
13.	Laborers in vineyard	20:1–16
14.	Two sons and obedience	21:28–32
15.	Man without wedding garment	22:11–14
16.	Straining gnats and swallowing a camel	23:24
17.	Wise and foolish virgins	25:1–13
18.	The great judgment	25:31–46

In Luke Only

1.	Physician heal thyself	4:23
2.	Two forgiven debtors	7:41–43
3.	Putting hand to plow	9:62
4.	Satan falling like lightning	10:18
5.	The good samaritan	10:29–37
6.	Friend at midnight	11:5–8
7.	Key of knowledge	11:52
8.	The rich fool	12:13–21
9.	Watchful servants	12:36–38
10.	Unwitting disobedience	12:47–48
11.	The barren fig tree	13:6–9
12.	The closed door	13:25
13.	The high and low seats	14:7–11
14.	Counting costs	14:28–30
15.	Appraising the enemy	14:31–33
16.	Lost coin	15:8–10
17.	Lost boy (prodigal son)	15:11–32
18.	Unjust steward	16:1–13
19.	Rich man and Lazarus	16:19–31
20.	Servants doing their duty	17:7–10
21.	Unjust judge	18:1–8
22.	The Pharisee and publican	18:9–14
23.	Sifting Peter as wheat	22:31
24.	Green and dry wood	23:31

Miracles in the Synoptics

In All Three Gospels

	MARK	MATTHEW	LUKE
1. Peter's mother-in-law	1:30–31	8:14–15	4:38–39
2. Cleansing of leper	1:40–42	8:2–4	5:12–16
3. Paralytic let through roof	2:3–12	9:2–8	5:18–26
4. Man with withered hand	3:1–5	12:9–14	6:6–11
5. Stilling the storm	4:37–39	8:23–27	8:22–25
6. Demoniac of Geraza	5:1–13	8:28–34	8:26–39
7. Jairus' daughter	5:22–24, 35–42	9:18–19, 23–26	8:40–42, 49–56
8. Woman with hemorrhage	5:25–34	9:20–22	8:43–48
9. Feeding of 5,000	6:35–44	14:15–21	9:12–17
* (10. Blind man of Bethsaida	8:22–26	9:27–31	18:35–43)
11. Son with dumb spirit	9:17–27	17:14–21	9:38–43
12. Bartimaeus	10:46–52	20:30–34	18:35–43

In Mark and Matthew

	MARK	MATTHEW
1. Walking on the sea	6:45–51	14:22–33
2. Syro-Phoenician woman's daughter	7:25–30	15:22–28
3. Feeding of 4,000	8:1–9	15:32–39
4. Cursing of fig tree	11:13–14, 20–21	21:19–21

In Mark and Luke

	MARK	LUKE
1. Man with unclean spirit, synagogue	1:23–26	4:33–37

In Matthew and Luke

	MATTHEW	LUKE
1. Centurion's servant	8:5–13	7:1–10
2. Blind and dumb demoniac	12:22–23	11:14–15

In Mark Only

1. Deaf-mute	7:32–35	
* (2. Blind man of Bethsaida	8:22–25)	

In Matthew Only

* (1. Two blind men   9:27–31)
   2. Dumb demoniac   9:32–34
   3. Stater in fish's mouth   17:27

In Luke Only

1. Escape from mob   4:30
2. Miraculous catch of fish   5:1–11
3. Raising of son of widow of Nain   7:11–17
4. Woman with infirmity   13:10–17
5. Man with dropsy   14:1–6
6. Ten lepers   17:11–19
7. Restoring ear of high priest's slave   22:47–53

* Whether these are variations of a common tradition or separate miracles is uncertain.

The Messianic Secret in Mark

1:25	Rebuke of demons
1:34	Rebuke of demons
1:44	Charge to leper
3:12	Rebuke of demons
4:11	Secrets given to disciples
5:43	Charge at raising of Jairus' daughter
7:36	Charge at healing of deaf-mute
8:30	Charge at Peter's confession
9:9	Charge after Transfiguration (Until after the Resurrection. This is the climax for the motif.)

Two further possible instances:

9:30	Jesus and the disciples pass secretly through Galilee
11:33	Jesus' refusal to answer question about his authority

Doublets and Repetitions in Matthew

3:2—4:17—10:7	The call of the kingdom
3:10—7:19	Ax laid to the root of the tree
4:23—9:35 (Mk. 6:6)	Teaching, preaching, healing
4:24—14:35 (Mk. 6:54–55)	Fame of Jesus
4:25—12:15	Crowds followed him
5:18—24:35	My word will not pass away
5:29–30—18:8–9	If eye, hand, foot offend, remove them
5:31–32—19:9	On divorce
5:33–37—23:16–22	Oaths
6:15—18:35	On forgiveness
6:26—10:29–31	More value than many sparrows (cf. 12:12)
7:12—22:40	All the Law and the Prophets
7:15–20—12:33ff.	Good and bad trees and fruit
9:13—12:7	Quotation from Hosea 6:6
9:27–31—20:29–30	Two blind men healed
9:32–34—12:22–24	Blind and dumb demoniac healed
9:36—14:14	Compassion on the multitude
10:6—15:24	Go only to lost sheep of Israel—disciples/ Jesus
10:17–25—24:9, 13	They will deliver you up
10:22b—24:13	He who endures to the end shall be saved
10:38–39—16:24–25	Cross bearing
10:40—18:5	He who receives you receives me
11:21–24—12:41–42	Cities which would have repented
12:34b—15:11ff.	On inner defilement
12:38–39—16:1–4	Sign of Jonah
13:12—25:29	To him who has shall be given (cf. Mk. 4: 24–25)
16:19—18:18	Binding and loosing
17:20—21:21	Faith which moves mountains
18:1–5—20:26–27—23:11–12	True greatness
18:7—26:24	On Judas' betrayal of Jesus
19:30—20:16	Last first, first last
24:45–51—25:14–15b	The servant and the absent master
26:25—27:11	You have said it
27:34—27:48	The drink offered to Jesus on the cross

Comparative Lists of the Twelve Disciples

MARK 3:16–19	MATTHEW 10:2–4	LUKE 6:13–16	Acts 1:13
Simon-Peter	Simon-Peter	Simon-Peter	Peter
James Zebedee*	Andrew his brother	Andrew his brother	John
John his brother*	James Zebedee	James‡	James
Andrew†	John his brother	John‡	Andrew
Philip	Philip	Philip	Philip
Bartholomew	Bartholomew	Bartholomew	Thomas
Matthew	Thomas	Matthew	Bartholomew
Thomas	Matthew the tax collector	Thomas	Matthew
James Alphaeus	James Alphaeus	James Alphaeus	James Alphaeus
Thaddaeus	Thaddaeus	Simon the Zealot	Simon the Zealot
Simon the Canaanite	Simon the Canaanite	Judas son of James	Judas son of James
Judas Iscariot	Judas Iscariot	Judas Iscariot	

* Boanerges.
† Andrew is identified as the brother of Simon-Peter in Mark 1:16.
‡ Luke 5:10 identifies these as sons of Zebedee.
Note: Levi is identified as the son of Alphaeus in Mark 2:14, and Matthew replaces Levi with Matthew in Matthew 9:9.

Index of Names and Subjects

Index of Biblical References

NEW TESTAMENT